Shrink Rap

SIXTY PSYCHOTHERAPISTS DISCUSS THEIR WORK, THEIR LIVES, AND THE STATE OF THEIR FIELD

Lee D. Kassan, M.A.

JASON ARONSON INC.
Northvale, New Jersey
London

Director of Editorial Production: Robert D. Hack

This book was set in 10 pt. Stone Serif by Alpha Graphics of Pittsfield, New Hampshire and printed and bound by Book-mart Press, Inc. of North Bergen, New Jersey.

Library of Congress Cataloging-in-Publication Data

Kassan, Lee D.
    Shrink rap : sixty psychotherapists discuss their work, their
lives, and the state of their field / by Lee D. Kassan.
        p. cm.
    Includes bibliographical references.
    ISBN 0-7657-0017-4 (hc : alk. paper)
    1. Psychotherapy. 2. Psychotherapists. 3. Psychotherapy—
Practice. 4. Psychotherapy—Vocational guidance. I. Title.
RC480.5.K365 1997
616.89'14—dc20   96-18541

Manufactured in the United States of America. Jason Aronson Inc. offers books and cassettes. For information and catalog write to Jason Aronson Inc., 230 Livingston Street, Northvale, New Jersey 07647.

Acknowledgments

This book would not have been possible without the participation of the sixty therapists who agreed to be interviewed and who spoke so openly and honestly about themselves and their work. I cannot thank them enough.

I also want to thank the following people for their help: Peter Kassan and Steven Bohall, for plowing through the manuscript and giving me their astute editorial feedback; Dr. Rena Subotnik, for help with the research for the references; my editor, Michael Moskowitz, for believing that this could be a book worth reading; C.B., for the personal support and tolerance while I was working on this instead of paying attention.

Contents

PART II—THEORY

PART III—PERSONAL HISTORY AND EXPERIENCE

PART IV—THE STATE OF THE FIELD

Introduction

This is a difficult time in the history of our profession. Different schools of treatment, with modifications of theory and technique, have proliferated to the point where there are now hundreds of competing therapies, each claiming greater efficacy or even greater truth. At the same time, pressures from third-party insurance carriers are forcing practitioners toward briefer treatments, and also demanding details of therapy and of patient disclosures that threaten the privacy and confidentiality on which most therapies are based. Recent legal decisions also invade the clinical setting, requiring the therapist to act as an agent of the state and report to authorities various situations, including child abuse, intent to harm, and other such dangers.

For reasons we may find difficult to understand, the field as a whole, including the professional organizations that represent the individual practitioners, seems to be going along with these changes and not challenging such incursions or protecting the territory in which we work. As you will learn from their responses, most of the therapists interviewed herein feel the pressure of these developments and are concerned about the effects on their profession.

In such a climate, we need to know what therapists do, feel, and think. Hundreds, if not thousands, of books tell us how to do psychotherapy and psychoanalysis: how to arrive at the correct diagnosis; how to formulate an intervention; how to deal with transference and resistance; how to handle countertransference; and so on. Very few books tell what the experience is actually like for the therapists themselves and what these therapists think about the various theories and the concrete specifics of the work. This book is an attempt to convey that experience in the practitioners' own words.

The book is directed at two audiences: professionals and patients. As a therapist myself, I know that one of the features of private practice is the isolation: We are alone in our offices, seeing only patients. Many of us wonder how other therapists deal with the situations and experiences that we encounter. I have found that while we are always happy to discuss a case with colleagues, we are sometimes hesitant to discuss ourselves and rarely get the information we need to understand how we fit in with the rest of the field.

Patients are also very curious about us and what we do. In the course of doing this book, I have come to wonder if many of the personal questions patients ask us aren't, at least to some extent, an attempt to understand how we do the work and what our experience is like. When a patient asks, "Where are you going on your vacation?" perhaps they are also asking, "How far away do you need to get from me and from this work?" I hope that the book will help patients better understand what their therapists are doing and thinking as they work.

Sixty therapists of various orientations and backgrounds were interviewed in person between May 1994 and January 1995. These interviews covered as broad a range of topics related to the practice of psychotherapy as could be covered in an interview of reasonable length. I'm sure every reader will be able to think of an additional question or two and wonder why it wasn't included. All I can say is that these seemed like the most significant areas to cover when I designed the questionnaire. The final version of the questionnaire included over 100 questions and lasted between an hour and an hour and a half, depending on how much the individual had to say.

Approximately 100 therapists were initially invited to participate in the interview. As former president of a small professional group affiliated with my training institute, I had access to a mailing list, and many of the first group to agree to the interview were people I had some personal contact with previously. These people referred me to other therapists I did not know personally. In most instances, those declining to be interviewed gave no reason, though some replied to the invitation by saying that they were too busy. Almost all interviewees were taped in their own offices; a few came to my office. Two were taped over the telephone.

Most of the therapists in the book live and work in the New York City area. Some work in other parts of the country and a few work in suburbs or small towns. Of the total sample of 60 therapists, 46 have offices in Manhattan, 8 in suburban locations, and 6 in rural areas outside the New York area. My impression is that geographical location has little (if any) bearing on what goes on in treatment. Once the door closes and it's just two (or more) people in a room, the work is pretty much the same no matter where it takes place.

This is not a random sample, and no claim is made for statistical validity. The group consists of 33 women and 27 men. Ages range from early thirties to mid-seventies. There are 23 M.S.W.'s, 21 Ph.D.'s (which includes Psy.D.'s), 6 M.D. psychiatrists, and 10 people with other degrees, which include M.A.'s in psychology, M.S.'s in rehabilitation, and pastoral counselors with religious degrees. The majority, 40 people, are in private practice exclusively, while 16 have some kind of other clinical position at an agency or hospital. I have also included 4 people who have no private practice but do only individual therapy in an agency setting.

Years of experience range from 1 to 50 and are distributed this way: three have 5 years experience or less; five have from 6 to 9 years; ten have from 10 to 14 years; sixteen have from 15 to 19 years; fourteen have from 20 to 24 years; four people have 25 to 29 years; three have from 30 to 34 years; and five have from 35 to 50 years experience.

I have tried to select a variety of theoretical orientations, although studies have shown that experienced clinicians are more like each other than like any particular school or theoretical orientation. As primary orientation (see Question 37), all the major schools are represented.

I have made every effort to conceal the identity of the therapists in this book so that they could speak frankly and candidly without concern about the effect on their patients or their practices. All references to specific persons, places, and other identifying facts have been removed. Quotations are identified only by gender, degree (M.S.W., Ph.D., M.D., etc.), and years of practice. I believe this will be enough information to orient the reader to the background of the speaker. References to specific cases have been disguised or generalized so that no patient is identifiable.

Specific topics have been grouped into four main areas: practice, theory, personal history and experience, and the state of the field. *Practice* includes those specifics that are the nuts and bolts of the hour: session length; fees; rules; and so on. *Theory* includes all the questions about causes and dynamics, beliefs and opinions about metapsychology. *Personal History and Experience* includes background, training, the therapist's own therapy and supervision. *The State of the Field* includes opinions and judgments about what's wrong and what's right in the field currently and attitudes toward the work as a whole. At the end, I try to summarize what the interviews reveal and imply and give some of my own opinions about what needs to be improved and changed in our field. Within each question, I try to discuss the range of responses as objectively as possible and to label my own experience and opinions as such in a "Comments" section, in which I also try to address the issues and controversies each topic raises. In most instances, no definitive answers exist for the issues raised, and the questions remain open.

In spite of its unfortunate associations with the medical model (see Question 97), I have used the term "patient" to refer to the people who come to see us professionally. It is the word used in almost all the literature, and other terms have their own drawbacks. Because informal speech, as in a taped interview, is so different from written prose, excerpts from interviews have been lightly edited for sense and readability. Since almost everything discussed here is opinion, phrases like "I think that," "I believe," and "I feel that" have been removed from most quotations.

Because a comprehensive list of all the relevant books and articles on all the many different topics included in the book would be as long again as the book itself, I have included at the end of each question only several books and articles relevant to that specific topic. In some instances, it was difficult to choose from many possible references; in others, it was difficult to find even one. If the reader wishes to explore further a particular topic, computers and CD-ROM now make searches on any subject easy and straightforward.

I want to thank all the therapists who spent time with me and shared the details of their experiences, for without them this book would not be possible. In almost every instance, the therapists who agreed to be interviewed spoke openly, honestly, and revealingly about themselves and their work, and I deeply appreciate their courage in doing so.

There are no superstars of the analytic community included here, and probably very few whose names professionals might recognize from their books or articles. The therapists who speak here are the skilled practitioners who do the work without fame or glory. I hope this book brings them, and all practitioners in the field of psychotherapy, a little more appreciation, recognition, and understanding.

Practice

This section contains those questions about the practical dimensions and structure of the session. While we would not be surprised to find diversity on questions of theory, even to these more basic questions there is usually a wide array of responses. Many of these aspects of the work also tend to be somewhat neglected in training and in the professional literature. (I don't recall instructors or supervisors ever discussing session length, or how to collect overdue fees, or the value of telephone sessions. They seemed to believe that only theory really needs to be taught, and these concrete particulars will take care of themselves.)

Question 1: How many patients do you see in a week?

There was a very wide range of responses to this question. In general, those with part-time or full-time agency positions had fewer patient hours than those only in private practice (although there was some overlap). This makes sense: Fewer available hours means fewer patient hours. One therapist made this comment about part-time practitioners:

> An awful lot of people who do part-time psychotherapy, who work in hospitals and clinics for the most part, and then have eight or ten hours a week of private patients, I'm convinced that their work is much lower quality than those people who do it more frequently. The reason is that you wear one cap in the hospital setting, and then you shift over, and it's a little bit like they're amateurs, and the public doesn't know if they're going to someone who's an amateur or someone who's a dedicated professional. Can you imagine a surgeon who only does one operation a week? And the rest of the time he's doing all kinds of other work? They don't know what they're doing. They don't have a solid body of knowledge that they're applying and perfecting and working with. They're flying by the seat of their pants a good deal of the time.
> [Male, M.D., 20 years practice]

Those therapists who are exclusively in private practice said that their patient hours ranged from 15 to 40 hours, with one person saying that he had 50 hours in a week, and more.

> At the moment, it's about fifty. Years ago, it was seventy.
> [Male, Ph.D., 40 years practice]

NUMERICAL DISTRIBUTION

One person had fewer than five hours; three people had from 5 to 9 hours; six therapists had from 10 to 14 hours; thirteen people had from 15 to 19 hours; eight therapists had from 20 to 24 hours; nine people had from 25 to 29 hours; nine also from 30 to 34 hours; nine again from 35 to 39 hours; one person had 40 hours; and one had 50.

COMMENTS

The issue here is whether there is an optimum number of patient hours, and whether a therapist can see too many patients, or too few. No patient would want a surgeon who does only a few procedures each year; practice makes perfect. On the other hand, no patient would want a surgeon who does so many procedures that he feels rushed, overburdened, or exhausted.

All of us have heard stories about therapists who start seeing patients at 7:00 A.M. or even earlier and who stay in the office until 9:00 or 10:00 in the evening. We might find it hard to imagine scheduling seventy hours in a week, and doing them well, and still having a life outside the office.

A full-time practice may be preferable to a part-time one. Switching roles in midday, as from administrator to therapist, can be confusing and difficult, and perhaps the potential is there for problems, if the therapist slips into his administrative role with patients. In addition, the therapist who sees only a few private patients may find it much harder to allow one to stop treatment.

RELATED READING

Seaburn, D. B., and Harp, J. (1988). Sequencing: the patient caseload as an interactive system. *Family Systems Medicine* 6(1):107–111.
Taube, C. A., Burns, B. J., and Kessler, L. G. (1984). Patients of psychiatrists and psychologists in office-based practice: 1980. *American Psychologist* 39(12):1435–1447.

⧆⧆⧆⧆

Question 2: How long is a session? Do you take a break between sessions?

A traditional psychoanalytic hour used to be 50 minutes, with a ten minute break for note-taking, returning phone calls, and a trip to the bathroom. At some point, therapists realized that if they made the session 45 minutes, they could see four patients in three hours instead of three, provided they took no breaks between patients. Whether this was done for financial reasons, or simply to accommodate more patients, is hard to say.

> If I can work back-to-back, I prefer it, because it's time saving.
> [Female, M.S.W., 20 years practice]

Of the group with the 50-minute hour, almost everyone said that they took a break in the ten minutes between sessions. Of the group with 45-minute sessions, only about six people said they took a break between each patient. Others described several different patterns.

I take a break between every two sessions. There's never more than two in a row.

[Male, Ph.D., 10 years practice]

I take a break not between each session, but between groups of sessions.

[Female, M.S.W., 15 years practice]

A session is 45 minutes, except with couples I spend a whole hour. I usually do four or five in a row, and then a break, and then another four or five in a row, but no break between sessions.

[Female, M.S., 15 years practice]

I do a group of sessions and then I take a long break, then another group of sessions.

[Female, Ph.D., 20 years practice]

I've found it better not to take a break. Somehow the breaks were more disruptive than just going on.

[Male, M.S.W., 25 years practice]

I used to take breaks, I stopped, and now I'm resuming. If you have a long day, it's so pressured that you can't even go to the bathroom or answer the telephone. I've decided to restore the interval.

[Male, Ph.D., 50 years practice]

I try to take a break. I don't have full control over my schedule. I might schedule breaks but have emergencies and medical things I have to squeeze in.

[Female, M.D., 15 years practice]

Other theoretical approaches also adjust session length. Family therapy sessions are often ninety minutes.

A session is 90 minutes. If it's in the evening, I begin at five, I can work straight through to eleven without a break.

[Male, Ph.D., 25 years practice]

Some cognitive/behavioral work can also make session length flexible.

Fifty minutes to an hour and a half. If it's an exposure session with someone with OCD [obsessive-compulsive disorder], or in vivo work [in the actual situation] with someone who's agoraphobic it's usually an hour and a half.

[Female, Ph.D., 10 years practice]

Because of the logistics of getting patients in and out of the consulting room, scheduling back-to-back with no break means either patients actually get less than the full 45 minutes, or else the therapist ends up running increasingly late. Starting late, or ending late, or extending session length, can unintentionally send disturbing messages to the patient.

> I'm more careful about starting on time and ending on time since working with a patient who would always come late, and since I was just starting my practice, I had all the time in the world. I'd give her extra time, and then one day she said, "What's the matter with you? If you don't know when the beginning of the session is, how am I supposed to know when the beginning of the session is?" She was absolutely right.
>
> [Male, Ph.D., 20 years practice]

NUMERICAL DISTRIBUTION

Twenty-one therapists said the session was 50 minutes; 34 said the session was 45 minutes; 5 said the session was some other length.

Twenty-six practitioners said they regularly take a break between sessions; 23 said they did not; 11 said sometimes they did and sometimes they did not.

COMMENTS

The issues connected to this question are: What is the optimal session length, for patient and for therapist? Is a break between sessions necessary? What are patient reactions to coming in as the previous patient is leaving?

I suppose that it doesn't matter what the session length is, as long as it is consistent, starts on time, and ends on time. The fifty-minute session is part of our legacy from Freud, and there's no reason not to change it. I find that one advantage of a fifty-minute session and a ten-minute break is that it enables me to start all my sessions at the same time and for patients to know that they can usually reach me in person by phone at the same time each hour. This makes it possible for people who want to speak to me directly to do so, and also for people who want only to leave a message to do that.

I find it hard to understand how therapists can go from one session to another without any break, without time to visit the bathroom, return calls, make notes, or just clear one's mind. Back-to-back sessions also increase the likelihood of sessions starting later and later through the day, since patients often take a few moments to leave the office. I have had patients complain about previous therapists who ushered them in as someone else was leaving; they told me they felt as if they were in a revolving door.

RELATED READING

Bierenbaum, H., Nichols, M. P., and Schwartz, A. J. (1976). Effects of varying session length and frequency in brief emotive psychotherapy. *Journal of Consulting and Clinical Psychology* 44(5):790–798.

Greenson, R. (1974). The decline and fall of the fifty-minute hour. *Journal of the American Psychoanalytic Association* 22:785–791.

Hammer. E. (1990). *Reaching the Affect: Style in the Psychodynamic Therapies.* Northvale, NJ: Jason Aronson.

🔁🔁🔁🔁

Question 3: Do you take notes during the session? Afterwards? What kind of notes do you make?

The stereotype of the patient on the couch and the analyst in the chair with notepad in hand no longer describes most of our work. Attitudes toward note-taking, both during and after the session, vary widely.

Here are some comments in favor of notes during the session:

> It was very difficult in the beginning to learn how to do it, but now I find that it's just part of how I do it. I find it very useful and I encourage my trainees to do it.
>
> [Male, Ph.D., 25 years practice]

> I write down if there is a strong emotional reaction to something, and I sometimes will very cryptically jot down notes that have to do with particular people, names, or incidents. I always re-read my notes before the next session, and it keeps me up to date.
>
> [Female, M.S.W., 10 years practice]

> I'm interested in language, so I'll write one or two words. It's for me a way of focusing also. Instead of having to make eye contact the whole time, I can really think about listening. The other thing I do is listen for themes, so if I hear a theme I'll write a note to myself to come back to it.
>
> [Female, Ph.D., 5 years practice]

It's a means for me to contain some of my countertransference reactions, so I can listen more, hold off, and postpone my intervention. I might also write dreams, data, and so on.

[Male, Ph.D., 20 years practice]

Things people say. Feelings, quotations. Lately I've been trying to put down goals.

[Male, Ph.D., 15 years practice]

One therapist described an unusual situation, where the patient requested notes during the hour.

I took notes recently with a new patient who actually made that request, and said that she had a lot of fear that I would forget significant things that she said. It was very reassuring to her that I took notes because I was making sense out of what she was saying. As she became less anxious and panicky over the six months she was here, my notes became sparser and sparser. I was almost taking notes more for her than for me.

[Female, M.S.W., 20 years practice]

A few therapists described taking notes with analytic patients on the couch.

I take notes during an initial consultation, and during sessions with patients where we're doing analytically oriented work and they're talking about dreams or experiences or fantasies where there's a lot of free association going on.

[Female, M.D., 15 years practice]

I sometimes take notes with patients on the couch. Not with patients who sit up. I usually write down dreams, associations to dreams, and perhaps a few words about other important events in the hour or the patient's life.

[Male, Ph.D., 40 years practice]

Some, with patients who are in analysis and on the couch. In those sessions I try to get as close to verbatim notes as I can. With other patients I generally take some notes, just a few notes at the end of sessions, key points.

[Female, Ph.D., 15 years practice]

A number of people said that they take notes only during the first session or two, to gather factual data, history, names, and so on.

I take notes usually in a first meeting, rarely after that. If somebody is telling me something very specific, I'll ask them if they mind my writing it down, but usually not. Occasionally after a session. Periodically I'll make several pages of detailed notes on a particular session.

[Male, M.S.W., 20 years practice]

In the beginning of working with people, the first session, I'll often take a few basic notes, and do a basic genogram, especially with a couple or family, and then I rarely will take notes during a session.

[Female, Ph.D., 20 years practice]

Several people mentioned that they write down dreams, often verbatim, when they are reported in a session.

The only things I do write down are dreams.

[Female, M.S.W., 5 years practice]

Only when a person has a dream, then I write that down in the session.

[Male, M.S.W., 15 years practice]

Many therapists also said that taking notes during the session is difficult, and diverts their attention.

I don't like to take notes during a session. I'm taking notes on my control [training] case, and it's distracting.

[Female, M.S.W., 45 years practice]

I don't think you can listen and write at the same time. Also, I think it gives misleading messages when the patient sees you write down certain things and not others.

[Male, M.A., 15 years practice]

Even those who never take notes during a session will usually make notes after the session or at the end of the day. Here are some of the usual contents for these notes:

About a dream or something that took place in the patient's life that was momentous, or a new perspective they might have on an old issue. In general how they were feeling, better or worse.

[Female, M.S.W., 10 years practice]

I would note significant events that they reported, but mostly I'd write down process changes in the interview, in other words, times when I felt they became defensive and why, and some things they might report about their own dynamics.

[Male, M.S.W., 15 years practice]

Dreams, key phrases, names and ages of significant people. Not a lot.

[Female, M.S.W., 20 years practice]

Afterwards I write a little factual stuff I want to remember, like a name, but mostly a general sense of what the content of the session was. I write down dreams right away, and I make a note about my own reactions, and what I might watch for in the next session, in the patient and in myself.

[Female, M.S.W., 30 years practice]

Usually I try to have a little process capsule in the note. The length of the note corresponds to the richness of what's happening in the session. Some brief running commentary on the content of the session, things I found significant, things I said that were significant, and dreams.

[Male, M.D., 15 years practice]

Afterward, my method is to record on a tape, because I find that quicker. I record new content that emerges, sometimes dream material. I used to do that a lot more, but I don't anymore because I don't use dreams as much as I used to in analysis. Variations in feeling states that I note, things that I want to think about, connections that I might have made that I don't necessarily bring directly into the treatment but that go on in my mind.

[Female, M.S.W., 15 years practice]

I usually try to remember what I consider to be the key emotional events of the session, the moments that really capture what was going on with the patient, and what it suggests in terms of their psychology that I might not have picked up before.

[Male, Ph.D., 5 years practice]

Two kinds of things. One is concrete information: dates, numbers, contacts. And the other things are themes, issues, things I might want to come back to, or look for in the future but don't handle immediately. Startling comments or remarks. Something that makes a real impression at the time.

[Female, Ph.D., 30 years practice]

I'll write down a lot about history, if they're taking medication, when they feel anxious, how anxious they rate their anxiety. I have them fill out self-rating forms which I usually keep in their file.

[Female, Ph.D., 10 years practice]

I would write down family history issues that might be relevant to what's going on, some significant outcome of a particular session, a homework assignment that I might have given them, things of that sort.

[Male, Ph.D., 25 years practice]

Afterward, I would certainly make note of a change in mood, or having reported a serious depression, or a loss. If I was going to refer somebody for medication I would note that. I would note the discussion I had with the psychiatrist about them. And I usually note the general focus of the session.

[Female, M.S.W., 10 years practice]

I write down how somebody presented affect [showed feelings], if they spoke a lot that day, what specifically they talked about that day. I was reviewing some case notes today and realized I wrote a lot about what she wears, because that reflects how she's changed a lot.

[Female, M.S.W., 1 year practice]

One therapist said that he waits a while before making notes.

They're very private, and only for me, so I make it a dialogue with myself. I've learned that it helps to wait a while, not to let it be too fresh from the session. In the morning, when my wheels are turning and I have some private time, I get back to sessions from the last couple of days, and make notes. And it's very rich. I see connections that leap out at me.

[Male, M.S.W., 10 years practice]

A few people said they usually don't take notes at all, during or after sessions.

Not during or afterward. My memory's pretty good. I only take detailed notes if I'm in supervision, and periodically I'll go into supervision.

[Male, M.S.W., 35 years practice]

Not during or afterwards. Sometimes I summarize, every few months.

[Male, Ph.D., 15 years practice]

Not during, and not afterward as a rule. Once in a great while, I might write down a very important dream, or some kind of breakthrough.

[Female, M.S., 20 years practice]

For insurance purposes, I do those write-ups. But I don't take very many notes. I have a very good memory.

[Female, M.S.W., 25 years practice]

I used to do it more, and now I find that I don't need to. Generally, when you do this work for a long time, you develop a memory for things, and I remember most things I want to remember.

[Female, Ph.D., 20 years practice]

Even those who never take notes for themselves recognize that, in today's litigious climate, notes might be useful.

If there's something that I think could be a major problem, like a risk of suicide, I'll want to document that I was aware of it. It's a cover-your-ass note.

[Male, Ph.D., 20 years practice]

NUMERICAL DISTRIBUTION

During the session: 16 people said yes; 9 more said first session only; 5 said dreams only; 30 said rarely or never.

After the session: 42 people said yes; 18 said no.

Six people said they never or rarely take notes of any sort.

COMMENTS

The issues here are: Can the therapist take notes during a session and still be fully attentive to the patient? What is the effect on the patient of writing down certain things and not others? Are notes after the session useful? Is documentation in this age of litigation necessary?

I have never understood how a therapist can take notes during a session and still be listening to the patient. Unless it becomes a kind of automatic writing, having to watch the pad while the therapist take notes means not watching the patient, missing gestures, body movements, and facial expressions. Thinking about what is being written means paying less than complete attention to what is being said. Having the patient watch the therapist write down some things and not others, as with dreams, gives added weight and reinforcement to specific topics, and may lead the patient, consciously or unconsciously, to provide more of the reinforced material in an effort to please the therapist.

Although note-taking during the session seems to me to be counterproductive, I think that brief notes after the session are extremely useful. A few lines and highlights from the session can consolidate in the therapist's mind the themes of the hour, and can serve the following week to remind of unfinished business. While I think we all develop good memories, it seems an unnecessary burden to have to carry a treatment of several years in one's head.

Session-by-session notes for the entire course of a treatment can also serve as a tremendous resource for the therapist, documenting trends and patterns over a period of years. This can be especially important when an impasse or stagnant period occurs. In the rare event of some kind of legal procedure, comprehensive notes can protect the therapist.

RELATED READING

Andrews, J. D., Norcross, J. C., and Halgin, R. P. (1992). Training in psychotherapy integration. In *Handbook of Psychotherapy Integration,* ed. J. C. Norcross and M. R. Goldfried, pp. 563–592. New York: Basic Books.

Hickling, L. P., Hicklin, E. J., Sison, G. F., and Radetsky, S. (1984). The effect of note-taking on a simulated clinical interview. *Journal of Psychology* 116(2):235–240.

Wolfson, A., and Sampson, H. (1976). A comparison of process notes and tape recordings: implications for therapy research. *Archives of General Psychiatry* 33(5):558–563.

🅁🅁🅁🅁

Question 4: How do you set fees?

Setting the fee can be a complex yet imprecise process. Many of the therapists interviewed had trouble articulating exactly how they arrived at a fee. One person described just how complicated it can be.

> Usually, the patient over the phone asks me what the fee is, and I'll ask them if it's okay if we meet and discuss it. The interview is ten dollars more than the fee that we set, because I see the patient for an hour initially. If the patient insists, I will tell them a fee, but nowadays with insurance and managed care, you have to know what the insurance

situation is, because the carrier may set the fee. When I set it, it has to do with my years of experience. I have an ideal fee in terms of what I consider my professional self-worth. I do have hours for low-fee patients, people in training and such.

[Male, Ph.D., 20 years practice]

Setting the fee can be almost a capricious decision, made on the spot.

When I was first starting out, I had only one patient I'd taken with me from my internship, and I got a call from somebody I had met, and she wanted to see me. I knew she had money, so I knew it was not a case where I had to worry about what she could afford. She asked me what I charge, and my mind spun around, and I just came up with a number. I remembered feeling that was a fee I could feel comfortable with, given that I was just starting out. As I began practicing, and knowing what my peers charged, I began adjusting upwards.

[Male, Ph.D., 5 years practice]

I basically operate on a sliding scale. Fees range from $25 to $100. I base it on people's finances, to large extent. There are times when even if their finances can warrant it, there's a lot of resistance to paying what I think the fee should be, and depending on my mood and on whether I like the person, I'll agree or not.

[Male, Ph.D., 20 years practice]

Another person pointed out that charging a very low fee can be as much of a problem as a fee that is too high.

My regular fee is set by asking around. I want to stay in the ballpark of what's reasonable. I don't want people not to come because it's too high, and I don't want people to think there's something wrong with me because I'm charging so little.

[Female, M.A., 20 years practice]

Most practitioners said they had some kind of sliding scale, a range of fees from which to choose, depending on several variables. The "sliding scale" can mean different things to different people.

My fees are on a sliding scale. I have a central number, and that's a combination of what I thought most of my patients could afford and also some sense of what I thought I was worth and what I think a therapy session is worth.

[Male, M.S.W., 15 years practice]

I have a sliding scale, and there's a big range in what I charge. I see some patients for $30 a session and some for $100. It depends on what they can afford, but also on how frequently they come, and when during the day they can come.

[Female, Ph.D., 15 years practice]

I tell the person what my fee is. I set that by finding out what the range of fees are for our profession, and settling on something that's comfortable for me. If someone indicates that they're really having a problem with that fee, and I feel that we can work together, I'll make an adjustment, but the range of adjustment is no more than $15 below the regular fee.

[Female, M.S., 15 years practice]

I think I have a regular fee, but I also have a sliding scale. I start out by telling people my regular fee. I set that by talking to colleagues, seeing what the going rate is, and then I decide what I'm comfortable with.

[Female, M.S.W., 30 years practice]

I try to gauge what's fair. I have a sliding scale, and if somebody's struggling and really needs consideration, I'll lower the fee, and if somebody's very well-fixed I'll charge them the top fee. I set that by what feels reasonable to me. I think I was also influenced by what my own analyst charged, which was a very high fee.

[Female, M.S.W., 20 years practice]

I have a range of fees. I try to sense what the patient's situation is in terms of finances and burden of living, like a single parent with a kid. And I also try to take into account what they're comfortable with. Sometimes I'll say what my top fee is and explain, knowing that someone isn't going to be able to pay that, that it's my top fee and I have a sliding scale, and what do you think you'd be comfortable with? They'll name a figure and I'll say it's a little lower than I was thinking of, do you think you could manage this figure?

[Male, M.S.W., 20 years practice]

I have a sliding scale that has worked very well for me through the years. I've seen people for a very low fee, but to them it's like a million bucks. I have an average fee, and I've negotiated down and negotiated up.

[Male, M.S.W., 15 years practice]

One person said specifically that the fee was a mutual decision.

> By mutual discussion. The school of thought to which I belong says you set fees, and frequency of sessions, by mutual discussion when you establish a treatment contract.
>
> [Female, Ph.D., 20 years practice]

A few people said that a sliding scale can be a problem for them, because it can create a practice filled with long-term low-fee patients.

> I have a range, and I have a regular fee that I want. I set that at what I feel is reasonable, and what I'm worth, and what I need to live on. I will ask for my regular fee, and if someone says that's a problem I'll ask them what they think they can afford. Sometimes I have reduced the fee and then felt resentful, so I have to feel okay about working at a reduced fee. I also have two pro bono cases.
>
> [Female, Ph.D., 5 years practice]

> I have a basic fee. I set that based on years of experience, the going rate, right in the middle of the market rate for this area. I do some sliding, especially with people I'm currently working with who change jobs, or lose jobs, or their family situation changes. I feel very responsible to the people I'm currently working with. I do very little sliding with new people, especially now. I used to, when I was building up a practice. Now I don't do any.
>
> [Female, Ph.D., 20 years practice]

> I've done it a few ways. I started out having a set fee. Then somebody introduced the idea to me that their therapist had a fee range, like a twenty dollar range, and within that they let the person pick. So for a few years I did that. More recently I decided I'm going to have a flat fee again, and the fee that I want. Right now I have a bunch of lower fee people from way back, so anyone new I want to charge what I consider a good fee, and then it helps carry some of the lower fee people. At this point, I don't want to start with someone where it's going to be a many-year commitment at a low fee.
>
> [Female, M.S., 15 years practice]

Many practitioners said they set the fee based on what they believe others are charging.

> I have a basic fee, which I set by getting a sense of the general marketplace, and I've had a problem because the usual fee in my area for my level of professional is a little higher than I have been charging,

and I've had trouble raising it up there. The second part of the process is after I establish the fee with the clients, we assess their ability to pay, the maximum out-of-pocket amount they can pay. That plus the insurance reimbursement becomes the fee.

[Male, Ph.D., 25 years practice]

I on principle believe, particularly after I had been practicing for a while, that I should charge at least as much as a recent graduate of a residency, some psychiatrist who didn't know anything. So I keep my fee at least in front of theirs.

[Male, Ph.D., 20 years practice]

My standard fee is set on the basis of what I consider to be the going rate for my work. If it's a matter of a patient not being able to afford that, then my way of adjusting it is to get some idea of what their gross income is, take ten percent of that and divide it up by the number of weeks and sessions in the year. If it's too low, I can't see them.

[Male, M.D., 20 years practice]

I have a usual fee, which I set based on my experience and what I determine is a usual fee for colleagues that have around the same amount of experience. And then I have a lowest fee, below which I really can't go because of having to earn income.

[Female, M.S.W., 10 years practice]

Some set fees based on their expenses and costs.

I have a set fee, which I set as a business thing. I thought about what my rent is, and my insurance costs, and so on. Then I do see people on a sliding scale, which to me means sliding down, not sliding up if people have a lot of money.

[Male, Ph.D., 10 years practice]

Frequency of sessions is sometimes a factor in setting the fee.

I have a range of the fee that I would like to have, and that's a narrow range. The typical way I set a fee now is this: If a person is coming once a week, and I don't have any reason to believe that they're impoverished, then they pay the full fee. If they decide they can come twice a week, it's lower by about twenty percent. Three times a week it's even lower, and so on.

[Male, M.D., 20 years practice]

> I have a range, the minimum and the maximum. I set my regular fee according to what I think other people are charging. My minimum is for somebody who's really in need, or is in analysis three or four times a week.
>
> [Male, Ph.D., 40 years practice]

All these factors are sometimes included in the process of setting the fee.

> I have what I call my regular fee. I set that on the basis of what I hear that my colleagues are charging, and on the basis of my degree, with the assumption that psychiatrists charge more. Then, when I meet new people, I tell them what my regular fee is, and then I also say that I work on a sliding scale. I will adjust the fee if they think it's necessary, and more often than not, when I allow them to choose the fee they're comfortable with, it's more than I would have charged. Which over the years has continued to surprise me, and I've learned to keep my mouth shut.
>
> [Female, M.A., 20 years practice]

For at least one practitioner, it was a matter of simple arithmetic.

> It's very simple. I decide how much I want to earn during the year, how many hours I want to work a week, calculate how many hours that is, and divide. That sets my fee.
>
> [Male, Ph.D., 50 years practice]

Some therapists said that the economic climate is sometimes a factor, and therapists may have some anxiety about setting higher fees.

> That's changed in recent years, with managed care, and the economic situation. I say "Such-and-such is my fee. Is that a problem?"
>
> [Female, M.S.W., 45 years practice]

> I set fees according to what I think I can get to keep my practice at a certain level. Right now it's harder to get patients, and as a result I've been reluctant to raise my fees for a long time.
>
> [Male, Ph.D., 15 years practice]

> Because I'm new at it I tend to be really sappy about it. I go on a sliding scale, where I start at a certain fee and then come down if I need to. I have two really low fees in my group just to keep the group going.
>
> [Female, M.S.W., 5 years practice]

What the person can afford. It's been hard because of the HMO's taking over, so I've had to slide my fee to what people can pay without insurance.

[Female, M.S.W., 15 years practice]

Several people said that it was important to them to keep at least a few hours for low-fee patients, and not to turn away a motivated patient because of inability to pay the usual fee.

I have a fee that I try to get for individual and one for couples. Right now only about a quarter of my practice is able to pay that fee. Usually I get a sense of what they can afford. I have lower fees for people who can come in during the day than for people who come during prime hours. I've dropped my fee sometimes even by half for a student who can come during the day.

[Female, M.S.W., 20 years practice]

Because I haven't finished my analytic training, I set my fees a little lower than peers. I lower the fee for students, or for patients who can't afford it.

[Female, M.S.W., 15 years practice]

It depends. My full fee is one amount and more for couples, whom I see for a full hour. It's quite arbitrary. I do have a philosophy that this shouldn't be only for people who can pay that amount of money, because it is a lot of money. So I like to keep a portion of my practice for low-fee people.

[Female, M.S., 15 years practice]

I have a set fee, which I'm told is rather low. Most of them pay that. I have some at a lower fee, actors, unemployed, and so on.

[Female, M.A., 15 years practice]

I have a range of fees. Basically, I try to charge the going rate as best I get a sense of it. I try to keep my fees on the low end of the going rate so that I'm competitive. I will, if the person needs a lower fee, make some allowance for that. I see some people for a very low fee, because it's a way to see some very disturbed people for intensive treatment.

[Male, M.D., 15 years practice]

Most of my work is on salary. In my private practice, which is very small, it varies. I have a particular fee that seems to be the going rate, but I'm pretty flexible. If a patient is interesting to me and I want to work with them, and they can't afford the going rate, I will charge them less.

> [Male, M.D., 5 years practice]

Some use high fees to keep unwanted patients away.

> Last winter I was very busy, with twenty-two hours and I was teaching, and I was exhausted, so I upped my fee and said I'm not going to see anybody else unless they're paying a very high fee. If they didn't want to pay that fee, that was fine. When I get overtired, I raise my fees.
>
> [Female, M.S.W., 25 years practice]

Finally, one person described an unusual situation, where the patient paid more than the set fee.

> I even had one woman who was constantly falling behind in her bills, not just with me, and I work with people around money, because I think it's so vital, and I like to bring it right into the room and handle it. We tried all different solutions, and I finally suggested that when she paid me, she add a little extra, I think it was only five dollars, and that became a credit on her bill. She's now up to ten dollars each session, and she has plans for the accumulated money. I'm her banker.
>
> [Female, M.S., 15 years practice]

NUMERICAL DISTRIBUTION

(Some people mentioned more than one answer.) Twenty-one people said they set the fee based on their sense of the "going rate" for their background, experience, and location; 28 people said they set fees on a sliding scale, based on ability to pay, frequency of sessions, and other factors, in discussion with the patient; 5 people use a formula based on hours and expenses; 4 people said the fee is based on their experience and self-worth; 2 people said their fee was based on what they could get. Seven people said their fees were set by a clinic or a professional group of which they were a member.

COMMENTS

The issues here are whether therapists can articulate how they arrive at the fees they charge, and whether that process is fair to the patient and the therapist.

Setting fees is a fairly complicated procedure, and it seems that many therapists are less than clear about how they do it. The question of whether raising fees is an ethical thing to do is an interesting one (see Question 6). I think it would feel much cleaner to set new fees higher than to raise fees already set, although I have done both. When a new patient is referred by a current patient seen at a particular fee, it may be impossible to set the new fee higher than the old one.

I try to keep some kind of fee parity with colleagues of similar background and experience. Setting fees too low can be just as problematic as setting them too high, because it raises questions about the quality of the service offered.

RELATED READING

Glennon, T. M., and Karlovac, M. (1988). The effect of fee level on therapists' perception of competence and non-possessive warmth. *Journal of Contemporary Psychotherapy* 18(3):249–258.

Inman, D. J., and Bascue, L. O. (1984). Fee policies of psychologists in private practice. *Psychotherapy in Private Practice* 2(2):3–12.

Lasky, E. (1984). Psychoanalysts' and psychotherapists' conflicts about setting fees. *Psychoanalytic Psychology* 1(4):289–300.

Schultz, K. (1988). Money as an issue in psychotherapy. *Journal of Independent Social Work* 3:7–21.

Tulipan, A. B. (1983). Fees in psychotherapy: a perspective. *Journal of the American Academy of Psychoanalysis* 11(3):445–463.

🔊🔊🔊🔊

Question 5: When do you collect fees?

Fees are collected weekly by about a third of the sample. For some therapists, this is an issue related to trust that the patient will actually pay the bill.

> I collect usually every session. There are people who pay me on a monthly basis, once I've established trust and feel confident that they're going to pay.
>
> [Male, M.S.W., 10 years practice]

> I like to get paid at the beginning of each session. This is something I learned from my own therapist.
>
> [Female, M.S.W., 10 years practice]

> I collect weekly unless there's a problem, and that way I don't have to do a lot of bookkeeping.
>
> [Female, M.S.W., 20 years practice]

About one quarter prefer to be paid monthly, often because of the billing involved.

> I collect once a month, although I have a few people who prefer paying me by session. I bill the others at the end of the month and ask that they pay the first week of the next month.
>
> [Female, M.S.W., 20 years practice]

> My suggestion is once a month, that's what I prefer. If someone wants to pay every week, I'll go along with that, it doesn't bother me.
>
> [Male, Ph.D., 10 years practice]

> I'm lazy, and would rather it would be once a month, but most people prefer to pay each week.
>
> [Male, Ph.D., 20 years practice]

One person saw the patient's choosing to pay every week as a control issue.

> I collect fees usually ideally at the end of the month. There are certain patients, though, that want to be in control, I suppose, and they pay me every session, or they pay me every two weeks, and I let it go until the moment comes up and we begin to work on the meaning of it. I do say in the first session I'd like them to pay at the end of the month, but some patients go on their own.
>
> [Male, Ph.D., 20 years practice]

Insurance coverage is sometimes a factor in determining when therapy bills are paid.

> About fifty percent of the time I get the copayment at each session, and fifty percent I wait until after the insurance is in and get the copayment afterwards.
>
> [Male, Ph.D., 25 years practice]

> I collect at the time of the appointment for self-paid patients. For insurance cases, I have a billing service and it comes in through the insurance companies or the managed care companies.
>
> [Male, Ph.D., 20 years practice]

It also depends on things like insurance. I collect at each session if the person is paying me directly. If it's insurance coverage, we'll sometimes submit it and I'll collect from the insurance company.

[Male, M.D., 5 years practice]

Many people left it up to the patient to choose the payment schedule.

When I start with someone, I offer them the option of paying monthly or by session.

[Female, M.S.W., 20 years practice]

Mostly I collect them once a month, and I write a bill. But there are some people who feel much more comfortable paying me every week. I used to be resistant to that because I had my own way, and I felt that was the way it should be done. But I've realized that in those cases that's the way they need to operate with money and some of them know well enough that they have problems with money. So now I'm very flexible, and if you want to pay me every week, that's just fine.

[Female, M.S., 15 years practice]

Several people said that it didn't matter to them what the payment schedule is, as long as the patient is consistent.

I make it so that it's whatever it is: every week, every two weeks, or once a month, and that's what it remains.

[Male, Ph.D., 15 years practice]

I don't have a system. All I ask is that we have a consistent arrangement about it.

[Female, M.S., 15 years practice]

I tell everyone in the first session that I don't care if they pay me every week, every two weeks, three weeks, or monthly, but I don't want them to run up a bill of more than a month.

[Female, M.A., 15 years practice]

NUMERICAL DISTRIBUTION

Twenty-three people said they prefer to be paid weekly; 14 said they prefer to be paid monthly; 23 said they do whatever the patient prefers.

COMMENTS

The issues here are whether there is an optimum arrangement for payment, and whether the therapist or the patient decides which payment schedule is followed. If the patient prefers to pay weekly, does the therapist insist on monthly billing?

The traditional pattern of giving bills monthly seems to be changing, as more patients wish to pay weekly, and more therapists feel more protected by accounts kept current. I'm sure many readers have noticed the change in their physicians' offices, who now ask for payment at the time of the visit and no longer send bills. Many patients seem to prefer keeping current, and not having the pressure of a large bill at the end of the month.

About ten years ago, I started collecting fees weekly for all new patients. I used to collect them monthly but I got tired of some patients building up a balance and then quitting, still owing me two months or more, and of finding I was unable to collect that money. If, after some time, patients demonstrate their reliability and responsibility, we may sometimes switch to monthly billing.

RELATED READING

Herron, W. G., and Welt, S. R. (1992). *Money Matters: The Fee in Psychotherapy and Psychoanalysis.* New York: Guilford Press.

Meek, C. L. (1987). Suggestions on the collection of fees. In *Innovations in Clinical Practice: A Sourcebook,* vol. 6, ed. P. A. Keller and S. R. Heyman, pp. 271–276. Sarasota, FL: Professional Resource Exchange.

Pasternack, S. A. (1988). The clinical management of fees during psychotherapy and psychoanalysis. *Psychiatric Annals* 18(2):112–117.

Raney, J. O. (1983). The payment of fees for psychotherapy. *International Journal of Psychoanalytic Psychotherapy* 9:147–181.

⊠⊠⊠⊠

Question 6: Do you ever raise or lower a set fee?

A fee is set at the beginning of treatment. If treatment lasts for years, the therapist may feel some pressure to raise the fee. Conversely, if the financial situation of the patient changes and the patient is earning less, there may be some pressure for the fee to be reduced. How do our therapists handle these situations?

Several therapists discussed raising fees after a period of time.

> Right now I'm in the process of raising all my fees, because I think I'm underpaid.
>
> [Female, M.S., 15 years practice]

> There are a handful of people that have been with me for a very long time, where I have had to allow for some adjustment because they started so low.
>
> [Female, M.A., 15 years practice]

> I do raise a set fee, when someone's been here for years, I'll bring my fee up five or ten dollars.
>
> [Female, Ph.D., 20 years practice]

> I'll raise a fee after what seems like an appropriate amount of time, say every couple of years. If someone has straitened economic circumstances I'll lower the fee, although frankly I'm less inclined to do that at this point.
>
> [Male, M.D., 15 years practice]

> I'm my own boss, so I have to give myself salary increases periodically. If a certain amount of time goes by, I'll bring up the question of a fee increase with the patient.
>
> [Female, M.S.W., 20 years practice]

> I haven't in about three years, but I might again. If the patient's financial circumstances have improved, I would increase the fee.
>
> [Male, M.D., 20 years practice]

> I would raise a fee with the passage of time. If someone's fee has been the same for two years, I might say I'm increasing the fee as of a certain date and then we talk about it.
>
> [Female, M.A., 15 years practice]

Others discussed lowering the fee temporarily under certain circumstances.

> People that I've worked with for a long time, like if they decide to go back to school and have little money, I would see them for a lower fee. It's a growth thing when patients do that, and I'm not going to punish them for it.
>
> [Female, M.S.W., 10 years practice]

If someone loses their job or their insurance changes or they go under a managed care plan under which they have no coverage any more, then I'll reduce the fee, and if their circumstances change again, I'll have the understanding with them that they'll pay the regular fee again.

[Female, M.S.W., 10 years practice]

Others said they would sometimes lower a fee and sometimes raise it.

I set the fee. If the fee is less than the fee I want, I tell the patient it's not my regular fee, and when they can afford to raise their fee, they should. Once I set a fee, I don't raise it unless I raise all my fees. Even then, I don't raise it with patients where I think it would form an economic hardship. The way I raise my fee normally is to raise my entrance fee, which is not to take any more patients at the old fee. In the fullness of time, if the subject comes up, I discuss it with my old patients, and if they're willing to raise their fee we come to an agreement.

[Male, Ph.D., 50 years practice]

I'll lower a fee in the case of a severe loss of income, with the proviso that it's not just their way of making me take care of them. I'll raise it if their income increases considerably.

[Male, M.S.W., 10 years practice]

If circumstances change, if finances change. I'll do it in either direction. I've also seen people for a token fee for six months or a year, if I thought it was necessary, and not someone trying to put something over on me.

[Male, Ph.D., 20 years practice]

It depends on circumstances. If they're unemployed all of a sudden, I'll lower it for a while. If they're at a low fee, and suddenly come into more money, I'll raise it.

[Female, M.S.W., 20 years practice]

Raising would be done in general, because of rising costs or because the demand for my services encourages me to raise fees. Lowering fees is due to a financial situation that a patient might have. I'm flexible in that area.

[Male, Ph.D., 30 years practice]

I do lower a fee, and will raise it, but I don't do it automatically.

[Female, M.S.W., 45 years practice]

If someone's been steadily employed, and getting raises, I might do it annually or every two years. If someone's been ill, or out of work, I'll lower the fee.

[Female, Ph.D., 30 years practice]

In the course of the treatment over a period of years, the fee usually goes up, but it has occasionally gone down as well.

[Male, M.D., 20 years practice]

One therapist brought up an interesting issue about raising fees.

I very rarely do that. I once consulted with a lawyer about that, and he felt it was unethical, a breach of contract.

[Male, Ph.D., 40 years practice]

NUMERICAL DISTRIBUTION

(This question was added toward the end of doing the interviews, so not everyone got asked.) Of the 11 people who did answer the question, 9 said they raised fees in some circumstances, and 10 said they would lower it in certain circumstances.

COMMENTS

There are several issues raised by this question: Is it ethical to raise a fee once it is set? What are the effects on the patient and the treatment of raising or lowering a set fee?

Most of the therapists I know will raise fees every year or two, for both new patients, who begin at the higher fee, and current patients in long-term treatment. Salaried employees expect a raise each year, and professionals often feel entitled to the same kind of increase.

The question remains of whether it is ethical to raise existing fees. I would prefer to raise the fee only for new patients, but some patients stay with me for many years, and carrying them at the original fee may be a problem for me if it's very much lower than my current fee. Most patients will agree to a fee increase periodically, but may feel that they actually have little choice about agreeing.

Lowering fees may be equally complicated. I have no problem lowering a fee for a temporary financial crisis, but the patient may feel guilty about accepting the reduction, demeaned by the charity, and obligated to "behave." What if the only alternative to reducing the fee is a break in treatment? This is a difficult choice for both patient and therapist.

RELATED READING

Citron-Baggett, S., and Kempler, B. (1991). Fee setting: dynamic issues for
 therapists in private practice. *Psychotherapy in Private Practice* 9(1):45–
 60.
Erle, J. B. (1993). On the setting of analytic fees. *Psychoanalytic Quarterly*
 62(1):106–108.
Gumina, J. M. (1977). Fee reduction as an aid to therapy. *Professional Psychology* 8(1):88–94.
Lien, C. (1993). The ethics of the sliding fee scale. *Journal of Mental Health
 Counseling* 15(3):334–341.

⧓⧓⧓⧓

Question 7: What do you do when a patient owes you money?

There are two different situations where the patient owes money. When
the patient is still in treatment, it usually becomes a topic of discussion in
the session, although most therapists acknowledge that they don't like
having to confront the problem. When patients leave treatment with an
unpaid balance, the situation is very different. Making it a therapeutic topic
of discussion in session is no longer possible, and contact is limited to
phone calls and mailed bills.

The first situation is that of the patient still in treatment. Many therapists said that they consider money a very important issue, and definitely
part of the treatment.

> I get the money. If they're in therapy with me I make it a therapeutic
> issue to resolve it. I've never terminated with a therapy patient where
> we had an unresolved bill. It's not just a rationalization, but I really
> believe that it's important for them to be in a relationship with someone
> where they take care of their responsibilities. It's just a metaphor for
> all their other responsibilities.
>
> [Male, Ph.D., 25 years practice]

> I'm better about it than I used to be. I talk about it, explore it. I had a
> patient a long time ago who owed me a lot of money, and she came
> in and told me that she had just bought an expensive bicycle. So I got
> some supervision, and in the next session I said, "Can you think of any
> reason I should buy you a bicycle?" And it was wonderful. She got it,
> and for the first time in her life began to look at money realistically.

We worked out a payment schedule, and that was a model for her to set up all kinds of realistic budgets and plans.

[Female, M.S., 20 years practice]

I ask for it. Every time I give them a bill or they give me a check, I bring it up.

[Female, M.S.W., 5 years practice]

I have a policy of not allowing debts to build up, which is not entirely foolproof but helps in the majority of cases. If it looks like someone is not going to be able to pay the fee, I'll either decrease the number of sessions, or lower the fee, so that they do not incur debt. It's not healthy for the therapeutic relationship for a patient to be in debt. Occasionally, like when an insurance claim is denied, people can owe a lot, and then I ask them to pay as much as they can over time.

[Female, M.D., 15 years practice]

I analyze it, but I learned that it's often helpful to break it down into a schedule of payments they can make every week. Structuring it and giving them guidelines.

[Female, M.S.W., 30 years practice]

I have a technique I call "nudging." I consider money a very important element of the treatment. I don't think of the money as an external business arrangement between us, but as a major issue in the way they live their life. So if there's a money issue, we talk about it a lot and analyze it a lot. None of my patients owe me any money, and I've almost always been paid, eventually. There have been occasional very disturbed people who have left me with a bill.

[Male, Ph.D., 50 years practice]

A few therapists acknowledged that collecting fees could be difficult for them, partly because of their own angry feelings or other reactions.

I have a failing in that area. I let it go too long. And yet it's been something that I can let go. I consider a bad debt one of the problems of business, or a misjudgment or countertransference on my part.

[Male, Ph.D., 30 years practice]

I don't have any problem raising it with people who just haven't paid for two months. With people who let it slide a week or maybe don't pay until the fourth week of the month, and I've got a lot of people who haven't paid yet, there's part of me that's very resistant to addressing that. I don't know whether I'm identified with their money crunch because I'm having a money crunch, or what it is exactly.

[Female, M.S.W., 20 years practice]

I don't like it, and I bring it up in the session. I've learned to bring it up in a gentle enough way so that even though I may feel angry, I don't act on it. I'm never going to get anywhere unless we analyze it and find out what it means.

[Female, M.S.W., 20 years practice]

I talk to them about it right away. I used to let things go, and I've gotten stiffed, so I don't let anything go any more. I think it was hard for me to ask for money, so I didn't bring it up, but now I'm very comfortable.

[Female, M.S., 15 years practice]

Several people pointed out that owed money can become a topic that dominates the session to the exclusion of other subjects.

It can dominate the treatment, and that's horrible. I hate to work as a bill collector.

[Male, Ph.D., 5 years practice]

It depends on who it is. I've learned through experience not to allow people to build up large debts. It doesn't work, because I get resentful and the person gets guilty. It floods the treatment, so I will terminate the treatment. Certain people have owed me money and paid it.

[Female, Ph.D., 20 years practice]

Several other therapists said they would also terminate a patient who built up a substantial balance.

If a patient owes me money, and the person has money, then we analyze it. If the patient has money and is just simply not paying then we terminate.

[Male, M.S.W., 35 years practice]

I have a policy where I will tolerate up to one month's debt, and beyond that I won't work with someone. That's how I protect myself from people who walk off owing one month. It pisses me off.

[Male, Ph.D., 10 years practice]

I haven't had too much problem with that. At the end of the month, I deal with it right away. I would terminate if the person got a month behind. This has changed over the years. I used to be very bad about it, and got stuck for lots of money. But now I'm on top of it, I don't have that as a problem. But it took me a long time to learn that.

[Male, Ph.D., 25 years practice]

I either make a contract with them that they have to pay a certain amount every month, or they have to take a vacation from therapy until they pay off their bill. Early on, patients would leave owing money. Now I see it coming and don't let it go on so long.

[Female, M.S.W., 20 years practice]

I always make it part of everything else that's going on in the treatment. If the bill becomes too much, I'm not going to let them build up a bill. I'm going to terminate.

[Female, M.S.W., 20 years practice]

At least one other person tried a different approach.

I try to be kind and generous, and not say anything, just wait patiently.

[Male, M.S.W., 10 years practice]

Others said that if a patient were having difficulty paying for treatment they would consider lowering the fee (see also Question 6).

You learn from when you're ripped off. It has taught me not to allow people to run up a debt. It's not good for the patient or for the therapist. If the person is really in financial straits, I'd rather reduce their fee, and then raise it back when the situation changes.

[Female, M.S.W., 15 years practice]

I don't have that situation, because I talk about it at the beginning and I make it clear, and they get billed every month. So people have to explain to me why they haven't paid, and if it's a realistic problem, there are times when I know I don't get paid, like if someone lost their job. If that happens, I'll say that the situation has changed, they're not working anymore, and don't they think we should talk about lowering the fee. I'd rather they paid less, but paid it, so they would feel that they were being honorable.

[Female, Ph.D., 10 years practice]

This therapist also suggested that the therapist must also bear some responsibility for the situation of the patient owing a large amount.

> When the situation happens that the client owes money, it means that the therapist has not been the adult in the situation in terms of talking about it and making it realistic. And setting limits too, that if you're not going to pay, I can't continue seeing you. I'll refer you to a low-cost clinic. I'm not going to wait for four months until your bill is huge. I'm going to talk about it in a week or two.
>
> [Female, Ph.D., 10 years practice]

The other situation is that of the patient who stops treatment owing money. There are different strategies for collecting these debts, but none of them is always successful and trying to deal with the patient under these conditions can be frustrating.

> There are times when I feel uncomfortable asking, as if I'm being crude, which is such an interesting reversal of reality. There have been times when I have refused to give up when someone owes me money, and have sent bills for as long as two years, and got the money. I felt like I won a war. I don't do that all the time. There are plenty of times when I just give up.
>
> [Female, M.A., 20 years practice]

> Call them, and tell them I'm wondering about that, what kind of arrangement we can make. I pursue it directly myself.
>
> [Male, Ph.D., 25 years practice]

> I pester them. I bill them regularly for a couple of months, and if they don't respond I call them. A couple of colleagues have sued patients, but I haven't even sent them into collection. I try to cleverly make them feel guilty.
>
> [Male, M.D., 20 years practice]

> I'm relentless: letters, phone calls. Generally I get it.
>
> [Female, M.A., 20 years practice]

> Try to get it. Find out what's going on. I have lots of people who've never paid me. I've discussed this with supervisors a lot. I don't send bills, because that gives a negatively suggestible patient an opportunity to defy you and never pay.
>
> [Female, Ph.D., 20 years practice]

Several people said that after pursuing debts for some time, they reach a point where it doesn't feel worth pursuing.

Most of all, I try to get it, one way or another. I've never used legal means. If it gets to that point I just drop it.
[Male, M.S.W., 25 years practice]

Send them some polite notices, bills. And then after a while, I drop it.
[Female, M.S.W., 15 years practice]

A few therapists give the unpaid accounts to collection agencies or lawyers.

Patients who are no longer seeing me, I tell them to pay me. They get three bills at thirty-day intervals, and a final notice, which is a letter indicating that they leave me no option. Ultimately I'll send it off for collection.
[Male, Ph.D., 20 years practice]

I've been through a lot about that over the years. I did go to small claims court once, and the threat of that made the person decide to pay me. I try to keep the bills from getting very big. I deal with it right away now, if someone owes money.
[Female, M.S.W., 15 years practice]

Very few practitioners said that collecting fees was rarely or even never a problem.

I very rarely have a bill. I've never been stiffed, ever.
[Female, M.A., 15 years practice]

I discuss it with them. I've had very few problems with patients owing me money. If it's in arrears, I discuss it with them and try to deal with it analytically.
[Male, Ph.D., 40 years practice]

NUMERICAL DISTRIBUTION

In those cases where patients are still in treatment, almost everyone said they would discuss the situation with them, although 7 people said this topic was a difficult one. Seven said they would try to work out a payment schedule for the unpaid amount. Only 2 people said they would not bring up the topic for discussion. Five people said they would reduce the frequency of sessions or have the patient stop treatment until the balance was paid. Another 3 people said they would reduce the fee.

In the case of the patient who has left treatment with an unpaid balance, 40 people said they would send bills, and another 10 said they would call. Only 2 people said they would take some kind of legal action or turn the bill over for collection.

COMMENTS

This question brings up several issues: What is the best way to deal with a patient whose bill is in arrears? What is best for the treatment? What is the best way to protect the therapist's income? Is it ethical to terminate a patient who owes money? Once a patient has left treatment, how does the therapist collect what is owed? Are lawyers and collection agencies ethical methods for the therapist?

Money is an area of some difficulty for many therapists: setting fees, collecting payments, pursuing debts. The patient who leaves treatment owing money is especially difficult to deal with because we have little if any leverage, and maintaining the debt is a way for the patient to maintain the connection with the therapist, as well as being able to passive-aggressively express anger not expressed during treatment.

Once a patient leaves, my experience is that it becomes exponentially more difficult to collect unpaid bills. Most therapists recognize that the occasional uncollected debt is part of the business, but it is still frustrating and sometimes infuriating. Several therapists mentioned that it is often easier to let the money go than to spend time and energy trying to collect it.

The situation of a patient currently in treatment who owes money is also difficult. The therapist may tend to let people go too long in arrears, and then they may terminate, perhaps partly out of guilt and the pressure of the accumulated debt. The therapist may resent having to deal with someone who isn't keeping even the most basic agreements, and the anger can make it hard to discuss the problem. On the other hand, most therapists don't like the idea of abandoning a patient in a temporary financial crisis. Lowering the fee until the crisis passes sometimes helps, but may create complications of its own (see Question 6).

RELATED READING

Klebanow, S., and Lowenkopf, E. L. (1991). *Money and Mind.* New York: Plenum Press.

Knapp, S., and VandeCreek, L. (1993). Legal and ethical issues in billing patients and collecting fees. *Psychotherapy* 30(1):25–31.

MacHovec, F. (1985). To sue (clients) or not to sue: is this a question? *Psychotherapy in Private Practice* 3(2):75–78.

🏵🏵🏵🏵

Question 8: How do you deal with insurance?

Insurance for psychotherapy has become a reality that almost all therapists have to deal with. Patients have come to expect reimbursement or insurance coverage and will sometimes stop treatment when the coverage runs out. Insurance companies ask for (sometimes demand) details of treatment and of the patient's personal life, with no way to guarantee the confidentiality of that material.

Most practitioners said that when insurance coverage is being used, they ask the patient to pay them directly first and wait to be reimbursed by the insurance company. Here are some typical responses:

> The patient pays me, and I give them the bill which they give to the insurance company.
>
> > [Female, M.S., 15 years practice]

> I like the patient to pay my fee and then I give them a bill every month for their insurance company.
>
> > [Female, M.S.W., 10 years practice]

In cases of hardship, practitioners will often make other arrangements.

> I fill out the insurance forms and give it to the patients to submit. I prefer for them to pay me directly, but I have patients who are financially tight, and as long as they pay me the difference, I will wait for the insurance to come through.
>
> > [Male, M.S.W., 20 years practice]

> Sometimes patients pay me and get reimbursed. There are some instances where they've waited to get paid and then paid me.
>
> > [Male, M.S.W., 25 years practice]

> Mostly I have clients pay me. But when it's really iffy for a client, if it would be a hardship—I don't think therapy should hurt, I don't think it should be pain and suffering. For some clients to front the money is too much of a burden.
>
> > [Female, M.S.W., 15 years practice]

> Those who don't have much money and depend on their insurance, I wait. I don't like to do that, though, because some companies are very slow.
>
> > [Female, M.S.W., 20 years practice]

Patients pay me usually. If someone's lost their job, I'll let them pay me a portion and get the rest from the insurance.

[Male, M.S.W., 10 years practice]

If the person has a decent income, then they pay me and I fill out the forms and they get reimbursed. There have been cases where the person is on disability, for example, and I collect from the company.

[Female, Ph.D., 30 years practice]

Several therapists mentioned that managed care was changing the rules in this area.

If a patient is using insurance I fill out the forms. It's becoming more of a problem with all of the managed care cases.

[Male, M.S.W., 35 years practice]

With managed care, I have to get paid directly from the insurance company. I never call the shots anymore. I deal with it the best I can but I don't deal with it very well.

[Male, Ph.D., 10 years practice]

It used to be that they would pay me and then they would get the insurance reimbursement. These days, with the managed care, you can't do that, because the patient has no choice, even if they want to pay, the insurance company insists that you get the co-payment, whatever it is, and the rest you get from the insurance company. That's the way they monitor things.

[Male, Ph.D., 20 years practice]

I have a very few people who are on managed care, and it's a total mess. I have more uncollected fees in one year of managed care than in the previous twelve years of practice put together.

[Female, M.D., 15 years practice]

A number of therapists said that their credentials sometimes made it difficult to get insurance coverage.

I accept insurance, but I have to tell people that I may not be covered with my credentials.

[Female, M.S., 15 years practice]

I don't. I'm not licensed, and I don't ask anyone to sign as my supervisor.

[Male, M.S.W., 10 years practice]

> I can't get insurance yet, because you have to be practicing five years.
>
> [Female, M.S.W., 5 years practice]

> I work with a psychiatrist who co-signs the forms.
>
> [Female, M.A., 15 years practice]

And a very few simply declined to accept insurance at all.

> I don't accept insurance, except for very rare cases, and so I don't deal with it all.
>
> [Male, M.S.W., 15 years practice]

A few people mentioned some of the difficulties of using insurance coverage (discussed in more detail in Question 9).

> I try to understand the influence of the insurance reimbursement on the treatment, especially the issues of breaching of confidentiality.
>
> [Male, M.D., 20 years practice]

> I'm very reluctant to reveal anything about a patient so I use the same diagnosis for virtually everyone and that's 300.40 depressive neurosis, which basically means that they're not very happy. It's the least stigmatizing diagnosis in the DSM.
>
> [Male, M.S.W., 15 years practice]

> Most of my patients are either anxiety disorders or dysthymia because I don't like revealing personal information. I know there's no such thing as confidentiality in medical records, that's just a bogus lie, so I use socially acceptable diagnoses.
>
> [Male, Ph.D., 25 years practice]

> Sometimes there's private insurance, and that becomes a problem because of confidentiality. I don't like to write personal information, but often the patient says "I need to be in therapy, I want to be here" and they give me the green light, and say "Write what you want, write what will keep me in treatment."
>
> [Female, M.S.W., 10 years practice]

NUMERICAL DISTRIBUTION

Thirty-nine people get paid by the patient, who then collects reimbursement from the insurance company; 4 of the above group added that in specific cases of hardship, they are willing to wait until the patient gets the insurance check to get paid themselves; 10 accept assignment and get paid directly by the insurance carrier; 6 get paid by a managed care plan; 3 do not accept insurance of any kind.

COMMENTS

The issues here are: Who is responsible for paying for therapy? What are the effects of insurance on the treatment?

The cleanest psychotherapy situation is one in which there are no outside intrusions. Insurance coverage was a minor intrusion until recently (see Question 9). I think most therapists prefer that the patient pay for treatment himself or herself, but few therapists could survive today with that requirement. Patients have come to expect that insurance will be accepted and used to pay at least some portion of the fee.

Insurance plans can become a problem with obvious effects when they ask for details of treatment, limit number of sessions, or terminate coverage. Unconsciously, using insurance may have meanings for the patient that affect the course of treatment in more subtle ways. For example, using insurance may symbolize dependency and not feeling fully adult, which could retard a patient's progress.

RELATED READING

Clamar, A. (1983). Third party payments: implications for practitioner and patient. *American Journal of Forensic Psychology* 1(4):3–10.
Halpert, E. (1972). The effect of insurance on psychoanalytic treatment. *Journal of the American Psychoanalytic Association* 20:122–133.
Small, R. F. (1992). How to maximize insurance reimbursement. In *Innovations in Clinical Practice: A Source Book*. Vol. 11, ed. L. VandeCreek, S. Knapp, and T. L. Jackson, pp. 227–239. Sarasota, FL: Professional Resource Press.

◙◙◙◙

Question 9: How have the changes in insurance coverage affected you?

In the good old days, patients who used insurance were given a bill at the end of the month, which they could submit to the insurance company for reimbursement. While some patients still do this, more and more patients are part of HMO, PPO, and managed care plans. The plan lists the therapists from whom the patient may select, determines the fee and the number of covered sessions, and demands details of treatment and of the patient's personal situation. None of the therapists in the survey group was happy about the changes.

Some therapists focused on the question of the limits of coverage and the length of treatment.

> Recently, I had a patient who had an eight hundred dollar limit, and when he reached that, he said he had to wait till next year to come back. He broke off for the summer. He may come back in the fall, but he'll have to pay all of it himself.
>
> [Male, Ph.D., 40 years practice]

> It's a problem, with all of the interference, and you've got to check with them beforehand, and there's always somebody who's practicing triage who's a damn clerk. Fortunately, the first time I had to deal with this, the person doing the triage was a clinical psychologist, so I was lucky.
>
> [Male, M.S.W., 35 years practice]

Some focused on the issue of confidentiality.

> One patient's employer switched over to an HMO, which wanted all kinds of personal details about the patient and the treatment. The patient and I discussed what I would and would not reveal. I was as vague and general as I could be.
>
> [Male, M.A., 15 years practice]

> I'm concerned about confidentiality, too. When I do these phone reviews that they've mandated, I always ask who I'm talking to, what's their discipline and licensure. Sometimes it's a clerk. Originally I refused to do it over the phone. I would only do it by mail, and one place went along with that, and that way I have more control. Many of these companies tape the conversations. Now that I've become part of the managed care, I've had to agree to do these reviews.
>
> [Male, Ph.D., 20 years practice]

> I have a few managed care cases now, where you have to call every ten weeks or so to ask for more sessions. I have some concerns about telling private information that is extremely current to people who are going to judge whether this person is going to be reimbursed. People have wanted the coverage and have asked me to do it.
>
> [Female, M.S.W., 10 years practice]

Some therapists focused on the problem of fees.

> I have many more people who don't have insurance that covers them, because they're in one of the managed care networks where they have to use specific practitioners and the number of sessions is very limited. So they choose to go outside the network, and wind up coming to me if I'm willing to see them at a lower fee. Many of the new patients I've gotten this year are lower fee, instead of getting hooked up with one of the managed care places. I find that I have to see many more people to make the same amount of money.
>
> [Female, M.S.W., 20 years practice]

> I have two managed care plans that I've picked up because current patients have been involved with them. I felt that I had to do it. I have eight people on managed care now, and that's far too many. My fees there are a third less than I normally charge.
>
> [Female, Ph.D., 20 years practice]

> My fees have dropped. A patient who went on a health plan, his fee dropped from ninety-five to sixty dollars.
>
> [Female, M.S.W., 25 years practice]

Several people mentioned the additional paperwork and the time on the phone with case managers and billing clerks.

> I spend several hours each week on additional paperwork, trying to organize myself. I'm not in a position to hire a secretary, so they have added a new dimension to my work: keeping records, insurance forms, photocopies, co-payments, and so forth.
>
> [Male, Ph.D., 20 years practice]

> It's affected me a lot. I'm in a couple of managed care plans. First, it's caused me to have to learn an entire new language, and to have to think about therapy in different ways than I ever did before. I'm not great at dealing with bureaucracy so I've had three or four screaming fights with one place. They have professionals as case managers, but the billing part is done by a clerk, so first you have to do a special report, which a professional reads and then they call you and discuss the case with you. Then the billing goes to another section. I was supposed to get a check, and received a check for less than half that amount. The clerk says, "You didn't put the CPT code on the form." I didn't even know what a CPT code was. I said, "There's no place on the form to put a CPT code." She says, "Oh, we know. We're changing the form."

I said. "How would I know to put the code on the form if there's no place to put it and you didn't notify me to add CPT codes to the form?" They automatically billed me at the lower rate instead of calling me and asking me.

[Female, M.S.W., 10 years practice]

I don't think I've lost anyone because of it, but I find it very irritating to have to fill out a lot of forms, and go after insurance companies that are reluctant to pay.

[Female, M.S.W., 30 years practice]

For some therapists, the problem was to get into the plans and get on the lists.

I can't get on any managed care lists, because they're closed. I think if I had a bigger practice it would be a real problem, but if I had a bigger practice, I'd probably be more actively trying to get on the lists.

[Female, Ph.D., 10 years practice]

Someone was referred to me who was on a managed care plan, but I wasn't on their list, so I didn't get the referral.

[Male, Ph.D., 5 years practice]

It's done some damage to my practice, because I was so reluctant to join up with the managed care networks that I held out too long, and now when it's clear that you can't function without them, they're closed. It's had a negative impact on my practice.

[Male, Ph.D., 20 years practice]

I haven't been able to get into the managed care plans. I've tried to get into them and they seem to be closed.

[Female, M.S.W., 15 years practice]

A lot of people are in plans where they can't get reimbursed for me. And I can't get onto plans because they're filled up, and they don't refer to me. I'm definitely adversely affected.

[Female, M.S.W., 15 years practice]

Some people who haven't been seriously affected yet are anticipating the future with some concern.

I'm not in any managed care programs. I really think they're unethical, and I have to deal with them for clients, but my practice has been so

bad, they really dictate treatment. If I have to continue dealing with
them, I'm going to have to come up with another way of working.

[Female, Ph.D., 5 years practice]

They're affecting my attitude and my future concerns rather than my
present situation. It's an everyday issue for me, because I tend to worry
about the future. I'm on one provider list, and it's a big company, and
they limit the fee, and you have to justify every five sessions. It affects
the nature of the therapy relationship. It makes me very discouraged,
because you can't really form a bond. You spend half the time talking
about insurance, and whether you're going to get authorization. It
becomes a medical necessity, so it's not psychotherapy. You're limited,
and so you can't just let something develop.

[Male, Ph.D., 15 years practice]

Some practitioners said they were hoping to be able to avoid getting involved in managed care, and that their practices would survive without it.

I've gotten solicitations from some of the HMOs to fill out their forms
and be on their panel, but I haven't done it. I don't know that I want
to get referrals that way. I get most of my referrals from my patients.

[Female, M.A., 15 years practice]

The HMOs exclude me because they get their own providers and they
pay very little. On the other hand, as my recent numbers have shown,
I'm still a viable entity in the marketplace.

[Male, Ph.D., 25 years practice]

I prefer not to accept insurance patients if I can. I find their requirements
onerous, in terms of the paperwork, and I find that they have no interest
whatsoever in long-term psychodynamic therapy.

[Male, Ph.D., 50 years practice]

I'm not a member of any managed care organizations. I prefer not to
do that. I'm very much concerned, as are all psychoanalysts, with the
effect that managed care is going to have on our profession.

[Female, Ph.D., 20 years practice]

I hate dealing with the insurance companies. I'd rather take half a fee
than deal with the managed care companies, and all that writing. I
recognize the need for it on a theoretical basis, but the way it's done,
there's something not right about it.

[Male, Ph.D., 20 years practice]

NUMERICAL DISTRIBUTION

Twenty-eight people said they had not yet been affected; 6 said managed care plans were closed to them; 12 mentioned the intrusiveness of the plan in terms of confidentiality or number of sessions; 4 mentioned that they had lost patients when they were not part of the managed care plan, or when the benefits ran out; 3 mentioned having to accept a lower fee; 6 mentioned the additional paperwork and telephone contact required by the managed care plans.

COMMENTS

Issues in this area include: What are the effects of managed care on patients and treatment? What are the effects on the therapist and his or her practice?

The changes in insurance coverage due to managed care are affecting every therapist's practice. Many therapists I know would prefer lowering their fees so patients could pay on their own to dealing with managed care.

Patients may have to stop treatment when insurance coverage ends or be unable to begin with the practitioner of their choice if that therapist is not covered by the insurance plan. Confidentiality is a shambles, with patient records and personal details available to the insurance carrier and sometimes revealed to the employer, intentionally or inadvertently. It may be very difficult for patients who know that the number of sessions covered by insurance may be limited to feel safe enough to engage fully in the process.

This entire situation of managed care seems to me to be an inevitable outgrowth of the medical model of psychotherapy. The emphasis on treatment plans and symptom alleviation makes long-term personality exploration and restructuring virtually impossible. An important question is whether the practicing psychotherapists in this country have to go along with the takeover of our field by the insurance companies.

RELATED READING

Austad, C. S., and Sherman, W. O. (1992). The psychotherapist and managed care: how will practice be affected? *Psychotherapy in Private Practice* 11(2):1–9.

Giles, T. R. (1991). Managed mental health care and effective psychotherapy: a step in the right direction? *Journal of Behavior Therapy and Experimental Psychiatry* 22(2)83–86.

Kisch, J. (1990). Psychotherapy: dilemmas of practice in managed care. *Psychotherapy in Private Practice* 11(2):33–37.

Sederer, L. I., and Mirin, S. M. (1994). The impact of managed care on clinical practice. *Psychiatric Quarterly* 65(3):177–188.

Todd, T. (1994). *Surviving and Prospering in the Managed Mental Health Care Marketplace.* Sarasota, FL: Professional Resource Press.

ⓇⓇⓇⓇ

Question 10: What do you tell patients about confidentiality?

This used to be an easy question. We told all our patients that everything that was said in the sanctity of the consulting room was completely confidential. Many therapists still see the question this way.

> I would never reveal anything that a patient told me in an individual session or in group. I wouldn't bring it up. I would never talk about patients to other patients. I would never reveal names to supervisors. I have strict rules because it's very important.
>
> [Female, M.S.W., 20 years practice]

> I don't talk about patients, unless it's in supervision. I try not to use any identifying information even then. I've never warned a patient that there are exceptions.
>
> [Female, M.S.W., 30 years practice]

> Everything that takes place in this room is confidential, and to talk about a patient and to identify a patient to anyone outside of here is a breach of their confidence. And I try to obey it religiously.
>
> [Male, M.S.W., 35 years practice]

> I tell patients whatever happens in here is totally confidential, and I wouldn't even tell anybody that you are in treatment. The only way that is changed is if they give me permission. The legal exceptions have never come up for me in my practice.
>
> [Female, M.S., 15 years practice]

> I tell them that if there is a third party who wants to communicate with me about them I will inform them before saying anything about them to anybody else.
>
> [Male, M.D., 15 years practice]

My own rules are pretty fixed. I don't discuss anyone by name. I do use examples, now that I'm teaching, but I never use any names. I don't discuss patients with other patients, which is important because many patients are interconnected. Over the years I see many more patient-initiated referrals than outside referrals, so people know each other, and they very often try to fish for information, and I have to confront them.

[Female, M.A., 15 years practice]

I'm pretty strict about that. I don't discuss patients by name with other therapists. If I work with two people who know each other I will not reveal anything to either of them about the other.

[Female, M.S., 15 years practice]

The only person I would speak to about a patient is my supervisor, and she's not affiliated with the clinic.

[Female, M.S.W., 10 years practice]

Anything they say doesn't leave the room, unless they ask me to talk to someone and I get their approval.

[Female, M.A., 15 years practice]

I tell them that what is said in here is strictly and completely confidential, that I do not disclose anything, even whether they've seen me or not, without permission.

[Male, M.D., 20 years practice]

I see individuals and families and groups, so the rules are a little different. Certainly an individual is free to discuss their therapy with anyone they wish. In group people can speak about their own reactions but not about other group members. I don't discuss my patients except if they're working with another therapist, say for medication, or group, or marital therapy, or in a supervision situation where the patient is never identified by name.

[Female, M.S.W., 10 years practice]

As suggested in this last remark, the question of confidentiality gets more complicated when working with more than a single individual: couples, families, groups.

Sometimes I'll meet with the parents of a child patient, and explain that I'll meet with them to talk about their concerns, but I'm not going to tell the child's secrets. Or I might ask the child for permission to talk about something.

[Male, M.S.W., 20 years practice]

Even with adolescents and children, I have certain boundaries about what I will and won't discuss with a parent. Sometimes I'll clear it with the adolescent, talk to them about what I will or won't discuss with their parents. I certainly don't discuss patients outside of my office. In supervision groups I will, but I keep identifying data very hidden.

[Female, M.S.W., 15 years practice]

Because I'm a family therapist, I've had issues with that, because often-times I'll do separate sessions with two people in a couple, or especially with an adolescent. My general rule for this is that if I learn something that I think is really salient for the other person to know, I say that I won't divulge what they've told me, but I feel it's imperative to let the other person know, and let's talk about how I can help them do that. With an adolescent, I tell them that everything is confidential unless I feel there's a danger, and if I do, I'm going to tell the parents. I'll never do it behind their back, I'll always tell them I'm going to do it.

[Female, Ph.D., 20 years practice]

With children, it's a little complicated. I tell them what we talk about is completely between the two of us. If they want me to say anything to their parents, I'll do that, but I'll tell them about it first and talk to them again afterwards. If I'm having a meeting with the parents, I'll talk about it beforehand with the child. Or if the parents have called with a specific question, I'll tell the child about that.

[Female, Ph.D., 15 years practice]

Because I don't usually work with individuals, if I see a person alone, we talk about it first in the context of the relationship system, and I get permission among all parties to do that. Although I don't necessarily inform anybody what we talk about, I let everybody know that I don't hold confidences, and if there's something that compromised the trust among us all, I would ask the person to reveal it, and if they wouldn't, I would discontinue my role with them.

[Male, Ph.D., 25 years practice]

When I work with couples I discuss it because I usually will see them individually, and whatever is said in those sessions will stay there.

[Female, Ph.D., 5 years practice]

Things are a lot more complicated these days, and currently there are two major problem areas affecting this question. The first problem is the limitations on confidentiality applied as a result of the *Tarasoff* case in California, and the court decision that the therapist who knows of a patient's intention to harm another person has a legal obligation to warn that other person. This has also been extended to include the instances of suicidal patients, whose intention is to harm themselves, not someone else. In addition, knowledge of child abuse is now also included in the legal obligation to report a situation.

The second problem is the increasing involvement of health insurance managers in the treatments of their clients. More and more, the insurance companies feel entitled to ask (or demand) personal details of the issues of treatment, projections of the length of treatment, diagnoses, and other previously private material.

How are we dealing with these intrusions? The *Tarasoff* issue appears to be considerably easier for many therapists to handle.

> I read them the psychotherapy Miranda act, which basically says everything you tell me is in confidence except if you tell me that you're going to hurt yourself or somebody else and I have to stop you. Or if you tell me about child abuse, and I have to turn you in, even if you're committed to treatment. I'm really unhappy about that last piece, but so be it.
>
> [Male, Ph.D., 25 years practice]

> Absolutely nothing that gets said in my office leaves my office, with the exception of child abuse, and I do warn people about that.
>
> [Male, M.S.W., 15 years practice]

> Everything is confidential provided you're not going to hurt yourself or somebody else. If I have a clear indication that you're going to do that, I like to get somebody to contact in case of an emergency.
>
> [Female, M.S.W., 10 years practice]

> Everything's confidential. I'm in a peer supervision group, so I'll use a first name in discussing a case. I have had to tell people that there are exceptions to the rule of confidentiality if they're a danger to themselves or others. It's usually that they're a danger to themselves.
>
> [Female, M.S.W., 25 years practice]

> There have only been a couple of instances over the twenty-five years where I felt the person was going to do something dangerous or illegal, and I said "I want you to know that if I really think you're going to murder your wife, then I'm going to tell somebody."
>
> [Male, Ph.D., 25 years practice]

> I tell them that everything they tell me is privileged, and that I am legally obliged to keep their confidences. I do tell them that I cannot

withhold information about a crime, and if the courts order me to, I would follow the instructions of the court.

[Male, Ph.D., 50 years practice]

I give a kind of standard spiel, that everything they say here is confidential, with certain exceptions. That I'm obligated by law, if I think that they're going to be a danger to themselves or others, and I may say something about the *Tarasoff* case.

[Male, Ph.D., 20 years practice]

Those therapists working in an agency setting or even a group practice may deal with this issue more concretely, by presenting a written explanation that the patient signs.

I read them a form which explains to them the limits of confidentiality, I have a pre-printed form that I use, and at the end of the first session I always have them sign a copy and I also make a note in the official clinical log, not my process notes but the clinical log, indicating that the patient has been informed of the limits of confidentiality.

[Male, Ph.D., 20 years practice]

I assume it, unless they bring it up. Patients that come through the clinic read and sign a release that discusses the exceptions.

[Female, M.S.W., 15 years practice]

I would never say anything about a client without a written release. At the agency, everything is written down and signed, so people know what the exceptions are to the rule.

[Female, M.S.W., 5 years practice]

It's very strictly enforced. I wouldn't tell anybody anything. We usually go over a form about what the confidentiality rules are when we first meet.

[Male, M.S.W., 15 years practice]

Some therapists decide never to raise the question of confidentiality unless the patient brings it up, or if some of the material coming up seems to require such a discussion.

Sessions are confidential. I don't explain that under the law there might be exceptions, unless it seems that it might be an issue.

[Male, M.S.W., 20 years practice]

I don't discuss it unless it comes up. They all know the exceptions.
[Female, Ph.D., 20 years practice]

I don't tell patients that there are some exceptions unless that topic comes up. I don't want to tell them a lot of different rules at the beginning. If it comes up, I'd have to warn them that what they're telling me now I might have to reveal.
[Male, Ph.D., 15 years practice]

I tell people it's confidential. I don't remember the exceptions ever coming up in my private practice.
[Female, M.S.W., 15 years practice]

I assure them that everything we're going to discuss is strictly confidential. It never comes up again.
[Female, M.A., 15 years practice]

If they don't ask about it, I would probably not bring it up. If they do ask, keeping in mind that I'm a psychiatrist so I see a spectrum of severity, I generally will say to people that there is complete confidentiality except in situations in which I feel somebody is in danger, either to themselves or someone else.
[Female, M.D., 15 years practice]

I tell them that what we say is confidential. I've never initiated that conversation unless I felt that it was a particularly dangerous situation.
[Male, Ph.D., 5 years practice]

I tell them as much as they need to know at the time. I generally make some statement during the first session about the time being for them and that what goes on in the session is private. Sometimes I wait until they raise the subject. You can mention it too soon and it raises anxiety.
[Female, Ph.D., 30 years practice]

A number of therapists said that the *Tarasoff* exceptions to the rule of confidentiality haven't come up in the populations they work with.

Whatever happens in the consulting room is between the patient and me, and that's it. Exceptions? I don't have those kinds of patients.
[Female, M.S.W., 20 years practice]

I'm strict about it. I've never told patients that there are exceptions.
[Female, M.S., 20 years practice]

I tell them that what they say here, stays here. I've never discussed the exceptions.

[Male, M.D., 20 years practice]

Everything we say here is confidential. It's never come up in private practice that I've worked with a suicidal patient, so I've never had to break that.

[Female, M.S.W., 5 years practice]

I've had occasion to have to talk about the exceptions but I don't explain it as a general introduction. Most people who come to me seem to have an understanding of it.

[Male, Ph.D., 10 years practice]

Whatever happens is confidential. I would tell a patient if I thought that person was potentially dangerous, either to himself or somebody else, that there are exceptions to the rule. I don't recall that I ever felt it was necessary to do that.

[Male, Ph.D., 40 years practice]

With many patients it's not an issue, and never even gets discussed.

[Female, M.S.W., 20 years practice]

Probably I have had to tell patients about the exceptions, but it's rare, because my patient population is such that it hasn't presented itself.

[Female, M.A., 20 years practice]

Some therapists would hesitate to act even if it were fairly clear that there was some likelihood of danger to someone else.

Everything's confidential. I would probably tell them about child abuse being an exception. I'm not sure what I would do about someone who was planning a murder.

[Female, M.S., 15 years practice]

The second problem, the demands of insurance companies and the breaks in confidentiality both actual and potential, is discussed in much greater detail in Question 9, but here are a few general remarks about the conflict.

I'm very rigid about confidentiality. The whole managed care issue infringes terribly on what I think confidentiality is. I might discuss a patient with the psychiatrist who's treating the patient with me.

[Female, M.S.W., 15 years practice]

I tell them that it's part of the process, but if they're getting insurance, sometimes the insurance company will want to know the diagnosis and occasionally some details.

[Male, M.S.W., 10 years practice]

I also say that at times I may have to give certain information to the insurance company. I say it's supposed to be confidential, but I don't think these days that it really is, so I try to keep things as impersonal as possible.

[Male, Ph.D., 20 years practice]

NUMERICAL DISTRIBUTION

Twenty-four people said they tell patients that everything is confidential; 28 do mention and/or discuss the legal exceptions; 8 say nothing unless the patient brings it up.

COMMENTS

The issue here is what we currently mean by confidentiality, and how the therapist can preserve the privacy of the therapeutic relationship.

We are assaulted these days with breaches of the walls of the consulting room. Although the situation of a patient threatening to harm someone else may come up only rarely, when it does it becomes an agonizing choice. How will I know whether this is a real danger? At what point do I contact someone, and who do I contact? Some therapists appear to have decided not to think about this possibility, hoping that their bright, middle-class patients would never make it necessary. I had the impression doing these interviews that many therapists would do nothing in any case, whatever the law, feeling that their role is too compromised by having to play policeman.

The situation of a suicidal patient is relatively simple compared to a potential threat to another person. (The problem of the suicidal patient is discussed in Question 29.) Therapists don't seem to have the same moral conflict about breaking confidentiality to protect and preserve the patient they are already working with.

As for the insurance companies' demand for the details of treatment, most therapists are actively trying to protect the privacy of their patients and still somehow comply with the requests for information, since, for many patients, staying in treatment is contingent on getting reimbursement. Many of my colleagues are using the same diagnoses for all patients, selecting the most innocuous categories, the ones that reveal the least personal information.

RELATED READING

Beck, J. C. (1990). *Confidentiality versus the Duty to Protect: Foreseeable Harm in the Practice of Psychiatry*. Washington, DC: American Psychiatric Press.

Nowell, D., and Spruill, J. (1993). If it's not absolutely confidential, will information be disclosed? *Professional Psychology: Research and Practice* 24(3):367–369.

Smith-Bell, M., and Winslade, W. J. (1994). Privacy, confidentiality, and privilege in psychotherapeutic relationships. *American Journal of Orthopsychiatry* 64(2):180–193.

Thelan, M. H., Rodriguez, M. D., and Sprengelmeyer, P. (1994). Psychologists' beliefs concerning confidentiality with suicide, homicide, and child abuse. *American Journal of Psychotherapy* 48(3):363–379.

⧉⧉⧉⧉

Question 11: What are your rules about cancellations?

As therapists, we sell our time and our clinical skills. Patients usually are seen the same time each week, a standing appointment that we change only for important reasons. While we may not feel entirely comfortable charging for services not given, it may be difficult to find an arrangement which is fair to both patient and therapist.

One therapist, in practice only a few years, described the conflicts he had in setting a policy.

> That's really a tough one. I've had battles with my own therapist about that. So on the one hand, he's my role model, and I want to be like him, and on the other, I want to kill him sometimes about his policy. It's gone through changes, but right now my policy is that as long as it's not at the last minute, when I've already left the house, if the patient calls me and gives me a little notice, I'll agree to reschedule. I used to say I'll reschedule within a week, and now I'll reschedule anytime. The latest thing I'm coming to is that I'm going to bill the missed hour. You can have the rescheduled hour whenever we can work it out, but meanwhile I'm going to bill you for this.
>
> [Male, Ph.D., 5 years practice]

The more psychoanalytically oriented therapists seem to be more likely to charge for every session, no matter how much notice of a cancellation they are given.

> The patient is leasing out my time, and they're responsible for the time. That's a basic line, and I try to stick to it.
>
> [Male, M.D., 20 years practice]

Another therapist found she had some difficulty keeping such a strict rule.

> This is an area I have trouble with. I'm really a pushover. I try to tell people it's like paying rent: You own this hour, it's yours, and I need to know that you're going to be there, I'm expecting you. However, I get very mushy about vacations, business trips, like that. If they tell me they're going to be away four weeks from now, and giving me lots of advance notice, I find that I get lenient, I'm not firm enough in my policy.
>
> [Female, M.A., 15 years practice]

Many therapists, even those that see the hour as leased by the patient, will offer a make-up if given notice in time, though there is much variation even within this group.

> The set policy is that if they're coming every week, then that's their responsibility, to make a session every week. If they can't make the session within the week, then they call up and let me know at least twenty-four hours in advance, and then we try to reschedule it. If we can reschedule it in that week or so, then that's a make-up session. If I can't do it, because I'm busy, sometimes I'll let it go.
>
> [Male, Ph.D., 15 years practice]

> My rule about cancellation is that the patient's responsible if they cancel the session, they're responsible for the fee, and I will try to make up that time if their schedule and my schedule permit.
>
> [Male, M.D., 20 years practice]

> If they don't give twenty-four hours notice, they have to pay. If they give twenty-four hours notice, I'll make every effort to reschedule. If I can't reschedule, they have to pay. I make exceptions for a few patients, like one who's out of town a lot for his job.
>
> [Male, M.S.W., 15 years practice]

The patient pays for every session he options. However, if he gives me sufficient notice, I will try to fill the hour with somebody else. If I succeed, then he's not responsible to pay for the hour. I don't require a patient to attend on any legal holiday or religious holiday. They're entitled to cancel, if they choose, without penalty.

[Male, Ph.D., 50 years practice]

I charge for sessions unless we've arranged beforehand, like if the patient is out of town. If they tell me a week in advance that they have to be in California on business, I won't charge them. I will try to reschedule.

[Female, M.S.W., 30 years practice]

I charge for all sessions that are scheduled, but I will make up sessions that are canceled by a certain time limit, usually twenty-four hours. Occasionally with children I'm a little more lenient. If a kid wakes up sick in the morning, and the parent calls me right away in the morning, I'll make up that session.

[Female, M.S.W., 15 years practice]

If you cancel you pay, with the exception of people whose work brings them out of town for weeks at a time, and I don't charge them. That's something we set up in the very first session.

[Male, M.S.W., 15 years practice]

The patient is liable for the session. If they know they're going to be absent, to let me know as soon as they can so I can, if it's possible, fill the hour. If I fill the hour, I don't charge. Also, if in that week I have an opening, they can make up the hour without a charge.

[Male, Ph.D., 20 years practice]

They pay. They're responsible. If I can reschedule the same week, or even the following week, when I have an open hour, we do that.

[Female, M.A., 15 years practice]

They have to pay if they don't show up. If they tell me that they're going to be away, we will try to reschedule at a time that's convenient for both of us, if I have a free hour. I do give them two weeks vacation.

[Female, M.S.W., 10 years practice]

For dire emergencies, that is, deaths, hospitalizations, no charge. Otherwise, I charge. If it's a business appointment in advance, then I give a make-up session.

[Female, M.S.W., 20 years practice]

The majority of the interviewees have a policy that requires 24-hour notice, often with some flexibility around emergency situations. Even within this group, some are more strict than others.

> Patients must give me twenty-four hours notice or they are charged for and expected to pay for the session even if they don't come. There's no such thing as a make-up session. The rationale is that without some notice I can't use the time for anything else. I have maybe once or twice in fifteen years not charged for a missed session when a patient was in an auto accident the same day, or a family member died, or something on that order.
>
> [Male, M.A., 15 years practice]

> Twenty-four hours, and I will try to give them a make-up if they request and if they can, but I let them know that I may not have an hour available. So they're still responsible if they don't let me know twenty-four hours in advance. If I have someone who cancels twenty-four hours in advance but does it repetitively, around social engagements or like that, then that becomes a treatment issue even though they've technically followed the rules.
>
> [Female, M.S.W., 20 years practice]

> Twenty-four hours in advance, and I will do everything I can to reschedule you within that week, so that there's no charge for that. Less than twenty-four hours notice, and I can't reschedule, then you're charged.
>
> [Female, M.S., 15 years practice]

> If a person gives me twenty-four hour notice, and I can reschedule an appointment in that same week, I will. If not, they pay for the session.
>
> [Female, M.S.W., 20 years practice]

Some therapists with the twenty-four hour policy are more lenient.

> Twenty-four hours without a charge. And it doesn't have to be rescheduled that week. And I sometimes will not charge for a cancellation at the last minute if there's a compelling emergency.
>
> [Male, Ph.D., 25 years practice]

> They're vague. Many insurance companies won't pay for missed sessions. I ask people to give me twenty-four hour notice. If somebody is sick, I won't charge them. I can make use of my time, and have other things to do.
>
> [Male, Ph.D., 40 years practice]

If they give me twenty-four hour notice, I'll let them reschedule. They have to pay me if it's less than twenty-four hours, or less than twenty, I give them a little leeway. If they want to come in anyway, they have to pay me for the missed session too.

[Male, M.S.W., 10 years practice]

People need to give me a day's notice, and we reschedule if they can. If it's a last-minute cancellation, then the person's responsible for that, but I would reschedule that also and not charge for the rescheduling. I don't charge people if they're on vacation.

[Female, M.S.W., 10 years practice]

I'm a little too flexible. I have a general twenty-four hour cancellation policy, which I try to adhere to. If there's a real crisis, I don't charge, and if it's somebody who never cancels, and they call at the last minute and say they're sick, I don't charge. With people on managed care, I charge for all cancellations, no matter what.

[Female, Ph.D., 20 years practice]

If they give me twenty-four hours notice, I don't charge them. People who cancel like twice a year, even if they give me ten minutes notice I really bend over backwards to try not to charge them and give them another time.

[Female, M.S.W., 25 years practice]

If somebody doesn't give me twenty-four hours notice they're responsible for the session. I will reschedule at a time when I have an open hour if I can, and then they're not charged. I'm flexible about emergencies, or illness.

[Female, M.S.W., 10 years practice]

Some may have a different time limit.

If I'm not informed within forty-eight hours I charge. If I'm informed before that I usually can reschedule.

[Female, M.S.W., 5 years practice]

I have a policy where if you give me forty-eight hours notice I do not charge. If you give me less, and I can't fill the hour, then I will charge. If I do fill the hour I don't double bill.

[Female, M.S., 15 years practice]

If you cancel in less than a week, I'll offer you two or three daytime make-up times, because I rarely have evening openings. If you can't make any of those, you're responsible for the session.

[Female, M.A., 15 years practice]

I have a very liberal policy there too. If patients give me at least a week's notice, they wouldn't be responsible to pay. If they cancel later than that, they pay. I also believe patients can take a vacation. I don't charge during vacations.

[Female, M.S.W., 20 years practice]

Others have a more flexible policy.

Many of my patients are in business, and businesses require travel or meetings, so I try to be flexible. When I spell out the initial contract I stipulate that if they're going to be away, or they have a meeting and they let me know in advance, I will be more than happy to rearrange the schedule. However, regardless of the cause, if it's a last-minute cancellation then they pay for it.

[Male, M.S.W., 35 years practice]

Twenty-four hour notification, and I'm flexible about that. If I can see them another time during the week, I won't charge them, and if there are mitigating circumstances I may not charge them either.

[Male, Ph.D., 25 years practice]

I expect cancellations to be made up. People pay for cancellations, but I offer a make-up session whenever possible. If they know they're not going to be able to attend they should let me know at least twenty-four or forty-eight hours in advance, unless it's an emergency. If they wake up with a hundred and four degree fever, and call me, then I understand that. I don't charge for planned vacations, when I'm notified in advance.

[Male, M.S.W., 20 years practice]

A few people have very loose rules about cancellations, or even no rules at all.

I don't charge for service that I don't give. It doesn't matter how much notice I get.

[Male, Ph.D., 30 years practice]

> I've never charged anyone for missing a session. If we can reschedule, fine. If we can't, then we don't.
>
> [Male, Ph.D., 5 years practice]

> I'm very flexible. As long as it makes sense to me, people can cancel any time. I actually feel that if someone tells me the day before, they can cancel for even a reason that's not very good. As long as it doesn't inconvenience me. If I have to come in, then I want a good reason.
>
> [Female, Ph.D., 10 years practice]

> Some patients, especially borderline patients, I'm a little more liberal with make-up sessions. If they cancel they have to accept a make-up. And with some patients who are more naive about the rules of therapy and the procedures of therapy, I will allow make-ups.
>
> [Male, Ph.D., 40 years practice]

> Very loose. As long as they call me before, they don't have to pay. Any time before.
>
> [Female, M.S.W., 15 years practice]

> I have a problem charging for cancellations, that if I'm not working I shouldn't be charging. Maybe it comes from my own analysis, where my analyst didn't charge. Most people don't miss sessions. Until it comes up, I don't make an issue of it.
>
> [Female, M.S.W., 20 years practice]

> I'm pretty flexible. I'm so busy that sometimes a cancellation is a welcome relief. If a patient lets me know ahead of time, then I don't charge.
>
> [Male, M.D., 5 years practice]

One beginning therapist found that not having a rule wasn't working.

> I started out not having a rule about it, and found that people weren't very responsible. So then I made a rule that people have to pay for missed sessions but I haven't been enforcing it. I think I'm going to have to make the rule that people pay if they don't come because I don't have that big a practice.
>
> [Female, M.S.W., 5 years practice]

Finally, several people said that the cancellation policy was different for different patients, depending on certain treatment issues.

> To some degree, they vary with different patients. Usually, my policy is that I charge for missed sessions, that I try to reschedule it if I have

the time and then I don't charge. If I can't, then I do charge. Then I have some bendings of the rules, where patients can't, for example, schedule a vacation at the same time as I do, and then I don't charge.

[Female, Ph.D., 15 years practice]

The basic rule is if you give me a day's notice, I don't charge you for the session. That isn't hard and fast, because there are people I do charge for sessions even if they give me two weeks notice. It has to do with the way I think they're using me as a commodity, or that they can do it at any time and it doesn't matter. Or with someone who has to be out of town all the time for their business, even though that's a legitimate reason, I can't hold that hour empty half the time.

[Male, Ph.D., 20 years practice]

I try to be pretty flexible. Most times, if I get a cancellation I can fill the time. If I have a patient who's coming twice a week, and they have a regular time, and they cancel, I expect them to pay for the session. Other people, depending on where they are in treatment and what I think they can understand or tolerate about a cancellation, it may be twenty-four hours. I never charge people for their vacations.

[Male, M.D., 15 years practice]

It depends on who it is. If it's someone who's fairly stable, I usually ask for a minimum of twenty-four hours notice. If it's someone who's ill, and who could be sick at a moment's notice, then we deal with that.

[Female, Ph.D., 30 years practice]

NUMERICAL DISTRIBUTION

Thirty people said they had a policy that required 24-hour notice; 6 required 48 hours or even longer notice; 7 said they didn't charge for a canceled session, even at the last minute; 17 said that the patient was billed for all missed sessions, although 10 of these offered substitute or make-up hours.

COMMENTS

Some issues raised by this question are: Is it ethical to charge a patient for missed sessions? Which cancellation policy is best for treatment? How does the therapist protect his or her income without being unfair to patients?

This is a tricky question, because there are good arguments on all sides. As a businessperson, the private practitioner needs some kind of structure to protect his or her income, and to maintain the integrity of the schedule. On the other hand, it may be hard to justify charging patients for services they don't receive, and hard for a patient to believe that the therapist has nothing to do with the time except sit and stare at the wall.

One of my first supervisors explained his policy, a strict responsibility for all sessions, as comparable to leasing an apartment. You don't ask the landlord for a rebate on your rent if you're going on vacation. My response was that you can, however, sublease an apartment if you know in advance you're going to be away.

Whatever the policy, it is important for the rules to be pefectly clear to the patient. Ambiguity and uncertainty usually create unnecessary anxiety and disruptive disputes.

RELATED READING

Blackman, W. D. (1993). Are psychoanalytic billing practices ethical? *American Journal of Psychotherapy* 47(4):613–620.
Furlong, A. (1992). Some technical and theoretical considerations regarding the missed session. *International Journal of Psycho-Analysis* 73(4):701–718.
Herron, W. G., and Sitkowski, S. (1989). Fee practices of different psychotherapeutic orientations. *Psychological Reports* 65(1):142–148.
Scanlon, P. (1982). Fees and missed appointments as transference issues. *Social Casework* 63(9):540–546.

⬙⬙⬙⬙

Question 12: Do you have any kind of physical contact with a patient?

This is another tricky area. Physical touch can easily be misinterpreted by the patient as sexual or seductive, or can be experienced as intrusive or invasive. In the best circumstances, touch can be comforting and reassuring. But many therapists believe that it's safer to avoid touching patients.

When patients have left treatment, it's never initiated by me, but sometimes they've kissed me. Physical contact is so loaded that I try to avoid it.

[Female, M.S., 15 years practice]

Almost everyone, regardless of theoretical orientation, shook hands at the beginning and end of treatment.

> We shake hands the first time they come, and sometimes again after a vacation break. Also at the last session.
> [Male, M.D., 20 years practice]

> A handshake perhaps, on first meeting.
> [Male, M.D., 20 years practice]

> Maybe a handshake once in a while, like before vacations.
> [Female, M.S.W., 15 years practice]

Some patients want to shake hands at every session.

> Some patients shake my hand. I have one guy who shakes my hand before and after each session, and that's a part of our connection.
> [Male, Ph.D., 5 years practice]

A slightly different perspective on handshakes was given by one person.

> With a new patient, I will shake hands. Or if a patient is finishing, terminating, I will shake hands. I had one very borderline patient who insisted on shaking hands every week, and that was very important to him. He was quite ill with HIV, and I felt that to refuse to shake hands would be very hurtful. When I tried to analyze it, and I really couldn't get anywhere with it, I compromised by allowing him that indulgence. Actually, it's a European custom. European analysts shake hands with their patients every time.
> [Male, Ph.D., 40 years practice]

Other kinds of contact, most commonly a hug, were also mentioned by various therapists as acceptable under certain circumstances.

> I've been embraced by and embraced patients.
> [Male, Ph.D., 10 years practice]

> Occasionally a hug. Sometimes hand-holding. Sometimes patients will sit at my knee, and I'll pat their heads.
> [Female, M.A., 20 years practice]

> I may have put my hand on someone's arm when they were having an anxiety attack in a public setting and I couldn't talk to them, just to establish that I'm sitting next to them.
> [Female, Ph.D., 10 years practice]

There are clients that I have hugged, or held their hand during an emotional cathartic moment.

[Female, M.A., 15 years practice]

If somebody's had a very rough time, I'll put my hand on their shoulder as they're going out.

[Male, Ph.D., 40 years practice]

If the person's crying or very upset, I've gone close to them and put a hand on their knee, or my arm around someone.

[Female, Ph.D., 20 years practice]

A few therapists make contact fairly regularly.

I have one patient that hugs me on a regular basis, and I hug back, and it feels completely comfortable. It began on the day her father died, and has continued since then.

[Female, M.S., 15 years practice]

I have a patient who wants a hug after every session, and I don't know how it started. Maybe once in a great while somebody shakes hands.

[Female, M.S.W., 10 years practice]

More analytically oriented therapists tend to regard all behavior as a kind of acting-out, and something that may need analyzing.

Only if they surprise me with an extended hand. My training was pretty much "hands off," and I believe in that.

[Male, M.S.W., 10 years practice]

I do not extend my hand, but if a patient does, in the beginning, I reciprocate, and down the road explore it a little bit, depending on the patient.

[Female, M.S.W., 45 years practice]

I shake hands at the end of the first session, usually, as a part of establishing the contract and the relationship. Other than that, no.

[Female, Ph.D., 20 years practice]

Others mentioned the importance of some kind of touch.

A lot of times people give me a hug at the end of the session. I'll shake hands at the beginning and at the end of a session. Contact of that kind is a very important acknowledgment of the relationship.

[Male, Ph.D., 25 years practice]

I originally worked in physical rehab, and those patients were often unable to express themselves with words, and I got used to giving them a hug when they indicated that they wanted one. I would comply without any problem. And it's just carried over. If patients need it or want it, we'll talk about it, but usually it's very spontaneous and I respond, and we'll talk about it the next time.

[Female, M.S., 20 years practice]

Patients who are physically ill present special problems.

I have worked with some AIDS patients, and when I feel it's appropriate I will give the patient a hug, for very specific reasons. I'm trying to make sure the patient knows that they're not like lepers.

[Male, M.D., 5 years practice]

Several people mentioned the awkwardness of physical contact with patients of the opposite sex.

Maybe at termination, I might, depending on how long I've been working with them, I might hug somebody goodbye. I don't know if I'd ever hug a male patient goodbye. I think I'd shake hands.

[Female, M.S.W., 10 years practice]

Once, when therapy terminated, a patient spontaneously hugged me. I will shake hands initially at the beginning of therapy. There are some male patients, macho types, who insist on it. I thought it was good for the therapy. With female patients, even before it was an issue, I was always quite cautious about it.

[Male, Ph.D., 5 years practice]

The occasional pat on the back while walking out at the end of the session, mostly only same gender. I don't touch women.

[Male, Ph.D., 20 years practice]

Finally, some therapists cautioned about the ways that touch may interfere with understanding.

I might have done this fifteen years ago: If someone's crying I might go over and put my arm around them, hold them, or something like that. In the good old gestalt days I might have done that. It's not that I'm more cautious now, it's that I'm more interested in what their experience is and their communicating that in words.

[Male, Ph.D., 25 years practice]

Contact may be more the therapist's need than the client's.

I certainly would shake hands, and I might pat someone on the shoulder. I used to have more contact, but I don't now. I began to feel that, first of all, that kind of encouragement or closeness doesn't help therapy at all. In some cases, it was as much for me as for the patient.

[Male, M.S.W., 15 years practice]

NUMERICAL DISTRIBUTION

Seven people said they have no physical contact at all; 23 said handshake only; 30 (20 women and 10 men) said that they make other kinds of contact. Most of these people emphasized that it had to be initiated by the patient.

COMMENTS

Issues here are: Is physical contact always problematic? Is it useful to try to distinguish between sex and affection?

These days, with so many stories of unethical therapists in the air, it may feel dangerous to do anything that might be misconstrued or misunderstood, and physical contact has a huge potential for such misreading. On the other hand, actively avoiding any physical contact sends its own messages, and may also be misunderstood.

In my own practice, I shake hands with everyone, male and female, at the first session, usually in the waiting room when I introduce myself. Some patients like to shake hands at the end of every session, and I do that without analyzing it. Every once in a while, a patient asks for a hug, and I do that. I never initiate physical contact, because it can be so sexually charged, but I think it's also important not to make patients feel rejected. I think that many patients do have difficulty distinguishing sex from affection, and clarifying the difference may be helpful.

RELATED READING

Burton, A., and Heller, L. G. (1964). The touching of the body. *Psychoanalytic Review* 51:122–134.

Goodman, M., and Teicher, A. (1988). To touch or not to touch. *Psychotherapy* 25(4):492–500.

Holub, E. A., and Lee, S. S. (1990). Therapist's use of nonerotic physical contact: ethical concerns. *Professional Psychology: Research and Practice* 21(2):115–117.

Woodmansey, A. C. (1988). Are psychotherapists out of touch? *British Journal of Psychotherapy* 5(1):57–65.

🔊🔊🔊🔊

Question 13: If a patient called for an emergency session, would you try to schedule one?

A situation that may arise only rarely is the emergency call. It may be possible to deal with the crisis in a brief phone conversation, or the patient may request an extra session. When a patient asks for an emergency session, does the therapist make room for one?

The vast majority answered simply, "Absolutely," without qualification. A few elaborated a little more.

> I will schedule emergency sessions or even extra sessions that are not an emergency if a patient requests it and I have an available hour. Once in a very great while, maybe three times in fifteen years, I have come in on a day I normally wouldn't be working for an emergency session.
>
> [Male, M.S.W., 15 years practice]

> I have, sure. Sometimes not at the best hours for myself.
>
> [Male, Ph.D., 10 years practice]

> If someone calls and wants to be seen before the next session, I do it, and if they can't come in or it's a day that I'm not in the office, we'd have phone contact or else a phone session.
>
> [Female, M.S.W., 10 years practice]

> I have no rules. If I'm working with someone who's going through a crisis, or severely disturbed, and they need an emergency session, then I'll provide one.
>
> [Male, M.S.W., 35 years practice]

> I let patients know that if they really need an emergency session, they should let me know, and will try to see them or at least speak to them on the phone.
>
> [Male, M.S.W., 20 years practice]

> Most of my patients have never requested an emergency session. When someone does, I will certainly go out of my way, work extra hours, to accommodate them. It doesn't come up very often.
>
> [Female, M.S.W., 20 years practice]

Some therapists encourage extra sessions during crisis or emergency situations.

> I offer people the freedom to contact me by phone if they need to, and I find that most don't. When they do, it's usually a crisis, and I encourage them that rather than deal with it on the telephone, that we set up another session.
>
> [Female, M.A., 15 years practice]

> I try to accommodate them. However, if there's a pattern to it, I talk about it with the patient and suggest that they're really in need of more sessions.
>
> [Female, M.S.W., 15 years practice]

And some discourage it.

> When I pick up the phone and they say it's an emergency, they'll usually tell me something about it, or I'll ask, and I may process it in terms of what happened in the last session, and ask them to hold it till the next time. It varies.
>
> [Female, M.S.W., 20 years practice]

> Normally they don't need it and I don't encourage it. Sometimes when someone's going through a major crisis I will set up extra appointments for them.
>
> [Male, M.S.W., 15 years practice]

Some therapists said they try to evaluate the emergency before scheduling an extra session.

> I would have to know the patient and know what's going on, and find out a little bit about it. But I'm not rigid about it.
>
> [Female, Ph.D., 20 years practice]

> I try to evaluate on the phone if it's indeed an emergency. I generally would encourage them to come at the appointed time.
>
> [Male, M.D., 20 years practice]

I guess it would depend on the patient. If the patient calls every day with an emergency, I would contain them and say that we'll talk about it in our next session. Someone who never calls, and suddenly does call, I'd see them right away.

[Male, Ph.D., 20 years practice]

NUMERICAL DISTRIBUTION

Five people said they would evaluate first; 3 said they would discourage it; 52 said that they would simply schedule the session.

COMMENTS

The issue here is whether the patient or the therapist is the best judge of what is an emergency, and whether the therapist respects the patient's judgment or decides on his or her own.

What the patient considers an emergency may not receive the same evaluation from the therapist. There are advantages and disadvantages to scheduling extra sessions in moments of crisis. The patient may feel cared about and supported when the extra session is scheduled, but may also feel contained and reassured when the therapist conveys confidence in the patient's ability to hold the material until the next regularly scheduled session.

Perhaps this question is analogous to the difference between scheduled feeding and on-demand feeding of infants. I tend to think that patients are usually the best judge of what they need, and if they request an extra session, I will accomodate them if I can find time in the schedule. If doing so has other meanings, conscious or unconscious, they will usually emerge and can be discussed later.

RELATED READING

Fish, S. L. (1990). Therapeutic uses of the telephone: crisis intervention vs. traditional therapy. In *Talking to Strangers: Mediated Therapeutic Communication*, ed. G. Gumpert and S. L. Fish, pp. 154–169. Norwood, NJ: Ablex Publishing.

Smith, V. A. (1980). Patient contacts outside therapy. *Canadian Journal of Psychiatry* 25(4):297–302.

☒☒☒☒

Question 14: How do you feel about telephone sessions?

Circumstances sometimes make it impossible for the patient to be in the office. One alternative to missed sessions is telephone sessions. (This question does not refer to brief telephone contact in a crisis situation, but to a full session, scheduled in advance and billed as a regular session.)

Some therapists have no problem with arranging telephone hours and working by phone.

> I've done them. I feel they're appropriate, and I'm comfortable with them. It's not my choice, I much prefer a patient being with me in the room, but sometimes situations militate against that, and a telephone session is much better than no session.
>
> [Female, M.S.W., 45 years practice]

> I do think they work, absolutely. One woman had phone sessions for six months because of a physical condition where she couldn't leave her bed, and I spoke to her once a week for that entire period. It's not my preference, but if the therapy is working, and issues are coming up, you can definitely deal with them over the phone.
>
> [Male, Ph.D., 25 years practice]

A therapist who was comfortable with an occasional telephone session felt differently about making that the norm.

> I feel fine about them once in a while. I did have someone call who wanted to see me, but couldn't come in to the office, and basically wanted a telephone treatment, and I said I was very uncomfortable with that.
>
> [Male, Ph.D., 5 years practice]

Sometimes telephone sessions do become the normal session.

> I have them. As a matter of fact, I used to have them regularly with three different patients around the country. I feel completely comfortable with them because in all these cases people were relocated and wanted to continue treatment with me.
>
> [Female, M.S., 15 years practice]

Others don't like telephone work, finding it difficult to focus.

I don't do as well because I wander. I know that I'm not as present, I look around, thinking of what I have to do later, look at the newspaper. I try not to do it. If someone's in desperate need, I'll tune in.

[Female, Ph.D., 20 years practice]

Many felt that they miss too much important information.

I feel like I miss too much, in the body posture. I'm very big on how you sit and what you do with your body while you talk, and how you evade or avoid. There's so much nuance in body language that I don't like to miss that.

[Female, M.S.W., 20 years practice]

I did once or twice and decided "Never again!" I absolutely will not do them. There's a lot that goes on that's non-verbal, that's sensory, and I think that's essential to the session. From my end of it, I'm not sure at all what I'm dealing with.

[Male, M.S.W., 25 years practice]

I've done it but I don't like it. I'll talk to someone on the phone briefly, but long telephone sessions, without the face-to-face, that doesn't do it for me, so I figure it doesn't do it for them either.

[Female, M.S.W., 15 years practice]

It's very difficult to work without any visual feedback, and I find it hard to pay attention on the phone. Those few patients who have had telephone sessions seem to find them helpful, however, and I guess they're better than no session at all.

[Male, M.S.W., 15 years practice]

One person said there was another risk in telephone work.

I've found over the years that the overwhelming majority of miscommunications and misunderstandings have occurred as the result of telephone contact. Either I didn't hear something, or they heard something a way I didn't mean it, and I find out three months later. So I'm wary of the telephone.

[Female, M.D., 15 years practice]

Many therapists think that telephone hours can be productive and valuable.

I do several telephone sessions a week at this point. I find that while it's not as good as somebody being in the office, it's better than having a disruption to the regularity of the sessions. With some patients, it loosens them up, and it's easier to talk on the phone than in person. Once they get over the discomfort of being quiet on the line for a while and giving themselves time to think, which usually takes them two or three sessions, it becomes just as comfortable.

[Female, M.S.W., 20 years practice]

I've been having two very long experiences with that which have worked out very well. One went on for eight years, and now that person is back in town and seeing me again. And another also for a long period of time. It's worked out better than I would have ever thought.

[Female, M.S.W., 30 years practice]

I've done telephone sessions with people who've moved away, or if it's somebody who needs intensive work but can't get out of their house, for whatever reason. Sometimes they're more effective than face-to-face interviews.

[Male, Ph.D., 40 years practice]

It's very variable. I have a couple of clients where it's been a turning point, and incredible things have happened through telephone sessions that have very much surprised me. I've had phone sessions with clients who relocated, and I finally have insisted that they find someone local.

[Female, M.A., 15 years practice]

I had one patient who was because of her career called out of town for long periods of time, three, four, five months, and it was an extremely stressful time. The other time a patient had just had a baby, and wasn't able to leave the house for a few months, and she really did need to talk about what it was like to be a new parent. I prefer in-person sessions, and there are certain things I won't talk about on the phone. I don't discuss dreams on the phone. I like phone work to be more concrete stuff.

[Female, M.S.W., 10 years practice]

Others find them not useful, or even negative experiences.

I've done two or three of them over the years, in emergency situations. I don't think they're ultimately helpful. They give the false impression that it's the content of the discussion that's relevant as opposed to the relationship and the transaction in a real, live way.

[Male, M.D., 20 years practice]

I don't really believe that therapy goes on in telephone sessions. But I've done them. I have a borderline patient who lives some distance from here, very phobic, often ill, and the treatment is strictly supportive. If she makes an appointment, and for some reason can't come in, but wants to talk on the phone, I will do it. But I don't consider it real therapy.

[Male, Ph.D., 40 years practice]

They're very unsatisfactory. I don't feel I get all the information I need from the patient. I don't get a sense of what to focus on, and it's not clear that the patient has a sense of how to proceed.

[Male, M.D., 20 years practice]

I will speak with someone over the phone, but I won't have a session over the phone. I don't like the fact that there's no personal contact. I can't see what the person is looking like. Especially in the area of drug and alcohol treatment, it's very important that the person be there. I'll do crisis intervention, but I don't do phone sessions.

[Male, M.D., 5 years practice]

Often, it's felt very intellectualized, as if they're talking about their own psychology. Somehow there was a chemistry that was missing that can happen in person. And I think reading the cues of what you're seeing is so important to knowing what's happening with this person.

[Male, M.S.W., 15 years practice]

A few people said that they had changed their attitude from negative to more positive.

I used to be more hidebound about it, and that would communicate to patients that I thought it wasn't the best thing, that it was better to talk face-to-face, and I put pressure on the patient to come in. I'm concerned about the resistance end of it. More and more, it's a way to deal with difficult clinical situations with somebody who really needs it.

[Male, M.D., 15 years practice]

I do telephone sessions now with three long-term patients that moved out of town. At first, I tried to get people to find a new therapist locally, and I've had experience that it doesn't always work, so if someone wants to continue with phone work I do it. I formerly had not been comfortable with phone sessions, but I've gotten comfortable. It feels okay now.

[Female, M.S., 15 years practice]

Some extreme circumstances almost require telephone work.

> I've done that occasionally, with one very disturbed patient when she was away on business trips and very frightened of going. Actually, I conducted an entire therapy over the phone with one patient, an adolescent boy who because of religious beliefs felt he couldn't sit alone in a room with a woman.
>
> [Female, Ph.D., 15 years practice]

Even those who feel comfortable and positive about telephone work would not do it if they thought the patient was using it as a resistance. But even if it is a resistance, it may still be possible to work this way.

> They certainly can be useful, but sometimes they're resistance, someone just doesn't want to come, and this is their way of resisting. I had a very depressed patient, who had seen many other therapists, and if they wouldn't do phone sessions she would quit. It didn't make any sense to me to try to stand by a rule and lose the patient. Ultimately, she's improved a lot. But I always doubt myself: Should I be stricter? Am I being too easy?
>
> [Male, Ph.D., 20 years practice]

> It depends on the patient, and on me, and my contact with them, and whether we can focus in on each other. If the purpose is to avoid coming in, then I discourage it. If it's someone who's moved recently, and is in the process of finding another therapist, then I'll do it.
>
> [Male, Ph.D., 15 years practice]

NUMERICAL DISTRIBUTION

Thirty-one people said they do telephone sessions and either like them or at least are not negative about them; 21 do them reluctantly, discourage them, and have reservations or negative feelings about them; 8 will not do full telephone sessions, although they will have brief phone contact.

COMMENTS

Several issues are connected to this question: Is telephone work useful, or does it give only the impression of therapy without the substance? Is it better to skip a session than to have a telephone session? With patients who have relocated at a great distance, is real therapy continuing by telephone, or is it resistance and denial by both patient and therapist of termination?

When circumstances make it impossible for the patient to be in the office, a telephone session can maintain the regularity of the schedule and the connection with the therapist. On the other hand, the therapist is obviously missing much, and the quality of the hour may suffer. This is clearly a very individual decision, and has a lot to do with the particular patient and the particular therapist. I don't like telephone sessions much, because I find it hard to stay focused only on the disembodied voice, but I do them when necessary, because I think they are better than no session at all.

When a patient terminates because of professional or personal circumstances, is it better for that patient's treatment to continue with a trusted professional familiar with the case or to find a new therapist in the new location? Is it grandiosity on the therapist's part to feel that the patient should continue by telephone, and that no new therapist could do as well? The situations of a patient moving to a large urban area with many professionals and of a patient moving to a rural area without professionals may be different.

RELATED READING

Grumet, G. W. (1979). Telephone therapy: a review and case report. *American Journal of Orthopsychiatry* 49(4):574–584.

Hymer, S. M. (1984). The telephone session and the telephone between sessions. *Psychotherapy in Private Practice* 2(3):51–65.

Rosenbaum, M. (1977). Premature interruption of psychotherapy: continuation of contact by telephone and correspondence. *American Journal of Psychiatry* 134(2):200–202.

🔊🔊🔊🔊

Question 15: Do you ever answer phone calls during a session?

On the whole, most therapists said simply that they never answered calls while working with a patient. Here is a somewhat longer response:

> Never. I'm religious about it. I had a therapist who used to answer the phone during sessions, and I hated it, and I really ragged on her for it. She said "Well, that's the way I work," and it drove me bananas. I don't

even have a phone in my office, because I didn't even want a machine clicking.

[Female, Ph.D., 20 years practice]

Several practitioners mentioned that while they generally don't answer the phone during a session, an emergency might arise that would cause them to do so.

Very seldom, unless I know there's an emergency, if I'm expecting something. Sometimes a patient will say that his or her spouse has to contact them.

[Male, M.S.W., 20 years practice]

Many people know if it's an emergency, they should call, hang up if they get my machine, and immediately call me back. That's a signal to me that it's an emergency.

[Female, M.S.W., 20 years practice]

It's usually an emergency if my receptionist calls me during a session, so I will.

[Male, M.S.W., 13 years practice]

Sometimes a less urgent situation might also be grounds for answering the phone.

It depends on where I am. In one location I have no secretary so I do answer the phone.

[Male, M.D., 5 years practice]

The only time I would is in my group, if somebody hasn't appeared, and I'm concerned about why they haven't.

[Female, M.S.W., 15 years practice]

I wouldn't, unless I had warned a client beforehand that something particular is afoot. For example, I had a carpet being delivered last week, and told the client that I might have to interrupt the session.

[Male, M.S.W., 10 years practice]

Occasionally, but mostly not. Only when I'm expecting something very important.

[Male, M.S.W., 10 years practice]

Either if I know I'm expecting a particular call that I want to take, or sometimes I'll forget to turn the volume down on my machine and I'll hear that it's someone I've been trying to get hold of for a while.

[Male, Ph.D., 20 years practice]

A small number of therapists said they did answer the phone when they started practicing, but have since changed their behavior.

I don't any more. My first therapist used to answer the phone during sessions, so I did for a while, but patients used to get so offended. My second therapist did not.

[Female, M.S.W., 25 years practice]

I used to, until I realized that it was really not fair to the patient to do that. I used to think that was part of the process and dealing with whatever went on.

[Male, M.S.W., 25 years practice]

Another small group of therapists still routinely answer phone calls during patient sessions.

I try not to, but I do.

[Male, M.S.W., 15 years practice]

I answer the phone, except if the patient objects.

[Male, Ph.D., 50 years practice]

If it rings I answer it, and would then get off immediately.

[Male, Ph.D., 20 years practice]

One therapist made a judgment about those patients who do object.

Yes. I want patients to know that I am always available. I may not do it, because some patients object and some patients don't object. The more narcissistic patients object.

[Female, Ph.D., 20 years practice]

Finally, another therapist, who also makes judgments about those who object, gives an unusual reason for answering the phone during a session.

Yes. I started doing that because I found that a lot of patients will use the fact that I have an answering machine to leave a provocative message that I won't be able to deal with. For instance, they want to quit therapy but they don't actually want to talk to me because then they'd have to take responsibility for it. So they leave a message and then I try to get ahold of them and of course I can't reach them. I like to answer the phone so I can handle anything that comes up at the moment it's happening. The other reason is in case there's an emergency. But I do get some problems with certain borderline or narcissistic patients who object to my answering the phone during their sessions, and I've lost a few patients because of it. I think I would have lost them anyway, because they just used that as a reason, and they would have used anything else.

[Male, Ph.D., 15 years practice]

NUMERICAL DISTRIBUTION

Thirty-seven people said they never answer the phone during a session; 9 said that they do; 9 said they do only in an emergency; and 5 more said they would only in some other specific situation.

COMMENTS

The issue here is: Whose needs take priority in the session?

I can't think of any valid reason to answer the phone during a session. Even emergencies can usually wait the twenty to forty minutes it might take to complete a session and call back. Answering the phone conveys the message to patients that the therapist's priorities and needs are more important than their own. Making pejorative diagnoses of the patient as narcissistic for objecting to that behavior is a real distortion of the reality that the patient is paying for the time and deserves the full attention of the therapist. Using the rationalization that answering calls conveys to patients that the therapist is "always available" seems to me to have more to do with the grandiosity of the therapist than anything else. And the frustration of having to deal with certain patients' taped messages is a poor justification for interrupting sessions, when balanced against our commitment and obligations to the patient in the room.

Part of our job as therapists is to create a safe space, free from outside influence or interruptions. Answering the phone while in session disturbs that space. It is unfortunate if a ringing phone creates anxiety in the therapist, but if we are to create Winnicott's "holding environment," and become the container for difficult feelings, we must include the ability to contain our own anxiety about incoming phone calls.

RELATED READING

Meek, C. L. (1986). Guidelines for using an answering machine in your practice. In *Innovations in Clinical Practice: A Source Book,* vol. 5, ed. P. A. Keller and L. G. Ritt. Sarasota, FL: Professional Resource Exchange.

🔊🔊🔊🔊

Question 16: Do you allow smoking? Eating? Coffee or other beverages? Do you do any of these yourself in a session?

The strict analytic position seems to be that, in the consulting room, anything other than talking constitutes resistance and avoidance.

> Certainly not. This is a talking room. Nothing but talking. No action, no touching, no sex, no violence, no eating, no drinking, no gum. I do none of those myself, either.
>
> [Female, Ph.D., 20 years practice]

> I want to set the frame that this is serious business, and we don't want any distractions.
>
> [Female, M.S.W., 20 years practice]

> I usually explain that something is going to go into the cigarette or the beverage or the food that I would rather they speak up about.
>
> [Female, M.S., 15 years practice]

Even without this point of view, these behaviors by the patient can be disruptive. It may be difficult to concentrate on what a patient is saying if we're watching the open cup of coffee balanced on the knee, or the burning ash about to fall on the carpet.

SMOKING

Smoking is perhaps the most intrusive of these behaviors, because if the patient smokes, the therapist also inhales. Cigarette smoke gets into everything, and a room starts to smell after a few weeks of cigarettes. Most therapists had a rule against smoking, except for those very few who still smoke themselves. These are some typical responses:

> I don't allow smoking, in the consultation room or in the waiting room.
>
> [Male, M.A., 15 years practice]

I have a sign in the waiting area saying "Please don't smoke," so they don't. No one's smoked in here in a long time.

[Male, M.D., 20 years practice]

Nobody smokes in the whole suite because one of the therapists has asthma.

[Female, M.S.W., 10 years practice]

A few people changed the rules when they changed their own habits.

When I smoked, I allowed smoking. When I stopped smoking I stopped them from smoking.

[Male, Ph.D., 25 years practice]

I don't allow smoking anymore. I used to when I was a smoker, and for a little while after that too, until it got very unpleasant.

[Female, M.S., 20 years practice]

Some therapists make allowances at the beginning of treatment.

I try not to allow smoking, but I have a patient now and sometimes she just has to have a cigarette. We limit it to one. I definitely discourage smoking.

[Female, M.S.W., 15 years practice]

Sometimes yes. When they first come, I'll allow it, because I think they're under enough tension and enough stress, and they don't need more from me.

[Male, M.S.W., 10 years practice]

I don't allow smoking, except perhaps in the first session, when a patient may be extremely anxious and having a difficult time.

[Female, M.S.W., 15 years practice]

I used to allow smoking in my previous office, because I had one patient who wasn't able to get started without a cigarette. When I moved here, I imposed a no-smoking rule and the patient thanked me for helping her stop.

[Female, M.S., 15 years practice]

Even the few therapists who allow smoking still discuss it with their patients.

If someone says they want to smoke, and usually it's a new patient, I'll say, "It's better if you can avoid smoking because it may drain off some of the information that might be helpful. So if you can not smoke, fine. But if you have to have that cigarette, then do it."

[Female, M.S.W., 20 years practice]

I discourage smoking. If I feel that somebody's level of anxiety is such that they would have trouble working in the session I would probably make an exception.

[Male, M.S.W., 20 years practice]

I ask folks to trust me that when I ask them not to smoke they try not to smoke. When I see them trying to bury some feelings I'll often ask them to hold that cigarette back, because I can watch them start to get agitated and reach for the cigarette. Ninety-nine percent will say okay, and then it's pretty interesting when they say "Fuck you" and light it anyway. I only have a few who smoke so it's less of an issue than it used to be.

[Male, M.S.W., 15 years practice]

EATING

Food was sometimes allowed.

I do allow beverages and occasionally food if the patient hasn't had any other time to eat. If it becomes a regular thing or a resistance we discuss it.

[Male, M.A., 15 years practice]

One patient who comes during the lunch hour eats lunch, and I'm perfectly comfortable with that.

[Female, M.S., 15 years practice]

Sometimes patients have come in and munched on something, but I don't make a big deal about it.

[Male, Ph.D., 5 years practice]

Sometimes if someone's coming on their lunch hour, they're conveniencing me by coming out here, so I allow it.

[Female, M.S.W., 25 years practice]

Eating yes, especially during group sessions, and sometimes people will bring breakfast in. I have coffee myself.

[Male, Ph.D., 40 years practice]

Eating—I never made a rule about it, and only one person has done it, and I let it go because she has low blood sugar.

[Female, M.S.W., 10 years practice]

I allow some of my child patients to eat, when they come directly from school and don't have time for a snack. Sometimes it's a way we can talk rather than play, and it allows a different kind of experience to occur.

[Female, M.S.W., 15 years practice]

And sometimes actively discouraged.

If they do bring something in, it becomes an issue of what's going on in the session, not just that they're hungry.

[Female, M.S.W., 10 years practice]

I don't disallow eating, but if the patient came in with food or coffee, I would try to understand why they need to eat while they're here.

[Male, M.D., 20 years practice]

Very few therapists eat during a session.

I'll share food with someone, or eat theirs with them.

[Male, Ph.D., 20 years practice]

BEVERAGES

The large majority of therapists had no rule against beverages in sessions.

I'm completely neutral about beverages. If someone brings in a can of soda or coffee, I don't even comment on it.

[Female, M.D., 15 years practice]

If a client needs to. So far I haven't found it distracting or intolerable.

[Male, M.S.W., 10 years practice]

Those who did not want patients to have beverages in session addressed it directly.

If somebody brings in coffee or a beverage I don't say, "You're not allowed to," I say, "Let's discuss it, and analyze the reason for it." In practice I find that nobody does it more than once or twice.

[Male, Ph.D., 40 years practice]

Most therapists did not themselves drink anything, although some had coffee, tea, or water, and a few offered to share with patients.

Sometimes I have tea and sometimes offer it to clients.

[Female, M.A., 15 years practice]

Sometimes if I'm seeing someone very early in the morning I have coffee, and I offer the person coffee.

[Female, M.S.W., 5 years practice]

I always drink water. Years ago I used to drink coffee. I wouldn't bring in a steaming cup of coffee in front of a patient.

[Female, M.S.W., 25 years practice]

I drink coffee and tea a lot, and I don't believe in double standards. In my waiting room, I have coffee and tea.

[Female, Ph.D., 20 years practice]

When it's really hot, I will offer people a cold drink: water or iced tea or something. I will have a cold drink myself.

[Female, M.S.W., 10 years practice]

Rarely, the therapist may try something unusual.

I've actually had a major breakthrough with someone when I've had a beer with them. It was very hard for me to decide to do that.

[Male, Ph.D., 20 years practice]

A few therapists raised the question of a double standard.

I drink water all day, so I think they should also do what they need to do.

[Female, Ph.D., 5 years practice]

I don't allow any of these. Sometimes I'm guilty of drinking coffee, or I'll chew gum. I try to do it quietly, and if a patient objects, I'll stop.

[Male, Ph.D., 15 years practice]

Finally, one person commented on the question of rules about such behaviors.

I try not to be too controlling, since I do have that tendency.
[Female, M.S.W., 20 years practice]

NUMERICAL DISTRIBUTION

By the Patient

Smoking: 50 said they did not allow it; 8 said they did; 2 more said they allowed it but would discourage it.

Eating: 33 said they did allow it; 7 more said they allowed it but would discourage it; 20 said they did not allow it.

Beverages: 47 said they did allow it; 5 more said they allowed it but would discourage it; 8 said they did not allow it.

By the Therapist

Smoking: only one person said that he smoked during sessions.

Eating: only 4 people said they would eat something during a session.

Beverages: 37 people said they would have water, coffee, tea, or soda during a session; 23 people said they would not.

COMMENTS

One issue raised by this question is whether it is useful to have rules about patient behavior, in or out of the office.

In dealing with these particular behaviors, we have to weigh the advantages of eliminating the distractions of cigarettes, food, and beverages against the disadvantages of more rules and more resistances. I have a rule forbidding smoking, to protect my office and my lungs, and no one ever challenges or questions it. I don't have rules regarding food or beverages, though sometimes patients do seem to use those as a buffer against certain feelings. If patients need the buffer, I don't see the value of removing it prematurely. Occasionally, as a patient spills his coffee over the chair and rug, I wish I did have a rule, but it starts to feel very parental and infantilizing to tell them they can't do in the office what they do everywhere else.

Another issue is raised by those therapists who provide or share food or beverages for patients. To many therapists, this would appear to be acting out, by therapist and patient, and therefore would be proscribed. To others, it might feel more like joining with or metaphorically feeding the patient, and would have a positive meaning. Personally, I would never offer food or beverages, because I believe the therapist feeds the patient with words, with insight, understanding, and interpretation, not with cookies and milk.

RELATED READING

Maiuro, R. D., Michael, M. C., Vitaliano, P. R., et al. (1989). Patient reactions to a no smoking policy in a community mental health center. *Community Mental Health Journal* 25(1):71–77.
Munetz, M. R., and Davies, M. A. (1987). Smoking by patients. *Hospital and Community Psychiatry* 38(4):413–414.

🖼🖼🖼🖼

Question 17: How do you feel about medications? Do you have any patients on medications? How does that affect the treatment?

Sometimes, in the course of a treatment, the therapist will begin to consider medication for certain patients: the depressed patient who doesn't respond to psychotherapy alone; the patient who is so anxious he doesn't function in or out of the session; the patient whose manic episodes become cause for concern. The therapist has to weigh the possible advantages of symptom relief and improved functioning against the possible disadvantages of blunting the affect and making the therapy more difficult, and the complications, at least for non-medical practitioners, of bringing in a third party.

More than half of the interviewees said they used medications and referred to psychiatrists when they thought it would help.

I believe that if someone is intensely anxious or very severely depressed, it would be sadistic not to provide medication. With all due respect to some of my non-medical colleagues who are anti-medication, I think to make someone go though a protracted period of time without medication is really brutal. What I find is that when the patient is on medication there's more of an available ego to work with.

[Male, M.S.W., 35 years practice]

I have several patients on medication, and they were all people I recommended to see a psychiatrist for medication, because I felt that the degree of their anxiety or depression was actually making it harder for us to work together. I have only one person who is not responsive to the medications and had to go into the hospital. Most of them, within two or three weeks, feel a lot more comfortable, and I think the work becomes much more productive.

[Female, M.S.W., 20 years practice]

Part of my training was with a psychiatrist, who suggested that it's a merciful thing, if someone is in terrible deep depression. If a medication can lop off the worst depths of a depression, why not?

[Male, M.S.W., 10 years practice]

It takes the edge off, and calms people down enough to be able to work on issues.

[Female, Ph.D., 20 years practice]

Some referred their patients only reluctantly.

I don't rush to medicate my people. I don't think that's a great idea. I'd rather work with them without a medication. If their pain becomes such that they really can't tolerate it, and it's interfering with their functioning, then I will send them. I do have several people on medications, but it wasn't mild complaints. It was serious incapacities. The reason I don't jump to send someone for medication is I want them to feel that I'm there, that I can tolerate their pain and I don't have to medicate their pain away. I just feel that it's better to talk about it. There's no negative effects on treatment, it has lifted several people's serious depressions, and they're more available to work.

[Female, M.S.W., 20 years practice]

If a person wants medication, I give them a referral to a psychiatrist that I'm affiliated with. I usually wait for them to suggest it, but I might initiate it. If the person was a danger to themself or to others, I would say that you need to admit yourself to a hospital or see a psychiatrist for medication because you're just too unsteady. That's the only time that I would recommend it. Otherwise I think it's better to try to fight through the feelings via therapy.

[Male, Ph.D., 15 years practice]

Basically I'm biased against it. I would rather deal with whatever symptoms the person is having. If somebody's not functional then, sure, I recommend them for medication. But if they're able to function, I'd rather just try to treat the symptoms and help them with it.

[Female, M.S., 15 years practice]

I would like it if nobody took medication. I would like it if everybody could have his or her feelings and talk about them and behave appropriately. If a patient needs medication in order to continue in therapy, and stay alive, then I refer them to psychiatrists. The effects are both positive and negative. In many cases, it enables them to stay in treatment, and, to be sure, it blanks some feelings out that don't come into the therapy.

[Female, Ph.D., 20 years practice]

None of my patients is on medication. I recommend medication if they're in great distress and they want relief. I educate them about psychotropic medication, and inform them that mostly it doesn't cure the problem, that it gives them relief, that it's toxic, and the sooner they get off the better. It doesn't change the treatment. The only medications that I'm really familiar with, Zoloft particularly, have been helpful when they work.

[Male, Ph.D., 50 years practice]

Several therapists said that while they had formerly been against medication, they had changed their position and were now in favor of it.

I've moved in a different direction. Even though my training is in pharmacology, I was always against using medications for psychological disorders. I am now in favor of it, if used judiciously. Because psychotherapy doesn't work for all things. I'm not that big on theory. I've studied all the different theories, but I believe the most important thing is to be a humanist, and relieve suffering. For schizophrenia, psychotherapy by itself isn't going to work. And for manic-depression it isn't going to work. And if somebody's in acute distress I have to weigh the situation.

[Male, Ph.D., 10 years practice]

I used to be really opposed to using medication, and now I have more mixed feelings. I have seen it really be a help in treatment at times, allowing people to get past some of their obsessive, depressive behavior so we can get to issues. So I've seen it be really valuable on a short-term basis.

[Female, M.S.W., 15 years practice]

I used to be very reluctant to recommend it. I was never against it, but I never was for it, either. I'm getting more training, and it's at a psychiatrically oriented institute. My supervisor is a psychiatrist, and he's talked a lot about medication with certain kinds of patients and how valuable it can be. There are times now when I'll ask the person if they're open to it, how they feel about it, and I might suggest it.

[Male, M.S.W., 15 years practice]

I've changed my views. I worked in a mental institution for years, and hospitals, and I thought that often medication was given too quickly, and abused. Now, I have a lot more respect for what it can do, that people don't have to be in as much pain, certainly with the new anti-depressants. When it's necessary, I refer them to one of the two psychiatrists I use.

[Female, Ph.D., 5 years practice]

I used to be much more negatively disposed toward ritalin, and I have found cases where it's really made a big difference for the child.

[Female, M.S.W., 15 years practice]

Most therapists have a very positive relationship with the medical person they use.

I love medication. I have a referring psychiatrist that I've worked with for fifteen years. Every time I've sent him someone for a second opinion, when I want medication considered or hospitalization. And every time I thought a client needed to be medicated so did he, and every time I think they didn't need to be, neither did he. And I never warn him ahead of time, and we've agreed every single time.

[Male, M.S.W., 15 years practice]

Two people cautioned about the importance of finding the right psychiatrist.

I have had patients on antidepressants and anti-anxiety medications, and it's all right if your psychopharmacologist is cooperative and doesn't interfere too much with the therapy.

[Female, M.S.W., 30 years practice]

I think there is room for medications. The effect, whatever it is, is grist for the mill. Sometimes it triangulates the transference. But what's important is to do some legwork and find a psychiatrist who will be psychologically minded, so he won't interfere with the treatment.

[Male, Ph.D., 20 years practice]

One person spoke at length about the effect of bringing in a third party, the psychiatrist or psychopharmacologist.

The effect on the treatment is that it complicates the relationship with you because of the additional relationship with the psychopharmacologist, who's asking them very personal stuff. In order to be evaluated you have to tell your history to someone you don't know, and they ask very carefully about symptoms and very private things, and they should, otherwise the assessment would be inadequate. And also in making the referral you've gotten their consent to speak with this other person, but then the pharmacologist might know something about them before they even get there, which people have feelings about, even if it's at their request.

[Female, M.S.W., 10 years practice]

Many therapists report significant improvement in those patients taking medication.

If somebody's very depressed, antidepressant medication takes the edge off of the depression and helps the psychotherapy work.

[Female, M.S.W., 25 years practice]

I work collaboratively with psychiatrists all the time, and it's really essential for some people. With anxiety disorders, if people are avoiding situations, if they need to take medication because they're not getting better with cognitive treatment, a little bit of medication will help them do what they need to do, and then you taper the medication off after they've dealt with the feared situation. These medications don't make people zombies, they just lower the level of anxiety so that they can cope.

[Female, Ph.D., 10 years practice]

I'm very pro-Prozac. In one instance, it affected the treatment marvelously. This patient really has done well on it, and well in the treatment. He's been much more responsive, much more integrated in terms of how he deals with the session. He used to be much more scattered. He suffered from agitated depression, and lots of times I had the sense he was flying around the room. He really settled in. It helped tremendously.

[Male, M.S.W., 25 years practice]

I'm real comfortable with them. I have many patients on medications. If it works, it helps the treatment. There are certain conditions, like OCD, where ignoring medication really borders on the unethical.

[Male, Ph.D., 20 years practice]

Mostly, I have clients on Prozac. I think it facilitates the treatment. I think it really helps them gain the confidence to look at more, their lives tend to go better, and they're less frightened, less depressed, less obsessive.

[Female, M.S.W., 15 years practice]

Generally the effect is a positive one, in that the patient feels that they're being heard and listened to and being taken seriously, and their suffering is being addressed. So it enhances the relationship, for the most part.

[Male, M.D., 20 years practice]

Some therapists don't see much improvement with medication, or even see some detriment.

I don't know how significant it's been, either positively or negatively. Some feel a little better, but nothing dramatically different.

[Male, M.S.W., 15 years practice]

The new SSRI [selective serotonin reuptake inhibitor] medications tend to even out the moods so it becomes harder for the person to generate a lot of feeling to motivate themselves. They have sometimes a placid affect, and it's harder to elicit more energy around those issues.

[Male, Ph.D., 25 years practice]

I had some experience in the past with people being on Xanax, which I would hope that no one does again for a long time because it's a horror show to get off of it. It's really very habit-forming.

[Female, M.S.W., 10 years practice]

In my clinic position, they use medication very freely. There may be instances where it's necessary, like an antipsychotic. But I'd rather not use antidepressants and anti-anxiety drugs, because they're like zombies sometimes, and it absolutely cuts them off from feelings.

[Female, M.S.W., 45 years practice]

My experience is that medication doesn't make that much difference one way or the other, either plus or minus. I suppose you could take the edge off intense anxiety, and in the chemically based things like manic depression lithium definitely helps, but I don't think generally it does a lot.

[Male, Ph.D., 25 years practice]

I do work with psychiatrists, or physicians, around the need for medication, or the altering of the medication, or the side effects that I may see. In most cases, it's a detraction from the treatment. It interferes with the depth of the therapeutic process. Exploration becomes a little more difficult, and resistances come up more easily.

[Male, Ph.D., 30 years practice]

I find that patients on medication are *less* available. It feels to me that it does mask certain things, and I don't like that. I'm not that afraid of intense feelings. I don't mind if somebody's very depressed—I can be with that. I have a patient right now who's very depressed, and with her I have actually asked her if she wants medication, because I think she might be helped by it, but she refuses and so I just go with it and stay with her.

[Female, M.S., 15 years practice]

In most cases, it's been very disrupting, because there's been anger towards me that I wasn't the one that was able to make them feel better. There's been anger toward the psychiatrist, that he's insensitive, he doesn't know what he's talking about. There's been anger at themselves, what do I need this for, I'm a real mess now and medicine is an indication of how sick I am. So there's a lot of disruption. But in spite of that, it's been mostly a positive in terms of the actual effects. But it brings up a lot of issues between the two of us, like why am I coming here to see you if this pill is going to make me feel better? On most occasions, I've suggested the medication, although a few times the patient has asked for it.

[Female, M.S., 15 years practice]

Some other effects that were mentioned are:

Patients have felt wounded when I question if they ever considered it.

[Female, M.S.W., 15 years practice]

It's different if the person brings it up or if I do, because it does seem as if you can't bear to hear their feelings if you bring it up.

[Female, M.S.W., 10 years practice]

I've seen it shorten the treatment, because people start to feel a whole lot better due to the medication. I encourage them to remain in treatment because I suggest that now that things are calm, this is a wonderful time to work on the issues. And sometimes they stay and other times not.

[Female, M.A., 20 years practice]

Clearly, there are times when it's used defensively, as a way of keeping themselves from feeling how distressed they are.

[Female, Ph.D., 15 years practice]

Most of the patients that are on medication feel taken care of, that I have noticed that they're in a lot of pain and made the suggestion about helping them feel more comfortable.

[Female, M.S.W., 10 years practice]

I have occasionally had people quit because I insisted on it.

[Female, M.S., 20 years practice]

Patients sometimes think that the medications should make them better, and then the obsession turns to why the medication isn't making them better.

[Female, M.S.W., 15 years practice]

The effect on the treatment is that the client comes with such a profound sense of hopelessness, and just the tiniest degree of belief that maybe, just maybe, they could change. And they spend two or three weeks with me and they want the miracle of Lourdes and it doesn't happen. I diagnose them, and send them for medication, and they get their miracle of Lourdes. And they credit me with that, rather than the psychiatrist.

[Male, M.S.W., 15 years practice]

Here are three psychiatrists speaking at some length about the use of medications and some of the effects on the treatment.

I trained in a very psychoanalytically oriented residency, one of the last years of that, ever. Actually, a really weak part of my training was psychopharmacology. I finished my residency much weaker in psychopharmacology than the average psychiatrist. The fact that I'm very comfortable with medication and really believe that it's useful and important has come not from training but from my own experience in the office. I educated myself in psychopharmacology after my residency. I don't use medicine with a lot of people, but I don't hesitate to use it if it would offer significant symptom relief, or even make a treatment work better. In the majority of cases, it facilitates the psychotherapy. In a handful of cases, it's used as a kind of defense, let's talk about the medicine instead of the problems. But that's a psychotherapeutic issue. I have never treated anyone who wanted to discontinue their psychotherapy because they felt better on medication. I have on occasion given medication and had problems, bad reactions, or it didn't work, and had that hurt the therapeutic relationship. In some cases, people having bad reactions to medication and dealing with me about it is very therapeutic, because they deal with the negative aspect of the transference. But there are occasions where it's ended the treatment.

[Female, M.D., 15 years practice]

As a psychiatrist, I use a lot of medications, when appropriate. I treat a lot of people for depression, I treat a lot of people for psychotic disorders, and I use medications for those reasons. For anxiety disorders, I don't use the anxiolytics, because they're all addictive, and it's so difficult to use them correctly. So for anxiety disorders, I would use other methods, psychotherapy, behavior therapy, other methods. Ideally, it enhances the treatment. With a person with major depression, you could treat that with cognitive therapy and with psychotherapy alone. You need to discuss that with the patient and it has to be the patient's choice. But my experience has been that if a person has a major depression, a clinical depression, usually with an antidepressant and therapy together, they're able to do better work in therapy, because they're emotionally available.

[Male, M.D., 5 years practice]

I still have my original prescription blanks, from twenty years ago. I haven't used them up yet. But there are two or three medications that I have found extremely useful and probably life-saving and helpful in the therapy. Lithium, especially, and occasionally some antidepressants. In these instances, I think it's a necessary adjunct to the treatment, because without the antidepressant, this one patient was almost silent in session. The antidepressant really helped them work and speak much more in the sessions.

[Male, M.D., 20 years practice]

NUMERICAL DISTRIBUTION

Thirty-five people said they had positive attitude toward medications; 6 more said they had changed their original attitude from negative to positive; 9 said they had mixed feelings; and 10 said they didn't like having patients on medication.

COMMENTS

The issues here are: Are psychotherapy and medication mutually exclusive? Does medication enhance or diminish the effectiveness of therapy? Is the patient on medication more available and more present, or are feelings muted and less accessible?

This is another complex area. If I suggest medication, it may mean to the patient that I've given up on psychotherapy, or that I can't tolerate what's going on in the sessions. If I don't suggest it, I may be extending their distress unnecessarily. A third party complicates treatment, with phone calls back and forth to the psychiatrist, and a possible split in transference.

In the last two years, I have had more patients on medication than in the previous ten. I have seen some of the newer antidepressants be very effective with some patients, and not at all effective with others. I have had several very anxious patients use anti-anxiety medications fairly well on an as-needed basis, and a few who overused them to avoid any disturbing feelings.

I used to be very reluctant to send a patient for a medication consultation, because I believed that the patient might conclude that I can't tolerate his or her feelings, especially the depression, and so I'm sending them to someone who will make those feelings go away. I've come to believe more in the usefulness of medication for some patients, though I still refer very cautiously. With a very depressed patient, therapeutic work may not be possible until the depression is relieved. A very anxious patient may not be able to tolerate the additional anxiety that therapy can elicit.

In general, I prefer to wait for the patient to ask about medication, which makes it much less likely that he or she will read anything into my recommending it. I will almost always set up a pharmacological consultation if the patient wants one, although I may in some cases say that I don't think medication will help much.

RELATED READING

Bascue, L. O., and Zlotowski, M. (1981). Psychologists' attitudes about prescribing medications. *Psychological Reports* 48(2):645–646.

Breggin, P. R., and Breggin, G. P. (1994). *Talking Back to Prozac.* New York: St. Martin's Press.

Gelenberg, A. J., Bassuk, E. L., and Schoonover, S. C., eds. (1991). *The Practitioner's Guide to Psychoactive Drugs,* 3rd ed. New York: Plenum Press.

Kramer, P. D. (1993). *Listening to Prozac.* New York: Viking.

🕃🕃🕃🕃

Question 18: Do you use the couch? Why?

The old stereotype of the analyst shows the patient lying on the couch while the analyst sits behind taking notes. Are there still valid reasons for using the couch?

About twenty percent of the sample said that they use the couch with most of their patients. Not surprisingly, these therapists tended to be more psychoanalytically oriented.

> It's easier for me to listen to the patient, and in most instances it helps the patient talk more freely. They're not watching me and trying to make eye contact and seduce, make me laugh, whatever. Of course, that can happen anyway. Patients listen for my movements, if I change position, you can't avoid that completely. But it is easier for me to listen. I can relax more and not worry about my facial expression, or if I'm twiddling my thumbs. And then I can also observe myself a little more freely, while I'm listening to the patient.
>
> [Male, M.D., 20 years practice]

> I like not having to look at the patient, or having the patient look at me. It can be distracting, and the patient can possibly regress more in that position.
>
> [Female, M.S.W., 45 years practice]

> Almost all of my patients are on the couch. I find that's the best method for me, because I don't feel comfortable looking at patients. And patients can look at you, like a paranoid patient, or a seductive patient, and make you feel very uncomfortable, and you wish you had a mask or something. Everything you do acquires significance, and it handicaps your ability to respond objectively and calmly.
>
> [Male, Ph.D., 15 years practice]

> It depends on the frequency of sessions. If I see someone more than once a week, I definitely use the couch. Even on a once-a-week basis, there are times we do use the couch, when an impasse is reached or there's a resistance that's difficult to overcome. It does help in effecting changes within the therapeutic situation.
>
> [Male, Ph.D., 30 years practice]

> It helps to free the patient from having to tune in to me. If a patient is very observant of me, and responding only to me instead of themselves, I'll suggest it.
>
> [Female, M.S.W., 20 years practice]

I use the couch if I'm seeing someone often enough and if the person is healthy enough. When patients sit up, they too often are looking for reactions in the face of the therapist. They're trying to get a response, to please the therapist, and it removes them from themselves. Often, when you put the patient on the couch there's a greater degree of introspection.

[Male, M.S.W., 35 years practice]

I encourage people to use it. I find it works wonderfully well. It facilitates people saying what's on their mind, and it loosens things up a bit. They can jump around more, it stays less in the present, people drift over time better. I like it. I never insist on it. I'll suggest it at some point into the treatment, when I think the relationship is set.

[Female, M.S., 15 years practice]

It has to do with providing the space and the opportunity for exploration. It allows the patient to relax and feel separate and not be distracted.

[Female, Ph.D., 15 years practice]

Although the couch is stereotypically associated with the silent analyst, one person pointed out that it is possible to be as interactive with someone on the couch as if they were sitting up.

I use it in a very interpersonal, intersubjective context. I probably talk as much with a patient on the couch as I do with one in the chair.

[Female, M.S.W., 15 years practice]

More than a third said they sometimes suggest the couch for specific situations.

Most of my people are sitting up. I suggest it when I feel that someone would be freer, would be able to contact more things and talk about them without looking at me. I also have someone sitting up who doesn't look at me for the past three years.

[Female, M.S.W., 20 years practice]

I suggest it with clients who feel like they've said it all, covered everything, and yet somehow know that there's more to see.

[Male, M.S.W., 10 years practice]

Only when I do hypnosis.

[Female, M.A., 20 years practice]

On occasion, if it's somebody who's pretty stable and not prone to regression, and where I think they can tolerate developing a deeper transference, so that by not looking at me they'd have to deal with their fantasies. For some people it might be more relaxing and allow them to introspect more.

[Male, M.S.W., 20 years practice]

This is a very small couch, so I've only used it with people who are short. I use it with patients who really understand the process. Where the patient feels comfortable with it and is able to free associate a little bit more.

[Female, M.S.W., 10 years practice]

Even those who rarely use the couch can occasionally have reason to use it.

I think the relationship is what's important, so I want them up and relating to me. That's also what they want. I very seldom have patients who want to lie down. There are times it's called for in terms of what's happening in the process, like when the patient needs to commune as much with themselves as with me. It provides an opportunity for me to be experienced as less intrusive.

[Male, M.S.W., 25 years practice]

Almost half said they never use the couch, or only once in a great while will suggest it. Some said they didn't see any value or advantage in using it.

No. I don't feel any particular need. I prefer working face-to-face, I like to use the relationship, and the couch is not a mode that I'm trained in.

[Male, Ph.D., 5 years practice]

I don't any more, because of my own experience on the couch and my moving away from the psychoanalytic, and wanting to do more here-and-now work.

[Female, M.S.W., 15 years practice]

I was never trained to do it, and I think seeing the person's face is incredibly important. Using the couch to speak freely when they can't do it face-to-face is a trick. If they can't speak freely, our job is to understand why not and work on that.

[Male, M.S.W., 15 years practice]

I don't any more. I was never that comfortable with it. My room is small and there's nowhere for me to sit behind them, so it always felt awkward. I also found it took so much time to get people comfortable with the whole process of lying down that I would give up.

[Female, M.A., 15 years practice]

A few people said that if the patient needed not to look at the therapist, two chairs could still accomplish the same goal.

I like to work face-to-face. Also, I like the model of two of the same chairs, and patients who don't want to look at me will swivel their chair away. So they have the option, and it accomplishes the same purpose as the couch.

[Female, M.S., 15 years practice]

People often use the wall as a couch, in that our chairs are usually at right angles, and they would have to turn their chair to face me, and some of them do that.

[Female, M.S.W., 10 years practice]

Several people suggested that the couch could be used to avoid something, or that it could create problems rather than solve them.

One of my patients uses the couch, but I think its an avoidance, avoiding me, he can just ramble on in his own way.

[Female, M.A., 15 years practice]

I'm finding that the patients I had on the couch were getting more stuck, that those patients needed the eye-to-eye contact.

[Female, M.D., 15 years practice]

I haven't used it in quite some time. If somebody wanted to use it, we would discuss what that was about, and if it made sense to me I wouldn't oppose it. I'd use it for people where looking at me distracts them, and they can't focus on what's happening with themselves. Then I'd do it on a temporary basis until that was no longer so.

[Female, M.S., 20 years practice]

NUMERICAL DISTRIBUTION

Twelve people said they use the couch with all or almost every patient; 23 said they use it some of the time; 25 said they never or very rarely use it.

COMMENTS

There are two main issues here: Does the couch do what is claimed for it, namely make it easier to talk freely? If so, is using the couch a facilitating strategy or an avoidance of confronting directly the difficulty of speaking freely?

There is a real mystique surrounding the couch, for patients and, I think, for therapists, too. Many analysts (and some patients, too) don't consider it real treatment unless the patient is on the couch. Something almost magical is expected to happen; regression and free association are expected to increase automatically. Many patients are afraid even to try lying on the couch, expecting something uncontrollable to happen.

The couch can, on the other hand, be useful in certain situations. I suggest it to some patients who spend much energy monitoring me, my movements, gestures, facial expressions, and so on, if exploring the whys and wherefores of their concern fails to relieve it. Although they may be initially anxious about not being able to see me, they usually find it very liberating.

RELATED READING

Goldberger, M. (1995). The couch as defense and as potential for enactment. *Psychoanalytic Quarterly* 64(1):23–42.
Reiser, L. W. (1986). "Lying" and "lying": a case report of a paradoxical reaction to the couch. In *Psychoanalytic Study of the Child* 41:537–559. New York: International Universities Press.
Searles, H. F. (1984). The role of the analyst's facial expressions in psychoanalysis and psychoanalytic therapy. *International Journal of Psychoanalytic Psychotherapy* 10:47–73.
Waugaman, R. M. (1987). Falling off the couch. *Journal of the American Psychoanalytic Association* 35(4):861–876.

🔊🔊🔊🔊

Question 19: What are dreams?

[While this question technically belongs in the section on theory, it is included here to avoid separating it from the next question, on how dreams are handled in treatment.]

No one knows for sure what purposes dreams serve, or even what they are. In psychoanalytic terms, they are wish fulfillments, or an attempt at conflict resolution. Recent physiological research suggests that they may be merely the product of random synaptic firings of the sleeping brain. How do the therapists in our sample think of dreams?

Many of our therapists saw dreams as psychological phenomena.

> They're what we've always said they are: thoughts of the unconscious. They're repressed memories, repressed feelings.
>
> [Female, Ph.D., 30 years practice]

> Dreams are a wonderful language that we have. We can take all our experiences and create something very concise and clear. Dreams are really much clearer than our day-to-day talk. I think dreams are an inner book about yourself, because they're so personal and so unique. It's one of the few things that's completely your own—no one else has the same dream.
>
> [Female, Ph.D., 5 years practice]

> Dreams are ways in which your mind is telling you what you couldn't face during the day.
>
> [Female, M.S.W., 20 years practice]

> Dreams play out unconscious conflict. It takes things we're thinking about, anxious about, to a deeper level, and keeps playing them out while we're sleeping.
>
> [Female, M.S.W., 5 years practice]

> They're a form of communication by the patient in terms of the meanings and conflicts that are going on in his life, and it's a problem-solving area.
>
> [Male, Ph.D., 30 years practice]

> Sometimes wish fulfillments, sometimes conflict, attempts at conflict resolution.
>
> [Male, M.S.W., 10 years practice]

> They're ways that our emotions get played out in stories when we're sleeping. They can be reflective of very concrete things that just happened, that we're just thinking about, or they can be other things that we haven't been dealing with but are present within us.
>
> [Female, M.A., 15 years practice]

> It's an ongoing mental process, that continues from daytime to nighttime. Our minds are constantly figuring things out, and projecting, all the things you do in the daytime.
>
> [Male, M.S.W., 25 years practice]

Dreams are a coded message having to do with unconscious wishes or unconscious fears, which of course are often the same thing. They're a residue of unresolved issues in one's conscious life that then become plots in the dream.

[Male, Ph.D., 15 years practice]

They are, like any other manifestation of the human mind, compromise formations. By manifestations of the human mind, I mean that they're the same as any other thoughts, feelings, or behaviors. Compromise between acceptable and unacceptable impulses, and between abilities to gratify and inhibit those.

[Male, M.D., 20 years practice]

Dreams are very loose fantasies, that indicate what the person wants, or is frightened of.

[Male, M.S.W., 15 years practice]

Others saw dreams as primarily physiological phenomena.

A dream is a physiological process of energy in the brain that somehow continues a process that's going on during the day in a way that's less controlled consciously, so that it can reveal what's going on better.

[Female, M.S.W., 30 years practice]

A dream is a rambling amount of neurotransmitters going on in the brain.

[Male, M.S.W., 15 years practice]

The best I've been able to get from the sleep research is that they are some fairly random brain-stem activity, possibly limbic activity, that then gets vaguely organized, probably more around day residue than anything else.

[Male, Ph.D., 20 years practice]

I'm not sure. I think they're mostly physiological. The body is reorganizing itself, and balancing itself. It's drawn from real life, and some of the issues a person lives with.

[Male, Ph.D., 25 years practice]

Others saw dreams as a combination of physiological and psychological elements.

Dreams are hallucinatory experiences. There's a whole range of things that stimulate dreams. Freud said that there is a sleep-disturbing stimulus. Anything that disturbs sleep is likely to stimulate a dream. But the stimulus of the dream does not account for the content of the dream. The content of the dream, the dream story, lends itself to interpretation, and the interpretation is undoubtedly related to what's going on in the person's life at the particular time.

[Male, Ph.D., 50 years practice]

Dreams are not purely biological, and not purely psychological. Sometimes they're disparate elements that just come up, random firings, but it's how we make sense of it, the higher cortical processing is our personality.

[Male, Ph.D., 10 years practice]

They're memories of something that happened during the day, that gets associated in the neurology of your brain to little bits and pieces of prior experience.

[Male, Ph.D., 15 years practice]

Sometimes they're manifestations of the unconscious, and sometimes residue of overworked brains firing off.

[Female, M.S.W., 25 years practice]

At least one person had changed his opinion about dreams, leaning more now to a physiological explanation.

Here's another area where I've changed. I'll still work with anyone who brings up a dream, but I no longer encourage people to bring me their dreams. I'm influenced by what I continue to read about the bio-chemical aspects of dreaming, and I'm not so sure that dream analysis wasn't just this amazingly inventive idea that Freud had.

[Female, M.A., 20 years practice]

NUMERICAL DISTRIBUTION

Forty-two people said dreams are a psychological phenomenon; 7 people said dreams are a physiological phenomenon; 6 people said dreams are a combination of physiology and psychology; 5 people said they didn't know what dreams are.

COMMENTS

The obvious issue here is whether dreams have meaning and purpose, and consequently whether analyzing them in treatment has any value.

Unfortunately, nobody knows for certain what dreams are and what purpose they serve. The latest research findings seem to indicate that dreams are a sequence of random firings of neurons. Even if that is true, it may be irrelevant, because there seems to be a secondary process by which they are organized and remembered and associated to, and that can become important material to work with in the session.

RELATED READING

Altman, L.L. (1969). *The Dream in Psychoanalysis*. New York: International Universities Press.

Freud, S. (1900). The interpretation of dreams. *Standard Edition* 4 & 5.

Solms, M. (1995). New findings on the neurological organization of dreaming: implications for psychoanalysis. *Psychoanalytic Quarterly* 64(1):43–67.

᠍᠍᠍᠍

Question 20: How do you work with dreams?

Most therapists, no matter what their theoretical orientation or belief about the nature of dreams, use them in treatment in some way. The patient recounts a dream, and then what?

Many therapists, especially analytically oriented ones, use the classical techniques of dream analysis and interpretation, although they may disagree about whether to tell the patient their own associations or interpretations.

> I work with them very classically analytically. I ask people to tell me the dream, and sometimes ask what their feeling was when they woke up, so that I know what the affect is. Then I'll ask them to pick out an element or elements and tell me their associations, and I might have to do a little education about how to do that. I give my own associations very, very rarely, only if it seems particularly relevant to a particular dream.
>
> [Female, M.D., 15 years practice]

> When they say they have a dream, I immediately pick up my pad, and it's like salivation. I listen to the dream, write it down. Sometimes they'll bring me a copy of the dream, and I like that the best because I get tired writing. Then I go over it piece by piece, and get their associations, their symbols, and the way they look at things rather than give them

my pat interpretations of it. If I know the person pretty well, I might bring up things that I know about them. I usually give feedback afterwards.

[Male, Ph.D., 15 years practice]

Usually, the patient will tell me the dream, a lot of people come in with it written down, and I'll listen to the whole dream, and if it's complicated I'll write it down. And I ask them what they make of it. Then I start at the beginning of the dream, and ask them to associate to the different elements.

[Female, M.S., 15 years practice]

I ask them to tell me the dream, and then I ask them to tell me again, and I listen for changes, how their voice is, and their body language. Then I go over it with them, and at certain points I'll ask them to tell me more about a certain image or situation. If I've been working with someone a long time, I will tell them what I think, and I'll also ask them to look at it in terms of conflict, and in terms of resistances, and in terms of their relationship with the therapist.

[Female, M.S.W., 10 years practice]

If a patient brings in a dream, I try to find out what they think precipitated the dream. I try to understand the context of the dream to begin with and then see if the dream itself and their associations to the elements of the dream will help further our understanding of what's going on with them. I do give them my own associations.

[Male, M.D., 20 years practice]

I encourage the patient to try to understand why he set up the dream in the way that he has, and its different meanings. I have him associate to the dream. I try to let him know that, as the dreamer, he has the key to understanding the full meaning of the dream and that he's trying to work out current conflicts through his dream material, which may have a bearing on antecedents in his growing-up years. I try to avoid telling the patient what I think the dream means.

[Male, Ph.D., 30 years practice]

One therapist described in detail how central dreams are to the way he works.

It's always presented within the context of the session. I always try to think about the dream on many levels, and one level is how the dream fits the session. There might be a correspondence between the structure of the session and the structure of the dream. I will ask for associations, and let the patient share with me what they think the dream is about. I also use dreams as markers in the development of the treatment. In my initial interview I always ask for a dream, and I always internally, to myself, refer back to that dream with the new material that's emerging, and I'm able to see the process, the vicissitudes of the treatment based on that dream. I don't give my own associations. I might use my association to formulate my interpretation.

[Male, Ph.D., 20 years practice]

A psychiatrist mentioned specifically how difficult it can sometimes be to get patients to work with dreams the way he wants to.

I try to work with it traditionally, but if I count the number of patients over the past fifteen years who could work with a dream traditionally, I would not run out of fingers and toes. It's very difficult to get patients to associate meaningfully. I'm very careful about giving associations of my own, but sometimes I will. I see many patients who are too defended to report their dreams or remember their dreams. I try to get across the message that this is a meaningful communication about the patient's inner life, and that it can be understood, and that it's able to help us learn something about the person. I always show interest in dreams and in talking about them. I have some patients where it's really been key to the therapy, to understanding them.

[Male, M.D., 15 years practice]

Different therapists emphasize different aspects of dream work.

I encourage people to keep dream logs. I use a combination of a gestalt approach and an analytic, even more Freudian, approach, looking at the symbolic representations of the dreams. Also looking particularly at the relationships in the dreams, that the characters have, and the objects in the dreams to the characters. So it's very much from a relationship focus. I'll have the patient first give their interpretation of what they think is going on and then I'll tell them what it really is.

[Male, Ph.D., 25 years practice]

I ask them what they think about it, what was the experience like, what did it feel like when they had the dream? Do they want to look at it? We look at the metaphors, and the words, which are so rich with meaning. I really enjoy working with dreams.

[Female, Ph.D., 5 years practice]

Several therapists said that they treat dreams no differently from any other material.

I work with them the same way as anything else: I listen and try to understand. I don't think of them as more significant than anything else the patient talks about.

[Female, Ph.D., 15 years practice]

I'm much less focused on dreams with patients than I used to be. In the beginning, I used to ask the patient to associate to the different elements, à la Freud. Now, I try to listen to it with not much more attention than I give any other material. With some patients the dreams are very useful, and with others not so useful. I used to try to figure out every dream a patient brought me, but now I'm much more humble. A lot of dreams are just not decipherable, and some key dreams are tremendously useful.

[Male, M.D., 20 years practice]

My way of analyzing them is that the patient will relate a dream and I will simply listen to whatever follows. I try not to analyze the dream item by item, what do you associate to this or that, which I find too mechanical. If you just listen well enough you'll find that what follows is definitely related to the dream. It doesn't even have to be in that same session. Sometimes a patient will tell you a dream at the end of a session, and everything that preceded it was an association to the dream.

[Male, M.S.W., 35 years practice]

Others use, or at least include, a gestalt approach to working with the dream.

Dreams can be really wonderful because they move people away from content, from reporting. They can be a doorway to other levels of material. It gives patients a new way to approach what they're thinking or feeling. I use basically a gestalt approach. I sometimes take notes when someone presents a dream, and that gives them the message that this is important.

[Female, M.A., 15 years practice]

I'm greatly influenced by the notion that all the characters in the dream are parts of the dreamer. Sometimes I use gestalt techniques if the patient can't quickly get in touch with that notion.

[Female, M.S., 20 years practice]

It depends on how they want to work with it. Some dreams are celebratory. A colleague talked about dreams that have to do with death. I ask people to put a headline to their dreams, to give me a focus of what they want to concentrate on. I ask them in a gestalt way to be someone or something the dream.

[Male, Ph.D., 40 years practice]

Dreams are an expression of the unconscious, and very helpful, and I like to look at dreams as expressions of the self. Every part of the dream is a part of who you are, which is something I've held onto from my gestalt experiences. I look most strongly at what the dominant feeling is in the dream, and then relate that feeling to what's happening in life.

[Female, Ph.D., 20 years practice]

Several people expressed the belief that the most important aspect of the dream is not the content, but the communication to the therapist.

I think of the dream as a communication, that the patient is telling me something. Why this dream on this day is really very important. And I ask the patient for his reactions to it, his associations, as much as possible. I try to make it, like everything else in therapy, a growth experience, so that they get something out of this dream, not just that it shows that they're conflicted. That doesn't mean anything.

[Female, M.S.W., 30 years practice]

With regard to my role as an analyst, dreams are a communication between the patient and me, and I try to work with them no differently than I would any other communication. Which doesn't mean I don't do typical standard dream exploration, because I do. But it's no different from what I do in exploration of what his wife said this morning.

[Male, Ph.D., 10 years practice]

I work with them according to what they mean to the patient. I ask them about what it means to them, what it means to be sharing the dream with me, why they thought it was important. I emphasize its meaning in terms of the shared experience of telling me.

[Female, M.S.W., 15 years practice]

A couple of people suggested that dreams in the context of treatment can be a resistance.

I work with them as a resistance. I believe that the telling of dreams is in fact a resistance to the patient telling directly what the dream is saying. So I listen to the dream, and to the message in the dream, and try to figure out how come that isn't coming up directly in the therapy, and eventually it will.

[Female, Ph.D., 20 years practice]

There are some patients who never bring in dreams, they say they never remember them. Some patients use them in a very intellectualized way that takes them away from the process, as a resistance.

[Female, M.S.W., 20 years practice]

People tell me their dreams and their associations. And again I have them do most of the work. They have to pull to get anything out of me. I've discovered over the years, I used to give these big interpretations but they go nowhere. A lot of patients will ask for interpretations, but they're just trying to flatter me or make me feel important. So I turn the question back to them and ask what they think it means.

[Male, Ph.D., 15 years practice]

When I was working more analytically, I would have them describe it and free associate. Now, I listen to the dream and to what the person makes of the dream. I ask the question, "Why is the person bringing the dream to me?" I had a patient who brought me three or four dreams every session, and I finally said, "Enough with the dreams! Let's get on to what's going on in your life." It can be an avoidance.

[Male, Ph.D., 10 years practice]

Our group was divided about the question of giving their own associations to a patient's dream. Many said they would not do it, particularly with a new patient who might be strongly influenced by those associations. Some said they would never give their own associations, even with long-term patients. Most seemed to feel comfortable giving, at least occasionally, some of their own associations after the patient had finished working on his or her own.

Some people tell you what they make of the dream, what they think, and what was going on that day, and what it might symbolize for them. Some people keep their dreams in a journal so they don't forget them. If a person has no idea what a dream might be about, I might get some idea from their associations, and see if that feels right to them.

[Female, M.S.W., 10 years practice]

I listen to it, I try to get them to just tell the dream from beginning to end, with whatever details they remember. I suggest that, taking the dream as a starting point, without trying to be logical, they just see what comes to mind about the dream. I try to get something general first. Then, we go on to the particular elements of it. I'll throw in some associations of my own, and when I let myself do that more, even when I don't know exactly why I'm saying it, it's allowed people to say some things they might not otherwise say. It's as if my unconscious stuff is in touch with their unconscious stuff.

[Male, Ph.D., 20 years practice]

With some people I just want to listen to their dream, and I don't want to talk very much about it, just get the associations. This would be with a person I don't feel very related to yet. Dream work might be experienced as an attack. If I'm having an idea about a dream I might say that I am, and give it, and ask what they think of it.

[Female, M.S., 15 years practice]

They tell me the dream, and I ask first for their ideas and associations, and then I'll say what I think.

[Female, M.S.W., 15 years practice]

They report them, and tell me their feelings, what the day residue was, and how they felt when they woke up. What they link it to, what they think it's about. After, I'll say what I think and we take another spin on it.

[Female, M.A., 15 years practice]

Generally, I try to get the patient to associate and try to come to some understanding of what they might mean, and I might introduce my own thoughts about something in the dream. But it's their dream and they should know what it means.

[Female, M.S.W., 15 years practice]

A few therapists said they didn't work much with dreams.

I think most people who think of therapy think of dream interpretation, so all of my clients come in and want to tell me about their dreams, because they want to be good little patients, and they learn pretty quickly that I'm not a dream interpreter. When someone has a pretty obvious, pretty powerful, pretty important dream we'll look at it, but it's not my thing.

[Male, M.S.W., 15 years practice]

I don't think there's much value in interpreting them. If a patient came to me and said they had a dream and want to talk about it, that's only important as a communication.

[Male, Ph.D., 25 years practice]

I don't really work with them. So many clients want a specific interpretation, and it's just not my field. But it's fun to talk about them.

[Female, M.S., 20 years practice]

I haven't had a lot of training in dream work. I will discuss dreams with people, but I don't make any heavy interpretations because I don't think I have the training for that.

[Male, M.D., 5 years practice]

One behavioral therapist, who does little work with dreams, still finds them valuable, but points out a danger in working with them.

The therapist shouldn't act as if they've got some secret way of understanding the dream. That's what makes people very suspicious of therapists.

[Female, Ph.D., 10 years practice]

NUMERICAL DISTRIBUTION

Almost two-thirds, 39 people, said they work with dreams in a fairly classical, psychoanalytic way. Of these, only 8 said they would never or very rarely give associations of their own; the rest said they would. Another 6 people said they work with dreams from a gestalt approach. Five people said they concentrate not on symbols and content but on feelings. Ten people said they generally don't work with dreams.

COMMENTS

How therapists work with dreams depends partly on the type of therapy they do, and partly on what they think dreams are. Behaviorally oriented therapists, or family and couples therapists, usually don't work with dreams because they often don't work with unconscious material or processes. Even psychodynamic therapists may be skeptical about dream-work if they have come to believe a neurological explanation of dreams. Therapists who do work with dream material, whether via free association, role-playing, archetypes, or some other method, may emphasize to different degrees the significance of such material.

Personally, I find dreams and dream analysis to be very powerful and always find it a little frustrating to work with a patient who doesn't remember his or her dreams, because we are losing so much potentially useful information. Obviously, treatment can be very successful without ever discussing dreams, but having them available adds another dimension to the process.

Another issue raised by this question is whether it is useful for the therapist to give his or her own associations and ideas about a dream, or if doing so would interfere with or contaminate the field.

I think that if the therapist waits until after the patient has finished associating or working over the dream before presenting his or her own ideas, the danger of interference is reduced, if not entirely eliminated. In working with dreams, I get associations from the patient, and, because so much of the way I work focuses on the relationship between the patient and me, often I will ask where I am in the dream. I will then sometimes give my own associations, based on what I know about the patient, suggest possible meanings, and even at times say that if this were my dream, it might be about this or that.

RELATED READING

Blechner, M. J. (1995). The patient's dreams and the countertransference. *Psychoanalytic Dialogues* 5(1):1–25.

Delaney, G. (1993). The changing role of dream interpreters in the understanding of dreams. *International Journal of Psychosomatics* 40(1–4): 6–8.

Kaplan, D. M. (1989). The place of the dream in psychotherapy. *Bulletin of the Menninger Clinic* 53(1):1–17.

Perls, F. (1969). *Gestalt Therapy Verbatim*. Moab, UT: Real People Press.

Van den Daele, L. (1992). Direct interpretation of dreams: some basic principles and technical rules. *American Journal of Psychoanalysis* 52(2):99–118.

🔊🔊🔊🔊

Question 21: What do you do when a patient tells you about alcohol or drug use?

These days, it is very common to hear about recreational drug and alcohol use from patients. It may be difficult to assess the extent of this use and where it crosses the line into substance abuse. How do our therapists deal with this situation?

Everyone said they would discuss the area with the patient and try to come to some evaluation of the seriousness of the problem.

> I analyze it, and assess whether the patient is in some sort of danger, like drinking and driving, or doing something self-destructive. I look at it more psychologically. I would refer them to a program if I really felt it was out of control, especially alcohol or cocaine. I've had more problems with the patients who smoke pot. It seems like they've been self-medicating.
>
> [Female, M.S.W., 15 years practice]

> We discuss it. If they're using it as a substitute or to escape, then that does become an issue to talk about in therapy. I might refer someone to AA.
>
> [Female, M.S.W., 10 years practice]

> I usually ask if the person thinks it's a problem, and explore it. I don't tell anybody not to, unless it develops in the course of the treatment that the person really needs to stop. I don't have a policy about working with someone who drinks or uses drugs.
>
> [Female, M.S.W., 5 years practice]

> We explore it: the amount, and when and where it happens, and their concern. I'm very sensitive to people who have a lot of substance problems, because at the hospital I saw a lot of those people. I'm very aware that there are some people you can see for years before they're ready to address their substance abuse problem. There are others for whom, to begin to do therapy, I would address it as the first priority, where it really sabotages their functioning. It depends on the severity. If people are drinking a little too much to relieve a social anxiety, I'll raise it as an area of concern, that it has potential to get out of hand, but I'm not going to say that they can't be in treatment. Whereas if someone is drinking to the point where their job is on the line, or their marriage is breaking up over it, I might say that they need to get treatment for the alcohol use before they start doing deeper therapy.
>
> [Female, M.S.W., 20 years practice]

Several people said specifically that they would not have a session with someone who was high on alcohol or drugs.

> I let them know I couldn't treat them if they came in intoxicated.
>
> [Female, Ph.D., 30 years practice]

If people come in here intoxicated, I won't work with them, and I tell them to go and take care of the problem and then call me back. Sometimes they do, and other times they never call back.

[Female, Ph.D., 20 years practice]

I always tell them that they cannot come to the session high, and in some cases I might start to push for a 12-step program.

[Male, M.S.W., 15 years practice]

One person mentioned how difficult it can be to treat substance abuse without a recovery program.

I haven't had anybody with an alcohol or drug problem in years. In the past, when I did have patients with drug use, I would try to analyze it and understand it and get to the roots of it. In most cases, it's very difficult.

[Male, Ph.D., 40 years practice]

Over two-thirds of the therapists said they would refer the patient with a serious abuse problem to a 12-step or rehab program (see also Question 68).

That's a major issue for a lot of my patients, because I see a lot of people in recovery. I've changed my thinking about alcohol, substance abuse, and overeating. I make it clear that this is not the place where we're going to deal with that one issue only, whether they're drinking or not drinking. I can't set myself up to become a punitive person in their lives. I will work with them for some time to get them ready to begin a recovery group like AA. Even overeating, I encourage people to do the weight loss work at some weight loss center. Otherwise I think it can become a resistance to therapy.

[Female, M.A., 15 years practice]

I always encourage people to go to meetings at 12-step programs. I will suggest rehab if it's necessary. I have psychopharmacologists that I use and sometimes medication will be warranted.

[Female, M.S.W., 10 years practice]

For some therapists, it is frightening or disturbing to work with substance abuse.

When they tell me about that, I realize I have stepped into an area that I really don't feel very able to help them in. If they're actively using, I'll tell them they have to get into some kind of program that deals with that problem because I'm not skilled in those areas. It's something that's intimidating and scary to me.

[Female, M.S., 15 years practice]

Several therapists said they would not work with a new patient whose presenting problems included substance abuse.

I've had one or two substance abusers, and I don't usually like to see them privately, because my office is in my apartment.

[Female, M.S.W., 45 years practice]

During my initial interview, I ask about that. I work out of my home, and I don't want heavy-duty substance abusers in my home. I can refer them to the agency and work with them there, but I don't want to do that alone. There's more support there.

[Female, M.S.W., 5 years practice]

I ask a lot of questions in the intake, and I won't see anyone who's using drugs. They have to have been in a program and been abstinent for at least six months.

[Female, Ph.D., 10 years practice]

If I hear that it's a real substance abuse case, I just don't take it. I'm not experienced with that and I'm not really into it.

[Female, M.S.W., 15 years practice]

All too often, however, the issue comes up not with a new patient, but with someone already in treatment, perhaps for years.

Usually, in the first two or three sessions I'll take a history, a pretty exhaustive alcohol and drug history. Often, folks who are recovering, that's a primary issue for them, but many other people will, six or nine months into therapy, begin talking about their use and we'll begin to explore it more and more.

[Male, M.S.W., 15 years practice]

Of the therapists who said they would refer such a patient to a program, a little more than half said they would, at least in certain circumstances, make remaining in therapy contingent on the patient going to that program.

I'm pretty strict about that. I'm a recovered alcoholic, and I don't like to work with drinking alcoholics. I've done it a couple of times, but

I'm no good with it. So I will tell people right away, if they tell me they have a drinking problem or I spot one, that if they want to work with me they have to go to a program at the same time. And some people I'll tell to go to AA for a year and then call me if they still want therapy.

[Female, M.S., 20 years practice]

My policy is that I can't treat such a person unless they're involved in some kind of 12-step program. The treatment is contingent on them going. I know from experience, because I've tried it the other way, that without that additional support my efforts are unsuccessful.

[Male, Ph.D., 25 years practice]

I would want the person abstinent by the end of the first year of treatment, much earlier than that if possible. I would work in a general way toward abstinence. I would encourage them very much to go into a recovery program as part of the process. And if abstinence was impossible I would terminate the treatment, which I have done.

[Male, Ph.D., 25 years practice]

I tell them it's a real problem and they'll have to take care of it, otherwise we're just talking to the drug. Nothing's going to happen until they stop. I insist that they go to AA, or NA, or whatever. I do make treatment contingent on them going, because otherwise it's a waste of time, and I think that's unethical.

[Female, M.S.W., 20 years practice]

We talk about it. If there's any psychotropic medications, I would discuss it with the psychiatrist, because of possible drug/alcohol interactions. And I would then spend a good deal of time talking specifically about alcoholism or substance abuse. If I felt it were a sufficiently central issue, I might make treatment of the drug issue central, that is, no other issues are discussed until this issue is resolved. I have, on several occasions, made treatment contingent on them getting into some kind of program.

[Male, Ph.D., 20 years practice]

I will try to investigate the extent and the circumstances, when they tend to do more, and so on. If I get to the point where I consider it advisable for the patient to be in a program, I will tell them that. I have told patients that they can't be in treatment until they take care of their substance abuse.

[Male, Ph.D., 20 years practice]

Insisting that the patient attend a program, however, can lead to dishonesty or even leaving treatment.

> I listen very carefully. Are they driving when they're doing it? I'll bring up AA from time to time. I have sometimes made treatment contingent on AA. I did it last winter and the guy left me. He was heavily into drinking and I didn't have enough of a transference built up. A supervisor told me not to do that, that the patients would be outwardly compliant but would lie about it.
>
> [Female, M.S.W., 25 years practice]

> I'm very stern, I'm very serious about it. I have a number of times over the years told patients that psychotherapy is no match for alcohol or drug addiction, and I would not continue to see them unless they became actively involved in a treatment program. What I have also learned is that sometimes people lie. They say they are and they're not.
>
> [Female, M.A., 20 years practice]

Slightly less than half said they would continue to work with the patient in therapy even if he or she did not go to the recommended program.

> I don't jump on anything, so I wouldn't jump on that either. I'd file it away, try to find out gradually if it's to excess, and talk about it, explore. I never demand that the person go to AA, NA, whatever it is. I don't think that's the right thing to do.
>
> [Female, M.S.W., 20 years practice]

> That's something I really explore. How much, is it a problem for them, or for someone else. If it is a problem, I have referred them to AA. I've never made the treatment contingent on them going.
>
> [Female, Ph.D., 5 years practice]

> I treat it like any other communication. If people come to me with that as the presenting problem, I tell them that, with respect to narcotics, they really can't be analyzed until they kick the habit. I'm willing to see them, nevertheless, but I feel it's my responsibility to tell them that not much is going to happen unless they kick the habit. I do advise them to go to a 12-step program.
>
> [Male, Ph.D., 50 years practice]

> If a person defines themself as someone who has an alcohol problem, we'll set our goal to look at what that's doing in their life. On numerous

occasions, I've sent them to rehab programs and 12-step programs. I never make treatment contingent on them going, because that's abandoning a patient, and that's unethical.

[Male, Ph.D., 40 years practice]

I become very alert, and I ask for details. I try to indicate by my level of curiosity that this is no small thing, and let's make sure we have a clear picture. I've suggested 12-step programs, and sometimes the person is already in a 12-step program when they begin with me. I hate contingencies, so I would probably just say to them, "Look, how can we keep working if you're doing that?"

[Male, M.S.W., 10 years practice]

Even when not threatening to terminate a patient who continues with substance abuse, a therapist can be very forceful in applying pressure.

It depends. I have one patient with a very serious alcohol problem, an immensely self-destructive guy. I eventually insisted that he go to AA, as I realized how serious it was. I didn't make the treatment contingent on him going, because he had been seeing me a long time. I didn't feel like I could say, "Go or else," but I did say "You have to do it."

[Male, Ph.D., 5 years practice]

A few people said that they do not usually refer patients with substance abuse problems to programs.

I do what I do with everything else they tell me about: I listen and try to understand what they're talking about. Are they asking for help? What does it mean to them? I generally don't refer to programs. I've pointed out the seriousness of some instances of alcohol or drug abuse, and have raised the question of what they've done or tried to do to address it. I haven't told them they should or need to go. I don't make treatment contingent on them going. I've helped a number of patients get off alcohol and drugs, with modest success.

[Male, M.D., 20 years practice]

I've only had this happen twice in my practice. The first time it was someone I was seeing analytically on the couch three times a week. So I simply dealt with that as part of the analysis. I did not make anything special of it. The second time I knew something was going wrong, but I couldn't pinpoint it. I kept asking questions and I kept getting denials, and then one day she came in in a very big state of anxiety, hid her face, and said that she's been using cocaine. And when she made the statement she pulled back as if she expected to be struck. All I said was that I knew something had been wrong, and let's deal with it.

[Male, M.S.W., 35 years practice]

NUMERICAL DISTRIBUTION

Everyone said they would explore the extent of the use/abuse. Five people said they would refer out a patient who was a heavy user; 42 said they would recommend a 12-step or rehab program. Of this last group, 23 said they would, in at least some circumstances, make therapy contingent on the patient attending the program; 19 said they would continue to see a patient even if he or she didn't take the recommendation.

COMMENTS

There are a number of issues here: Is individual psychotherapy the best treatment, or even an effective treatment, for substance abuse? What special parameters of treatment become necessary with such a patient? Is it ethical, or even productive, to require the patient to attend a 12-step program (see Question 66)? Is it ethical to terminate a patient who keeps using drugs or alcohol?

As with most of the therapists here, my own approach in dealing with a patient who mentions alcohol or drugs is to try to learn the dimensions of use: how much, how often, for what purpose? If it seems out of control, I will inquire if the patient has ever considered a 12-step program. I've never required a patient to stop using as a condition of treatment, or even required that they go to meetings of a 12-step program, although they know I will not have a session with them if they're obviously high. Unfortunately, it's not always obvious, and patients have told me later about having a couple of beers or smoking a joint before a session.

I have found that some patients stop drinking and using drugs almost spontaneously in the course of a successful treatment, even when that issue is not specifically the focus of treatment. As their anxiety level drops and conflicts are addressed and resolved, they seem to no longer need the substance.

I don't like to terminate patients while they continue to want treatment, no matter what their behavior, and as long as they come to sessions and pay their bills I usually will continue seeing them.

RELATED READING

Fleming, M. F., and Barry, K. L., eds. (1992). *Addictive Disorders: A Practical Guide to Treatment*. St. Louis, MO: Mosby Year Book.

Jarvis, T. J., Tebbutt, J., and Mattick, R. P. (1995). *Treatment Approaches for Alcohol and Drug Dependence*. New York: Wiley and Sons.

Levin, J. D., and Weiss, R. H., eds. (1994). *The Dynamics and Treatment of Alcoholism: Essential Papers*. Northvale, NJ: Jason Aronson.

🔊🔊🔊🔊

Question 22: What do you do when a patient tells you about unsafe sex?

The spread of AIDS and other sexually transmitted diseases has made this subject a highly charged one for many therapists. It may be especially difficult to listen to a patient tell about behavior that puts him or her at risk. How do we deal with such material?

There was a significant split between those practitioners who thought that patients needed to be educated about the facts, and those who thought that patients already know the facts and don't require education.

Here are some responses that emphasize education.

> We do a lot of talking about it, and I have always talked about using condoms. Now, I will discuss particular activities in even more detail. I believe it's important to do a lot of education.
>
> [Female, M.S.W., 10 years practice]

> If I feel they're having unsafe sex, I question them about it, find out if they know it's unsafe, and encourage them to be safe. I try to do a little education, in a subtle way without giving a lecture, just asking questions.
>
> [Male, Ph.D., 15 years practice]

> I ask them direct questions, and ask them what they know, and I give them information and handouts.
>
> [Female, Ph.D., 10 years practice]

And here are some responses from therapists who don't believe the problem is one of knowledge and education.

Usually it's not an issue of lack of knowledge. I've never run across a patient who didn't know when they were having unsafe sex that it was unsafe. So it's not a question of education.

[Female, M.S.W., 20 years practice]

I analyze that. It's not a problem of education. It's a self-destructive urge, particularly with adolescents. Grandiosity is part of it, but there's a self-destructive underpinning to that grandiosity that I have to address.

[Female, Ph.D., 20 years practice]

I inquire about it and try to understand what is driving that sort of self-destructive behavior. I might include some factual comment in the inquiry, something like "You know, women are the fastest-growing segment of the AIDS population," but I always assume the patient is aware of that because most of my patients would be.

[Female, Ph.D., 15 years practice]

I question it, explore it, find out what's going on. They all know they shouldn't be doing that. In New York City, everyone knows what unsafe sex is.

[Female, M.S.W., 15 years practice]

Some therapists believe it is important to be aggressive in responding to reports of unsafe sex.

I point out the reality of that, and try to vigorously move in and discuss why he or she would be taking such masochistic risks with their lives.

[Male, Ph.D., 40 years practice]

I'm very directive about AIDS, and cut-and-dried about facts and the foolishness of unsafe sex.

[Female, M.A., 15 years practice]

I immediately say they really have to stop it, and I will educate them about safer sex, and/or send them to [agency name] for a workshop.

[Female, M.S., 20 years practice]

I deal with that, because I believe it's both suicidal and homicidal. I deal with it very definitely.

[Female, M.S.W., 45 years practice]

I confront them and exhort them not to do that. I say, "Are you crazy? Do you think you're the one person who's immune?"

[Female, M.S.W., 25 years practice]

I lecture them very strongly. I think it's a matter of education and maturity. Sometimes it's masochistic behavior.

[Female, Ph.D., 20 years practice]

I tell them that I think they're stupid, and that I can't control what they're going to do, but I'm disappointed, I think it's wrong.

[Female, M.A., 20 years practice]

I've counseled them about it. I've been very upfront about it. Even if they cognitively know it, they sometimes need a kind of parent figure to remind them. I cite the statistics. I tell them they're playing Russian roulette.

[Male, Ph.D., 5 years practice]

And others respond no more aggressively than to any other material.

I would work with it like anything else, try to understand what's going on about that. Because everybody's informed at that this point, so why, if you have the information, aren't you taking care of it?

[Female, M.S., 15 years practice]

I haven't had people telling me about unsafe sex. I do ask them about it, and find out if they're aware of the issue, and are they concerned about it. Usually it doesn't go beyond that.

[Male, M.S.W., 20 years practice]

A number of therapists emphasize the self-destructive aspects of such behavior, or the fantasies behind it.

I try to analyze the self-destructiveness involved.

[Male, M.S.W., 35 years practice]

When they're talking to me about unsafe sex they're talking about risking suicidal behavior. And it's often in the context of people who are not taking care of themselves in a lot of ways, and doing slow suicidal actions. We try to explore it and see what goes on right before that situation.

[Female, M.S.W., 20 years practice]

I will try to investigate the fantasies, which usually go to some kind of grandiose, omnipotent thinking, or to be special, or issues of denial.

[Male, Ph.D., 20 years practice]

One person saw it as a problem of impulsivity.

If I think it's appropriate, I'll try to do something about shoring up the patient's impulse control. First, there may be informational issues, and then what's the impulse control like, and then the question of consequences. The way I'd approach problems with an acute concern about someone's impulsivity getting them into trouble.

[Male, M.D., 15 years practice]

Two therapists dealt with unsafe sexual behavior as a kind of addiction.

With unsafe sex, there's almost an addictive quality to it, because you have people with certain kinds of feelings, and they run to anonymous or cut-off sexual situations where they get to play out something that's going on for them. It doesn't soothe them for very long, and then they have a need to repeat the behavior elsewhere. I treat it like any other kind of addictive behavior.

[Female, M.S.W., 20 years practice]

There are a lot of things that come up in mind, like moral issues. I think sexual behavior can also be equivalent to an addiction, and I may work with it in that way. But it's suicidal, homicidal stuff, and I treat it as such.

[Male, Ph.D., 10 years practice]

Several therapists have made treatment contingent on the patient stopping unsafe sexual behavior.

I have struggled with this! I consider unsafe sex, to people who are educated to the issues, to be both suicidal and homicidal. I contract them to work on it with me, and if that behavior doesn't stop, I can't continue to see them.

[Male, M.S.W., 15 years practice]

I counsel them heartily about it, do some education. In one case I refused to see a patient because I felt she was taking risks in terms of her life, and I told her if she continued acting out that way that I would have to reconsider working with her.

[Female, M.S.W., 15 years practice]

Others mentioned the frustration of not being able to prevent such dangerous behavior.

> I talk about it with the person, but I'm not in control. I see people who have unsafe sex, and there's nothing I can do about it.
>
> · [Female, M.S.W., 20 years practice]

> It depends who it is. If it's somebody who does it all the time, what am I going to say? I certainly try to bring up the subject, some education. With some people, you can get into the why, the self-destructive aspects. With others, that just drives them away.
>
> [Male, Ph.D., 20 years practice]

Or the uncertainty about how to deal with the issue.

> I will ask them what their idea is of safe or safer sex, and we'll go over what is known. But I rarely bring that up, even though most of my patients are gay men. It's a dilemma I haven't resolved in my own mind, whether that's right. Sometimes I will bring it up, depending on whether they've been tested or not, and what they say about their sex life.
>
> [Male, M.S.W., 15 years practice]

Even a sex therapist can feel some frustration in dealing with this subject.

> I yell at them a lot. I will go over it with them, but that's as far as I'll go. If there was any question of violating confidentiality on a public health level, I wouldn't go that far. But I certainly will talk with the patient about it. Because I do sex therapy, this is a fairly common topic of discussion anyway.
>
> [Male, Ph.D., 20 years practice]

NUMERICAL DISTRIBUTION

Two people said they did nothing special and treat it as they would any other communication from the patient; 13 said they would explore it; 14 said they would emphasize the self-destructive aspects of the behavior; 11 said they would be very confrontational about it. Twenty-two people said they do some concrete education, while 6 said they didn't think lack of education was the problem.

COMMENTS

The issue here is: What is the most therapeutic role to take with patients in these situations?

Although no one mentioned this, it seems obvious that therapists must first educate themselves about the facts and realities, in order to know how to handle what patients tell them, to know what is true and what is not, what is safe and what is not.

I don't know that it is necessary, or useful, to berate patients for unsafe sexual behavior. Asking the right questions and pursuing the topic can intrinsically convey concern and serve the purpose of confrontation. As with any other questionable behavior, taking a position which forbids the patient to do something can lead to the patient not stopping the behavior, just concealing or not discussing it.

I think it is important to pursue the self-destructive elements of any behavior, and the grandiose or masochistic fantasies that may underlie such activity. My experience has been that when these are uncovered and dealt with, the behavior usually stops.

RELATED READING

Erickson, S. H. (1990). Counseling the irresponsible AIDS client: Guidelines for decision making. *Journal of Counseling and Development* 68(4): 454–455.

Gold, R. S., Skinner, M. J., Grant, P. J., and Plummer, D.C. (1991). Situational factors and thought processes associated with unprotected intercourse in gay men. *Psychology and Health* 5(4):259–278.

▨▨▨▨

Question 23: How do you end the session?

It can be easy to fall into the habit of ending the session in the same way, with the same phrase. Most of the therapists said that they did use the same words in most sessions. Many used some variation on one of these phrases:

Usually I say "We have to stop here today."

[Male, M.D., 20 years practice]

"I'm afraid our time is up today."

[Male, Ph.D., 40 years practice]

"I'll see you next week," or "We'll take it up next week."
[Male, Ph.D., 10 years practice]

Three people mentioned using this phrase:

I've picked up a phrase from one of my own therapists: "To be continued."
[Male, M.S.W., 10 years practice]

Some combined a physical movement or gesture with their words.

People tell me that I have a hand motion that I do, and they know it's time. What I usually say is "It's about that time," or "We have to stop here."
[Male, Ph.D., 20 years practice]

I usually tip over closer to the end of my seat, and say "Well, we have to wind up now. Time is about up."
[Male, Ph.D., 15 years practice]

Different ways with different people. Sometimes I give non-verbal cues. I lean forward in my chair, and say, "Well . . ."
[Female, Ph.D., 20 years practice]

A few found that a movement alone was enough to signal the end of the hour.

I usually just stand up.
[Male, Ph.D., 50 years practice]

It's usually some movement that I make, or my tone of voice.
[Male, Ph.D., 20 years practice]

I've got everybody trained, just like Pavlov. Nearly all of my patients lie on the couch. My chair makes a loud squeak when I lean forward, and they get up. I don't have to say anything.
[Male, Ph.D., 15 years practice]

Or that patients could tell from a facial expression.

It's funny. They all know by a certain look that comes over my face, and they may ask if the session's up now. I do find myself saying

"Unfortunately" if the patient is in the middle of something, or "I'm sorry, we have to stop."

[Female, M.S.W., 5 years practice]

One person analyzed using only a movement this way:

I've changed with that. It used to be all body language. I think I was afraid to say that time was up. Like somehow it was impolite or uncaring. Now, I'll just say our time is up, or that's all we have time for.

[Male, M.S.W., 15 years practice]

Several therapists try to warn the patient about the coming end of the session.

I let them know a little in advance, because for me initially, time was an issue and setting limits was quite hard.

[Female, M.S.W., 5 years practice]

I don't like to do that abruptly, so I'll usually say, "We just have a few more minutes" and do it gently in that way maybe five minutes before the end of the session.

[Female, M.S.W., 10 years practice]

I don't cut somebody off in the middle of a sentence or a thought. I wait until they're finished and I might even comment back, and sometimes I might even say, "We only have a minute or two more, and I wanted to ask about such-and-such." So they're prepared.

[Male, M.S.W., 20 years practice]

"We have to stop now." With children, if it's a play session, I usually give them a little warning that we're going to have to put the play things away.

[Female, M.S.W., 15 years practice]

Finally, several people said they tried not to use the same words each time.

I used to have a phrase. I used to look at the clock and say, "Well, we only have a minute or two more." Now, I end sessions all different ways, usually by connecting up things in the session.

[Female, M.S., 15 years practice]

I'll try to draw it together by asking a tie-up question, or asking them to think about something.

[Female, M.S.W., 5 years practice]

NUMERICAL DISTRIBUTION

Thirty-three people said either "We have to stop" or "Our time is up for today"; 11 use some other phrase. Eight people stand up or use some other non-verbal cue. Eight people warn of the impending end of the session.

COMMENTS

Issues here include: Are some ways to end the session better than others? How do we weigh interrupting the patient in order to stop on time against letting the patient complete what he or she is saying and running late?

While patients may learn our routines, and even make fun of them occasionally, I think they are reassured by the consistency and dependability implied. Some patients always seem surprised by the end of the session and express concern about being interrupted, so a gentle warning about the impending end of the hour may soften the blow.

I think it is extremely important to stop (and start) on time, although doing that in the middle of a sentence seems awfully rigid and unnecessary to me (not to mention obnoxious). The structure of the hour, and the boundaries between the session and the rest of the week, imply a lot about the therapist's ability to handle and contain the material patients bring with them.

Several therapists mentioned having a clock the patient can see, but I can imagine patients finding this distracting. My own experience is that some long-term patients begin to know when the time is almost up and wind themselves down in anticipation. Knowing how much time is left can sometimes be an interference, as when patients ask how much time is left because they don't want to begin discussing a topic if they will be interrupted soon.

RELATED READING

Freeman, D. S. (1977). The use of time in family therapy. *Family Therapy* 4(3):195–206.

Winestine, M. C. (1987). Reaction to the end of the analytic hour as a derivative of an early childhood experience: couch or crib. *Psychoanalytic Quarterly* 56(4):689–692.

⧢⧢⧢⧢

Question 24: Do you work with groups? What are the tasks of the group therapist?

In addition to seeing patients individually, many private practitioners also have a therapy group. There are a number of different approaches to group therapy: psychoanalytic, gestalt, systems, and so on. How do the therapists who run groups see the role and tasks of the group therapist?

Slightly more than half the sample have therapy groups. Of these, half said that the primary task of the group leader is to make it possible for people in the group to talk and relate to each other.

> To facilitate communication between the group members, to observe the interaction, to look at the whole group dynamic.
>
> [Female, M.S.W., 30 years practice]

> My job is to be there and to promote group discourse between the members. To intervene if a masochistic patient presents themselves as a group scapegoat. I intervene if there's a group monopolizer. I manage things.
>
> [Female, M.S.W., 25 years practice]

> The main task is getting people to talk to each other, and to help analyze the ways that people don't really relate to each other. Recently, I've been focusing on helping people focus on their affective experience, what they're feeling, and I've been doing that in a much more systematic way, because I think I've been taking that for granted, and denying that most of the time people are not aware of what they're experiencing. I'm also doing a lot on communication, because we miss each other much of the time. I work with the resistance too. Also, if there's a theme that's coming up, I may take one person and work individually with that person around that theme, knowing that it's relevant to several other people.
>
> [Male, Ph.D., 25 years practice]

> I usually try to facilitate relationships between people, so they can help each other see that lots of people have the same problems, and encourage them to help each other.
>
> [Female, Ph.D., 10 years practice]

> To help the group members talk and say everything.
>
> [Female, M.S.W., 45 years practice]

To facilitate the interaction, to serve as the counterbalance between the intense affects that come up in the group, to explore the transference that may occur, not only with the therapist but between the patients.

[Male, Ph.D., 20 years practice]

One third said that the most important task is to make the group a safe place for the members.

To set up a structure in which members feel safe and protected, and allowed to interact with each other, so that they can gain understanding about themselves and work through issues related to their family and their present.

[Male, Ph.D., 15 years practice]

To help make the environment safe and secure, and allow things to happen in a context where patients know they can take risks and feel that they won't be harmed. To pay attention to the needs of the various patients, to make sure that they're not getting injured by the process of the treatment. Sometimes by contractual agreement prior to the group, I will help the patient overcome the difficulties they have by an agreement to be there to help them. To facilitate the entry of a patient into the group.

[Female, M.S.W., 15 years practice]

The task of the group leader is to help the group to feel safe and to form. Knowing when to get into the group and when to step out.

[Male, M.S.W., 15 years practice]

Another third said the primary task is to keep the group moving and intervene if things get stuck. This can sometimes mean expressing something that is unexpressed directly by the group, or intentionally stirring things up.

To facilitate interaction among members of the group, monitor what's going on in terms of roles people are taking. To move the group along.

[Female, M.A., 15 years practice]

I think it's to facilitate the process, and that sometimes means to shut up and let it happen. Every now and then you need to intervene to do something that isn't being done by the group or to make an interpretation of a transference that the group is getting stuck on. I often see myself as a provocateur in group.

[Female, M.A., 20 years practice]

To let his or her presence be known. To facilitate reactions from the people in the group.

[Male, Ph.D., 10 years practice]

The task is to try to help make the connections that are there more visible. I see the group therapist as a conductor.

[Male, Ph.D., 40 years practice]

To keep the group going in a constructive way. To be aware of the dynamics of the group, and interpret it judiciously.

[Male, M.D., 20 years practice]

In more advanced groups, the group therapist is a moderator, a guide. If the group is working well, they can work on their own with a little direction from the therapist.

[Female, M.S.W., 5 years practice]

Some people said that the primary task is to keep the focus of the work inside the room, so that patients deal directly with each other about things that are happening between them.

My job is to bring the discussion back into the room. Sometimes I use my own feelings very directly, and might disagree strongly with an expressed feeling.

[Female, M.S., 15 years practice]

To facilitate interaction between the members, and to try to work within the group rather than on the outside problems. To try to make it alive within the group.

[Female, M.S.W., 20 years practice]

A number of people said that it was important for the therapist to see that everyone in the group got the time and attention they need.

Once it's running, people talk about their present life and the impact of the past, but also their feelings about one another. I would guide them to facilitate that, if anyone were intimidating someone else, or they weren't sharing time well. I like people to feel like they're equally participating, and they aren't there to take care of other people.

[Female, M.S.W., 10 years practice]

Several people said the therapist can function as a role model to the group members.

> To lead a group to be therapeutic to one another by modeling, where your attention is going, by encouraging. Most of what I do as a group leader is what my own group therapist does. He's been a model for me.
>
> [Male, M.S.W., 10 years practice]

> As facilitator, as role model. You use yourself in a different way in groups, less removed, more exposed. People get to see others' reactions to you, and yours to them.
>
> [Female, M.S.W., 20 years practice]

One person pointed out that the tasks of the therapist begin even before the group convenes.

> It starts even before you begin the group, in choosing the people. Is this going to be a good mix? Trying to get people at the same level of working on themselves, so that no one is a loose cannon, or doesn't fit. I think that sometimes people aren't ready for a group. You might not know that from individual because people behave differently and you're different, and they don't have to share you in individual. So you're making sure that the composition of the group is as appropriate as it can be.
>
> [Male, Ph.D., 25 years practice]

Several people mentioned how difficult running a group can be.

> The task for me was surviving the experience. Even though I love group, I felt very flooded by all the input. There's so much going on, so to try to stay on top of it was my task, and not get overwhelmed.
>
> [Female, M.S., 15 years practice]

> Running a group is hard work, because my need to understand what's going on with everybody moment to moment made me feel sometimes very flooded and I had a hard time prioritizing what to go after. There were always too many choices, and I always felt like I was missing things that I should be dealing with.
>
> [Female, M.S.W., 20 years practice]

> Because it's a number of people, a very important dynamic is added. It requires an alertness to body language, and gestures, and innuendo.

You have to have eyes all over the place. You have to deal with your countertransference even more strongly because it's so much more likely to be engendered, because you get more involved.

[Female, M.A., 20 years practice]

NUMERICAL DISTRIBUTION

Only 35 people said they worked with therapy groups. Of these (some gave more than one response): 18 said the primary task was to facilitate people talking and relating to each other; 10 said to make the group a safe place; 10 said to mediate or help if the group gets stuck; 5 said to make sure everyone gets some attention and time; 4 said to be a role model; 4 said to keep the focus inside the room, in the here-and-now; and 1 said to select the right people for the group.

COMMENTS

The question here is which elements of group therapy are significant to treatment outcome and must be carefully handled by the therapist.

There are many important tasks for the group therapist: to select the right members; to make it a safe place; to make sure everyone gets the attention they need; to help them if they get stuck. But I think the most useful task is to make conscious the group dynamic, to say, "Right now, I think this is what is happening in the group."

My experience in running groups is that patients get the most out of the experience when the focus of the discussion is what is going on in the room among the group members. This is when there is the most energy and immediacy to the discussion and when group members are most engaged by the interactions.

It's not possible to do everything in a group. Each therapist has to select an approach and keep the focus there or he or she can easily be overwhelmed by all the material.

RELATED READING

Bernard, H. S., and MacKenzie, K. R. (1994). *Basics of Group Psychotherapy*. New York: Guilford Press.

Halperin, D. A. (1989). *Group Psychodynamics: New Paradigms and New Perspectives*. Chicago, IL: Year Book Medical Publishers.

Yalom, I. D. (1970). *The Theory and Practice of Group Psychotherapy*. New York: Basic Books.

▨▨▨▨

Question 25: Do you work with couples? What are the tasks of the couples therapist?

Some practitioners work only with individuals, and some also see couples. There are a number of different approaches to couples therapy, many of which were mentioned by these therapists.

Thirty-five of the sixty said that they work with couples. The largest portion of this sub-group said that when working with a couple their primary task is to improve the communication between the partners.

> With couples I don't try to interpret the unconscious. I keep the focus primarily on the here-and-now and the interaction of the couple, and try to open up the channels of communication, pointing out to them how they relate to each other.
>
> [Male, M.S.W., 35 years practice]

> The task is always to help the patients to say everything. It's not my job to separate people or to bring people together. I help them to talk, and then they have to decide what they want from their lives.
>
> [Female, Ph.D., 20 years practice]

> To facilitate communication. To help them hear one another, because mostly they're talking to themselves, about the other, about what's wrong.
>
> [Female, M.S.W., 20 years practice]

> I generally see myself as an interpreter with two people who speak different languages. I interpret what they're saying to each other.
>
> [Male, Ph.D., 50 years practice]

> It's completely different, as different as doing behavioral work. When I work with couples, although I use my psychodynamic ways of understanding things, I'm not there to use myself as a transference object with them. I'm there to facilitate their healthy use of each other as transference objects, and so my work with couples is kind of simplistic. I teach them how to be each other's analyst, how to talk to each other.
>
> [Male, Ph.D., 10 years practice]

> To try to help each person hear what the other is saying. And as a therapist once said to me, to reduce the duologue and increase the dialogue.
>
> [Male, Ph.D., 10 years practice]

It all depends. Sometimes it's to get them to sit in the same room without screaming at each other. I try to get them to listen to each other.

[Female, M.S.W., 25 years practice]

Sometimes that approach may not seem to have enough impact.

I used to think that my task was to help them talk to each other and then get rid of me. But lately I feel like I'm missing something. But it's often too long term. I want to find something shorter.

[Male, M.S.W., 15 years practice]

The next largest segment of our group said the task was to identify and clarify the problems and issues in the relationship, and the ways that conflict arises.

The first task is to clarify what the problems are in the couple.

[Female, M.S.W., 5 years practice]

My task generally is to define both the issues that are current, and how much of the individual pathologies of the couple are playing into the current issues, and how the couple wants to work on these issues.

[Male, M.D., 20 years practice]

I see my task as helping them to understand what the problem is, and that can take a long time. Once we know what it is, we can decide, do you want to solve this or not?

[Female, Ph.D., 5 years practice]

I tend to be a little more active in terms of pointing out things and doing some negotiation, or being a go-between in terms of communication where the couple can't communicate directly. Sometimes they can hear it through me rather than from each other.

[Male, M.S.W., 20 years practice]

To help the couple see that they are individuals and the couple is a third entity. I try to help them see how they trigger each other off, to see what steps they could take to have more understanding of where the other one is.

[Female, M.S.W., 20 years practice]

My view is to diagnose what the issues are. What are the conflicts between the couple, and what are the conflicts that each one is struggling with, and how they interact and mesh and create difficulty.

[Male, M.D., 20 years practice]

To help both parties understand why they're having the problems, and perhaps come to the best solution they can make about the problems.

[Male, M.S.W., 25 years practice]

Even a behavioral therapist will often work with couples, and identifying the problems in the relationship is part of the work.

I work a lot with couples, because with anxiety disorders the spouse is very involved. Often the spouse will accompany them in doing the tasks. The spouse may care very much, but often either pushes them too fast or infantilizes them, and hasn't been educated how to best help someone with a phobia. Plus there are often marital problems underlying the anxiety that need to be made explicit. I always have the spouse come in at the beginning of treatment to talk about their perception of what's going on, and to make clear that we all have a common goal. If I thought the marriage was in serious trouble, I would tell them that I think there are serious problems and the anxiety is not going to go away until the two of them have worked on the marriage. And then I'll refer them to someone I know who specializes in marital problems.

[Female, Ph.D., 10 years practice]

An equally large group said the primary task was to identify the partners' roles and their historical antecedents and how they relate to each other now.

In the relationship, we look at what they each had with their parents, and how the parents related to each other and to the clients. Also, at what the parents personality types were and how that connects to who they've chosen to be with.

[Female, Ph.D., 20 years practice]

I've had couples where there's so much pathology, I do what I call "analysis in the presence of the other." There are other couples where trying to let them have all their feelings about each other in the presence of a neutral observer is very facilitating.

[Female, M.S.W., 15 years practice]

To help each of them get a sense of how they react out of their personal history with each other.

[Female, M.S.W., 20 years practice]

To help them to relate to each other by understanding what they're doing to prevent an authentic relationship from occurring, how they're resisting each other, how they're transferring to each other.

[Male, Ph.D., 15 years practice]

I would want them to learn to be sensitive to who the other is, and to realize that some of their disagreements may be based on much earlier relationships.

[Female, M.S.W., 10 years practice]

To differentiate between the family of origin of each partner of the couple and their own relationship, because the problem that most couples have is that they bring their own parental relationships into the new relationship, so there are six people there together. It's very crowded. Also, the effects of projective identification, how the other plays out the particular role, how you get the other to be what you want them to be.

[Male, Ph.D., 20 years practice]

Several people said their task was to direct the couple in specific ways, even to develop homework assignments.

I'm the teacher. I'm teaching them some skills related to the communication process between them. And I'm probably going to be doing modeling and role-playing.

[Female, M.A., 20 years practice]

Working with couples has to be more structured and less open-ended than individual therapy. Without structure, people can just use it for a catfight.

[Female, M.S.W., 5 years practice]

Sometimes couples need tasks, tasks that give them boundaries, that help them structure their relationship.

[Female, M.S.W., 15 years practice]

I work around problem-solving, after defining what the problems are, giving homework. With sexual problems, using some of the more standard treatment techniques.

[Male, Ph.D., 20 years practice]

A few people said the primary task was to create a safe environment for the couple to work in.

To create and preserve the climate in which they can work.

[Male, M.S.W., 20 years practice]

Other points of view were that the therapist can be the mediator or the role model for one or both of the individuals.

Sometimes I'm a mediator, to keep them from killing each other, and let them talk. A patient said to me recently, "So now you're the referee, right?" I said, "Thank you for seeing that."

[Female, M.S., 15 years practice]

My job varies. I used to make them talk directly to each other. My job is to get them to hear what they're not hearing due to their own stuff. On the other hand, I just worked with a couple where my job really was to show her by modeling how to deal with her overbearing, verbally abusive husband.

[Female, M.S., 15 years practice]

Neutrality becomes important when working with a couple. Taking sides can make progress impossible.

The things that I pay attention to are maintaining neutrality, and supporting the alliance with both. I try not to be the individual therapist for one, or for both. I try to be just the couples therapist.

[Female, M.D., 15 years practice]

Of those who said they don't work with couples, several gave reasons why they don't.

I don't work with couples if I can possibly help it. Because the blaming that goes on in the beginning is such an irritation to me, and I don't have skills to get around it or under it or whatever you do.

[Female, M.S., 20 years practice]

I'm not very happy working with couples usually, because it's often so negative, just fighting.

[Female, M.S.W., 30 years practice]

I don't work a lot with couples, only three or four times. I don't have therapy as the goal. I'm not a good couple person, I don't do that well. I work largely with communication.

[Male, Ph.D., 25 years practice]

Even those who see couples don't always like it.

I'm not too fond of couples, because usually by the time they come, they're ready to kill each other, and it's just murder and mayhem. I usually see so much behind it, that I'm immediately thinking they need their own therapy. It's a challenge, and I don't think I've mastered it. I take them, but I sort of dread it.

[Female, M.S.W., 15 years practice]

I don't like to work with couples. I don't get it, and I've read a lot and had a lot of supervision. A lot of couples got a clearer idea of why they couldn't stay together, and maybe that's valuable. I've never had the sense that I helped the couple get better in their relationship.

[Male, M.S.W., 15 years practice]

I've had some of my most frustrating experiences with couples who came in not ready to be in therapy, but just wanting a place to fight, and refusing to calm down. My feeling is "I don't need this."

[Female, M.A., 20 years practice]

NUMERICAL DISTRIBUTION

(Some people gave more than one response.) Fifty therapists said they worked with couples; 10 did not. Twenty said the primary task is to improve the communication; 9 said to identify the issues and problems; 9 said to identify roles and ways of relating to each other; 9 said to identify the individual historical antecedents; 5 said to give specific tasks and develop homework assignments; 2 said to be a role model; 2 said to be a mediator; 1 said to be a provocateur, to generate imbalance; and 1 said to maintain neutrality and not take sides.

COMMENTS

As with the previous question, the issue here is: Which elements of couples therapy are significant to treatment outcome and must be carefully and competently managed by the therapist?

Working with couples is very different from working with an individual patient, and each of the roles mentioned above is at times one for the therapist: mediator, interpreter, instructor, role model, provocateur. Generally, though, when I work with a couple, I work almost exclusively on the communication, on how they talk to each other, what they say and what they are too afraid to say, and on conveying what the behavior of one means symbolically to the other. I find that the way the couple communicates is usually where the problems lie, and if you can understand and improve that communication, everything else improves. Historical material is sometimes relevant and can help partners understand the other's reactions and interpretations, but emphasis on the present meanings and modes of communciation are more significant.

RELATED READING

Freeman, D. S. (1992). *Family Therapy with Couples: The Family-of-Origin Approach.* Northvale, NJ: Jason Aronson.

Haldane, D., and McCluskey, U. (1981). Working with couples: psychiatrists, clinical psychologists, and social workers compared. *Journal of Family Therapy* 3(4):363–388.

Martin, D., and Martin, M. (1983). An analysis of private practice in marital and family therapy: implications for training. *Psychotherapy in Private Practice* 1(4):65–68.

Scharff, D. E., and Scharff, J. S. (1991). *Object Relations Couple Therapy.* Northvale, NJ: Jason Aronson.

Wile, D. B. (1981). *Couples Therapy: A Nontraditional Approach.* New York: Wiley and Sons.

🦋🦋🦋🦋

Question 26: What do you do with a boring patient?

Although we may not want to admit it, every therapist has occasionally had the experience of being bored with or disconnected from what a patient is saying. Some patients have a style of presentation that may actually encourage this response in the therapist. How does a therapist deal with the experience of being bored?

One therapist described at length dealing with a boring patient who was his first patient, which was very difficult.

> This particular patient was a major influence. He was very obsessive-compulsive, always complaining about relationships and people leaving him, and he was boring me to tears in the way he presented it. He complained, with whining, and I was struggling with saying something about this boring quality to him. It was more than just a quality, it was pervasive. And finally after struggling and feeling guilty about being bored, you shouldn't be bored if you're a good therapist. And what if I said anything? Isn't it the worst insult in the world to have your therapist say that you're boring? So finally after months I got up the courage to say, "You know, I've got to tell you, the way you relate and the way you present, you're very boring." And I had my heart in my throat when I said it. He looked very hurt, and then he said, "You know, other people say that too." And it turned around the therapy totally.
>
> [Male, Ph.D., 25 years practice]

Another person also described the experience in some detail and how feeling bored can create a cycle of inactivity.

> Sometimes I feel like I've been working too long, or I'm stuck. To me, a boring patient is someone who doesn't make any movement, and comes in week after week with the same shit. When I start wandering, I know I'm pretty bored, because I'm usually tuned in. But there are some people I could just go to sleep with. It's a bad feedback loop, because the more bored I get, the more I just sit back and don't do anything. The way I try to change it is to sit up and start asking some provocative questions, and start pushing a little bit, to try to shake things up. Some people are boring because they're bored in their lives, and therapy is a reflection of what happens in life.
>
> [Female, Ph.D., 20 years practice]

Many people said they try to understand the experience as information about the patient and to use the feeling of boredom as a bridge to the patient.

> I take it very seriously, because the fact that the patient is boring is a communication. The first thing I do is try to become aware of the fact that I'm feeling bored, then I stop and pay close attention to the patient to see what the patient is doing to me to make me feel bored.
>
> [Male, M.S.W., 35 years practice]

> Try to understand why they're boring. Most people are not boring, most are quite interesting. To me it's a tip-off that they're disconnected from their feelings.
>
> [Female, M.S., 15 years practice]

Another therapist suggested that being less connected to some patients than to others is inevitable and not necessarily a sign that something is wrong.

> I try to figure out why they're boring. I allow myself to accept the reality that I will like some people more than I do others, and it's not necessarily an aspect of their psychopathology.
>
> [Female, M.A., 20 years practice]

Some practitioners said they try to confront the situation quite directly.

> I tell him he's boring. I might say, "I'm not sure why this is happening, but for some reason there's something that's making me feel bored. What do you think it could be?"
>
> [Male, M.S.W., 25 years practice]

Yawn. Try to talk about it, or try to refocus the session. Give the message that they're not talking about the central issue, that they're avoiding.

[Female, M.S.W., 15 years practice]

One of the ways I deal with it is to say to the patient, "You're talking in a dull, flat monotone, which is virtually hypnotic, and I was not sleepy or drowsy before you came here. What do you suppose is behind that?" And invariably hostility is. And I would do it repeatedly. After a while the patient would internalize it, and be able to say, "I sound boring to myself," or "I'm talking in a dull monotone. What am I angry about?"

[Male, M.S.W., 35 years practice]

I sometimes ask them if they think they're getting enough out of the session, and do they feel like it's useful to them. In extreme cases, I've told them they're not making me work hard enough.

[Female, Ph.D., 30 years practice]

I've talked with a patient about how difficult it is to sit with him, because of how little he gives. I try to address it. It might be very difficult to address with some people because it would be so wounding, but if I can I try to address it, and find out what it means to them to be the way they are.

[Male, Ph.D., 5 years practice]

Patients use the word, and I always ask them to explain what they mean by it. I do have patients who drone, and I tell them directly that something is happening to me, and I report it in a way that's not accusing.

[Female, M.S., 15 years practice]

I will rarely say I'm bored, but more encourage whether we can work on something new. I will sometimes say things like, "It seems to me that we've been through this before," or "We seem to keep talking about the same thing."

[Female, M.A., 15 years practice]

I think you have to be challenging with your patients, because otherwise therapy can get quite boring, and I don't like to be bored. I might try a different approach, like a gestalt approach, and really move things along. Or ask a very challenging question. Or even be, not in an unkind way, a little confrontational.

[Male, Ph.D., 10 years practice]

I may come to the conclusion that what's going on is that the person is making it impossible to engage. I will definitely address that with them.

[Female, M.D., 15 years practice]

I might raise a question about that, not that it's boring so much as to say that I'm not sure what they're talking about is that relevant, or I'm not sure what we're getting at, something like that.

[Male, Ph.D., 25 years practice]

Others try to wait it out, until the patient moves on to something more engaging.

A boring patient is usually someone into repetition. That's what generally gets to me. I keep myself busy thinking my own thoughts. I'm tuned in, but mostly I'm waiting.

[Male, Ph.D., 50 years practice]

I bite my inner lip. I realize that probably there's a lot of repressed rage going on, or repressed something, otherwise it wouldn't be so boring. I try to tune in to whatever it is.

[Female, M.S.W., 20 years practice]

My tendency is to allow it to continue. I see a boring patient as someone who's lacking insight, but sometimes I don't confront it because I think that's just their full capacity. I don't think I challenge that.

[Male, M.S.W., 15 years practice]

I try to stay awake. I fight the urge to transfer them to somebody else.

[Female, Ph.D., 10 years practice]

If I have someone who's boring, I go with it, and realize that I'm being as sincere as I can be. I will sometimes stop people and say, "Let's get to the feeling," and move right in there and be directive, but sometimes I just have to let something go on.

[Male, Ph.D., 15 years practice]

Sometimes I go off into my own fantasies, and sometimes I get very sleepy and it's hard to stay awake. I might verbally discharge something, say something, but more often I fantasize.

[Female, M.S.W., 45 years practice]

One therapist said she tries to educate herself so that she can join patients in whatever they're discussing.

I have a patient who's obsessive. I try to get into whatever he's into, and I try to educate myself so I can do that with the patient.
[Female, M.S.W., 15 years practice]

Our group was divided between those who see feeling bored as something originating in the patient and those who see it as a countertransferential reaction originating in the therapist. Here are some who understand it as the therapist's issue.

I examine my countertransference. Why should a patient be boring?
[Female, M.S.W., 30 years practice]

I've had the experience of feeling that it's very hard to pay attention, and consider that my countertransference, and when I notice that's happening, I try to think about what the patient is talking about and why I might be feeling like that.
[Female, Ph.D., 15 years practice]

If somebody's really boring, most of the time I think it's my fault. I try to figure out what's bothering me. Some clients I feel tired with, and I wonder if it's because of the time of the day, or whether their life is just not that interesting. I try to make eye contact, and really be present. I'd bring it up in peer supervision.
[Female, M.A., 15 years practice]

I don't believe in boredom. Boredom is a shield for aggression. If I had a countertransference that a patient is boring me, I would investigate what that is about, what is the patient repeating for me.
[Male, Ph.D., 20 years practice]

And here are some who see it as originating in the patient.

The first thing I try to do is understand the boringness of the resistance, try to figure out how to get around that resistance, and interpret it, and how to confront it. Sometimes that works, sometimes it doesn't. And if it doesn't, usually the patient doesn't stay too long.
[Male, Ph.D., 40 years practice]

I try to listen even more carefully. I have to think about why he's trying to put me to sleep, and what's so dangerous that he needs to have me out of commission. That wakes me up.
[Female, M.S.W., 20 years practice]

I don't consider them a boring patient. I see a lot of patients where the nature of their defenses is such that they need to withdraw affectively. Some patients are just not that connected, and that'll come across as a boring patient. I try to understand its dynamic meaning, and interpret it if I can, draw the patient's attention to it.

[Male, M.D., 15 years practice]

I try to figure out why they're boring. Sometimes it's because they're so depressed, and they speak in a monotone. Sometimes they're anxious, and they hold back a lot of what might be interesting because they think that you'll think they're crazy, so they're boring on purpose. Some people worry a lot about being boring, and they tell you entertaining stories, and that can get frustrating also, because they're not in therapy to entertain you.

[Female, M.S.W., 10 years practice]

I try to determine what's going on that I'm bored. The patient might be very angry and not saying it. The patient might be avoiding something else between us. They're disconnected from what they're saying, and I'm bored. Or the patient may be very full of themselves, very narcissistic, and I need to know that I'm in the room.

[Female, M.S.W., 20 years practice]

I've had that experience frequently. I consider boredom a manipulation, both on the part of the therapist and of the patient. I address it as a manipulation. Stilted, slow, willful speech is a maneuver on the part of the patient to control, to defend. And once it's brought up, there's a loosening of affect which shifts the work. I persist at it until a change takes place.

[Male, Ph.D., 30 years practice]

Others said they understood feelings of boredom as an interaction between patient and therapist.

I feel if I'm bored, it's partially about the patient, but there's got to be a piece of me, that's not pulling something out or guiding them in a different way.

[Female, M.S.W., 5 years practice]

I don't think it comes from them or from me, but from the space between us. I respond to boring patients, and I've never been bored by a patient for very long, because I always wonder what makes them so boring.

[Male, Ph.D., 10 years practice]

Several people suggested that the solution to this situation is to become more active.

> When it reaches a certain point, I try to tell myself that the next session I'm going to go in and do something specific. And the specifics aren't so important as the decision to try to take a certain amount of control over what's going to go on. It shakes something up, breaks into whatever they're doing, and even more important, it frees me. The boredom is when I don't feel free. Then even if they're still boring, I don't feel bored, because it's changing my reaction and consequently changing something in the interaction.
>
> [Male, Ph.D., 20 years practice]

> I think about what's going on, and then I'll start asking questions, getting more involved, try to get out of the rut.
>
> [Female, Ph.D., 5 years practice]

Not everyone saw becoming more active as a positive thing to do.

> Usually if someone's boring it's because they're self-involved, so I help them get to what's going on behind that. Sometimes out of countertransference I try to be funny, try to draw them out, try to make the session more interesting for me.
>
> [Female, M.S.W., 20 years practice]

One behaviorally oriented therapist saw boredom as a positive sign.

> Doing what I do, I don't really get that bored, because I'm very active. If I am, it probably means that we've begun to achieve what the person is looking for, because we're searching for things to talk about.
>
> [Male, Ph.D., 20 years practice]

And several therapists denied ever being bored while working with patients.

> I've never been bored in my life.
>
> [Female, M.S., 20 years practice]

> Nobody bores me.
>
> [Female, M.S.W., 10 years practice]

> I don't have any boring patients.
>
> [Male, Ph.D., 25 years practice]

I don't think there's such a thing. There are patients who have great difficulty speaking. I try to be as analytical as I can. I try to engage them as much as I can.

[Male, M.S.W., 10 years practice]

I have to tell you that I don't have boring patients any more. Since I don't care any more whether someone comes back, I take more risks. I don't feel restricted, so I can confront it directly.

[Male, Ph.D., 40 years practice]

I like minutiae, and I'm very detail oriented, so I don't get bored very often. You can tell me all the details and I don't mind it, I'm very interested.

[Female, M.S., 15 years practice]

NUMERICAL DISTRIBUTION

Seventeen people said they become more active and try to confront the patient directly in some way; 10 said they try to wait out the patient. Another 23 people said they try to use the experience of feeling bored to understand the patient. Ten people said they are never bored when working with patients.

COMMENTS

The issues here are these: Are some patients objectively boring or is the therapist reacting countertransferentially? Is a reaction of boredom somehow induced by the patient, or is the therapist disconnecting due to some personal unresolved problem? If the patient somehow induces boredom, is getting the therapist to feel bored a defense or a manipulation?

I think that most of the time, when the patient seems boring to the therapist, it's due to the patient's lack of connection to what he or she is saying. Boring patients are hard to connect with because they're not connected to themselves. I don't often have the experience of being bored because there are a number of ways to cut through it. Usually I'll address it directly by saying that they don't seem to be connected to what they're talking about. Their disconnection seems to me usually to have the defensive function of avoiding charged subjects or material and rarely to be an intentional manipulation.

Actually, this is an issue that comes up quite often in group, where group members may individually feel bored when a person is talking, but they don't know that everyone else is bored too because no one reports the experience. In almost all instances, it turns out that the person who's talking isn't connected to what they're saying either, that they're just filling up the silence because of their own anxiety.

RELATED READING

Altshul, V. A. (1977). The so-called boring patient. *American Journal of Psychotherapy* 31(4):533–545.

Gerardi, D. L., and Natale, S. M. (1987). The bored and boring patient. *Psychotherapy Patient* 3(3–4):31–41.

Golden, G. K., and Hill, M. A. (1994). Only sane: autistic barriers in "boring" patients. *Clinical Social Work Journal* 22(1):9–26.

Tabin, J. K. (1987). Some lively thoughts on boredom. *Psychotherapy Patient* 3(3–4):147–149.

Taylor, G. J. (1984). Psychotherapy with the boring patient. *Canadian Journal of Psychiatry* 29(3):217–222.

🔁🔁🔁🔁

Question 27: What do you do with a hostile patient?

Most patients will get angry at the therapist eventually, and working with both the anger and the reluctance to express it is a central part of treatment. Occasionally, the therapist encounters a patient who seems actively hostile, always angry, and it is often unclear why. Dealing with such patients can be difficult, because everything the therapist tries seems to evoke more anger. As one person put it:

> Patients have called me all kinds of names, and attacked me personally, the way I dress, the way my office is set up, the way I look. It's part of the job.
>
> [Male, Ph.D., 40 years practice]

Most of the sample said they would try to join the anger and validate it in some way.

> I'm pretty good with hostile patients. I listen to them. I acknowledge their anger, I let them know I want to try to understand what it's about. I don't imply that it's all psychological. If you're angry about something, maybe there's a good reason.
>
> [Male, M.S.W., 20 years practice]

I try to understand the hostility as some kind of empathic failure on my part.

[Female, M.S., 15 years practice]

If you're talking about the hostile, borderline person, always complaining, never give you any gratification no matter how hard you work with them, that's when I pray to Kohut. And it always works, it's amazing. Whenever I remember to join the person, and say, "Well, I really haven't helped you enough with this problem," if I have enough sense to validate them, everything calms down. But if I get involved with my countertransference and try to straighten this person out, then I'm dead.

[Male, Ph.D., 25 years practice]

I first have to understand if they're really being hostile, or is this just my reaction. People are often hostile for very good reasons, and if I understand their reasons, and say, "You seem upset. What's happened? Is it anything I've done? Anything that's been done here?" then it usually handles it. I've never had the experience of someone being angry at me and it made no sense and was totally their problem.

[Female, Ph.D., 10 years practice]

It depends on what's needed. Sometimes hostile patients need hostility back. Sometimes it has to be mirrored and reflected. Sometimes people just need to have somebody hear them.

[Female, Ph.D., 20 years practice]

Some therapists said they feel comfortable with hostile patients, and may even enjoy the energy of the engagement.

I enjoy them. I listen carefully to the verbalizations, and try to reflect what might be going on. I do enjoy the passion.

[Male, Ph.D., 30 years practice]

I try to have fun. I try to make love to them.

[Male, Ph.D., 10 years practice]

I encounter it, directly. Oftentimes, a hostile patient is most ready for change. It's an opportunity.

[Male, Ph.D., 25 years practice]

I'm very tolerant. I tell them to go ahead, that the rule is you can say anything, and I really mean that. You can't hit me, but you can be as verbally abusive as you need to be. I can take it.

[Male, M.S.W., 10 years practice]

Therapists may develop strategies for handling hostile patients. One such tactic is to tell themselves that it isn't about them.

> I don't have a big problem, because I know it has nothing to do with me. The anger and the feelings, I don't take it personally.
>
> [Female, M.S.W., 10 years practice]

> I don't take it personally, and I don't mind their being hostile. I try to investigate it with them.
>
> [Male, Ph.D., 50 years practice]

> I've had hostile patients, and they interest me. I can't say I love someone attacking me, because I don't. I try not to react personally, and remember that this person is probably coming from a lot of pain.
>
> [Male, Ph.D., 10 years practice]

Another tactic is to try to use humor to lighten the situation. This strategy can sometimes backfire.

> I try to use my sense of humor. Sometimes that works with hostile patients and sometimes it doesn't. I had a patient who left me because of some joke she didn't like. I listen to them and try to let them get it off their chest and soothe them down, and try to make a joke here and there.
>
> [Female, M.S.W., 15 years practice]

On the other hand, many therapists find angry patients hard to work with. Several described the difficulty of staying with a very angry patient.

> My heart starts to pound when there's that open hostility. If I have the courage, I will sometimes say that they seem to be seething and it seems to be directed at something I said or did. I try to bring it into the room.
>
> [Female, M.S., 15 years practice]

> They probably wouldn't come to me. I'm really not good with it. They wouldn't stick it out.
>
> [Female, M.S.W., 15 years practice]

> It's hard for me. I work a lot on my own fear, because it can feel scary, and settle myself down.
>
> [Male, M.S.W., 15 years practice]

> I try to hang in there with the patient. Sometimes I feel like pulling away, I don't want to be there, leave me alone. I may feel things like that, but I try to stay with it.
>
> [Female, M.S., 15 years practice]

I don't enjoy that, and I've really had to work on not being intimidated when someone's really angry. What I do is go with it, and I don't fight it. I don't let anyone abuse me, but I don't feel I have to control it.

[Female, Ph.D., 5 years practice]

What I need to do is say that I feel that they're hostile, be direct and then go from there. But my tendency is to try to make them feel better.

[Female, M.S.W., 5 years practice]

I've not had too many hostile patients, but I think it's that I don't allow patients to be as hostile as they should be. It's a countertransference issue, and I've explored it in my own therapy.

[Female, M.S.W., 10 years practice]

At the beginning, that was really hard for me. It scared me a lot, if someone has no remorse for the things they do. In the [drug abuse] population I work with, there are a lot of people like that.

[Female, M.S.W., 5 years practice]

One person who is aware of his difficulty with hostile patients uses the feeling directly with patients.

I confront the hostility in a non-threatening manner. I'm often feeling intimidated, anxious about their reaction, and on guard. I let them know how I'm feeling, and it usually helps to moderate the hostility.

[Male, M.S.W., 15 years practice]

Therapists can feel assaulted, and may need to draw boundaries.

Nobody can yell at me. They can tell me what they're upset about, but there are certain parameters of what they can do and not do. I had a borderline patient who would get very flooded and start yelling at me in a very loud voice, and I would tell her that I can't permit her to do that, because there are other offices, but that I want very much to understand what's going on for her when she gets so flooded and angry. It's not always enough to do that once or twice, but eventually she hears me.

[Female, M.S.W., 20 years practice]

I hold on to the edge of my chair, and talk about their hostility. And I have to tolerate it. If I think it's productive, I'll work on it. If they're hostile just for the sake of abusing me, I won't let that continue for very long. I'm not here to be abused. And I'll suggest that perhaps we're not cut out to work together.

[Female, M.A., 15 years practice]

I try very hard to keep applying boundaries. Sometimes the hostility is okay, and I let them do it and I just do whatever I need to do, but if it gets out of bounds in terms of my limits, I probably would end the session.

[Female, M.A., 20 years practice]

Hostility is a psychotherapeutic issue, and I'll work with it the way I work with anything else. Hostility in a form where I'm starting to feel uncomfortable, a little threatened, or it starts to feel abusive, then I will say to the patient that we have to find a way to talk about this that doesn't make me scared.

[Male, M.D., 5 years practice]

It depends what kind of hostility. There's gratuitous hostility, and you don't have to sit there and be insulted, you don't have to be a punching bag. If it's hostility coming out of something, not gratuitous, I'll try to engage it. They can be as hostile as they want as long as we're engaged together.

[Male, Ph.D., 20 years practice]

It depends where we are in the treatment process. If a patient is abusively hostile at any point in the process, I'll say that I don't want to be abused.

[Female, M.S.W., 45 years practice]

A few people pointed out that hostility is sometimes expressed in passive ways, not just in overt anger.

Overtly hostile are not the more difficult patients. It's the ones that are so nice, and really want to kill you underneath it all, those are the trickier ones.

[Male, M.D., 20 years practice]

I've had patients who've been screaming at me, and I've had patients who've been chronically late and it clearly is a passive-aggressive acting out. In both cases, I try to understand what they're so angry about.

[Female, Ph.D., 15 years practice]

Finally, several people said that they see hostility as a defense, and so they try to get behind the hostility and anger.

Up to a point, I try to be empathic to the anger and the disappointment in me. When I feel it's being used defensively, I ask them what else might be there that the anger and hostility are protecting.

[Female, M.S.W., 25 years practice]

If their hostility is a very slight cover for their fragility, I'm very careful about it, because they may need to show me that they're more in control than they really are, that they're tough.

[Male, Ph.D., 40 years practice]

NUMERICAL DISTRIBUTION

Thirty-nine people said they would try to validate the feeling and investigate its meaning and function; 17 said they would confront the hostility and set boundaries; 4 said they usually divert the hostility or try to smooth it over.

COMMENTS

The issues in this area are: Is the patient hostile because of something in the patient, or is it a reaction to something the therapist has said or done? What are the best ways of responding to such hostility?

In either case, when a patient expresses a lot of anger, I think it is most useful to try as much as possible to accept the anger. I may say to an angry patient that I can see that they have a lot to be angry about, which often takes them by surprise, because no one has ever validated the anger before. If it's directed at me, again I try to validate it and acknowledge whatever I did that set it off. That alone can be very healing. Much as I may want the patient to understand my reasons and motivations, becoming defensive and trying to explain or justify my own behavior has never been useful in repairing the break in the therapeutic alliance. My experience is that therapists who dismiss patient anger by labeling it "narcissistic" or calling it a "negative therapeutic reaction" are asking for trouble, and only escalating the problem.

I think patients who express anger directly, no matter how unpleasant or even frightening that may be, are much easier to work with than patients who express anger indirectly, by coming late, or paying late, or being silent, and who deny (or are unaware) that they might be angry about anything.

RELATED READING

Strean, H. S., ed. (1985). *Psychoanalytic Approaches to the Resistant and Difficult Patient.* New York: Haworth Press.

Reich, W. (1949). *Character Analysis.* New York: Noonday Press.

Teitelbaum, S. (1994). Treatment issues of patients who engage in power struggles. *Clinical Social Work Journal* 22(3):263–276.

🆂🆂🆂🆂

Question 28: What do you do with a seductive patient?

Just as hostility can be tricky to address, seductive behavior can also be difficult. One therapist addressed the question of how to identify such behavior.

> It's been very hard with this one patient, because her seductiveness is so very subtle that I was never entirely sure about it. She's very attractive, and I found her a turn-on, but how do I know that she's being seductive? I was able to open up the subject very gently, and we're exploring how important it is for me to be turned on to her.
>
> [Male, Ph.D., 5 years practice]

Seductiveness is not always limited to the sexual arena.

> Seduction is not always a sexual seduction. There's a more subtle kind of seduction where the patient is trying to please you, lull you into some kind of entertainment.
>
> [Male, Ph.D., 50 years practice]

Even when the therapist is certain that the patient is being sexually seductive, how to handle it presents a number of options. Many therapists regard some kinds of seductive behavior as a normal part of treatment, a development of positive transference. These therapists said they would try to ignore seductive behavior and only address it if it became absolutely necessary.

> The good news about the seductive patient is that after a while it falls off by itself. The bad news is they may turn out to be crazy. If that's the case then even the best legs in the world don't matter.
>
> [Male, Ph.D., 25 years practice]

It's a tricky situation. I either try to ignore it, or try to use it. I make a decision about whether I need to do anything about it.

[Male, Ph.D., 15 years practice]

If it's blatant erotic seductiveness, I think I would ignore it until I understand it and can tie it in to other things that are going on in the person's life, like their way of gaining control or power, or of maintaining self-image, or whatever. I wouldn't confront someone and say, "You're being seductive."

[Male, Ph.D., 20 years practice]

If it's part of the development of a positive transference, I'll let it alone.

[Male, M.D., 15 years practice]

A couple of people said that seductive behavior by the patient made them more alert.

I would be on guard, very much on guard.

[Male, Ph.D., 40 years practice]

I have a lot of trouble. I'm easily seduced, which is one reason I don't work a lot with individual patients.

[Male, Ph.D., 25 years practice]

On the other hand, many others in our group said they would address it directly.

I talk about it. I've learned to do that. "What do you think is going on here? That's not going to happen. I'm uncomfortable if you dress that way, or act that way. I hope you didn't misinterpret what our situation is." We talk about it.

[Female, Ph.D., 10 years practice]

If it's really obvious I would definitely talk about it with them.

[Female, M.A., 15 years practice]

Talk about what's going on that they need to be seductive.

[Female, M.S.W., 20 years practice]

The first thing is that I wonder why they're trying to seduce me, and I would probably ask them that.

[Male, Ph.D., 10 years practice]

Different therapists react differently to seductive behavior, depending on the meaning that they assign to it.

> I pay close attention to the seductiveness, because seduction is really an attempt at power, and it's a cover-up for hostility. It's an attempt to take over the power of the situation.
>
> [Male, M.S.W., 35 years practice]

> I'm very aware of it. It can be because they're very needy, and want you to embrace and love them. I have to assess the nature of it.
>
> [Female, M.S.W., 45 years practice]

Several therapists said they would try to analyze with the patient the meaning and function of such behavior.

> It depends on how it presents. I've had patients where there have been erotized wishes towards me that I've missed, which have erupted in some way. When it's a clinical problem like that, I've tended to interpret what I think is going on. When a patient starts to express wishes for a sexualized relationship, then I try to address the underlying fantasies.
>
> [Male, M.D., 15 years practice]

> I've said things, commented on how important it is to them for me to like them. I try to translate it, make sense out of it.
>
> [Female, Ph.D., 30 years practice]

> I would address it with them in terms of what it is that they would like in the relationship with me.
>
> [Male, M.S.W., 20 years practice]

> I'd try to understand and interpret it. It can be the patient's way of diverting my attention.
>
> [Male, Ph.D., 20 years practice]

> Understand when they're being seductive and why. Usually, it signals a great deal of anxiety and feeling very frightened on their part.
>
> [Male, M.S.W., 15 years practice]

Sometimes addressing it directly means clarifying the boundaries of the therapeutic relationship.

> I set limits. If they want to meet for coffee, I tell them that's not okay.
>
> [Male, M.S.W., 10 years practice]

I set very firm limits. I've certainly had patients be seductive toward me, and we discuss the need for professionalism, and their need for a professional, not a boyfriend.

[Male, M.D., 5 years practice]

It depends on the seductiveness. I've had patients tell me they have feelings for me, and we talk about that. I have to explain sometimes about the therapeutic relationship, and how it might be common to feel those things.

[Female, M.S.W., 5 years practice]

If it's overt, we talk about it. I frankly explain that I'm flattered, but that they don't know me from a hole in the wall, all they know is this persona. And then we talk about whether it's too difficult for them to continue with me, or if they want to go on.

[Male, Ph.D., 20 years practice]

With borderlines, I do very clear limit setting, and clarify the purpose of our meetings. And I let them know that I believe that those feelings are there in order to mask other feelings.

[Male, M.D., 20 years practice]

Others said they would try to join it in a way that would prevent it from becoming dangerous.

Part of what goes on is often a seduction or a flirtation, and depending what the bounds are, there are times where I'll be mildly flirtatious, with either male or female patients. I can have fun with it, within certain bounds, with male or female. It can be helpful, and the energy can be very useful.

[Male, Ph.D., 20 years practice]

It depends. If they're "strutting their stuff" I would try to help them enjoy it. If it's a threatening seductiveness, I would ask them how they think it's making me feel.

[Female, M.S., 15 years practice]

Addressing it directly, however, can be difficult. Suggesting that the patient is engaging in seductive behavior may easily feel critical and rejecting.

I enjoy that, but it's more troublesome for me [than anger], much more difficult, because there's a thin line between criticalness and condemnation, and I have to be very careful. I have to let the behavior unravel itself so that what I say doesn't become a condemnation. I don't want to lose the patient, or have an injury to their self-esteem.

[Male, Ph.D., 30 years practice]

Sometimes the behavior becomes so overt that it has to be addressed directly.

After one session in which a female patient was really quite distraught, she came up to me, and I could see by the look in her eyes and her body language that she was going for a big passionate kiss. I saw this coming, and I said let's sit down and talk about this.

[Male, Ph.D., 10 years practice]

The gender of the therapist and the patient may be a factor in how the issue gets addressed, as in this instance of a female therapist and a male patient.

I remember one seductive patient who used to ask for hugs at the end of each session, and I stopped giving him hugs because I felt uncomfortable with that.

[Female, M.S.W., 25 years practice]

In addition, the age of the therapist may be a factor. Two older male therapists said it was much easier now to decline the invitation.

I have a feeling that it's changed because of my age. I don't think women are openly seductive with me anymore the way they were when I was a young man, when I was really hard-pressed to decline a patient's open invitation. It's hard to do, if you're young and the woman is attractive.

[Male, Ph.D., 50 years practice]

At my age, they're barking up the wrong tree.

[Male, Ph.D., 40 years practice]

Several people mentioned the danger of taking the attraction at face value and of certain kinds of responses.

I try not to take it personally and respond in kind.

[Female, M.S.W., 30 years practice]

A few in our group suggested that seductive patients can induce reactions in the therapist, some of which may be difficult to tolerate.

I had a patient once where as soon as he entered the room, I would start getting the most kinky bizarre fantasies. He had been court-ordered into treatment for something sexual with boys. He was disowning his own sexuality, and it was bouncing around the room and I was picking it up.

[Male, M.S.W., 10 years practice]

I had a court-ordered patient who was remanded to treatment for molesting his daughter, and at one point he said, "I notice you're not married. You're the kind of woman I like to go out with." I didn't trust him and I was uncomfortable. I tried to move the discussion toward what's stopping him from meeting women.

[Female, M.S.W., 10 years practice]

Some people emphasized the adaptive value of such behavior for certain patients.

Sometimes I'll want to get away from it, because it feels too intense for me. But I try to hang in there and use my intellect to calm my anxiety, and keep trying to figure out what is going on, what's this about. That helps me feel more removed, so I'm not as nervous. This is where the self psychology stuff comes in handy, with the perspective of trying to see everything as adaptive. I had one very seductive patient, and it was his only point of contact with people. He didn't know how to talk any other way.

[Female, M.S., 15 years practice]

Occasionally, the seductive behavior can become so dominant in the session that therapy becomes impossible.

I had that once, and I told him I couldn't work with him, because he really crossed the line.

[Female, Ph.D., 5 years practice]

NUMERICAL DISTRIBUTION

Thirty-five people said they would address the behavior gently and try to investigate its meaning; 12 people said they would generally ignore such behavior unless it became very blatant; 8 said they would confront such behavior with limit-setting and possibly termination. Five people said they never have encountered seductive patients.

COMMENTS

Some of the many issues raised by this question are: How do we decide that a patient's behavior is seductive? If the therapist is having sexual feelings, is that somehow induced by the patient, or is it the therapist's unresolved problem? If we decide that the patient is in fact being seductive, is it better to work with it directly or to ignore it? What are the best ways to work with such behavior directly? Is it necessary to set explicit limits?

It may be difficult to decide with any confidence that a patient's behavior is seductive. For example, I have noticed with women raised in the South that they seem to flirt almost automatically, a style of relating that is culturally reinforced quite strongly, and it might be unfair to ascribe any particular motive to that behavior.

In general, I don't say anything about seductive behavior for a long time. Maybe it's something she (or he) does when nervous, and as she gets to know me and feel safe she'll stop doing it. Maybe it's a test to see if I can tolerate it without responding. After she stops, I would try to address it more directly. I've never had a situation where it didn't taper off after a while.

I think it's important to note that there are other kinds of seduction than just sexual seduction. The patient who continually tries to amuse and entertain is also trying to seduce the therapist into a collusion to ignore and overlook issues.

RELATED READING

Gregory, B. A., and Gilbert, L. A. (1992). The relationship between dependency behavior in female clients and psychologists' perceptions of seductiveness. *Professional Psychology: Research and Practice* 23(5): 390–396.
Sniderman, M. S. (1980). A countertransference problem: the sexualizing patient. *Canadian Journal of Psychiatry* 25(4):303–307.

🔊🔊🔊🔊

Question 29: What do you do when a patient talks about suicide?

A suicidal patient is every therapist's worst nightmare. Such patients require a great investment of time and energy, and usually need action outside our usual boundaries.

The first step for most practitioners is to try to assess the risk.

I listen even harder. Is it the first session, or have I been seeing them for years? What else is going on? If it's the first appointment, I'm going to find out about suicidal history. I'm going to consider the possibility of a psychiatric referral for medication. I'm going to ask if they can control themselves, and do they have actual plans, and do they think they need to be hospitalized?

[Female, M.S.W., 20 years practice]

If they talk about suicide, I gather all the pertinent information if I haven't already done that. They may have a history. If I don't already know a lot about them, I go into it quite intensively. And if I feel it's indicated, I would use medication, or refer them to someone who hospitalizes patients.

[Male, M.D., 20 years practice]

I try to evaluate the seriousness of the intention. I use whatever information I have about their suicidality, past attempts, lethality of those attempts, etc. And then if someone is talking seriously, I try to sell them on hospitalization.

[Male, Ph.D., 20 years practice]

I work very closely with our staff psychiatrist, so I will have the patient seen immediately by the psychiatrist. I'll explore the suicidal thoughts further, find out if they have a plan of action, if they've had a history. I found it to be helpful to have them rate suicidal thoughts from zero to ten. Anything seven or above is very serious.

[Male, M.S.W., 15 years practice]

I explore it very carefully: do they have a plan, has it happened before? I look at the family history, too. I'll send someone for a medication evaluation. I might call their family.

[Female, M.S.W., 10 years practice]

One psychiatrist thought that she would be more likely to hospitalize a patient than nonmedical therapists.

In patients I know really well, and am familiar with the underlying issues, I may well just let it unfold. With someone I don't know well, I'll shift gears and ask a lot more questions. In either case, if they're talking about it in any other than a thematic way, I will, sooner than a nonmedical person, ask if they feel they need to be in the hospital.

[Female, M.D., 15 years practice]

Many therapists acknowledged that suicidal patients elicit intense anxiety.

> I had one, at the beginning of my training, and I got very frightened. I shifted into a response of, "I'll do anything, just don't kill yourself." My impulse was to ask her to come and live with me.
>
> [Female, M.S.W., 20 years practice]

> That's what raises my anxiety level the most. I'll never be able to feel like it's not in some way my fault. It's the most anxiety-provoking thing a patient can tell me.
>
> [Female, M.S., 15 years practice]

> It always makes me nervous. It doesn't throw me as much as it used to. I don't think I have to rush and call 911, or hospitalize someone. I'm more likely now to take it very seriously, but to talk about it at length, and to be calmer about it. I realize it doesn't necessarily mean someone's going to do it, it's really just a thought and not an action. Still, in private practice, when you're alone, it's still my least favorite thing to hear.
>
> [Female, Ph.D., 5 years practice]

> I get scared when I hear people seriously talking about suicide. I don't like to hear it. Also, I think that if a person is really going to do it, there's really very little I can do to stop that. I would try, of course.
>
> [Female, M.S.W., 5 years practice]

> I get scared. I might refer them elsewhere. I might bring the family members in, and have them watched. I would make them a priority in my practice, and see them before I'd see anybody else. I get very anxious about that. It's the scariest thing of all.
>
> [Male, Ph.D., 25 years practice]

> I get real worried, but we talk about it. When I hear the word it does make me worry, because I feel very responsible.
>
> [Female, M.S.W., 10 years practice]

A therapist who has had a suicide in his or her practice can be especially anxious about another.

> That's a real problem for me, because I had a patient who committed suicide when I was a student. It has affected my life forever. Now, I

have to make a determination about whether that patient is just talking, because many people talk about committing suicide, or whether it's serious. If it's serious, I have a legal obligation to inform a member of the family, and I have done that. I send them for a psychiatric consultation. I would not continue to see them unless they agreed to have the psychiatric consultation.

[Female, Ph.D., 20 years practice]

Some therapists try to help normalize the feelings, so that they are not so frightening.

I try to help them tolerate the thought, and say, "Who wouldn't want to be delivered from the sheer work of life? It's a burden." I haven't yet had anyone sound like they're collecting the material to do it.

[Male, M.S.W., 10 years practice]

I don't get freaked by it. We talk about what it means. It very often has to do with a certain belief system that's set up a certain way that it can't be changed. And within that belief system, suicide makes perfectly good sense to me. I used to be less compassionate with that issue years ago, but I've had enough of my own pain and other people's pain to know that if you're in a situation and you believe that things can't be changed and you're in total anguish all day long, after a certain period of time who wouldn't think of suicide?

[Male, Ph.D., 25 years practice]

Several therapists said that when a patient mentions suicide, they try to get an agreement with the patient not to act on the feeling.

I essentially tell them that we have to have a contract that they're not going to do it, and that they're going to call me if they think they're ever going to do it, or else I will not be able to work with them.

[Male, M.S.W., 25 years practice]

Ultimately, I insist that they make a bargain with me that they will not kill themselves while they're working with me.

[Female, M.S., 15 years practice]

If they don't agree to being hospitalized, then we have a safety plan, where they agree not to kill themselves before the next session, or they'll call if they feel desperate, or go to emergency rooms.

[Female, M.S.W., 10 years practice]

If it's less serious, we'll just explore, and we make a contract that they're not going to do it as long as they're working with me.

[Female, M.S., 20 years practice]

If they're only thinking about it, I have them write out a contract with me that if they start to think about it, they'll call me.

[Female, M.S.W., 5 years practice]

Several people said they would emphasize the contradiction between being in therapy and planning suicide.

I tell them they're entitled, but if they're planning to commit suicide they should discharge themselves from treatment, because the contract is that they want to get well, and if they've decided they don't want to get well anymore, they should discharge themselves from treatment and go and do what they want with their life.

[Male, Ph.D., 50 years practice]

Very early on, I let people know that I have very little tolerance for suicidal behavior, that I'm inclined to do something soon. If it's a patient who's testing to see if I'm going to rescue them, I try to get across that if they want to commit suicide, they're perfectly entitled to do that, that many people do that, but they don't need to see a therapist for that. But if they're coming to me for therapy, the assumption is that they're interested in getting help with this, and that involves some kind of commitment to keep themselves alive. I try to get that commitment, but you can't always get it, and then you're left dealing with a chronically suicidal patient.

[Male, M.D., 15 years practice]

A number of people pointed out that many patients who want to discuss suicide actually have no intention of doing it, and that it is useful to stay calm and convey to the patient that it is safe to talk about.

I don't want the patient's emergency to become my emergency. But certainly we talk and we discuss it, we consider the severity and whether the patient will consider hospitalization.

[Male, Ph.D., 20 years practice]

So much of it is just talk, with no intent. I really try to normalize the feelings, and tell the client not to scare themselves to death focusing on it, and get them to focus on the fact that they'll never do it.

[Female, M.S.W., 15 years practice]

I don't get alarmed by it. It's an opportunity for me to have the patient attend not only to their death wishes, but to the crisis in their self-esteem. From that, it becomes an opportunity to understand the deep dislike for themselves, or the deep intolerance for their pain.

[Male, Ph.D., 30 years practice]

I do investigate it, and I use words like "killing" that I'm not afraid to use. I explore the extent and the depth and the thoughts and fantasies. I tell them it's their choice. I tell them it's a trump card, and they need to be sure when they play it. It comes up a lot with my AIDS patients.

[Female, Ph.D., 30 years practice]

I'm very active in questioning them about it, and finding out what it is. Is there a plan, or is this just a vague feeling? I don't overreact to it. I do it in a very nonthreatening, nonanxious kind of way. A patient told me that she left a therapist because the therapist overreacted to her depression, and she was not suicidal, and she didn't want to have to take care of the therapist's anxiety. I'm very calm, because I've worked with very disturbed patients. I would cancel my sessions and go with them to the emergency room.

[Female, M.S.W., 15 years practice]

Some therapists find humor useful, as it conveys to the patient that the therapist is not afraid to discuss the topic.

The first time the patient mentions it I have a phrase I use, and it always works. I say to the patient that I understand how despairing they feel but I want them to know that if they commit suicide I'm not going to treat them. And the patient cracks up laughing and says it's ridiculous, but the phrase reaches the patient on an unconscious level. What I'm doing in effect is making a counter-threat. After that, we start dealing with what's underlying all of it.

[Male, M.S.W., 35 years practice]

NUMERICAL DISTRIBUTION

Eighteen people said they would discuss the feelings and investigate the risk; 15 said they would refer the patient to a psychiatrist for medication evaluation; 15 others said they would discuss hospitalization; 7 said they would get a contract or agreement with the patient not to act on the feelings; 5 said they would contact family or friends of the patient.

COMMENTS

Some of the issues in this area are: What are the best ways to assess suicidal risk? Are suicidal threats a manipulation of the therapist? If a patient is at risk of suicide, what is required of the therapist? What are the most useful responses that the therapist can make? Does a person have the right to terminate his or her life?

Suicide is a very tricky subject. I'm not sure that there is any way to be certain whether a patient will or will not act. I think that the patient is probably the best judge and can decide whether hospitalization is necessary. I haven't had anyone commit suicide, or even make an attempt, while in treatment with me. One patient did kill himself several years after treatment ended. When people express suicidal feelings, I ask them to make an agreement with me not to do anything until we've talked, although I'm not certain how much influence that contract actually has. I have learned over the years that most people want to be able to discuss the subject without feeling that they're frightening me and that most of them haven't any intention of doing anything, they just want to be able to talk about it. It's a relief to be able to explore the feelings with someone who isn't afraid to talk about it.

The subject of suicide comes up much more concretely in working with HIV+ and AIDS patients (see also Question 94), where patients know what lies ahead and see suicide as an option that maintains some control over how much of the physical (and sometimes mental) decline they want to experience. A therapist who is morally opposed to suicide may convey that attitude to the patient and make it impossible to discuss the subject. A fear of many AIDS patients who are considering suicide is that they will wait too long, to the point where they are no longer able to act and must ask for assistance in dying, assistance they cannot be sure of getting. This fear may prompt them to act prematurely.

Since I do not believe in any sort of afterlife, I have no moral objection to rational suicide, especially in cases of terminal illness. On the other hand, I know that patients often anticipate that they could not tolerate what they actually can handle fairly well, and so I certainly don't encourage suicide either.

RELATED READING

Giovacchini, P. L. (1981). *The Urge to Die: Why Young People Commit Suicide*. New York: Macmillan.

Jacobs, D., and Brown, H. N., eds. (1989). *Suicide: Understanding and Responding*. Madison, CT: International Universities Press.

Kolodny, S., Bindr, R. L., Bronstyein, A. A., and Friend, R. L. (1979). The working through of patients' suicides by four therapists. *Suicide and Life-Threatening Behavior* 9(1):33–46.

Litman, R. E. (1994). The dilemma of suicide in psychoanalytic practice. *Journal of the American Academy of Psychoanalysis* 22(2):273–281.

Ruben, H. L. (1990). Surviving a suicide in your practice. In *Suicide over the Life Cycle: Risk Factors, Assessment, and Treatment of Suicidal Patients*, ed. S. J. Blumenthal and D. J. Kupfer, pp. 619–636. Washington, DC: American Psychiatric Press.

Widiger, T. A., and Rinaldi, M. (1983). An acceptance of suicide. *Psychotherapy: Theory, Research, and Practice* 20(3):263–273.

ﱠﱠﱠﱠ

Question 30: What do you do when a patient seems to make no progress?

Some patients move by leaps and bounds, and some seem not to move at all. It can be difficult to tolerate the apparent lack of movement, for it attacks our self-image as the effective healer.

Many therapists acknowledge the frustration of such an impasse, and how it can make them question themselves.

> That's when I really wonder about whether I'm in the right profession.
>
> [Female, M.S.W., 5 years practice]

> If I didn't have enough successes with other patients I'd begin to doubt my competence.
>
> [Male, Ph.D., 10 years practice]

> I question my competence. I feel self-critical, and I talk about it in supervision.
>
> [Female, M.S.W., 15 years practice]

> I worry. I go to see my supervisor for a consultation, because there I can also examine what's going on. What am I doing or not doing? What am I missing? Sometimes I ask if I'm the right person for this patient.
>
> [Female, M.A., 15 years practice]

When the frustration level gets high enough, certain feelings toward the patient can emerge.

> Sometimes I wish they would leave treatment.
>
> [Female, M.S.W., 10 years practice]

Some regard the feelings of impatience and frustration as indications of a countertransference problem in the therapist.

> If a patient seems to make no progress, then I'm probably feeling some kind of countertransference. If I have a need for there to be progress, that's a countertransference problem.
>
> [Male, Ph.D., 15 years practice]

For many, the situation leads to a consultation with colleagues or a supervisor.

> That's when I would talk to a colleague, run something by a colleague. That something's wrong here, and I can't handle it, and sometimes just talking about it helps.
>
> [Female, M.S., 15 years practice]

> I went back into supervision around a patient I had been seeing in analysis for six years, and had supervision of that case until it terminated two and a half years later, because I felt that I just wasn't able to work through certain resistances.
>
> [Male, Ph.D., 40 years practice]

> Sometimes I bring in another therapist: first in consultation outside the session, and then to come into the session with me, as an active participant.
>
> [Female, M.A., 20 years practice]

> I discuss the work with a colleague. In a couple of instances, it's helped to move it along.
>
> [Male, M.D., 20 years practice]

And some will try to address it directly with the patient.

> I think about it a lot, and sometimes I would even bring it up with them, that there's not much movement going on, and maybe we have to try something different. Sometimes bringing it up stirs things up and things get moving again.
>
> [Female, M.S.W., 10 years practice]

> I address that with them. I see it as a resistance, or a fear, and I ask them what they might be afraid of dealing with.
>
> [Female, M.S.W., 25 years practice]

I would raise my frustration with them, and my concern that I'm not helping them. That usually motivates some kind of effort.

[Male, Ph.D., 25 years practice]

In a few instances, I've explored if the patient wanted to discontinue therapy, or if they'd prefer another therapist. Some of my patients are very low functioning, and they tend to fix on me and won't leave.

[Male, Ph.D., 10 years practice]

I increase the frequency of sessions. Generally, if I feel the patient is making no progress, the patient feels that too. So we talk about what might be going on, and often as a result of that discussion they decide that they're really not coming frequently enough.

[Female, Ph.D., 15 years practice]

I might wait it out for a while. Then I might point out to the patient that we've been talking about the same thing over and over and do they have any sense of what that's about. Sometimes they'll come back and say they've been scared to go beyond where they are.

[Female, M.S.W., 5 years practice]

I bring it up quite directly with the patient. I'll ask them if they have the same impression, and if they do, I wonder what we should make of this. I'll wonder with them if there's something I'm not doing, and if not, whether we need a consultation.

[Male, M.D., 20 years practice]

Some will refer the patient to another therapist or consider termination.

Usually, I will reach a point where I say that we're not getting anywhere, and I've used up my bag of tricks, and I try to convince them that it's not their fault. I take the responsibility for it. I would try to convince them to transfer to somebody else who could come in with a fresh look.

[Male, Ph.D., 20 years practice]

Sometimes, I will discuss with the patient that we've been trying and trying and not getting anywhere, and then I owe the patient a proper referral.

[Male, Ph.D., 20 years practice]

I try to bring it to light, in as temperate and patient a way as possible, because I have a low threshold for too much time going by and very little happening. I would also seriously consider terminating, unless something happens.

[Male, Ph.D., 30 years practice]

Usually I get rid of them. I will discuss with them the fact that we don't seem to be getting anywhere in the therapy. If that helps the therapy to move along, fine. If it doesn't, then we come to a mutual agreement that we're not going to continue the therapy.

[Male, M.D., 5 years practice]

I have terminated patients, several times, where after a period of time it felt like nothing was happening and I wasn't feeling good about it and neither were they. Sometimes I've referred them to someone else, sometimes advised that they take a break from therapy. It's been positive every time I've done that.

[Female, Ph.D., 20 years practice]

But another therapist pointed out the possible danger in making such a referral or in terminating.

I don't know what progress means. You can define it in terms of clearly defined goals. I would initiate a discussion about their progress, and I might suggest that they see someone else. You have to be careful, because you don't want it to seem like you're rejecting them. I have a patient whose previous therapist thought he didn't need therapy any more, and he was devastated, because he has so much stuff to work on.

[Male, Ph.D., 15 years practice]

Others also pointed out that the patient may have a different assessment of the situation than the therapist does.

Do they think they've made no progress? Sometimes I may think they haven't and they really think they have. There are also some people who have a limited capacity for insight, and they use therapy as maintenance, as a way of checking in with another person, and that's okay too.

[Female, M.S.W., 10 years practice]

I ask them if there's something that I'm not doing that would be more helpful to them. They may not perceive that they're not making any progress. Those may be your own issues and your sense of timing. If you're feeling that way and they're not, they're spending money and coming in regularly, then they're getting something that may not fit with your agenda.

[Female, Ph.D., 10 years practice]

> I check out with them if they're really feeling that way. I may feel that they're not making progress, and check it out with them and they're feeling fine and dandy.
>
> [Female, M.S.W., 20 years practice]

Sometimes the roles are reversed, and the therapist may see progress where the patient does not.

> I usually think they are making progress. Sometimes they think they're not. I point out to them where I think they are making progress, and ask them if that's really true. I ask what they think we can change. I usually think things are going better than they do.
>
> [Female, M.S.W., 15 years practice]

> We keep working on it. There is progress, it's just in such small increments. There are those who can never admit that things are better. So I point out the changes that they've made.
>
> [Female, M.A., 15 years practice]

Some people try to be more active, or to shift gears and change their approach.

> I will often think a lot about whether it's something in the treatment or in the patient, and I'll sometimes try to approach the treatment differently, shift something from analytic to cognitive, rethink some of the symptoms. I'll present it to my peer group, and get some supervision. Then, I'll suggest a consultation, though I find that those consultations are usually not helpful.
>
> [Female, M.D., 15 years practice]

> I always take it to supervision, but sometimes the way I work with it is to get hold of what the feelings must be for the patient, and try to explore the feelings with them. I try to engage the person's aggression, their anger at me, their disappointment in me for not helping them, and sometimes that can move the treatment to another place.
>
> [Female, M.S.W., 15 years practice]

Others try to be less active.

> I may bring it to their attention if I think they have the capability of doing a lot more. I might decrease the frequency of visits for the time being—it might not be the right time.
>
> [Male, M.S.W., 15 years practice]

A few therapists said that they had never had the experience of no progress.

> I've had slow progress, but I've never had no progress. I get supervision, and I'm sometimes reminded of how far this person has actually come, and how hard true intimacy is for them.
>
> [Female, M.S., 15 years practice]

> It hasn't happened yet. I tell people in training that my technique is basically ruthless. I'll do whatever I can to get change.
>
> [Male, Ph.D., 25 years practice]

Several others said it is important to define the goals of treatment and to recognize that, for some patients, simple maintenance may be significant and valuable.

> There are patients where the engagement process takes a very long time. Sometimes just the continued coming to therapy is getting somewhere. I usually feel like I'm getting someplace with patients.
>
> [Male, M.D., 15 years practice]

> You have to carefully measure what that means. With some people, making no progress but staying where they are and not getting worse could be progress. If the person was suicidal and self-destructive, and is now stable, and without therapy would deteriorate again, is that making no progress?
>
> [Female, Ph.D., 30 years practice]

NUMERICAL DISTRIBUTION

Twenty-nine people said they would address this situation with the patient; 24 said they would discuss the case with a supervisor or colleague; 7 said they would refer the patient elsewhere.

COMMENTS

Some issues in this area are: What does "progress" mean? Does the therapist have an agenda for the patient, and why? Who is the best judge of therapeutic results? Is "maintenance" a valid goal in therapy?

I think the most useful definition of "progress" is movement toward the patient's goals. Usually, the therapist knows what these goals are and can assess whether the patient is closer to achieving them, but ultimately the patient must be the judge of the results and effectiveness of treatment.

Working with a patient who, over some period of time, seems to be getting nowhere is very frustrating. I have learned that sometimes I can think that patients are making no progress and they don't feel that way at all, which would imply that I have an agenda or a schedule of my own that does not match the patient's. I have even been in a situation in which I hear from a colleague who's seeing someone close to my patient that he or she is changing a lot, though I don't see it in my office. But when both the patient and I feel that way, I try to get a consultation, some feedback from a colleague, some supervision, some suggestions about what might be going on, or about what I might try, and that usually opens it up and leads to some new movement.

With some very damaged patients, therapy that prevents them from regressing or decompensating, although it may not produce much "progress," may be very helpful and valuable.

RELATED READING

Elkind, S. N. (1992). *Resolving Impasses in Therapeutic Relationships.* New York: Guilford Press.

Kendall, P. C., Kipnis, D., and Otto-Salaj, L. (1992). When clients don't progress: influences on and explanations for lack of therapeutic progress. *Cognitive Therapy and Research* 16(3):269–281.

Weiner, M. F. (1974). The psychotherapeutic impasse. *Diseases of the Nervous System* 35(6):258–261.

🔊🔊🔊🔊

Question 31: How do you handle termination? How do you feel when a patient leaves treatment?

Virtually every patient leaves treatment, sometimes when they have accomplished whatever goals they came in with, sometimes prematurely. How does the therapist deal with these two situations, and what are the effects on the therapist of loss of a patient?

Most therapists said that they prefer for termination to take place as a process over some time.

I think it's one of the most fruitful things that happens in therapy, the whole process. I like doing a long, long termination with a lot of feelings expressed.

[Female, M.S.W., 30 years practice]

I like a termination period of anywhere from two to six months, and consider that as a special part of the treatment, the termination phase. Often, a lot of things tend to get dragged up again.

[Male, Ph.D., 40 years practice]

Usually people agree to set a date, and work towards that, and we review where they were when they started, and where they got to, and what might bring them back to therapy at some point, what they might struggle with in the future. I think termination is really important.

[Female, M.S.W., 10 years practice]

At the time when the patient has made enough progress and thinks they want to stop, when the patient and the analyst agree that most or all of the goals of the treatment have been met, we set a termination date in a few months. I've found that a rule of thumb is for every year of treatment, one month. If they've been in treatment for four years, we set a date four months away. It works very nicely.

[Male, M.D., 20 years practice]

Some people will begin to talk about feeling better and stronger, and ask if I think they're stronger, and I'll say that it seems that they're thinking about leaving. Then we go through a process. Maybe a weaning process, where we cut down to every other week, or even take a break for a few weeks.

[Female, Ph.D., 30 years practice]

I like a good healthy termination to last a while, so that we can have a feeling of recapitulation of the treatment and a review of the relationship, and with enough room in it that the patient can shift the boundaries of the termination if they need to, that they know they have the latitude to say they're not ready if they want. I always let a patient know they can come as long as they want.

[Female, M.S.W., 15 years practice]

Many therapists wait for the patient to bring up the subject of termination.

I like to wait for the person to bring it up. Then we can have a discussion about the goals and progress, and I can give them feedback about what I see. When people bring it up, I'll give them an evaluation, but they make that decision for themselves. I'm very open to people taking breaks.

[Male, Ph.D., 15 years practice]

Usually what I do is go over how therapy was for the patient. I don't think I would ever suggest termination, but I might ask them to do a review of where they were and where they've come, and is there anything more they want?

[Male, M.S.W., 15 years practice]

When it's time, it's usually brought up by the patient, not by me. I never raise it. They may not be ready for it. If they're ready, you trust them to bring it up.

[Female, M.A., 15 years practice]

Periodically, patients will bring it up, and whenever they do, we talk about it and understand whether it makes sense or not. And sometimes it becomes clear to the patient that they're afraid of getting involved further in some next thing that's coming up. Sometimes they feel like they've really gotten what they came for, and it makes sense to stop. And sometimes there are practical reasons, like they're moving, or they have a new job and don't have the time, or they don't have the money and it doesn't seem worth it any more.

[Female, Ph.D., 15 years practice]

Other therapists may suggest termination to the patient when it appears the work has been completed.

If I have to bring up termination, because I feel that the work is essentially completed, I'll say that I think it's time for us to talk about stopping treatment and what their thoughts are about it.

[Male, M.D., 20 years practice]

I start to bring up the issue by saying that they're starting to get much better, and they probably don't need to see me as often, and how do they feel about that. It depends on the person. They may say, "You're right, I'd like to start coming once a month." Then I terminate very slowly. They know they can always come back, and they can always call me. They usually let me know when they're ready, and I just have to listen for it.

[Female, Ph.D., 10 years practice]

I might suggest termination, because that's part of what they came in with, the whole separation thing, and they do need to separate.

[Female, M.S.W., 20 years practice]

Usually, I'll say that I think things are going very well, and let's try every other week, and we do that for a few sessions, and then we drop to once a month once or twice, and that's the end of it.

[Male, Ph.D., 20 years practice]

Some therapists said they would try to talk a patient out of quitting prematurely.

Sometimes people will just quit suddenly. I ask them why they're telling me now, and why they're breaking our agreement. We've made a contract to do it on a gradual basis. If someone's transferred for their job, there's not much you can do.

[Male, M.S.W., 10 years practice]

When people want to leave, it's always okay, even if they're not ready to leave. I may talk about why they want to. I encourage people not to be precipitous. I always ask them not to do it today, whether it's appropriate or not. I want people to stay so we can talk about it for a period of time.

[Female, M.A., 15 years practice]

I like to give it some time, rather than this'll be the last session and have a nice life. Sometimes they come in that way. I might give them the recommendation that I don't think it's the greatest idea to stop. Based on what I know about them, I would incorporate that into my suggestion that they give it some time and check it out.

[Female, M.S.W., 20 years practice]

If it's premature, in my professional judgment, I do everything that I possibly can to help the patient to stay.

[Female, Ph.D., 20 years practice]

If they suggest it, and I'm against it, we'll talk about it. I'll wonder why they want to do that at this point.

[Female, M.S., 20 years practice]

Others said they would not try to talk a patient into staying in treatment.

I'm very good about that, because I had an experience with a therapist who wouldn't let me go. I'm very open, talk it over, and see it as a very healthy part of the process. If somebody's had a lot of therapy, it's fine with me even if everything's not settled.

[Female, M.S., 15 years practice]

I tend to let clients go. Clients can make a lot of progress outside of therapy. One of the worst things is to hold them in when they don't want to be there, even if there's more work to do, and there often is. I want to empower them to make decisions.

[Female, M.S.W., 15 years practice]

I know people get scared that you'll hold on to them when they're ready to go, that's one of the things that they've heard. I think you have to treat people with respect about this. Sometimes people feel okay for now, and they would like to leave, and they would like to go with your blessing, not with your conviction that they're going to relapse and come back in five weeks.

[Female, M.S.W., 10 years practice]

If it's not planned, and somebody wants to leave, there's nothing I can do. I've found that out over time. Let them go, be gracious, and maybe they'll come back.

[Female, M.S.W., 20 years practice]

Sometimes people will come in and say they want to leave next week. I'll explore that, and usually I'll accede to it. I'll say that I think they have the strengths, and that the door is always open if they want to come back. I don't try to talk people out of it.

[Female, M.S., 20 years practice]

A narcissistic injury to the therapist may be part of the effect of a sudden termination.

I had one termination recently where the patient just wanted to stop, and not set a date. If they just quit, I feel like I failed or I missed something.

[Female, M.S.W., 15 years practice]

Sometimes I feel that the work wasn't completed, or I could have done better.

[Female, Ph.D., 5 years practice]

Termination can be a problem for the therapist exclusively in private practice who depends on the income.

> I feel happy for them when they leave. It's not my main salary. It's a problem when it's your main salary, and they're getting better and they don't need to see you any more, but you need their money.
>
> [Female, Ph.D., 10 years practice]

Most therapists acknowledge that they have mixed feelings when a patient terminates, even when the treatment has been very successful.

> I often feel both sad and very gratified because I feel that I've really helped this person.
>
> [Male, M.S.W., 20 years practice]

> It's an especially difficult phase of treatment because it arouses some of the most difficult feelings for me: separation, loss, the limitedness of life. I try to be as grownup about it as I can.
>
> [Male, Ph.D., 10 years practice]

> I don't feel when somebody leaves that it's an endpoint. And if they do continue somewhere else, it's not necessarily a comment on our treatment, but rather a developmental process, and I've become more comfortable with that. I used to feel like I didn't fix them well enough, and I don't think that anymore. I'm also more comfortable with the idea that I may not be right for everyone, or have what it takes for every person.
>
> [Female, M.A., 15 years practice]

> If I feel that it was a nice piece of work, then I feel good when someone leaves. When someone just quits, I'm usually totally surprised, and a little angry.
>
> [Male, M.S.W., 10 years practice]

> It's still an area I have some difficulties with. Sometimes I feel relieved when someone leaves, sometimes I feel like I lost a friend.
>
> [Male, M.S.W., 15 years practice]

> When they leave, I feel happy for them if they're going on to something they want to do, but I feel sad because I've been attached.
>
> [Female, M.S.W., 15 years practice]

I've told people that they can write me, or call me from time to time, and it would be nice to hear from them. Because it's odd, with people who don't, you're in this intimate situation and all of a sudden they're gone, and you have no idea. That's one of the hardest things about this profession, to be that close, and then not to know anything about the person, and they're finished.

[Female, M.S.W., 20 years practice]

If I really like the patient, I miss them. I've had a few patients where I really enjoyed my sessions with them, they were wonderful people. Usually I feel pretty good when they finish. I mean, that's what I'm trying to do, put myself out of business.

[Male, Ph.D., 20 years practice]

If they've left feeling like they've really been helped and they got what they were coming for, then I feel good. I feel sad, but I'm glad that I've been helpful.

[Female, Ph.D., 15 years practice]

If I think they're leaving at the right time and not doing something premature, I feel okay about it. If they leave in the middle, I feel unfinished.

[Male, M.S.W., 25 years practice]

If it's someone that I'm very attached to I feel a loss, sad. I feel good about the work we've accomplished and sad to lose them. It's the child's job to leave, and it's the job of the parent–analyst to contain their own pain about it, and not to burden the child with it.

[Female, M.S., 20 years practice]

Several people said that they regard termination more as a temporary hiatus than as a final separation.

I don't consider ending therapy as a termination. Once I'm a person's therapist, I see myself as their therapist from here on in. That's the nature of our contract.

[Male, Ph.D., 25 years practice]

I make them aware that it doesn't have to be the end, that I'm available if they want to come back, and tell them that termination itself can be a growth experience.

[Male, M.S.W., 20 years practice]

I don't like to call it termination in a final sense. It can happen for many different reasons. If it's because the patient is satisfied with the way they're functioning, then I'm fine with it.

[Female, M.S.W., 45 years practice]

NUMERICAL DISTRIBUTION

Twenty-five people said they would, at least in some instances, suggest termination; 35 said they would wait for the patient to bring up the subject.

COMMENTS

Some issues here are: Who decides when treatment is finished? What are the effects of the therapist suggesting termination? Is it useful to try to change the mind of a patient who has decided to stop treatment?

Ideally, termination is a process that occurs over some period of time, although patients often have their own schedule in mind when announcing that they're ready to stop treatment. I prefer that people let me know when they're thinking about it. I never suggest it myself, because I think it's presumptuous of me to tell patients they're ready to leave and can be hurtful if they don't agree and feel as if I'm trying to get rid of them. I believe that they'll know when they're ready and they'll let me know. I prefer to set a date that gives us time to wrap up, but people will sometimes just quit abruptly, and I've learned never to argue with them or try to convince them they should stay, because if I make it easy for them to leave, there's a good chance they'll come back if they need more therapy, but if I make it hard for them to leave they'll never come back.

I feel good when someone leaves after a successful treatment, but also a little sad, because they've been an important part of my life and I'll miss them. I feel disappointed in myself when someone quits suddenly, because in those circumstances it is almost always due to some serious error on my part.

RELATED READING

Blum, H. P. (1989). The concept of termination and the evolution of psychoanalytic thought. *Journal of the American Psychoanalytic Association* 37(2):275–295.

Firestein, S. K. (1974). Termination of psychoanalysis of adults: a review of the literature. *Journal of the American Psychoanalytic Association* 22:873–894.

Fortune, A. E., Pearlingi, B., and Rochelle, C. D. (1992). Reactions to termination of individual treatment. *Social Work* 37(2):171–178.

Goldberg, A., and Marcus, D. (1985). "Natural termination": some comments on ending analysis without setting a date. *Psychoanalytic Quarterly* 45(1):46–65.

Kupers, T. A. (1988). *Ending Therapy: The Meaning of Termination.* New York: New York University Press.

Martin, E. S., and Schurtman, R. (1985). Termination anxiety as it affects the therapist. *Psychotherapy* 22(1):92–96.

ᘯᘯᘯᘯ

Question 32: When would you refer a patient elsewhere?

A new patient calls, and we either make an appointment for a consultation or immediately refer them elsewhere. On what basis do we make that decision?

Often, current patients refer other people in their lives: spouses and other lovers, friends, relatives, and so on. Sometimes we may feel that the new referral is too close to the current patient, and refer them elsewhere.

One person felt that this situation was not a problem.

> I hardly ever refer. I take almost anyone who calls.
>
> [Female, Ph.D., 20 years practice]

But most therapists had some guidelines in this area and made referrals to other therapists.

> I refer when I feel there'd be a conflict, like a sibling or a relative. It's too incestuous, because they get together and they talk about it.
>
> [Female, M.A., 15 years practice]

> I refer out when someone can't fit my schedule, or when someone is a close relative or friend. They say it doesn't bother them, but it really does, and you can't put your own needs of wanting the new patient ahead of your patient's needs.
>
> [Female, M.S.W., 30 years practice]

> I make referrals when I'm working with a husband and it's the wife, or boyfriend and girlfriend, that kind of thing, or a very close friend,

then I would make a referral. Some people tend to be very possessive of me, so I'm loath to take referrals from them.

[Male, M.S.W., 35 years practice]

If it's somebody too close to someone I'm working with, I'll usually refer to another therapist. What I do when they first say that someone wants therapy is I talk it over with the patient in regard to how they feel about the person seeing me. I would do it if my patient would prefer it, or if I feel there would be a complication.

[Female, M.S., 15 years practice]

I wouldn't see close friends or relatives of patients, even for a consultation. I'd chat with them informally and then refer them to a colleague.

[Male, M.D., 20 years practice]

Several people mentioned that they prefer to keep couples therapy and individual treatment separate.

If I work with a couple together, I then refer them out for individual treatment.

[Male, M.D., 20 years practice]

If I've seen someone individually and they now want to do couples work I'll refer them to someone else.

[Female, Ph.D., 5 years practice]

Many people said they would refer elsewhere a patient with a problem they didn't feel able to deal with effectively. Sometimes this might be due to lack of training or experience with a particular problem.

When I feel that I'm out of my league, like if a patient had a severe eating disorder.

[Male, M.D., 20 years practice]

I had a very obsessive-compulsive patient, and she saw someone simultaneously with me for that specifically.

[Male, M.S.W., 10 years practice]

If somebody is actively suicidal when they first call, I'll refer them out. I don't want to deal with someone coming in that way, who's going to require that much attention.

[Female, M.A., 15 years practice]

And sometimes it might be due to some personal issues or feelings.

> I'd refer if I felt I couldn't work with the patient. If the patient had a specific issue that I couldn't deal with, and that I'm not trained to deal with. I couldn't work with a man who was abusing a child.
>
> [Female, M.S.W., 15 years practice]

> When I don't feel qualified, or when something throws me. I don't like to work with an eating disorder, because I've had it in my family.
>
> [Female, M.S., 20 years practice]

> I would not take on a psychotic patient, or someone likely to become psychotic. I wouldn't take an acutely suicidal patient. I would refer someone who looks classically borderline. I can sometimes tell on the phone whether someone's going to be a management problem for me.
>
> [Female, M.D., 15 years practice]

> If I feel I'm not the right person for them. If I'm afraid of physical violence, or of getting involved in a situation that's too difficult. If I'm seeing a couple, and realize that the husband is having an affair, then I have to get out of that situation.
>
> [Male, Ph.D., 15 years practice]

Another situation where a therapist might refer a patient elsewhere is when the treatment feels stuck and is not progressing.

> When the negative transference is out of hand, and we're at a stalemate.
>
> [Female, M.A., 20 years practice]

> When I felt we were not getting anywhere, when there seemed to be some problem we couldn't resolve.
>
> [Male, M.S.W., 25 years practice]

> I would refer a patient out if we weren't getting anywhere. We might have gotten somewhere for a while and sort of plateaued. If we plateau for long enough, and the same kind of issues keep coming up and I can't come up with anything new, nothing I do or say seems to make a difference, then I'll consider referring them out.
>
> [Male, Ph.D., 20 years practice]

> If I feel that I'm not working well with the patient.
>
> [Male, M.D., 5 years practice]

NUMERICAL DISTRIBUTION

Twenty-four people said they would refer a patient who was closely connected to a current patient; 14 said they would refer a patient whose problem was something they were not familiar with or trained to treat; 6 said they would refer patients elsewhere if their schedule was full; 5 said they would refer a psychotic or suicidal patient; 5 said they would refer out someone they knew personally; 5 said they would refer someone who could not afford their fees; 1 person said she would refer a patient who wanted a male therapist.

COMMENTS

Issues raised by this question include: Which patients should be referred to other therapists? How close can patients with the same therapist be without undermining their treatments? What are the effects on patients of referring them to other therapists?

Therapists are bound by a code of ethical behavior that includes a section about practicing only within areas of expertise, and every therapist will meet some patients whose problems lie outside that expertise. These patients must be referred elsewhere.

I also believe that it is important to have boundaries between patients. Whenever current patients make a referral of someone from their lives, we discuss why they're making the referral and whether they really want me to see that person. Sometimes patients feel unable to refuse the other person themselves and want me to turn them away.

If it's really acceptable to both parties, seeing a couple both together and individually has advantages and disadvantages. It can be very useful to have the dual perspective and the intimate knowledge of both people. It can also, at times, be very complicated and difficult, for example, when there are secrets from the partner that the therapist knows, and many therapists make revealing such secrets a condition of treatment.

Giving away a patient may be difficult, especially when the caseload is down and the therapist needs the money. I think it helps to have a network of other therapists, familiar and trusted, to whom one can refer patients with some confidence, knowing that referrals will come back when the other therapist is in a similar situation.

Referring out a current patient, because of an impasse or for whatever other reason, may feel very damaging and rejecting to the patient, and should be absolutely the last resort, only after supervision and consultation have failed to break the impasse.

RELATED READING

Cheston, S. E. (1991). *Making Effective Referrals: The Therapeutic Process.* New York: Gardner Press.

Mayer, E. L., and deMarneffe, D. (1992). When theory and practice diverge: gender-related patterns of referral to psychoanalysts. *Journal of the American Psychoanalytic Association* 40(2):551–585.

Tryon, G. S. (1983). Why full-time private practitioners refer patients to other professionals. *Psychotherapy in Private Practice* 1(2):81–83.

⬡⬡⬡⬡

Question 33: Have you ever advertised? With what results?

In the old days, many professionals, including physicians and lawyers, were prohibited by their codes of ethics from advertising. Over the past few years, however, professional advertising has mushroomed, and every newspaper has a column filled with ads for psychotherapy and counseling.

Most of our group had never advertised their services. Of those who tried it, there were mixed results.

On the positive side, a few said that advertising did bring in some patients.

> When I do something new I get the newspaper to cover it. All that stuff is useful.
>
> [Male, Ph.D., 25 years practice]

> I've advertised as part of a group. It's been very helpful.
>
> [Female, M.S.W., 15 years practice]

> Recently, I advertised as part of a group. There have been some results. I haven't personally seen any of those patients, but there have been some calls and my colleagues in the group have gotten some referrals.
>
> [Male, Ph.D., 10 years practice]

But most who tried advertising found it was not a productive source of new patients.

> I wanted to get more homosexual patients, so I advertised in one of the gay papers, but I didn't get a single answer.
>
> [Male, M.S.W., 25 years practice]

I tried to advertise in the Yellow Pages, and haven't gotten a single call. In the past, I've advertised in some local papers and some gay newspapers, and I've gotten one or two patients from that.

[Male, M.S.W., 15 years practice]

One time, as part of a group. We took a name, and placed ads, but we only got a couple of referrals. This was many years ago.

[Female, M.S., 15 years practice]

I think ten years ago I put an ad into one of the neighborhood papers, and nothing happened.

[Male, M.D., 20 years practice]

As part of a group, with poor results.

[Female, M.S.W., 15 years practice]

I'm not too crazy about it. I've tried the local newspapers, but I don't think it brings very much. The usual channels are better, from colleagues or from another patient.

[Male, M.S.W., 10 years practice]

One therapist who had not tried advertising thought it might be useful.

I should. I should be a better businessperson.

[Female, Ph.D., 5 years practice]

NUMERICAL DISTRIBUTION

Only 10 people said they had tried advertising in newspapers, the Yellow Pages, or elsewhere. Of these, only 4 felt it was useful in acquiring patients.

COMMENTS

The issue here is: Given that it is now considered ethical, is advertising productive of new patients?

There may still be some stigma attached to advertising, a remnant of the days when professional advertising was prohibited. (Only one-sixth of this group had tried it.) In addition, advertising may indicate to some a kind of failure, an inability to acquire patients in the more conventional ways.

I have myself tried advertising a couple of times. The first instance, in the local MENSA newsletter about ten years ago, did bring in one patient, who stayed for several years. The other ad, which appeared more recently in a local newsletter for parents, referred to my earlier book about high IQ children and was aimed at parents of bright adolescents. I got no responses, not a single call.

For me, the main question about advertising is this: do I want patients who choose their therapists from an advertisement? That kind of situation suggests to me people who are so isolated from others and/or ashamed of their need for treatment that there is no one in their lives that they could comfortably ask for a referral or recommendation, and that therapy with such patients might be very hard work indeed.

RELATED READING

Dyer, A. R. (1988). *Ethics and Psychiatry: Toward Professional Definition.* Washington, DC: American Psychiatric Press.
Hite, R. E., and Fraser, C. (1988). Meta-analysis of attitudes toward advertising by professionals. *Journal of Marketing* 52(3):95–103.

℞℞℞℞

Question 34: How and where do you set boundaries? How do you deal with self-disclosure? How much do you tell patients about yourself?

At some point in every treatment, the patient will ask questions about the therapist, and the therapist has several options in responding.

One person spoke at length about some of the issues involved.

> I don't have a rule about it. I tend not to talk a lot about myself because that's not usually how things go. I believe that the anxiety and concern about self-disclosure among analysts stems from the fear of contaminating the transference, and I don't believe that the transference can be contaminated. Transference weaves around whatever is there. I think we mystify unnecessarily. I hate when I hear analysts respond to patients who ask a simple question like are they married by saying mechanically, "How do you feel about that? Do you have any thoughts about that?" What kind of answer is that? There's something mystifying and dehumanizing, and it smacks of a certain kind of power play. Yesterday a patient asked me at the beginning of a session if I had children. And I had about a half second's hesitation, and I decided in

that half second to go with what I don't know, and to not even know what I want to do and just do whatever I did. And I said, "No I don't have children," and it felt so natural in that moment to do that. The session went beautifully. I know why he asked, I found out afterward. I think the dogma around self-disclosure stems from the doctor–patient power play originally.

[Male, Ph.D., 10 years practice]

Questions about professional credentials are usually answered directly.

I'm very open about professional questions: my educational background, where I trained, and so on. I feel they deserve to know.

[Female, M.A., 15 years practice]

Many therapists tend to believe that self-disclosure is usually a mistake, that it blurs the therapist's role and makes it more difficult for transferences to develop.

I don't see the need to tell people about myself. My interpretations might let on something about me, but in general I don't think it's constructive or useful. The task is to help the patient understand what they're talking about, not to let them know something about yourself. To the degree that you're doing one, you're not doing the other. Also, it's an appeal to an authority that I think is misleading, because instead of telling them this is the meaning of what you're talking about, and you can cite the reasons, you're saying this is what you're talking about because I know it from my own experience. That's a different role, not the role of the therapist.

[Male, M.D., 20 years practice]

I have to be selective, and be very careful not to contaminate the transference or countertransference, which becomes a kind of posing, a lack of authenticity on my part that bothers me. In the long run, it works well, because I point out that it's awkward for me, with the promise that if it's really necessary I wouldn't hesitate to reveal it. I don't often feel the necessity, just their curiosity.

[Male, Ph.D., 30 years practice]

In the beginning, if a patient asks me questions, I analyze that. Any questions about my personal life, I analyze that.

[Female, Ph.D., 20 years practice]

For the most part, I don't disclose much, because that can get in the way of the therapy. The less they know about me the better. There are

times patients find out that I'm also in recovery, because I go to meetings myself. In that sphere, sometimes it's unavoidable.

[Male, M.D., 5 years practice]

I will tell them that I will hold off on answering, because I think it's a
helpful tool if they can bear it. We can use the information, and let's
play around with their imaginations.

[Female, M.S.W., 20 years practice]

One therapist described "loosening up" in this area.

I tend to work very privately, because I don't want it to intrude. I have
a supervisor who talks about himself a lot with patients, and at first I
thought, "Oh, my God!" Since I've been working with him, I've been
able to disclose more to patients. When patients ask me directly things
like, "Do you have children?" I'll answer them.

[Female, M.S., 15 years practice]

Another therapist, who sees patients for a very long time, said that self-
disclosure was better saved for late in treatment.

I think that self-disclosure is more appropriate after you've been with
a patient for twenty or thirty years than it is in the first few years of
treatment.

[Male, Ph.D., 50 years practice]

Sometimes sexual orientation is the area of the question.

If they ask me if I'm gay, and they come from a gay referral service, I
will tell them that, but that's about it.

[Male, M.S.W., 15 years practice]

I've had patients who are looking for a lesbian therapist, and somebody
may have told them that I'm gay, but I wouldn't generally tell someone
what my sexual preference is. I have lesbian patients who have no idea
that I'm a lesbian. I've seen them at certain social events and felt like
I needed to leave. I just don't see the point unless it's a real treatment
issue.

[Female, M.S.W., 10 years practice]

Other therapists believe that in some instances patients may need to
receive a direct answer to such questions.

> If a patient thinks they're the only one in the universe who has done or thought or felt something, I might tell them that I've done that too.
>
> [Male, M.S.W., 10 years practice]

> I'm more apt to self-disclose a little bit with couples. And with kids, I'll do it even more, because kids can be so mistrustful.
>
> [Male, Ph.D., 10 years practice]

> If I feel that the patient really needs to know for some reason, and wants me to answer first, either because they don't like to play my game, or they're tired of it, I will answer first. I don't like to be withholding for withholding's sake, arbitrarily. But I will keep a lot back, not because I don't want to be known, but because I want it to evolve organically.
>
> [Male, Ph.D., 5 years practice]

> I might tell a patient where I'm going on vacation, if they ask, or if I'm married. If they have some distorted impression of me that's causing some anxiety, I might correct that.
>
> [Male, M.D., 20 years practice]

Even a very psychoanalytic therapist can sometimes bend the rules.

> I tell them virtually nothing. Once in a blue moon, for some very, very special reason I might tell a patient something about myself. For example, I'm seeing a patient who's dealing with an elderly mother, and she's really struggling with it, and I'm helping her analyze her conflicts around it. But there are also certain realities, so I have shared with this patient dealing with my own elderly mother.
>
> [Male, M.S.W., 35 years practice]

One person said that too much self-disclosure was sometimes a sign of fatigue.

> When I'm exhausted and ready for vacation, I will often say things I wish I hadn't.
>
> [Female, M.D., 15 years practice]

Another therapist said that sometimes patients don't really want to know.

> I've had a patient who told me that the first year in therapy she didn't know a thing about me and she didn't want to know anything about me.
>
> [Male, Ph.D., 10 years practice]

Several people made the distinction between information about the private life of the therapist, and information about the therapist's thoughts, feelings, and experiences in the room with the patient.

> I'm much more likely to talk about what I'm feeling in the here and now than I am about personal things, but occasionally if it seems appropriate to me I'll divulge something about myself. If it's very important for someone to know where I'm going to be when I'm away, I will answer that.
>
> [Female, M.S., 20 years practice]

> I tell a lot about my inner processes. I use that very often as an interpretive tool. I don't tell a lot about my real life.
>
> [Male, Ph.D., 25 years practice]

> As you get older, you feel a lot more free to use yourself, and I like doing that. I don't mean revealing a lot of personal stuff, but I mean using your own reactions spontaneously, and sometimes when it seems indicated to give a little personal information.
>
> [Female, M.S.W., 30 years practice]

A number of people said they saw great value in revealing themselves.

> One of the most powerful things I do is to talk about myself and let people know me. I don't mean indiscriminately, but it opens up all kinds of stuff that never would get opened up if it was strictly a professional literal office. I believe in a more egalitarian relationship, and being willing to show my weaknesses and vulnerabilities.
>
> [Male, Ph.D., 20 years practice]

> Because I see the process as interactive, with equal reciprocal roles, I tell them quite a bit.
>
> [Female, M.S.W., 15 years practice]

> I will let them know if I'm married, if I have kids, where I went on vacation. I'm pretty self-disclosing. I'm a real person, and they can connect with me. I really believe that, as a therapist, I am their friend to some extent.
>
> [Male, M.S.W., 15 years practice]

> I'll tell a lot, especially my failures, partially to indicate that we all have our issues. I'll use myself as an example both positively and negatively.
>
> [Male, Ph.D., 20 years practice]

I might sometimes bring something out about my own experience, but it's more as a parable, a kind of modeling.

> [Male, Ph.D., 40 years practice]

I would reveal myself to them. I talk about my kids a lot. Sometimes I use it as a modeling thing.

> [Male, Ph.D., 25 years practice]

Some mentioned the usefulness of sharing similar experiences.

If there's something that might help someone with something they're going through, like a career thing, I might tell them of a similar experience.

> [Female, M.S.W., 5 years practice]

If they're there for panic attacks, and they ask me if I've had a panic attack, it's important to tell them I have, and this is what I did to overcome it. I know you're scared, and I don't know it from books, but because I've felt one myself. People who are talking about problems with their children often need to know that I've raised children.

> [Female, Ph.D., 10 years practice]

I'll talk about myself if it's appropriate, give them an example where the same thing may have happened to me, and how I was affected.

> [Female, M.A., 15 years practice]

I'll sometimes tell them what my own experiences were, to let them know that I understand what they're going through.

> [Male, M.S.W., 10 years practice]

I will use myself when it's appropriate, and it's sometimes very appropriate. I will often reveal my sexual orientation to someone who's also gay, for positive role modeling. I've also raised two kids, and when I see parents who are talking about childrearing I will always reveal that I have kids and know what it's like to be a parent. I've even revealed to a patient who was breaking up a long relationship and was having a hard time that I've been through that and recovered from it.

> [Female, Ph.D., 20 years practice]

One person used her own experience as a patient as a model.

My experience with my first therapist was that I didn't feel comfortable telling him everything about me if he didn't tell me *something* about himself. He went against his training and did tell me enough about himself to make me able to do it. I always remember that.

[Female, M.S.W., 15 years practice]

Several people suggested that it may be futile to try to conceal oneself, that the patient will always know who we are.

I tend to disclose very little, and people don't ask me very much. But I think that people get a sense of who you are by how you are.

[Female, M.S.W., 10 years practice]

Everything about us is a form of self-disclosure: the way the office is set up, the way we dress, the way we speak, whether we take a phone call or not.

[Male, Ph.D., 10 years practice]

They get to know me by how I work and who I am in the room.

[Female, M.S.W., 15 years practice]

NUMERICAL DISTRIBUTION

Seven people said they reveal nothing; 17 said they reveal very little; 28 said they reveal occasionally, when appropriate; and 8 said they reveal a lot.

COMMENTS

Some of the many issues here are: How does therapist self-disclosure affect treatment? Is self-disclosure damaging or productive? How does the therapist decide what to reveal and when to reveal it?

The old stereotype of the blank-screen analyst, who says little and answers no questions, still survives, and patients are often surprised when the therapist reveals, intentionally or inadvertently, that he or she has a personal history and a life outside the office.

It's not always clear when patients ask a question whether they really want to know the answer or if it's a kind of test to see if the therapist will keep his problems, issues, and history out of the treatment. I think that every small boundary violation or ambiguity raises questions for patients as to whether there will be more significant violations.

In my own practice, I make a distinction between knowing me and knowing about me. My patients all know me very well, because I'm very much myself with them. They know very little about me, because I've found that revealing personal facts from my private life can be very intrusive, and that even when they say they at first that they want to hear it, weeks or months later they often tell me they wish I hadn't told them.

Sometimes, on the other hand, a patient has a personal question about the therapist, and no matter how much they may analyze it and explore it, the patient still wants it answered. On those occasions, I will usually give some answer, because otherwise treatment stalls. Once in a great while the patient will wait until the end of treatment for the answer, but usually not.

RELATED READING

Dowd, E. T., and Boroto, D. R. (1982). Differential effects of counselor self-disclosure, self-involving statements, and interpretation. *Journal of Counseling Psychology* 29(1):8–13.

Goldstein, E. G. (1994). Self-disclosure in treatment: what therapists do and don't talk about. *Clinical Social Work Journal* 22(4):417–433.

Hill, C. E., Mahalik, J. R., and Thompson, B. J. (1989). Therapist self-disclosure. *Psychotherapy* 26(3):290–295.

Lazarus, A. A. (1994). How certain boundaries and ethics diminish therapeutic effectiveness. *Ethics and Behavior* 4(3):255–261.

Weiner, M. F. (1978). *Therapist Disclosure: The Use of Self in Psychotherapy.* Woburn, MA: Butterworths Press.

🖎🖎🖎🖎

Question 35: When patients ask how or why you do this work, what do you tell them?

I think all therapists at least occasionally get asked by patients, "How can you do this all day? Listen to problems, and pain, and unhappiness all day long. Doesn't it get you down?" Different therapists respond different ways to this question and address differently what lies behind the question itself.

Many therapists try to answer the question directly, with some variation of the idea that they do it because they like it and are good at it.

> I usually say that I discovered as a teenager that I was incredibly nosy, and I discovered this job where nobody can tell me it's not my business to ask all these nosy questions. And I get paid for it.
>
> [Male, Ph.D., 25 years practice]

I would ask their fantasy about it first, and then I would tell them I do it because I enjoy it. It's the creativity, the use of the mind, the great contact with people.

[Female, M.S.W., 20 years practice]

What I often tell them is exactly what I feel, which is that this is fun for me. To this day, I cannot figure out for the life of me why people pay me for this, and it feels like cheating because at work you're supposed to sweat and slave and hate it. The fact is that I do something that I love.

[Male, M.S.W., 15 years practice]

I don't necessarily ask why they're asking the question. Sometimes the patient is just making small talk, and I will usually give them a short answer, like I enjoy it.

[Male, M.D., 5 years practice]

I say that I don't find it difficult at all, I don't find it tiring, I find it rewarding, I don't get drained from working with people.

[Female, M.A., 15 years practice]

The general point I make to patients is that this is what I like to do, that I don't find it onerous, and that I'm really appreciative that I have the opportunity to do it, which is true.

[Male, Ph.D., 50 years practice]

I usually chuckle, and say that I like my job, and there's good and bad with every job, but I like talking to people.

[Female, Ph.D., 20 years practice]

I have an answer that comes out automatically, so I know it's true. I tell them I can do it because I enjoy being with people in this kind of one-to-one setting. The other thing is that I feel very privileged to be in their lives in this unique and special way.

[Female, M.S., 15 years practice]

I tell them something one of my supervisors told me, which I have come to realize is true for me as well as for him, and that is that when I'm here, I'm one-hundred percent here, and it's only you I'm thinking about. But when I leave I don't carry the burdens with me, I've learned to compartmentalize, so when I walk out of my office, only if there is some emergency will I think about it.

[Female, M.A., 20 years practice]

I tell them it's extremely gratifying to meet with them, that I don't feel burdened, and that if I did I'd give it up and we wouldn't be working together.

[Male, Ph.D., 30 years practice]

I'm honest. I tell them it might be hard if this was all I did, because I like to talk to people about my life, and if I spent all day not talking that would be hard for me. I tell them I don't do this all day. And then I talk about the fact that I don't find people boring, meaning, whether I say it or not, I don't find you boring.

[Female, Ph.D., 10 years practice]

Some respond by saying that the work feels meaningful to them, and suits them in some way.

Sometimes I'll say that I do get gratification out of helping people and seeing them grow.

[Male, M.S.W., 20 years practice]

One thing I tell them is that working with people is the most exciting and varied work there is. Also, I might say that being in a helping position meets certain needs of mine.

[Female, M.S.W., 10 years practice]

I tell them it's not always easy, but that people are very important to me, and that each person is unique.

[Female, Ph.D., 30 years practice]

I tell them that life is hard, and this is one way to make life more tolerable, more livable, because I know how helped I was in my own life. I tell them that I listen differently than they might to their friend on the telephone, that I listen with a perspective, with a different ear.

[Female, M.A., 15 years practice]

I tell them that sometimes it really beats the crap out of me, and sometimes it's the most gratifying thing anybody could possibly do. And that mostly I have learned, as best I possibly can, to leave it in the office.

[Male, Ph.D., 20 years practice]

I usually say that I'm most alive when I'm working. That everybody's born to a purpose, and I don't think I could do too much else in life.

[Male, Ph.D., 40 years practice]

Some people try to convey to the patient that the work is not so difficult as it may seem to them.

> I used to have a stock reply, that what's difficult is not listening to what
> the problems are, but really getting a grip on what the person is all
> about, and why the person has these problems, and why they want
> me to give them advice or solutions.
>
> [Female, M.S.W., 5 years practice]

Most people said that they try to explore the motivation for asking the
question before they answer it.

> First I would explore why they're asking it, what does that question
> mean, and get them to tell me a little bit more. Eventually, if they
> persist, I tell them that this is the profession I went into because I enjoy
> doing it.
>
> [Female, M.S., 20 years practice]

> Most of the time, I would respond to that as to anything else, which
> means I would inquire where the question is coming from, and why
> are they asking it. I have told people that I find the work absolutely
> exciting to do.
>
> [Female, M.D., 15 years practice]

> I say that it's my training, that's what I do. Before I do that, I'll ask
> them about what they think I'm feeling when I listen to them.
>
> [Female, M.S.W., 20 years practice]

Several people said they try to turn the question around and put it back
on the patient.

> I say that obviously that means that you wouldn't be able to do this,
> and I turn it back to them to get them to try to explore what they're
> feeling, how they would feel about doing this work. And what do they
> think about me doing this, am I pretending or what.
>
> [Male, Ph.D., 15 years practice]

> Sometimes I ask them how they can do what they do all day.
>
> [Male, M.D., 20 years practice]

> I'll say, "It's a living," if there's bullshit going on and I want to cut
> through the bullshit. If we've gotten through all the possible ways they

might be resisting with that comment, I tell them that it's the most interesting time of the day for me.

[Male, Ph.D., 25 years practice]

Sometimes I've made light of it, and said to them that I could never do what they do.

[Male, Ph.D., 10 years practice]

A number of people suggested reasons that the patient might ask this question.

They're asking if I can stand them, if I have faith in their ability to change, if I like them, if I love them.

[Female, M.S.W., 15 years practice]

They're talking about their own misgivings about themselves, that they're boring, that they're not interesting people.

[Male, M.S.W., 10 years practice]

It usually comes up when I see people back-to-back, when the client comes in and they see the other one leave. It often has to do with their feelings that they're just replaceable, they're a nonentity.

[Female, M.S.W., 15 years practice]

I may say to the patient that they must think that I suffer the way they suffer, as part of their own dynamic.

[Male, Ph.D., 20 years practice]

With a new patient, I might say that they must be wondering if I'm interested in you, or if I'm with you when I just saw someone else and they walk out and you walk in.

[Male, Ph.D., 20 years practice]

I ask them what they think. How can I stand to listen to people like you all day long?

[Female, Ph.D., 20 years practice]

Sometimes that is the person's thinking about becoming a therapist themselves, and they're wondering if they could tolerate the work. Maybe they just told you something that's so painful they can't stand to hear it, and they're afraid that you can't stand to hear it.

[Female, M.S.W., 10 years practice]

I might interpret that they're feeling like I can't stand them, or I might laugh with them.

[Female, Ph.D., 15 years practice]

I ask them, when they say that, how difficult they think they are. That's usually the subtext of that question.

[Female, M.S.W., 30 years practice]

One patient recently seemed to be saying, "I'm never going to be your equal. No matter how hard you try to make me be your equal, I will always be inadequate next to you. And I need you to play some kind of sadistic power game with me."

[Male, Ph.D., 10 years practice]

Oftentimes they're asking if I'm really giving them my full attention.

[Female, M.S.W., 20 years practice]

In some cases, it's envy that I'm doing something that they would like to do, and sometimes it's hostility, and sometimes it's a compliment.

[Male, M.D., 20 years practice]

NUMERICAL DISTRIBUTION

Thirty-five people said they answer the question; of these, 23 say they do it because they like or enjoy it, and 12 say they do it because the work is important or meaningful. The other 25 people said they don't answer the question directly, but try to investigate where it comes from in the patient and what the patient is thinking.

COMMENTS

The issue here is whether the patient is really asking a question, and, if so, whether it is productive to answer it.

At some point in the treatment, most patients seem to ask some form of this question. I think they are almost always asking about themselves and not about the therapist or the work when they do. (Once in a while, this question comes from a patient who is considering becoming a therapist.)

Patients often have the idea, left over from childhood when their parents seemed overwhelmed by the task of raising children, that telling someone how you feel, and needing something from them in response, is burdensome to that person. And consequently they think of themselves as burdensome and difficult and needy. I ask them what they think is so hard about listening to them and what could be so difficult for me in responding to their needs. The resulting discussion can lead to a real breakthrough in the therapy, because it often reveals that they have been "protecting" me from a lot of feelings and wishes and fantasies, which they now feel able to express.

RELATED READING

Mathews, B. (1989). The use of therapist self-disclosure and its potential impact on the therapeutic process. *Journal of Human Behavior and Learning* 6(2):25-29.

Simon, J. C. (1988). Criteria for therapist self-disclosure. *American Journal of Psychotherapy* 42(3):404-415.

Stricker, G., and Fisher, M., eds. (1990). *Self-Disclosure in the Therapeutic Relationship*. New York: Plenum Press.

Wells, T. L. (1994). Therapist self-disclosure: its effects on clients and the treatment relationship. *Smith College Studies in Social Work* 65(1): 23-41.

🔊🔊🔊🔊

Question 36: What do you wish patients knew about therapy that they don't seem to know?

When patients first walk in the door, they have whatever knowledge and experience they have accumulated to that point. Those experiences may have created expectations and beliefs, some of which may be an advantage to the process of therapy, and some may retard the process. Sometimes we may wish that patients knew more about the process when they first arrive, so that the treatment could go more easily.

While a quarter of the group said they had no such wish, most therapists said there were things that they would like patients to know. The largest portion of the group said that they wished patients knew that therapy was a process, something that took place over time, often a long time, and that it was sometimes difficult.

> That it might take longer than they would want it to, that they have to have a lot of patience.
>
> [Female, M.S.W., 20 years practice]

That it's a process, that it unfolds and takes some time, and it can offer rewards and gains in ways they may not have even expected, that can affect the rest of their lives.

[Male, Ph.D., 15 years practice]

I think people come into therapy, especially if they haven't had it before, with the wish/hope that each session's going to give them something that they can take away with them and hold on to, and it's going to help them cope in a better way. It takes a while for people to get the idea that it's a process, and there are going to be sessions where they walk out saying they don't even remember what happened, and others where they're going to walk out more anxious, and that it doesn't mean necessarily that it was a terrible session.

[Female, M.S.W., 20 years practice]

It takes time. It can't be done very quickly. There are some people who are extremely naive about what the therapeutic process is about, and they're expecting concrete rules about what they should do and then the problem will be solved. It's kind of like they went through school, they're educated people, but they never took a psychology course, they never had a conversation about feelings, and their experience and vocabulary and way of seeing the world, you wonder why they're in a therapist's office. They don't have the substructure yet, and it's frustrating and difficult.

[Female, M.A., 20 years practice]

For some patients, that it's going to be a struggle, and it's going to hurt sometimes, and that it takes a long time to see change.

[Male, M.S.W., 15 years practice]

Some people wished that patients knew that they had to put in most of the effort.

That it's work! That it's tedious, hard work, and there's no magic wand that they all want.

[Female, M.S., 20 years practice]

That it's all up to them. That they're the responsible agent, and nothing's going to happen unless they want it to happen. And I can't really do anything for them.

[Male, Ph.D., 50 years practice]

That it takes a lot of work. It's not just coming in and talking on a social basis. That it's hard work, that the person has to be able to bear discomfort and anxiety. That the therapy isn't necessarily going to make them feel better, but is going to help them learn about themselves, know themselves better.

[Male, M.D., 5 years practice]

A number of people wished that patients knew more about the process and how it works.

That there's something called transference that goes on between patient and therapist.

[Female, M.S.W., 15 years practice]

I wish they knew that there are no real rules, other than coming on time, and the rules of appropriate behavior, like they can't come in and take their clothes off. But that there are no other rules, that they can say whatever they need to say, and that they can't know what I'm thinking and feeling. A lot of people try to figure out what is the right thing to do.

[Female, M.D., 15 years practice]

I guess it would help if they knew that it's about the relationship.

[Female, M.S., 15 years practice]

A lot of the people I work with are not sophisticated therapy clients, so they don't know that they have to be on time. I have to work with that right away. I work with people who have a lot of taboos about talking about their feelings. If they talk about fears, that would make it happen. A kind of superstitiousness. I work with many people who are African-American, and they often don't know that I've worked with many African-Americans, and they need to know that. They don't know that it's okay to talk to me about anything. If they don't bring up the issue of what it's like to work with a white therapist, then I will.

[Female, Ph.D., 10 years practice]

I wish they knew a little more about free association, how to do it and let it happen.

[Male, Ph.D., 40 years practice]

Always, the question is how to help a person get enough observing ego so that they can think of their behavior as motivated in some way, as opposed to being the product of forces acting on them. That's a tough idea to get across to a lot of patients, and takes a lot of work. I wish the patients were more psychologically minded.

[Male, M.D., 15 years practice]

> That it's fascinating. I remember in training seeing my own therapist, telling him that I always find the process fascinating, and my clients don't always seem to be as fascinated in their own dynamics as I am in mine. And he just said, "Resistance."
>
> [Male, M.S.W., 10 years practice]

Several people mentioned a wish that patients knew that the therapist is a benign and generous figure, not someone to be afraid of.

> I've had patients who had a really distorted image of what the therapist must think of them, especially when I really like a patient and they think that I must think they're some sort of a dope, or terrible. I wish they knew that I liked them.
>
> [Male, M.S.W., 20 years practice]

> How dedicated and concerned and caring the therapist usually is. Patients mistake our professionalism for not being caring. They want instant solutions and gratifications, and they don't understand that because we don't have them doesn't mean that we care less, or that we're withholding something.
>
> [Male, M.D., 20 years practice]

> I would like them to know that therapists, in general, do have good intentions, and that we are human, and that it's a hard job being a therapist and we deserve to be paid for it.
>
> [Male, Ph.D., 15 years practice]

> I wish there was some way they could be less afraid of revealing themselves, and that we two could work as a team.
>
> [Female, Ph.D., 20 years practice]

> That I am really interested in knowing whatever they want to tell me, that I don't feel judgmental, and that I am really interested in engaging in the process. I feel ready to work, and sometimes some of the work is getting them ready to work, and I wish they would come in knowing that's what we're here for.
>
> [Male, M.S.W., 25 years practice]

> That it's very important for them to look at their stuff, and that I don't want to know it in order to attack them, but that it's really important for them to make progress. Because too many people spend too many years in therapy defending unnecessarily.
>
> [Female, M.S., 20 years practice]

A few therapists wished for a little more trust.

> That they go through bad times and good times, and it would be easier if people had a little faith in what we're doing.
> [Female, M.A., 15 years practice]

> I wish they could handle not knowing, that it's okay not to know. That they don't need to know. In other words, trust. It's part of the process to get to that point.
> [Male, Ph.D., 20 years practice]

A few people suggested that it would be helpful if patients knew that they were allowed to relax, laugh, or even have fun.

> I wish patients knew that it's okay to laugh and have fun, that they don't always have to be solemn and talk only about what's wrong. And that it doesn't mean we're wasting time and being frivolous.
> [Male, Ph.D., 15 years practice]

> That it's fun. That it's not about suffering. A good session is not a session where you come in and thrash and cry and carry on and have this moment of catharsis, but one in which you have some fun.
> [Male, M.S.W., 15 years practice]

Several people mentioned that it would be helpful if patients knew more about how to choose a therapist in the first place.

> I wish people knew more about qualifications and credentials, and what training is. I'm sick and tired of hearing about people who go through 12-step programs and they put out a shingle. I wish people knew not to choose them as therapists.
> [Male, Ph.D., 10 years practice]

> That they be better consumers. That they recognize that there are many ways to do it, and not every way is appropriate for them, and for them to be informed enough to find the appropriate therapist for them.
> [Male, Ph.D., 25 years practice]

> I still find that some patients think that therapy is what only M.D.s do.
> [Female, M.S.W., 20 years practice]

On the other side, many therapists said it didn't matter what patients knew about therapy or that what they know may actually be an impediment.

I think they know what they need to know.
[Female, Ph.D., 15 years practice]

I think it's my responsibility to teach them. In fact, when people come in thinking they know about it, usually we have to get around that. Their preconceptions are either wrong or it's a different style from mine.
[Male, Ph.D., 20 years practice]

I don't care what they know. It's the feelings that count.
[Female, M.S.W., 45 years practice]

They do know, they come to me prepped, with previous therapy. I wish they knew that I may work differently than other therapists, that eventually we're going to have to leave that person on the side of the road so we can go on.
[Male, Ph.D., 40 years practice]

I think if patients knew everything about the process of therapy they'd probably be cured and not need to see you in the first place.
[Male, M.S.W., 35 years practice]

NUMERICAL DISTRIBUTION

(Some people mentioned more than one answer.) Nine people said that it takes a long time; 8 said that it's a process, not a simple solution; 6 said that the therapist has good intentions and likes them; 6 said that it's hard work; 5 said that the therapist doesn't have all the answers; 4 said that it's all right to have fun; 4 said that it's worth doing; 3 said that it's all right to say anything; 3 said that credentials are important; 2 said that being in therapy doesn't mean you're crazy; 2 said that it's all about the relationship with the therapist; 1 said more about how to free associate. Thirteen people said they don't wish for patients to know anything in particular.

COMMENTS

The issue here is whether it is necessary or even productive for the patient to be knowledgeable about therapy.

Not too long ago, patients in psychoanalysis were often cautioned against (and sometimes prohibited from) reading about treatment or discussing their therapy with anyone, with the explanation that this would somehow compromise the therapy. While most therapists no longer make such rules, many seem to think that the sophisticated patient is hard to treat because he or she uses such knowledge as a resistance. I find it hard to believe that knowledge could be a liability.

This question literally asks about a fantasy of the therapist's. In the real world, patients know what they know and the therapist deals with it, whatever it is. Often what patients think they know about therapy is erroneous, and we must spend time correcting the misunderstandings. All this is part of the treatment. If patients really knew all the things mentioned in the responses above, most treatments might be simple and straightforward.

I think if I had to choose one thing that I wish patients knew about therapy, it would be that the most productive and useful work, and the healing part of the treatment, takes place in and around their relationships with me, and that if we talked about nothing else, that could still be a complete therapy.

RELATED READING

Braaten, E. B., Otto, S., and Handelsman, M. M. (1993). What do people want to know about psychotherapy? *Psychotherapy* 30(4):565–570.

Melnick, J. (1978). Starting therapy: assumptions and expectations. *Gestalt Journal* 1(1):74–82.

Zwick, R., and Attkisson, C. C. (1985). Effectiveness of a client pretherapy orientation videotape. *Journal of Counseling Psychology* 32(4):514–524.

Ⅱ
Theory

This section deals with issues of theory and meaning, those ideas and concepts usually included under the heading of metapsychology. It also includes questions of opinion and attitude about the various conditions, situations, and other phenomena that therapists encounter in their work. Here again, just as in the section on practice, there is a tremendously wide range of responses on almost every question, and not always is this attributable to theoretical orientation.

Question 37: What is your theoretical orientation?

Most therapists train in a certain school of thought, which sometimes becomes their orientation and sometimes is replaced by other systems of thinking. I asked these therapists to label themselves as to orientation and metapsychology. Although almost everyone gave a primary orientation, most also included several other approaches in their self-definition, and, as we shall see, different people often meant different things by the same label.

Almost a third said that they were psychoanalytically oriented, often with modifications.

> I'm eclectic psychoanalytic. I felt that there were good things about the various schools of therapy and analysis, and it really wasn't helpful to me to just adopt one particular approach or one particular theoretical posture. One posture didn't seem to work with everybody.
>
> [Male, Ph.D., 15 years practice]

> When asked I say I'm trained as a psychoanalytically oriented psycho-therapist. Sometimes that's true and sometimes it's not true. Over the years, my theoretical point of view has changed as the result of experience.
>
> [Female, M.A., 20 years practice]

> What I go by for my neurotic patients is the concept of the dynamic unconscious, and the fact that there are forces at work within the individual which are shaping and sometimes primarily determining their behavior, of which they are unaware. And that the therapeutic work that I do with patients will help them become more aware of these things and therefore better able to understand themselves. It's basically psychoanalytic.
>
> [Male, M.D., 20 years practice]

> I believe that psychoanalysis can be applied to emotional and mental conditions not hitherto treated by psychoanalysis, such as schizo-phrenia, preoedipal disorders, impulse disorders, and so on. I also believe in working with more than one person in a family, which classi-cal analysts do not. I work with husbands and wives, with parents and children. I'm treating seven members of one family. It's an extension of the theoretical basis of psychoanalysis to the preoedipal disorders.
>
> [Female, Ph.D., 20 years practice]

I'm Buddhist psychoanalytic. I believe in the unconscious, in transference and countertransference and resistance, I basically believe in psychoanalytic developmental theory, but I also believe that life is taking place right now. I believe that being awake and present and alive at the moment is really crucial, and any of the other stuff that takes you away from that, all the other stuff has got to be filtered through that awareness, otherwise it doesn't change anything.

[Male, Ph.D., 25 years practice]

It's basically Freudian, but at the same time I'm eclectic, and will be reasonably practical because of practical concerns. If a person is available for in-depth analysis, then my Freudian approach remains Freudian without any modifications, without any parameters, without any let-up.

[Male, Ph.D., 30 years practice]

A related group defined their orientation as "object relations."

I'm probably more someone who gets their orientation from classical ideas. I'm not really a Freudian. I see myself as more of an object relations or self psychologist.

[Female, M.S.W., 15 years practice]

I guess object relations, with a little bit of self psychology at this point. My original training was fairly Freudian, but after being in groups and reading and going to conferences, and seeing what works, gradually you change your approach.

[Female, M.S.W., 30 years practice]

The official words for it are British and American object relations with a heavy dose of self psychology.

[Male, M.S.W., 10 years practice]

I think I do operate a lot within a separation/individuation model. So that object relations model is fueling my thought a lot. Developmental issues. That's a characteristic of any theory I have, that it feels very developmental. My work with children influences that a lot.

[Female, M.S.W., 15 years practice]

Broadly, I'm in the realm of psychoanalytic, heavily toward the ego psychology/object relations area, some of self psychology. But also eclectic. On occasion I'll do some hypnosis, I'll do some behavior therapy. But in terms of understanding a patient I come from the ego psychology/object relations point of view.

[Male, M.S.W., 20 years practice]

Another related group identified themselves with Kohut and the self psychologists.

At my institute, you could study everything, and I tended to gravitate towards self psychology, because that tended to make the most sense to me. But I'm more eclectic than that. I don't want to plug anybody into some formula. But the focus on the patients' experience, that's what influenced me.

[Female, M.S., 15 years practice]

I'm not very articulate about how I work. I guess I'd have to call myself a cognitive self psychologist. It's our belief systems that influence our lives, and a lot of that is subconscious. I believe in positive reinforcement, expressing confidence in someone. Most people didn't get enough nurturing.

[Female, M.S.W., 15 years practice]

If you had to categorize me, I'm probably more Kohut than anyone else. I often think that what we're seeing is preoedipal stuff, I don't think there's much oedipal stuff, although every now and then you see someone who's oedipal and intellectualized.

[Female, M.A., 15 years practice]

A quarter of the whole sample said that they thought of themselves as eclectic, including several different orientations in their approaches, although the word "eclectic" seems to mean different things to different people.

It would be easy to say eclectic, and that's probably what it is. It's a little bit of everything. Sometimes I worry that it's such a hodgepodge. I used to be cleaner years ago, I'm not pure anymore. I was also much more involved in maintaining a theoretical orientation. I think I'm expedient and pragmatic now. I still do a lot of gestalt work, because I think it really works. It moves people along, it gets them involved in the treatment. I like it because it's active, and I can be an active participant.

[Female, M.A., 15 years practice]

Eclectic, as everyone says. My training in residency was very biologically oriented. They called it eclectic, but it was much more medical and biological than psychodynamic-psychological. That certainly influenced me. I'm more knowledgeable working with medications than in any particular type of therapy. We did have psychotherapy training throughout the residency, but that was weaker than the medication. The thrust was learning how to diagnose, and how to use medications. My therapeutic approach is not any particular orientation.

[Male, M.D., 5 years practice]

Eclectic. I see the personality as a grid, with little squares running down. Certain issues are right at the surface, and they just need mentioning for the person to hear them, and they resolve themselves, or become satisfactory enough that they don't need dwelling upon. Other issues may have just a coating over them, and take a few sessions to get to. Others may have a layer of steel over them, or reinforced concrete. And some are just like a volcano, they almost have to erupt on their own.

[Male, M.S.W., 10 years practice]

Five people defined themselves as behavioral or cognitive therapists.

Behavioral/cognitive, with a strong emphasis on classical and operant conditioning, and equally strong attention to cognitive elements: thought patterns, assumptions, and the like.

[Male, Ph.D., 20 years practice]

My training was psychoanalytic, psychodynamic, object relations, typical New York training, and that's basically how I understand people's development in terms of personality and ego defenses. In terms of treatment, that's only appropriate for some people. Most of my work is cognitive-behavioral in orientation. Which doesn't work, in my opinion, unless you can be analytic, because if every patient did what I told them to do, that this is how you get over your problem, I'd be out of business. They'd be cured, they could just read a book and know what to do. People don't do it for all of those psychodynamic reasons that you need to be able to work with. Good cognitive-behavioral therapists have a very good analytic sense of people, or they wouldn't be able to establish rapport to work with them.

[Female, Ph.D., 10 years practice]

Three said their orientation was family systems theory.

I'm a family systems therapist, although about half my practice now is individuals and couples. I wish I could get more families. I appreciate the strategic approach, and I'll do something structurally, so I'm more eclectic than I used to be, I'm not as pure. And I also do the Ericksonian work, which has expanded my work a great deal, and fits quite naturally with systems therapy.

[Female, Ph.D., 5 years practice]

Systems therapy. And a strong emphasis on language. The way people say things to each other is so responsible for how they behave. I work with the relationship. Through the relationship, whether it's an individual in the relationship with me, or the couple and how we develop the relationship among all three of us, something is going to come out of that.

[Female, M.A., 20 years practice]

I was trained in family systems theory, and I used to feel more rigid about deviating. I feel at this point that when I read books or go to workshops I incorporate whatever feels right in my own experiences. I'll incorporate anything at this point. My orientation is still basically family systems, even when I work with individuals. I believe in interactive work, and I'm quite active as a therapist. I push people, I don't sit back. And then there are times I do, depending on who I work with.

[Female, Ph.D., 20 years practice]

Another two said their orientation was developmental.

Developmental, psychoanalytic. Margaret Mahler—I rely very much on that separation/individuation stuff. And Masterson.

[Female, M.A., 15 years practice]

There was also a scattering of other definitions.

I would never call myself a gestalt therapist, but I'm probably closest to gestalt. I'm a garbage pail. I use what works. With a few people, I even go back to some of my traditional psychoanalytic training, but I use what works.

[Male, M.S.W., 15 years practice]

It's what now is being called relational-developmental. It's a psychoanalytic approach that's influenced by Gill and Hoffman, and people like Mitchell.

[Female, M.S., 20 years practice]

I think I'm really in the cultural school. Erich Fromm and Harry Stack Sullivan. I see our psychology intricately affected and involved in the culture that we grow up in.

[Female, M.S.W., 5 years practice]

I think it would be called interpersonal-existential to interpersonal-phenomenological.

[Male, Ph.D., 10 years practice]

At this point, it's humanistic, experiential. I use where I am and where I think the patient is. Technique is a rear-view mirror. I've had a lot of · training, and I don't have to think about it very much.

[Male, Ph.D., 40 years practice]

I'm relationship systems based. That's not necessarily a kind of therapy, but an acknowledgment that all self-development arises out of a context of relationship, therefore it's in the primary significant relationships that I prefer to work. Secondly, I consider that most of the problems people have come out of the history of their experiences, and the habits that relate to them, and the issues in their lives establish certain kinds of ways of being in the world. So if they could learn new ways to do that, that would help them change more effectively than any kind of insight they might have, even though insight is useful for motivation.

[Male, Ph.D., 25 years practice]

Several people suggested that in a thorough treatment it may be necessary to incorporate many different orientations.

The theoretical orientation is where the patient is. There's a wonderful paper on the four theoretical orientations, and depending on where your patient is, that's your orientation. If the patient is into a narcissistic injury, then you're dealing with Kohut and you respond that way. If the patient is now in an oedipal stage, then you're a Freudian. To be stuck in any one orientation is to reify or rigidify treatment, and then in a way you're duplicating what the patient experienced originally.

[Female, M.S.W., 20 years practice]

Eclectic, although I started off as classically Freudian. I'm firmly convinced that there are patients who fit the classical Freudian mold. There are Kohutian patients, and Kernbergian patients, and I don't think every single patient will fit the mold, and I don't think any one theory explains everybody. I think in the course of an analysis, if it's done properly, you do classic id drive work, you do work with narcissism, you deal with ego psychology, you do object relations. And I don't see how you could successfully treat somebody in a full-blown analysis and not do all of that.

[Male, M.S.W., 35 years practice]

Only three people declined to select a label for their orientation.

I don't have this great big theoretical orientation. I'm there, I think I know what I'm doing, but I don't have a big theory.

[Female, M.S.W., 20 years practice]

I was trained fairly classically analytically, from Freud through object relations theory, having been influenced primarily, up to a couple of years ago, by the object relations writers. Then I got very influenced by Kohut's work, and since then by Joyce McDougall and some of the Paris people. In the last few years, though, it's been changing a lot, and I'm not sure how to describe my orientation now. I've been doing a lot of work on dissociation and consciousness, and it raises some very serious questions about the structure of the mind, and how we know what we know. I don't find Freud's structural model very useful any more, and I think more about dissociated experience rather than unconscious, and I'm still working out what the difference is. I see things less as pathology, and more as adaptation. People can do outrageously patho-logical-looking things, and it's actually strength and health that make them do those things. There's a kind of paradoxical shift.

[Female, M.D., 15 years practice]

I don't fit into any category anymore. I've evolved my own frame, which has its roots in psychoanalysis, and passes through all of these other frames that I've experienced, and arrives at some personal synthesis.

[Male, Ph.D., 50 years practice]

NUMERICAL DISTRIBUTION

This is complicated to quantify, because most people mentioned several schools as influencing them or as being part of their orientation.

As their primary orientation, 16 said they were psychoanalytic; 15 de-scribed themselves as eclectic; 5 said object relations; 5 said cognitive or behavioral; 4 said self psychology; 3 said family systems; 2 said develop-mental; 2 said interpersonal; 2 said relational; 1 said humanistic; 1 said cultural; 1 said gestalt; and 3 said they were unable to label themselves.

Overall, the following orientations were mentioned as additional influences: psychoanalytic, 20 times; Freudian, 10 times; modern psychoanalytic, 5 times; Kohut/self psychology, 15 times; object relations, 15 times; ego psychology, 5 times; eclectic, 10 times; family systems, 5 times; behavioral, 3 times; cognitive, 4 times; developmental, 3 times; relational, 4 times; gestalt, 2 times; interpersonal, 2 times. The following were mentioned once each: humanistic; existential; cultural; Sullivanian; Ericksonian; strategic; and structural.

COMMENTS

Some issues in the area of theoretical orientation are: What do we mean by "eclectic"? Is a coherent theory necessary for effective treatment? Is one theory somehow more accurate, or more productive of effective treatment?

I have some trouble with the label "eclectic," because it so often seems to mean "without a coherent theory." What therapists do may seem only distantly connected to metapsychology, yet a theoretical basis gives meaning and purpose to our actions and interventions.

Assigning a label to oneself may be difficult to do, although most therapists do seem to have some body of theory from which they work. Patients often ask what orientation I am or what kind of therapy I do, and I have trouble knowing how to answer them in a way that will have meaning for them.

My own orientation is psychoanalytic, in that I believe in a dynamic unconscious. If I had to select a label, I'd label myself what seems now to be called relational or interpersonal, by which I mean that point of view described and influenced by people like Robert Langs, Merton Gill, Harold Searles. It's psychoanalytic, but it recognizes the truth of the patient's perceptions of the therapist and doesn't dismiss them as "transference."

RELATED READING

Herron, W. G. (1978). The therapist's choice of a theory of psychotherapy. *Psychotherapy: Theory, Research, and Practice* 15(4):396–401.

Herron, W. G., Ginot, E. R., and Sitkowski, S. (1987). Validity of self-designated therapeutic orientation. *Psychological Reports* 60(3):797–798.

Hiede, F. J., and Rosenbaum, R. (1988). Therapists' experiences of using single versus combined theoretical models in psychotherapy. *Journal of Integrative and Eclectic Psychotherapy* 7(1):41–46.

Pulver, S. E. (1993). The eclectic analyst: or the many roads to insight. *Journal of the American Psychoanalytic Association* 41(2):339–357.

Schwartz, B. D. (1978). The initial versus subsequent theoretical positions: does the psychotherapist's personality make a difference? *Psychotherapy: Theory, Research, and Practice* 15(4):344–349.

🔊🔊🔊🔊

Question 38: How did you choose an orientation?

How do we arrive at a particular orientation? How do we decide from what perspective we view and understand patients? Sometimes finding a theoretical orientation that makes sense and feels right can be a long process. Two people described it in detail:

> My first orientation, before I was a psychotherapist, was behavioristic. I worked with the retarded for many years. I went to school wanting to learn strict Skinnerian behaviorism. After a few years, that began to seem ridiculous to me. It just didn't explain human behavior. It explained some behavior of some retardates and some rats, and maybe a few minuscule behaviors in normal people. As a system of doing therapy, it seemed ridiculous. Then, over the years, I got involved in gestalt therapy, partly because it's very humanistic, and liberal, and partly because it accepts homosexuality. It came out of a '60s mentality. Then I went to a gestalt institute, and was very disillusioned and unhappy. Theoretically speaking, I don't understand gestalt therapy. It's a very complex and arcane theory and I haven't understood how to apply it to sitting and talking to somebody. I have colleagues who say it does apply, but I could never understand it. It led to a bad ending at the institute. I didn't finish, and I left. Now, I lean more toward the Masterson model, which is an object relations model, which makes a lot more sense to me. I look for an overarching theory that explains the work to me. I don't like what some people call "seat-of-the-pants therapy." I don't like sitting for months, going from session to session with whatever comes up, which for me is very uncomfortable.
> [Male, M.S.W., 15 years practice]

> Between college and graduate school, I worked for a year at a program that was doing experimental operant conditioning of schizophrenic and autistic children. And I found it to be quite remarkable, to say the least. I was much more impressed with what we were doing than I was with what Bettelheim, say, was doing. Spending five years to get eye contact from an autistic kid, when we could do it in five days, struck me as a gigantic waste of time. That kept evolving, as I read more and

more, and I also got interested in medical stuff, behavioral medicine, which is the interface of the emotional and physiological interaction. The cognitive side I was doing for a long time before anyone called it cognitive therapy. I used to call it "challenging people's assumptions." Then someone told me that it's called "cognitive restructuring."

[Male, Ph.D., 20 years practice]

Many people said it was simply how they were trained.

I think everybody was psychoanalytic at the time I entered a training institute. But also because all of the therapists I had seen were analysts.

[Male, M.S.W., 20 years practice]

It was what was being served up at the institute where I was trained.

[Male, M.S.W., 10 years practice]

The people who first taught me in school happened to be of that orientation.

[Female, Ph.D., 20 years practice]

The mentors I had in my training, and where I ended up in terms of the patient population I started working with and what was effective. I work with a lot of people who don't have money, and don't have years to get better. You need to start giving them techniques to cope right away.

[Female, Ph.D., 10 years practice]

I grew up at a time when there was a general consensus that Freudian psychology was correct. I trained at a place that was a bastion of psychoanalytically oriented training. Their goal was to teach medical residents how to do psychoanalytically oriented psychotherapy. If you could do that, you could learn to do anything else you needed to be a psychiatrist. Although there were some weird things that I encountered there, basically I felt that the model was a valid model, and I still do.

[Male, M.D., 15 years practice]

Others said it was their experience as a patient that influenced their choice of orientation.

The process of my own therapy, more than anything else.

[Male, M.S.W., 10 years practice]

Many others said it was the system that made intellectual or emotional sense to them, that something "clicked" for them.

> It's what rang true for me, a certain kind of respect for the other person. What appeals to me is the empathic approach, the concept of intersubjectivity.
>
> [Female, M.S., 15 years practice]

> My initial negative experience with an analytic therapist led me away from analytic training. Also, in social work school, very early on, I took a course in family therapy with a very dynamic instructor, and that totally turned me on, and I pursued that.
>
> [Female, Ph.D., 20 years practice]

> I started at the family therapy institute as a video consultant, when I had another career, and I was enthralled by the work they were doing. It was the heyday of family therapy. And where the psychoanalytic therapy never felt right to me, this language was something that felt right to me, that I could understand.
>
> [Female, Ph.D., 5 years practice]

> I was open and willing to hear out many different theories and different orientations from my internship days on, and I was exposed to many different styles and kinds of people, and the ones that impressed me the most time and time again were the analysts, classical Freudian analysts.
>
> [Male, M.D., 20 years practice]

> The process was that early on, when I started studying theoretical material, I had an immediate affinity for the basic philosophical under-pinnings of interpersonal theory.
>
> [Male, Ph.D., 10 years practice]

> I felt uncomfortable with the psychoanalytic approach because of my own experiences. I found the cognitive style of working was the one I felt more comfortable with.
>
> [Male, M.S.W., 15 years practice]

Others said they arrived at their present position after many years of different experiences.

> After the Jungian analysis I became more Freudian. In my rehab work I used a lot of people like Rogers, those counseling people. And when

I went to the institute I had people on the couch. I tried a more traditional approach, and saw its inadequacies, and began exploring other ways, first Robert Langs, then Merton Gill.

[Female, M.S., 20 years practice]

I had a tremendous amount of disappointment in Freudian application, which made me go into other theoretical rationales, and I experimented with a lot of other things, and swung full circle after many years to be more Freudian than eclectic.

[Male, Ph.D., 30 years practice]

NUMERICAL DISTRIBUTION

Twenty people said that their orientation comes out of what they were taught in graduate school or at a training institute; 15 people said their orientation comes mostly out of their experience in treatment as a patient; 10 said it comes out of their experience doing treatment as a therapist. Fifteen people said their current orientation is simply what feels right to them.

COMMENTS

One issue here is whether the therapist chooses his or her theoretical orientation for conscious or unconscious reasons.

It seems that many therapists choose for themselves whatever orientation is taught where they study. This may be college, graduate school, or the training institute. Of course, those who know what orientation they prefer will choose the school that teaches from that perspective. Others may choose the orientation of their own therapists.

What I have observed over the years is that therapists, as they acquire more experience, seem to be less and less attached to any one particular theoretical orientation and more and more inclusive of ideas and techniques from many different orientations. The advantage is obvious: a wider range of tools and responses to draw on. The disadvantage may be less obvious: lack of consistency and coherence.

Personally, having been raised in a psychoanalytic household, I was already well acquainted with that frame of mind, and pursued that approach in my training. Since then, I have become less traditional and more flexible in my own thinking.

RELATED READING

Cummings, N. A., and Lucchese, G. (1978). Adoption of a psychological orientation: the role of the inadvertent. *Psychotherapy: Theory, Research, and Practice* 15(4):323–328.

Guest, P. D., and Beutler, L. E. (1988). Impact of psychotherapy supervision on therapist orientation and values. *Journal of Consulting and Clinical Psychology* 56(5):653–658.

Havens, L. L. (1978). The choice of a psychotherapeutic method. *Journal of the American Academy of Psychoanalysis* 6(4):463–478.

Jacobs, D. (1993). Theory and its relation to early affective experience. In *Human Feelings: Explorations in Affect Development and Meaning*, ed. S. L. Ablon et al., pp. 305–316. Hillsdale, NJ: Analytic Press.

Syeiner, G. L. (1978). A survey to identify factors in therapists' selection of a therapeutic orientation. *Psychotherapy: Theory, Research, and Practice* 15(4):371–374.

Tremblay, J. M., Herron, W. G., and Schultz, C. L. (1986). Relationship between therapeutic orientation and personality in psychotherapists. *Professional Psychology: Research and Practice* 17(2):106–110.

ʀʀʀʀ

Question 39: Is there anything in your personality that is reflected in or determines your choice of theory or technique?

There must be some compatibility between who we are and the way we work, if we are to present ourselves with any authenticity. What do our therapists identify in themselves as influencing their choice of approach to treatment?

Many people said their personalities were such that they could not work in the traditional psychoanalytic mode.

> I have a strong personality, I'm very verbal, and I'm very active. To be a good family therapist, you need to have those characteristics. You can't just sit back. If you try to, you just get swallowed up. I also can't shut up for very long. I couldn't be quiet enough to get through an analytic session.
>
> [Female, Ph.D., 20 years practice]

> I couldn't work the way a lot of classical analysts work. I couldn't, for instance, be a non-involved therapist. I couldn't sit silently.
>
> [Male, Ph.D., 5 years practice]

I tend to be emotionally reactive. It would be very hard for me to be a sit-back, listening-type therapist.

[Female, M.S.W., 20 years practice]

I talk a lot, so I couldn't be a silent analyst. I think a lot of patients want more feedback, more interaction, and I need the connection too.

[Female, Ph.D., 30 years practice]

I am action oriented and I'm a risk-taker. I believe that unless you're willing to make changes in your life nothing is going to happen. I believe that being conscious of life decisions, this is how I live my life, and my therapy reflects that. I challenge patients to take risks. I realize the anxiety I experience doing new and different things so I appreciate the anxiety, recognize it with my patients, but also encourage them to go through it. I'm experientially oriented, I learn through experience, and I encourage patients to participate in experiential growth workshops that are available out there. I appreciate the resistance that people have to change, so I use bibliotherapy, support groups, as ways to maintain the therapeutic momentum.

[Male, Ph.D., 25 years practice]

Being interactive, because I can't be a blank screen. I don't have the face for it.

[Female, Ph.D., 5 years practice]

I think therapy *is* your personality, to a large degree. I like to participate, I can't sit back and be quiet, so I have to pick a theory that allows me to be active. Otherwise, it would be agony. I still have to tell myself at times, "Be quiet. You don't need to say anything."

[Female, M.A., 15 years practice]

I think part of my personality is that I find it very difficult to remain silent for fifty minutes, so that certainly influences my choice of technique. And I'm theatrical, so anything that involves role playing and participation in the session would appeal to me.

[Male, M.S.W., 15 years practice]

Others said their personalities were well suited to that psychoanalytic technique.

I think that there's something that may be a character flaw but is helpful to me as a therapist. I do psychoanalytic-type therapy, and patients are lying down facing away from me, and I find that often during a session I'm really half paying attention to them. I'm thankful that many of them just like to talk and I don't have to say much and I don't really want to say much. From that standpoint, I really give patients a lot of space, I'm not intrusive. In fact, I'm probably frustrating, because they have to question me, they have to dig a little bit to get anything from me. And that helps the therapy, because they're figuring out things for themselves. They get the message from me that I don't really need to say anything. My character has determined this a little bit, because I'm often in a mood where I don't want to relate to anybody. I'm a bit of a recluse, so this psychoanalytic method is good for me.

[Male, Ph.D., 15 years practice]

I'm a reflective person, and I'm a creative person. I like to look beyond the surface of things, so this is a perfect job for me.

[Female, M.S.W., 20 years practice]

I'm very sensitive to the feeling of intrusion, the boundary issues, and the need for people to have the opportunity to get in touch with themselves and their own inner processes and thoughts, so this way of working really provides that in a way that doesn't complicate it by giving directions or opinions.

[Female, Ph.D., 15 years practice]

I'm a very good observer, I can sit back and observe, being maybe passively involved in the situations.

[Male, Ph.D., 20 years practice]

I've learned to be patient, where at one time I thought my impatience was more a factor in my criticisms of Freudian therapy. Then because of changes I made, and my own experiences, I decided that my own willingness to work gradually, and be patient, helped determine the allegiance to the Freudian way.

[Male, Ph.D., 30 years practice]

Except at home with my children, I'm a very patient person, and I'm not with the kids because I use it all up in here. My personality is one of being patient and tolerant, and that's very helpful. Another thing that's part of my personality that very much affects my work is a real need to always be inquiring, to look closer and closer and closer, and smaller and smaller.

[Female, M.D., 15 years practice]

I'm not a confrontative or very aggressive person. I would steer away from some of the models where you need to be that way.

[Female, M.S., 20 years practice]

Several people talked about feeling a need to be open and engaged, emotionally active and responsive.

> It fits in with my temperament. I think it's important to be there for clients, not to be cold. I'm a warm, empathic person basically.
> [Female, M.S.W., 15 years practice]

> My mothering, nurturing inclination.
> [Female, M.S.W., 15 years practice]

> I think probably what I said about women is true about me, that I find it easy to join people in their experiences and easy to come out of it, and so probably that's something about me that affects my way of working.
> [Female, M.S.W., 15 years practice]

> I'm not a mild-mannered person. I've been able to learn to use my feelings in the conduct of the therapy so that I can get angry if I need to get angry, and that's easy for me because I'm an angry person. I'm not an opaque-mirror kind of therapist. I can be kind, I can be whatever.
> [Female, Ph.D., 20 years practice]

Others mentioned specific character traits that affect the way they work or the system they chose.

> Probably the old liberal/radical background. I don't really like set systems. I don't want to think that I have to follow a system.
> [Female, M.S.W., 30 years practice]

> I'm extremely wary and skeptical of authority and how it can be abused, and issues around power, how power is so perverted in society. Psychoanalysis is as vulnerable as anything else to that perversion, and I think that of all the theoretical models the interpersonal model is the least susceptible to that.
> [Male, Ph.D., 10 years practice]

> What drew me to this profession was the need to be heard, for someone to really listen to me. One of the major things in my personality, and patients have told me this, is my unique ability to remember them in a meaningful way.
> [Female, M.S., 15 years practice]

I think that in my own family, I did have a childhood in which my parents kept things from me. My passive-aggressive response was to ask a lot of questions to embarrass them. But I think also I was always inquisitive. I remember my parents saying, "How come you're always asking questions?" And the answer was, "Because you're not telling me." And I think that's where it comes from.

[Female, M.S.W., 10 years practice]

I'm insecure. I have some definite deficits interpersonally. These things can cause me to be a better relationship therapist than an individual therapist. I'm rigid, and that's a detriment too.

[Male, Ph.D., 25 years practice]

If I think about myself, I think a lot of my personal issues have been about having a strong sense of self and being able to affirm that and feeling mirrored. That's been a very important part of my experience.

[Male, M.S.W., 25 years practice]

Two behaviorally oriented therapists said this:

I'm not that patient. I like to see people get better and feel better quickly.

[Female, Ph.D., 10 years practice]

I question everything. Anything that doesn't have sufficient controlled experimental support gives me pause.

[Male, Ph.D., 20 years practice]

NUMERICAL DISTRIBUTION

Fifteen people said they were too active or impatient to be a traditional silent analyst; 6 others said their personality was suited to the psychoanalytic approach. Five people said they were always introspective, and 5 others said they were always questioning everything. Six people said they were good at nurturing or joining emotionally; 4 others said they were good at listening or observing. Three people said they were sensitive to boundaries; 2 people said they were sensitive to power issues. Two others said their strong sense of self was a factor in their choice of orientation. Twelve people said they didn't know or couldn't identify those elements in their personality.

COMMENTS

This question and the previous one refer to the issue of how the therapist chooses the orientation from which he or she works.

As therapists must feel comfortable intellectually with whatever theoretical and clinical approach they select, so there must also be some emotional compatibility between theory and the other aspects of the therapist's personality. Many therapists report that their personalities make it impossible for them to be the "silent analyst." That role also seems to me to be too disengaged, and I need to be more actively involved and participatory. In addition, I believe from my own experience that patients are not so fragile and don't need so much protection from the therapist.

There are a number of orientations available today that seem to work well and produce effective treatment, and I wonder if it matters whether the therapist selects his or her orientation consciously or unconsciously, as long as it fits comfortably and allows him or her to work effectively.

RELATED READING

Barron, J., ed. (1978). The theory and personality of the therapist. Special Issue. *Psychotherapy: Theory, Research, and Practice* 15(4).
Baudry, F. (1991). The relevance of the analyst's character and attitudes to his work. *Journal of the American Psychoanalytic Association* 39(4):917–938.
Tremblay. J. M., Herron, W. G., and Schultz, C. L. (1986). Relation between therapeutic orientation and personality in psychotherapists. *Professional Psychology: Research and Practice* 17(2):106–110.
Vasco, A. B., and Dryden, W. (1994). The development of psychotherapists' theoretical orientation and clinical practice. *British Journal of Guidance and Counselling* 22(3):327–341.

₪₪₪₪

Question 40: What is your opinion of classical psychoanalysis?

Classical Freudian psychoanalysis, the original treatment, now competes with hundreds of other approaches. How is it regarded by our group of therapists?

A little more than a third said they still believe in the basic premises of psychoanalytic theory and do psychoanalytic treatment.

> It's the basis of everything: uncovering, and looking at the unconscious, letting the person be, free associations. It's really very helpful.
>
> [Male, Ph.D., 15 years practice]

Everybody, if you ever have the time and the money, should have a classical analysis. I don't think it cures neuroses, but it gets to some interesting parts of the psyche.

[Female, M.S.W., 25 years practice]

It has its place. There are people who had early childhood experiences which were good, and they didn't get stuck until the oedipal period, and you have to work that way with them.

[Female, M.S.W., 20 years practice]

I used to not buy it at all. I'm very much the other way now, and think there are useful ideas, especially understanding that drives can definitely influence behavior. Freud's language, the translation made him more mechanistic, and the translators have done him a disservice. Once you get beyond some of the language, there's some very useful information.

[Female, M.S.W., 15 years practice]

Many people raised questions about specific elements of psychoanalytic theory or technique.

I always felt that lots of the theoretical framework about women never sat right with me. I think it was also that I was learning it during the whole feminist movement.

[Female, M.A., 15 years practice]

There are so many things about it that have been proven to be so wrong. The whole thing of using physics to explain psychology, like psychic energy.

[Female, M.S.W., 5 years practice]

I really don't accept the whole drive model, and I don't think it's helpful to people.

[Female, M.S.W., 30 years practice]

Several people said that classical psychoanalysis doesn't treat the patients we get in our offices today.

Classical analysts won't work with the kinds of patients I work with. They won't work with pre-oedipal people. And they don't work with people and their aggressive drive. Everything's oedipal and above, and people just aren't like that.

[Female, Ph.D., 20 years practice]

I don't understand why people work that way. My understanding in terms of drives and defense mechanisms is that it works at an oedipal level mostly, and most people's problems are not at an oedipal level. They're at a pre-oedipal level, so most of that wouldn't be effective, although people with pre-oedipal problems have lots of post-oedipal problems as well, so you can work on that. I've had a number of patients who've had nine or ten years of couch psychoanalysis and said they were finished, and came in to me and seemed very seriously narcissistic. They were at the beginning. You say one word different from theirs and they're in an outrage. It didn't seem like it had even identified the problem, much less fixed it.

[Male, M.S.W., 15 years practice]

A number of people thought that classical psychoanalysis is simply archaic, better replaced by new discoveries and developments.

I think it's out of date, that it's based on old paradigms and models. I feel kind of sad about having outgrown it. In co-leading a group with a very Freudian therapist, I saw unmistakably how it wasn't working.

[Female, M.S., 20 years practice]

It's over. It's to be honored and respected and all that, but it's over. We've learned a lot since then. But without that, you're stuck with a very limited, constricted, black-and-white world view. I don't want to sound like those who are dismissing Freud and psychoanalysis. It's one of the three or four greatest breakthroughs of humankind, and I have profound respect for it.

[Male, Ph.D., 25 years practice]

Freud was brilliant, and he certainly gave us an enormous amount to jump off from. He worked in the Victorian era. A lot of his basic stuff is forever incorporated, but a lot of his specific stuff is outdated and we need to move beyond it.

[Female, Ph.D., 20 years practice]

I see it as somewhat of an anachronism in today's world, because people don't come to therapists five days a week. And people are very resentful of not being responded to. We all know the theory, that it will develop the transference and all the acting-out and whatever, but I'm not sure it's worth it at all.

[Female, M.A., 20 years practice]

They're holding on to some theoretical ideas that just don't hold up any more, and it's really a drag on them.

[Male, Ph.D., 5 years practice]

Several people distinguished between the theory and the technique.

Classical analysis as a therapeutic technique is dead. Classical analysis as a theory of human development and human behavior, and a methodology for investigating and interpreting human behavior is very much alive.

[Male, Ph.D., 50 years practice]

Many others expressed serious reservations about the traditional psychoanalytic approach.

I think there's an elitism about it. The assumption is that the patient has the language skills and the time, and in that way it's very restrictive. It can be enormously helpful, and I know people who've gone through psychoanalysis, and it's something informative in their lives. But it's not practical, and it's limited. I don't like the language—I find the language very pejorative and negative. Freud was a genius, but there are limitations. I think his views on gender are really off.

[Female, Ph.D., 5 years practice]

It's kind of a luxury. It's there if you've got the time and the money to do it. I like to think of my own training as psychoanalytically oriented, the focus on the unconscious. What I don't like is playing doctor, in the sense of not being a collaborator with the client. To speak from an authority as if you were practicing medicine is inappropriate. The attitude that I'm the expert in the room, and I'm the only one who's competent to clean up the mess that you are, so shut up and do what I say.

[Male, M.S.W., 10 years practice]

The American analysts have dramatically misunderstood Freud's own orientation, and have used it badly. That's the part of psychoanalysis I abhor. Many of Freud's basic concepts are part of what I do, the developmental orientation. But they distort it, especially the role relationship between therapist and patient. That's where it's been distorted the most.

[Male, Ph.D., 25 years practice]

I never could make much sense of Freud, it never made sense to me. I never believed in the oedipal complex. I think that's already pathology, there I agree with Kohut. I don't think people can be blank screens. Our biases come through, and it's better to get them out on the table and let the clients deal with them. You can hide a lot of pathology and insensitivity behind being the blank screen. I'm not saying that all psychoanalysts do. I'm sure there are very sensitive psychoanalysts.

[Female, M.S.W., 15 years practice]

Some said that psychoanalysis has become a closed group, and a closed system, for some of its practitioners.

I've been at institutes which were very psychoanalytic, and it was too religious, too much like a mantra. Any orientation that imposes itself as the whole truth and nothing but the truth gets in the way of thinking. It probably doesn't hurt, but I don't think by itself it works. I think you need more than understanding. I strongly believe that the patient needs feedback from the therapist, and occasionally direction.

[Male, Ph.D., 10 years practice]

It depends on where one enters it, and what one makes of it. It's an elite school that is sometimes so exclusionary that it's difficult to comprehend it if you're not in the school. I read papers or go to presentations where it's in a jargon that only the people who have studied in a particular way understand it. However, I don't throw out concepts like the interest in aggression as an important force. And in terms of technique, the classical methodology is not the treatment of choice for most people.

[Female, M.S.W., 15 years practice]

A few were more thoroughly negative and skeptical.

I think classical psychoanalysis is a bunch of crap. These people live in this arcane little world based upon an unproven and unproveable theory. Classical psychoanalysis is nonsense. If Woody Allen wants to go for fifteen years, fine, I don't care. If he's got the money and nothing better to do with his life than contemplate his navel, that's okay. But as far as psychoanalytic therapy for the treatment of most things, it's unproven, it's inefficient.

[Male, Ph.D., 20 years practice]

Most of the research I've read is that psychoanalysis doesn't work in the long run. Insight becomes the booby prize. I have so many people who come to me in various degrees of fucked-up lives who've spent five, ten, or fifteen years in psychoanalysis, and I wonder what the hell did they do there? They just stared at their navel while somebody went "Um hmm." That's pretty sad.

[Male, M.S.W., 15 years practice]

NUMERICAL DISTRIBUTION

(Remember that 17 people identified their primary orientation as "psychoanalytic," and 13 additional people included it as part of their orientation.) Twenty-three people said they had only positive attitudes toward it; 37 people said there were serious problems or flaws in the theory or the practice.

COMMENTS

There are several issues here: Is psychoanalytic theory still coherent and applicable? Is psychoanalytic technique still a valid therapeutic method?

As a theory, psychoanalysis hasn't incorporated the latest research findings about infant and child development, which appear to raise serious questions about many of Freud's basic premises. The old hydraulic model of mental energy seems to me very antiquated. I think there's also a lot wrong with psychoanalysis as a technique: it's not interactive enough, it assumes too much about the neutrality of the analyst, it emphasizes fantasy far too much over reality. We've come a long way since psychoanalysis was developed and we need to include what we've learned since then in our present approach. Traditional Freudian psychoanalysis often seems to me much like astrology, in that all the "truths" are already known; it's a closed system. On the other hand, the basic Freudian idea of a dynamic unconscious still seems valid to me, especially when combined with recent research and technical developments.

RELATED READING

Eagle, M. (1984). *Recent Developments in Psychoanalysis*. New York: McGraw-Hill.

Freud, S. *The Standard Edition of the Complete Psychological Works of Sigmund Freud*. 24 vols. London: Hogarth Press, 1953–1974.

Levine, R. (1979). Metapsychology and the psychoanalytic theory of technique. *Psychoanalytic Review* 66(3):367–382.

Stern, D. (1985). *The Interpersonal World of the Infant*. New York: Basic Books.

ছছছছ

Question 41: What is your opinion of self psychology?

One of the most powerful modifications of psychoanalytic theory and technique recently has come from Heinz Kohut and the self psychologists. How do our group of therapists regard Kohut and his followers, their theory and their technique?

Many people, not necessarily those describing themselves as self psychologists, were extremely positive about it.

> I always felt very comforted that Kohut made me believe that things can change, that we can change, and if we're able to discover what it was that we missed or didn't get that we needed, that there's a way of being able to provide that for ourselves now. It's optimistic.
>
> [Female, M.S., 15 years practice]

> He made an enormous impact on classical analytic theory. His way of approaching the narcissistic patient is something I've found very helpful. And even with other patients, the whole way of understanding their experience.
>
> [Female, Ph.D., 15 years practice]

> One of the most useful things I learned from this approach is that with a borderline patient, when they get angry, it's iatrogenic. It's the therapist's break in empathy. What you have to do is go back and re-establish the selfobject. Also, their whole intersubjectivity approach, that it's two people interacting, and that's where a lot of healing happens.
>
> [Female, M.S.W., 15 years practice]

> I like self psychology, and I sometimes use some of that when I think it fits. I had a supervisor who was a self psychologist, and from her I picked up a way of phrasing things so that you see behavior as adaptive, and it's a less accusatory style. And sometimes the idea of mirroring is useful with some people. It can give you something to do when you don't know what to do.
>
> [Female, M.S., 15 years practice]

> If I'm understanding him correctly, it seems very true. The image that occurred to me once for transmuting internalization is when you get a jump-start from someone else's battery. You get a relationship with someone who's motor is running fairly well, functioning well, and in

the context of that relationship you get to the disintegrated parts of yourself.

[Male, M.S.W., 10 years practice]

In my old training, the point of view was that if anything goes wrong, it's the patient's fault. With self psychology, if anything goes wrong, it's the therapist's fault. It could be somewhere in between. I like the whole emphasis on empathy, and it's worked well for me.

[Female, M.S.W., 15 years practice]

Kohut brings to light the healthy narcissistic needs of people, and he's helped me appreciate the narcissistic personality disorder. A lot of therapists have trouble working with patients with those issues that are so prominent. It gives me a better understanding of what might have been missing, and how to work with patients. And also that it's a healthy need for everybody.

[Female, M.S.W., 15 years practice]

With a very narcissistic patient, it may be the only way he can be helped.

[Female, M.S.W., 20 years practice]

Many others had positive attitudes in some ways, toward specific aspects, but with reservations that are sometimes serious.

When I worked with psychotic patients, there were aspects of his work that appealed to me. The whole idea of empathic failures. I think it's been elevated to a technique. But he's really very close to Freud.

[Female, M.S.W., 5 years practice]

I like the empathic approach. But I think it's limited, and there are people you can't use it with. My biggest criticism of self psychology is that they don't look at their own countertransference, ever. If you attend one of their workshops, that's what's missing. The patient will be saying things like, "I felt you were doing this," and they'll just say, "Gee, that must have been a terrible feeling. It must be awful to have your therapist do the same things as your parents." But they never own up to it.

[Female, M.S., 20 years practice]

It's got some useful ideas, but it's a kind of dogmatic theory, and it appeals to people who need that kind of structure to adhere to. Clinically, it involves the observation of particular kinds of transferences emerging, and I can't say I've done enough work with those kinds of patients to say that I've been impressed with the clinical phenomena that match what he describes. On the other hand, the people who do it might say that if I were doing it right, I would see that. It's the same thing in psychoanalysis.

[Male, M.D., 15 years practice]

They do excellent work with many narcissists. I don't understand from reading it, though, how you get into the painful stuff. It makes it safe, but it never creates the emergency. From their theoretical point of view, of course, that's not what you get into. I don't, at this moment, agree with that. But I think their ability to engage a patient like that, the very narcissistic patient, is incredible, and maybe they're the only ones who speak to how you do that.

[Male, M.S.W., 15 years practice]

Several people said they thought that Kohut had been heavily influenced by Carl Rogers.

I think it's basically where it's at, some variation of that. All Kohut does is say that this is what narcissism is, and to help someone grow out of it, you have to appreciate them and care for them, and let them know that they're cared for. But Rogers said that basically thirty years ago. Kohut brought those two influences together.

[Male, Ph.D., 25 years practice]

I think Kohut stole a lot from Carl Rogers, who stole from other people also. They've made a god out of Kohut. It's another religion, and they've replaced Freud with another god.

[Male, Ph.D., 10 years practice]

A number of people also mentioned how difficult Kohut is to read and understand.

I think it's very interesting, but very difficult to read him. I would like to be more involved with it.

[Female, M.S.W., 10 years practice]

He's impossible to read. Of the more analytic approaches, it's one that makes sense. If I were more analytic, that's probably the approach I would use.

[Female, Ph.D., 5 years practice]

I started studying it at one point, and found it too complex. I even went to a supervisory group about it, but I never really got it.

[Male, Ph.D., 15 years practice]

If I read an article by a Jungian, they're describing the same psychological phenomena, but the person seems like they're talking gibberish to me. I get that feeling sometimes when I talk to a self psychologist: I don't know what they're talking about.

[Male, M.D., 15 years practice]

Some others question Kohut's basic premises, and don't find his formulations useful.

I believe in drive theory, and the aggressive drive is very important in my work, and Kohut always seems to me to be too kind, too loving, too empathic, and you don't get to the aggression.

[Female, Ph.D., 20 years practice]

I think the self is just another name for the ego.

[Male, M.S.W., 10 years practice]

Kohut and self psychology are a major manifestation of avoidance and resistance to truths about the unconscious, namely sex and aggression. They think that problems of aggression and sexuality are secondary to problems of the integration of the self.

[Male, M.D., 20 years practice]

Several people said that the self-psychological approach encourages the therapist to be inauthentic.

They're too wedded to a view that you have to be a certain way with the patient, to be always affirming. The problem with it is that it encourages the analyst to be false. You may not feel that way toward the patient. You may want to give the patient a kick in the ass, but you've got to be the all-confirming, mirroring analyst. That might not be a good way to be, for you with that patient at that time. It could be horribly inauthentic.

[Male, Ph.D., 5 years practice]

Some of it has stayed with me in terms of making a more conscious effort to understand the patient's experience and be empathic, but some of it borders on play-acting, on making nice to the patient, and it's a little patronizing.

[Male, M.D., 20 years practice]

Several people said that, while they find the theory useful, the technique was not.

> I like the theory very much, I think it's obviously a very empathic way of viewing people. My observation of people who are doing it is that on some level it's easier for them because they never have to make an interpretation. A patient can be in treatment with them for years, and the patient hasn't really grown all that much because the therapist doesn't make too many interpretations. Also, it's my observation that the people who do it are really very worried about patients getting mad at them or losing patients, so it sometimes serves the therapist's needs more than the patient's needs. When you're doing therapy, sometimes you have to take a risk. And it's okay for a patient to feel anxious sometimes.
>
> [Female, M.S.W., 10 years practice]

> I think Kohut had a lot of good and interesting things to say about narcissism on a theoretical level. But self psychology as a clinical approach is misguided, because to me it's in the same ballpark with Jung and Carl Rogers. This kind of therapy, where you're just trying to be supportive and empathic, a lot of therapists can misuse this and not give patients space to be aggressive, to express their negative feelings.
>
> [Male, Ph.D., 15 years practice]

> My sense of self psychology is that you use yourself, but in a way that you don't interact that much, and I still grapple with the idea of how much I do or don't interact. I guess I feel that with Kohut, there's not enough interaction.
>
> [Female, M.S.W., 5 years practice]

> I haven't found the Kohut approach sympathetic to my point of view. I think it underestimates the role of insight and of interpretation.
>
> [Male, Ph.D., 40 years practice]

NUMERICAL DISTRIBUTION

(Keep in mind that in Question 37, four people identified themselves primarily as self psychologists, and 11 more included self psychology in their description of their orientation.) Forty-eight people said they found at least something positive and useful in Kohut's work; 9 said they did not. Three people said they didn't know enough about it to comment.

COMMENTS

The issue here is whether self psychology is a coherent theory and an effective approach to treatment.

Kohut presents probably the most significant challenge to the premises and beliefs of traditional psychoanalysis. There are many therapists who now identify themselves as self psychologists, and many more who have incorporated at least some of his teachings and techniques.

My own experience with self psychology is that it's certainly useful in dealing with certain narcissistic or preoedipal patients who need a different kind of response from other kinds of patients. But Kohut himself is virtually unreadable and a lot of his concepts simply don't make sense to me. I also think that although he responds to anger by validating it, he never really deals with the anger by analyzing and understanding it and by engaging it directly.

RELATED READING

Kohut, H. (1971). *The Analysis of the Self.* New York: International Universities Press.

Stolorow, R., and Lachmann, F. (1980). *Psychoanalysis of Developmental Arrests.* New York: International Universities Press.

White, M. T., and Weiner, M. B. (1986). *The Theory and Practice of Self Psychology.* New York: Brunner/Mazel.

Panel discussion. (1988). The relationship of models of the mind to clinical work: self psychology. *Journal of the American Psychoanalytic Association* 36(3):741–748.

🔊🔊🔊🔊

Question 42: What is your opinion of behavior therapy?

In the recent world of managed care, concrete solutions are increasingly expected by insurance companies. Medication is one (see Question 17), and behavior therapy is another. How do these therapists regard the behavioral approach?

Fully two-thirds of the group said that behavior therapy is useful in certain ways in certain situations.

There's a place for it, certainly with phobic patients, and addictive patients. There are times when you need to use a behavioral approach, and I do integrate that into my sessions from time to time.

[Male, Ph.D., 15 years practice]

It's very effective with phobias and certain kinds of symptoms.

[Male, Ph.D., 25 years practice]

I don't think it can be used as the sole form of treatment, but it's useful with some diagnoses, like obsessives, certain kinds of behavior. It can be very useful with the mentally retarded, developmentally delayed.

[Female, Ph.D., 30 years practice]

With some kinds of problems, like panic attacks, it can be useful.

[Female, M.S.W., 15 years practice]

I've had some training in it, though I'm not really comfortable doing it. Like the systematic desensitization, and the relaxation techniques. I've had patients go to a behavior therapist at certain points, and it's been helpful.

[Male, Ph.D., 15 years practice]

It's very helpful for phobic problems that don't need medication. It's very useful in some of the more severe disturbances where you need to get control over behaviors.

[Female, M.D., 15 years practice]

I don't think you need to go to a therapist to do behavior therapy. It takes a lot of discipline and stick-to-it-iveness.

[Male, M.D., 20 years practice]

If someone wants to change something, and they want to change it right here, and they're indoctrinated to change that, then behavior therapy works. If it lasts them a year or the rest of their lives.

[Female, M.S., 15 years practice]

Many of those in favor of behavior therapy included a caveat.

In a training program in counseling, I tried a behavioral approach with an alcoholic patient. I used a very traditional approach, with operant conditioning, so I know how to do it, and I know the theory, and it didn't work. It doesn't work with alcoholics.

[Female, M.S., 20 years practice]

It's wonderfully useful, and it's dangerous in the wrong hands. Any therapy that can modify people's behavior is open to however you want to modify their behavior. But it's useful, because in the addictive population I work with, it's behavior change that results in self-esteem, not self-esteem resulting in behavior change.

[Male, M.S.W., 15 years practice]

It seems to help people with phobias, and with people with subtle neuro-cognitive deficits. But as a treatment for psychological conflict, even behaviorists will say that it's the quick fix.

[Male, M.D., 15 years practice]

Having worked as a school psychologist, I used it very effectively in symptom relief, and in helping children and adolescents deal with their fears. It had a place, and was quite effective. But in terms of any depth kind of therapy, no.

[Male, Ph.D., 30 years practice]

Sometimes we need to use some of the techniques in treating patients who do a lot of acting out destructively. In general, it's not a treatment of choice, except for some addictions, like overeating, or phobics.

[Female, M.S.W., 45 years practice]

One person emphasized the interpersonal relationship, even in behavior therapy.

I think behavior therapy has value. One of them is not always acknowledged by behavior therapists, which is that there is a relationship that involves interpersonal dynamics as well, and I think that when it works, it does so because those are involved in addition to the mechanisms that are employed in the treatment. I think that thinking too much in behavioral terms really misses the dynamic issues, and it can be very symptom-oriented and never get to those things that are underlying the symptom. At the same time, I think that symptom relief is very important, and so it has a place.

[Female, M.S.W., 15 years practice]

One person, who did see the value of behavior therapy, said that he himself could not use that approach.

It's interesting, it's useful. I personally find it boring. It would be deadly to me to do anything like that.

[Male, M.S.W., 25 years practice]

An equal number were strongly positive about behavior therapy as were strongly negative. Those very much in favor said there was much of value in behavioral and cognitive approaches.

> There's some very helpful techniques there. Behavioral rehearsal, running through whatever you're anxious about, really desensitizes the person. There's lots of helpful things in it. Also, cognitive therapy, reframing it and looking at it from a different perspective.
>
> [Female, M.S.W., 25 years practice]

> I think the methods they've developed are very helpful and very effective, and I use them a lot in my work.
>
> [Male, Ph.D., 25 years practice]

Several therapists had a very strongly negative opinion.

> I don't think of it as therapy. I think it can be useful as an interpersonal tool between people, but it's not therapy to me.
>
> [Male, Ph.D., 10 years practice]

> I think that it reduces symptoms. I don't think it helps someone, in the long run, to understand themselves any better. I don't even know if it improves relationships.
>
> [Female, M.S.W., 10 years practice]

Those against said primarily that behavior therapy fails to address the real problem, that it simply isn't deep enough, and omits understanding.

> For people who will not under any circumstance become involved in any of the more verbal therapies, it's workable. I don't think it can get to the core of the problem.
>
> [Female, M.S.W., 10 years practice]

> In certain areas, it's worthwhile, but it also needs to be in addition to other therapy. These days, with managed care, everyone wants behavior therapy because then they don't have to pay for anything beyond twelve sessions. It's helpful, because you can help someone to get started, but it's not enough and they need to do other work with it.
>
> [Female, M.S.W., 5 years practice]

> It has very, very good effect on symptoms. Because it doesn't use transference or resistance as a theoretical underpinning, it doesn't attack causes of behavior.
>
> [Female, Ph.D., 20 years practice]

I think it's shallow and superficial.

[Male, Ph.D., 20 years practice]

I'm not very in favor of it. It's more of a surface thing. You get people to act better, but they really aren't better.

[Female, M.S.W., 15 years practice]

It's not of great interest to me. I'm sure it's helped a lot of people, but I'm interested in understanding, and they're not.

[Male, Ph.D., 5 years practice]

I think it's not harmful, but it's of very limited usefulness. As the years go on, it'll be dropped, just as the original behavior therapy was dropped. Now it's cognitive/behavioral, which is a little more encompassing. I don't think it explains the things that most of the people who come to me are looking for. If someone walks in the office with phobias or obsessional things, and that's how you see their main problem, then you might use it.

[Male, M.S.W., 15 years practice]

Others said that they believe the gains in behavior therapy can be temporary.

It's like crisis intervention. It has no real lasting benefits, except for phobias.

[Female, M.S.W., 20 years practice]

Beneficial in the short run, but not so effective in the long term.

[Male, M.S.W., 15 years practice]

I'd like to be kind about it, but any patient I've seen who's gotten frustrated with psychotherapy and tried behavioral therapy finds that it doesn't work. It really doesn't work long term.

[Female, M.S., 15 years practice]

NUMERICAL DISTRIBUTION

(Keep in mind that 5 people identified their primary orientation as behavioral/cognitive, and 2 more included it in describing their orientation.) Ten people said they had a positive attitude toward it; 10 people said they had a negative attitude toward it; 40 people said they thought it was useful in certain situations. In addition, 9 people said they thought it addressed only symptoms and not underlying causes.

COMMENTS

The issues here are: Is behavior therapy an effective treatment? For what kinds of problems? How permanent are the results? What about the underlying dynamics?

The advent of managed care has meant an increased reliance on brief, more focused therapies. Behavior therapy is one such approach. I know that many psychoanalytic therapists still believe in the likelihood of symptom substitution, but I have never heard of that actually happening. Many of the therapists in our sample seem to think the gains of behavior therapy are temporary, but I'm not aware of that happening either.

I have very little experience with this kind of treatment. I think many psychodynamic therapists probably do at least some cognitive work with their patients. I'm sure that behavior therapy is useful in certain concrete situations, like phobia, but given its structure I can't see it applying to anything more diffuse than that.

RELATED READING

Bandura, A. (1969). *Principles of Behavior Modification*. New York: Holt.
Kaplan, S. J. (1986).*The Private Practice of Behavior Therapy: A Guide for Behavioral Practitioners*. New York: Plenum Press.
Wolpe, J. (1969). *The Practice of Behavior Therapy*. Elmsford, NY: Pergamon Press.

◎◎◎◎

Question 43: What is your opinion of hypnosis?

Another option for the therapist is the use of hypnosis. The definition of what constitutes a hypnotic state and the applications in therapy have recently been tremendously expanded by Milton Erickson and his followers. How do our therapists think about hypnosis?

In some ways, response to this question was similar to the question about behavior therapy. More than half the group expressed positive attitudes toward the use of hypnosis with patients, at least in certain situations.

I don't do it myself, but I have suggested it for things like relaxation, migraine headaches, like that.

[Female, M.S., 15 years practice]

I do favor hypnosis, for smoking. The kind of hypnosis I like to do is more relaxation.

[Female, M.S., 20 years practice]

It can be very helpful in certain kinds of cases. I have a patient with a conversion disorder, and she has a lot of trouble accepting that there's a psychological basis, and we've gotten very deep into her psyche but the conversion disorder hasn't changed. I've thought about hypnosis and self-hypnosis as ways to help the treatment along.

[Female, M.S.W., 15 years practice]

Several people said they didn't really understand the nature of hypnosis, or how it is supposed to be used.

I don't get it. I don't get what hypnosis is all about. I've been hypnotized and it's nice, but I don't know what it does or how it works. It doesn't make any sense to me. It's like reincarnation: maybe you're right but I don't get it.

[Male, Ph.D., 25 years practice]

My attitude towards hypnosis is, why hypnotize when you can just sit down and talk?

[Male, Ph.D., 10 years practice]

I still find the inductions difficult, I'm not comfortable with doing it, so I do it more indirectly.

[Female, Ph.D., 5 years practice]

A third of the group expressed mostly negative attitudes. Many suggested that the results may be temporary, or that the real problem doesn't get addressed.

For certain specific kinds of problems, it could probably be effective, but it might not be long-lasting.

[Female, M.S.W., 5 years practice]

I just don't see the results lasting. It's like a temporary high.

[Female, M.S., 15 years practice]

Everyone's jumping on the bandwagon, everyone's going to hypnosis for behavioral problems. If it can be used in psychotherapy, not just "I'm overweight and I want to lose weight," or to stop smoking, but in the context of being immersed in a therapy, it can be useful. Otherwise, the issues are masked and come up again.

[Female, M.S.W., 10 years practice]

As with behavior therapy, I'd be concerned about symptom substitution, and I don't think its effects are very lasting.

[Male, Ph.D., 40 years practice]

I think it's useful for a certain group of people. I got into it for a while, although I wasn't very good at doing it. I don't know how sustaining it is. I think it's more temporary than long term.

[Female, Ph.D., 30 years practice]

It's superficial.

[Male, Ph.D., 20 years practice]

One person saw a patient's request for hypnosis as a resistance to treatment.

Hypnosis has been helpful to people I know personally. Patients have asked me if I would send them to a hypnotist, but I see that as a resistance.

[Female, Ph.D., 20 years practice]

Several people saw it as useful in bypassing resistances.

There are times when a patient can't remember, as with a sexual abuse memory, and you could just use hypnosis for a session or two as a tool to go back and get those memories.

[Male, Ph.D., 15 years practice]

It's useful if used carefully and selectively, by someone who really knows what they're doing. It's similar for me to an amytal interview, in that the purpose of it would be to help a person relax, and get to the point that they can discuss issues and get in touch with issues that they're too anxious and defended to discuss normally.

[Male, M.D., 5 years practice]

Others expressed discomfort with the idea of bypassing resistances, and with the apparent imbalance of power and control in the relationship.

I don't like hypnosis, because I don't like the feeling of somebody being in charge of another person, telling them what to do. That really bothers me.

[Female, M.S.W., 30 years practice]

I've had very extensive training and experience with it. I've tried to use it myself for pain, and I think that sometimes it's helpful. I don't use it with patients. I don't like the inequality of the relationship.

[Female, M.S., 20 years practice]

I don't think it's good to use it all the time, because then the patient becomes dependent on you in a primitive, childlike way. You're the authority who's actively hypnotizing him all the time, and he doesn't develop on his own and become his own person.

[Male, Ph.D., 15 years practice]

I don't do it myself. As a person who decided early on that I was comfortable with techniques that encouraged people to take responsibility for behavior, it was hard to practice a technique which was essentially a manipulative technique.

[Male, M.D., 15 years practice]

Someone else suggested that there may not be any such imbalance of power.

I went to a very interesting workshop, which presented an idea of hypnosis much more acceptable to me, sort of Ericksonian ideas, although I still have a little trouble with the concept of the unconscious. I'm not sold yet, I'm not sure what that means yet. But one of the things the instructor pointed out is that all hypnosis is self-hypnosis. That one sort of decides to follow along.

[Male, Ph.D., 20 years practice]

Some people suggested that in today's climate doing hypnosis might be risky.

It can be useful for some post-traumatic things, although these days you have to worry about getting sued.

[Female, M.D., 15 years practice]

The whole thing about suggestibility that's coming out around the false memory is kind of scary.

[Female, M.S.W., 15 years practice]

NUMERICAL DISTRIBUTION

Thirty-four people expressed a positive attitude toward hypnosis; 12 people expressed a negative attitude; 14 people said they didn't know enough about it to have any opinion.

COMMENTS

Some of the issues here are: What is going on in the hypnotic state? What is the role of the hypnotherapist? Is bypassing resistance useful?

I took some training in hypnosis early in graduate school and was fairly effective at doing it. But I found that I don't like it, and even though I'm trained in it, I would never use it. I don't like the power imbalance or the passivity of the patient, and I don't like the element of magic. I haven't seen anything done with hypnosis that couldn't be done better without it. I don't see the value of bypassing resistances without exploring and understanding them.

In particular, the use of hypnosis for memory retrieval seems to me to be very risky, because there is no way to tell the accuracy of this material. The desire to please the hypnotist and maintain the relaxed state is very strong, and patients may only be coming up with whatever they think the hypnotist wants to hear.

RELATED READING

Cheek, D. B. (1994). *Hypnosis: The Application of Ideomotor Techniques.* Boston: Allyn and Bacon.

Haley, J. (1973). *Uncommon Therapy: The Psychiatric Techniques of Milton H. Erickson, M.D.* New York: Ballantine.

Kenworthy, R. J. (1987). Clinical hypnosis: a description of some uses of hypnosis in both behavior modification and psychotherapy. In *Current Issues in Clinical Psychology*, vol. 3, ed. E. Karas, pp. 217–226. New York: Plenum Press.

≋≋≋≋

Question 44: What is your attitude toward diagnosis?

The *Diagnostic and Statistical Manual* of the American Psychiatric Association has become the basis for making diagnoses, and almost all therapists are trained to use it. Insurance requirements make this necessary for reimbursement. How useful are the diagnoses that we find in the DSM, and how do they affect the way we do treatment?

Half of our group said that diagnosis was minimally useful, or not useful at all.

> The labels don't mean too much to me. They're not alive enough for me.
>
> [Female, M.S.W., 20 years practice]

> I was taught that it should be crucially important because you don't know how to treat if you don't have a diagnosis. But other than writing the numbers down on an insurance form, or discussing a patient in a peer supervision group, I rarely think about it.
>
> [Female, M.A., 20 years practice]

> I'm sacrilegious about that. I think they're for insurance purposes, and medication, and otherwise irrelevant.
>
> [Female, M.S.W., 5 years practice]

> I don't use it. I find it irrelevant. I use it only for insurance forms. I'm not trained like that, and I'm not interested in it.
>
> [Female, Ph.D., 20 years practice]

> The only practical use is for insurance forms. It's like the jargon of any profession: you can impress people with it. I thought once I should learn to speak fluent DSM, but I can't.
>
> [Male, M.S.W., 10 years practice]

> Not at all important, not a bit.
>
> [Male, Ph.D., 10 years practice]

> I think it's very important to know what it is so you can throw it away and never use it again.
>
> [Female, M.S.W., 20 years practice]

Some people said specifically that DSM categories are not accurate or descriptive of actual patients and that other kinds of diagnosis were more useful.

> The diagnosis that I'm concerned with is precisely the diagnosis of what are the unconscious conflicts that the patient is struggling with. DSM

is very superficial. They're misguided attempts to bring order, to re-assure ourselves that we know more than we really do.

[Male, M.D., 20 years practice]

I don't particularly prize the DSM. It's a consensus, and very politically correct at times, exclusionary of pathologies that offend people's sense of individuality. I prefer interpersonal diagnoses, how is the person with me. There's too much mutability that diagnosis doesn't completely account for.

[Male, Ph.D., 40 years practice]

I don't really use much diagnosis, the DSM stuff. I use more what's happening in the present. I'm not into the medical model.

[Female, M.S.W., 15 years practice]

I think more of a dynamic diagnosis than a clinical diagnosis from the DSM. I prefer not to categorize people that way. I'd rather give a description of areas of functioning, and developmental blocks, and so on.

[Male, Ph.D., 15 years practice]

I think of it more in terms of pre-oedipal and oedipal, rather than DSM.

[Female, M.S.W., 45 years practice]

If I'm using an object-relations model, I diagnose more in terms of what their internal world might be like, or how healthy their relationships have been. I look at it more in a developmental way.

[Female, M.S.W., 15 years practice]

I don't find that people fit the DSM labels very well.

[Female, M.S., 15 years practice]

I'm forced to use it for insurance purposes and at the clinic. And for supervisory purposes, I use it to teach because some of the behavior is predicted, like with a borderline personality. But for myself, I'm working with a person, not with a borderline personality.

[Female, M.S.W., 10 years practice]

A number of people said that they did not find diagnosis useful because, with rare exceptions, it did not lead to any particular treatment strategy. They pointed out that, while it is important to know if a patient is severely impaired in a way that might be treated with medication, other diagnoses were less clear and less pragmatic in determining a treatment approach.

I don't depend on it, unless I think there's an organic component. If someone's schizophrenic, I want to know about it. Otherwise it's just a label. It doesn't change my work, I don't work differently because of a diagnosis. In fact, it gets in the way.

[Female, Ph.D., 5 years practice]

What's best is to take someone where they are and work with the material they're bringing in, because even if a diagnosis can tell you something about them, you can't really do anything with that until it's somehow there in the session.

[Male, Ph.D., 20 years practice]

Most of the DSM diagnoses don't have much to do with the people that I'm seeing. I don't think the standard diagnoses have much role to play in the treatment. They don't lead to any particular methodology.

[Male, Ph.D., 50 years practice]

The label doesn't mean a damn bit of difference in terms of the therapy. I don't work any differently with a schizophrenic than I do with a neurotic.

[Male, Ph.D., 10 years practice]

On the other hand, several therapists said that diagnosis did, in fact, help them devise a treatment strategy with patients.

I do believe in diagnosis. It's useful to organize what people are showing you. If a diagnosis includes a dynamic understanding, then it helps the therapist work.

[Male, M.S.W., 15 years practice]

One of the big disadvantages of diagnosis is that it's too much theory. It imparts some kind of fixed expectation of behavior and even motivations. So it can be limiting. Too much attention to it biases you about the treatment process. However, in some instances, understanding something about the psychopathology from a perspective of a body of knowledge can keep you from making certain kinds of mistakes.

[Female, M.S.W., 15 years practice]

It's useful if you can be cognizant of staying flexible about it, because it can help and guide you in your approach.

[Female, Ph.D., 30 years practice]

Sometimes, when I'm having difficulty with a patient, if I think about them diagnostically, it can help me understand why they're where they are.

[Female, M.S., 15 years practice]

A few people said that diagnostic categories were sometimes useful in discussions with other professionals.

> It's useful sometimes in the therapeutic community to have a language which describes something, but it's not useful to patients.
>
> [Male, Ph.D., 25 years practice]

> When I'm dealing with colleagues, especially psychiatrists, they're real big on pigeonholes, it does make a difference.
>
> [Male, Ph.D., 20 years practice]

> It's useful between clinicians, maybe, to discuss the patient, and talk about a treatment plan, but it gets overused, especially in in-patient facilities, and the diagnosis can follow those people around.
>
> [Female, M.S.W., 5 years practice]

Only one-sixth of the group said that diagnosis was very important or useful, particularly with certain conditions or presenting problems.

> In order to do effective treatment, it has to begin with a comprehensive and accurate diagnosis.
>
> [Male, M.S.W., 15 years practice]

> Diagnosis is essential to proper treatment. That's one of the things drilled into me in training, and something that I do believe.
>
> [Male, M.D., 5 years practice]

> It's very important. Our diagnostic categories are grossly inadequate to the clinical pathology that exists. As a person who deals with a lot of psychotic patients, that's especially apparent. But diagnosis, in terms the therapy, in terms of trying to form an accurate idea of dynamic, genetic diagnosis, it's crucial.
>
> [Male, M.D., 15 years practice]

> It's very important in working with anxiety disorders, because there are different techniques to use with different ones, and you don't want to be treating someone for panic disorder who has obsessive-compulsive disorder.
>
> [Female, Ph.D., 10 years practice]

> I find I've gotten more and more pro diagnosis. Years ago I was more leery of pigeonholing people into boxes. The more I'm in practice the more they fit into boxes. Problems of living don't lend themselves very

well to diagnoses, but when people come in who've got a lot of dysfunction, then I have found it very helpful to try to put that person into a category.

[Male, M.S.W., 15 years practice]

I believe in it wholeheartedly. Too many colleagues that I've met don't do it, and I think it's a big mistake, because the treatment gets off on the wrong foot. If you don't have a sense of their diagnosis, if you don't know you're dealing with a manic-depressive, for example, or a borderline, then forget it. It's essential.

[Male, M.S.W., 25 years practice]

Several therapists said that it was important to diagnose schizophrenia or other conditions that might require medication.

If one is considering medication, and if one is perhaps doing an analysis and you need to know if the patient is out of touch with reality.

[Male, M.D., 20 years practice]

It's helpful, sometimes, and useful, particularly with affective disorders where people need medication.

[Female, M.A., 15 years practice]

With some people it's very important, especially with people who need medication. I think it's important for therapists to be able to recognize patients that they can't help. If someone is very psychotic, or in a manic state, I think we need to be able to recognize that, and not try to use ordinary techniques to work with it.

[Female, M.S., 20 years practice]

If somebody is schizophrenic, or is depressed, or is a substance abuser. I like to have some general idea of where they fit, and use that with them.

[Female, M.S.W., 10 years practice]

I had a patient who initially we saw as a panic disorder with some depression, and then we changed our minds and saw more as a bi-polar, and we changed the medication and things got much better. So there is some value there, probably more in terms of psychotropic medications than in what I do.

[Male, Ph.D., 20 years practice]

The other third fell somewhere between and were generally ambivalent about diagnosis.

DSM is in some ways important, because we can't deny that there might be certain kinds of syndromes or conditions that are unique and distinctive. On the other hand, my inclination is to see people in terms of developmental levels and adaptation and so on, and from that point of view, it doesn't make a damn bit of difference what the diagnosis is.

[Male, M.S.W., 20 years practice]

Where diagnosis is useful is in diagnosing the people who want to complain versus the ones who are really committed to change. Some people come in with presenting problems that are pretty serious, but I'm usually pretty good at diagnosing the ones that are going to be easy to work with. It's a kind of diagnosis. I can make my treatment plans and have a sense of how long it's going to take. Versus the ones who are going to be a long haul. I look at the secondary gain from the symptoms, and how enmeshed it is in the person's whole life pattern. I also look at diagnosis from the perspective of if I think medication would be useful, what kind of a depression they might have, which ones would be responsive to medications and which ones won't. I also need to know whether the person is going to decompensate on me, whether the person is neurotic versus schizophrenic.

[Male, Ph.D., 25 years practice]

I had a teacher who believed in it very strongly, and thought that it was crucial for us to make a diagnosis and have a sense where the patient fit in the scheme of things. I respect the effort. I'm always trying to diagnose my patients, in the sense of trying to understand their dynamics. But to diagnose them a la DSM seems less crucial to me.

[Male, Ph.D., 5 years practice]

Several people pointed out that making a diagnosis was a continuing process, not a one-time decision.

It's an ongoing process. As things go on, I'm always re-evaluating what the basic dynamic is and the situation is that we're dealing with.

[Female, M.S.W., 30 years practice]

It's constantly changing. Your diagnosis at the beginning of treatment is not necessarily the one you'll have three months, six months, or three years later. It's a guideline as to what's going on in the patient at the time the diagnosis is made.

[Male, M.S.W., 35 years practice]

DSM-III is practically worthless with most patients. It's okay for the very severe disturbances, but for most patients we get, it's not subtle enough. I think diagnosis, with most patients, starts with the first hour, and continues through the last hour, and all of your work is diagnostic. Putting labels is mostly for insurance purposes.

[Male, Ph.D., 40 years practice]

In a way, I'm diagnosing throughout the treatment, and always modifying, always surprised.

[Female, M.S.W., 25 years practice]

Most of the people I see don't fall into any particular category, so diagnosis is always in flux.

[Female, M.S.W., 20 years practice]

One person suggested that it may be valuable to throw out diagnosis, that to stop thinking of the patient as being a particular diagnosis may help the patient stop thinking of himself that way.

It's generally not useful. There are times I criticize myself for that attitude, and times I go through a rush of learning all different kinds of technical things, but basically I haven't found it an important part of my work. Sometimes I forget that someone's crazy, because I'm so into their stuff and it seems so interesting. I forget they're crazy, and they forget they're crazy too and they stop being crazy.

[Male, Ph.D., 25 years practice]

NUMERICAL DISTRIBUTION

Ten people found diagnosis very useful and important; 21 people said it was somewhat useful; 29 said it was minimally or not at all useful or important.

COMMENTS

Some issues here are: What does diagnosis actually describe? How useful is it in treatment? Does it lead to effective therapy?

When assessing a new patient, in terms of diagnosis, I think it is important to know whether a person is psychotic or not, to know if there are major affective disorders or other conditions where medication may be useful, and to know if there are any organic conditions. Other than that, diagnosis seems to me to be irrelevant. Emphasis on diagnosis is one of the more prominent features of the medical model. But most people don't come to therapy because they're "sick," they come because they're unhappy and have gotten a glimpse of the probability that they are somehow creating, or at least contributing, to their own unhappiness. Diagnosis is completely irrelevant to the exploration of this possibility.

RELATED READING

Diagnostic and Statistical Manual of Mental Disorders (1994). 4th ed. Washington, DC: American Psychiatric Association.

Kutchins, H., and Kirk, S. (1988). The business of diagnosis: DSM-III and clinical social work. *Social Work* 33(3):215–220.

—— (1992). *The Selling of DSM: The Rhetoric of Science in Psychiatry.* New York: Hawthorne Press.

Lamson, A. (1986). *Guide for the Beginning Therapist: Relationship between Diagnosis and Treatment.* New York: Human Sciences Press.

Setterberg, S. R., Ernst, M., Rao, M., et al. (1991). Child psychiatrists' views of DSM-III-R: a survey of usage and opinions. *Journal of the American Academy of Child and Adolescent Psychiatry* 30(4):652–658.

🐚🐚🐚🐚

Question 45: What is a borderline patient?

"Borderline" is a very common diagnosis these days, but it isn't always clear what the term refers to.

Some therapists identify the borderline patient by certain specific characteristics.

> They're more than very severe neurotics, more than people who just suffer too much. They're individuals who have difficulties controlling certain intense affects, given a reasonable intact reality-testing. People whose sense of themselves is very distorted, whose body image in terms of the ego is really a core issue for them, and which often goes hand in hand with certain hypochondriacal symptoms. They have certain very specific kinds of ego difficulties.
>
> [Male, M.D., 20 years practice]

I would think of someone who heavily uses splitting as a defense, and denial, and projection.

[Female, Ph.D., 15 years practice]

They usually have at least five out of the eight things in the DSM. I had one who couldn't look at me, and she's had therapy before. They're so demolished as people. They're not schizophrenic, they can relate, but there's so much damage.

[Female, M.S.W., 15 years practice]

Somebody with a tendency toward really obsessive relationships. A tendency to splitting. They either overly glorify or overly denigrate people in their lives, including me. Usually someone with unstable or very problematic relationships. Possibly someone who can slip in and out of psychotic states. They grab your guts. They figure out where your soft points are very effectively, and then they work them.

[Male, Ph.D., 20 years practice]

I use the criteria from the DSM to define it. I don't know that it's so concrete. Irrespective of their professional development, there's a line of emotional inadequacy that interferes with their ability to perceive life in a way that's going to be useful and effective. They get in their own way constantly.

[Female, M.A., 20 years practice]

A person who's got such a deep belief in their unlovability and their worthlessness, they're so filled with shame, that they live in constant terror that they'll be exposed as not worthy of living. Most of their behavior, the unpleasant behavior, is a panic behavior in response to the terror that they'll be exposed as not worthy to be alive and they'll be killed.

[Male, Ph.D., 25 years practice]

A narcissistic, angry patient. I see a chaotic life, I see anger, hostility, some ego functions that are deficient.

[Male, M.S.W., 25 years practice]

Patients who are very angry at their original mother, and can't get beyond it. They resent everything you do, and oppose you every step of the way.

[Female, M.S., 20 years practice]

Very concrete, something is either black or white, good or bad. They don't have the capacity to see gradations or mixtures. A lot of rage and anger.

[Female, M.S., 15 years practice]

Someone who has poor ego boundaries, who cannot tolerate ambivalence, whose ego is very fragmented and filled with anxiety. They're often very helpless, unable to believe they can master things. They have a lack of self-object representation.

[Female, M.S.W., 15 years practice]

Patients who reproach, and blame, and are angry, and don't want to take any responsibility for themselves.

[Female, M.S.W., 5 years practice]

Some identify the borderline by a shift in the attitude of the patient, from idealization to denigration.

A patient that is highly volatile, impulsive, and the moods tend to fluctuate. Their self-esteem fluctuates. They tend toward splitting, so they're highly ambivalent towards you from one moment to another. They can idealize you and then devaluate you, and that is really hard to take sometimes. They can seem to be the greatest patient you ever had, they idealize you, and you're going to save them, they've finally found the right person for them, and you can get pulled into that. Once you get pulled in, then the next moment you're a total creep. You're completely devalued, and you can feel enraged.

[Male, Ph.D., 15 years practice]

People who make everything very black and white. A little hysterical. You're wonderful today and you're a lousy therapist tomorrow.

[Female, M.S.W., 5 years practice]

Some identify the borderline by their own reactions to the patient.

I seem to at any given time have at least one borderline patient, where as soon as I start to dislike them, that's the key. When I realize that, it helps me do much better work, because now I know.

[Male, M.S.W., 15 years practice]

Someone who is so chaotic in the room that they make me feel like I have just jumped out of not just my skin but theirs too. They make me feel like I just don't want to be here.

[Female, M.S., 15 years practice]

I know when I've had one, because they're so difficult, so horrible. It's a character disorder of a particularly difficult type to work with, because there's a lot of splitting, and of manipulation. Whatever you give isn't good enough. There's a lot of projective identification, and it's very difficult to keep your feelings about yourself intact.

[Female, M.S.W., 30 years practice]

I'm sure that I have seen some, that after a session or two I say, "Hmm, I think that's a borderline." They're the hardest. I don't know if I'm coming or going with them. It's very hard to read them.

[Female, M.A., 20 years practice]

Several therapists said that they thought of borderline patients as being literally on the border between neurosis and psychosis.

I like the original definition: the borderline between neurosis and psychosis.

[Female, M.S.W., 15 years practice]

It's on the border, and sometimes they go over into psychosis.

[Female, M.S.W., 45 years practice]

A borderline has an ego which can sometimes seem to break down right in front of your eyes, not react in a normal way to interpretations and so on. It's usually a neurotic, sometimes with psychotic features.

[Male, Ph.D., 40 years practice]

A few therapists said they had a problem with the diagnosis.

I know what it is technically, but I don't think of them that way. That label is used to distance from them.

[Male, Ph.D., 10 years practice]

The type of defenses, the splitting. But I don't find people who fit into categories so easily.

[Female, M.S., 15 years practice]

I harken back to what they used to call pre-schizophrenic. I think a lot of what they call borderlines are really ambulatory schizophrenics. The schizophrenia has been kept in check.

[Male, Ph.D., 5 years practice]

NUMERICAL DISTRIBUTION

(This question was added in the middle of doing the interviews, so only 31 people answered it.) Eight therapists mentioned the tendency to splitting; 7 mentioned the hostility; 3 mentioned the instability. Three people emphasized the projective identification that can arise in the therapist. Four people said they saw "borderline" as indicating an area of the spectrum between neurotic and psychotic. Two people emphasized the terror and extreme anxiety, and 2 others emphasized the unstable relationships these patients have. One person emphasized the narcissism, and one person emphasized the shame.

COMMENTS

The issue here is: What does this diagnostic label actually refer to?

I have a lot of trouble with this diagnosis. I think this whole diagnostic category is judgmental, accusatory, and pejorative and is often used to excuse the failures of the therapist. I always wonder how much of the rage attributed to so-called borderline patients is iatrogenic.

RELATED READING

Kernberg, O. (1975). *Borderline Conditions and Pathological Narcissism*. New York: Jason Aronson.

Marziali, E. (1992). Borderline personality disorder: diagnosis, etiology, and treatment. *Smith College Studies in Social Work* 62(3):205–227.

Masterson, J. F. (1976). *Psychotherapy of the Borderline Adult*. New York: Brunner/Mazel.

Miller, S. G. (1994). Borderline personality disorder from the patient's perspective. *Hospital and Community Psychiatry* 45(12):1215–1219.

Wile, D. (1984). Kohut, Kernberg, and accusatory interpretations. *Psychotherapy* 21(3):353–364.

ßßßß

Question 46: What causes schizophrenia?

Most therapists have been taught in their training that mental illness exists on a continuum, from neurosis through character disorder past borderline to psychosis. The group of disorders known collectively as schizophrenia comprise the largest portion of the psychoses.

Recent research and technology like PET scans, which can show differences in brain functioning between normal individuals and those diagnosed with schizophrenia, seem to suggest that schizophrenia is a physiological condition of genetic or other biological origin. Psychoanalytic theory suggests that it is the result of bad parenting, of mixed messages and double-bind situations. What do our therapists think?

Many therapists believe that schizophrenia is a purely biological condition.

> I'm very clear at this point that it's biological. I don't buy any of this object relations stuff.
>
> [Male, Ph.D., 10 years practice]

> It's a brain disease.
>
> [Female, M.D., 15 years practice]

> I think it is a genetic metabolic disease.
>
> [Male, M.D., 20 years practice]

> I think it's a physiological issue. I don't think it's a schizophrenogenic mother any more. I feel very strongly that it's a biochemical disorder.
>
> [Female, M.A., 15 years practice]

> I think it's a genetic disease that is exacerbated by environment. Many people with schizophrenia can function if there's a good fit, if they get the resources they need. But the fundamental cause is physiological.
>
> [Female, Ph.D., 5 years practice]

Some therapists still believe in the psychodynamic explanation.

> I believe in the psychoanalytic theory that schizophrenia is environmentally caused, that it has to do with schizophrenogenic treatment by probably schizophrenic parents. The parents are themselves schizophrenic, most probably not diagnosed, and the treatment of the child is so confusing and so attacking in a subtle way that the child has to withdraw. I think this begins in earliest infancy when the child first gets confusing messages from the mother. The mother may be hugging the child but is looking at the child in a hostile way. There's double messages like that from the beginning that cause the child not to be able to form a cohesive ego. As far as the genetic component, I believe there's a trend nowadays to try to make everything genetic. We don't want to take responsibility for what man does to man. I think there might be a genetic predisposition towards schizophrenia, but I don't think it's the crucial factor.
>
> [Male, Ph.D., 15 years practice]

> More often than not, it's a breakdown in parental nurturance prior to age five.
>
> [Male, Ph.D., 30 years practice]

> Families. Family interactions, and parents.
>
> [Female, M.S.W., 5 years practice]

Some therapists include the possibility that the explanation is psychodynamic, along with other factors.

> I think there are probably numerous causes, many things feeding into it. It may be genetic, maybe biochemical. There may be environmental factors. I don't think it's only a schizophrenogenic mother, but sometimes maybe it is.
>
> [Female, M.S., 20 years practice]

> It's partly biological and partly environmental. Like having a borderline parent.
>
> [Female, M.S.W., 10 years practice]

Family systems theory has its own explanation.

> I don't believe in the schizophrenogenic mother. As a family therapist, I believe it's the whole family system. A lot of mixed messages in childhood, and a lot of inconsistency certainly move toward it.
>
> [Female, Ph.D., 20 years practice]

> Some schizophrenia is biological. Some is created by the family dynamics. You tell the child that the way you can maneuver and get out of craziness is to be crazier yourself. Or that your craziness will hold your family together. It's an adaptive mechanism to craziness in the family.
>
> [Female, M.S.W., 20 years practice]

Most of the therapists in our group felt it was a combination of these factors.

> It's a complex process. It's a complicated interaction between genetics, physiology, parenting, social interactions.
>
> [Male, Ph.D., 20 years practice]

> A combination of some kind of genetic diathesis and fucked-up really early childhood experiences. I've worked with a large number of schizophrenics, and the number where there wasn't a major, major dis-

turbance in early childhood is virtually nil. I know that's not politically correct. The environment has played a very big role in the etiology.

[Male, M.D., 15 years practice]

I think it's probably a mixed bag. It could be partly genetic, and it could be parents who will not help the child make any sense out of the world, who undermine whatever the child's perceptions are, because the parents are quite disturbed themselves.

[Female, M.S.W., 20 years practice]

I do go along with the genetic factor, and with, either intrauterine or from birth on, a very malignant relationship with the mother.

[Female, M.S.W., 45 years practice]

I really think that there's a continuum, in which physiology plays a very important role, but that environment intersects with physiology. And that when you get a lot of organicity, a lot of biological predisposition, and a little environmental insult, you can have a schizophrenic reaction. In other cases, you can have a little organicity and a lot of environmental impact and get the schizophrenia. But I think there's an interface between the two.

[Female, M.S.W., 15 years practice]

My school of thought believes that schizophrenia is a combination of biological and environmental forces. We believe that there is a tremendous amount of internal rage that contributes to the development of schizophrenia.

[Female, Ph.D., 20 years practice]

I think some of it is biological, and some of it is generated by the dysfunctional family, by the communication.

[Female, M.S.W., 10 years practice]

It's a combination of a certain genetic predisposition with the integration of developmental experiences in early childhood.

[Male, M.D., 20 years practice]

I think it's a medical condition. It's exacerbated by dysfunctional families.

[Female, M.S.W., 25 years practice]

One behaviorally oriented therapist allowed for some environmental influence.

> Let me preface my comment by saying that I'm extremely reductionistic. I'm very much physiological in my thinking. There is probably, as with a lot of other things, some constitutional predisposition, whether it's genetic or congenital, and possibly some environmental events, but I doubt that they're the environmental events which have traditionally been considered schizophrenogenic. Possibly even something as simple as a sufficiently high stress state, caused by almost anything, could act as a trigger or a releasing mechanism.
>
> [Male, Ph.D., 20 years practice]

Several therapists discussed the diagnosis itself, and the role that goes with it.

> Schizophrenia is a whole system, that we identify at this point, with genetic components and variations of the cognitive patterns. Some people have been marginalized both by society and by their families, and this becomes the only acceptable role, and so they act out the role.
>
> [Male, Ph.D., 40 years practice]

> I share Thomas Szasz's belief and Ronald Laing's belief about it. However, what that means to me is that the entity "schizophrenia" has not been defined. Do I think there are certain organic conditions which lead to hallucination and thought disorder? Yes, I do believe that. But the diagnosis of schizophrenia is made carelessly, and most people who are diagnosed as schizophrenic should not be called schizophrenic. Although the designation of that label is a good descriptive, if you don't get tied down to the notion that when you describe someone as schizophrenic you're making an organic diagnosis.
>
> [Male, Ph.D., 50 years practice]

NUMERICAL DISTRIBUTION

Twenty-five people said schizophrenia was a biological, physiological, or genetic illness; 7 said it was entirely a result of family or environmental situations; and 28 saw it as a combination of these factors.

COMMENTS

The issue here is whether schizophrenia is a physiological or a psychological condition and what treatment is appropriate.

I think it's very clear these days that schizophrenia is a biologically determined condition. It's not the bad mother or the double bind or anything like that that causes it. Those situations can make people crazy, but not in this particular way. CAT scans and MRIs show that the brains of people with schizophrenia are different from the normal brain. It is also clear that stressors trigger it in some people and not in others, but I wonder if it is even possible to create schizophrenia without the pre-existing genetic condition. I think it's terrible that parents of schizophrenics, who go through hell with those children, are made to feel responsible for the condition.

Even if we believe that schizophrenia is physiological, psychotherapy may still be helpful in dealing with family and individual dynamics.

RELATED READING

Gershon, E. S., and Cloninger, C. R., eds. (1994). *Genetic Approaches to Mental Disorders.* Washington, DC: American Psychiatric Press.

Leff, J. P. (1980). Developments in family treatment of schizophrenia. *Advances in Family Psychiatry* 2:313–333.

Matthysse, S., and Holzman, P. S. (1987). Genetic latent structure models: implication for research on schizophrenia. *Psychological Medicine* 17(2):271–274.

Neill, J. (1990). Whatever became of the schizophrenogenic mother? *American Journal of Psychotherapy* 44(4):499–505.

Szasz, T. (1961). *The Myth of Mental Illness.* New York: Horber.

🧶🧶🧶🧶

Question 47: What causes depression?

Every therapist, no matter what orientation, deals with depressed patients to some extent. What we mean by the term "depression" can cover a wide range of syndromes. Several practitioners described the situation this way:

> Depression actually is a wastebasket diagnosis, and it covers a lot of territory. People are on a spectrum of biological vulnerability and psychological and environmental factors. I see a lot of different kinds of depression, from mild to severe and psychotic. Most psychotic depressions are a biological disorder in someone who had that vulnerability and circumstances. I see lots of depression in people who are biologically vulnerable, but I don't see it as an illness necessarily.
>
> [Female, M.D., 15 years practice]

The word covers a tremendous range of feeling states. Anyone can get depressed, but then there are people whose early experience gives them a groove that they can get into when they get down, where they get stuck. Then there are people who probably have some kind of genetic or biochemical predisposition that gives them that groove to go to, with the help of experience.

[Male, Ph.D., 5 years practice]

Many therapists see some depression as purely biological, and some as psychological.

Bi-polar disorder, manic-depressive illness, is absolutely a biochemical disorder. I think there is also situational depression that may not necessarily be of chemical origin.

[Female, M.A., 15 years practice]

I think there's a lot of biological input into depression, or some depressions at least. But you certainly can be depressed for psychological reasons.

[Male, M.S.W., 20 years practice]

I'm always looking at the interaction between what we call the emotional state and the physiological. There are probably some people who are pure straight form biological depressions, where there are no clear psychological referents, or triggers. Somebody's just going along and they just get really depressed. With others there are clearly external referents: a loss of some measurable proportion, a death, the loss of a job, something of that nature, that may trigger off a process.

[Male, Ph.D., 20 years practice]

I think there's an inherited factor, that it is chemical. I think that in major depression, medication brings the patient back to an even keel. But I also think there's the kind of depression that can be talked through, and that's more the blue, out-of-sorts kind.

[Female, M.S., 15 years practice]

I think some depression is definitely caused by biological forces, but I've also worked with enough depressives, and achieved enough very good results psychologically, to feel a lot of it has also been caused psychologically.

[Male, M.S.W., 35 years practice]

Major depression is probably a biological predisposition. But I think the analytic concept of depression as internalized aggression is valid, too, for a lot of people.

[Female, M.S.W., 30 years practice]

There's a strong genetic component to depression, and research bears this out. We see that it definitely runs in families. But there are a number of different types of depression. The major depression, or classic melancholic depression, is the most strongly genetically caused. More atypical depressions, dysthymic disorders, those are more caused by life circumstances and experiences.

[Male, M.D., 5 years practice]

There are different kinds of depression with different causes. The primary factors for less severe and less prolonged depressions are more in the psychological realm, and the causes for very severe intractable depressions are more within the biological realm.

[Male, M.D., 20 years practice]

Many therapists see depression as an interaction between physiological and psychological factors.

I think there's a biological component, but it also has a lot to do with early history.

[Female, M.S., 15 years practice]

I think that some recent studies suggest that there may be some genetic basis for depression. But as Freud said, there is an overdetermination where there's an element of genetics and an element of the psychological, and when the two hit a threshold, you get an illness.

[Male, Ph.D., 40 years practice]

There's a genetic propensity for depression, but that's much more psychologically influenced. It's deprivation of love and emotional supplies.

[Male, Ph.D., 25 years practice]

There's a diathesis for it in many people. If you look for it, there's a history of depression in the family. But also it obviously correlates with object loss, deprivation, and experiences of faulty parenting.

[Male, M.D., 15 years practice]

It's probably biochemical, and sometimes triggered by loss, major loss.

[Female, M.S., 20 years practice]

I think that there are genetic, biological predispositions that are activated in some people under a very small amount of stress, and some in which there needs to be a lot of environmental stress before it activates the depression.

[Female, M.S.W., 15 years practice]

A combination of factors. I'm beginning to think that some people are born more depressive than others, and develop that way. It's also long-standing losses and low self-esteem, and learned helplessness, feeling that they can't really do anything about life. And also pain, a lot of pain and anger, emotional pain and loss.

[Male, Ph.D., 15 years practice]

More practitioners see it as predominantly psychologically based.

There might be a genetic predisposition, but it's hard to say whether it's that or prenatal stuff that predisposes. I think it's a loss in earliest childhood that isn't mourned completely, something like that.

[Male, Ph.D., 15 years practice]

Maybe some biological predisposition, but I think more often it is really rage turned inward, in my experience.

[Female, Ph.D., 15 years practice]

It's unrealistic to expect that people are not going to experience some depression at some point in life.

[Female, M.A., 15 years practice]

It comes from a sense of hopelessness, that continues on a downward spiral.

[Male, M.S.W., 10 years practice]

In almost all the cases I've seen, the causes of the depression are apparent, and the person has plenty to be depressed about. I've not seen many cases of people who seem to be randomly depressed for no reason at all.

[Male, Ph.D., 50 years practice]

It manifests as lack of self, people out of touch with who they are. Again, lack of attunement, not getting the supplies they needed. There's probably a biological predisposition.

[Female, M.S.W., 15 years practice]

I think it's an experience of loss of the primary object.

[Male, M.S.W., 25 years practice]

Absent parents, and an unattuned environment. Loss.

[Female, M.S.W., 20 years practice]

It's a breakdown in parental nurturance prior to age five.

[Male, Ph.D., 30 years practice]

I really feel it's emotional deprivation, unempathic parenting.

[Female, M.S.W., 25 years practice]

I think some of it is learned behavior, if there are depressed people in the family.

[Female, M.S.W., 10 years practice]

Families and family interactions. I really believe people cause mental problems.

[Female, M.S.W., 5 years practice]

Loss. Loss of all kinds.

[Male, M.S.W., 10 years practice]

One therapist saw some depression as possibly not curable.

Sometimes lifetime patterns and lifetime deprivations have caused chronic depressions that I'm not sure are healable. In my early years of practice, I thought everything was treatable, and now that I'm a grownup, I don't think that. I've seen people come with intense depressions that I don't think are ever going to change drastically, medication or no medication, because of their backgrounds.

[Female, Ph.D., 20 years practice]

NUMERICAL DISTRIBUTION

This is hard to quantify because most people said there are different kinds of depressions with different causes, or that there are usually a combination of factors in any depression. Overall, 27 people mentioned biological or physiological causes; 18 included genetic predisposition as a cause; 14 mentioned family influences, bad parenting, and object loss; 12 mentioned other psychological dynamics, such as rage and learned behavior; 22 emphasized situational stress. Only 2 people said it was exclusively biological and only 10 said it was exclusively early parenting failures.

COMMENTS

Some issues here are: What condition(s) does "depression" refer to? What are the most effective treatments? What are the implications for therapy of putting a patient on medication?

There is a tremendous range of patient syndromes labeled "depression." Analytically trained therapists tend to look for psychological explanations, and these are rarely absent. Life is stressful and sometimes overwhelming. The question remains as to whether these external stressors are the cause of the depression.

The new antidepressants work more effectively with fewer side effects than the previous generation of medications, and patients appear to be less resistant to taking them. Treatment of depression is more likely to include antidepressant medication, often at the patient's request.

I really don't know what causes depression. Some appears to come almost out of nowhere, but most seems to be reactive to some difficult situation. Since medication can often relieve the depression once it has appeared, I see no reason not to use it, provided the patient also investigates how the stressful situation led to this particular reaction.

RELATED READING

Beck, A. T., Rush, J., Shaw, B., and Emery, G. (1979). *Cognitive Theory of Depression.* New York: Guilford Press.

Beckham, E. E. (1990). Psychotherapy of depression research at a cross-roads: directions for the 1990s. *Clinical Psychology Review* 10(2):207–228.

McGuffin, P., and Katz, R. (1993). Genes, adversity, and depression. In *Nature, Nurture, and Psychology*, ed. R. Plomin and G. E. McClearn, pp. 217–230. Washington, DC: American Psychological Association.

Tennant, C., Hurry, J., and Bebbington, P. (1982). The relation of childhood separation experiences to adult depressive and anxiety states. *British Journal of Psychiatry* 141:475–482.

図図図図

Question 48: What determines sexual orientation?

For many years, our field assumed that sexual orientation was a choice, conscious or unconscious. The DSM classified homosexuality as a mental disorder. Although that diagnosis was removed from the DSM, many therapists maintained the belief that homosexuality was a psychological distortion of normal sexual development. In the past few years, some researchers have suggested that sexual orientation may be biologically determined. This question was included to find out how therapists think about sexual orientation now.

One very experienced therapist described the difficulties in this area.

> In general, sexual orientation is determined by education, cultural education. The boys are taught to be like their fathers, and the girls are taught to be like their mothers. I'm a little puzzled by certain cases in the literature, such as transsexuals who seem to be driven almost from the day of their birth to act out in a certain way. I've learned to be highly skeptical of most reports, so I don't really know the story there. The homosexuals that I've dealt with, I'm at a loss to explain their gender choice. I can't find a common theme.
>
> [Male, Ph.D., 50 years practice]

In spite of the complicated nature of this question, most people lean toward one or another explanation. Some think it's psychologically determined, and they mention several different possible influences.

> My observation is that it's really about people's early relationships and what they did and did not get from parents and significant others. I don't see it as pathology. Every choice we make in life is based on our early relationships. I think that it's one of the choices. I don't think people are even conscious of the fact that it's been a choice.
>
> [Female, M.S.W., 10 years practice]

> In all of the cases I've worked with, everything I've seen indicates that it's psychological determinants. For political reasons, I do go along with removing it from the DSM as being pathological. But on the basis of individual psychology, I do believe it's psychological.
>
> [Male, M.S.W., 35 years practice]

If the primary identification with the mother is complete, it frees the individual to select a sexual orientation. The relatedness with the primary person, the mother, is crucial in determining the preference.

[Male, Ph.D., 30 years practice]

I've never understood why people would think that sexual object choice would be determined before birth, when there are no objects before birth. It has to happen as you develop.

[Male, Ph.D., 10 years practice]

I think it's a combination of, on one hand, the fact that we're all poly-morphous perverse, and, on the other hand, when you have very early sexual experiences in terms of behavior and of psyche, that can then determine the sexual orientation.

[Male, M.S.W., 25 years practice]

Partly role modeling, sometimes seduction by an older, trusted person.

[Male, M.S.W., 10 years practice]

I think that it's the communication in the family, unconscious messages that are given, not only to the child, but everyone in the family has a role. The biological might be a factor, but very small.

[Female, M.S.W., 10 years practice]

I think that something goes on in early childhood having to do with trauma, either on a reality basis or a fantasy basis.

[Male, Ph.D., 40 years practice]

I lean more toward the environmental and less toward the genetic. There could be some brain thing, but it just doesn't make sense to me. I don't understand how you would be born with a brain that turns on to one sex or the other. Why aren't you born with a brain that's turned on to blonds with short haircuts?

[Male, M.S.W., 15 years practice]

I think it has a lot to do with identification. I had a childhood friend who was very much, compared to aggressive macho boys, kind of feminine, and I learned that he was homosexual. His father was dis-appointed in him because he was very athletic, the director of the day camp, and a macho guy. My own father was not athletic, much more intellectual, more "feminine" himself, and I realize that I could identify myself as heterosexual, even though I was very much like my friend, because I had a different definition based on my circumstances.

[Male, M.S.W., 20 years practice]

At the age of between two and three, there is a phase of sexual orientation development when the child discovers the difference in the anatomy of the sexes. How the parents react to the child's curiosity, how they react to it's feelings about it's own gender, determines whether the child wants to be that gender or would rather be another gender.

[Male, Ph.D., 15 years practice]

Some think it's biologically determined.

There's a multi-factorial component here, but recent research and thinking would lean toward some kind of biological predisposition. I don't think that a person is homosexual or heterosexual due to the way they were raised. We've see a lot of children raised in homosexual households that are heterosexual, and obviously vice versa. There's some environmental stuff there, but it's not where the money is.

[Male, M.D., 5 years practice]

I remember some research where they looked at all the childhood configurations that were supposed to be producing gay kids, and none of them held up consistently. So we're probably looking at some kind of congenital thing.

[Male, Ph.D., 20 years practice]

From what I see in my own children and their friends, and many homosexual patients and friends, these people seem to develop their orientation at around five, which would not be inconsistent with psychoanalytic theory, but I think it's more genetically determined than anything else.

[Male, Ph.D., 25 years practice]

I believe it's inborn. People arrive in the world gay or straight. I also believe that no two people in the world have exactly the same sexual orientation. It's a spectrum.

[Male, M.S.W., 10 years practice]

I think you're born with it.

[Female, M.S.W., 10 years practice]

Many think it's an interaction between biology and psychology.

I think there's a biological substrate somewhere, whether it's hormonal during pregnancy, or genetic, there's something there in addition to what goes on in the person's life.

[Female, M.S.W., 30 years practice]

I think it's nature and nurture. I think there's a predisposition to sexual orientation, and then there's a fit and a choice. What people are able to deal with in their lives, what makes them feel good, and what they're able to tolerate.

[Female, Ph.D., 5 years practice]

Primarily, I think that biology determines that, but I do think that there can be a heavy impact of certain environmental conditions. In particular with male patients, how mothers deal with sexuality. I think that among many gay men, they've had mothers who've been unable to respond to them with the normal enjoyment and pleasure in the son's being male.

[Female, M.S.W., 15 years practice]

I think there's biology to it, there's a predisposition. But then I see clinically certain things in the environment, almost the caricature of the overbearing mother and the absent father. My clinical experience backs that up.

[Female, M.S., 15 years practice]

I'm sure there are some genetic factors there, but when I look at family of origin issues in the lives of homosexuals, it just seems to me that there are too many factors there to discard their influence.

[Male, Ph.D., 25 years practice]

Some therapists think that the explanation is biological for certain individuals and psychological for others.

I think the notion that there's a part of the brain, that it's genetic, probably has a certain legitimacy in the homosexual population. I think there are kids who are prone to becoming gay as kids. With other people, I think it's more situational.

[Female, M.S.W., 20 years practice]

It might be a genetic factor, or it could be the relationship of the parent of the same sex that's fraught with a lot of hostility and problems.

[Female, M.S.W., 45 years practice]

Some are born and some are made.

[Female, M.S.W., 20 years practice]

A combination of both nature and nurture. It's not necessarily mixed together. It can be either way. There's also a certain choice involved.

Some people know they're gay from the time they're born, and others make clear decisions at different points in their life.

[Female, M.A., 15 years practice]

Two female therapists said that the explanation differs in men and in women.

It's not identical in men and women. It's not the same factors. There's probably some biological component that is then modified by life experience. It seems to me that more women are more comfortable with the crossover, that more women have had relationships with women and men who don't need to be with women their whole life. Whereas most of the men I've worked with, some are ambivalent, but with the majority of men it's a very strong feeling. They may have enjoyed a relationship with a woman, but there's no question in their mind. It has a sense of much more clarity. Developmental issues make women more able to have a sexual contact with another woman, and it doesn't have the same meaning as with men.

[Female, M.D., 15 years practice]

I think in women it could be more sociological. I've noticed that women who've been sexually abused become lesbians, and I know that women are sexually abused at a higher rate than men, and the male has then become aversive to her. It's also easier for women to be in a close cuddly relationship where the sex isn't that important.

[Female, M.S.W., 25 years practice]

NUMERICAL DISTRIBUTION

Forty-one people said it was either a combination of factors: physiological (genetic/biochemical/hormonal in utero) plus psychological, or that some cases were physiologically determined and others psychologically determined. Only 12 people said it was exclusively psychological factors, and only 7 said it was exclusively physiological.

COMMENTS

The main issue here is whether sexual orientation is determined before birth by something physiological or if family dynamics and other situational influences create sexual orientation. The explanation that the therapist holds determines the way this issue is handled in treatment.

For many years, sexual orientation was assumed to be psychologically determined, and it is only recently that the field has seriously considered the possibility that the crucial factors may be genetic or biological. At this point, there is no decisive evidence in either direction and we are left with our own individual attitudes and beliefs.

My own practice has always included a large percentage of gay men and women. Despite all that experience, I still am unsure of the answer to this question. My tentative explanation right now is that sexual orientation is genetic and innate. Most gay patients I have seen tell me they knew they were gay their entire lives, which does not rule out the psychoanalytic explanation but seems to me to make it less likely.

In addition, I have seen the same family constellations that are supposed to produce homosexual children, for example, the passive father and domineering mother, with many heterosexual patients, as well as the reverse. No particular pattern appears to be consistently associated with either sexual orientation, and so I conclude that there must be something else that causes it.

RELATED READING

Baer, R. (1981). *Homosexuality and American Psychiatry*. New York: Basic Books.

Bancroft, J. (1994). Homosexual orientation: the search for a biological basis. *British Journal of Psychiatry* 164:437–440.

Gallagher, B. J., McFalls, J. A., and Vreeland, C. N. (1993). Preliminary results from a national survey of psychiatrists concerning the etiology of male homosexuality. *Psychology: A Journal of Human Behavior* 30(3–4):1–3.

Rosenberg, K. P. (1994). Biology and homosexuality. *Journal of Sex and Marital Therapy* 20(2):147–151.

Ross, M. W. (1984). Beyond the biological model: new directions in bisexual and homosexual research. *Journal of Homosexuality* 10(3–4):63–70.

Socarides, C. W. (1978). *Homosexuality*. New York: Jason Aronson.

Troiden, R. R. (1989). The formation of homosexual identities. *Journal of Homosexuality* 17(1–2):43–73.

⧽⧽⧽⧽

Question 49: Should a gay patient see only a gay therapist?

Recently, the issue of similarity and fit between patient and therapist has gotten very politicized. This question and the next two questions address some aspects of that issue. One person put the problem this way:

If that were so, I would only see people who are exactly like me.

[Female, Ph.D., 20 years practice]

Our group felt overwhelmingly that there was no particular reason for a gay patient to see only a gay therapist, unless the patient insisted on it.

I think that one of the problems gay people have in our culture is that dichotomization of people by sexuality and identity defined by sexuality does damage, does violence to the internal self. I think it's really good for people to try to transcend those identities and categories.

[Male, Ph.D., 10 years practice]

It irritates me when people say that, when professionals say that. I think they should be back in therapy if they're saying that. We're all sexual beings, but we're treating a person, not a sexual problem. It has to do with a whole personality.

[Female, M.S.W., 10 years practice]

The feeling that "I can only live within this group" is what creates a problem to begin with.

[Female, M.S., 15 years practice]

It's not necessary, or necessarily the best idea. They shouldn't know the orientation of the therapist.

[Male, M.D., 20 years practice]

One female therapist described how the issue can come up with a patient.

My first control patient was a lesbian, and we worked together for two years. A male student came into the treatment room inadvertently, and she went into a severe anxiety state, and then was very angry, and expressed a lot of feelings about men. I joined her, but perhaps not strongly enough, because after that she questioned whether I was the right therapist for her. She wanted a lesbian therapist, and eventually she left.

[Female, M.S.W., 45 years practice]

Three people mentioned the importance of a straight therapist being knowledgeable and open to gay issues.

A gay patient should see a therapist they can work well with, and the therapist has to be gay-sensitive, and understand the issues and work with their own homophobic attitudes.

[Female, M.S.W., 15 years practice]

A gay patient should not see a homophobic therapist.

[Male, Ph.D., 50 years practice]

There are some straight therapists who shouldn't work with gay patients.

[Female, M.D., 15 years practice]

One straight therapist acknowledged his difficulty working with gay patients.

I'm probably not the best therapist for some gay patients, because some of the histrionics are uncomfortable for me.

[Male, Ph.D., 25 years practice]

Two gay therapists discussed some of the pros and cons.

I think when they come to me it's often from somebody who's not describing me as a gay therapist, who doesn't know whether I'm a gay therapist. Sometimes people ask for a gay therapist. I think that people sometimes need to identify with a role model, or want to respect themselves as a gay person by being close to someone they see as successful. If those people are identifying a need in themselves then that's fine, but I think there are many patients who are gay who feel more comfortable talking to somebody outside of the community, whose fear is that they don't want to be talking to somebody that they'll bump into in a club. It's more anonymous with someone who's outside the community.

[Female, M.S.W., 20 years practice]

Sometimes gay patients are entering treatment around gay issues and sometimes because they're depressed or some other issue that's got nothing particularly to do with being gay.

[Female, Ph.D., 20 years practice]

Several therapists suggested that gay therapists are not automatically good with gay patients.

I used to think that gay patients should see only a gay therapist, but I've changed my mind. I've met gay therapists I wouldn't send a dog to, and I've met some straight therapists I would myself go into treatment with.

[Male, M.S.W., 15 years practice]

I've had gay patients who've told me they wouldn't go near a gay therapist.

[Male, Ph.D., 20 years practice]

One person brought up the way the issue is handled in a clinic setting.

> I hate that kind of restriction. . . . In some clinics, if you say you're gay, you're automatically assigned a gay therapist. I think that's wrong.
>
> [Male, Ph.D., 40 years practice]

Several straight therapists suggested that there are significant advantages for gay patients who enter treatment with straight therapists.

> I've had a gay patient come to me specifically because he wanted to be able to relate to other men, to not feel cut off from the rest of mankind, and that was an important part of our relationship.
>
> [Male, M.S.W., 20 years practice]

> I had one come to see me specifically because they thought it was a predominantly straight world, and they wanted to learn to function in it.
>
> [Male, M.S.W., 10 years practice]

> It's very good for some gay patients to form a good relationship with a straight therapist. They feel more accepted.
>
> [Female, M.S.W., 30 years practice]

> A lot of gay men often prefer to see a woman rather than see a straight man, and that to me is very questionable. Their identification with women is a problem, and they really need to work out a lot of issues with men.
>
> [Male, M.S.W., 25 years practice]

Several others believe there are advantages to gay patients seeing gay therapists.

> It depends on what the patient needs. A gay patient may need to see a gay therapist as a role model.
>
> [Female, M.S.W., 5 years practice]

> If the person feels they would be most comfortable with someone who's gay, or that someone who isn't gay wouldn't understand them. I don't think that's true, but if that's their perception, they're the consumer and they're the ones who need to be comfortable.
>
> [Female, Ph.D., 10 years practice]

A number of people pointed out the dangers of unconscious collusion or blind spots.

There's the possibility of a gay therapist colluding with a gay patient, sharing the same viewpoint. I find that a lot of gay patients who come to me have a chip on their shoulder about being gay. They have inferiority feelings about being gay, but they attribute it all to society being prejudiced against them, but it has also to do with their own narcissism, and that can never be resolved if they go to a gay therapist who has the same view.

[Male, Ph.D., 15 years practice]

For some people, it's probably important, because there are certain things that they feel will be understood. On the other hand, that plan involves a decision to reinforce certain resistances and to regard certain issues as nonexistent, which is a disservice to a lot of people.

[Male, M.D., 15 years practice]

A gay therapist probably has a countertransference in terms of working through all the dynamics of a gay patient.

[Male, Ph.D., 40 years practice]

In spite of changes in the DSM, some therapists still have negative attitudes about homosexuality.

I'm more in the classical Freudian corner on this. I still believe that homosexuality is a deviation. I make a distinction, in that I think that everybody's sexual orientation should be respected, and people should be treated with equal respect no matter what their orientation is. But I still think that homosexuality should be regarded as a deviation and should be treated as such. It's more than a choice of orientation. It's also a lifestyle, it is an ideology, it is many things that I think are destructive to society. The whole question of whether homosexuality is destructive to society and to the people who practice it now being obscured under the banner of human rights. This tends to discourage any objective inquiry.

[Male, Ph.D., 25 years practice]

NUMERICAL DISTRIBUTION

Almost everyone said "not necessarily" or that it depends on the fit between patient and therapist. Only 4 people said that certain patients may need to identify with a gay role model, and 23 mentioned that if it's important to the patient, then he or she should be accommodated. Nine people said no, emphasizing the possibility of collusion or countertransference.

COMMENTS

This question and the next two refer to the issue of patient–therapist match. How important is it to ensure that patient and therapist share the same qualities, experience, or background?

This issue has become somewhat politicized, with some groups insisting that only a gay therapist can understand a gay patient and be free from bias in treatment. Many homosexual patients have a lifelong history of feeling different and estranged from others, and I think that it is very healing for many gay patients to have the experience of being understood and accepted by a therapist who does not share their sexual orientation.

I think it is crucial for all therapists, regardless of sexual orientation, to examine their own beliefs and prejudices in this area, both before and during treatment of any patient with such issues. Bias toward may be just as disruptive of good treatment as bias against.

RELATED READING

Beutler, L. E., Clarkin, J. F., Crago, M., and Bergan, J. (1991). Client–therapist matching. In *Handbook of Social and Clinical Psychology: The Health Perspective,* ed. C. R. Snyder and D. R. Forsyth, pp. 669–716. New York: Pergamon Press.

Nash, J. L. (1993). The heterosexual analyst and the gay man. In *Affirmative Dynamic Psychotherapy with Gay Men,* ed. C. Cornett, pp. 199–228. Northvale, NJ: Jason Aronson.

Silverstein, C., ed. (1992). *Gays, Lesbians, and Their Therapists.* New York: Norton.

🔊🔊🔊🔊

Question 50: Should a patient see only a therapist of the same ethnic group?

This is another question that has become politicized, and group identity sometimes overrides treatment considerations. The feeling that "only someone who is like me can understand me" is sometimes the deciding factor in choosing a therapist.

Our group felt overwhelmingly that there is no compelling reason for an ethnic patient to see a therapist of the same background, unless it is so important to the patient that treatment will not otherwise begin.

Not unless there's some kind of issue where they really have to have it, they're so stuck on it. If you really struggle to listen to a person, and get into their perspective, as a therapist you can work with anyone.

[Male, Ph.D., 15 years practice]

It depends on where they're at and what issues they're working on. If you have a good therapist it doesn't matter.

[Female, M.A., 15 years practice]

The relationship is between the patient and me, period.

[Female, Ph.D., 20 years practice]

I think that a therapist who can maintain objectivity, and can handle transference issues, and who can use an interrogatory approach, can work with anyone.

[Female, M.S.W., 15 years practice]

At least one therapist disagreed.

I treated a black man once, and whenever we got near his issues, it was my "racial problem." Whenever you get political resistances, you know that can be used as a cover.

[Male, Ph.D., 25 years practice]

Many emphasized that the issue has to be discussed.

I have a number of minority patients, and if they haven't thought about it, I would keep raising it from time to time so that they would know that it wasn't a taboo subject. Just like you might have a patient who's three hundred pounds, and they feel, "What could you know? You've never been obese." I would raise the question, "What does it feel like to work with someone who's white?"

[Female, M.S.W., 10 years practice]

I can work with anyone, but if someone comes in and is disappointed that I'm not what they expected, if you just talk about it, just bring it up. How do you feel about talking to someone who isn't black? That usually handles it.

[Female, Ph.D., 10 years practice]

And others believe that it is incumbent on the therapist to become informed about the patient's cultural milieu.

I think for anyone to treat someone who's culturally different requires that the therapist do a tremendous amount of work to understand. I need to understand that culture thoroughly.

[Male, M.S.W., 15 years practice]

I think that if you're going to work with someone from a different culture, you really need to inform yourself.

[Female, M.S., 20 years practice]

I think I've probably fallen short there because I don't really know the essence of another culture, and it sometimes makes me simplistic, or even naive, about something basic and essential to their lives. With those patients, I will deliberately ask them to explain more to me, and that helps, and I check out with them regularly how I'm doing.

[Female, M.S., 15 years practice]

Some white therapists said that there may be some usefulness in matching ethnic or racial background in terms of identification.

In my limited experience working with black patients, my sense was that it never quite worked out right, and it would have been better for them to see a black therapist.

[Male, M.S.W., 25 years practice]

I certainly think that a person should be comfortable with the person they're seeing, and there has to be a wavelength that they can connect on. So if you have a real inner-city black with an upper-class white, it's not going to work.

[Female, M.A., 20 years practice]

All things being equal, if the therapist is of the same group, it probably, at least initially, makes a big difference. But there's more to being a good therapist than having the same cultural background as somebody. You have to be really willing to learn from your patients, and patients know when you really don't share their experiences.

[Male, Ph.D., 10 years practice]

Sometimes black or minority patients should see a therapist of the same background particularly for role modeling if the issues are upward mobility or professionalism, and they need a role model they can identify with.

[Male, Ph.D., 25 years practice]

In some cases, it would be better for a black patient to see a black therapist because of identification, having the therapist as a role model, say for a child or adolescent.

[Male, M.S.W., 20 years practice]

In general, yes, they should, because they will receive a fair understanding. I had a black woman patient once, who I put in a group of white people, and it was embarrassing to me how transparent their racism became. It just hurt me. They were totally unconscious of it. They liked her, but they talked to her as if she didn't have the same experience of the world that they did. And she left.

[Male, Ph.D., 50 years practice]

Increasingly, I see the value of sending black clients to black therapists. There are identity issues. One woman I did an intake with really wanted a black therapist. She felt that only a black female therapist could understand the identity issues that she had.

[Female, M.S.W., 15 years practice]

We've underestimated the role of identification in treatment, and how big a part the real relationship plays in the effectiveness of psychotherapy. It's almost impossible for a black person in this culture to identify with a white person, except pathologically. It's really asking a lot.

[Female, M.D., 15 years practice]

One person suggested that selecting a therapist from a different background may be part of a process for the patient.

There are people, especially first generation, who feel that seeing a therapist who's not the same ethnic group is part of their moving out, so that it's not only not a negative, I become a safer person. It's part of their process of assimilation, and the transference to whatever negative experiences they had is less obvious.

[Female, M.S.W., 20 years practice]

Several other therapists suggested that there may actually be disadvantages in matching racial or ethnic background, or that matching is no guarantee of good therapy.

If a black patient has a lot of anger at whites, and thinks that whites are prejudiced against blacks, and that all the problems of blacks are the result of whites, and he goes to a therapist that feels the same way, there may be a lot of characterological stuff going on that will never be resolved.

[Male, Ph.D., 25 years practice]

If a black person feels that they need to see a black therapist, it may be the only way they'll be able to work on what they need to work on. On the other hand, there may be collusion between the therapist and the patient that certain issues are not issues.

[Male, M.D., 15 years practice]

I'm black, and the worst therapist I ever had was black. He wasted the best years of my life. The two best therapists I ever had were Jewish.

[Male, M.S.W., 35 years practice]

It could be a sign of a resistance, or "only someone like me can understand me" could be a major narcissistic defense.

[Male, Ph.D., 20 years practice]

There's the danger of losing your objectivity, of overidentifying with the patient. Also, the patient can say, "Well, you know what I mean," and feel that they don't have to explain it.

[Female, Ph.D., 30 years practice]

NUMERICAL DISTRIBUTION

Virtually everyone said either "not necessarily" or "it depends on the patient and the therapist." Five people said that it was a good idea, at least some of the time, for reasons of understanding and identification, but 12 others pointed out that it can sometimes lead to a kind of collusion.

COMMENTS

Again, the issue here is how similar in background and experience patient and therapist must be for effective treatment.

Obviously, if a patient wants a therapist of a particular ethnic background, it's their choice. They may believe that this is what they need in order to feel comfortable enough to reveal themselves. It may be difficult to convince them that other considerations are more important.

Assuming that a therapist of the same background will automatically understand is often a mistake. I was asked by a black patient once for a referral to a black therapist, which I gave. The patient returned to me after a few sessions, saying that it had not worked out because "his black experience was not my black experience." This patient continued in treatment with me and, I think, realized that the racial question was perhaps not so significant as she had thought.

RELATED READING

Jones, E. E. (1978). Effects of race on psychotherapy process and outcome: an exploratory investigation. *Psychotherapy: Theory, Research, and Practice* 15(3):226–236.

Mehlman, E. (1994). Enhancing self-disclosure of the African-American college student in therapy with the Caucasian therapist. *Journal of College Student Psychotherapy* 9(1):3–20.

Sue, D. W., and Sue, D. (1990). *Counseling the Culturally Different: Theory and Practice.* New York: Wiley and Sons.

Turner, S., and Armstrong, S. (1981). Cross-racial psychotherapy: what the therapists say. *Psychotherapy: Theory, Research, and Practice* 18(3):375–378.

Wolkon, G. H., Moriwaki, S., and Williams, K. J. (1973). Race and social class as factors in the orientation toward psychotherapy. *Journal of Counseling Psychology* 20(4):312–316.

⬧⬧⬧⬧

Question 51: Should a patient see only a therapist of the same gender?

Again, the large majority of our therapists said there was no compelling reason to match gender, and that good therapy was possible in either case.

> Over time, if you're dealing with transference, no therapy is going to be perfect and no therapy is going to be complete, but if you have a good human being who really gets into things, and loves you a certain way, you're going to do what you need to do for yourself.
>
> [Male, Ph.D., 25 years practice]

> I don't think that women are necessarily best served by seeing female therapists, or males are best served by seeing male therapists.
>
> [Male, M.S.W., 35 years practice]

On the other hand, patient preferences usually determine the choice.

I have had a number of men call over the years and ask for a referral to a male therapist, particularly heterosexual men, who sometimes feel that seeing a woman is too infantilizing, or is too threatening on some level.

[Female, M.S.W., 20 years practice]

Patients bring a certain need. They will decide. They may feel they can only work with a therapist of a particular sex, and that has to be discussed.

[Female, M.A., 15 years practice]

It's up to the patient. If the patient is very clear that they want to see a woman, why would I insist that they see a man?

[Male, Ph.D., 20 years practice]

A few practitioners mentioned the advantages of having both male and female therapists at different stages of treatment.

I think for some people, male or female, having experiences with both male and female therapists would be very useful. I used to lead a group with a male co-therapist, and he would bring most of the men and I would bring most of the women, and we'd see them individually as well, and sometimes in the middle of treatment we would switch and give them that experience.

[Female, M.S.W., 30 years practice]

Sometimes you're working on certain issues, and it might be helpful to work with one sex or the other.

[Female, M.A., 15 years practice]

I think that people need two therapists. Just like you need a mother and a father, you need a male and a female therapist as part of your experience.

[Male, Ph.D., 50 years practice]

A significant minority said there were some general advantages to matching gender.

Sometimes I feel it's very helpful for a woman to be seeing a woman therapist, particularly if she's had very bad mothering. Women can do extremely well with female patients.

[Male, Ph.D., 40 years practice]

I think it's sometimes very important for women to see women and men to see men. Because of trust, being able to set up a trusting relationship. If a man has never had a trusting relationship with a man, and only relates to women, it might be very helpful to form a thera-peutic relationship with a man.

[Male, M.S.W., 15 years practice]

There are times when it's clear that the issues relate more to a man or to a woman.

[Female, M.S., 15 years practice]

It depends on the issues involved, and the sophistication of a male therapist to their own biases. There can be a pathologizing by male therapists of syndromes, such as when a woman doesn't have a primary relationship in her life. I think that body issues are sometimes prob-lematic with male therapists and female patients, on both sides. I'm not sure women can be as open with male therapists, nor are men as free to explore body issues with female patients because of the taboos that are involved.

[Female, M.S.W., 15 years practice]

It's often helpful not to have to make that leap, at least during the initial stages of therapy.

[Female, M.D., 15 years practice]

There's a slightly reduced risk of misunderstanding a hug, for example, with a female therapist than with a male therapist, and that can be very powerful and valuable.

[Male, Ph.D., 20 years practice]

And several therapists mentioned specific kinds of patients as benefit-ing from a match in gender.

Occasionally, I have felt with some of my male patients who did not have enough fathering, that they needed input from a male.

[Female, M.S., 15 years practice]

I don't think lesbians trust male therapists.

[Male, M.S.W., 10 years practice]

I do think young male adolescents do better with a male therapist because they often need a father figure.

[Male, Ph.D., 25 years practice]

If a female patient has a history of sexual abuse, it might be better for her to see a woman.

[Female, M.S., 15 years practice]

One woman suggested that there may be risks for female patients with male therapists.

I think a lot of male therapists, if they get a young, pretty girl in the office, forget they're therapists in a certain way. I'm very concerned about the sexual acting out between therapist and patient.

[Female, M.S.W., 25 years practice]

NUMERICAL DISTRIBUTION

Again, virtually everyone said it depends on the individuals involved. Thirty-two people mentioned specific instances where it might be better, as with adolescent patients, or women who'd been abused, or where there were other specific issues. Only 3 people—2 men and 1 woman—said specifically that they thought female therapists understood female patients better than did male therapists.

COMMENTS

Once again, the issue is the similarity of patient and therapist, and whether one gender is capable of understanding the other. To a lesser extent, the question is also about patient comfort and ease of self-disclosure. Another dynamic here is the situation of male therapists and female patients, where power and sex may become problems.

Again, patients must decide how important gender of the therapist is for them, but we as professionals can support or dissuade this kind of thinking. If we encourage the female patient to seek only a female therapist, aren't we reinforcing a negative stereotype of men? A woman who has had damaging experiences with men, such as an abusive father, could benefit tremendously from a safe and nurturing experience with a male therapist. Some women don't trust or feel safe with men, though, and will need to see a woman first. Conversely, a man may not feel that a woman will be capable of understanding or accepting him, and it would be healing to have that experience.

I know from my own experience in treatment that different issues come up with male therapists than with female therapists, and believe that every patient would benefit from both experiences (see also Question 52).

RELATED READING

Erickson, B. M. (1993). *Helping Men Change: The Role of the Female Thera-
pist.* Newbury Park, CA: Sage Publications.
Jones, E. E., and Zoppel, C. L. (1982). Impact of client and therapist gen-
der on psychotherapy process and outcome. *Journal of Consulting and
Clinical Psychology* 50(2):259–272.
Kaplan, A. G. (1985). Female or male therapists for women patients: new
formulations. *Psychiatry* 48(2):111–121.
Meyers, H. C. (1986). Analytic work by and with women: the complexity
and the challenge. In *Between Analyst and Patient: New Dimensions in
Countertransference and Transference,* pp. 159–176. New York: Analytic
Press.
Mogul, K. M. (1982). Overview: the sex of the therapist. *American Journal
of Psychiatry* 139(1):1–11.
Person, E. S. (1983). Women in therapy: therapist gender as a variable.
International Review of Psycho-Analysis 10(2):193–204.

⬧⬧⬧⬧

*Question 52: Is there a difference between the way male therapists and
female therapists work?*

The responses were almost evenly divided between those who think that
there are differences in the way male therapists and female therapists work
and those who believe there are no such differences by group. The latter
said that whatever differences exist are individual.

First, those who see no significant between-group difference.

> I think that good therapists are all alike. Good therapists all tend to do
> similar things. When you get to a state of health to the extent of healthy,
> mature equilibrium in your own life, you tend to respond in typically
> healthy ways to the things that patients bring to you, and whether
> you're male or female you'll respond in that way.
>
> [Male, Ph.D., 15 years practice]

> The biggest difference is between beginning and experienced
> therapists.
>
> [Female, M.S.W., 15 years practice]

> There has to be some difference, but I don't think it's very great. If the
> person is well trained, and they're listening to the dynamics of the

patient, they're going to work with those dynamics. It might be a slightly different style.

[Male, Ph.D., 40 years practice]

One person said that men and women may take different routes to get to the same place.

I think very good therapists, males and females, work more similarly, in that they're very empathic and attuned to the patient. I think that men have a harder time getting to that point because of the way male socialization occurs. Women may have more difficulty getting to proper boundaries.

[Female, M.S.W., 25 years practice]

In general, those who see a difference between male and female therapists described women as being more empathic, more engaged, and more accepting.

My sense about that is that it's similar to the difference between fathers and mothers with their kids. You can have an extremely caring, involved, nurturing father, but many, many people will say that there's this place where they can draw a line, and fathers are able to stay on the other side of it, and mothers can't quite do that, they're just sort of in there. That probably happens in psychotherapy, and I don't mean blurring the boundary or being overinvolved, it's just a kind of feeling of being somehow more inside. It has to do with early gender development issues for girls, in the sense that from so early on, girls are tuned in to what people are feeling and thinking and needing.

[Female, M.D., 15 years practice]

In general, female therapists tend to be more warm and more emotionally available, and male therapists tend to be more, not authoritarian, but authoritative and emotionally abstinent.

[Male, M.D., 15 years practice]

I suspect that female therapists tend to get more into detail, tremendous emotional detail, and men will do that less.

[Male, Ph.D., 20 years practice]

Men and women are very different. We see the world through different-colored glasses. I hesitate because of stereotypes. We all come as therapists using our life experience, and who we are, with the experience of being a man in the world or being a woman in the world, and bring that to our patients. There are certain things that women just don't have to say that I understand.

[Female, Ph.D., 20 years practice]

I think that it's possible that women could be more gentle, more empathic, more of a holding environment. And men might be more investigative, more active in that way, interpreting, and less easy for them to hold on.

[Female, M.S.W., 20 years practice]

Women are able to share in a very intimate way that would embarrass men, and that makes therapy for women with women more effective, because there's not some of the defensiveness that there would be with a man.

[Male, Ph.D., 25 years practice]

I think, because of my own experiences, that women are more nurturing. I think because of being a mother, I'm much more developmentally oriented. I've learned as much from raising children as from being in school about developmental issues and phases. I see so clearly how patients are struggling through certain developmental crises.

[Female, M.A., 15 years practice]

I think some male therapists are not as sensitive or as nurturing as some female therapists.

[Female, M.S.W., 30 years practice]

I think, in my limited sample, that women have an easier time allowing themselves to enter the space of the patient, to let something about the emotional boundary go, with the full knowledge that they can come out of the enmeshment. I think that's a developmental issue with women, that this is a by-product of a different development than men, and I do think it affects the therapeutic work. The danger of that is that some women may use that and not know how to come out of the enmeshment, and that's very dangerous.

[Female, M.S.W., 15 years practice]

A patient said that in general women therapists are more nurturing in their style, not necessarily in their theoretical orientation, but just in how they are. Women and men are very different, so how could it not be different?

[Male, M.S.W., 15 years practice]

I think women are a little better at this. In our culture, women have kind of a head start, a focus on interpersonal emotional things. My experience in supervision and therapy is that I've done better with women therapists myself.

[Male, M.S.W., 10 years practice]

There might be a slightly higher degree of informality when a woman works with another woman, and possibly a little more self-disclosure by the therapist. Maybe a little more connectedness. I also see in the female therapists I know a little more warmth.

[Male, Ph.D., 20 years practice]

Several therapists suggested that although differences between groups may exist, men who choose to be therapists may have more "feminine" qualities.

Most therapists are female, even if they're men.

[Male, Ph.D., 40 years practice]

Maybe the men who become therapists think more the way women do, in terms of not being linear, and being a caretaker and thinking of the impact of your words on the other person.

[Female, M.S.W., 10 years practice]

A few people suggested that there are other kinds of differences.

I think male therapists can do things female therapists can't do, and vice versa. Male therapists can get away with being a little more out-rageous, a little more confrontational. Female therapists can extend themselves more emotionally, and male therapists would run the risk of being misunderstood.

[Female, Ph.D., 5 years practice]

Female therapists in general have a tendency to do more counseling than psychotherapy. It seems to deteriorate into that kind of thing. Also, they often misinterpret transferential phenomena. Female therapists do that more often than male therapists, at least in the seminars I've been in or have given. They seem to lack the full appreciation of what transference and countertransference is all about.

[Male, Ph.D., 30 years practice]

Males have an easier time with the business aspect of the profession than women. Men have an easier time asking for and feeling entitled to a certain fee.

[Female, M.S.W., 15 years practice]

My belief is that men often have much more interest in the power thing than women do.

[Female, M.A., 20 years practice]

Sometimes I think men are more into being directive and authoritative, but that works well with some clients. Some clients want that.

[Female, Ph.D., 10 years practice]

Female therapists tend to get off into feminist issues more, and so it's harder for me to be open because I feel I have to be something as a woman talking to a woman that I don't have to be with a man. It's a political agenda.

[Female, M.S.W., 5 years practice]

I think that women therapists are much more nurturing and much more process-oriented, and male therapists have to work hard to get rid of product-oriented thinking. Men are very conditioned to work and see results, and if you're not getting well quick enough that means I'm not working hard enough, and I need to see the product coming off the assembly line.

[Male, M.S.W., 15 years practice]

NUMERICAL DISTRIBUTION

Thirty-four people said that they thought there were significant differences; 26 people said they thought that there was no difference along gender lines, and that differences were individual.

COMMENTS

This question raises the issue of whether women and men are intrinsically and fundamentally different and how those differences might affect treatment.

This is a tricky area. I don't want to reinforce the stereotype that women are more openly supportive and empathic and emotional, while men are more analytic and confrontational, yet perhaps there is some truth to that generalization. Women are socialized differently from men, and both genders develop different aspects of their personalities. As with all generalizations, it is of no value in describing a particular individual, and I know many exceptions to the generalization on both sides.

RELATED READING

Cantor, D. W. (1990). *Women as Therapists: A Multitheoretical Casebook.* Northvale, NJ: Jason Aronson.

Kulish, N. M. (1989). Gender and transference: conversations with female analysts. *Psychoanalytic Psychology* 6(1):59–71.

Person, E. S. (1986). Women in therapy: therapist gender as a variable. In *Between Analyst and Patient: New Dimensions in Countertransference and Transference,* ed. H. C. Meyers, pp. 193–212. New York: Analytic Press.

Ruderman, E. B. (1986). Gender related themes of women psychotherapists in their treatment of women patients: the creative and reparative use of countertransference as a mutual growth experience. *Clinical Social Work Journal* 14(2):103–126.

Shafter, R. (1988). When the therapist is female: transference, counter-transference, and reality. *Issues in Ego Psychology* 11(1):32–42.

🔃🔃🔃🔃

Question 53: How do you think therapy works?

In many ways, this is the most significant question in the interview. All the other questions follow from this one. What is it in the process of psychotherapy that changes people's feelings, behavior, and experience?

Two-thirds of these therapists said that it was the relationship with the therapist that created change.

> Therapy offers a person an opportunity to experience the major issues in their life, the major conflicts, in a nonthreatening relationship with someone whose job it is to help them understand those issues and conflicts, who's dedicated to that alone. In that relationship, if it's established and safe enough, they can re-experience and then learn what the major issues and conflicts have been and are in an ongoing way.
>
> [Male, M.D., 20 years practice]

> It works mostly because of the relationship. Something gets changed inside because of something that's happening outside, and it's in the relationship. All the techniques, and all the things that you say, are all in the service of the relationship.
>
> [Female, M.S.W., 30 years practice]

> Probably through the relationship between the analyst and the patient. It's the most important tool. There's a gradual buildup of trust, and

gradual opening up, and that's how it works. It's magic! It's working it through with your therapist, right there in the transference about whatever it is.

[Female, M.S.W., 20 years practice]

Therapy works by having an intimate, trusting relationship with another human being who has special training to deal with issues. Making an intimate connection with another person.

[Male, M.D., 5 years practice]

Through relationship, as someone comes to therapy, and forms some kind of dependent relationship on the therapist. Sometimes it's an intense transference and sometimes it's just a respect. In short-term work, people don't get hooked in in terms of that dependent transference, but they get hooked in in terms of a relational respect, to trust that person's guidance and consultation.

[Female, Ph.D., 20 years practice]

I think it's the relationship and the attachment. The sense of comfort, and being understood by someone, and being able to share things that are old and painful or disturbing. Or current things that are troubling, or even exciting, good things. I know there's two hundred or three hundred different approaches to therapy, and what it comes down to is the relationship. If you go to a person and you feel comfortable talking to them, and if something felt off or wrong you could say that, then you'd be okay.

[Female, M.S.W., 10 years practice]

Fundamentally by the experience of relationship. There's a relationship that two people have together, and if that relationship is a nurturing, healthy one, then it'll tend to work.

[Male, M.S.W., 25 years practice]

First of all, I think it's in conversation, in language, that we understand ourselves and our world. That's a very effective way to help people because they're using language to describe their experience. People, in order to have a hold of their own understanding of themselves, need to be acknowledged by another person. And then the security of an intimate, trusting relationship can help a person feel more confident and secure.

[Male, Ph.D., 25 years practice]

I think therapy works because they develop a more objective relationship, a very intimate, very loving relationship, with someone who's not caught up in their lives. They get to say things that they can't say in any other space, whether it's work or family or friends or lover. They can say to me, "I love my children but I wish they all were dead," or "My mother just died, and I inherited a lot of money, and I'm so glad she died," and they can't say that anywhere else. I think it's real important to be able to say to another human being the stuff that circles our head and our heart.

[Male, M.S.W., 15 years practice]

I think it works by the steady connection with the therapist. It's someone you know that every session will maintain a continuity, and help you in your continuity of self. You begin to discover that you have a continuity via this other person who is there for you and whose attention belongs to you. An intelligent attention.

[Male, M.S.W., 10 years practice]

For some people, they can hear something that they wouldn't hear by themselves. If you can get the person's attention, if they want to hear you, then some people can use the session enormously well, and go away and reflect on it. Other people will use you, mirror you, use you as an alter ego who will sustain them during the week. Sometimes strength comes from that. It's like learning to dance: at first you copy the other's steps.

[Female, Ph.D., 30 years practice]

I really think it's all about the relationship: forming a relationship with another human being that is different from any other relationship that you've had. Most people have never been in therapy before, so it's teaching people how to look at themselves very differently. But if you can't have that relationship, it doesn't matter what you're going to teach them, they won't be able to take it in.

[Female, M.S.W., 10 years practice]

The bottom line is that it really is about the relationship, and about having a different kind of relationship with someone. I wouldn't have said that three years ago, but I'm coming to that conclusion.

[Female, Ph.D., 5 years practice]

It's a real mystery. One of the things I try to do as a therapist is take the mystery out of it, to make it accessible to people. It basically has to do with the relationship. If there's not a relationship of trust, nothing's going to happen. The relationship is the primary part of the process.

[Female, M.S.W., 10 years practice]

Two things. What's primary is the relationship, that helps people to heal, to understand. The other is insight. It helps people to observe their lives, and make choices, and organize experience. But the relationship is the first thing.

[Female, M.S., 15 years practice]

Sometimes it works because there's someone there who really listens for an hour a week. I've certainly had a lot of patients, probably more women than men, whose partners don't pay much attention. I probably pay more attention to them in fifty minutes than they actually get, in terms of intense focus, all week. So I think it can be a very nonspecific diffuse kind of effect.

[Male, Ph.D., 20 years practice]

Therapy is best when it doesn't feel like you're doing therapy, when you're just hanging out bullshitting, with some known goal in mind, and you don't always have to be focused on interpreting and understanding. And that there's something that someone absorbs from you and your way of being. There's a certain kind of acceptance that gets communicated over time, regardless of any content that you do or don't say. And somebody feels that what they have to say is worthwhile and meaningful and important, and you can get into it, and you can laugh with them and cry with them, and that's very helpful.

[Male, Ph.D., 20 years practice]

Several others in this segment said specifically that therapy was a "corrective emotional experience."

Love is not enough, but without it, nothing cures. The only thing that cures is love. It's ultimately a corrective emotional experience. It's the process that cures.

[Male, Ph.D., 50 years practice]

In general, it works as kind of a re-healing. You allow yourself to establish an intimate relationship, and establish trust, and then all of the things come up that came up before, and you give yourself an opportunity to experience it in a way that isn't the toxic way that happened initially.

[Female, M.A., 15 years practice]

Therapy provides a corrective emotional experience. There are several steps. First you have to be able to have your feelings, then your behavior changes, and then your feelings change after that. There has to be an atmosphere in which you can talk and not be judged.

[Female, Ph.D., 20 years practice]

It is a corrective emotional experience. In self-psychology terms, it is getting the selfobjects and using them more wisely. It's the inter-personal connection established between two people that gives the supplies that were needed that the client didn't get. And then the client can go out and get them for themselves.

[Female, M.S.W., 15 years practice]

It works because you have a relationship, and it's a reparative rela-tionship. The therapist is, hopefully, together, and he's therefore able to model to the patient how a together person handles his feelings, how he thinks, and so forth. All of this is conveyed, also, in the way the therapist relates to the patient in the relationship. The patient discovers somebody who doesn't react in the same way that other people react to him, but gives him more healthy reactions that allow him to get out of stuck places, and then he changes.

[Male, Ph.D., 25 years practice]

I think it works in the relationship, and therefore I think the trans-ference/countertransference relationship is imperative. But within that, I really have a developmental model in my mind. It's not just that it's a friendly relationship and people like each other. It works because the relationship contains in it a great deal that renegotiates develop-mental issues in a good way for the patient. For example, that the therapist can tolerate anxiety, and helps the patient tolerate anxiety in the way that a good-enough parent/child relationship would have made the patient able to. And the importance of having a therapist who can tolerate in a positive way the patient's negative transference.

[Female, M.S.W., 15 years practice]

It works because the therapist offers a totally different experience. There's no agenda that the patient has to fit into. And that gives the patient the opportunity to see that there's something different in the world. The frame provides an enclave in which the patient can try out different things without threats of recrimination.

[Female, M.S.W., 20 years practice]

Because we get paid, and because we have established a regular treatment hour and a contract with the patient, the kinds of things they would do with the other people in their life don't happen the way they would happen with those people. We will talk about feeling pushed away rather than just being pushed away. Because it's been set up in that way, we can use ourselves to help them mirror what's going on for them, in a way that those other people won't do. That's the piece that's therapeutic, that they can begin relating differently to one human being, in a way that hopefully gets transferred to the other people in their life.

[Female, M.S.W., 20 years practice]

For the most part, in psychotherapy and a good part of psychoanalysis, what eventually transpires is that through the positive transference and the love of the analyst, the patient gets better.

[Male, M.D., 20 years practice]

Others said that it was the insight gained, or the development of a greater self-awareness.

A person in the course of therapy learns something about the reasons for the way they react emotionally or behave in certain kinds of situations. That's a key part of the process of successful therapy. However, what becomes conscious, or the way it becomes conscious, isn't limited to intellectual or cognitive contents. It's an important part of the therapy, for a person to be able to have some idea about what's different, and what the basis for it is, and what about their past experience relates to their way of handling conflicts. But at some level, a process of the development of emotional insight, or the freeing up of certain anxieties, also occurs.

[Male, M.D., 15 years practice]

Nobody really knows how it works, because it's about change, and we don't know what makes people change. My feeling is that therapy works by shifting emphasis from the external to the internal, and then the patient develops some kind of awareness of their own internal process, how they function. They become curious about themselves, and in that process of becoming curious about themselves, there is a liberation, because rather than being critical of themselves, they start asking questions: Why do I do this? Why do I prefer that? Why do I have this fantasy? There develops a respect for oneself, one's impulses, one's opinions, one's thoughts, one's body.

[Male, Ph.D., 20 years practice]

In childhood, parents and schools and everybody puts so much attention on the child's performance and activity and thinking, and there's such a neglect of how the child is feeling. We tend as adults, because our emotions have been so neglected, to have problems. Therapy is a place where people really get to know their feelings, to understand their emotions, and where people are helped to appreciate those emotions and pay attention to them. People who are helped in therapy, and not everyone is, usually come away feeling more connected to themselves, to their emotional selves.

[Female, M.S.W., 15 years practice]

I think it works primarily through insight. It's a cognitive practice. The hardest thing to do in therapy is to listen, and to hear the conflicts that are in the material, and to tease out the fantasies that are misleading the patient, causing the patient trouble, and sharing them with the patient, giving them insight into what their conflicts are.

[Male, Ph.D., 40 years practice]

A smaller group said that it was the technical elements of the treatment that led to change. In psychoanalytic therapy, these include "interpretations," or "transference."

At the beginning, the narcissistic transference is very important. Treatment centers on the transference, from the negative to the positive. In the course of treatment, countertransference feelings are induced, some of which are subjective, because of the life experience of the analyst, and some are more objective. The use of these feelings in understanding what's going on in the room is very important, and providing the emotional communication that's necessary to resolve the transference resistances.

[Female, M.S.W., 45 years practice]

The existence of transference and the process of working out the transference is what brings about the fundamental changes in character structure that account for the results. It takes time and it takes hard work.

[Male, Ph.D., 30 years practice]

Being permitted to talk provides a form of discharge of anxiety. And on the basis of the data presented, you start making the unconscious conscious. If the patient is well enough, this helps the patient in resolving conflicts, and helps that patient to feel integrated, and gives him a sense of mastery over his own emotions. You demonstrate to the patient how his mind works.

[Male, M.S.W., 35 years practice]

Once there's been the establishment of a sense of safety and trust, the patient really looks at themselves in relation to other people, and their dreams, and everything about their experience of life. Also, in the transference, seeing these very same things occur in relation to the therapist, and feeling them very intensely there, there's the opportunity to understand and unravel and rework whatever these habitual patterns and ways of thinking have been. A choice is opened up that didn't exist before, and a patient can understand that they don't have to feel guilty, for example. Changes are made in their lives and it sort of starts to snowball.

[Female, Ph.D., 15 years practice]

In behavioral therapy, the technical elements may be called "conditioning" or "re-learning."

Certain kinds of therapy work because of the application of specific behavioral principles and fairly well-proven techniques based on operant and classical conditioning principles.

[Male, Ph.D., 20 years practice]

It's a combination of reparenting and teaching. There are people that don't have friends in their lives, they don't have anyone they're close to. They may seem to have friends but there's no one they really talk to. It's a unique experience, a safe environment. It's also teaching people new ways to deal with situations. At times, depending on the therapy, it can also be a place of limit-setting, which may not be done in the home where in that person's life things are out of control. It's very much parental in all of those ways.

[Female, Ph.D., 10 years practice]

A few people said the most important part of the process was the element of self-disclosure.

Therapy works when a therapist provides an atmosphere where a person takes a chance to really make public what she really believes, deep down, and continues to discover increasingly the deepest beliefs that have formed and informed her entire life. And in the process of revealing that, in a totally accepting context, has a chance with an ombudsman of her spirit, to rethink her life.

[Male, Ph.D., 25 years practice]

Having someone with whom you can be really open with yourself is a tremendous thing for a lot of people. Someone who really listens to you, and tries to understand you, just being in the presence of someone like that is really powerful because it so enables you to be with yourself in a different way.

[Male, Ph.D., 5 years practice]

A few people said that the most significant element was the regularity and dependability of the process.

> By coming, showing up. Just coming starts the process that's already halfway there by walking through the door.
>
> [Male, M.S.W., 15 years practice]

> I really believe that probably fifty percent of its effectiveness is just showing up, just the willingness to be helped.
>
> [Male, M.S.W., 15 years practice]

NUMERICAL DISTRIBUTION

Thirty-one people said it works primarily through the relationship; 9 more said specifically that it is a corrective emotional experience; 10 said through insight and/or reflection; 4 said it was the technical aspects, whether interpretation or operant conditioning; 3 said it was the continuing self-disclosure; 3 said it was the regularity and ongoing nature of the process.

COMMENTS

This question refers to the primary issue of our whole enterprise: What is happening in therapy? How does merely talking lead to change? Which are the significant dimensions and which are irrelevant to outcome? How important is the therapist's personality? How important is technique?

This really is the central question: What are we doing and how do we do it? Much of the time the process seems mysterious and almost magical. We have our volumes of theory and arsenals of techniques, yet I often feel as though neither of those fully accounts for the personal transformations I observe day after day in my office.

I think the effect and importance of insight have been overemphasized, and that the "corrective emotional experience" has been unfairly deprecated. For patients to be with someone who treats them differently from anyone else they've ever encountered has tremendous impact. Obviously, cognitive understanding of one's own motivation and choices is useful, but I think the healing element is the emotional one. This makes the personality and availability of the therapist more significant than any technique he or she might use.

RELATED READING

Alexander, F. (1948). *Fundamentals of Psychoanalysis*. New York: Norton.

Chessick, R. D. (1969). *How Psychotherapy Heals*. New York: Science House.

Fromm, E. (1991). Causes for the patient's change in analytic treatment. *Psychoanalysis and Psychology* 27(4):581–602.

Kohut, H. (1984). *How Does Analysis Cure?* Chicago: University of Chicago Press.

Mahoney, M. J. (1991). *Human Change Processes: The Scientific Foundations of Psychotherapy*. New York: Basic Books.

Rothstein, A., ed. (1988). *How Does Treatment Help?: On the Modes of Therapeutic Action of Psychoanalytic Psychotherapy*. Madison, CT: International Universities Press.

Weber, J. J., Bachrach, H. M., and Solomon, M. (1985). Factors associated with the outcome of psychoanalysis. *International Journal of Psycho-Analysis* 12(2):127–141.

Winstead, B. A., and Derlega, V. J. (1994). The therapy relationship. In *Perspectives on Close Relationships,* ed. A. L. Weber and J. H. Harvey, pp. 325–339. Boston: Allyn & Bacon.

▧▧▧▧

Question 54: What are the tasks of the psychotherapist?

All therapists see themselves as having a certain job to do. How they see the job depends in part on their theoretical orientations, how they understand the process of therapy, but certain common elements may show up in responses from therapists of very different orientations.

Most people combined several or all of the different tasks in their responses, but the largest number of people said the primary task of the therapist is to be present, as completely with the patient as possible.

> To be as present in each session as I possibly can be. To be able to make sense out of not only this session, but to link it up to others in some way.
>
> [Female, M.S., 15 years practice]

> You have to be there, and be alert. To have an emotional availability. To be free enough of my own stuff, and to be taken care of in my own life, so that when the patient comes in I'm able to listen to them and not look to them to take care of me. I don't have to give any brilliant

solutions, just indicate that I'm pretty close to understanding how they're feeling, which I think works miracles.

[Male, M.S.W., 10 years practice]

To be very present. To be as alert as possible. To respond to each and every cue.

[Male, Ph.D., 40 years practice]

My task is to be there, truly be there.

[Female, M.A., 20 years practice]

To be there for the patient in the sense of sitting there, listening to the patient to see where their hurts or traumas are at, the general assessment of them.

[Female, M.S.W., 25 years practice]

To be where the patient is at, and not to bring your own agenda. To facilitate the process, so the patient can do the work, by being with the patient.

[Male, Ph.D., 20 years practice]

To be in the room with the person, and help them understand what goes on for them, what the issues are.

[Female, M.S., 15 years practice]

An extension of that task is the need to listen and to understand. This is obviously connected to being present, since it is impossible to listen well without focusing one's full attention on the patient.

It's really important for the therapist to be a good listener.

[Male, Ph.D., 25 years practice]

I tend to adapt to the person I'm with. It takes a while, but I try to learn the language of the person so we can talk to each other, and I take that task on myself. I don't want people to have to learn my language.

[Female, M.S., 15 years practice]

To listen very carefully to what the patient is saying. To try to understand the central experience that's being talked about, and articulate that and see where it goes.

[Female, Ph.D., 15 years practice]

Related to both of these responses are those that said the task is to be empathic and to create a safe place in which the patient feels accepted.

> To create safe, secure boundaries in which a patient can say anything, and feel secure in doing that.
>
> [Female, M.S.W., 15 years practice]

> You provide a safe space, in which trust can develop, and allow the maturational process to proceed. What cures is being able to say everything. So you create a situation that makes it safe to say everything.
>
> [Male, Ph.D., 50 years practice]

> To provide a safe, nonjudgmental environment for the person to freely explore whatever issues they want.
>
> [Male, M.S.W., 15 years practice]

> To provide the frame, with consistency, availability, what Kohut calls empathic observing. To be responsive and not reactive.
>
> [Female, M.S.W., 20 years practice]

> To provide the atmosphere, and lend themselves to the relationship, and make it safe enough for anything to come out of the patient. Not to lead the patient anywhere, like a good lawyer who's not allowed to lead the witness but will get to the essence of the issue.
>
> [Male, M.D., 20 years practice]

> To set up an atmosphere of trust, and safety, and regularity. To allow for exploration of the person's experiences. To offer accurate feedback and genuine support.
>
> [Male, Ph.D., 15 years practice]

> To provide an atmosphere in which a patient can say everything. The physical setting should be comfortable. I have to, in my own demeanor, act like a professional, act interested, caring, and connected, as if I want to do the work with the patient.
>
> [Female, Ph.D., 20 years practice]

> To set ground rules and a framework. Certain basic rules within which people can work, from the time structures to the expectations, and to lay them down very clearly.
>
> [Female, Ph.D., 30 years practice]

Related to this last group of responses is that of developing the relationship with the patient.

First of all, to develop an alliance with the patient, and help the patient feel safe, and help the patient work within the process.

[Female, M.S.W., 15 years practice]

The first task always is to develop that relationship, and that takes anywhere from a fairly short period of time to a very long period of time, sometimes as much as a year or more.

[Male, M.S.W., 15 years practice]

To observe the difficulties in creating a positive relationship, which may stem from either the patient's past or one's own past, and to try to interpret them, to try to eradicate them, to try to bypass them if necessary, in order to create communication that is actually positive and affirming and healthy on both sides.

[Male, M.S.W., 25 years practice]

Another group, primarily psychoanalytic therapists, said the main task is to interpret the meaning of the patient's behavior and communications and to deal with the transference and countertransference.

To clarify what the issues are. A patient will come in and summarize his or her experience and give you his or her interpretation of what's gone on. But that leaves the therapist completely in the dark. All you know is what the patient thinks, but that is colored by his own characterological drives and needs. So how do we open up the events and experiences in the person's life so that he or she can encounter what's really going on?

[Female, M.S.W., 5 years practice]

I think there are four phases to therapy: the first is to listen; the second is to think about what you're hearing; the third is when you think you understand what you're hearing to share it with the patient via an interpretation; and the fourth phase is to listen to the patient's reaction to the interpretation. And start the cycle all over again.

[Male, Ph.D., 40 years practice]

The tasks are fairly clear: to try to help the patient develop a situation with the therapist that they can both see something that is going on within them, and then to be able to look at it and come to some sort of mutual understanding as to what's going on, what factors are going into it. I would ask questions, I would suggest possible motivations and meanings, explanations, otherwise known as interpretations, both genetic and dynamic.

[Male, M.D., 20 years practice]

Helping the patient get a different perspective on their behavior. By pointing out what I see. They talk and reveal certain things, and I interpret it.

[Female, M.A., 15 years practice]

To be hearing the patient with an understanding of how what they're saying indicates pain and defense against pain, anxiety and defense against anxiety. Then, to begin to introduce at some point, which could be two sessions or two years, your understanding of the pain in a way that feels like an assistance, and to help them stay with that, and feel safe enough to tolerate it and work through it.

[Male, M.S.W., 15 years practice]

To be alert and aware of the how and when of transference, and to examine and scrutinize the behavior of the patient within the sessions. And to also look very seriously at the outcome of that transference in real-life situations, and see how it bears on the functioning of the patient in life. The scrutiny needs to be given to both: the work that's done within the office, and what happens outside.

[Male, Ph.D., 30 years practice]

You want to get a person thinking about what makes them tick, without imposing a theoretical model on them. I'm interested in understanding how earlier life experiences create particular conflicts, which later become persistent bugbears for the person dealing with later relational issues. So from a technical point of view, I'll be encouraging the patient to address those kinds of issues and look at them. Now, lots of patients can't do that, but that's another question. I'm trying to help the patient think about how early life experiences affect the way that they deal with their life now. At another level, however, that material is present and evident in the nature of the relationship with the therapist, so I'm also trying to encourage some awareness that there's a transference, and to interpret whatever needs interpreting.

[Male, M.D., 15 years practice]

To make the unconscious conscious. To show the patient how his mind works.

[Male, M.S.W., 35 years practice]

Another group, primarily (but not exclusively) the behaviorally oriented therapists, described the tasks as having to do with goals, or with showing new choices and options.

I want to help the patient define what they want from treatment, in my case, in fairly operationalizable terms. In short, to set goals regarding change, and then help the patient to achieve the change. I see it as a contractual relationship: you tell me what you want different in your life, and I'll try to help you get there.

[Male, Ph.D., 20 years practice]

I try to help the person who's come in to recognize that they have choices about how they can live their lives that they haven't considered before. Sometimes the choices are very obvious.

[Female, M.A., 20 years practice]

With all clients, their judgment is impaired, so I try cognitively and emotionally and psychodynamically to clear up any problems in judgment so they can make accurate assessments of themselves and other people and situations. If they can do that, then they can make a plan.

[Female, M.S.W., 15 years practice]

Education is the first part, to teach them where we're going to go from here, how it's going to work. Then the task is gradually to make interpretations, and most of all to help them understand that they have choices in life, that they don't have to do it the way they've always done it.

[Female, M.S.W., 10 years practice]

Another cluster of responses related to the need for the therapist to be well trained, and to make accurate diagnoses and evaluations of the patient.

There was a time when you could be a psychotherapist, and you didn't have to know a lot about biology, or medical stuff, and only had to know your own school of thought. The task of the therapist now is to be fairly well-informed about the variables, to know when to refer to a medical person, to know when to pay more attention to cognitive functioning than to conflict, to know about development. Therapists have to recognize that even well-meaning, well-educated people have to think about boundaries, that there are lots of situations to be aware of countertransference issues, where you don't even see that you're headed into trouble.

[Female, M.D., 15 years practice]

To discern, diagnose, as quickly as possible, what the patient needs, and to find a way of supplying it.

[Female, M.S., 20 years practice]

> To be well trained, number one. To be constantly growing in their profession.
>
> [Male, M.D., 5 years practice]

> It's not enough to be a nice person, you have to be skilled.
>
> [Male, Ph.D., 10 years practice]

And to be patient and compassionate, consistent and dependable, honest and ethical.

> To be responsible, and reliable, and ethical, and skilled. If you aren't familiar with the issues that the person brings to you, you have an obligation to learn about them. Compassion, skills, techniques.
>
> [Female, M.S.W., 10 years practice]

> To have patience and not to rush. To be gentle, caring, intelligent.
>
> [Female, M.S.W., 20 years practice]

A number of people said that an important task is to keep the therapist's own issues from contaminating the treatment, and to manage counter-transferential reactions.

> I think we all have to work pretty hard to keep our own lives out of the session, and to keep the treatment as uncontaminated as we can in terms of our own needs and images of ourselves that we don't want wrecked.
>
> [Female, M.S.W., 20 years practice]

> First, you have to know yourself very well, and you have to know when it's your issue and not theirs. Second is that money shouldn't come first. If money comes first, this isn't the right profession for you. If you start seeing people for a half hour back to back, one after the other, and you're tired and you're not listening to them, go into business—this isn't the field for you. I don't know how many hours you can really listen to someone back to back. You're there to help them, and that has to stay very clear.
>
> [Female, Ph.D., 10 years practice]

> I believe in the importance of saying the thing that it frightens you to say as a therapist. When I train therapists, I tell them when you feel the increased pressure of your back against the chair, it's a good kinesthetic cue that you're leaning back from something you probably

need to lean into and confront and deal with. Just like with downhill skiing, if you're scared and you lean back, you'll wind up on your ass, and if you lean into the fall, you gain control. It's the same principle.

[Male, Ph.D., 25 years practice]

NUMERICAL DISTRIBUTION

This is hard to quantify, because almost everyone mentioned several things. Fourteen people said "to be present"; 12 emphasized "listening"; 11 said "interpretation"; 10 said "to empathize" or "to be compassionate"; 10 mentioned patience and neutrality; 9 said to be skilled or well trained; 7 said to understand; 7 emphasized consistency and dependability; 5 said to show choices; 4 said to develop the relationship; 3 said to confront and challenge; 3 said to be honest; 3 said to be ethical; 2 said to be a role model; 2 said to educate; 2 said to diagnose; 2 said to use your own reactions as a vehicle for understanding; 1 said to be flexible; 1 said to define the goals of treatment.

COMMENTS

The issue here is: What is the therapist supposed to be doing in effective treatment? The answers to this question are contingent on how the previous question is answered: Our views of the tasks of the therapist depend on our conceptualizations of the significant dimensions of treatment.

A supervisor early in my training said that one of our most important tasks was to challenge the patient's assumptions, and I have come to believe that this may be the most important one. Obviously, it's important to understand and convey that understanding to the patient, and to be empathic and accepting, and to be nonjudgmental. All of these behaviors may in fact be challenging the assumptions of the patient, if the patient assumes that no one will ever understand or that they will never be safe enough to talk freely. But I still believe that questioning what someone else takes as obvious may be the most useful thing I can do.

RELATED READING

Finke, J. (1990). Can psychotherapeutic competence be taught? *Psychotherapy and Psychosomatics* 53(1–4):64–67.

Hill, C. E., and O'Grady, K. E. (1985). List of therapist intentions illustrated in a case study and with therapists of varying theoretical orientations. *Journal of Counseling Psychology* 32(1):3–22.

Llewelyn, S. P. (1988). Psychological therapy as viewed by clients and therapists. *British Journal of Clinical Psychology* 27(3):223–237.

Marziali, E. (1984). Three viewpoints on the therapeutic alliance: similarities, differences, and associations with psychotherapy outcome. *Journal of Nervous and Mental Disease* 172(7):417–423.

℞℞℞℞

*Question 55: When you listen to the patient, what specifically are you
listening for?*

Depending on his or her theoretical orientation, the therapist may listen
for different kinds of material, emphasizing certain elements and ignoring others.

The largest group of therapists said they listen for feelings.

> Mostly feeling. When they laugh where they ought to cry, or cry where
> they ought to laugh. What are they telling me, and what are they not
> telling me.
>
> [Male, M.S.W., 15 years practice]

> Feelings. Part of my orientation is that feelings inspire all behavior,
> therefore any expression which is a guide to understanding it is how
> a person feels.
>
> [Male, Ph.D., 25 years practice]

The second-largest group of therapists said they listen primarily for
content, for the specific facts and features of what the patient is saying,
and their meaning.

> I'm listening to hear events that I can open up to real exploration. In
> order for me to understand why the client is bringing things up in the
> first place, I have to be able to imagine the whole interaction.
>
> [Female, M.S.W., 5 years practice]

> I look mainly for meaning. I translate a communication into not only its
> literal form, but the source of it, and the meaning has to be understood
> in terms of fundamental characteristics and patterns that the patient has
> displayed from early on in life to their current situation. When those
> patterns are obvious and transparent, they have a certain meaning, and
> the timing is important, when that is shared with the patient.
>
> [Male, Ph.D., 30 years practice]

One person suggested that there may be a problem listening for content.

> Patients are always wanting you to get involved in content, and some-
> times it's a real struggle to convince them that it's not going to get us
> anywhere.
>
> [Female, M.A., 15 years practice]

Another group said they listen primarily for themes, for recurring patterns.

> For themes that recur, for something that resonates with my own
> preconscious/unconscious and intellectual understandings of what
> might be important to the patient.
>
> [Male, M.S.W., 20 years practice]

> I'm listening for themes, and how someone uses language, their
> internal language, so I'm always listening for patterns, repeated
> patterns, metaphors, code words.
>
> [Female, Ph.D., 5 years practice]

> I listen for themes, more than anything, for connections to past and
> present events. Someone said that doing crossword puzzles was one
> of the best ways of training to be a therapist, and what that means is
> that you get remote associations.
>
> [Male, Ph.D., 40 years practice]

> Over time, I'm listening for patterns, of thinking and behavior. If I look
> over time, it can help them to piece things together.
>
> [Female, M.S.W., 5 years practice]

The next group said they listen for unconscious material, issues and
conflicts not directly expressed but implied by the conscious content.

> I'm listening for the unconscious material. Are they too quick to say
> they're not angry about something? Or that they *are* angry about
> something?
>
> [Female, M.S.W., 10 years practice]

> For what they don't know they're saying. I'm always reading between
> the lines and making the connections.
>
> [Female, M.A., 20 years practice]

> I'm listening for what's not said, what's between the lines.
>
> [Female, M.S.W., 20 years practice]

All the verbal and nonverbal cues to what's going on with that person at the moment. What a person is saying at the moment is often not what's going on. You have to try to get beneath that, and help the person get beneath that.

[Male, M.D., 5 years practice]

I listen for what are the essential conflicts, what are the unconscious conflicts that determine the manifest behaviors and problems that the patient is having, with an understanding that many if not all of them probably originate in childhood, and some in experiences that were not verbalized or verbalizable, yet are finding expression in current events. I listen for the unconscious conflicts that are still actively operating.

[Male, M.D., 20 years practice]

Another group said they listen primarily for references to the therapist and the treatment.

Often, it's stuff about what's going on between the patient and me, and what's going well, what if anything I've done wrong. Where is the anger, where is the sadness, stuff like that.

[Female, M.S.W., 20 years practice]

The main thing is the development of the relationship and how we both act with each other. I'm listening for trust. I'm listening for references to the treatment.

[Female, M.A., 20 years practice]

References to me and to treatment, explicit or implicit, disguised material.

[Female, M.A., 15 years practice]

I listen a lot for references to me. If what they're saying about what their friend did might have anything to do with something I've done.

[Female, M.S., 15 years practice]

Who and where are they placing me in the realm of their social contexts and social contacts. And what their fantasies are about the therapy.

[Female, M.S.W., 10 years practice]

Some people said they pay the most attention to their own reactions to whatever the patient is discussing.

What I listen for most with everyone is my reaction to them, and that ends up being the most important thing. I obviously talk about their content, but my reactions are much more important. Am I involved, or am I distant? What is it that's happening that's making me be that way?

[Male, Ph.D., 20 years practice]

I don't do it like that. Whatever comes in, I hear. I hear it on many different levels: in terms of transference, and in terms of my own feelings.

[Female, M.S.W., 45 years practice]

Behaviorally oriented therapists tend to listen more concretely than psychodynamic therapists.

The pain, and their sense of responsibility for their lives, for how they've created whatever it is they're complaining about. So that then I can have some leverage in pointing out to them the consequences of their not changing, and also put them in the direction to remove the pain.

[Male, Ph.D., 25 years practice]

I listen for problems in judgment. That includes cognitive and emotional. Impaired, faulty beliefs.

[Female, M.S.W., 15 years practice]

What do they want help with? Not what I think they should change. What they want comes first, and if I think that's something I can help them with, that's what we're working on. If I can't help them, then I should help them find someone who can.

[Female, Ph.D., 10 years practice]

I probably tend to focus in on trying to take the concepts that they're talking about, and define them in operational or behavioral terms. I'm listening for desire for change, motivation, but really a focus on what do you want to be different about your life? And if after two or three sessions I can't make it fit my mold, I might then refer them to a more psychodynamically oriented therapist.

[Male, Ph.D., 20 years practice]

I listen for what's troubling them, what they want to change, what they're contributing to this dilemma that they're not aware of.

[Female, M.S., 15 years practice]

A number of people said that how they listen depends on how they see the patient.

> It depends on who the patient is, and where they are developmentally. With a lot of patients, I'm listening for the child.
>
> [Female, M.S., 20 years practice]

> That varies partly by the diagnosis, partly by the goals. Sometimes you listen for the unconscious material exclusively, and sometimes you're being very literal and listening to the actual content.
>
> [Male, M.S.W., 25 years practice]

Others said that the most significant thing for them was the relationship between the different elements of the patient's communications, most of all the discrepancy between cognitive and affective aspects.

> I don't only listen to what the patient's saying, I also listen to what the patient's not saying. I observe how they posture themselves, how somebody phrases something. A person can be saying one thing verbally and another thing nonverbally. I'm trying to cut beneath what the person is saying.
>
> [Male, Ph.D., 10 years practice]

> I'm listening for fragmentation. I'm listening for the difference between the behavior, the feelings, and the verbalizations.
>
> [Female, Ph.D., 30 years practice]

> I'm listening to what they're not saying, and where they may be discrepant between what they're saying and how they're acting. Like if they say they're not having trouble with the therapy, but they're always coming late or rescheduling a lot or just not having much to say.
>
> [Female, M.S.W., 20 years practice]

Some people gave unique and individual responses to this question.

> I'm listening for creative experience. I'm listening for something I can hear that says, "Aha!" I listen for the light to go on.
>
> [Male, Ph.D., 10 years practice]

> I listen for the level of damage. For danger signals, like suicidal stuff. I listen for whether they have childhood amnesia, gaps in their memory. I listen for bigotry, because that also tells me about damage.
>
> [Female, M.S.W., 25 years practice]

I'm listening for five things in every session: past life, present life, dreams, sexual thoughts and feelings, and thoughts about the analyst. So I'm listening to see how many of those come up, and how they come up.

[Female, Ph.D., 20 years practice]

Several people said they don't listen for anything in particular.

I'm not listening to anything. I'm just letting the patient talk, and I know that as he talks he will be attracted to certain themes, and these are the knots in his life. And he'll keep going back to them and he will naturally unravel them if I just give him a supportive space to do that in.

[Male, Ph.D., 15 years practice]

On one hand, nothing in particular, and then suddenly something will catch my attention. Something dissonant, a discrepancy, something that emerges.

[Male, Ph.D., 20 years practice]

I'm not listening for anything in particular. I'm trying to understand what the patient is trying to communicate to me.

[Male, Ph.D., 50 years practice]

I'm not specifically listening for anything. I'm listening for what is it this patient is trying to tell me that has something to do with what's making them miserable.

[Male, M.D., 20 years practice]

I listen for everything. Not only do you listen to the words, you listen to the tune. There was a time when I was listening only for what I was familiar with, and I missed too much.

[Male, M.S.W., 35 years practice]

NUMERICAL DISTRIBUTION

(A number of people gave more than one response.) Twenty-five people said they listen mainly for feelings; 18 said they listen for content; 12 said for themes and patterns; 9 said for unconscious material; 8 said for references to the treatment or the therapist; 4 said for goals and motivations; 4 said for conflict; 3 said anxiety; 3 said transference; 2 said resistance or defenses; 2 said their own reactions or countertransference; 1 said for something new. Five people said they don't listen for anything in particular.

COMMENTS

Again, the answers to this question depend on the way the therapist conceptualizes effective treatment, and on what he or she believes is significant in the process.

As I said in Question 36, I believe that the central part of the work in therapy takes place in the relationship between the patient and me. Therefore, I listen most of all for encoded references to me and my behavior, and to my impact on the patient, things the patient may not be able to tell me directly. Secondarily, I'm also listening for contradictions and inconsistencies that may reveal an internal conflict, which will tell me where the patient gets stuck.

RELATED READING

Blau, T. H. (1988). *Psychotherapy Tradecraft: The Technique and Style of Doing Therapy.* New York: Brunner/Mazel.

Chessick, R. D. (1989). *The Technique and Practice of Listening in Intensive Psychotherapy.* Northvale, NJ: Jason Aronson.

Chrzanowski, G. (1980). Reciprocal aspects of psychoanalytic listening. *Contemporary Psychoanalysis* 16(2):145–156.

Scharff, J. S., and Scharff, D. E. (1992). *Scharff Notes: A Primer of Object Relations Therapy.* Northvale, NJ: Jason Aronson.

Usher, S. F. (1993). *Introduction to Psychodynamic Psychotherapy Technique.* Madison, CT: International Universities Press.

Watts, F. N. (1989). Listening processes in psychotherapy. In *Psychotherapy. Directions in Psychiatry Monograph Series*, vol. 5, ed. F. Flach, pp. 114–124. New York: Norton.

▧▧▧▧

Question 56: What is the significance of insight?

One of the premises of psychoanalytic theory is that insight is crucial to personality change, while behavior therapy suggests that insight is irrelevant to changes in behavior. How do our therapists see insight functioning in the therapy they do now?

Almost half the group said that insight was very important, or even crucial, in the process of therapy.

Insight is absolutely crucial. Without insight, there's no therapy. People define insight differently. I think some therapists call awareness insight.

It's when you're not just appreciating it intellectually, but emotionally too.

[Male, Ph.D., 10 years practice]

If the patient doesn't have insight, then I don't have a patient. I don't think I can work with somebody who doesn't show some insight. I think some people who don't have it initially can develop it, but some of them won't.

[Female, M.S.W., 5 years practice]

It's crucial. It's the key. When it happens, it's what liberates people.

[Female, M.A., 20 years practice]

If you're not going to work in a behavioral way, insight really is everything. It's an unbelievably beautiful thing when somebody begins to understand. It has at times brought me the verge of tears.

[Female, M.S.W., 10 years practice]

When the patient feels and understands and sees the connections between what they're talking about in the moment and with the past and other similar feelings and thoughts, then that has a very organizing effect.

[Female, Ph.D., 15 years practice]

It's extremely valuable. I have a lot of patients who have no insight, and therefore we have very little productivity in our sessions.

[Male, M.S.W., 15 years practice]

Even those therapists working in a behavioral framework can see insight as important.

It's important in treatment of anxiety disorders, as well as with others. Because anxiety symptoms don't come out of the blue, they're not genetic, they're due to catastrophic thinking, and you need to understand why you as a person have that way of thinking and behaving.

[Female, Ph.D., 10 years practice]

And even a therapist who recognizes that insight doesn't always lead to change can see it as extremely important.

That's what I'm hoping to develop in the patient. That's the ballgame, the key thing that they will learn about themselves. The problem often is the translation of that insight into changes in real life. That step is the most difficult step in therapy. But insight is still the central product that we're trying to develop.

[Male, M.D., 20 years practice]

A group almost equally large said that insight was only somewhat important in therapy and that other factors were as important, or more so, in creating change.

Insight becomes a beacon, a light, but insight without behavior change is pointless. But it becomes a light, this is where that comes from, this is why that happens, now what do you want to do about it?

[Male, M.S.W., 15 years practice]

I think it's important. I don't think it's necessary for change. You can have a lot of insight about why and what causes it, but it doesn't necessarily lead to change. Change can lead to insight sometimes. It's not the major goal for me.

[Female, Ph.D., 5 years practice]

Insight is meaningless if you just leave it on the table, and don't look at how you're going to use this new information.

[Female, M.S.W., 10 years practice]

Other therapists emphasized the emotional aspect of insight, as opposed to intellectual understanding.

It's useful to the degree that it's emotional insight, not just intellectual. It doesn't make a damn bit of difference what they understand if they don't feel it and go through what it means to them on a gut level. And that can change a person's view of the world, or of themselves.

[Male, M.S.W., 20 years practice]

People feel very good when they get insight, so it has to be valuable. The cognitive is important. It's not the whole thing, and if insight is only cognitive it's very limited. But the kind of feeling of, "That's right, and it makes sense, it feels right," that's very powerful.

[Female, M.S.W., 30 years practice]

It's important, but without other things it's not change-inducing. Because it's too grounded in intellect, and intellectual experiences aren't the change-inducing agents.

[Female, M.S.W., 15 years practice]

A true insight combines the intellect and the feelings. They can have one or the other at different points, but when they put it together, it has so much meaning. Operationally, it can help alter attitudes, and that may change some behavior.

[Male, Ph.D., 15 years practice]

Several people suggested that change precedes insight, not the other way around.

It's crucial, but it generally comes after change has occurred, or in the process of occurring. By examining, by all kinds of interventions on this level, things begin to change inside. And when that happens, sometimes all of a sudden you see something you haven't seen before. That's very important, and very exciting and stimulating, and it stirs up all kinds of other stuff down there too. But the change precedes the insight.

[Male, Ph.D., 25 years practice]

It's very important, but it's an outcome. It's what the patient gets if the treatment is working, not what leads to the effect.

[Male, Ph.D., 50 years practice]

I don't think it's crucial, but it's helpful. A person can grow and make changes without it. Insight often comes way after the change, often years down the road.

[Male, M.D., 5 years practice]

Another person said that the therapist can't always be sure when and where insight is occurring.

It is important to have the experience of insight, but insight can be very subtle, and we may often miss seeing it in the patient. I often ask at the end of treatment what was the most significant moment or experience in the course of the treatment, and I have my own ideas about that, and patients will very often mention something that would never occur to me as so important.

[Male, Ph.D., 20 years practice]

Several people said that insight was not very important in treatment.

I'm mixed on it, because I don't think it's crucial at all. I've seen people in therapy for twenty-five years, three times a week in analytic therapy, with all the insight in the world, and they're nuts, and they don't change their behavior. Insight is helpful, particularly for people who think intellectually. Sometimes people have to understand in order to make changes. The way I work is I push change, and I believe people are happiest and most productive when they change their lives, and not just when they understand. I've also worked strategically in family therapy, where insight is totally irrelevant, and sometimes I find that you can help people to get to another point without insight, and that's fine.

[Female, Ph.D., 20 years practice]

It's sometimes overrated. People are learning something about what they're doing, but I don't know that it produces change.

[Female, M.A., 15 years practice]

I don't think it's a big deal.

[Female, M.S., 20 years practice]

Minor. Where it's important at all, it's a first step. But people have to change, and they have to be willing to change, and it's part of our job to encourage that process.

[Female, M.S., 20 years practice]

It's a first step. It doesn't always lead to anything.

[Female, M.A., 15 years practice]

NUMERICAL DISTRIBUTION

Twenty-nine people said insight was crucial or very important; 24 said it was only somewhat important, especially if it did not lead to change; 7 people said it was not important.

COMMENTS

The issues here are: What does "insight" mean? How necessary is it for effective treatment? Does it or does it not lead to change?

I think it's hard for someone to change behavior without some insight into what drives it in the first place. So it's necessary but not sufficient, because insight alone doesn't create change. People usually have to make a conscious choice, at least for the first few hundred times, to do something differently.

RELATED READING

Appelbaum, S. A. (1976). The dangerous edge of insight. *Psychotherapy: Theory, Research, and Practice* 13(3):202–206.

Baranger, M., and Baranger, W. (1966). Insight in the psychoanalytic situation. In *Psychoanalysis in the Americas,* ed. R. Litman, pp. 56–72. New York: International Universities Press.

Bloom, P. B. (1994). Is insight necessary for successful treatment? *American Journal of Clinical Hypnosis* 36(3):172–174.

Munson, E. (1975). Insight versus feeling. *Journal of Primal Therapy* 2(3):230–238.

Smith, B. L. (1989). The transitional function of insight. In *The Facilitating Environment: Clinical Applications of Winnicott's Theory,* ed. M. G. Fromm and B. L. Smith, pp. 159–178. Madison, CT: International Universities Press.

🔁🔁🔁🔁

Question 57: What does "transference" mean to you?

The concept of transference is the cornerstone of psychoanalysis and psychoanalytic therapy. Freud defined it in his earliest work, and his understanding of it did not change much. How do therapists conceptualize it today?

Many analytically oriented therapists use the classical definition, and find that it still works for them.

> A re-experiencing, currently with the therapist, those issues that are important in your central previous relationships. It's universal, and there's not more in the relationship with the therapist, it's just that we focus on the transference, we want to understand it.
>
> [Male, M.D., 20 years practice]

> That the patient sees me as some figure in their life, and attributes to me characteristics based on that figure.
>
> [Male, Ph.D., 15 years practice]

> I still have a pretty classical concept. It's the configuration of internalized experiences, objects, and representations that gets translated into the therapeutic relationship. Except in certain instances, such as psychotic transferences, it's not pure, but is sort of clouded.
>
> [Female, M.D., 15 years practice]

It's the classical meaning: to transfer onto the present situation emotional and cognitive elements from the past.

[Male, Ph.D., 50 years practice]

Kohut and the self psychologists defined the concept in a somewhat different way.

In the self-psychological model, there are different kinds of transference. It's what function you serve for the person, which can be a clue to what was missing in their earlier experience. It can also be a replay of what happened earlier.

[Female, M.S., 15 years practice]

We all have transference reactions to everyone in the world, and we reenact our early relationships with our parents. Maybe it's the wish to get something that was missing in early childhood, the wish that our partners, our friends, our co-workers would see us in a certain way. Or wishing for some appreciation. Something that was missing in childhood.

[Female, M.S.W., 15 years practice]

Others have also refined, expanded, or modified the original definition.

It can mean that the person is taking on aspects of me, wanting to incorporate a piece of me, become a part of me, to merge in some way.

[Female, Ph.D., 30 years practice]

Everything that the patient feels with the therapist. It's manifestation of how they are with all of their object relations.

[Male, M.S.W., 15 years practice]

It's responding to me the way the patient has allowed himself to respond to other people. The rigidity of the response is the transference.

[Female, M.S.W., 20 years practice]

I used to think it was the projection of early object relations on to the therapist. There's more to it than that. The projection isn't just about a past relationship, it's a continuation of that past relationship in the patient's fantasy and imagination. So that frequently, in one sense, it's happening with you.

[Male, M.S.W., 25 years practice]

It's where a lot of the life of the therapy is. It's all the projections onto me from the patient, every feeling that they have based on history, all kinds of things converging in the moment in the session.

[Female, M.S., 15 years practice]

Some therapists emphasize the distortion that transference implies, that the patient is not experiencing the therapist accurately.

It's the ideas and fantasies that the patient has about me that are not accurate, that are the product of certain kinds of fantasies that the person has about what the world is, and that are based upon certain kinds of early experiences.

[Male, M.D., 15 years practice]

The person bestows on the therapist symbolic meaning above and beyond the reality of his person.

[Male, Ph.D., 30 years practice]

A repetition from the past in the present. It's a means of establishing with the therapist an important connection with an object from the past in the present. It's a distortion.

[Male, Ph.D., 20 years practice]

My experience of transference is that it's not personal. I don't have a sense of the person really transferring onto me and getting into a transference neurosis. When a person gets into a transference neurosis, that's more of a psychotic state to me than a neurotic state. . . . All their crazy beliefs come out. . . . I don't believe it's a transference neurosis about me. Maybe if I worked with the person five days a week like Freud did, I would. Maybe he drove them crazy by doing that.

[Male, Ph.D., 25 years practice]

Some other therapists question the idea of distortion inherent in the idea of transference.

It's not a distortion, to my mind, it's a further development of a relationship, and these developments are constantly happening. In therapy, it's a second chance to relive some of the feelings. It's continuity that can be worked with.

[Male, Ph.D., 40 years practice]

Responses generally were fairly consistent, including the patient's history and the projections onto the therapist.

It's the place of projections. It's an opportunity for me to experience who the important figures in the patient's past were. I get to be these things as they're projected onto me.

[Female, M.S.W., 20 years practice]

That the patient develops an emotional reaction to the therapist predicated on the patient's original emotional reactions to the parents. The term has become so broad lately that it means anything the patient feels toward the therapist.

[Male, M.S.W., 35 years practice]

When somebody's taking an earlier experience, and bringing some of those same emotional feelings into the room and playing them out with the therapist in some way.

[Female, M.S.W., 20 years practice]

It's a very helpful tool. I think of it as what reenactments a client is having in the therapeutic relationship, what's being repeated, and the phenomenon of them working it out with me, using me to reenact that, ideally in a positive way this time.

[Male, M.S.W., 15 years practice]

Several people stated that transference occurs in all relationships, not only with the therapist. The difference is that in the relationship with the therapist, transference phenomena get discussed and understood.

It means bringing something from the past into the present, and it happens in all relationships and not just in therapy.

[Female, M.S., 20 years practice]

Transference is bringing your life experience into a relationship, and it happens in all relationships. The value of it happening in the psychotherapeutic relationship is that it happens with the understanding that it's happening, and the therapist has the insight to see it as something that reflects the patient's inner life and experience. So it becomes useful, whereas in other kinds of relationships it may not be useful.

[Female, M.S.W., 15 years practice]

A number of therapists said that they didn't work much, or even not at all, with transference and its manifestations.

Transference is everything and everywhere. I don't think of it anymore when I work.

[Male, Ph.D., 10 years practice]

I differ with the psychoanalysts in that I don't see that as the place to work. I'd rather use natural transference in their primary relationships as the alternative.

[Male, Ph.D., 25 years practice]

Yet even a behavioral therapist, who does little work with transference per se, may find it useful.

It's what people do all the time. They have strong reactions to people because they remind them of people who have influenced them in the past. People with anxiety disorders often see the therapist as a parent, and they can depend on you, and they trust you, and at the beginning of therapy that can be very helpful. The transference is that I'm somehow going to keep them from having a panic attack or I'm going to take care of them. Eventually, I'm going to teach them how to soothe themselves, but at the beginning, if you want to see me as someone who can do that, that's fine.

[Female, Ph.D., 10 years practice]

NUMERICAL DISTRIBUTION

Fifty-three people gave a fairly traditional definition of transference as a repetition of past relationships in the present with the therapist. Three others use the self psychology definitions. Four people said they don't work with transference and declined to define it.

COMMENTS

The issue here is: What is transference distortion and what is real perception? How do we distinguish one from the other?

The concept of transference, to my mind, implies a distortion of reality and of experience. If therapists start with that assumption, it may be difficult to see the ways in which they are very much like the earlier figures in the patient's life. I think it's much more useful to regard transference as the spin a patient puts on the therapist's behavior. There's always some reality to the perception, but it's filtered through the particular prism of that individual and his or her history. I think it's necessary to acknowledge the reality before moving on to the exaggeration or distortion.

I know from my own experience that the therapist is not perfect or unimpeachable, and so I try to find the truth in what patients are seeing and saying, and acknowledge it, and not automatically dismiss it as a transference distortion.

RELATED READING

Bauer, G. P. (1994). *Essential Papers on Transference Analysis*. Northvale, NJ: Jason Aronson.

Bird, B. (1972). Notes on transference: universal phenomenon and hardest part of analysis. *Journal of the American Psychoanalytic Association* 20:267–301.

Gill, M. M. (1982). *Analysis of Transference*, Vol. 1. New York: International Universities Press.

Zetzel, E. (1956). Current concepts of transference. *International Journal of Psycho-Analysis* 37:369–376.

ಔಔಔಔ

Question 58: What does "resistance" mean to you?

Another basic concept of almost all psychotherapies, resistance classically meant the patient's refusal or inability to follow the basic rule of free association and was seen as essentially an unconscious process. Today, it also appears to include any hesitation on the part of the patient to follow the directions of the therapist, and it is regarded as more conscious.

The majority of our group saw resistance as a healthy and positive response of the patient, one that needs to be respected and accepted, and emphasized the protective and constructive purposes of resistance.

> A very healthy way of defending against things that are scary. I don't think it's an obstacle at all. I think you have to find ways of helping the patient to use it and understand it. It's not a negative thing at all to me.
>
> [Female, M.S., 20 years practice]

> Resistance is always in the service of trying to protect themselves. It's not a bad thing. When it happens, I try to understand where the person's sense of self is threatened.
>
> [Female, M.S., 15 years practice]

> Resistance is a way of keeping things in check so the person doesn't get flooded, so I feel very respectful of resistance when I see it. The patient's giving me a message that things are going too fast.
>
> [Female, M.S., 15 years practice]

> I think it means just not wanting to do something, not wanting to think of something or feel something, and that can be in relation to me, or

in coming, or in life outside. Sometimes I think that people who've just done a lot of powerful work in therapy will then put up some walls and say, "No more." I understand and encourage that. I think people need to take breaks from therapy, and come back when they're ready to go to work again.

[Male, M.S.W., 15 years practice]

Some respondents saw resistance as more of a problem than an asset.

Resistance is the problem. It's the only problem we're treating, because resistance is character, resistance is knowledge and belief and values. Resistance has to do with the repetition compulsion, which is staying the same, resisting change. The whole endeavor is to produce a change. The opposite of resistance is change. Therapy is to produce change, so it has to resolve resistance.

[Male, Ph.D., 50 years practice]

Anything that the patient is doing that interferes with the therapy process.

[Male, Ph.D., 15 years practice]

Everything that opposes the fundamental rule, which is to share with me whatever comes into your mind.

[Male, Ph.D., 20 years practice]

An avoidance of developing insight or developing a transference.

[Male, M.S.W., 20 years practice]

Those forces in the patient that are operating against the coming into consciousness of the fantasies that are underlying the transference.

[Male, M.D., 15 years practice]

There are certain people who really seem to not want to engage in the work as I see it. I'm not sure how much of it has to do with them and me, and how much to do with how painful it is for them to move out of a certain psychological set. It's hard to say where it comes from, but what it feels like is that the patient doesn't want to engage in the work.

[Male, Ph.D., 5 years practice]

I would tend to see it more as non-compliance.

[Male, Ph.D., 20 years practice]

One therapist explained at length how she had changed her thinking about this concept.

> My thinking on resistance has been changing from a classical concept of resistance being an internal maneuver to ward off unpleasant affects, or awareness of information, to assert control, to now as a demonstration of something that's not being taken care of before you get to what you need to get to. I see it as a message to the therapist to wait a minute, that there's something that needs to be done before it feels safe. It's the patient teaching me how to do my job.
>
> [Female, M.D., 15 years practice]

A number of people emphasized the fear and anxiety behind resistant behavior.

> A normal experience in which the various fears and anxieties of the patient become in some way enacted between two people. It's a normal response to an experience which is perceived as having threats in it.
>
> [Female, M.S.W., 15 years practice]

> It's fear. Resistance is healthy, and I try to go with it.
>
> [Female, M.S., 15 years practice]

> It means to me that the patient is frightened about something: a feeling, a thought. Sometimes it's a way of asserting themselves.
>
> [Female, M.S.W., 20 years practice]

And some emphasized the ambivalence about change.

> It's the patient wanting to get better but fighting tooth and nail not to make any changes.
>
> [Male, M.S.W., 10 years practice]

> The patient's having fears about his movement, in terms of his awareness, in terms of his growth, and it's almost a reasonable, rational attempt on his part to slow down or stop the very thing he has come into treatment for.
>
> [Male, Ph.D., 30 years practice]

> Usually it means that they're trying to do the therapy and another part of them is trying not to do the therapy. Like the patient forgets the

appointment, and says that they really did want to come. Well, they did, but part of them didn't want to come.

[Female, M.S.W., 15 years practice]

One person emphasized the communicative aspects of resistance.

It's the experience of some block in communication. There's some kind of misunderstanding, a block of the free flow of the relationship. Recently, I find less and less resistance. If you and the patient are really in tune with each other, it's not the big problem that you think it's going to be.

[Male, M.S.W., 25 years practice]

Several people objected to the concept and the term.

I hate the word, because I think it's overused, and accusatory, and judgmental. Sometimes people steer away from certain things because those things are not what's most important to them right now, and it doesn't have to do with not wanting to deal with those things, but with feeling directed and taken away from what's more vital to their interest right now.

[Female, M.S.W., 20 years practice]

I think it's a term that's convenient for therapists, about someone who may be approachable by another therapist or another style of therapy. It's someone saying, "I'm not ready to trust who I am with who you are."

[Male, Ph.D., 40 years practice]

I don't like the word, because it sounds kind of pejorative. You're bad if you're resisting. People develop defenses because they need them in their lives, and you have to respect them. And what we call resistance is probably just someone who's not ready to take the chance of experiencing something without knowing what's coming up next.

[Female, M.S.W., 30 years practice]

I'm uncomfortable with resistance in the psychotherapeutic literature because I see it as the therapist's projection onto the patient of the responsibility for something the therapist should own.

[Male, Ph.D., 25 years practice]

I don't like the term, because it's denigrating to the client, it's disempowering. I prefer "self-protection" and then you help the client understand why they're protecting themselves, where it comes from, and you help them see how smart and clever they are to have come up with their own way of protecting themselves, and that they can do that as long as they need to.

[Female, M.S.W., 15 years practice]

That's what happens when people don't do what they need to do to get better. I think sometimes therapists are obnoxious, and clients have reactions, and it's interpreted as resistance. Therapists need to know what their personalities are and what clients normal reactions to them are. If someone's reacting differently than most people do, then you can start calling it resistance.

[Female, Ph.D., 10 years practice]

NUMERICAL DISTRIBUTION

Twenty therapists defined "resistance" as being self-defense or self-protection; 13 said it was avoidance of insight or awareness; 12 said it was anything that interferes with the process of treatment; and 10 said it was the avoidance of change. Five therapists objected to the term and said that it usually reflected a failure on the part of the therapist.

COMMENTS

Some issues in this area are: Resistance to what? Is it an intrapsychic mechanism or an interpersonal phenomenon? Is it an indicator that the therapist is "on target" or a sign of therapist error?

I think of resistance in psychotherapy as analogous to what the word means in physics, where it refers to electricity flowing in a circuit. Resistors are put in a circuit to modulate and adjust the level of voltage, because certain electrical devices will only work at a specific voltage, and it's often important to prevent an overload that may damage the components. Clinically, resistance is whatever impedes the flow of energy, either within the patient or between them and me, and it often has a similar protective function.

It disturbs me that the word is sometimes used to dismiss the self-protective reactions of a patient to the intrusive or critical interpretations of the therapist, and that the patient is deprecated for refusing the help of the purely benevolent therapist.

RELATED READING

Strean, H. S. (1985). *Resolving Resistances in Psychotherapy*. New York: Wiley and Sons.
Verhulst, J. C., and Van de Vijver, F. J. (1990). Resistance during psycho-therapy and behavior therapy. *Behavior Modification* 14(2):172–187.
Wile, D. (1984). Kohut, Kernberg, and accusatory interpretations. *Psycho-therapy* 21(3):353–364.

🗟🗟🗟🗟

Question 59: What does "countertransference" mean to you?

Originally, countertransference meant the unresolved conflicts of the thera-pist as they come up in response to the patient and the patient's transfer-ence. This definition has been expanded to include much more and now can mean all the responses of the therapist to the patient, including those induced by the patient.

Many therapists still use the classical definition.

When the therapist's conflicts are transferred onto the patient, so the patient represents a figure from the therapist's past, on some level. It always exists. The job of the therapist is to keep it under control, and not allow it be active in the therapy. If a patient is an acting-out patient, then certainly the patient can induce a reaction, an emotional reaction of annoyance, of anxiety. But that's not what I mean by countertrans-ference. I mean something unconscious.

[Male, Ph.D., 40 years practice]

It's when you're having an experience with a patient triggers something in your own history, so that something's tapped your own vulnerability, and your ability to be objective may be compromised at that point.

[Female, M.S.W., 20 years practice]

Whatever stuff I'm doing with the patient that may really be about me, that I may be imposing to or reacting to inappropriately, the feelings they're stirring in me.

[Female, M.A., 15 years practice]

Whatever there is about me that interferes with my hearing what the person's spirit is saying. Sometimes I'll feel defensive, sometimes I'll feel angry, or impatient. They're obvious ways, but I'm sure there are less obvious ways where it takes me a long time to get around to hearing something.

[Male, Ph.D., 25 years practice]

Others use the more inclusive definition.

I think of that in its broadest sense, as including the particular thoughts and feelings that are engendered in the therapist in the work with the patient.

[Female, Ph.D., 15 years practice]

It's my total reaction to what the patient brings up, whether it's my own feelings about what the patient's presented to me, or my associations.

[Male, Ph.D., 20 years practice]

I see it in the global sense. Not just my feelings that have to do with my relationships with my parents, but any emotional response, induced or not.

[Female, M.S.W., 15 years practice]

One person gave a specific example.

I have to be particularly careful with certain clients, when the client is especially resistant, because I was myself such a rebel. I can assume they're acting the way I used to act, and usually that's not the case.

[Male, M.S.W., 15 years practice]

Two people suggested that even when the countertransference comes out of the therapist's personal history, it can still be useful in dealing with the patient.

If I'm having that reaction, then I should take care of that myself. But sometimes if it's interfering with the treatment, I can discuss it. If someone is very, very angry, and I have a reaction where I confuse them with someone from my past and am afraid they're going to hurt me, then I can talk about it. I can say, "You're scaring me. I know what it's like to be a child and be screamed at. I can't work with you if you're scaring me. Let's try to change this interaction."

[Female, Ph.D., 10 years practice]

It's when I get hooked, which happens to all of us. It's so important for us to be aware of our own issues so we don't get hooked, or can understand it when we do and get unhooked. A certain kind of person can hook you in. Sometimes it can actually be positive, like the patient who was like my own child and I grew her up.

[Female, Ph.D., 20 years practice]

Another portion of the group emphasized the induced feelings created somehow by the patient, and the potential value of becoming aware of those feelings and the process that creates them.

Patients induce strong feelings in you, and if you can get a handle on that, which is very hard, you can understand what's going on with the patient.

[Male, M.S.W., 15 years practice]

It's a useful tool. If you start to feel something that you're not comfortable with about your patient, you better look at what's going on with yourself. On the other hand, it can also be that the patient is bringing up something that can be useful diagnostically, an induced reaction.

[Female, M.S.W., 30 years practice]

Most of the therapists answering said they believed that feelings could be induced by the patient. Others said that they did not believe in the notion of induced feelings, and saw that idea as shifting responsibility for the therapist's reactions onto the patient.

I don't believe countertransference can be induced. I have more than enough issues of my own and can have very strong reactions to people. You have to take responsibility for your own feelings.

[Female, Ph.D., 10 years practice]

The idea of "induced" never made a whole lot of sense to me. Either it's there or it isn't.

[Female, M.S.W., 15 years practice]

It takes two to tango. Transferences and countertransferences are a two-way street, and they can be encouraged or discouraged or modified by the other person. Certain patients are more likely to evoke certain patterns in us that are determined by our past.

[Male, M.D., 20 years practice]

A few people emphasized the importance, and the difficulty, of distinguishing personal responses from induced feelings.

One way is how is this patient making me feel, and how can I use that to help them to change? The other way is when there's something unresolved in me. I have to distinguish them, and if I'm having trouble doing that, I bring it up in supervision.

[Female, M.S.W., 20 years practice]

I think there are subjective and objective countertransferences. I can, by maintaining a certain objectivity, separate the subjective from the objective ones, and I find that most of them are objective, and are induced in the relationship with the patient.

[Female, M.S.W., 15 years practice]

NUMERICAL DISTRIBUTION

Forty-two therapists define countertransference as being those responses of the therapist to the patient originating in unresolved personal issues; 14 others said countertransference is all the reactions of the therapist to the patient; 4 others said they don't work with countertransference and didn't define it. Twenty-five people said countertransference could be induced; 5 said it could not.

COMMENTS

Some issues here are: What is the most useful definition of countertransference: unresolved issues in the therapist or all therapist reactions to the patient? Can countertransferential feelings and difficulties be induced by the patient, or must these issues preexist in the therapist?

Countertransference in the broadest sense of the term, that is, all the reactions of the therapist to the patient, is inevitable and necessary. The therapist would have to be totally disengaged to have no reactions to the patient's material. Countertransference is an impediment only if the therapist is unaware of it or fails to see it as a potential resource. I think it's useful and important for the therapist to know his or her usual (in a sense, normal) countertransference patterns, so that, if and when an exception to the normal pattern occurs, the therapist can realize the likelihood that this exceptional reaction is in some way being induced by the patient. Knowing this can give some significant clues to the patient's patterns and psychodynamics.

RELATED READING

Hedges, L. E. (1992). *Interpreting the Countertransference.* Northvale, NJ: Jason Aronson.

Lorion, R. P., and Parron, D. L. (1987). Countering the countertransference: a strategy for treating the untreatable. In *Handbook of Cross-Cultural Counseling and Therapy,* ed. P. Pedersen, pp. 79–86. Westport, CT: Greenwood Press.

Maroda, K. J. (1994). *The Power of Countertransference.* Chichester, England: John Wiley and Sons.

Racker, H. (1968). *Transference and Countertransference.* New York: International Universities Press.

Searles, H. (1965). *Countertransference and Related Subjects.* New York: International Universities Press.

——. (1987). Countertransference as a path to understanding and helping the patient. In *Countertransference,* ed. E. Slakter, pp. 131–163. Northvale, NJ: Jason Aronson.

🐍🐍🐍🐍

Question 60: What is anxiety?

Anxiety is perhaps the most common complaint of new patients: distress, worry, fear of the future. Overwhelming anxiety, in the form of panic attacks, can lead to agoraphobia. But what is anxiety? How do our therapists conceptualize this state?

One portion of our group of therapists emphasized the signal function of anxiety.

> I pretty much agree with Freud's 1926 paper on anxiety, that it's an unconscious perception of a dangerous situation, one which the unconscious ego thinks could be dangerous.
>
> [Male, Ph.D., 40 years practice]

> I define it as a tool of the body telling you something's wrong, real or imagined. It's a body signal saying, "Careful, there's a car heading at you coming down the street." If there really is a car heading at you, then anxiety is a helpful tool. If the car is parked on the side of the road, however, that tool has become dysfunctional.
>
> [Male, M.S.W., 15 years practice]

> It's a signal of danger. It could have to do with a psychic conflict coming to the surface. Some feeling of threat or danger is going on and there are some underlying feelings.
>
> [Male, Ph.D., 15 years practice]

It's an affect which signals some form of danger, so the ego can get prepared. If anxiety is overwhelming, it floods the ego and doesn't serve as a signal but is more annihilating.

[Male, Ph.D., 20 years practice]

Another segment of the group suggested that anxiety is the result of an underlying conflict.

Anxiety is a reflection of conflict, and it's normal. We all have anxiety because we all have various kinds of conflict. In pathological anxiety, there's an inability to understand that, and there's an inability to contain the anxiety.

[Female, M.S.W., 15 years practice]

The fear of the consequences for certain wishes.

[Male, M.D., 20 years practice]

I believe that anxiety is anger turned inward, which is unacceptable, so that the ego erects a symptom or a defense so as not to feel the force of that aggression. So you get a phobia, or a compulsion, a variety of physical symptoms, so you don't feel the unacceptable, almost irresistible, unconscious impulse. Anxiety is a cover-up.

[Female, Ph.D., 20 years practice]

I really believe in the Freudian definition, that it's a conflict between superego and an id impulse.

[Female, M.S.W., 25 years practice]

Anxiety is a signal of some conflict going on on a deeper level, an ambivalence or conflicting feelings.

[Male, Ph.D., 15 years practice]

One person offered a slightly different way of thinking about anxiety.

The person I like most on anxiety is Sullivan. He talks about it in terms of the relationship between the mother and the infant, and the infant picks up on the anxiety. It usually relates to a feeling of being disapproved of, or upsetting somebody, or a generalized feeling that you're bad.

[Female, M.S.W., 5 years practice]

Behavioral therapists tend to emphasize the physiological component.

It's a warning signal. It's somewhat biological, somewhat genetic, to be a high-strung person, and then you add a lot of stress and a lot of maladjustment. It's very common. You have to normalize it at the same time as you say it's a problem.

[Female, Ph.D., 10 years practice]

I would define it in physiological terms. It's the cognitive perception of a dangerous situation, which then translates into a physiological set of events that have to do with sympathetic arousal. I would attack it on both fronts: I would teach the person to control the physiological side of it, and also talk with them about reorganizing the way they think about the particular situation.

[Male, Ph.D., 20 years practice]

NUMERICAL DISTRIBUTION

Nineteen people defined anxiety as simply nervousness or irrational fear; 19 defined it as a signal of danger, actual or imagined; 9 others said it is a signal of internal, usually unconscious, conflict. Thirteen people defined it simply as a physiological response.

COMMENTS

The issues here are: What is the most useful definition of anxiety? Is it normal or pathological? How does the therapist best deal with patient anxiety?

I think that anxiety is like a warning light on a console. It says, "Here comes something dangerous." Of course, some patients are so flooded with anxiety that the light is on all the time and ceases to be of much use. Most people in our culture experience some level of anxiety some of the time, so it is normal in at least the statistical sense. While it seems theoretically possible to live free from anxiety, I doubt that this is a realistic goal for most people, and far more useful would be to learn ways of dealing with anxiety when it arises.

Fritz Perls used to say that anxiety was the gap between the present and the future, that if our attention were focused in the present anxiety would be impossible, and I have found this to be a useful way of thinking about the problem of anxiety. Techniques that focus attention in the present, such as meditation or hypnotic relaxation, are very good at reducing or even eliminating anxiety as a symptom.

RELATED READING

Perls, F., Hefferline, R., and Goodman, P. (1951). *Gestalt Therapy.* New York: Julian Press.

Schafer, R. (1983). *The Analytic Attitude.* New York: Basic Books.

Tuma, A. H., and Maser, J. D., eds. (1985). *Anxiety and the Anxiety Disorders.* Hillsdale, NJ: Lawrence Erlbaum Associates.

⧈⧈⧈⧈

Question 61: What are patients most afraid of in therapy?

Patients arrive in therapy with various worries and fears about the process itself, and these fears may impede the process. Newcomers may have no idea what is expected of them and what they are free to say or do.

The most common response to this question was the fear of intimacy, of getting too close and too dependent.

> They're afraid of what they most need, which is emotional intimacy.
> [Female, M.S.W., 20 years practice]

> Their longings for intimacy, their longings to be taken care of.
> [Male, M.D., 20 years practice]

> Being too close.
> [Female, M.A., 15 years practice]

> That they'll be here forever.
> [Female, M.S.W., 10 years practice]

> Getting too attached, dependency.
> [Male, Ph.D., 15 years practice]

> What they used to say was that they were afraid they were going to care about me too much and never leave therapy. I don't hear that so much any more.
> [Male, M.S.W., 25 years practice]

A corollary fear is that of being swallowed up or controlled by the therapist.

> Expressed or unexpressed is a fear of being taken over by another person. Certainly for patients who have separation issues and where

there's been a lot of enmeshment and symbiotic attachment, that's a very big fear, that the therapist is going to make them into something that they don't want to be, or invade them and take them over.

[Female, M.S.W., 15 years practice]

Losing their identity, losing themselves.

[Male, Ph.D., 50 years practice]

Being too vulnerable, being controlled.

[Male, Ph.D., 25 years practice]

That you're going to make them do things that they don't want to do.

[Male, Ph.D., 20 years practice]

Being too dependent can lead to another fear, that of being then abandoned by the therapist.

That if they really tell the ugly, terrible thoughts and feelings in their heads, that I won't love them.

[Female, Ph.D., 5 years practice]

Being judged, and being rejected by the therapist.

[Male, M.D., 5 years practice]

That you'll throw them out.

[Female, M.S.W., 15 years practice]

Abandonment by the therapist.

[Male, Ph.D., 30 years practice]

Several therapists said that the most prevalent patient fear was of discovering something unacceptable about themselves.

I think people are afraid that there's a monster inside. And there isn't, of course. A lot of people are afraid they're going to find out something terrible about themselves.

[Female, M.S., 20 years practice]

One of the things I see is that people are afraid of what's lurking inside: aggressive impulses, intense feelings, things that they usually defend against a lot. They're afraid of uncovering it, and that if you let yourself feel something it's going to lead to action.

[Female, M.S., 15 years practice]

Loss of defenses, and awareness of stuff that they've worked very hard not to be aware of.

[Male, M.S.W., 10 years practice]

Learning the truth about themselves.

[Female, M.A., 15 years practice]

Really getting in touch with their unconscious fantasies of murder. Their most deeply unconscious wishes and fears.

[Female, Ph.D., 15 years practice]

Patients can also be afraid of going crazy, of being overwhelmed by their own thoughts or feelings.

There's usually some kind of underlying fantasy that certain kinds of situations will trigger intolerable affect.

[Male, M.D., 15 years practice]

A lot of them are afraid of losing control, of going crazy. They're afraid of finding out things that they're ashamed of, finding out they're really bad or unacceptable.

[Female, M.S.W., 30 years practice]

Another commonly mentioned worry is of being misunderstood.

That they're going to bare their soul and they won't be understood, or they'll be misunderstood.

[Female, M.S., 15 years practice]

Many therapists mentioned a fear of change.

They come in wanting to change but when they get close to it they take a step back because they don't know what's going to happen when they leap off the edge.

[Female, M.S.W., 5 years practice]

Change is pretty scary, no matter how superficial it might be. What will I be like on the other side?

[Male, Ph.D., 20 years practice]

They want things to change for them but they're afraid of making the changes themselves.

[Male, Ph.D., 10 years practice]

One patient said, "If I change now, I'll regret all those years that went before, and that would be too hard." Change.

[Female, M.A., 15 years practice]

Some are afraid that their lives will change in ways they won't be able to handle, that changes will disrupt their lives too much.

[Female, Ph.D., 20 years practice]

Several therapists reported that fears of being shamed, embarrassed, or humiliated were also powerful worries for some patients.

The very biggest thing is of feeling ashamed.

[Female, M.D., 15 years practice]

I think they're afraid of humiliation most, shame and humiliation.

[Male, M.D., 20 years practice]

Being made fun of in some way. Being admonished on some level around something painful.

[Female, M.S., 15 years practice]

They think that we are mind-readers, and that we'll see something about them that will be incredibly embarrassing.

[Female, M.A., 20 years practice]

NUMERICAL DISTRIBUTION

(Some people gave more than one response.) Eighteen people said getting too close, being dependent, or being controlled; 13 people said being judged, criticized, rejected, or abandoned by the therapist; 15 said of finding out something awful about themselves; 10 said of being shamed or humiliated; 8 said of changing; 4 said of being unable to leave; 3 said of going crazy or losing control; 2 said of being misunderstood; 2 said of the unknown; and 1 said of separating from parents.

COMMENTS

There is no major controversy behind this question per se, except as it refers to the therapist's conception of the human psyche.

While it may be true that patients are afraid of all of the various things mentioned above, I think that patients are most afraid of discovering that there really is something bad about them, something really terrible that they would be devastated to know and to let the therapist know. And I think that a lot of the psychoanalytic literature encourages that belief, the notion that we're all secretly seething cauldrons of ugly, awful, primitive stuff.

RELATED READING

Bugental, J. F., and Bugental, E. K. (1984). A fate worse than death: the fear of changing. *Psychotherapy* 21(4):543–549.

Giles, S., and Dryden, W. (1991). Fears about seeking therapeutic help: the effect of sex of subject, sex of professional, and title of professional. *British Journal of Guidance and Counselling* 19(1):81–92.

Kushner, M. G., and Sher, K. J. (1989). Fear of psychological treatment and its relation to mental health service avoidance. *Professional Psychology: Research and Practice* 20(4):251–257.

Rothstein, A. (1990). On beginning with a reluctant patient. In *On Beginning an Analysis*, ed. T. J. Jacobs and A. Rothstein, pp. 153–162. Madison, CT: International Universities Press.

℞℞℞℞

Question 62: How much personal therapy should a psychotherapist have?

This has always been an important issue in training: How long until someone is fully trained and ready to do treatment? How necessary is it to resolve one's own issues in order to work with someone else's issues?

Most of our group thought that a therapist needs some long-term experience as a patient. Some emphasized the aspect of attempting to resolve his or her own conflicts.

> Enough therapy to have gone through the entire process, whatever that may be. To work on your own self so that when you're working with a patient, you're not putting your stuff on the patient.
>
> [Female, M.S., 15 years practice]

> I think it depends on the individual. But we all have to be careful not to use our patients to resolve our own problems, or to get them to deal with things the way we would like to deal with them. When you take care of that in your own therapy, you free up the energy to address somebody in a less contaminated way.
>
> [Female, M.S.W., 20 years practice]

Others emphasized the need to know in depth what the patient's experience may be.

> There's no specific number of years. It takes as long as it takes. It's necessary to do this work, to be on the other side.
>
> [Female, Ph.D., 5 years practice]

> A therapist who's had no therapy is lacking in some way, so it's worthwhile to have experienced it, so you know what goes on. It's hard to say exactly how much.
>
> [Female, M.S.W., 5 years practice]

> He should certainly have a little bit more than anything he does. If he sees people once a week, he should have had some therapy at twice a week. He should never see people three times a week if he's never been a patient three times a week. He shouldn't do group therapy if he hasn't been in group therapy. I'd say three, four, five years, to really have a chance to get in and look around. There's no crime in doing it longer.
>
> [Male, Ph.D., 25 years practice]

> They should certainly have a bunch of years, if nothing else, to know what it feels like, even if they're not solving problems. Presumably, that will make them more attuned.
>
> [Male, Ph.D., 20 years practice]

A few people said that whatever therapy a person is doing, he or she should experience an analytic treatment of some sort.

> There has to be a foundation, some real therapy, not est or primal scream or body work. I'm not saying people shouldn't experience those. I have and they've been helpful, but the basic foundation is Freudian.
>
> [Female, Ph.D., 30 years practice]

And another pointed out that, because of institute requirements, a training analysis may not be the place to do it.

> Some people go through their real therapy after they finish their training, because then they don't have to worry about being evaluated. At many institutes, there are a lot of boundary violations.
>
> [Male, Ph.D., 20 years practice]

A number of people see therapy for therapists as a lifelong, if not continuous, part of their professional qualifications.

Therapy is a lifelong experience. You can end it, but you can't finish it. There's no reason why you shouldn't continue to grow and learn for your entire life.

[Male, Ph.D., 50 years practice]

I don't think you have to be in therapy for your whole life, I think you can come and go with it.

[Female, M.S., 15 years practice]

I don't think there's an amount. But I have come to think that it's good for therapists to have treatment at different points in their life stages, both in terms of their development as therapists and their own personal life stages. Because things change internally, and our life experiences impact on us differently as we live.

[Female, M.S.W., 15 years practice]

As much as possible. You're always in therapy. Once you start the process, the process takes hold, and whether you're with another therapist or with yourself, you're always processing.

[Female, M.S.W., 20 years practice]

As long as they breathe!

[Female, M.S.W., 45 years practice]

A few people mentioned specific amounts.

I think every therapist should have analysis, three to five times a week for four to six years.

[Male, Ph.D., 40 years practice]

A therapist should have analysis. Five times a week for the course of the analysis, whatever that might be.

[Male, M.D., 20 years practice]

I think you have to be in therapy at least three years before you begin to do treatment, and you need to be in treatment even as a therapist in an ongoing way.

[Female, M.S.W., 10 years practice]

At least three to four years of intensive therapy before they're ready to do good, effective work.

[Male, Ph.D., 30 years practice]

A lot of therapy. Over the lifetime of a therapist, it should be at least eight years.

[Male, Ph.D., 15 years practice]

Only one person, a behavior therapist, said it was not necessary for a therapist to have treatment himself.

I don't think it's necessary to have therapy. I don't see it as a necessary precursor. How much? It depends on what you're going in for. If it's a long-term dig into your personality, then it'll be long-term. If you have a compulsive hand-washing habit, then you should go to a behavior therapist and it should be as short as possible.

[Male, Ph.D., 20 years practice]

And another saw life experience as comparable to treatment in enlightening a practitioner, suggesting that too much personal therapy could actually be a liability.

It's really hard to say. I think life experience is valuable, if not more valuable. Sometimes therapy can make a person not so helpful, because therapy is a kind of religion, and if you get into that framework those beliefs affect your work. If you get out in the world more, sometimes that's more helpful.

[Male, Ph.D., 25 years practice]

NUMERICAL DISTRIBUTION

Sixteen people said "as much as he or she needs"; 13 people said "a lot" or "plenty"; 9 said "it depends on the individual"; 6 said practitioners should return to treatment at various stages of life; 4 said treatment should be ongoing; and 5 others were unable to say. Only one person said personal therapy was not necessary.

Of those who offered specific amounts, one said "3 to 5 times a week for 4 to 6 years"; one said "3 years minimum"; one said "3 to 5 years"; one said "5 times a week for years"; 2 others said simply "years."

COMMENTS

The major issues here are: Is it possible to do therapy without having been a patient? What does it mean to suggest that the therapist "resolve" personal issues before doing treatment?

I think the answer to this question is analogous to what Lincoln is said to have answered when asked how long a man's legs should be: he supposedly replied, "Long enough to reach the ground." A psychotherapist needs to have enough personal therapy to give him conscious awareness and control of his own problems and issues, which might take a very long time.

Lurking inside some of the responses to this question is the myth of the totally analyzed therapist, who has resolved all personal issues and can now do uncontaminated treatment. I don't believe this is a realistic goal, no matter how much therapy the therapist-in-training has.

In addition, no matter what personal issues or problems the therapist needs to work on, I think it is important to have the experience of being the patient through all the various stages of a long-term treatment. I find it hard to imagine how a therapist could be empathic to a patient without knowing first-hand the experience of being a patient.

RELATED READING

Corey, G., Corey, M. S., and Callanan, P. (1993). *Issues and Ethics in the Helping Professions*. 4th ed. Pacific Grove, CA: Brooks/Cole Publishing Co.

Herron, W. G. (1988). The value of personal psychotherapy for psychotherapists. *Psychological Reports* 62(1):175–184.

MacDevitt, J. W. (1987). Therapists' personal therapy and professional self-awareness. *Psychotherapy* 24(4):693–703.

Norcross, J. C., and Guy, J. D. (1989). *Ten Therapists: The Process of Becoming and Being*. London: Tavistock/Routledge.

◈◈◈◈

Question 63: Do you think it's possible to take patients into areas where you yourself still have problems or unresolved issues and work with them there?

This question refers to an old controversy: Must the therapist have resolved his or her conflicts to be able to help patients resolve theirs? In some ways, this question is related to Question 62, about how much therapy a therapist should have. Both address the issue of whether one must have completed one's own treatment before treating others and whether progress will be possible otherwise.

One person described some difficulties for the therapist working in a problem area.

One can, depending on how deep one is going to go. If the therapist feels that the area is too vulnerable for them, they can try to circumvent it. But what can happen is that the therapist, and this is not on a conscious level, can begin to identify with patient, identify with the problem, or even use their intellectual understanding of the problem for themselves, and that's not going to make good therapy for the patient.

[Female, M.S.W., 10 years practice]

Perhaps surprisingly, since so many people said in response to Question 62 that a therapist needs a lot of therapy in order to do good work, most of the group said that they thought it was possible for therapists to work successfully in unresolved areas.

I do it all the time. I deal with marriages, and divorces, and children, and I've never been married and have no children.

[Female, M.S., 15 years practice]

I've had the experience of seeing patients deal in the therapy with issues that I haven't dealt with as well or haven't resolved as well.

[Male, M.D., 15 years practice]

Those are examples where the student teaches the teacher. Where you go in together and both benefit, even though the patient doesn't know that may be happening.

[Female, M.A., 20 years practice]

Yes. You have to be, because there are always unresolved things in the therapist.

[Female, Ph.D., 20 years practice]

Absolutely, and I resent the hell out of them when I do, when they do better than me. Often with couples, they work out a communication style that I still struggle with. I can teach it, but I can't live it. And with money issues too. I think it's quite possible.

[Male, M.S.W., 15 years practice]

I say it all the time. It's difficult to do it, and you're unlikely to do it, because you don't even know it's a path to take. You don't even know you're not doing it. It's possible to vicariously help your patient through something you yourself have never experienced by empathy.

[Male, Ph.D., 50 years practice]

You have to. You don't have a choice. There are areas where you can slow down, like with dealing with death with AIDS clients. It was really hard, but I had to go there, because they were going there. You can decide not to, but then you can't do the work, and then you have to say to the client, "I can't do this work." Sometimes the most exciting thing about this work is that you can realize that you've gone into an area that you had previously avoided, and really been there and felt okay.

[Female, Ph.D., 5 years practice]

I remember someone saying once that you're going to find out sometime that some clients are healthier than you are.

[Male, M.S.W., 10 years practice]

Several people pointed out that it is important, even crucial, to know where the unresolved conflicts reside, and to continue working on them.

You can, provided you work with them side by side as you go along. Sometimes you can be very creative, and it can be wonderful. It's a very tricky thing. You have to be aware that you're dealing with something that's much more problematic.

[Male, M.S.W., 25 years practice]

It's always possible; it may not be productive. If you know that there are certain things that you still struggle with, if you're very aware of that and what the issues are, then it's okay.

[Female, Ph.D., 30 years practice]

If I'm aware of the unresolved issues, and I can struggle with person in the same area, they may even get further than I've gotten.

[Male, Ph.D., 15 years practice]

It's a very delicate work, but I think it can be done, providing that you analyze the area in yourself as much as you can. You want to wait for the patient to bring those areas up.

[Male, Ph.D., 20 years practice]

A few people suggested that there may be some value in letting the patient know when the issue is a problem for the therapist.

The answer is probably yes, but only if you're also actively seeking to work on the issue in yourself. It could help you, actually, to go into that area with your patient, because it can force you to confront things of your own. I don't think it's terrible to admit to certain patients at certain times that you have conflicts around an issue too.

[Male, Ph.D., 5 years practice]

It's possible. First, you need to know what your unresolved issues are, and, at times, to admit that. To say, for example, as I did with someone, that something I was recommending to her was a hard one for me.

[Female, Ph.D., 10 years practice]

You have to be careful that you don't impose your own inadequacies, or use it as a kind of voyeuristic thing to work out your own stuff. I would tell the patient I have an issue in a certain area.

[Male, Ph.D., 30 years practice]

You can do it if you're willing to go there yourself and be vulnerable and essentially be in therapy yourself in the room with the patient. So there are limits, but I know it's happened with me.

[Male, Ph.D., 20 years practice]

If you have to be a blank screen, I don't see how you can. We do it with our kids all the time. If I'm allowed to be myself, then I can.

[Female, M.S.W., 15 years practice]

Others suggested that we may do such work all the time without even knowing it.

If it's not possible, I wouldn't know about it. The typical answer is no, you can't. But how do you recognize that? The fact that you haven't had that experience doesn't preclude your helping the patient understand that experience. There are two kinds of blind spots: intellectual, cognitive blind spots, where you don't know about it, or your emotional conflicts that interfere with your hearing something. The work might actually be helpful to the therapist.

[Male, M.D., 20 years practice]

It's probably easiest to do that. If I have an unresolved issue, I'm probably more or less unaware of it, which tends to be a defensive style of mine.

[Male, M.D., 20 years practice]

On the other side, a significant minority said it was not possible.

It would pollute the therapy if the issues were unresolved in the therapist. I can't imagine how you'd do the work.

[Female, M.A., 15 years practice]

I don't think you can take a patient past where you are yourself, in your own development. If you haven't handled relationships, recreational time, enjoyment and having fun, you can't teach your patients and they can't get there either.

[Male, Ph.D., 25 years practice]

You can take them into those areas, you don't always make much progress in them. I always find that I've made a big growth step in my own life and am suddenly aware of something new, suddenly within the next two months all of my patients are starting to deal with the same area. I don't think it's coincidence.

[Female, M.S.W., 20 years practice]

I think that's one of the most true factors in treatment. If I haven't dealt with the issue, I can't take people farther than I've at least tried to work with myself.

[Female, M.A., 15 years practice]

Others, while not completely ruling out the possibility of some productive work, said that such gains would be limited by the therapist's unresolved issues.

It's more difficult, and you might not be able to help the person quite as much. For example, before I was in recovery myself, I was able because of my training to work with alcoholics and tell them what they needed to hear, and guide them correctly. But it was only after I was in recovery myself that I was able to go to a new level with the patients.

[Male, M.D., 5 years practice]

It's possible, but very difficult. The therapist is trying to walk barefoot on a gravel road: You can do it, but you might fall down. You have to walk very gingerly. You have to go very carefully, because you can hurt someone in that area. You need to give yourself permission that in this area, you're not going to be too helpful to the patient, and that's a mature, healthy approach.

[Male, M.S.W., 15 years practice]

I think there are people who may use where they go in ways that are more effective than I do. They may touch the same issue and then do things with that that are more than I'm able to. But they may have been made possible by what we went through together.

[Male, Ph.D., 25 years practice]

Sometimes patients have done things that I'm not sure I could have done. But I haven't taken them to that. There's something about the comfort of the relationship that allows them to test out certain things, just as my daughter can do some things that I couldn't do. Creating the therapeutic environment may allow a patient to do some things.

[Female, M.S.W., 25 years practice]

You have to. Who has it all resolved? You have to go where they are. There's a limitation when you go into those areas where you're unresolved. You just have to do the best you can.

[Female, M.S.W., 15 years practice]

NUMERICAL DISTRIBUTION

Fourteen said no, or probably not; 46 said yes, or probably.

COMMENTS

This is another question that, in part, refers to the myth of the totally analyzed analyst, that the therapist must completely resolve his or her own conflicts before helping anyone else.

The answer to this question depends in large part on how the respondent conceives of the role of the therapist. If the therapist is the teacher and the guru, handing out his or her accumulated wisdom, then it's clearly not possible to teach something that the therapist doesn't know well himself from his own experience. But if the therapist conceives of the role as one who follows wherever the patient needs to go and tries to make sense of whatever the patient discovers, then personal issues and experiences become less relevant and less limiting.

If the therapist knows that he (or she) has issues in a particular area, I think he can still do meaningful work with a patient in that area. It's when the therapist doesn't even know that it's a problem area for him that he won't be of any help and can even be hurtful.

RELATED READING

Fausel, D. F. (1988). Helping the helper heal: co-dependency in helping professionals. *Journal of Independent Social Work* 3(2):35–45.

Guy, J. D., Poelstra, P. L., and Stark, M. J. (1989). Personal distress and personal effectiveness: national survey of psychologists practicing psychotherapy. *Professional Psychology: Research and Practice* 20(1):48–50.

℞℞℞℞

Question 64: How common is sexual abuse?

This is one of the current major controversies in the field specifically and in society generally. Together with the next question, about recovered memories, they constitute one of the thornier issues facing every therapist today: how to regard reports of sexual abuse in the patient's childhood experience.

There was some division in the group of interviewees on this question. Although about two-thirds said that sexual abuse was either very common or fairly common, a quarter said that it was not common at all and that the incidence of actual abuse had been seriously exaggerated.

Here are some responses from those who thought there was a lot of sexual abuse.

> It's incredibly common! I have a whole group of women patients who are victims of sexual abuse of various kinds. I think it's a huge phenomenon, and that's a change in my awareness since I first began practicing.
>
> [Female, M.A., 15 years practice]

> It's very common. A lot of people that I've worked with have reported childhood sexual abuse, and have gotten back to the issues. It's so much more present in the media that I hope there's less of it happening today. A lot of people certainly have suffered sexual abuse.
>
> [Female, Ph.D., 20 years practice]

> At least thirty percent of my patients have been sexually abused.
>
> [Female, M.S.W., 10 years practice]

> I think it's much more common than has been reported. Now whether we're talking about sexual abuse as meaning actual sexual intercourse is another issue. That happens some, but what I'm perceiving more is kids who have definitely been sexually molested by a parent, by an uncle, by an older brother. It feels like it's about eighty percent of the females in my practice and about ten to fifteen percent of the guys. I think it's pretty high.
>
> [Female, M.S.W., 20 years practice]

> At least one out of three women. The proportion of thirty percent of my practice has always borne up ever since I've been working. If anything, it's more than that, but it's at least that.
>
> [Female, M.S.W., 10 years practice]

And here are some who thought there was less than reported.

> I don't think it's anywhere near as common as it's being portrayed in the media right now. There's an hysterical exaggeration of it, often fostered by some of our colleagues.
>
> [Male, Ph.D., 20 years practice]

> I've not had it in my practice at all. I do believe that the diagnosis of sexual abuse has gotten out of hand.
>
> [Male, M.S.W., 35 years practice]

> I get very wary of something that starts to surface as an issue, and becomes the catchall word or phrase. I worry about using the word "abuse" within the session. I hear more psychological abuse than actual sexual abuse.
>
> [Female, M.S., 15 years practice]

> I think much less common than most people think. I've seen very little evidence of childhood abuse in my practice, in forty years, very little. I've seen fantasies about it, and thoughts about it, but not any evidence that it's very common.
>
> [Male, Ph.D., 40 years practice]

A few people said that it would be necessary to define what is included under the heading of sexual abuse before deciding how common it is.

> It depends on how you define it. It's been overly loosely defined lately. I'm so lacking in confidence in most of the research. It's reached a point where definitions are so loose that they've become unbelievably overinclusive.
>
> [Male, Ph.D., 20 years practice]

> There are things that I consider sexual abuse that no court of law would identify as sexual abuse, but affected the patient just as much as sexual abuse.
>
> [Male, Ph.D., 20 years practice]

> There's a very big range. Many experiences between parents and children are experienced by the children as sexual abuse, and could be classified that way, like leering. I think that kind of thing is very common.
>
> [Female, Ph.D., 15 years practice]

> It depends what you include in sexual abuse. There are instances that have deleterious effects on people and come up as problems later

on that don't necessarily sound like abuse. Things like overexposure, too much intimacy, permitting the child to be privy to primal scene stuff, things like that that are really very abusive and have a detrimental effect on people but aren't commonly considered abuse. They're not overt instances of an adult taking advantage of a child. If you include all of those, it's fairly common. If you limit yourself to actual instances of an adult doing something to a child, then they're not that common.

[Male, M.D., 20 years practice]

Specific patient populations, such as substance abusers, may have a higher incidence of sexual abuse in their backgrounds.

It's much more common than most people would think. It may be the populations I work with. With people who are addicted, there tends to be a history of abuse. When you work with a specific population, you tend to think the whole world is that way.

[Female, M.S.W., 5 years practice]

I think it's very common. I work a lot with families with alcohol abuse, and think sexual abuse and alcohol abuse are hand in hand. I see probably a disproportionate amount.

[Male, M.S.W., 15 years practice]

I work primarily with a substance-abusing population, and it's a much more common event with that population. So I would say that with the caseload I have, it's probably fifty percent. Primarily women, but men also.

[Male, M.S.W., 15 years practice]

The population may be skewed, because a lot of them are in recovery. Out of that population, I would say seventy-five percent have been molested.

[Male, Ph.D., 15 years practice]

On the other hand, several practitioners said that, given all the current publicity, they were surprised not to encounter more of it in their own patients.

It's a surprising thing that in my practice, there's no one with a history of sexual abuse, which I cannot explain, I can only report it.

[Male, Ph.D., 50 years practice]

I don't know. Apparently, more common than we thought. Among my own patients, I haven't really heard it that much.

[Female, M.S.W., 15 years practice]

I have very seldom run into it, in terms of my patients, even though it's obviously so prevalent. I think it's quite common, not because I've encountered it in the therapy session, but from everything else one hears.

[Male, M.S.W., 25 years practice]

Several people said that they were concerned that the rash of publicity had created an atmosphere of hysteria.

I'm concerned that it's become the movie of the week.

[Female, M.A., 20 years practice]

In the past it was underreported. Maybe now a bunch of people are jumping on the bandwagon to identify sexual abuse when it's not there.

[Female, M.S.W., 20 years practice]

I think sexual abuse is common, and I think that it happens frequently, and that it certainly needs to be looked at and dealt with. But I think there is a lot of hysteria about sexual abuse and sexual harassment, which causes there to be a kind of a witch-hunt fervor about it that gets in the way of reality.

[Male, Ph.D., 15 years practice]

One person spoke at length about the difficulty of discussing this subject in the current climate.

When I started practice, it was thought of as nonexistent. Now, I think it's gone a little too far in the other direction. I would say it's a factor in about twenty-five percent of people's lives. I'm not altogether persuaded how negative a factor it is. I think it's one of those PC topics where we don't really have a chance to explore the positives and the negatives. This is a bad thing, and these are the good guys, and these are the bad guys. We don't really know what goes on. There may be a vast number of people out there who had sexual experiences with adults who are perfectly fine. We just don't know.

[Male, Ph.D., 25 years practice]

NUMERICAL DISTRIBUTION

Fourteen said it was very common; 25 said it was fairly common; 3 said it was only somewhat common; 9 said it was not common or that the incidence had been exaggerated; and 9 said they didn't have any sense of it and couldn't say.

COMMENTS

There are several issues here: How do we best define sexual abuse? How do we accurately determine the frequency of its occurrence? Are psychotherapy patients a skewed sample? How do we evaluate the accuracy of what patients report?

Sexual abuse is a difficult area to discuss in the current climate. We have no way of accurately knowing what the prevalence is, especially when the question is complicated by the possibility that actual occurrences may be repressed from memory (see also Question 65). Additionally, because we see a selected population, it is impossible to generalize. If 30 percent of our patients have a history of sexual abuse, that does not mean that 30 percent of the general population have a similar history. I have no idea how common sexual abuse is or has been, and I don't think anyone else knows either.

RELATED READING

Bass, E., and Davis, L. (1988). *The Courage to Heal.* New York: Harper and Row.

Maltz, W. (1992). *The Sexual Healing Journey.* New York: HarperCollins.

Mennen, F. E. (1992). Treatment of women sexually abused in childhood: guidelines for the beginning therapist. *Women and Therapy* 12(4):25–45.

Nuttall, R., and Jackson, H. (1994). Personal history of childhood abuse among clinicians. *Child Abuse and Neglect* 18(5):455–472.

⧆⧆⧆⧆

Question 65: Do you have any opinion about the controversy over recovered memories and false memory syndrome?

This is perhaps the most controversial topic right now, with a number of experts publishing books on both sides of the question. On one side are those who accept the validity of recovered memories of sexual abuse as they come up in treatment. On the other are those who question both the reality of such material and the political agenda of the therapists who practice such therapy.

There was another tremendous split in our group of therapists, with about a third believing in recovered memory, another third being very skeptical about recovered memory, and the last third undecided.

Here are some responses of those who believe in the return of previously repressed memory of sexual abuse.

> My understanding is that people have been in therapy and talked about sexual abuse for many years, and there wasn't any controversy, and there wasn't any such thing as false memory syndrome until the laws changed in a number of states to where you could sue the perpetrator many years after the abuse. Because it entered the legal statutes and it would cost somebody, and the perpetrator can be forced to pay for the survivor's therapy, the false memory foundation was formed by parents who had been accused of sexual abuse. I don't know any therapist who would tell someone that this happened if it didn't. It's not uncommon for a person to come in and remember a lesser abuse, like a brother or a neighbor, and later on recover other memories. And I would look at that and say that they had evolved more trust, and that more of their repressed past had come back, that they had felt safe enough to talk about it. The FMS [false memory syndrome] people would say that it was created by the therapy.
>
> [Female, M.S.W., 10 years practice]

> I have never felt that a patient is coming up with a false memory. I think it's possible, but in treatment, when you see people go through the kind of pain they go through to recover a memory, I've never felt that anyone is making stuff up.
>
> [Female, M.S., 15 years practice]

> I think the "false memory" thing is false. I think it's rare, and I think therapists who induce these things are rare, and got a lot of publicity. I think it's awful that other people are having doubts about whether they suffered, when they obviously did.
>
> [Female, M.S.W., 20 years practice]

> I tend to go much more with what the patient is saying. If the patient is traumatized, I tend to believe them. I believe the memory. I suppose false memory is possible. I myself work in a very nonintrusive way. I wouldn't introduce an idea to a patient.
>
> [Female, M.S.W., 15 years practice]

I wonder why anyone would make that up. I do believe it's possible, if the therapist is a maniac about it and sees sexual abuse everywhere, through suggestion and so on, you can create false memory. Most of these cases are not false memories.

[Female, M.S.W., 25 years practice]

The patients who have reported sexual abuse to me, there was no false memory. They really knew very clearly what had happened.

[Female, M.S.W., 10 years practice]

I think that anything can be misused, even memories, but this new thing about false memory is very destructive. It's really reproducing the situation of people not believing about abuse in the present. We need a lot more research on the nature of memory, especially traumatic memory. But if a patient comes in and starts to remember something, I'm going to believe it and listen to it. I'm not going to push them to go to court and get money for it, but that's a whole other thing. I do think it's possible to create false memory with suggestible people.

[Female, M.S.W., 30 years practice]

I don't subscribe to the notion of false memory. People generally remember pretty accurately. I'm not using hypnosis, I'm not encouraging or providing those ideas. These are issues that people are coming in with, knowing that this is what happened. I've also had patients where there was parental alcoholism, and it raised the question that perhaps there was some sexual abuse within the alcoholism.

[Female, M.A., 15 years practice]

I wonder about it. How do you create a false memory? I'm not sure it's possible. When the memory begins to emerge, it's consistent with the way they've been behaving.

[Female, M.S.W., 20 years practice]

Other therapists find it hard to believe in recovered memories, and they recognize the possibility of false memory.

I do think that many of the people who have been recovering these false memories have been prompted to do so. In the work that's been done, it seems pretty clear that it's suggestion.

[Male, Ph.D., 50 years practice]

I'm very skeptical that people will recall very flagrant, blatant, dramatic sexual abuse so many years later. The patients I have who were sexually abused remember their abuse. They don't connect it with their current problems, but they usually remember the abuse.

[Male, M.D., 20 years practice]

I think most of the time they're false memories and that therapists don't know what they're doing. That ends up making people who actually are having real repressed memories being doubted even more. It needs a lot more investigation, and therapists who do work that they're not trained to do are irresponsible.

[Female, Ph.D., 10 years practice]

I think that false memory is much more more common than we recognize. I think that therapists have to be very careful not to instill it or inject it. I know about this because it's occurred in my family.

[Female, M.S., 20 years practice]

I think there's a lot of false memory, and a lot of suggestion from certain therapists who believe in childhood sexual abuse, and make suggestions to their patients who, if they're borderline, want to please the therapist.

[Male, Ph.D., 40 years practice]

I don't trust recovered memory. My reading of the research about memories in general suggests that the memories that are elicited are elicited mostly by the conversation in the present, and are not really a product of past experience.

[Male, Ph.D., 25 years practice]

I think it's a lot of hogwash, the recovery and all of the things that suddenly come out. It's steered in that direction of recovering abuse, which may or may not have occurred. I think it's the flavor-of-the-month ailment.

[Female, M.A., 15 years practice]

I think that there's a lot of hysteria going on now. I think this recovered memory stuff, a lot of it is iatrogenic. I think the psychotherapist can create it. So I'm skeptical of some of it. There's a lot of hysteria on both sides. It's definitely possible to create false memory, especially with hypnosis. The strength of the therapist is very potent. I'm very careful not to plant seeds in someone's head.

[Male, Ph.D., 10 years practice]

I get suspicious when all of a sudden too many people are having memories about sexual abuse. I think too many innocent people have been hurt by that.

[Male, M.S.W., 35 years practice]

I do feel that there's been a kind of hysterical overinclusion of a lot of situations as being from sexual abuse that I think is overplayed at this point. There's a lot of sexual abuse going on, but I think that a lot of the cult situations, the satanic things, and the women who say they blocked out ten years of their life and they're sure they were abused during those ten years, in my knowledge of repression it doesn't operate that way. I can see people blotting out an incident, a traumatic incident, but it's hard for me to believe that they can repress years of their lives.

[Female, M.S.W., 20 years practice]

Several people mentioned their questions about the nature of memory and whether it is possible to create false memory.

I've been involved in Ericksonian hypnotherapy in the last few years, and I have a lot of concerns about practitioners who are doing this. My opinion right now is mixed. We have to understand the process of memory and how people remember. Normal day-to-day events are different from trauma, it's really a different kind of memory. We have to be guarded about it, but not throw it out completely. I do think it's possible to create false memory.

[Female, Ph.D., 5 years practice]

Those who found it hard to decide about this issue explained the difficulty.

There is such a thing as repression, and therapy can help lift repression. Patients are also very vulnerable to suggestion, and if therapists have a pet project or suggest that they're probably forgetting, some patients will say, "You're right, I did forget." Some will say, "No, you're wrong, and you're pushing me in the wrong direction," but some won't.

[Female, M.S.W., 20 years practice]

I think there's some truth to it, that people can have a memory and then realize that it was a fantasy. It's difficult to really pinpoint it right now. There's so much hoopla right now with the self-help groups that say if it happened, it happened, and put your father in jail, and all that garbage. And some professionals are jumping on the bandwagon and saying everyone was abused and everyone had dysfunctional families. People are abused, and it's real. But it's sometimes exaggerated, and I wonder what the communication with the family is at the time.

[Female, M.S.W., 10 years practice]

I've been reading some of the literature, and I think there are some a priori assumptions being made based on unproven theory that disturb me. Because people show certain adult characteristics, psychodynamic or psychoanalytic theory says that there should have been child abuse, and I wonder about the potential for self-fulfilling prophecy.

[Male, Ph.D., 20 years practice]

You do arrive at certain narratives, or likely ways that things occurred, or stories that seem to make everything make sense, that you really can't know the truth of, not just in regard to sexual abuse, but of anything. Not that I would ever say that to a patient. But you might arrive finally at some conclusion that maybe this was a chronic way that a parent behaved toward the patient. And those narratives might not even be true, but they have a sense of conviction for the patient. Sometimes they help to make things make sense, but are also sometimes seen as a stopping point when they in fact are just a certain story that the patient tells themselves that defensively covers over some other aspect of the story. It's not so terrific to stop there.

[Female, Ph.D., 15 years practice]

It's a shame that it's become a polarized issue, that it has to be one or the other. That there are people who say there's no such thing as repression, and therefore there's no such thing as the possibility in adult life of "recovering" a memory, being able to focus on something you were never able to focus on before, and realizing that you always sort of knew that. And people who are on a crusade to convince the world that everyone has been sexually abused and has these unrecovered memories. A plague on both their houses!

[Male, Ph.D., 5 years practice]

I certainly believe it is possible for some therapists to elicit false memory. I don't believe that everyone who comes into therapy and remembers that abuse happened is actually a recovered memory. But it's also a reaction to how much we are uncovering in terms of sexual abuse and incest in America. The belief that false memory exists allows us to distance from the fact that this is actually happening.

[Male, M.S.W., 15 years practice]

Several therapists discussed the political agendas underlying this issue.

On one level, my take is that this is a political struggle that has nothing to do with memory. That the false memory association is an organization I'm extremely suspicious of, and have reason to believe is founded for all the wrong reasons. And what makes it complicated is the rest of us who do work with people who are recovering memory all know that there are memories that are unreliable. We don't consider memory to be reliable. So we're put in this position of true versus false, when I've never taken the position that this is true. I've only taken the position that this is a complex phenomenon. We know a lot more now then we did before about how the brain processes information. We know that we don't know enough to answer this question, but one can account for ways in which information is confused. My position is that I look for a general integrity to the picture of what someone is describing, and that depends not just on their memories, but on their symptoms, on their life experience, on the constellation of their family, on what other members of the family have experienced, corroboration, all of those things go into it. Sure, you can create false memories. You can induce false memories under certain circumstances in certain people. The statistics are that in maybe twenty-five percent of people you can create a false memory, which means in maybe seventy-five percent you can't. I don't think psychotherapists, the majority of therapists who are trying to sort through this stuff with people, except for a handful of really incompetent therapists (and there are some really incompetent people out there), can create false memories. They can make mistakes in treatment, but not false memories.

[Female, M.D., 15 years practice]

I do believe in the possibility of recovered memory, and I do believe that it's possible that memories that people recover in therapy don't necessarily represent reality. I do believe that they could be induced by the way the therapist works. You really have to draw a strict line between the usefulness of this in therapy and the use of going to sue someone for something that the patient believes happened.

[Male, M.S.W., 20 years practice]

Now you have the hysteria about always looking for sexual abuse on one hand, and then you have this reactionary hysteria that is accusing therapists of putting thoughts and memories into patients' minds. I believe that there are some therapists, perhaps some radical feminist therapists for instance, who have an ax to grind, who join with the patient, and encourage the patient to get revenge. And it then becomes some kind of ritual of revenge rather than pure therapy, and I think that's bad for the profession.

[Male, Ph.D., 15 years practice]

On the other hand, patients may also have personal agendas.

> I'm more inclined to think that families can be pretty shitty places for a lot of people. Where there are false memories, I'm not so sure they're really false memories, they're attempts at getting even. There's a purposeful characterological thing, like, "I'll show them." I don't think therapists push for it, but if the opportunity is there, some people will take it as a way of getting back, getting even.
>
> [Male, Ph.D., 40 years practice]

> It's become such an "in" thing to have a history of sexual abuse. A few patients have said to me that they think they were sexually abused, and I ask them why, and they say that they've been told that everybody has been sexually abused. That kind of stuff drives me nuts. There's too much hype that everyone was sexually abused. To some degree, every woman I know has suffered some sort of sexual abuse or molestation, but it's often very minor. Whether it's traumatic, and how it gets built up, is overplayed sometimes. It's possible to create false memories, especially with stories.
>
> [Female, Ph.D., 20 years practice]

> There are some people who have a sense, and think that it might be the problem, but it may not be. It's possible to create a false history, and they may do that in order to cover up the truth, because they don't want to admit they've been living a lie.
>
> [Male, M.S.W., 10 years practice]

NUMERICAL DISTRIBUTION

Overall, 17 people tend to believe in the accuracy of recovered memories; 22 people would tend to doubt their accuracy; and 21 have no particular leaning either way. Almost everyone believes that it is possible, given a suggestible patient, to create false memories, either accidentally or because of some personal or political agenda. Only 3 people said they thought it was not possible to do so.

COMMENTS

The very controversial issues here are: What is the nature of memory? What is the mechanism of repression? How do we regard patient memories recovered in treatment? Is it possible to create false memories, in treatment or elsewhere, intentionally or inadvertently?

While we have only partial answers at best to most of these questions, one thing we do know is that it is possible to intentionally create false memories experimentally (Loftus and Ketcham 1994), although we still don't know whether this can happen unintentionally in therapy.

I think it's risky to use hypnosis to recover memories because it's so easy to implant suggestions, especially with dissociative patients, as so many abuse survivors seem to be. Sometimes I feel like we're back at the Salem witch trials, with some of the stories of satanic abuse, where even the details are so similar. On the other hand, I think some patients don't remember things that have happened until they get into therapy and start talking about the issue, often for the first time.

RELATED READING

Loftus, E., and Ketcham, K. (1994). *The Myth of Repressed Memory.* New York: St. Martin's Press.

Wright, L. (1994). *Remembering Satan.* New York: Knopf.

Yapko, M. D. (1994). Suggestibility and repressed memories of abuse: a survey of psychotherapists' beliefs. *American Journal of Clinical Hypnosis* 36(3):163–171.

◧◧◧◧

Question 66: How do you feel about 12-step programs?

The 12-step philosophy and the various 12-step programs have proliferated in the last few years. Some therapists use these programs as adjuncts to treatment, and sometimes patients come into therapy already involved in a 12-step program.

Most of our group felt positively about the 12-step programs and would refer patients when they thought it appropriate.

> I think it's useful for people, people who are from alcoholic families, or are recovering from alcohol abuse. I basically insist that they go, that they give it a try. I would make the treatment contingent on them giving it a try. But once they have, if it isn't something they wish to continue that would be all right. But I feel that they should try it.
>
> [Female, M.S.W., 10 years practice]

I think they're very, very helpful. People who are addicted have lost their sense of humility about themselves, so that the 12-step program helps them regain the sense of humility and vulnerability, which helps them cope with addictive habits. I like the supportive nature of it, that you can go to a group every night, and that's very necessary because these are people who don't have the internal controls. The drawbacks are that, like any religion, it can become too dogmatic. And for some people, because of the dogmatism and religious orientation, it just isn't appropriate.

[Male, Ph.D., 25 years practice]

They're very, very useful. They help people tremendously. In some ways, they make clearer what is the essence of therapy, that there's something about faith and belongingness to something that's bigger than yourself.

[Male, Ph.D., 20 years practice]

I think they keep people clean and sober. I don't think they're a replace-ment or a substitute for therapy. If people go, they do what they say they're going to do as far as sobriety. I also think they provide some people who might otherwise be very isolated with a very good social support network.

[Female, M.S.W., 10 years practice]

I think they're wonderful, and I think they're going to grow in popu-larity and usefulness to society because of the lack of cohesive values and the sense of alienation that people live in, and 12-step programs are an antidote to that.

[Male, Ph.D., 10 years practice]

Several therapists had been educated about the programs by their patients.

I think they can be very useful for some people. I have suggested them to some people. Earlier in my practice when I wasn't as aware of them, I had a number of patients tell me that they had joined one awhile ago and it had been helping them, and I asked them about it and concluded that it was helping them.

[Male, M.S.W., 20 years practice]

I think better of them now that I have a patient who goes to AA and I see that it's really helping. I've been educated to see why they're so popular: it's such a support for her. She can go every day, and it's free. I think they get a little too much with their slogans.

[Female, M.S.W., 15 years practice]

Some people said the 12-step groups were an important adjunct to therapy.

They do different kinds of things, and some of it overlaps, and some is quite different. I think they can work together quite nicely.

[Male, Ph.D., 25 years practice]

They provide a structure for dealing with an addiction, and always available support, which people giving up an addiction really need. Even if you're seeing them twice a week, you can't cover the kind of affective instability they feel for a while.

[Female, M.S.W., 20 years practice]

I hear a lot of good things about them, and a lot of therapists come to me who are in recovery, so I see the benefits. People who go to them and are in the psychotherapeutic process and are therapists themselves are often very enlightened, highly evolved people.

[Male, Ph.D., 15 years practice]

I'm very impressed with them, because if you look at the steps, a lot of them are very consonant with the stages of psychotherapy.

[Male, Ph.D., 25 years practice]

I feel like they're a partner to therapy. I feel very comfortable with people being in 12-step programs. I encourage them to participate. I think sometimes people really need that kind of outside ongoing available support, also as a social support system as much as a therapeutic community.

[Female, M.A., 15 years practice]

A few therapists seemed to think that with some patients, the 12-step programs may even be preferable to therapy, at least for treating substance abuse.

I think they're fine for alcoholics, or people with certain kinds of problems. There's a limitation to them. It's not the same as analyzing the psychodynamics, but that's not indicated with some patients. To get them off of the harmful substances is really as much as you can hope for.

[Male, Ph.D., 40 years practice]

Sometimes people in the programs can be very dogmatic with them, but if someone has a serious addiction problem, it's the only thing that works.

[Male, M.S.W., 10 years practice]

Other therapists saw a conflict between the 12-step programs and psychotherapy.

I believe that 12-step programs are good for helping addictive personalities take the first step toward getting off the drugs and staying sober. But I believe that after that they may do some harm, because then they tend to cultivate a life-long dependency on the program. They also have kind of an antagonistic attitude towards therapy, and it's almost the same attitude that parents have towards therapy.

[Male, Ph.D., 15 years practice]

They direct their people to trust in whatever and it will happen, and I'm trying to tell them that you can direct certain things to happen, so it was very hard because I felt like we were butting heads.

[Female, M.A., 20 years practice]

For some people, they're very useful. They make it difficult for patients to be in psychotherapy. Patients need to feel that they don't fully buy the 12-step program, they have to maintain a split between the two.

[Male, M.D., 15 years practice]

I have patients involved in that now. If it helps, it helps. Whatever works is okay. I have been more accepting of those programs than they have of me, and those programs have felt more competitive and threatened by me than I have felt towards them.

[Male, M.S.W., 35 years practice]

Even therapists who have generally positive feelings about the 12-step programs may have reservations, sometimes serious ones.

They serve a very important purpose. People who drink and drug are very isolated people, and 12-step programs give them a large community. They're also so needy that they would drain one person. Here, they have a lot of people to call on. It helps to reinforce abstinence. The disadvantage is that you can get trapped in the program, if it becomes the new addiction.

[Female, M.S.W., 20 years practice]

I have mixed feelings. I sent one patient to AA, and I've rescued a couple from AA, because they can become addictive. And some people get caught up in a pattern of thinking that is dictated by the recovery movement, that you have certain ways you're supposed to think about certain problems that you have. And people get locked in, and they use the language, and the language becomes habitual, and they lose their ability to let their feelings inform their thoughts. There's this almost dictatorial pressure to think that certain way.

[Male, Ph.D., 5 years practice]

I do not think that they are answers to solving deep psychological issues. I think that for some people with addictions that 12-step programs offer them structure and boundaries that they are sorely in need of, as well as a place, an extended family kind of place, where they feel safe and identified. The drawback is that they can purport to supplant deeper treatment. Also, I think they emphasize deprivation too much, without a lifestyle adjustment.

[Female, M.S.W., 15 years practice]

I love them and I hate them. They work best for most, and they provide a twenty-four-hour, seven-day-a-week net for people who are in deep trouble and who would never be able to come off whatever they've been using with just therapy alone one hour a week. What's wrong is that, here in New York, they're full of psychobabble and full of very dangerous people, and very dogmatic people.

[Male, M.S.W., 15 years practice]

They can be useful, but I think that one of the problems is that people tend to rely on them for rules about how to live, instead of searching for that for themselves.

[Female, M.S.W., 5 years practice]

They're essential for the population I work with, the substance abusers. I find them very beneficial. The only drawback is the fact that they don't get feedback. They'll bring up a lot of information but they won't get the feedback.

[Male, M.S.W., 15 years practice]

They're very positive. The only drawback I know of is the possibility that some people may be suggested into believing that things like incest happened to them when it never did. I've not seen much of that, but there is a little bit.

[Female, M.S., 20 years practice]

I think that they're really worthwhile supports. A lot of people who are addicted don't have great support systems, or they're associating with other people who are addicted. It helps them not to isolate and gives them that network. Sometimes people believe that 12-step programs are the only way to go and it becomes almost cultish, a new addiction.

[Female, M.S.W., 5 years practice]

I think they're enormously helpful. However, I worry that people make it their identity, that they're always in recovery. That's a very limited identity, and definition of yourself.

[Female, Ph.D., 5 years practice]

I have mixed feelings about them. On the one hand, I think they're the single best thing for keeping people off of drugs or alcohol. Better than therapy or anything else. On the other hand, they're quasi-religious, there's a bit of cultism in some of them, and people in the groups much too freely dispense analysis and solutions. These folks aren't trained therapists, and they're giving really bad advice. Also, I don't buy the whole disease model.

[Male, Ph.D., 10 years practice]

Several people pointed out that the programs don't work with everyone.

I think they help some people. I think some people cannot relate to them. It's not good for everybody. Someone who's not ready to disclose a lot of personal stuff may not be ready for a 12-step program.

[Female, M.S., 15 years practice]

They're incredibly important for someone who is trying to get clean and sober, and trying to get into recovery. Now, not everyone will relate to or hook into the 12-step program, but many will, and I'm in favor of them. The spirituality is a strong component, and some people are turned off by that.

[Male, M.D., 5 years practice]

I find when I send patients that sometimes they come back and say they don't get it, or they feel isolated. I feel really disappointed when it doesn't work for them once I get them to go.

[Male, Ph.D., 15 years practice]

A few people in the sample were very negative in their comments about the 12-step programs.

They probably help a lot of people. I think a lot of them are full of crap. AA makes claims that it can't support, it asserts things. AA has no room within it's very rigidly defined rules for anything other than AA. There is a certain tunnel vision, and an almost religious fanatical belief in the system. I also don't like the first tenet of most of the programs, which is that you're powerless. I don't want that to be the first thing I communicate to somebody. I also have a problem with the recovery movement assuming a certain level of "this is not my fault." Now that may be a misinterpretation on my part of what they're presenting, but it comes across an awful lot that way.

[Male, Ph.D., 20 years practice]

It works for some people. It works for people who don't need it, and what I mean by that is people who can really utilize therapy, and can use therapy and use the steps to recover from their problem. However, with some people who use the steps it becomes a cult. There's a lot of splitting. If they don't like what their therapist says, they go to their sponsor, who's usually very poorly educated about psychological dynamics. I see it as another addiction. People use it either for their social milieu, and don't learn how to communicate outside of it, or as a crutch, going to two or three meetings a day.

[Female, M.S.W., 10 years practice]

NUMERICAL DISTRIBUTION

Forty-three people said they had generally positive attitudes toward 12-step programs; 13 said they had mixed feelings; and 4 said they had strongly negative feelings about such programs. In addition, 4 people said there was a conflict between the programs and psychotherapy.

COMMENTS

There are several issues connected to the 12-step programs: What does "disease" mean as applied to addiction? Are 12-step programs compatible with and supportive of psychotherapy?

I think that 12-step programs such as AA can be very helpful as an adjunct to therapy. Exploration of a client's addictive behavior is part of psychotherapy, but I don't want to spend the whole treatment on that one topic. With a 12-step program, patients can deal with that part of their lives and we can get on to other things.

I think that the main shortcoming of the 12-step programs, from a therapist's point of view, is that people get no feedback about what they say, and are not questioned or challenged. I understand that such response is not possible in that context, and the programs would not work that way. Because therapy does provide the feedback and investigation absent from 12-step programs, the combination of psychotherapy and a 12-step program can be very powerful, much like the combination of individual and group psychotherapy.

I think many therapists also have trouble with the premise of the first step in the 12-step programs, in which people acknowledge that they are "powerless" over alcohol (or whatever the group is dealing with). As therapists, we try to give patients an increasing awareness of personal responsibility and control, which this principle seems to undermine.

RELATED READING

McCrady, B. S., and Miller, W. R., eds. (1993). *Research on Alcoholics Anonymous: Opportunities and Alternatives.* New Brunswick, NJ: Rutgers Center of Alcohol Studies.

Ogborne, A. C. (1989). Some limitations of Alcoholics Anonymous. In *Recent Developments in Alcoholism,* vol. 7, ed. M. Galanter, pp. 55–65. New York: Plenum Press.

Powell, T. J. (1987). *Self-help Organizations and Professional Practice.* Silver Spring, MD: National Association of Social Workers.

Todres, R. (1982). Professional attitudes, awareness, and use of self-help groups. *Prevention in Human Services* 1(3):91–98.

III

Personal History and Experience

This section examines the various areas of the therapist's life, in and out of the office, in training and in practice. These include personal therapy and supervision, how personality impinges on style and orientation, and feelings about patients, colleagues, and the work itself. This section also includes the effects of outside influences on the work and the effects of the work on the therapist's life.

Just as many of the questions and issues in the first two sections were unaddressed during training, I don't recall in my training much coverage of many of these topics, either. Occasionally, a supervisor would suggest a vacation, or mention the effect of the schedule on his family, but this was very rare.

☒☒☒☒

Question 67: What was your first awareness of the profession?

For most therapists, somewhere in their background there is a moment of first awareness of the profession, that certain people get paid to sit in a room and talk to others. As one person put it:

> When I was a kid, somebody told me that there was a job where you got to sit and listen to people's problems. And I said, "And they pay you for this?"
>
> [Female, M.S., 15 years practice]

Some became aware of psychotherapy in childhood, when a relative or family friend was in the field.

> I was 10½ years old, and my brother had to take a course where he had to volunteer at an agency. One time, he took me with him, and that was it. Even though I was very young, they let me come back. And I knew that when I got out of college, I wanted to go to social work school.
>
> [Female, M.S.W., 10 years practice]

> My father was a psychotherapist. I've been aware of it my whole life, since I was about 9 years old.
>
> [Male, Ph.D., 15 years practice]

> Very early in my life, around 11 or even earlier. My father was a social worker, and he taught in a school of social work, and he had a private practice. I was in family therapy when I was 10.
>
> [Female, M.S.W., 10 years practice]

> I had some relatives that were therapists, so I always knew about it.
>
> [Female, M.A., 20 years practice]

One person said it was his religious background that first suggested therapy as a profession.

> I was raised as a Christian Scientist, and there were people who were known as practitioners, and I thought that would be a great thing to do, because you got to talk to people who were having troubles.
>
> [Male, Ph.D., 40 years practice]

Some became aware of therapy because a family member or friend was in treatment.

> I had a cousin who was about twenty years older who was probably schizophrenic. She was a patient with [name], and my aunt, her mother, was very interested in psychoanalysis and read a lot about it. This was my favorite aunt, so I got interested in it at about 12 years old.
>
> [Female, M.S., 20 years practice]

> My sister is twelve years older than me, and she was in therapy when I was young, so I always knew that people did that. I took a psychology course in high school, and I was in high school when I went to my first therapist.
>
> [Female, M.S.W., 5 years practice]

> When I was a little girl, my mother baby-sat for a woman who was very rich and who went to a psychiatrist. And my mother liked the woman, and she would have these stories. When I finished college, and was working, my best friend there, who was funny and interesting and bright, was going to a psychiatrist three times a week.
>
> [Female, M.S.W., 25 years practice]

> When I was about 8 years old, my mother's friend's daughter went to a therapist, and I asked what that was. I was told that she had problems and she talked to a lady about them.
>
> [Female, M.S.W., 20 years practice]

> When I was a kid, probably a teenager, my sister was going to therapy. My mother was in therapy, and when I was about 17, she wanted me to go and sent me to a therapist.
>
> [Male, Ph.D., 20 years practice]

> When I was a kid I knew about it. I know that my mother pressured my father to go into therapy at one point, and I know that he went to group therapy and hated it and quit. By that time, I already knew that it existed. I was probably an adolescent.
>
> [Male, Ph.D., 5 years practice]

> My first awareness was when I was about 16, and my father went to see a psychiatrist because he had ulcers.
>
> [Female, M.S.W., 45 years practice]

Many became aware through the movies.

From the movies when I was a teenager.

[Male, M.S.W., 35 years practice]

Maybe watching Woody Allen movies when I was young. Something in the media, movies or TV.

[Female, M.S.W., 15 years practice]

When I saw the movie *David and Lisa.* I was about 13. I ran out to get the book, and all sorts of other psychological books.

[Female, M.S.W., 10 years practice]

It was definitely before college. It may even have been *Spellbound.*

[Male, M.S.W., 25 years practice]

Others had their first awareness at junior high school age.

My first awareness was when I was in junior high school, and I got something in the mail advertising the collected works of Sigmund Freud, and I got it and read through it and thought the stuff in it was too much! I was hooked.

[Male, M.D., 20 years practice]

In eighth grade, I was in a psychology class I found really interesting, and it made me decide that's what I wanted to do.

[Male, M.S.W., 15 years practice]

When I was in high school, maybe even junior high school. I have an older sister, and she was having problems, and Lucy Freeman wrote a book called *Fight Against Fears* and that's when I fell in love with the profession.

[Female, M.A., 20 years practice]

I read Freud's *General Introduction to Psychoanalysis* when I was 13 years old.

[Male, Ph.D., 50 years practice]

Some learned about therapy in their high school years.

I realized I wanted to be a psychologist when I was in high school. There was an expectation that I would be a professional of some sort. I had been considering dentistry because I liked working with my hands. But then looking into people's mouths just turned me off. But I've always been fascinated with people, and I've always been the one that friends came to with problems, and I was always interested. Then I found out there was this business where you could do that. In high school I took courses at [name of college] at night in psychology, and then I went to [name of university] knowing I was going to be a psych major. A lot of people want to get into this business because of their own therapy experience, but that was not my case at all. I never had therapy up to that point.

[Male, Ph.D., 25 years practice]

I was 17 years old, and I met some people who were studying psychology. They were first and second year students, so they were always using the jargon, and some were in therapy. I became curious about that. I also remember reading Freud in high school, the theory of dreams, and it was very interesting.

[Male, Ph.D., 20 years practice]

Probably my first encounter with a school counselor in high school.

[Female, Ph.D., 5 years practice]

Some found out in college.

It was later than most people, I was in college. I didn't start college with the intention of being a psychologist. I was going to be a lawyer. Then I took a psychology course and realized that this was the stuff that was in my brain all the time, and they actually studied it! I learned about psychotherapy in the course of that.

[Male, Ph.D., 25 years practice]

I must have heard something about it in college, because that was when I decided that when I was earning money I would give it a try for my own problems. I'm from a small town, so I don't think I heard about it much before then.

[Female, M.S.W., 15 years practice]

My first awareness was when I was a freshman in college, my first psych course, and realizing that I was very depressed, and asking to see the teacher for treatment. That was my first insight into what it meant to be "in therapy," what it meant to get help in that kind of way. Even those few sessions made me aware that this was a very important way for people to deal with feeling and problems.

[Female, M.A., 15 years practice]

I was in college, in a class with Abraham Maslow, abnormal psychology. I loved the field and majored in it, but I never thought I could be a psychologist. Everyone was in education or social work. Always in the back of my mind it was what I wanted to do. I went back to school when my children were in high school and college.

[Female, M.A., 15 years practice]

Some people didn't learn about psychotherapy until graduate school.

My first awareness was when I was in medical school and did my psych rotation. Where I grew up, in the South, going into therapy wasn't something that people did.

[Male, M.D., 5 years practice]

Many in our group became aware through their own therapy, often at a very early age.

When I was a pretty young kid and was brought to a child analyst. I was a very resistant patient too.

[Male, M.S.W., 20 years practice]

When I went into therapy when I was 12. They started early in my family.

[Male, M.S.W., 15 years practice]

Not until I was in therapy myself. I had always wanted to be a writer, and I felt that being a writer was very close to being a psychologist because you had to understand people. It wasn't until I had been therapy for a few years. I had always thought that I was too messed up to be a therapist, and then I found out that it's one of the prerequisites.

[Male, Ph.D., 15 years practice]

When I was in my first analysis. I come from a rural background, so this was not high on our list.

[Female, M.S.W., 20 years practice]

Several people tried other careers before becoming aware that they could be a therapist.

Growing up, people always came to talk to me, so I knew that I had some kind of ability to effect change in the life of another person, and I thought that meant I was to be a priest. I went into the seminary only to find out that it was not the place for me. In college, I moved more and more into psychology and sociology. I never saw myself in private practice, because I was much more into community organization, starting programs, teaching. A friend and colleague pushed and pushed for me to be in private practice. Coming to work with people who were motivated was something I loved, so I continued.

[Male, M.S.W., 15 years practice]

I was working as a language and speech therapist in a hospital, and I was in a unit which had a child psychiatrist as a consultant, and he began to treat me as if I had some special talent in working with diagnostic and emotional issues in children. He started funneling all the children with those kinds of problems, like autism, schizophrenia, and emotional dysfunction, to me. And he gave me the books of Selma Fraiberg, saying that I should become a therapist. It took me a long time to take that on. Later I began to do research in the area of the mother–child relationship, and that's where it hit me in a personal way that I really could do this.

[Female, M.S.W., 15 years practice]

As a teacher, I took a free course that was taught by a psychoanalyst, and my mind was completely and utterly blown away. I sat in total amazement. It was a psychoanalytic approach to teaching, which is absolutely correct in my mind. The trueness of it was what struck me, because I had been a teacher for many years, and I had to know more.

[Female, Ph.D., 20 years practice]

I got into this profession by accident. In school I was interested in sociology and helping the poor, and I had no idea when I went to graduate school of becoming a therapist. I had never been in therapy and I didn't know anyone who had, except growing up I had known two people who had made serious suicide attempts and were hospitalized, and they had therapy afterwards of course. So I thought that unless you had overdosed or tried to run your car off the road that therapy was not for you. I had no idea that ordinary life situations were something you would talk to a therapist about.

[Female, M.S.W., 10 years practice]

NUMERICAL DISTRIBUTION

Twelve people said they learned about therapy first in college; 8 said in high school; 3 in graduate school or medical school, and 3 while working at other careers. Nine people had a professional in the family; 8 had a family member in therapy. Nine learned about therapy from being a patient in their own treatment; 3 more from friends who were in treatment. Five first learned about therapy from the movies.

COMMENTS

There are no great controversies raised by this question. We might ask whether learning about the profession at age 7 has a different effect from learning about it at age 23, and to what extent choice of this career is unconsciously affected by the first awareness and its context and meaning. There is, for example, probably some difference between those who, as children, learned of the profession because they saw family members in treatment and those who learned of therapy as a profession as adults only through their own treatments.

In my own situation, because both my parents were therapists and almost every adult who came to the house was also in the field, I was always aware of psychotherapy as a profession. I can't remember not being aware that it was a way to make a living. I did work in several other fields before turning (actually, returning) to this one.

RELATED READING

Dorr, A., and Lesser, G. S. (1980). Career awareness in young children. *Communication Research and Broadcasting* 3:36–75.
Hunter, V. (1994). *Analysts Talk.* New York: Guilford Press.

🖾🖾🖾🖾

Question 68: What experiences in your background led you to choose this profession?

Obviously, something influences a person to choose a particular profession. There are a lot of theories about what leads someone to choose psychotherapy. What influences do the therapists in this group identify as significant?

The stereotype is that the therapist is reenacting some family situation. A number of people did cite their family dynamics as a strong influence. Some said that "therapist" was, in some way, their role in the family.

> It's kind of classical really. I came from a family that was disturbed in a number of ways, and no one talked about anything, and I was the emotional caretaker, and didn't get noticed for having any personal needs. So I'm very interested in secrets, and what makes systems work, and all that.
>
> [Female, M.S.W., 10 years practice]

I was born into an alcoholic family, and I was a therapist from the age of 5.

[Male, M.S.W., 15 years practice]

One of the difficulties in my own childhood was that my mother was an alcoholic, and was often not emotionally available. When I started doing the work, it began to help me try to understand her and my experience, and that attracted me to the profession.

[Male, M.D., 5 years practice]

In my family it's the role I play of being the one people go to, especially my mother and an aunt of mine. And these two women started when I was very young to rely on me and come to me. It was very natural for me to become a therapist.

[Female, M.S., 15 years practice]

I knew pretty early on that I wanted to go into psychiatry, and it had to do with the dynamics within my family. My father had polio as an infant, so his whole life he was in the position of having a physical defect. He was a middle child, and his siblings were much more successful than he, and better loved by a very bitchy, narcissistic mother. He was always a guy who presented himself as a very strong, self-made man. He had some narcissistic problems, and we all felt we had to defend him and support him. I was hoping to heal him in some way.

[Male, M.D., 15 years practice]

In my background we didn't know about psychotherapy. I got my Ph.D. without having any therapy. I'm a rescuer. I was the youngest in my family, my mother's last hope, and I was going to become a priest and save the world. But as I got older I had problems intellectually with that, and I couldn't hold on to the theology too well. But I didn't give up the rescuing. I'm like a secular priest. I also have a very deep curiosity about how people work.

[Male, Ph.D., 25 years practice]

The whole world revolved around my father and his moods. You always had to read and be aware of what was going on inside him, so there was always a focus on the other, and attuning to the other, for your own survival. And my wants and needs were basically irrelevant. I was supposed to fulfill all of his expectations, and be the greatest musician and scholar and athlete and everything else, whether I wanted to or not.

[Male, Ph.D., 20 years practice]

Even though my sister is a few years older, I always had the feeling that I had to take care of her. I was always very worried about her. I thought if I could learn about psychological stuff, somehow she'd be okay. When I first went to college, I didn't think I would be a psychotherapist. I thought it would be too hard, or too long. It was a pipe dream.

[Female, M.A., 20 years practice]

I knew that I was a therapist from age 3—not necessarily by choice! It was clear that that was what I did. I had so much practice doing it, I thought I might as well make a living from it. I was in my family the family therapist, the peacemaker. My parents were very young when they had their kids, and so for various reasons I took on the role.

[Female, Ph.D., 5 years practice]

At the time I went to school, I was working more with kids, and I was out of touch with what a disturbed kid I had been. I think it had to do with the disturbance in my own family. My father was never in any kind of treatment, but was a pretty paranoid guy, and that had impacted very strongly on me. I didn't think at the time I went into the field that it was an influence, but I do now.

[Female, M.S.W., 20 years practice]

Others said that there were other kinds of family influences, not necessarily of the family pathology.

My father was a social worker and had a private practice. I couldn't imagine myself doing anything else. I was always very fascinated with the human condition, and what made people tick, and everybody's life, and how they conducted it, and what they thought and felt about things. Even as a child I was always very inquisitive.

[Female, M.S.W., 10 years practice]

It has a good deal to do with the Holocaust, and the idea that such a crazy thing, such a mind-boggling, intolerable idea motivated people and seemed to be the norm. I lost a lot of my family, so it became a very personal issue. I have followed the thread through my analysis. The idea of figuring out the mishegas that we all suffered was an important motivation.

[Male, M.D., 20 years practice]

I was the kind of kid who wanted to be a checkout girl at the A&P, because you stood there and you got to see what everybody was buying, you got to see who was eating what. You got a glimpse into other people's lives. I always was interested in people. I was a red-diaper baby, and my parents were devout Marxists, and they believed in the goodness of people. Of course, they believed in the masses, not individuals. It occurred to me one day that the masses, who were so revered, were nothing more than individuals such as myself. It appealed to me that people were talking about feelings, and that was a valid thing to talk about, and individual feelings were important.

[Female, M.S., 15 years practice]

I think it's my parents' perceptions of what kind of personality I had, and my strengths. I think they perceived me as someone who people could talk to easily, as someone who was very smart and patient, nonjudgmental, good sense of humor, and that this would be a good field for me.

[Female, Ph.D., 10 years practice]

When I was a child growing up my uncle and aunt had children that were very neurologically impaired, and they absorbed a lot of family time, and I was resentful of that. My first reaction was that I'd never want to do anything like that with children, but I found myself years later doing it.

[Female, M.S.W., 15 years practice]

I went to social work school not to be a therapist, but to help the world. My father was tremendously helped by the Henry Street Settlement, and he always talked about the social workers, how important they were to him, and that was where I first wanted to be a social worker and to help. Then I was working in a women's prison, and then with very disturbed adolescents, and it was like knocking your head against a wall. The administration, and the financial problems, made it very hard to do what I wanted to do. So I left that and went into training to become a private practitioner.

[Female, M.S.W., 30 years practice]

Some people said that being a psychotherapist was an extension of certain lifelong characteristics and ways of thinking.

I've always had the tendency to be questioning and wondering, why is this the reality, what is this all about? It's always the central question in my mind from very early childhood. A lot of my experiences in childhood that I was trying to figure out kind of led me to be psychologically oriented and therefore very interested in people and what makes them tick.

[Male, M.S.W., 25 years practice]

Most of my experiences growing up were that I lived in other people's heads, and figured out what they wanted and gave it to them. I ended up giving away so many parts of myself that I had nothing left. I don't live in other people's heads any more, but I still have that skill.

[Female, M.S.W., 20 years practice]

I always say you have to be nosy to be a good therapist, and I've always been nosy. I've always been a talker, and I've always been involved in intense relationships from when I was a little girl, my best friends. It's not a surprising field for me to be in.

[Female, Ph.D., 20 years practice]

It's my life story. I was a very sensitive and very shy child. And I was always searching for what helps, when I feel better, and when I don't. I was always aware of feelings, and troubling feelings.

[Female, M.S.W., 45 years practice]

For some reason, I've always been interested in how people tick: what motivates them, why they do what they do. I always looked beneath the surface of things, and the fact that I did not have an easy time emotionally in the world as a child probably contributed to my thinking that way. My curiosity on that front, I think, was there even without the troubles I had.

[Male, Ph.D., 5 years practice]

Many others mentioned their own personal issues, and the experiences in their own treatment, as being the major factors.

In high school, I did think about being a social worker, though I didn't actually do it until much later. I was into helping people. But what made me want to be a therapist was my own therapy.

[Female, M.S.W., 15 years practice]

My own experience as a patient at age 30. I was very unhappy, and somatizing to beat the band. The world opened up, and there were dramatic results, even in my physical health. I was awed by my therapist's skill and training. She said I might have an aptitude for it, but I regarded that only as something nice to hear. Years later, another therapist, who was himself a Jesuit priest, told me that there was training available for someone like me who wasn't a doctor, which I didn't know.

[Male, M.S.W., 10 years practice]

I had therapy as a teenager, which I found helpful. I also knew that my mother went to therapy once or twice a week. And I think she talked about it as helpful. In college I enrolled in introductory psychology and loved it, and decided to become a psych major.

[Male, M.S.W., 20 years practice]

Sometimes it was a negative experience that led to the idea of becoming a therapist.

My husband's interest in his work [as a therapist] was a factor. Then my own therapy, and one therapist was so awful that I thought, "I could do this better."

[Female, M.A., 20 years practice]

Others saw the major influences as being intellectual, even situational, leading to psychotherapy as a kind of compromise solution.

I came from a somewhat poor family that was full of intelligence but not highly educated. Not very psychologically minded, not open to exploring psychological experience. It wasn't part of my childhood, to think about, "How does this feel?" However, both my parents were open to ideas, so there was a lot of support for thinking. I never thought about being a psychologist. I went to medical school with the idea of being a family practitioner. But I also have this strong intellectual pull, and family medicine is not very gratifying on that level, and psychiatry is one of the more intellectual areas, so that was appealing. I was very interested in the ideas and the theories. Later I found that the people part of it was also very attractive and appealing. That's what led to psychiatry. The fact that so many doors were closed to my mother made it important for me to have the feeling that I could be in the position of opening doors for others, because it felt like such a tragedy not to have that available.

[Female, M.D., 15 years practice]

There's no doubt. In college, I was initially a philosophy major, and I enjoyed immensely the intense intellectual exercise of coping with ambiguity and abstraction. I naively believed that in order to be in a field you have to make an original contribution, and after my first year in philosophy I came to the conclusion that, while I could understand what I was reading and could extrapolate from it, I didn't think I could make an original contribution. I got interested in psychology because of the theoretical nature of a lot of what I studied, and I found it to be extremely stimulating in the same way philosophy was but it had a practical application. It was a way of taking these very abstract ideas, and the intellectual stimulation I enjoyed, and applying them in a practical way.

[Male, Ph.D., 20 years practice]

I sought treatment myself when I was accepted to medical school in Europe, and I was about as emotionally prepared to go to medical school as I was to fly the next space mission. I was always humanistically oriented, and always interested in science, and psychology combines the two.

[Male, Ph.D., 10 years practice]

There were issues about myself that I didn't understand. It was not my original vocational choice. I thought I was going to be a physician, and then, from meeting some other people, I realized you don't have to be a physician to get inside people.

[Male, Ph.D., 20 years practice]

I had to be a doctor, so it was a matter of what kind of doctor I was going to be. By the time I got to medical school, it was a choice between surgery or psychiatry. And the on-call schedule for surgery was too much, so I chose psychiatry.

[Male, M.D., 20 years practice]

NUMERICAL DISTRIBUTION

Twenty-six people said that being a therapist was their role in their family; 17 people said that their own treatment led them to become a therapist; 6 said that a role model inspired them; 6 people said it was their own personal issues that led them to this field; and 5 people said it was their curiosity and voyeurism about others that made them choose this profession.

COMMENTS

Some issues in this area are: To what extent are motivations to become a psychotherapist conscious or unconscious? Is there any truth to the notion that therapists enter the field to resolve their own issues?

I think we could safely say that, in almost every significant decision, some of our motivations are conscious and some unconscious, and choice of profession is unlikely to be an exception. The fact that some of the motivation for a choice may be unconscious doesn't necessarily make it a bad choice. The stereotype of the "troubled therapist" who works out his or her own problems on the job probably refers to the correlation between a troubled childhood and the development of many of the interpersonal skills that make a good therapist.

In my own case, both my parents were therapists, and I've been in therapy much of my life, so in a way I've been in training to become a therapist since I was a child. I tried several other occupations, but they all got boring after a while, because in most jobs you learn to do something you don't know how to do well, which is challenging, and then you keep doing it forever, which is very repetitive. This is the only job I ever had that's continually challenging and never boring.

RELATED READING

Eber, M., and Kunz, L. B. (1984). The desire to help others. *Bulletin of the Menninger Clinic* 48(2):125–140.

Frank, H., and Paris, J. (1987). Psychological factors in the choice of psychiatry as a career. *Canadian Journal of Psychiatry* 32(2):118–122.

Lackie, B. (1983). The families of origin of social workers. *Clinical Social Work Journal* 11(4):309–322.

Marston, A. R. (1984). What makes therapists run? A model for analysis of motivational styles. *Psychotherapy* 21(4):456–459.

Sussman, M. B. (1992). *A Curious Calling: Unconscious Motivations for Practicing Psychotherapy*. Northvale, NJ: Jason Aronson.

▧▧▧▧

Question 69: What was it like to see your first patient?

No matter how much training a beginning therapist has, the first patient is new territory, and usually evokes some intense anxiety.

He was an obsessive-compulsive, who repeated a million things, and I had no idea what it was about. I went into the staff room of the clinic after that session, and I met a colleague and said I'd like to transfer a case to you, because I can't help this person, I don't know what I'm doing. And he said how long have you been seeing this person? And

I said once! And he said to give it a few more sessions. An anxiety-producing experience!

[Female, M.S.W., 20 years practice]

The anxiety can be very constricting.

It was a patient I would do much better with now, because he needed someone who could be a little loose to help him loosen up, and I was very strict with the rules, very rigid. I think I was helpful to him, but I felt very bound.

[Male, Ph.D., 20 years practice]

It was scary. It was such a big responsibility, and will I know enough to do this? I would keep my mouth closed, because I was scared that maybe it wasn't right.

[Female, M.S.W., 20 years practice]

Self-doubt and feelings of inadequacy often come up.

I felt like an impostor. I was nervous, afraid to be doing the wrong thing, to make a mistake. I sometimes feel that way today.

[Male, M.S.W., 15 years practice]

My first patients were quite ill, so there wasn't that feeling of working with someone who was like me. In my training, I felt like I was a kid and I was pretending to be an adult, and they would catch on. I also felt that if I were them, I wouldn't talk to me if I didn't have to. I could understand that they would want an older, more experienced person. I always talked to them about how they felt working with a trainee who didn't have a degree yet, mostly because they didn't have money to go to someone private. My supervisor said it's best to talk about it.

[Female, Ph.D., 10 years practice]

It was very frightening, a real identity crisis. Who am I to present myself this way? I felt like a little kid dressed up in the parent's clothes. This is what my doctor does. Pretending. There was a lot of anxiety. I had even more anxiety doing group than individual. But I took to it right from the beginning and enjoyed it right from the beginning. I often felt that I didn't understand what was going on.

[Male, Ph.D., 25 years practice]

I felt like I had no business being a therapist, like I was a fake. People were coming to me to help them, and they thought I knew what I was doing, and I didn't know anything. I was just sitting there pretending that I was wise. I used to go home at night thinking I shouldn't be taking money for this, I should be paying them to use them as guinea pigs like this. I took me a while to feel like I was worthy.

[Male, Ph.D., 15 years practice]

Therapists often feel that it is important not to let the patient know how inexperienced they are.

I was very aware of trying not to let them know that they were the first patient. I was anxious, very concerned about my intelligence, about whether I would have anything to say that sounded the least bit smart.

[Male, M.S.W., 10 years practice]

I was uncomfortable because she was someone I had known at an agency, and she expected me to be the way I had been there, more casual and more counseling than therapy. I was uncertain because I was playing with what my style should be. With my first new patient, I felt really intimidated because she was my first patient, and God forbid she knows that! I was uncomfortable that I was taking money and unsure that I would be able to give good treatment.

[Female, M.S.W., 5 years practice]

On the other hand, at least one person thought it was useful to let the patient know he was just a beginner.

When I did my psych rotation in medical school, my first patient was an adolescent girl. I was nervous. I felt completely incompetent. I know that I was no more than someone to just come by and talk to, for her to complain about her psychiatrist to. We were very up-front that we were students and in training, and I was trying to just get used to talking with patients.

[Male, M.D., 5 years practice]

Being so anxious, the therapist may be preoccupied with herself, and forget that the patient has his own anxieties.

It was terrifying. I kept thinking, "What am I doing? What am I doing here? Who am I to be doing this?" Actually it went fine, because the patient was thinking the same thing.

[Female, M.A., 20 years practice]

I was very anxious. I wanted very much to be perceived as brilliant, as competent, as knowledgeable. It was very important to me to be perceived in a certain way, so that probably I was less involved with what was going on with the patient, because I was so involved with myself.

[Female, M.A., 15 years practice]

The patient was very depressed and in that one interview opened up a ton of stuff, and I was very proud that she talked so much and told me all these problems. It was a very moving interview. Then she never came back! I couldn't believe it!

[Female, Ph.D., 30 years practice]

Therapist anxiety may also interfere with seeing the patient's progress.

I was very insecure, did not at all have a sense in my value to my patients. They were all very disturbed adolescent girls who were not very verbal, and had no notion of where they had problems. They came in more to complain, and there was a real discrepancy between my sense that I wasn't accomplishing very much, and didn't have much relationship with the kids, and my supervisor's perception that they were changing and I was being helpful. I just couldn't see it. I wasn't able to see small gains. I was looking for transformation, for the kids to stop acting out, and I couldn't see the small changes that were happening.

[Female, M.S.W., 20 years practice]

Sometimes the supervisor or the referring colleague is a presence in the room.

I don't remember, but I'm sure it was terrifying. I was filled with performance anxiety, and whether I would be able to help them, and whether I'd understand what was going on. I was concerned about the referral source, and whether they would continue sending patients.

[Male, M.D., 20 years practice]

I felt that I had to have a storehouse of information from her that I could bring to my supervisor. So there was a phantom presence there.

[Male, Ph.D., 40 years practice]

I was terrified! There was this honest-to-God human being sitting in front of me, for whom I had this responsibility. Meanwhile, I have this incredibly long list of questions that I'm supposed to get answered, because my supervisor said that. And my professor and some of my classmates are sitting on the other side of a one-way vision screen watching me. I remember not getting through my list of questions because my instinct told me there were certain answers I had to follow.

[Male, Ph.D., 20 years practice]

I was really nervous, because the referral came from my mentor, and it was a couple, and I was very nervous. I wanted to be sure that I sounded appropriate, that I sounded like I know what I'm doing. It turned out that the man was very challenging, so I really had to shift gears. But I was really afraid that I'd let my mentor down if I didn't do a good job.

[Female, Ph.D., 5 years practice]

Several psychoanalytically oriented therapists said the classical model of the silent analyst helped them manage their anxiety.

My first patients were in graduate school. I was very uncomfortable seeing patients, very nervous, because I didn't know what to say and what to do. By the time I saw my first patient in private practice, I had already adopted a classical model which didn't require much, so I just remained silent, mostly.

[Male, Ph.D., 50 years practice]

I was really scared. I felt like it was the blind leading the blind. I was still in training, and I just felt so incompetent to think that I had any answers. It went amazingly well, because I learned that keeping quiet, saying less, the person would assume I was having all these brilliant thoughts. And I was just not knowing what to say.

[Female, M.A., 20 years practice]

Some therapists begin their private practice in their homes, since they don't yet have enough patients to afford office space. This situation can sometimes produce unanticipated complications.

I was very anxious. I wanted to impress the patient, and I was working for a low-cost referral service, and I saw the patient at home. The people in the apartment above cooked with huge amounts of garlic, and my place was reeking of garlic, and I was embarrassed, so before I saw the patient I would burn incense in the room.

[Male, M.S.W., 35 years practice]

It was very exciting, wonderful. I saw her in my apartment, and my cat chased her around the couch, and I just laughed. And then she wanted to come back, which made me very happy.

[Female, M.S.W., 15 years practice]

In a sense, many practitioners have two sets of first patients: those from training or agency work, and those from private practice. Some anxiety and self-doubt can reemerge when a therapist opens a private practice.

I remember being very scared. What was I doing, and did I know how to do this? In social work school, my supervisor told me to put my hair up so that I'd look older. I remember feeling insecure, and too young. When I started my private practice, after years of agency work, I felt again like maybe I didn't know what I was doing, as if I had forgotten how, because I was in my own office and there weren't people all around me.

[Female, Ph.D., 20 years practice]

I was already comfortable working with people from my agency job. Having someone come to my private office put a little more pressure on me. I was more self-conscious or nervous.

[Female, M.A., 15 years practice]

A very few people said that they felt very quickly comfortable in the role of therapist.

I was excited, and very happy to be doing what I always wanted to do. I was very optimistic, and felt very competent. I always had very strong feelings of competence.

[Male, Ph.D., 15 years practice]

I remember it exactly! She was my control case. I was very nervous, but I had been a rehabilitation counselor for many years, so I knew how to have an interview with someone. I was very at ease with that. I was nervous because I knew I was going to talk to a supervisor. Am I going to be able to understand what this person's telling me and then be able to describe it to a supervisor? I also had in mind, because I didn't know if they would talk or not talk, what would I do if they didn't talk? I knew as a therapist you're supposed to allow silence. As a counselor you don't have to. She turned out to be very talkative. I felt anxious but very excited. I was very thrilled to have a crack at it and see how I did. I had been to classes, and seen my supervisor beforehand, so I was sort of primed for it. And I remember her parting line. Before she left the office she said, "I'm a strange case!" And she was.

[Female, M.S., 15 years practice]

Several people spoke of having found their "true calling."

I was an intern. It was an adolescent anorexic girl in a hospital setting. It was a very difficult patient. For me, it was like I had found my calling. I wasn't sure when I started my internship what I was going to choose as a specialty. I began in the emergency room, and that was terrific, exciting, very frightening but very exciting. My second rotation was psychiatry, and suddenly I found myself getting there early, and at the end of the day I wasn't tired. It really solidified my choice.

[Male, M.D., 20 years practice]

There was a lot of anxiety associated with seeing patients for a lot of years into my training. My first outpatient was a young girl with epilepsy, and she was extremely needy. We established a connection that was clearly useful to her. I learned certain things about the nature of communication in therapy that stuck with me. I regarded the experience as confirming that this was something I liked and really wanted to do.

[Male, M.D., 15 years practice]

I was so excited I had a headache! I couldn't believe it when I got the referral. I was sitting in the session thinking, "I love this work." Then I thought, "What if I'm terrible at it?" It was very exciting.

[Female, M.S.W., 25 years practice]

I was a little scared. One of the reasons I had not become a therapist before was that I wasn't sure I wanted the responsibility of fucking around with anybody's head. I didn't know whether I was going to be good, and if I wasn't going to be very good I wasn't going to do it. Once I started, it was hard, but I absolutely felt that I had a gift and loved it.

[Female, M.S.W., 10 years practice]

Several therapists described their first case in some detail.

It was very frightening. I didn't know what I was supposed to do. It was before I had been in therapy so I really had no actual experience. But I always knew I was a good listener, so I listened. I was being trained in a very analytic model at the time so I wasn't actually supposed to do anything except listen, maybe make interpretations. But I'd always been action-oriented, so I wanted to do something, to make an impact, to help this guy deal with what he was complaining about.

[Male, Ph.D., 25 years practice]

One of my first cases was an Irish Catholic exhibitionist who had been referred to me by the courts. I was seeing him three times a week on the couch. His impulses were so severe. I realize now that he was probably a borderline, but I didn't know that at the time, and it's

probably just as well because it might have interfered with my judgment at the time. He used to time it so he would exhibit himself in
front of little girls just as he was ejaculating, and I felt such revulsion
I wondered why I was working with him, and what good I would do.
And then it hit me, and I said, "You're trying to get me to kick you out
of therapy, aren't you?" and he said yes. He had been seeing a world-
famous psychiatrist, a man who had written books about criminal
behavior, and this person had kicked him out of treatment.

[Male, M.S.W., 35 years practice]

My first patient in the walk-in clinic had just been released from a
psychiatric hospital, and she was obese and dirty, and she told me that
she could see that I'd had a hard life too. And then she asked me to
hold her. I said, "I'm not sure. Could you wait a minute?" And I went
out to ask some colleagues what to do, and one said, "Tell her in
therapy we hold each other with words." So I went back in, and I said
that, and it worked.

[Female, M.S.W., 5 years practice]

My first client at the agency was an old man, hard of hearing, and I
had a little cubbyhole office, and I had to shout at him. I didn't know
what I was doing, and kept trying to ask him about his sex life. And he
kept saying he wanted a job. He said to me that I was too young to
understand his problems. I went to my supervisor, who told me if I
stayed in the field long enough, someday someone would tell me I
was too old.

[Female, M.S.W., 30 years practice]

My first patient was one of my most difficult patients, and the one I
probably learned the most from, because she stuck with me in spite of
the fact that I was very much a neophyte. From the beginning, I remember thinking that what helped me the most was all the work I'd done
in communication, because there was so much that I got in spite of all
my anxiety from her nonverbal communication. I felt at ease with her
because I understood something about her before I tried to engage in
the long therapeutic process that we'd be in together.

[Female, M.S.W., 15 years practice]

It was the most terrifying experience. I remember picking the patient
up in the waiting room, and thinking, "What the hell am I doing? They
must be out of their mind to come and talk to me." After four or five
weeks, I did make a rather large error, and I knew it as soon as I said
it, and I spent a good portion of the next two days crying and thinking,

"Why did I say it?" It happened to be a correct interpretation, but it wasn't something the person was ready to hear. I really beat myself up severely for it.

[Female, M.S.W., 10 years practice]

NUMERICAL DISTRIBUTION

Forty-five people said they were very anxious seeing their first patient; 13 said they were not. Two people could not recall the experience.

COMMENTS

Some issues here are: What makes it easy for some therapists to feel comfortable and legitimate in the role and very difficult for others? Is it a good idea to let patients know that they are working with a beginning therapist?

I think the answers to both this question and Question 63 come from the way the therapist conceives of the role of therapist. If "therapist" means "expert who dispenses wisdom" then it will be very difficult for a beginner to feel entitled to that status, and equally difficult to reveal to the patient that the therapist is no expert; if the word means "companion/guide" it may be easier to feel comfortable both in filling the role and in revealing level of experience to the patient.

Most therapists actually have two first patients: the one at the agency and the one in private practice. In my own experience, my first agency position, right out of graduate school, was at a halfway house for discharged psychiatric patients. The very first day I had to hospitalize my first patient for a suicide attempt. Riding to the hospital in the cab, with the patient holding his bloody wrist, I remember thinking, "What the hell am I getting myself into here?"

With my first private patient, I was surprisingly calm. Having grown up in a household where both parents were therapists, I felt like a knew a lot and was ready to do the work. The patient was a young woman, bright, a good sense of humor, lively and attractive, and she seemed to be comfortable with me right away. We did good work together, and I saw her for about two years.

RELATED READING

Cade, J. (1993). An evaluation of early patient contact for medical students. *Medical Education* 27(3):205–210.

Howe, B. J. (1975). The practice of psychotherapy as a do-it-yourself treatment for a beginning therapist. *Family Therapy* 2(2):123–128.
Irwin, E. C. (1986). On being and becoming a therapist. *Arts in Psychotherapy* 13(3):191–195.

🐚🐚🐚🐚

Question 70: What was your experience in supervision?

Every trained therapist begins treating patients under the guidance and feedback of a supervisor. Agencies usually have supervisors overseeing the work of staff therapists. This question explores experiences in supervision, both good and bad.

A surprising finding here is that so many therapists had such negative experiences in supervision, at least with certain supervisors. More than two-thirds of the group said that they had had at least one supervisory experience that was hurtful, damaging, unpleasant, or simply a waste of time. Only about a quarter of the group had consistently positive experiences.

For the lucky ones, good experiences were often nurturing and educational at the same time.

> I was very lucky, because I had some very good supervision. My first supervisor's style was so knowledgeable, but she made me think for myself. She did not offer what she thought one should do, but really encouraged me to explore myself and what I could do. I've continued with her over the years and seen her change, and that's been important too, because it gives me the confidence to change, the way I think, the way I do things, that I'm not stuck in one place, that it's okay to try other things. With my case control supervisor I learned a lot about countertransference, about experiencing myself. And also a lot about setting up the tasks of treatment. I never had any negative experiences, only less dynamic.
>
> [Female, M.A., 15 years practice]

> The new supervisor was all over me in the first session. He criticized everything I did, but I loved him because he also somehow made me feel that he thought I was a terrific therapist and that it was a pleasure for him to work with me. So he was giving me a huge amount without ever making me feel put down, and I felt very respected by him.
>
> [Male, Ph.D., 5 years practice]

> My current supervisor conducts the supervision as if it were a session, not that I'm a patient, but she's given me a lot of different ways of

looking at things. She's very helpful. There are times when she says, "Could you have asked that a different way?" but she doesn't ever point her finger and say, "How dare you say that?" which a supervisor has actually said to me.

[Female, M.S.W., 10 years practice]

The best taught me more than anyone has ever taught me about looking at my own issues in the session, about looking away from the textbooks, and about humanizing this process. Stop looking for the answer on page thirty-four in the textbook on casework, it's not there. She really taught from a good–better–best perspective, and you had to do something really egregious, like steal from a client or punch a client or have sex with a client to get her to say that was wrong. Even then she might have you look at what that meant. She provided such a space, so that instead of supervision being a place where I felt I would be caught and made wrong, or that was a test and someone else knew the answers, it became this huge excitement of something I couldn't wait to get to. I learned so much. She would bring in the theoretical perspective after we had looked at the human stuff.

[Male, M.S.W., 15 years practice]

I had four supervisors. One I hired privately since I was doing therapy on my own. The first three were through the institute and the clinic. I had very good experiences with them. I tend to feel very threatened, afraid I'm going to be blamed or criticized, but actually with them I could say or do anything. It was a very freeing experience, which surprised me, because I thought I would not feel that way. I liked being in supervision.

[Female, M.S., 15 years practice]

My institute supervisors were very good. It wasn't where I felt I had to protect myself. They weren't critical, they were really on my side, and whatever I did was fine, and let's see what we can learn, and how we can help you and your patient.

[Male, Ph.D., 20 years practice]

I had excellent experiences in the counseling program, and I was able to be a child and say I know nothing and I'm in your hands and I'm here to learn, and not to be defensive at all. And that was wonderful.

[Female, M.S., 20 years practice]

The best supervision was my toughest. It was supervision of an analysis of a clearly borderline patient who was barely accepted at the treatment center. The patient was accepted on the contingency that this analyst supervise the case, because he broke the vote on accepting. I learned the most from this because he was confident that he could help me deal with and understand this patient, and that was true. This supervisor focused almost exclusively on negative transference, any kind of indication that this patient was harboring some kind of hostile, aggressive feelings toward me in the transference or toward significant others in the past. As it happened, that approach worked particularly well with this patient. It was this patient that gave me the best sense of how to deal with the unconscious in the psychoanalyst's office, and it was the supervisor who helped me translate that into my own voice and my own style in interpreting, and to be able to hear certain things that I wasn't in tune with.

[Male, M.D., 20 years practice]

I've had supervision over many years, and I've enjoyed it and found it very helpful. A good supervisor is someone who has something to tell you that you didn't know, who sees something in the material you're presenting you didn't see, or structures it in such a way that you have a new insight into it. Someone who can do that with a sense of neutrality and friendship, who isn't critical of your errors.

[Male, Ph.D., 40 years practice]

While some people stressed the accumulated experience of the supervisor, at least one person had a very positive supervision with a beginner.

Good supervision comes from the same thing that makes a good patient/therapist match: respect for your difficulties, and an appropriate pride in your accomplishments. My first supervisor was a beginning supervisor, and in reflection I think that my unconscious helped me choose her, because I was a beginning therapist. I wasn't so afraid to put out my own ideas. She was very sharp, but she was also a beginner, so we learned together.

[Female, M.S.W., 20 years practice]

Some people emphasized the intellectual aspects of the experience.

Some of it was good, when the person was smart. I need smart people who know what they're talking about, and who will also engage in discussion about what's going on, and make me think.

[Female, Ph.D., 30 years practice]

Supervision was a mixed bag. It's generally pretty anxiety-provoking for me, because I feel like I've always been a maverick, from the very beginning. It's been hard to trust my own judgment, and so many supervisors are so critical, they're so caught up in their own way of doing it, they can't see what you're doing. The good supervisors have really tuned in, and expressed confidence in me. And yet have also been able to cut to the chase when I've been off, and say that something wasn't too good. One of my best supervisors helped me clarify a lot of concepts. I'm a feeler, not a thinker, so this was really helpful.

[Female, M.S.W., 15 years practice]

One supervisor was a wonderful experience, because it was very interactive, and she was warm and very caring about patients. She had a lot to offer me that worked. She would give me books to read. I also have been supervised by a psychiatrist, and I learned an awful lot about medication from him.

[Female, M.S.W., 10 years practice]

I've had mainly good supervisors. My very first was a good match for me. What was helpful was that they helped me to clarify theoretical material, and then translate that into what you do when you're sitting in the room with the patient. We would role-play, and that made it less ethereal and more practical. And she was a nice lady.

[Female, M.S.W., 20 years practice]

I've hired supervisors, chosen people, who've been very good. People who could push me, and ask me provocative questions about why I'm doing something, and challenge me in ways that make me think. Who give me new ways to work with someone if I'm stuck.

[Female, Ph.D., 20 years practice]

I've had some excellent supervisors. My current guy really knows what he's talking about. He can organize what I present to him very quickly, and with considerable certainty. Now, ten years from now I may decide he didn't know what he was talking about, but right now it feels very good and it helps me. I'm reading a book on computers, and I feel like a disk that's being formatted. He can let me know what he's thinking about my work without being critical.

[Male, M.S.W., 15 years practice]

Others emphasized the emotional aspects.

The good supervisor was the same as makes a good therapist: to listen, not to rush into things, to let the process evolve without being critical, to try to understand what I do and why I do this instead of that rather than telling me what to do. So when the process of supervision mirrors the process of therapy, that's the way we learn. I know the supervisor/supervisee relationship is different from the therapist/patient relationship, but there are commonalities.

[Male, Ph.D., 20 years practice]

One of the great supervisors I had was one of the early proponents of nondirective psychotherapy, a Rogerian. Rogers really knew what it was about, and so did my supervisor. He was the most accepting, understanding, kind person I was ever supervised by, and it was very helpful to me, to feel understood.

[Male, Ph.D., 50 years practice]

I love supervision. A good supervisor is somebody who has the same belief system I have about doing the work, somebody with whom I can feel comfortable to talk about my mistakes, and who isn't going to make me feel defensive, and somebody who will put things in perspective for me, because I can get flooded around certain issues. I like a supervisor who is good at de-escalating it for me.

[Female, M.S.W., 10 years practice]

A couple of people said that it was possible for a supervisor to be too supportive.

In social work school, my first supervisor was incredibly supportive, and her support felt like it was very far from what my own perception was of myself. It was not a helpful kind of support. I experienced it as kind of dismissive. She kept saying everything was great and I was great, but it didn't have any impact on me because it was so extreme.

[Female, M.S.W., 20 years practice]

It was basically a very positive experience, in the sense that the supervisor was very supportive of me. Too supportive, actually, and at one point I complained to him that he was not critical enough. And he said he didn't have to be, and that was very nice, but I don't think he was right.

[Male, M.S.W., 25 years practice]

Several people stressed the importance of feeling respected by the supervisor.

The supervisors I liked almost from the very beginning made me feel like a colleague. It was like talking to a friend and colleague who's going to help you and fill you out, as opposed to talking to someone who says, "What do you know?"

[Male, M.D., 20 years practice]

I've had some wonderful experiences. I've had supervisors who let me practice the kind of therapy that I wanted to practice, and said, in effect, how can I help you? Just like a good therapist. They respected me as a colleague, and that was terrific. That's the kind I learn from.

[Male, Ph.D., 10 years practice]

One person, who comes from a social work background, suggested that there are differences in the nature of supervision depending on the training background of the supervisor.

Analytic supervision was a blessing. Social work supervision was a fucking bitch. I was in analytic supervision for fourteen years with various people, and in all those years, none of these people ever did anything as intrusive, hostile, or anxiety-provoking as in social work supervision. And it is noteworthy that I've supervised psychologists, psychiatrists, and social workers doing therapy, and it's only the social workers who are fearful and anxious and defensive. In social work, if you had any kind of countertransference problem or you missed anything, the supervisors invariably made you feel as if you had committed some sort of psychological sin. With the analysts, it was, "You have a problem here. Deal with it."

[Male, M.S.W., 35 years practice]

The vast majority of our group had some really hurtful experiences with supervisors. As one person pointed out, it may be difficult to admit the reality of the situation while it is occurring.

You value those things a lot more when you're going through them than afterward, because you have such an investment in seeing the supervisor as having something to offer you.

[Male, M.D., 15 years practice]

Here are some typical examples of bad supervisors.

Through the clinic where I trained it was not great. They liked to talk about themselves, not about the patient, or the case, or me. They liked to talk about wardrobe, their house in the Hamptons. And I went to the director and tried to get out of it, but there was no way, so I stayed and made the best I could.

[Female, M.S.W., 20 years practice]

During the first year with my first patients, I distinctly felt that the supervisor did not like me and did not trust me, and did some projecting of concerns about unethical behavior onto me that were not coming from me.

[Male, Ph.D., 10 years practice]

The supervisors during my internship were not very good. They were quirky, had personality problems, they were contemptuous, overbearing. They weren't really professional in their attitude toward the supervision. They weren't really engaged in the process: It was something they had to do and they were marking time.

[Male, M.D., 15 years practice]

My second supervisor was someone who was extremely analytic, and I hated it. I was doing family therapy for the first time, and knew nothing about doing family therapy in terms of theory, and instead of giving me something helpful, a better intervention, or showing me why I got led down the wrong path, which is really what I needed, all she was focusing on was my anxiety in the session, how anxious was I with this couple. I felt like I was ready to kill her. I wanted to say that I was very anxious with the couple and could we help me with the anxiety by telling me what I should be doing? And if we weren't talking about that, we were talking about my wearing black stockings, and how could anyone have respect for a therapist who was wearing miniskirts and black stockings? So we spent a lot of time in a mother–daughter haggling about stuff like that.

[Female, M.S.W., 20 years practice]

My worst was when I was working in a nontraditional high school, and I was working well with the kids, and they loved me and I loved them. I work really well with that kind of kid. And the supervisor called me at home, and asked me to meet her at a bar, and I knew something was up. She asked me if I was gay, and I said yes of course I'm gay, and she warned me not to mess with the kids. And I told her that if she didn't fuck with any of her clients, I wouldn't fuck with mine, and I warned her that if she ever tried something like that again I would have her in court so fast her head would spin. For the next year, supervision was a nightmare.

[Male, M.S.W., 15 years practice]

I have had two experiences that were very negative. One was very authoritarian. I had had four early terminations and was very worried about it. The first thing the supervisor told me when I made an appointment to see her was that I can't use the bathroom. She sees patients and supervisees in her house. I walked in and she says, "You're losing your patients. What do you think your problem is?" I became totally defensive, and wound up becoming very passive-aggressive with her. I switched to someone else, but she was also very directive and very nasty. I know I become visibly anxious when I feel threatened, and I did that with her, and she thought it was how I was with the patients. She was always accusing me of doing something wrong.

[Female, M.S.W., 10 years practice]

I've had attacking supervisors, and it was sometimes unbearable. I'm not good at that. At the gestalt institute, we had to be in group supervision with the director for a year, and it was very hard. She was attacking, she never had anything good to say, she would become enraged to the point of trembling if you disagreed with her. So I left.

[Male, M.S.W., 15 years practice]

At the institute, my first supervisor was not so good. I would bring in a tape, and he would listen for about two or three minutes and then say, "Well, this is what's going on," instead of playing the whole thing and getting into it. It wasn't that he was wrong, it just wasn't useful for him to tell me that way. It never helped me. The second supervisor there was very harsh and critical, so that wasn't any good either.

[Female, M.S.W., 5 years practice]

The first one was quite infantilizing. I don't like taking notes in a session, but it was all process oriented, and I had to present sessions word for word. I even began to tape sessions, but that made me feel like an actor. I was probably more conscious of the tape than the patient was. I was on my "best behavior" but I wasn't a very good therapist. I hated it. Several supervisory experiences were heavily theoretical, psychoanalytically theoretical, whether it was more Freudian, or object relations, or self psychology. And I hated that, because I don't belong to any "church." One supervisor insisted I take notes in the session, and I switched supervisors. I had several supervisors that I think were threatened by the fact that I already had a doctorate and they didn't, they were M.S.W.s.

[Male, Ph.D., 10 years practice]

Some supervisors seem to think that being judgmental and critical is helpful to the supervisee.

It was always communicated to me that there was a correct way and I just couldn't get it. I would present to a supervisor and I was completely confused and he would say that this meant that and so on, and how the fuck did he know? Monday-morning quarterbacking is the easiest thing in the world to do, and he would do this. And so I'd always be depressed and feel horrible about myself and unworthy, and I remember the year after I stopped supervision was such a relief. It was very intrusive, and demanding. But necessary. It's necessary to talk to somebody about your work. They all were knowledgeable and helpful and I learned a lot from all my supervisors, but they all were full of shit in that no one told me it's impossible, and no one told me how difficult it is, and no one told me it's okay to feel shame.

[Male, Ph.D., 25 years practice]

I had someone recently, a very famous analyst, who was a sadistic jerk. In our first meeting, I started to present a case, and he interrupted me and said, "Who taught you to do therapy that way!" From that point on, I was on edge with him every session, but I was required to have him as my supervisor. His method was to give him a dialogue of each session, step by step, and then he would jump on everything I said and was very judgmental.

[Male, Ph.D., 15 years practice]

In school, there was too much power play by the professor. The professors had to find something wrong with you, and until I realized that that was their job, it was difficult.

[Male, Ph.D., 15 years practice]

When I was a young therapist, being told what to do and being criticized was much more narcissistically difficult for me to handle. Now, I can take it with a grain of salt and try to figure out what they're trying to help me with. My worst supervision had so much of that invasive critical stuff that it was hard to experience myself as growing in the experience, and that was with someone who was very well-schooled, but very dogmatic in a classical Freudian tradition, and there was not much room for differences.

[Female, M.S.W., 15 years practice]

I had a supervisor who was a training analyst. His whole focus was countertransference, and people would leave his office in tears. He would only take you if you were in therapy. He figured someone else would put you back together again. His job was to point out every piece of countertransference that he saw. Sometimes he was wrong but he figured that was okay. I always argued with him. I said he was sadistic and he said he was benevolent. Because it was painful.

[Male, Ph.D., 25 years practice]

Some supervisors tell their supervisees what to do, and how to do it.

> I had some of what I consider bad supervision in graduate school. It was undermining and restricting. For me, bad supervision was when I was told, "You have to use this language, you have to think in this way," and there was no flexibility. They tell you what to do. This orientation is the only orientation, and you can't veer from that. What I would do is make up the process notes to give them what they insisted on.
> [Female, Ph.D., 5 years practice]

> I had a terrible experience in graduate school. My supervisor was totally into process reports, but had no idea of the case itself. She was into the words that were said. I found after a while that I couldn't be honest with her.
> [Male, Ph.D., 40 years practice]

> I had very bad supervisors at the analytic institute. One guy told me what to do. He never once asked me how I would handle it, what my rationale would be. Then I had someone who supervises by telling you about himself, not only how he would do it, but also his personal reactions to things. It's totally narcissistic.
> [Female, M.S., 20 years practice]

Some supervisors approach supervisees as if they were patients.

> There's that concept of therapeutic supervision, where you want to learn something, but the supervisor wants to get into your head, and it's frustrating. Some supervisors have poor boundaries in that way, that they're not clear what's therapy and what's supervision.
> [Female, M.S.W., 10 years practice]

> My school experiences were not good, and it had to do somewhat with my own feelings about myself, confidence issues, and feeling that I was the student and the peon. I felt more like the baby, and unsure of how to negotiate that. In the beginning, I was very worried about how they were going to see me. A good supervisor is one who works collegially and doesn't try to be your therapist. In school, we had to reveal a lot of our countertransference issues and personal material, and I found that the supervisors tended to use that a little bit.
> [Female, M.S.W., 5 years practice]

Sometimes the supervisor bends over backward to avoid being critical or judgmental, but acting like the silent psychoanalyst can be less than helpful.

One supervisor was a woman who would, week after week, sit looking at me with unblinking eyes and say very little. I had the feeling she was treating me like my worst fantasy of what a classical analyst was like. I kept trying to tell her that I was a student and it was my first case, and could she maybe teach me something? She didn't know what the hell I was talking about. I was lucky that the head of the clinic liked me and allowed me to change supervisors.

[Male, Ph.D., 5 years practice]

I had a really horrible supervisor early on. It was a guy who was classically analytic, and did not speak, and would periodically ask me how I felt about something. It was a nightmare. I used to fear going, and I used to call in sick. Finally, after a year, I asked the director for a new supervisor, and she said she couldn't believe I had worked with him for so long, that no one else had been able to.

[Female, M.A., 15 years practice]

At the institute, I had a lot of senior psychiatrists as supervisors. They would not say anything. They would comment if they thought you were doing something wrong, and say that they thought it was a mistake. If you asked them a question they would try to answer it, but otherwise if you presented a process, they just listened. If they didn't say anything, you figured you were doing all right.

[Male, M.D., 15 years practice]

I think my supervision was lousy. They just let me talk about my cases and how I handled them, and they never criticized it, or told me to do something else. I don't recall having a really good supervisor. In my case control, I had to do process notes for every session, what I said and what the patient said, and then I had to read them to the supervisor, but he never said anything about it. I said that it was not a perfect patient/therapist interaction, and he said it was fine. He seemed to be interested, but he never gave me his opinion.

[Female, M.A., 15 years practice]

I had supervisors I now see as having problems with aggression, because at the end of our time together, they'd say that there were all these issues that I didn't want to work on, things that they knew about, but they didn't say anything, they didn't tell me.

[Male, Ph.D., 20 years practice]

Because beginning therapists are sometimes very anxious about their competence and ability, they are not always able to use the resources of the supervisor.

Early on, I did not find it very useful, because I was terribly concerned with being found out as incompetent. So I didn't really trust the supervisors, that they would truly understand. I was still thinking that these people were going to grade me, and what's the right answer. The most important parts of my professional development came out of just experiencing patients in the room, and my professional readings.

[Female, M.A., 20 years practice]

Some found group supervision a happier experience than individual.

I like group supervision, because it can be easier to take it in when it's directed at somebody else.

[Female, M.S.W., 15 years practice]

And some found group supervision less than wonderful.

I had bad supervision in group, whenever there was more than one of us, because it stultified the clarity of what we were doing, too much competition, too much posing.

[Male, Ph.D., 30 years practice]

NUMERICAL DISTRIBUTION

Sixteen people said they had had only positive experiences in supervision. Of the others, 43 people said they had had both good and bad supervisors. Only one person said he had had totally negative experiences in supervision.

COMMENTS

The issues here are: What is good supervision? Is it useful to treat supervisees the same way as patients?

I think that what makes a good supervisor is the same as what makes a good teacher: asking the right questions and occasionally supplying some suggestions and even possible answers. Simply telling trainees what to do and how to do it makes it harder for them to find the solutions that work for them. Criticizing, embarrassing, or humiliating supervisees seems so obviously counterproductive that it is difficult to imagine how it happens. Yet according to this sample it seems to happen a lot.

One of the big surprises to me in doing this book was discovering how many therapists had bad therapy (see Question 72), and how many had bad supervision. Personally, I never had any really bad supervisors, just some that were less than helpful. My first supervisor was very good, supportive and noncritical, respectful of my point of view, and made me think about what I was doing without creating the anxiety that I was doing it wrong. My next supervisor was obsessed with diagnosis, which I usually find completely irrelevant, and we used to argue about that. Otherwise he was good enough, though I don't think I discovered much while I was with him. It was more just filling the training requirements. Another wasn't interested in anything but the affect, which isn't my own way of working, so that wasn't much help. I had one other supervisor who was very good. I respected him very much, and he showed me that you could loosen up a lot and use yourself in creative ways, which was very helpful. Good supervision can feel like a safety net when you're walking the high wire with patients, especially those first few patients. Bad supervision can be a nightmare.

I don't understand the rationale for treating supervisees like patients, even to the point of putting them on the couch. This blurs the boundary between therapy and supervision and, if the supervisee internalizes such blurring, might lead the trainee to blur other boundaries later on. I think it is perfectly valid for a supervisor to point out an issue that the supervisee needs to work on in his or her personal therapy, but to leave it at that and not try to do therapy with the trainee.

RELATED READING

Kennard, B. D., Stewart, S. M., and Gluck, M. R. (1987). The supervision relationship: variables contributing to positive versus negative experiences. *Professional Psychology: Research and Practice* 18(2):172–175.

Pruitt, D. B., McColgan, E. B., Pugh, R. L., and Kiser, L. J. (1986). Approaches to psychotherapy supervision. *Journal of Psychiatric Education* 10(2): 129–147.

Sherry, P. (1991). Ethical issues in the conduct of supervision. *Counseling Psychologist* 19(4):566–584.

Wallerstein, R. S., ed. (1981). *Becoming a Psychoanalyst.* New York: International Universities Press.

🔊🔊🔊🔊

Question 71: Have you ever supervised other therapists? What's that like?

At a certain point in their careers, many therapists get the opportunity to supervise other therapists and teach some of what they have learned.

Everyone who had done supervision described it as a very positive experience for them.

> It's the thing for which I feel most well-trained, the thing I do the best, and that I get the most gratification from.
>
> [Female, M.S., 20 years practice]

> It challenges me, and makes me think about cases in different ways, how I might have handled it differently, why I think what they did was good. It reinforces my own skills.
>
> [Male, M.S.W., 15 years practice]

> A lot of what I do with my patients is basically teaching, so communicating complex ideas in a variety of ways to different people is a lot of fun for me.
>
> [Male, Ph.D., 20 years practice]

> It gives me the chance to reflect on material without having to be directly involved in it. It gives me a breadth of latitude and freedom that I wouldn't have with a patient.
>
> [Male, M.D., 20 years practice]

> Our business is very lonely, so to talk about our work with someone who's in the same ballpark is wonderful. I'm a teacher, and I know a lot about this, and that's very exciting, very gratifying. I'm very tough on them about standards and reading and so on, but I want them to let their patients know that we're all in this together and it's very difficult and very mysterious.
>
> [Male, Ph.D., 25 years practice]

Some people specified particular aspects of doing supervision as most enjoyable.

> It's wonderful because I have to go back and remember why I do something, the foundations, and explain it. It's very challenging to work with students who are really interested in learning.
>
> [Female, Ph.D., 5 years practice]

> I find it fascinating to hear what other people do. Sometimes I'm aghast, and sometimes it's very gratifying to hear what other people are doing. I enjoy teaching stuff that I'm interested in.
>
> [Female, M.D., 15 years practice]

It's easier than working with patients, because I don't have the same responsibility. It's more of a peer relationship, the people I'm dealing with are not as disturbed and so it's much easier to relate.

[Male, Ph.D., 50 years practice]

I have a tendency to make patients out of my supervisees, and I find that's the best form of supervision.

[Male, Ph.D., 30 years practice]

Some supervisors said there were aspects of supervising that were hard for them.

I like to see people work. I need to be careful, though, because I sometimes lose perspective of where someone is in their professional development, and I can have expectations, and I talk to them as if they know more than they do.

[Female, Ph.D., 30 years practice]

Students don't understand that you're still working on your technique and your skills all the time, even after many years. They think that you learn it and that's it, then you have all the answers and all the responses and interventions as if they were in a file, and you just go to the right one.

[Female, M.A., 15 years practice]

At times I get a real charge out of it, because they're hungry for knowledge. At other times, I may feel inadequate, because I feel that I can't give them what they need.

[Male, M.D., 5 years practice]

I don't know if I'm a very empathic supervisor. I'm not critical, but it's hard to hear mistakes, and my impulse is to tell them what to do.

[Female, M.S.W., 15 years practice]

A few people mentioned the occasional difficulty of some supervisees.

It depends on the student. I've had a couple of psychiatric residents that I told they shouldn't be psychiatrists.

[Male, M.D., 20 years practice]

I had a bad experience with a supervisee who cried every session. After four sessions, she became enraged with me and left, accusing me of being insensitive.

[Male, M.S.W., 25 years practice]

It depends on the supervisee. Some don't think they have much to learn, and some are open. Some are arrogant, some view me as someone who doesn't have much to teach them. Some people are very fixed on one approach, they don't want to learn another approach. And that's frustrating.

[Female, Ph.D., 10 years practice]

NUMERICAL DISTRIBUTION

Twenty-six people said they had done supervision, and all described it as a positive experience for them.

COMMENTS

The issues here are the same as the previous question: What makes a good supervisor? How does being a supervisor integrate with being a therapist? So many of the therapists in this group had bad supervision—does anyone ever admit that he or she is a bad supervisor?

Personally, I've always enjoyed doing supervision, which can be a positive experience in several ways. First, it is an opportunity to pass on accumulated knowledge and experience to someone who can use it productively. Second, it can be a nice complement to doing therapy, another variation on the theme. Third, it's a way of being involved in treatment, but one step removed. As one interviewee said, it's "sort of like being a grandparent."

RELATED READING

Gandalfo, R. L., and Brown, R. (1987). Psychology interns ratings of actual and ideal supervision of psychotherapy. *Journal of Training and Practice in Professional Psychology* 1(1):15–28.

Lane, R. C., ed. (1990). *Psychoanalytic Approaches to Supervision.* New York: Brunner/Mazel.

Shanfield, S. B., Matthews, K. L., and Hetherly, V. (1993). What do excellent psychotherapy supervisors do? *American Journal of Psychiatry* 150(7):1081–1084.

Tasman, A. (1993). Setting standards for psychotherapy training: it's time to do our homework. *Journal of Psychotherapy Practice and Research* 2(2):93–96.

🔊🔊🔊🔊

Question 72: What was your experience as a patient?

Virtually every therapist is a patient at some point. For many, the experience in therapy is the deciding factor in choosing to become a therapist. Most therapists are required to have some treatment as part of their training.

Another surprising finding of the survey was how many of our therapists had negative experiences in their own treatment, with someone who was actively harmful or simply not helpful. Only seven people said they had had only good experiences in treatment, while everyone else said that there were some therapists who were either not good or actively bad.

Let's start with the good experiences.

> Even my first contact with therapy was very positive, because it made me feel hopeful. . . . At about age 24 I went into therapy because I was again very depressed, and that was a turning point for me. I was with a much older woman therapist who really helped me to explore my own childhood, my family, my parents, do the work that I had never even considered doing. It was very thorough, and group was also very useful. I always felt a very deep and profound connection to my first therapist. I really cared about her and I knew she cared about me.
>
> [Female, M.A., 15 years practice]

> When I got sober, I went into therapy with someone who was both a social worker and a certified alcoholism counselor, and I stayed with her for eight years, and that was an incredible experience. I trusted her, and I was able to talk with her about stuff that had happened all my life, issues that I thought about, and I was able to talk them through, to see them from different spaces. She could be with me. She was very confrontative and nurturing at the same time.
>
> [Male, M.S.W., 15 years practice]

> After my marriage broke up, I was miserable, and I went to a very good therapist, and was in individual and group with her, and that was a very good experience. She was very smart, and interactive, and there as a person. She was a very good role model for me. I was looking for a different kind of mother, and found one with her.
>
> [Female, M.S.W., 30 years practice]

> I went to my physician, who was a well-known specialist in psychosomatic medicine, and he referred me to his own analyst, who was a

very sweet, wonderful man who had been himself analyzed by Freud and was at that time head of New York Psychoanalytic. I went to him for five years, on the couch five days a week, and for the first three months I didn't say a word, and neither did he. But after that it was a very positive experience. He did very unusual things, that Freudians don't do. For example, I was physically ill, and he put me to bed upstairs in his apartment, because he was afraid for me to go home. Another time, he took me to the corner drugstore to get a prescription for me, and another time, after I had moved out West, he came out and visited me in the hospital. And that was marvelous. When I came back to New York a few years later, I went back to him for another year.

[Female, M.S., 20 years practice]

One of my better experiences was with a man who, after my convoluted stories, was able to pull out the essentials and present me with them. And the clarity of that really helped a great deal. My best experience was with a woman who was just the best mother, and I got the reinforcement of accepting who I am as being okay.

[Female, M.S., 15 years practice]

My very first experience was very good. She talked to me like I was a human being. She was understanding. She was very analytic, but able to help me understand why I was feeling, and why my behavior was what it was, and why my family might have been treating me this way. Later I was in psychoanalytic therapy with a man for about fifteen years, and that was very good. I was able to talk, to feel, and to learn, and he was able to move with me. I learned a lot about myself. I was able to see that not all adults are like my parents.

[Female, M.S.W., 10 years practice]

I was with someone who was eclectic, who really understood me, and was compassionate. He wasn't averse to advising me when I really needed advice. He was always there when I needed him, early in the morning or late at night. And then I was in a group therapy experience, where the leader used things I had previously thought were off the wall, like gestalt therapy, and it was fantastic.

[Male, Ph.D., 10 years practice]

The woman I saw next was extremely significant in my life, she did help me leave the marriage, and I did orient myself as an independent woman who could live without a man taking care of her. I truly identified with her, and she was an extremely important role model for me.

[Female, M.A., 20 years practice]

I had three four-year stints of therapy. They had positive aspects. I figure I could have gotten along all right with just the first four years. The other two were a reaction to a crisis in my life. One was with a psychiatrist during the sixties, three times a week on the couch, and by the end he was wearing beads and I was sitting on his lap. It was a wonderful experience, because he really cared, he was present, and he encouraged people to tell the truth, to get stuff out, really let it out. I really felt encouraged to be who I was, and I felt very cared for.

[Male, Ph.D., 25 years practice]

Probably the best person was a social worker who was gay, and asked immediately if I had a problem with that. I thought that was wonderful, that she said, "This is who I am, is that okay with you? Is this going to be a problem?" She was very reassuring, very maternal, very smart, patient, and was not averse to giving advice to a teenager.

[Female, Ph.D., 10 years practice]

It's kind of interesting, because the therapy I was in was as far from what I do as anything could be. What was wonderful about it was that there was this person, separate from my family, who cared a great deal, who was a kindly and concerned person. That was amazingly important.

[Male, Ph.D., 20 years practice]

I went into therapy with an analyst, and ultimately into analysis, and that changed my life. It was the most consistently reliable thing I'd ever experienced, the structure of it. She was always there. She was sick maybe once in five years. And also what was good, and at the time it worried me, was that she was quite interactive for an analyst. She talked a fair amount, and I kept thinking, "Something's wrong here." In retrospect, I realize that she was an older, more experienced person, and she knew what she was doing. I wish I could have appreciated it more at the time, instead of having the obnoxious doubt of a psychiatric resident, thinking maybe I should do better. She wasn't overly warm. The only thing that was bad about it was that I had to work extra hours to pay for it, and I was exhausted.

[Female, M.D., 15 years practice]

My second therapist, who I spent the major part of my treatment with, was very sharp. He was also very approving of me, and that was mind-blowing for me. I was okay with him, and most of my life had been spent trying to get that.

[Female, M.S.W., 20 years practice]

My second analyst was a child analyst, a kind of ego-psychological background, and he understood my difficulties as more of an earlier problem. He had some real problems in terms of his technique, that all these guys rationalize away and try to impose on you and to make you feel that it's your problem. But basically he understood the nature of my difficulties and was able to identify and interpret them. At this fundamental level, diagnosing the problem correctly was the key to the therapy.

[Male, M.D., 15 years practice]

My second analysis, which was with a fairly well-known self psychologist, where the main focus was on my perceptions and the validity of them, which allowed me then to look at what I was doing. She didn't have to make me do that. I'm smart enough and into the field enough to know that's what I'm supposed to doing. But I didn't feel accused, and I didn't have to be defensive.

[Male, Ph.D., 20 years practice]

I've had only one individual therapist, and also am in a group with the same person. She's very well trained, very insightful. I feel very comfortable opening up to her, very safe with her. She's very solid. She keeps a good professional distance. I don't like therapists who are too mushy.

[Male, M.D., 5 years practice]

My third therapist, who I've been with the longest, who is an analyst, has been terrific for me, and has been a great role model for me as an analyst. He is very sharp, and uses himself in the treatment very well. He's a real presence, without being an intrusion. He's very good at finding what's central emotionally at any given moment.

[Male, Ph.D., 5 years practice]

Sometimes even "positive" experiences can seem less than helpful looking back later on.

I had a wonderful analyst, a very sweet man. In retrospect, I don't think he was particularly helpful, because confrontation was missing about certain of my behaviors. I was very passive-aggressive in those days, and very out of touch with my anger and very unable to deal with it. Particularly towards my wife, that whole situation. I think what happened was the analyst only had a daughter and I became countertransferentially his son. My father was a very quiet, very noncommunicative man who was dying at the time, so the analyst became my father. Not by transference, but really by almost tacit agreement. So he never confronted me and I never confronted him.

[Male, Ph.D., 25 years practice]

I never had a bad experience. As a child, I had a very good family therapist, and my fantasy at the time was that she would marry my father. I thought she was extremely glamorous. She used a cigarette holder, and I was extremely impressed. I also saw her as a teenager and she was very helpful in explaining certain sexual issues. She did something that in retrospect I'm not sure how good it was. I wanted to apply to some experimental colleges and she told my father not to send me to those schools, saying that I would only sit around smoking pot and flunk out. She was probably right, but now I wonder what would have been the big deal if that had happened? Did that mean my life would have been ruined? Maybe I would have done something else and gone back to school. I think that she was very directive, and I maybe got deprived of an experience.

[Female, M.S.W., 10 years practice]

My first experience was with a very nice man who was not that much older than me, and I was with him for five years. It was traditionally psychoanalytic, he did very little talking. It was helpful, although not as helpful as it could have been. Although I was not yet myself a therapist, I did think he could have been more active, and I struggled with him on that issue.

[Male, M.S.W., 25 years practice]

It helped me a lot. It changed my life. I was able to find out the cause of my problems, that I wasn't a bad person, and that they didn't just come from outer space, that I was obsessive-compulsive and depressed. What made the experiences good was their understanding, their support, and their seeing things that I couldn't see. The therapist I've been with for such a long time, I became very reliant on her, and thought that she knew me better than I knew myself, and so there were a few instances where she made big mistakes and she wasn't right, and I listened to her instead of to myself and went through something that was needless. That happened about three times. I know she meant well, she just made mistakes. Now I listen to myself before I listen to her.

[Female, M.S.W., 15 years practice]

In medical school, I was in therapy with someone who was very oriented to family therapy, and that was about two years, and was absolutely liberating. I worked well with that person, and felt all sorts of possibilities were opening up that I didn't know about, things I could think about and start to deal with, and it was very, very positive. In my internship, there were things going on in my life that made me want to go back into therapy, and I went back to that therapist, but realized that, as great as it had been, she wasn't going to be able to work with me the way I needed, and I realized that I wanted a more analytically oriented treatment. I understood what the difference was.

[Female, M.D., 15 years practice]

My experience as an analysand was that it helped me to save my marriage, to be a better wife and mother, and opened a whole new profession and new life for me. If I had it to do over again, I would have wanted my analyst to talk more, instead of being so silent. I would have been able to tell him not to sit there silently.

[Female, Ph.D., 20 years practice]

I thought my first therapist was the greatest thing since sliced bread. In retrospect, I might feel differently. He was great for where I was at the time. He listened to me, and was the first person to do that. He seemed to respect me. I didn't feel criticized or put down. I think he liked me. He was supportive, and he had a sense of humor, and I felt good about him. It was an amicable parting. I often said that I built his swimming pool, because I referred so many people to him. When I came back to therapy, it was with a woman, and I saw her for about nine years. She was very bright, very sensitive, she was much more analytic than he was. There was something more mature about her.

[Female, M.A., 15 years practice]

Being understood is the most important. My first treatment was with an internationally known analyst, and she was a very generous woman who saw me at a low fee. At that time, if you were affiliated with a quality agency, the first question they asked was if you were in analysis. So I went to her, and it was a traditional Freudian analysis, three times a week, but I think that if more had been known about the narcissistic transference, and about modern techniques, I would have been helped more. Interpretation was not helpful. Emotional communication is much more important.

[Female, M.S.W., 45 years practice]

On the other hand, retrospect can sometimes bring a more positive evaluation.

During the time of my analysis, I was not sure it was helping me that much. In fact, it was a difficult time for me. During the years of my analysis, I was going through a lot of turmoil. It was two or three years later, when I had some perspective, and thought back a lot to what kinds of issues had come up and what we had discussed, that somehow things fell together, and it made more sense to me. But during the analysis, I wasn't sure that he was all that helpful, except for the idea of him seeming to be very, very tolerant and encouraging that I just continue. It was a little bit of a surprise, to realize that we covered much more territory than I had thought.

[Male, M.D., 20 years practice]

He was a Reichian, and we did a kind of therapy that was not talk, but breathing, and being nude, and hitting pillows, and screaming and carrying on. It was not so good, but in the course of time I really became appreciative of the changes that took place in me as a result of that experience, even though it was very unsatisfying to me at the time. I think it opened me up in some sort of way.

[Male, Ph.D., 50 years practice]

Some treatments start off well, but turn out badly in the course of treatment.

I found a female therapist I saw for ten years, who was very good when you were very depressed, but when you got less depressed and more autonomous she was too controlling. The last three years were not so good, and it ended badly.

[Female, M.S.W., 25 years practice]

My second therapist was a wonderful woman, very spiritual. She really got me pointed in the right direction. She got me through my twenties. She got me married, and she got me started in this profession. We separated over transference issues. I felt at the time she couldn't deal with those. Maybe it was just time. I think you can only work with a therapist for so long, then you need to move to someone else who has a different take.

[Female, M.S.W., 15 years practice]

Some therapists can be very helpful and effective, in spite of obvious problems.

I found a gestalt therapist, and stayed with him for many years, and he was okay except for time. He would stop exactly on time, no matter what was happening. I'd be talking and he'd say "Time," and I was right in the middle of a sentence. Other than that, he was a very good therapist, and I spent a lot of years with him and got a lot out of that therapy. He was terrific. It was interesting to work with a man. I found out a lot about myself.

[Female, Ph.D., 20 years practice]

My first therapist in many ways opened up the world of psychology to me: what as going on with me, and what was going on between me and other people. It was a very exciting adventure for me in many respects, but he also failed me too, because he was a very narcissistic guy who thought he was a world-saver of some kind, and was over-identified with me, and didn't see me as I needed to be seen. I was in my twenties and really looking for direction, and could have used some direction, instead of doing that, he helped me to worship him and think of him as terrific and want to be like him.

[Male, Ph.D., 5 years practice]

Most of the people in our group also had some negative or even de-structive experiences. These sometimes had to do with the perceived pas-sivity, distance, or rigidity of the traditional psychoanalyst.

I think that my other analyst was not active enough, and wasn't that good. He wasn't analyzing the transference, or confronting me on a lot of things, being stricter about money. I always paid, but I didn't pay on time, he never required that I pay on time, he had a very low fee. He was not professional in that regard.

[Female, M.S.W., 20 years practice]

In graduate school, I figured that I should be in analysis. Not therapy, because therapy is for plebeians. I went to a service that provided low-cost analysis, and was seeing this guy three times a week who had just gotten out of his training institute. It was one of the most horrible experiences of my life. It was really awful. For me, being on the couch, not having somebody respond to what I was saying, not giving me any kind of feedback whatsoever other than clearing his throat twice during the session, was abuse very much like what had gone on in my family. I felt not like he was giving me the space to be, I felt like I was floating out there by myself. I stuck with it for a year and a half, because I kept feeling it was my fault. And the analyst did too, he kept talking about my resistance to the process, and I began feeling angrier and angrier. I was coming in with incredibly rich dreams, that were almost gifts to him, and I wanted something back, and he said things that I couldn't even connect to, they were so far away from where I was. They may have been true, but they had nothing to do with me. So I quit, and it took me a few years to get back into therapy.

[Female, M.S.W., 20 years practice]

I did see someone when I was in analytic training, and I look back on that, even though she was very well known, as one of my least positive experiences. I don't remember accomplishing anything there. I don't think that she ever really reached me. She was a woman who was probably very skillful in theory, and was very much the Freudian analyst, very much the blank screen, offered very little of who she was, and I got nowhere fast with her. It did not help me to look at myself. I felt we never touched each other, and I had no regrets on leaving. It felt more like an academic pursuit. I came away no more connected to myself. It just went nowhere.

[Female, M.A., 15 years practice]

My first experience was in graduate school, and was with a classical Freudian analyst. He was a very nice man, but I was lying on a couch a couple of days a week, free associating, and he'd say, "Um hmm," and somehow he helped me a bit because even though he didn't say much, he was a loving presence, an accepting nonjudgmental presence. But it was not, as I look back now, such a great therapeutic experience. He was too uninvolved. I got into a marriage that was really just acting out the transference, and he never stopped me. He never picked up on it. He was also ill, he had throat cancer at the time, which I didn't know, but it made him very low-energy.

[Female, M.S.W., 30 years practice]

My first therapist was very Freudian, he sat behind me and took notes. I remember he wouldn't touch me no matter what. One time I had a headache, and he gave me two aspirin. He put them in the cap and turned it over in my hand to avoid having to touch me.

[Female, M.S.W., 10 years practice]

Some therapists were very limited in their approach. Some were extremely impersonal, very analytic, and that disturbed me. I asked one therapist where they were going on vacation, and the only thing he would say was, "What's your fantasy?" I understand that the question might elicit some useful material, but at least try to connect with me when I'm trying to connect with you. They were too rigid in their approach. I don't think I've gotten very much from being in therapy, not much useful feedback from my therapists, aside from having a forum to explore and ventilate.

[Male, M.S.W., 15 years practice]

My first experience was three years with a male psychiatrist, and I have tried since then to find some gain or value in it, and I think there was none, that it was truly useless. I don't think he ever got it. I don't think he ever really understood what I was dealing with. And I was in a very bad marriage, and he sided with me, and that didn't help. He was the very Freudian analyst, and he didn't say much. He didn't help me get out of my marriage, and he didn't help me develop any further insight about what was going on. I just don't think he was competent.

[Female, M.A., 20 years practice]

I went to a man, three times a week, an analyst. I think this one was counterproductive, and reinforced aspects of me and held me back, scrambled my brain a little bit. He was much more perfect by analytic standards, a high position in analytic circles, but this guy couldn't relate to a lox. One time I went into his office, where everything was always perfect, and I moved his chair a couple of inches, and tilted a painting a little. And he sits down, and you can see that he's uncomfortable, and then he notices that the picture is off, and he's trying to listen to me but he can't let it go, and after five minutes he says, "Excuse me," and gets up and straightens the picture and before he sits down again he moves the chair. This guy drove me out of my fucking mind. He wasn't a bad man, he never did anything bad to me, but he didn't put himself out on the line. It's not going to work, and it's going to make you crazier, because it looks perfect, but you're getting crazier and crazier, and he's more and more perfect, and it can drive you crazy.

[Male, Ph.D., 25 years practice]

My second therapist was someone who was not an orthodox classical Freudian, but who had advanced from that to resistance analysis, and that was mostly his being silent and me talking. I can't say very much happened. I never thought of it as therapy, but as a training analysis. I was putting in time in order to prepare myself to practice analysis.

[Male, Ph.D., 50 years practice]

I basically had two long-term therapies. The first was with a reasonably well-known, traditional analyst, who was basically a very nice man, but it wasn't what I needed. Every interpretation felt accusatory. One example was when I had a very difficult supervisor, authoritarian and controlling, and I'd come to therapy and talk about it, and without acknowledging my perceptions, he'd always ask why I was reacting that way. I don't think he was particularly bad. He was fairly traditional, and at heart was a nice man, but he wasn't flexible enough.

[Male, Ph.D., 20 years practice]

Sometimes the problem came from the therapist's inability to deal with certain material.

Then I saw a psychiatrist, who I fell in love with, and really obsessed about for seven years. I'm not sure I would call that therapy. It was very peculiar. I'm sure it was very difficult for him. He just didn't seem to know how to handle it. When I did go back to see him years after therapy ended, I said, "I've come to say goodbye, because I've thought about you for seven years." And all he could say was, "I knew transference was powerful, but I didn't know it was that powerful." And I thought, "You jerk!" What an impersonal thing to say to me.

[Female, M.S.W., 5 years practice]

It could have been a hell of a lot better. What was wrong with it was that it was a training analysis, which means that I don't think there was enough interpretation of the negative transference. I'm not sure why, but he didn't do it. I don't think he was big on negative transference. Perhaps he was afraid of it. This was in contrast to a supervisor who was very big on negative transference, and who had a profound influence on the way I work.

[Male, M.D., 20 years practice]

Sometimes there were other countertransference problems.

I was a terrible patient. The therapist I went to said that. He said I was the most difficult patient he ever had, and I was proud of that. He was very psychoanalytic and well-known in the field, the traditional classical analyst, and I was with him for about two years, individual and group. I was ready for my own career, and I had an opportunity to do my doctorate out of town, and he saw that as my not being a good patient because I was leaving therapy. I recognize now that there was a countertransference issue on his part.

[Male, Ph.D., 25 years practice]

My first therapist was a very superanalytic woman. I was referred by my first supervisor. I had an incredible transference to my mother. She had a very strong countertransference to me as well. I was leaving a marriage, and she couldn't stand that I was doing that. I don't think she realized how much countertransference she had until afterwards. She really yelled at me.

[Female, Ph.D., 20 years practice]

I saw one therapist when I was dealing with a close relative dying of cancer, and dealing with feelings of loss and anticipation. And all along the therapist keep saying, "You don't know that she's dying." And of course she died, and when I confronted him, he confessed that it was a countertransference issue, that he had been diagnosed years before with something that was commonly thought to be something fatal, and he refused to believe it was fatal, and he was convinced that this was why he survived. But for me it was not very helpful.

[Female, M.S., 15 years practice]

Some therapists seem to have their own agenda for the work, and it may conflict with what the patient needs.

In graduate school, we were very strongly encouraged to go to therapy. I saw a psychoanalytic psychiatrist who was horrible, who spent years talking about early childhood and never dealt with marital problems and real things that had to be dealt with.

[Female, Ph.D., 10 years practice]

My first analyst was a guy with a sterling reputation, who a friend of mine characterized as being the National Bureau of Standards in analysis. He was at an institute that was very classically Freudian. He was a standard classic analyst, and he interpreted my problems oedipally. There were areas where he helped me, particularly my relationship with my father, but he was wrong about the level at which he was interpreting. I was trying to please him, to be a good patient, but it wasn't helpful to try to integrate an understanding of myself that was wrong. He kind of missed the boat.

[Male, M.D., 15 years practice]

I left one analysis feeling that it was unresolved, that in the end it did not help me. Looking back now, I feel that wasn't true, that I was just very, very angry, and we were at an impasse, and there were problems with the way this person worked. He was an interpersonalist, and it got to a point where I was screaming that this was not about us, this was about transference. And he was taking what I said about him to be more concretely real, and so it could not be discussed. It was very frustrating.

[Female, Ph.D., 15 years practice]

Sometimes, the therapist was very intrusive or controlling, even hostile.

My second therapist didn't like what I was doing in my private life, and insisted that I change, and then threw me out of therapy for not changing, for not following some advice he had about staying in a particular group. It was supposed to be a learning seminar, and then I realized that the guy who was running it was making it group therapy, which I did not agree to be in. And my analyst was in it also, and then all the boundaries were getting blurry. I quit the group, and he told me if I didn't stay in the group he would not treat me anymore.

[Female, M.S.W., 20 years practice]

My first analyst had very good credentials, but he was a lousy analyst. He could not handle my hostility, he could not handle the transference. He was trying to foist upon me his own defensive system, rather than analyzing whatever was going on. Because of his inability to understand and analyze, he made certain demands on me that really affected me very deeply. Being the good obsessional that I am, I used the obsessional's hostile defense against the analysis. Lots of intellectual stuff, lots of theory. The damn fool didn't know how to handle it, so his way of dealing with it was to forbid me to read anything theoretical or technical. I've since learned that was a common thing to do in those days. Now, I had a father who was a self-made businessman who was anti-intellectual, who viewed reading as something you did for school. But if I read for pleasure it annoyed him, because he would refer to me as sitting on my ass doing nothing, like some of his intellectual friends. After my analyst told me no more reading, I developed a severe reading block for many years that I'm just starting to get over.

[Male, M.S.W., 35 years practice]

My first experience reaching out for help was when I was realizing I was homosexual, and I freaked. I went to see a psychologist who told me that there was hope for me, that he could change me, and that all homosexuals were child molesters. He told me that I would also begin to molest children, which really frightened me, because I believed him. I started to have anxiety attacks, and he put me on valium through his psychiatrist. I stored them up and overdosed, and went into a psychiatric hospital, where I learned to get away from him.

[Male, M.S.W., 15 years practice]

My worst therapist was a man who developed a strong countertransference. I went to see him one time and he was angry at me, and I was angry too, and he wouldn't let me talk. Whenever I started to say what I was angry about, he would interrupt and say he had to talk about what he was angry about. He wouldn't hear me. Throughout the course of seeing him, he would treat me like I was some kind of monster that he had to control, and it made me feel even angrier. I went to see a former supervisor for a consultation about this, and was advised to leave him. When I told my therapist I was going to leave, he apologized profusely and said he realized that he had been mistreating me. He convinced me not to leave him, but two weeks later he turned on me again and totally lambasted me. So I left him, but I was so distraught I lost ten patients in the next few months.

[Male, Ph.D., 15 years practice]

My first experience was a counselor at college, who had been analyzed by a famous Freudian, and she sent me to him. He couldn't see me so he referred me to someone else, also a well-known Freudian. I was scared of him because he was very dictatorial and very like my crazy father, and I stayed with him about a month. When he insisted that I must masturbate, which I never did up to that time, and that I tell him about my masturbatory experiences, when I didn't have any, I left.

[Female, M.S., 20 years practice]

The woman I worked with for a couple of years was much older and a mother figure, but a rigid and unaccepting mother. She was my mother all over again, and I couldn't work things out with her. I always recall this incident: I had taken my coat and put it over one of her chairs and then sat down, and during the course of the session she commented that my hair was "long and out of control" and also that I had taken my coat and thrown it over her "very fragile chair." I remember thinking at the time that I was the one who was fragile, yet she was more concerned with the chair. At that point I remember thinking that this was never going to work. It was painful, excruciating. I finally quit by leaving a message on her machine at the end of her vacation, and apparently she didn't like the lateness of the hour of my message, because she wrote me a letter admonishing me even for that.

[Female, M.S., 15 years practice]

I had a very difficult, very destructive experience. I went into analysis and I felt the therapist didn't see any of my strengths, he intimidated me into dependency on him, he needed money. I think the value in it was that it got me out of the psychoanalytic model. I needed to reject that, because it's not me. One thing he taught me: he taught me the consequences of denial and avoidance. I think it could have been done more gently. It's taken years to get over the anger at him.

[Female, M.S.W., 15 years practice]

When I was 16 years old, I asked my mother to take me to therapy, and she took me to my sister's therapist. He was this big, fat psychiatrist who sat there smoking Turkish cigarettes at his huge desk, and I sat next to him, and I remember in the consultation he asked me, "So, all you like to do is suck cock?" And it was mortifying, that he would use words like that with me.

[Male, M.S.W., 15 years practice]

My first therapist was not so good. I was 21, in my first marriage, which was terrible. I was somebody who was never allowed to complain about my life, and therapy was the first time I allowed myself to say that things were not that good and I don't feel so good. And she made fun of me and accused me of always complaining. One time, I came to see her and I thought she motioned me into the office, so I went in and sat down. And a few moments later, she came in and said, "There you are! How do I know you're not looking at my papers?" Another time I was telling her a long important dream, and she just faded out, and then snapped back, picked up the phone, and ordered tea with lemon. At which point I left treatment.

[Female, M.S., 15 years practice]

Other therapists were unaware of, or casual about, boundary issues.

My therapist, a woman, would do things like give me hugs. I would ask her and she would at first refuse and then relent and hug me, and I thought that was weak of her, to give up her principles. And she'd tell me things about herself, about her divorce, and about her dating adventures, that I didn't need to hear.

[Male, Ph.D., 15 years practice]

In my analytic training I had one of the poorest treatments I ever had. I felt that my analyst was not herself. I think that she hadn't worked out some of the same issues she was trying to work on with me and wasn't able to keep it to herself. Therefore it made the treatment feel very muddy. Also, I believe that there was a lot of judgmental stuff going on in my institute. She was also one of my supervisors. Boundaries were not kept carefully and well, and it really did interfere with the treatment process a lot. I had another treatment with someone that I felt was truly damaging, because again boundaries were not kept. It made me feel that there was something terribly wrong with me when I tried to insist on maintenance of boundaries and my analyst accused me of that being one of my problems.

[Female, M.S.W., 15 years practice]

I had a negative experience in college, my only experience with a social worker. She was an Adlerian, and a very stereotypically social worker type, Jewish, a mother who nagged me, and there wasn't any sense of psychological understanding, just follow the rules, like Freud didn't exist. Forget the dreams, forget your parents. Then she thought it would be very good for me to be in a group, which was also a disaster, with another Adlerian. There were no boundaries. He was friends with the patients, and encouraged everyone to be friends, to have them at your house and at parties.

[Female, M.S.W., 10 years practice]

My very first therapist, when I was twenty-four, kissed me on the mouth before a vacation, and I never went back to him. I'd only been seeing him about two months.

[Female, M.S.W., 25 years practice]

My first analyst was very unprofessional. The telephone would ring and he would answer the phone, three or fours times a session, or the bell would ring and he would get up to open the door. It was very distracting. Then I found out he was not a real analyst, he was only a psychiatrist. I was very disillusioned, and felt that I didn't get the real thing. The second one, this woman was a chain smoker, so the room was filled with smoke all the time! Now I realize how anxious the woman must have been.

[Male, Ph.D., 20 years practice]

I had a group therapist who said once, "I'll have to ask your husband about that," and I couldn't believe that he would say that when I was sitting right there.

[Female, M.S.W., 20 years practice]

At times, the therapist would not allow the patient to separate and leave.

I was in a very long-term therapy with a man who I think helped me a lot but had a lot of trouble with separation issues and would not help me leave him. I met a woman therapist in a group workshop and I made a very nice connection with her and started treatment with her, and she helped me separate from him. I had already left individual treatment with him because he did something I considered unethical. He started to have a relationship with a former patient, and wound up marrying her. But I was still in his group, where I stayed for about thirteen years, and I had a hard time leaving the group. And it was always blamed on me, that I couldn't work out my problem with him, not that he did something wrong. I'm still seeing her after about two years, and having a wonderful experience. She allows me a lot of autonomy, which I realize now he did not. I was a compliant child, and he tapped into that part. And she's not interested in doing that.

[Female, M.S., 15 years practice]

I got depressed, and went with a woman from the Spotnitz school, and saw her once a week for another four years. She lifted my depression just like that by telling me that she cared for me and that I was having a really tough time. I could have left after three weeks but I stayed for four years. But the Spotnitzians don't believe in termination, they're lifers, so it took me four years of fighting to get out. She resisted that like crazy.

[Male, Ph.D., 25 years practice]

My second therapist only lasted for nine months. He was, as far as I was concerned, an unmitigated disaster. I never felt as if he helped me to get to a deeper spot in myself. If I expressed any problem or upset, or brought up any issue, he immediately had a response to that issue, he immediately categorized it, classified it, told me what to do about it. There was never a sense of delving, of unfolding, of getting closer to yourself, of even getting closer to each other. And when I wanted to leave, that was horrible too. He blew up. It was absurd. He really helped me in a way, by his ridiculous response to my wanting to leave, because it confirmed that I was making a good decision.

[Male, Ph.D., 5 years practice]

NUMERICAL DISTRIBUTION

Everyone said that they had had at least some good experiences, but only 7 people said they had not also had negative experiences, where the therapist was either not very good or actively bad.

COMMENTS

This question raises several issues: What makes therapy good, and what makes it bad? How do negative experiences in treatment affect a therapist's work with his or her own patients?

Personal experience in treatment is probably the most significant part of the therapist's training, the experience with the most impact on his or her own way of doing treatment. Again, I was very surprised to learn how many of these therapists had had negative, hurtful, and destructive experiences in their own therapy. In my own case, I had some good experiences and some not so good. The negative ones happened as often as the positive ones.

I wonder what the effect of bad treatment is on the therapist and how much of what is consciously rejected as destructive and hurtful may be unconsciously internalized and repeated with future patients.

RELATED READING

Buckley, P., Karasu, T. B., and Charles, E. (1981). Psychotherapists view their personal therapy. *Psychotherapy: Theory, Research, and Practice* 18(3):299–305.

Kaslow, F., ed. (1984). *Psychotherapy with Psychotherapists.* New York: Hawthorn Press.

Pope, K. S., and Tabachnick, B. G. (1994). Therapists as patients: a national survey of psychologists' experiences, problems, and beliefs. *Professional Psychology: Research and Practice* 25(3):247–258.

▧▧▧▧

Question 73: How does your experience as a patient affect the way you work as a therapist?

Obviously, a therapist's experience as a patient is going to affect the way he or she does therapy. This question tries to get at the nature of the influences and effects.

Many people said that their good experiences as patients are internalized, that they identify themselves with their own good therapists and often act the same way.

> It affects you in ways, like a response you might make if it was something that was meaningful to you, that was said to you, or a way that you understand things in therapy. Just things that feel customary, even things like appointments, or phone contact, or emergencies, how you were treated that feels very right or very wrong. It seems like a way you would want to work, or not.
>
> [Female, M.S.W., 10 years practice]

> There's always some immediate identification that I notice, both conscious and unconscious. I find myself doing things, and then catching

myself and thinking, "Oh, that's what my analyst does." As my relationship progresses with my analyst, something happens where I individuate and I become very different.

[Male, Ph.D., 10 years practice]

The analysts I had were a model to me, the respect they had for me as a patient, the neutrality they exhibited, their insights, all helped me a great deal.

[Male, Ph.D., 40 years practice]

I hear myself, especially working with dreams, using the same phrases as my therapist would use. He taught me a lot about how to understand behavior, and look at the whole picture.

[Female, M.S.W., 10 years practice]

I'm still new at this work so I still play with it. If there's something a therapist has done or said that I liked, I might integrate that. I feel okay about suggesting things to a patient because my own therapist made some suggestions to me, things I didn't know about, that were very helpful to me.

[Female, M.S.W., 5 years practice]

As a patient, I'm not only a patient, but I'm also sitting and evaluating, and there are certain things that either work with me or seem like they might work with a particular client.

[Female, M.A., 20 years practice]

That's where your sense of what was therapeutically helpful for you contributes very strongly to what you do with patients: what you look for, what you try to accomplish. In a very fundamental way, my theory of therapy is heavily influenced by what I found therapeutic.

[Male, M.D., 15 years practice]

I feel very lucky to have a therapist who is very like me, and he's been a terrific role model for me. When I was in graduate school, I felt very calm while the other students seemed very lost, and I think it was because they didn't feel that their therapists were role models for them. They thought they were good, but they didn't know if they wanted to work that way.

[Male, Ph.D., 5 years practice]

There's a model established by my analyst that I probably follow to some degree unconsciously, and sometimes I catch myself thinking and remembering the kinds of things he did, sometimes by doing them differently and sometimes the same way. There's a certain amount of identification.

[Male, M.D., 20 years practice]

Sometimes a positive experience can teach some theoretical material.

The Jungian analysis affected the way I work with dreams, because that analyst was the first one to introduce the notion that all the characters in the dream are a part of yourself, and I've certainly used that in my own work.

[Female, M.S., 20 years practice]

It made me very empathic, and all of my different experiences have made it possible for me to approach different patients in different ways, and to make use of a variety of different interventions.

[Male, Ph.D., 50 years practice]

Several people said that their own treatment helped them resolve personal problems and issues, and therefore made them a better therapist.

The good therapy that I've had, and the training, has helped me get to the point where I can be a better therapist. In my early years as a therapist, I was very easily injured, and very prone to get angry, and my therapy has helped me change those patterns.

[Male, Ph.D., 15 years practice]

Others said that having been patients themselves allows them to understand and identify with whatever their patients are going through.

I've been on the other side, and I know what it's like, and I can identify with a lot of things that my patients do.

[Female, M.S.W., 10 years practice]

At this point, I have a real appreciation for how difficult it is to change, how hard it is, and how committed you really have to be, not just go through the process.

[Female, Ph.D., 5 years practice]

That's very complicated, and it brings to mind very concrete details, of suddenly being aware that books are piling up on my desk exactly the same way as they were piled on my analyst's desk! Or that I've arrived at a similar policy about missed sessions. It seems like it's mine, and then it turns out it's really theirs. Clearly, there are identifications that take place. It's very hard to do analytic work, actually it's impossible, without having been in analysis.

[Female, Ph.D., 15 years practice]

My success as a psychotherapist hinges very much on my ability to be empathic, to really get what the person is trying to tell me. That comes out of many different experiences, including how I felt in the patient chair.

[Female, M.A., 20 years practice]

In brief, it gives me an ability to know what it was like to be on the other end, so perhaps it makes me more sensitive to the patient's difficulty in hearing what I'm saying. I'm not sure that it affects my style or technique so much.

[Male, M.D., 20 years practice]

Others said that the negative experiences as patients had equal if not greater impact on their own styles as therapists.

It affected me very badly, because I've discovered that I have a tendency to identify with whomever I was in treatment with, and it really messed me up.

[Male, M.S.W., 35 years practice]

I think I became very aware of what I didn't get from my very analytic therapist, and how that did not work for me, and so I adopted a kind of posture that allows me to be much more real with patients. I don't talk about my private life, but I try to be who I am. I'm comfortable engaging people in a more familiar way.

[Female, M.A., 15 years practice]

Well, I certainly decided not to be Freudian, that it wasn't useful to spend hours in silence.

[Female, M.S., 20 years practice]

I am extremely aware of boundaries and the need for good boundary-keeping, especially because of the treatment in which they were so badly kept. My bad experience also taught me that one needs to listen to patients' experiences of the treatment as it's going along, because there can indeed be real things going on, not just projection. One has to be willing to encounter that possibility, and not to determine everything as transference-countertransference.

[Female, M.S.W., 15 years practice]

It makes me hope not to be overbearing, and know-it-all, and clumsy as some of my own experiences have been. Also, I learned that when a patient tells me about something that's going on in the room between us, I need to take it seriously, as opposed to throwing back at them and making them leave the room thinking it's all them.

[Female, M.S., 15 years practice]

From the bad experiences I've had with the very impersonal approach, I think I'm much more personable in my sessions.

[Male, M.S.W., 15 years practice]

Some people mentioned specific aspects of the work that they had learned to deal with in a particular way.

I never fight anyone who's terminating. I really believe this is a very powerful thing we have here, and people get into it, and we have to make them comfortable about getting out. Even though that makes me anxious sometimes, if my practice is down.

[Male, Ph.D., 25 years practice]

I have a lot more understanding of clients' feelings of powerlessness, and the need to treat them with respect and dignity. The psychoanalytic experience taught me that you have to be careful not to recapitulate the situation of childhood, with all the rules. People have their own lives and their own time constraints, and it isn't just about the therapist. It's infantilizing, and refusing to recognize them as separate, independent, autonomous adults.

[Female, M.S.W., 15 years practice]

I model a lot of my work on what I learned from my therapist, both the good and the bad, the things that I liked and the things I didn't like, like to be so overbearing or to answer the phone during a session or be late all the time, things that I hated.

[Female, M.S.W., 15 years practice]

One person said that his negative experiences had made him more careful.

It certainly made me more concerned for competence. I believe that one of our dictates, as in the medical profession, is to do no harm. I come from a place where it would be very difficult for me to think of myself as doing harm to a client, but I could do harm in terms of not knowing enough, and it's made me continue to go to school, and to learn and to learn and to learn.

[Male, M.S.W., 15 years practice]

Another person said that her bad experiences had perhaps made her too cautious.

My experience messed me up as a therapist, because I was so concerned that therapy not be the center of someone's life the way it had been for me, that I deliberately underplayed my impact on patients. I think therapy is limited, but it can be helpful, and it's taken me a long time to figure that one out.

[Female, M.S.W., 5 years practice]

Several people said that their experiences in treatment helped them decide to be more active, flexible, or authentic as a therapist.

I have to be a real human being. I have to not hide my craziness. I don't have to broadcast it, but I have to communicate however I can that I'm not superior in any way to my clients. I just have a certain craft that I'm doing that may be able to benefit them. And I got this belief on both ends: from therapists who did it and therapists who didn't do it. It's a human enterprise, and a wonderful enterprise, and a loving enterprise, but it's just my craft and my skills, and I'm no different from you.

[Male, Ph.D., 25 years practice]

I think of my first therapist, who was relatively silent, and I certainly don't want to be like that. Essentially, after giving it a lot of thought, I've come to believe in having a much more interactive relationship.

[Male, M.S.W., 25 years practice]

More in the past than now. In the first five or six years as a clinician, there was a certain amount of modeling. My therapist had a forty-five-minute hour, so that's what I had. I was extremely careful about consistency, and tried very hard not to make unnecessary changes. My own experience of having gone from a place that was very painful so much of the time to a place that was much more centered and calm was useful in working at difficult moments with people, when one doesn't know, when one has doubt about what's going to be helpful, how suicidal is this person, how much pain and suffering can a person endure. It gave me a sense that there is a process you can go through.

[Female, M.D., 15 years practice]

> I know what it's like to be on the other side, to have someone study
> you. And also to know what it feels like to not be on an equal basis,
> where the therapist wants to keep separate, and act like they have it
> together and you don't. I work with patients in more of a collaborative
> way, that they know as much as I do about their problem, and let's
> work together, investigate together, study the problem and come up
> with a plan together.
>
> [Female, Ph.D., 10 years practice]

A few people said that the identification with their analysts changed over
time.

> It affects me tremendously. For a while, I was more advice-giving and
> controlling, as my first therapist had been. And then I saw with my
> second therapist that it was much better to just stay with the feelings
> and trust that the person is going to work things out.
>
> [Female, M.S.W., 25 years practice]

NUMERICAL DISTRIBUTION

Twenty-nine people said that they internalized their experience with a good
therapist and tend to work that same way; 16 people said they intentionally avoid the mistakes that were made with them by bad therapists; 11
people said their experience in treatment allows them to identify with their
own patients and understand them better. Two people saw themselves
sometimes internalizing negative behaviors of previous therapists. Two
others said they saw little effect on the way they work.

COMMENTS

The issues here are similar to those raised by the last question: What are
the effects of good and bad experiences in treatment on the therapist's own
style and technique?

I think every therapy experience affects how we do treatment, what has
worked with us and what hasn't worked, especially the therapy that we
undergo as part of our training, at which point we are more sophisticated
and are watching very carefully and evaluating everything the therapist
does. Our experiences in therapy also give us whatever understanding we
may have of our own patients' experiences with us, their wishes and fantasies, their fears and anxieties.

My own experiences, good and bad, have made me more aware of what

I do and what I had better not do. Most important of all, I've learned not to be defensive and not to try to justify and explain my actions and behavior when the patient finds them not useful or even hurtful.

RELATED READING

Dryden, W., and Spurling, L. (1989). *On Becoming a Psychotherapist.* London: Tavistock/Routledge.
Norcross, J. C., Strausser, D. J., and Faltus, F. J. (1988). The therapist's therapist. *American Journal of Psychotherapy* 42(1):53–66.

🦎🦎🦎🦎

Question 74: How did you set up and establish your practice?

No matter how much training one has, or how much agency experience, it is always a bit of a leap to open one's own office. There are several ways of making this transition.

Many therapists open their offices as part of their analytic training, and are assigned patients whom they see in those offices. Those patients can form the core of the practice, which then expands to include other referrals.

> When you leave my institute, you're allowed to take the patients you worked with while you were there with you. That was the nucleus of my practice. They referred other people to me. I did whatever I could to make everyone I knew aware that I was in practice.
> [Female, Ph.D., 20 years practice]

> I was working with an agency full time. I went to part-time and left two days a week to build my practice. I got referrals from the institute.
> [Female, M.S.W., 20 years practice]

> First I rented by the hour, from someone who was established, and as the practice increased, I would debate if I was ready or not. I got patients through the training institute, and from colleagues.
> [Male, Ph.D., 20 years practice]

> At my training institute, we were assigned patients, but we were required to have our own office space. So I sublet somebody's office part-time, and then I gradually got more people.
> [Female, M.S., 15 years practice]

Other therapists may find office space to see patients after hours of the regular agency job, keeping a part-time practice until they feel ready to move completely on their own.

> I had a hospital job thirty hours a week, and I began my practice by renting an office and seeing patients in the evening and even on Saturdays. I started with two patients from my residency days, at very low fees, and then told everybody I was in practice. It took about five years until I took the plunge and went into full-time private practice.
>
> [Male, M.D., 20 years practice]

> I let all of my teachers, and professors, and colleagues know that I was opening a practice. I wanted to set up an analytic practice primarily, but I knew I would have to see other kinds of patients to support myself. It was going to be a part-time practice. One of my supervisors rented me space in his office suite. I sent out announcements.
>
> [Male, M.D., 20 years practice]

> I did it slowly. I went from full-time agency work to part-time. My first client was a referral from a colleague at the agency, a patient who didn't want to be seen at the agency because he was embarrassed. And then it went on from word of mouth, and then I put it out more.
>
> [Female, Ph.D., 20 years practice]

> The first thing I did was take out an ad in the local paper for a group, thinking that a group would get me a bunch of clients, and that's been slow, but the group is working well. I'll probably take out another ad soon. I've put up flyers, and also word of mouth. Occasionally, I've done a talk at a meeting.
>
> [Female, M.S.W., 5 years practice]

One person described in detail the gradual development of successful private practice.

> After working at a group home for adolescents, I went to work at a private clinic. I was there for a very long time, got ripped off mercilessly, but learned my craft, and began to develop a reputation in the community. After a while, I was bringing in my own cases, pretty much filling my own schedule as well as other people's schedules. When I left, I took a small number of patients with me, about seventeen, and sent out notifications, mostly to the physicians who were referring people to me, and they continued referring to me when I opened my own office. I also was getting referrals from my colleagues, especially

the psychiatrists who were getting a lot of referrals for medication consults, and they would hand them out for therapy.

[Male, Ph.D., 20 years practice]

Others prefer to keep the agency job and leave the practice as a part-time pursuit.

It came mostly through the institute I trained at, where they had a clinic. I'm not willing now to devote my whole life to building a practice.

[Female, M.S.W., 20 years practice]

I shared an office with somebody else. I'm still renting three nights a week from someone at my institute. It's easier because I'm not supported by my practice.

[Female, M.S.W., 15 years practice]

Opening a practice requires some self-publicizing, letting colleagues, supervisors, and others know that the therapist is available for private referrals. In some cases, a single connection can become a rich referral source that helps establish a practice.

I got my referrals from faculty at my graduate school. I specialized in adolescents because I was running an adolescent unit at the time. Since few people like working with adolescents, I got referrals from colleagues at the hospital where I was working. It became a word-of-mouth thing, mostly by reputation from other patients. For a while there was a local private school in my neighborhood, and I got one referral there from a professor who was doing evaluations of acting-out adolescents, and then I got a reputation at some of the private schools as being good with these kids.

[Male, Ph.D., 25 years practice]

Sometimes, at the very start of a private practice, there are not enough patients to support a private office, and patients are seen at home.

At first I saw patients in an office I set up in my apartment, and then when the number of referrals got to where I could support the cost of an office I did that. Patients came from former supervisors and from peers.

[Female, Ph.D., 15 years practice]

I started in my apartment, and my first referral was given to me by my therapist. After that, I got referrals from friends who were also therapists, and then from patients. I rented a place by the hour, here and there. I got out of my apartment pretty fast. Then I got my own office.

[Female, M.S.W., 15 years practice]

.I started getting referrals from my training institute, and I had an office there. Then I had to find one of my own, and I couldn't find it quickly enough, so I saw patients in my house. And this is still where I work.

[Female, M.A., 15 years practice]

I had to have some private patients as part of my training, so I let people know, friends and acquaintances, that I needed patients. I was working full-time during the day and going to school at night, so I saw three or four patients privately at my apartment. As my practice expanded, I got an office for myself.

[Female, M.S., 20 years practice]

Some people found that joining a group practice, or some kind of loose association of other therapists, made the transition easier.

I just jumped into it. Not the best time, in the middle of a recession. But I was doing some part-time work for my supervisor, who was retiring from private practice, and she wanted to put a group together to refer to, and she invited me to be part of that group. So I began as . part of a group. I was very lucky.

[Female, Ph.D., 5 years practice]

My institute gave me patients in the beginning, and then I met someone who was a therapist at a center near my home, and he asked me to join the center.

[Female, M.S.W., 25 years practice]

I joined a group practice that was already running and successful.

[Female, M.A., 20 years practice]

My training institute sent me patients, and then word of mouth, and then some colleagues and I formed a group. We advertise together. It's been a long process.

[Female, M.S.W., 15 years practice]

A few therapists took over the practice of someone who was retiring, or deceased.

A friend knew he was dying, and he wanted me to take over his practice, and I resisted and resisted. Finally he offered me the office for next to nothing. He had been in practice for a long time, and he told me it takes five years to get the practice beginning, and another ten years before it gets established, and you have to advertise always, and you have to put your business card in every person's hand: the milkman, the postman, everyone. And that at any time your clients can take off and then you have none, and you have to constantly be treating this as a business. I never advertise. I never put my card in the hand of anyone who didn't ask for it. Ninety percent of my clients have come from other clients. I have never not had a waiting list.

[Male, M.S.W., 15 years practice]

I was working for the state as a social worker. I started taking some classes at an institute and seeing some patients there, and a friend who was very sick and winding down his practice referred someone to me. But I didn't have an office, so he offered to let me see them in his office when he was finished for the day. So it was about 9:30 at night. Some of the patients where I was working referred some friends to me, and I saw them in my apartment, which was very difficult. I had two dogs, and I would lock them in the car. After my friend died, I took over the office.

[Female, M.S.W., 10 years practice]

One person said she had a special kind of support in making the transition.

Someone I knew had extreme confidence in me, more than I had in myself, and they said they were going to rent an office for me even if I wouldn't do it for myself. And that was extraordinary for me, because I've been extremely successful at this.

[Female, M.A., 20 years practice]

Some people said it was a smooth transition, that the times made an individual practice easy to establish.

I saved up a year's worth of income, and I just took the leap. I had only five hours of patients, but I decided that I was going to try it, and if I don't manage I'll get a job again. What happened was within six months I had a full practice, and I had all the money, so I bought a fur coat. I think I started my practice at a good time. There was a lot of money around, and once I sent out announcements I had all these patients.

[Female, M.S., 15 years practice]

I started off on a part-time hourly basis. I found someone who had office space to rent on an hourly basis. It was very easy getting a practice started in 1959. I'm glad I'm not starting today. By 1960, I had an office all to myself, close to the agency where I worked, so I could duck out for morning, lunchtime, or evening hours.

[Male, M.S.W., 35 years practice]

And some said it was very difficult.

I began at a community mental health center, and had been working part-time as a private practitioner when I left there. I had some con- sultation contracts of my own which helped me start. But it was very hard.

[Male, Ph.D., 25 years practice]

It was very slow, over a long period of time. Too slow.

[Male, M.S.W., 15 years practice]

NUMERICAL DISTRIBUTION

Not everyone was asked this question. Of the 44 people who were: 16 started by getting patients from their training institute; 22 started at an agency or clinic and then rented office space and let colleagues know; 3 more started in their apartment before getting an office; and 3 took over someone else's practice.

COMMENTS

There is no major issue here, only the questions of the best way to start and establish a practice and of what makes someone feel ready to open a practice.

When I started training at an analytic institute, it was affiliated with a referral agency that furnished patients to us at fairly low fees. Although they didn't pay much, they were at least plentiful. At one point I was seeing twenty patients from the agency plus others gathered from other sources. When I finished my training, I maintained my connection with the agency for several years, and many of those patients continued with me during that time. When the last one terminated, I left the agency permanently. It was a fairly simple way to start the private practice.

I think the times were different when many of the therapists in this book began their practices. Because of the changes brought by managed care, and the huge competition among new therapists for patients, I think it would be much harder to try opening and establishing a private practice today.

RELATED READING

Coche, J. M., and Coche, E. (1986). Leaving the institutional setting to enter private practice: a mid-life crisis resolution. *Psychotherapy in Private Practice* 4(3):43–50.

Roosa, L. W. (1982). The prodigal school psychologist: one psychologist's journey into the world of private practice and back. *School Psychology Review* 11(4):442–446.

Williams, L. M. (1991). A family therapist's guide to marketing: misconceptions, truths, and implications. *American Journal of Family Therapy* 19(3):206–214.

🐚🐚🐚🐚

Question 75: How long do you generally see people?

Psychoanalysis and psychoanalytic therapies can last many years. In behavioral or cognitive therapy, the goal is often as few sessions as possible. Recently, managed care organizations have limited length of treatment for all kinds of therapy.

Some therapists work from a theoretical framework in which short treatment is the goal.

> With a few notable exceptions, maybe ten to twenty appointments.
> [Male, Ph.D., 20 years practice]

> I average three to six months, and many I see on a periodic basis thereafter, usually at their initiation.
> [Male, Ph.D., 25 years practice]

> It varies. There are people I've been seeing for years, but the way I work the average is ten to fifteen sessions.
> [Female, M.A., 20 years practice]

Analytically oriented therapists tend to see patients for a long time.

I see them as long as it's helpful to them. Sometimes that can be years. One patient has been seeing me for fifteen years. Psychoanalytic therapy sometimes takes a long time.

[Male, Ph.D., 15 years practice]

As long as we both think there's continued growth. I have patients for over fifteen years.

[Female, Ph.D., 20 years practice]

My average, not including people who leave after two or three sessions, is about two years. And I've found, in reflecting afterwards, that people who leave after being engaged with me, there was usually some kind of impasse.

[Male, M.S.W., 15 years practice]

If someone's coming to me for something characterological, it's going to take years.

[Male, M.D., 15 years practice]

A few patients have left because they moved, and I've had some premature terminations. But it's years. I'm into long-term treatment.

[Female, M.S.W., 15 years practice]

Most of the therapists asked this question said that there was a wide range of treatment duration in their practices.

I've seen people for as little as three months, usually problem focused, and I also have people for thirteen years.

[Male, M.D., 20 years practice]

I still see the second patient I ever saw, but I think she may be a life patient. I see some people a short time, six to nine months, but I'm also working for sixteen years with someone. And everything in between. Mostly it's several years.

[Female, M.S., 15 years practice]

Couple work is an average of three to eight months, and half my practice is couples. Individuals I see about six months to three years, but I have a few people I've seen eight or ten years.

[Female, Ph.D., 20 years practice]

Some people don't stay very long at all. Then, I've got one person I've been seeing fourteen years, and another eight years.

[Female, M.S.W., 15 years practice]

It's really changed a lot. I saw one couple four times, and thought they had done what they wanted to do. But I also have seen some clients for five years.

[Female, Ph.D., 5 years practice]

Several people expressed surprise at how long patients chose to stay in treatment.

A long time, and it came as a surprise to me. Through school, I was horrified and thought of long-term therapy as a rip-off, that it was wrong, bad, unethical. But my clients are often damaged, very damaged, and when people had a life that comes out of a Stephen King novel, that doesn't lend itself to recovery in eight weeks. Some people stay with me for years.

[Male, M.S.W., 15 years practice]

Somewhat to my surprise, it does take years. One of the things that makes it so hard when you're training therapists is that it takes so long before you can see that what you're doing really works.

[Male, M.S.W., 10 years practice]

Several therapists said that they see patients at different points in their lives, as they deal with different issues.

A few people I see a long time. I see a lot of people intermittently, who come and go and come back.

[Female, M.S., 15 years practice]

I believe in lifetime treatment, so I have people ranging from one year to thirty years. Sometimes people come back to me after being out for twenty years, to work on problems that you have at sixty or seventy. It's very gratifying to me.

[Male, Ph.D., 50 years practice]

I've seen someone for seventeen years. I've had people come in for four years, leave for ten years, and come back in. I don't have an average.

[Female, M.S.W., 25 years practice]

NUMERICAL DISTRIBUTION

Most people said it varied so much that it was hard to specify with any accuracy. Of those who did specify a range: 8 said treatment was usually less than one year; 4 said one to two years; 12 said three to five years; 5 said five to ten years; 8 said over ten years.

COMMENTS

The issue raised here is: Is there an optimal length of treatment for each type of therapy?

There is a great range of responses to this question, since different approaches require different time frames. While there is no intrinsic correlation between length of treatment and quality of outcome, in general those who stay longer appear to get more accomplished. We might assume that personality exploration and reorganization is going to take longer than treatment of a phobia. The patient may also have some idea of how long treatment will last. I had a patient once who came into therapy with the intention of staying a year and left a year later, almost to the day.

In my own practice, individuals seem to stay either a relatively short time, a year or two, or a fairly long time, nine or ten years or even longer. Many patients come in and out of treatment, a year or two at a time, with absences in between of six months to several years. Couples therapy is usually briefer, though not necessarily, and I have seen some couples for five weeks and others for four years and longer. Patients in group either leave after a short time or tend to stay for many years.

Unless the therapist believes in suggesting termination (see Question 31), the length of treatment is determined by the patient.

RELATED READING

Binder, J. L., Henry, W. P., and Strupp, H. H. (1987). An appraisal of selection criteria for dynamic psychotherapies and implications for setting time limits. *Psychiatry* 50(2):154–166.

Burlingame, G. M., and Behrman, J. A. (1987). Clinician attitudes toward time-limited and time-unlimited therapy. *Professional Psychology: Research and Practice* 18(1):61–65.

DeBerry, S., and Baskin, D. (1989). Termination criteria in psychotherapy: a comparison of private and public practice. *American Journal of Psychotherapy* 43(1):43–53.

Howard, K. I., et al. (1986). The dose–effect relationship in psychotherapy. *American Psychologist* 41(2):159–164.

Koss, M. P. (1979). Length of psychotherapy for clients seen in private practice. *Journal of Consulting and Clinical Psychology* 47(1):210–212.

Strassberg, D. S., Anchor, K. N., Cunningham, J., and Elkins, D. (1977).

Successful outcome and number of sessions: when do counselors think enough is enough? *Journal of Counseling Psychology* 24(6):477–480.

☜☜☜☜

Question 76: Have you ever had a patient make threats toward others or toward you?

When a patient makes threats toward someone, we are legally obliged to warn that person, but evaluating the seriousness of the threat can be difficult (see also Question 10). Most private practitioners have never had to deal with this situation, for which they are extremely grateful.

A few therapists did encounter this problem, and described in detail just how difficult it can be.

> I've had a guy who stalked his ex-girlfriend. He verbalized that he could see killing her, killing her boyfriend. This was a guy I don't think would do it, I'm fairly certain he wouldn't do it. But I was apprehensive. Am I supposed to do something? Is this the case I'm supposed to report?
>
> [Male, Ph.D., 20 years practice]

> One situation was probably the most stressful I've had as a private therapist. That line where you're mandated to do something besides just explore it is not as clear cut before the fact as one would like to believe. Unless you're being very grandiose, there's no way of totally second-guessing what somebody might do. In my situation, I was telling the person that we would have to monitor how they felt, and that there was a real possibility that if this continued or escalated I would recommend that they go into the hospital, because I didn't want them to do something that would jeopardize their life, or their freedom. I was able to get them to start medication, so those feelings dissipated, and we were able to talk about them. But I was really not breathing for a couple of weeks there, and had quite a few anxious moments at home where I was wondering whether I was being grandiose in not having them hospitalized, and whether I was taking on more power than I should, and hoping that the relationship with me would get them through. It's very scary stuff.
>
> [Female, M.S.W., 20 years practice]

> One time a guy came for an evaluation, and he was on crack and alcohol, and he came with two friends. I said I couldn't work with him because he was obviously high. He said I *had* to work with him and I

had to save his life. I had to call 911 while he was there, and I called them twice and they never showed up. It was very scary.

[Male, Ph.D., 15 years practice]

Once, a patient said, in a very diffuse way, that he was going to hurt someone, that he "could feel the bones breaking." This guy was about three times my size, but when I confronted him and said, "You're not going to hurt anyone," he got very meek. He didn't stay in treatment very long.

[Male, Ph.D., 10 years practice]

I had a patient threaten to take out a contract on my life. This was about twenty years ago. He came into the session drunk, and I asked him to leave. He called me before the session time was over, and he told me that he had arranged to have me killed. I did see him again after that, though I had decided that I didn't want to work with him anymore. He had spoken to the bartender in a mob place, and the guy turned it down. He told the guy that you don't kill your therapist. But I was scared for a couple of weeks. He came in later on, had sobered up, and apologized, but when he decided to stop treatment, I didn't try to stop him.

[Male, Ph.D., 25 years practice]

I've had a patient who was HIV positive, very borderline guy, and when he found out he was HIV positive was really in a rage, and was going to get back at the whole gay community, and was out there having unsafe sex with as many people as he could get. My countertransference was I really wanted to turn this guy in. It was very scary to me, because I had to keep this secret. I thought there was something sadomasochistic in his revealing the secret to me knowing I can't do anything about it.

[Female, M.S.W., 20 years practice]

I had a man hold a huge crystal ashtray over my head for twenty-five minutes in a group, threatening to smash my head in. I've had a patient try to break into my house, and he broke down the door, but we had already moved. My office partner was killed by a patient. I have been stalked by a few patients.

[Male, Ph.D., 40 years practice]

Because we are usually alone in the office with the client, threatening behavior can be really frightening.

A man was referred to me and I saw him in the office once a week, and he was having problems with sexual orientation. He said he had lost a leg in Vietnam. I saw him for eight weeks without any recognizable signs of psychosis. Then he canceled for a month so he could go into the hospital to get fitted for a prosthesis, and he came back without any limp at all. I was staggered by the improvement, and he said it really fit quite well and rolled up his pant leg and I saw it was his real leg. There was no artificial limb, it was all a delusion. I knew at that point that I was in way over my head, and I began to talk to him about making a referral, and he started to threaten to kill me.

[Male, M.S.W., 15 years practice]

I had one patient, a schizophrenic patient, who would occasionally come in with a pair of scissors and make threatening gestures, and there were times when I was prepared to stop her if it was necessary. It never came to any actual act, but I was glad when she terminated.

[Male, Ph.D., 40 years practice]

The fear and danger may be even greater for the female therapist.

I had a parent of a child that I saw who was going through a difficult divorce, and she was quite psychotic at times, and she left very threatening messages on my machine. She began to believe that her husband was having an affair, and threatened her husband, and then she began to be paranoid about me and her husband, and was sure that I was having an affair with him. And she threatened bodily harm to me, to stand outside my door and tell everybody how I was not ethical and trustworthy. I handled it by speaking to my lawyer, and trying to contact her own therapist, who was not receptive to me.

[Female, M.S.W., 15 years practice]

I have felt a little frightened of a patient. I had a patient who saw some insecticide in my hallway on the way in say that he thought about blinding me with it, and I felt afraid of him. I'm in the process of transferring him to another therapist because I feel afraid of him again.

[Female, M.S.W., 25 years practice]

One therapist described an even more unusual situation.

I had my life threatened by the patient of a colleague with whom I was sharing office space.

[Male, M.S.W., 35 years practice]

Sometimes a confident response from the therapist can be reassuring and calming to the patient, or can help establish limits.

> I once had someone pull a knife out. I got very motherly, and said, "Put that thing away!" and he did. I chose not to see him, and terminated the treatment in the next session or two. I've had couples who've bordered on violence with one another, and I've physically intervened and stepped in between, and said they have to stop, that they can't do that here.
>
> [Female, Ph.D., 20 years practice]

> I had a patient once who told me he had a gun, and he told me about an incident where he had gotten very angry at a clerk and thought about getting his gun and shooting him. So I asked him if he would turn in his gun to me, and he did.
>
> [Male, Ph.D., 15 years practice]

> I was working with a couple, and he was just furious about what was going on, not so much with me as with his spouse, and he turned around and said he was going to get me. And I said I don't work in a climate like that and they would both have to leave. And they did.
>
> [Female, M.A., 20 years practice]

NUMERICAL DISTRIBUTION

Eight people said yes, toward someone else; 12 said yes, toward me; 40 said no, never in private practice.

COMMENTS

The issues here are: How does the therapist in private practice ensure his or her safety? What is the therapist required to do when threats are made?

These situations, in which clients threaten the therapist or some other person, are rare in private practice but can remind us of our vulnerability and sometimes our grandiosity. We may like to believe that we know who's dangerous and who isn't, but that can be a difficult call, and there are few guidelines to help us decide (see also Question 10).

In my own experience at an agency that treated psychiatric patients following their discharge from the hospital, I worked with many schizophrenic patients, some of whom were very paranoid, and with a few patients in the middle of a full-blown manic rage. I have been occasionally threatened and assaulted by such patients. I am happy to say that I don't recall ever having a patient in private practice make threats toward anyone else or toward me.

I remember being taught that in setting up an office, the furniture should be arranged so that both the patient and the therapist can easily get to the door and neither feels trapped or confined, and this has always seemed like good advice.

RELATED READING

Beck, J. C. (1988). The therapist's legal duty when the patient may be violent. *Psychiatric Clinics of North America* 11(4):665–679.

Mezey, G., and Shepherd, J. (1994). Effects of assault on health-care professionals. In *Violence in Health Care: A Practical Guide to Coping with Violence and Caring for Victims,* ed. J. Shepherd, pp. 1–11. Oxford: Oxford University Press.

Oppenheimer, K., and Swanson, G. (1990). Duty to warn: when should confidentiality be breached? *Journal of Family Practice* 30(2):179–184.

Tryon, G. S. (1986). Abuse of therapists by patients: a national survey. *Professional Psychology: Research and Practice* 17(4):357–363.

🅡🅡🅡🅡

Question 77: Have you ever been sexually attracted to a patient? How did you handle that?

In the current climate of increased awareness of sexual violations and transgressions by therapists, sexual feelings toward patients can be disturbing to the therapist. Feelings themselves may seem dangerous, and the therapist, especially in the early stages of practice, may feel the need to suppress or eradicate these fantasies.

> I bring it to supervision. I was very careful about how I dressed to make sure I was as unseductive as I could be. It can feel dangerous to me.
> [Female, M.S., 15 years practice]

> Once, and it scared the hell out of me. I never had that experience before, and I was able to talk it over in supervision.
> [Female, M.S.W., 10 years practice]

> One of my first patients was a beautiful Eurasian woman, and much to my dismay, I realized that I was sexually attracted to her, and I talked

about it with colleagues and supervisors, and once I realized that she really was objectively attractive, then it really was okay to feel attracted.

[Male, Ph.D., 25 years practice]

I try to find a supervisor, or a peer, to discuss it with. I want to make somebody aware of it, I feel like I need to do that.

[Male, M.S.W., 15 years practice]

My first time I thought, "Oh, Christ!" I took it up in supervision and in therapy, tried to understand. In some instances it was a transference from someone I had known. In some instances, it was just that the patient was very attractive. You don't respond to it. You have to appreciate that there are going to be patients you're going to be attracted to.

[Male, Ph.D., 10 years practice]

With more experience, therapists seem to become more comfortable accepting sexual feelings toward patients and to feel less threatened by their occurrence.

Haven't we all? I was more troubled by it in the first years than I am now. I acknowledge them to myself, own them, and don't act on them.

[Female, M.S., 20 years practice]

I enjoy it. It's fun. I've felt it toward men and women. I'm so strict about the boundaries that it doesn't feel dangerous to me. I'm not afraid of it.

[Female, M.S., 15 years practice]

I haven't found that too hard. In the early stages of my career I was susceptible to being affected by that. I've since learned that any dual relationship with a client is potentially hurtful, so I'm very careful about that.

[Male, Ph.D., 25 years practice]

I've been attracted to patients and had fantasies about patients. I try to understand the origins, and figure out the meaning. It's an interaction. There's a certain element of sexual attraction to any other human being, positive and negative.

[Male, M.D., 20 years practice]

At some point, if I'm working with someone over a long period of time, I'll probably be sexually attracted to everyone. It reflects something about what's going on. It can only be helpful, it has to be. It's not that it's bad, or that they're doing something and I'm doing something, it's that there's something about everyone that is attractive and sexual and engaging in that way. I'll just sit with it, and not feel like I have to do anything about it.

[Male, Ph.D., 20 years practice]

I think everybody's sexually attracted to their patients, whether they admit it or not. Some people are in total denial—they don't even know it. They're not lying about it, they really don't know it. It's part of normal life.

[Female, Ph.D., 10 years practice]

Some people are just attractive. But if there's an intense feeling of attraction, I try to understand a combination of what's going on in my own sex life plus what's going on with them and why are they doing this to me.

[Male, M.S.W., 15 years practice]

I try to enjoy it if I feel attracted. I try not to be seductive, not to feed into it. But I can be attracted to anyone. I think part of the therapy process is loving who you're with. I can't work with someone who I can't find something lovable about. I can enjoy looking at someone, and having feelings towards them, but I don't have to do anything with them.

[Male, Ph.D., 15 years practice]

I'm supposed to think about it and not act on it. Actually, I enjoy it. I can have a good time if I'm not afraid of it.

[Female, Ph.D., 20 years practice]

I don't think it's all that unusual. It's a very intimate situation. And even my female patients, I find them very beautiful, and I think about them. But there's no temptation to act out with any of them, so it's safe to feel the feelings.

[Female, M.S.W., 20 years practice]

Many people believe that it may still be useful to treat sexual feelings as countertransference and address them in supervision.

I was sexually attracted to one of my patients, and I inadvertently blurted it out, and he got so anxious he didn't show up for the next session. But he did come back the following week, and I was very relieved. I took it to my own therapy, and in talking about it I realized that I wasn't really attracted to him, it was something out of my own neediness.

[Female, M.S.W., 5 years practice]

I have someone now in one of my groups who's superattractive, and I'm sometimes distracted by his looks. I would talk about it in supervision.

[Female, M.S.W., 5 years practice]

I bring it to my therapy, and to my supervisor. It's not disturbing. I recognize that they're there, and they're human feelings.

[Female, M.S.W., 10 years practice]

I try to stay conscious. There's a very clear example of analyzing the countertransference. Freud says you have to constantly analyze the countertransference. You have to keep reminding yourself what a disaster it would be if you allowed yourself to act out on desire. You can easily make the mistake of thinking that outcome is really the desired outcome, when really nothing could be further from the truth. Even though the effort is being made, the outcome is not desired.

[Male, Ph.D., 50 years practice]

I saw one guy who was very cute. I felt like it was a similar thing to being bored. When I feel something different than I usually feel with patients, that's very interesting to me. If I felt myself very sexually aroused, I'd be very upset and go see somebody because I'd want to talk about it. That hasn't happened.

[Female, Ph.D., 15 years practice]

Even an experienced therapist can occasionally have difficulty with this kind of feeling.

If it gets out of hand, I would seriously consider terminating with the patient. That's happened only once. It is meaningful material, meaningful data, and I work with it as much as I can.

[Male, Ph.D., 30 years practice]

It changes one's attentiveness. It's distracting. I'll often think about it in terms of what I know about whom I'm sexually attracted to, and see what it tells me about this person.

[Female, M.D., 15 years practice]

Several people said that it was important not to let patients know about such feelings.

> Not with the patient! I deal with it in my own supervision. I try to understand what it is about this person. It hasn't happened very often. It's inevitably going to happen occasionally.
>
> [Female, Ph.D., 20 years practice]

> I try to be very careful in my reactions, and be very aware and keep in mind that I have to be as neutral and objective as I can.
>
> [Male, Ph.D., 40 years practice]

> I tell myself it's okay to feel that way, but I must make sure that I don't let the patient know that, and not let that interfere. It hasn't happened that often.
>
> [Male, M.S.W., 25 years practice]

At least one other person said they might discuss the feelings with the patient.

> I accept it, acknowledge it. Depending on the client, we may or may not talk about it. I don't panic. It's okay.
>
> [Female, M.S.W., 15 years practice]

Several people said that while they might feel sexually responsive to a new patient, after a short while such feelings receded.

> I'm like Searles on that. When I first see the patient, no matter how attractive, I concentrate on why the patient is there. I may make a note that the patient is attractive. And I can truthfully say that I get caught up in the patient's problems.
>
> [Male, M.S.W., 35 years practice]

> There's a funny phenomenon here, and it argues for a dynamic concept of superego. After about two or three appointments, even the most attractive patients, there is something about their vulnerability that removes them as sex objects. In fact, I'm not even comfortable generating sexual fantasies about them. It just doesn't work.
>
> [Male, Ph.D., 20 years practice]

> Usually, once I'm getting into the therapy part, I'm not. It's more at the beginning. I had one patient who was very handsome, with a very

good body, but as I got to know him, it wasn't that his good looks
diminished, but I was there to do the work and the feelings diminished.

[Female, M.S.W., 10 years practice]

Other therapists described having such feelings arise later in treatment,
and pointed out the diagnostic usefulness of such reactions to patients.

I've had patients where I haven't at all been attracted to them, and as
they get better, I find them more attractive. I see that as part of the
growth process.

[Female, M.S.W., 15 years practice]

I had a patient who would treat therapy like a date: He would talk
about what I was wearing, or he'd tell me that I looked good, and I
was aware that he needed to do this. I became uncomfortable when
I became aware that I enjoyed his doing it, and when he didn't do it
I'd wonder why he wasn't doing it. What we began to look at was
whether this went on with all the women in his life, and why his way
of dealing with women was so seductive. I used my feeling attracted
to him as awareness of something being induced, and used myself as
a barometer of what he was doing.

[Female, M.S.W., 20 years practice]

It's that old distinction between feeling and doing. At this point I use
it almost diagnostically. I can have a beautiful patient and I'm not
sexually attracted, and I find that as they become more intact and
resolved with the conflicts they came in with, I feel more attracted to
them as people. But not sexually. It doesn't happen any more.

[Male, Ph.D., 25 years practice]

Several therapists, five women and one man, said they had never experienced what they would call sexual feelings for a patient.

I've thought, "This person is attractive-looking," but not to the point
of thinking anything could ever happen.

[Female, M.S.W., 30 years practice]

I think some people are really interesting, I could see them as a friend,
but not sexually.

[Female, Ph.D., 5 years practice]

At this moment, I can't think of anyone. I'm sure I have, but it's very mild.

[Female, M.A., 20 years practice]

Not if you mean fantasy and whatever. I have maybe dressed a little better if I knew that a particular patient was coming in.

[Female, M.A., 20 years practice]

I'm gay myself, and most of my clients have been gay men, and often a generation younger than myself, and sometimes spectacularly handsome. But I've worried too much. I can see him and think, "What a nice-looking kid." I feel professional, and I don't feel that I would cross that boundary.

[Male, M.S.W., 10 years practice]

NUMERICAL DISTRIBUTION

Only 6 people, 5 of them women, said they had not been sexually attracted to patients. Everyone else said they had, at times, experienced sexual feelings toward patients.

COMMENTS

Some highly charged issues here are: How does the therapist best handle sexual feelings for the patient? Can patients induce such feelings? Are such feelings dangerous to treatment?

I think one of the benefits of practicing for a while is that I'm no longer thrown by this kind of feeling. It's part of the work sometimes, and I've been sexually attracted to both men and women and so what? It's just a feeling, and I don't have to be scared of it. I know I'm not going to act on it.

Sexual feelings toward patients can have a diagnostic value. If I start a treatment by having sexual feelings or fantasies toward a new patient, that can indicate something about the way they present themselves or a way that they function in the world. If I begin sometime later in the course of treatment to have sexual feelings toward a patient who never elicited those feelings in the past, that may indicate a shift in the patient, an increased accessibility, a heightened liveliness and energy, even an increase in self-esteem, or, on the other hand, that something has possibly frightened the patient and she (or he) is reverting to a defensive seductiveness.

RELATED READING

Pope, K. S., Sonne, J. L., and Holroyd, J. (1993). *Sexual Feelings in Psychotherapy*. Washington, DC: American Psychological Association.

Rodolfa, E., Hall, T., Holms, V., et al. (1994). The management of sexual feelings in therapy. *Professional Psychology: Research and Practice* 25(2): 168–172.

Tansey, M. J. (1994). Sexual attraction and phobic dread in the counter-transference. *Psychoanalytic Dialogues* 4(2):139–152.

▨▨▨▨

Question 78: Have you ever felt that you were falling in love with a patient? How did you handle that?

Feelings in therapy can be intense for the patient and for the therapist. A deep level of emotional involvement is part of the process and is almost necessary. Sometimes, this can take the form of a powerful countertransferential reaction, of falling in love in the romantic sense, with all the attendant fantasies. We know that this sometimes happens, and we have all heard of therapists who fell in love with and married their patients.

Only five of our sample said that they had experienced such a reaction.

> I did at one time early in my career feel like I was falling in love with a patient in the romantic sense. It was a time when my marriage was very rocky and I was feeling very needy and unhappy. And this was a woman who was very much my type, that I could easily have dated if she had not been a patient. I dealt with it by discussing it in supervision. I don't think she knew. I was quite conscious of the need not to act it out in some way, and I don't think I did.
>
> [Male, M.S.W., 15 years practice]

> I did, with one particular patient. I felt that if I had known this person in another context, I would have declared myself and I would have said this is how I feel and what do you think we can do about it. Instead, I sublimated it, and this was a patient who needed a lot of nurturing, so that's what I did with it.
>
> [Male, M.S.W., 25 years practice]

> I was in therapy and I'm sure I spoke about it there. But I fall in love with a lot of patients. I have very loving feelings toward many of them.
>
> [Male, Ph.D., 25 years practice]

> I think so. It's part of the process. It's not a big deal. I'm not afraid of acting on it. It energizes the sessions.
>
> [Female, M.S.W., 15 years practice]

Several others mentioned that they often have a different kind of love for their patients.

> I feel very loving toward my patients. I hug my patients, male and female, females more gingerly these days. Actually, I don't hug any female patients any more these days. It's too dangerous, it's not worth it. I feel very warmly toward them, but it's not love. It's paternal.
>
> [Male, Ph.D., 25 years practice]

> I've felt a strong attraction, and sometimes I'm very attracted to the person, not in a physical way, but to who they are. It feels more like a teacher's pet than a love object. A favorite, like a favorite child, but not a romantic love.
>
> [Female, M.S., 15 years practice]

> There are some patients I love, but not romantically.
>
> [Female, Ph.D., 5 years practice]

> Not in the sense that I would ever do anything, but in the sense that the person came up in my fantasy life.
>
> [Male, M.S.W., 15 years practice]

> Not romantically. There are patients who I've been working with a very long time, and the real relationship involves a great deal of regard, and that's an important part of the therapeutic matrix.
>
> [Male, M.D., 15 years practice]

> I remember one patient where I was aware of tremendous admiration for them.
>
> [Female, M.S.W., 45 years practice]

> Part of the therapeutic process is loving who you're with. So if you're loving someone who you're with, you're giving out love and feeling love. I can't work with someone I can't find something lovable about.
>
> [Male, Ph.D., 15 years practice]

NUMERICAL DISTRIBUTION

Only five people said they had fallen in love romantically with a patient. None of them acted on it.

COMMENTS

The issue here is: What do feelings of "falling in love" with the patient mean, and how does the therapist best deal with them?

This is another of those "forbidden" feelings, like hate, boredom, and envy, which can feel so dangerous to the therapist's equilibrium. In addition, we have all heard stories of therapists who fell in love with and married their patients, so we know it is possible to be "swept away" by such a feeling.

Although not in the conventional romantic meaning of the phrase, in a very real sense I believe that I fall in love with every patient. I have to open my heart and allow them to become important to me, so that working with them becomes significant enough for me to tolerate all the vicissitudes and difficulties of a long-term, in-depth treatment. I have to allow them to matter to me, in a deep and personal way, or the work is hollow and mechanical and of little use to either one of us.

RELATED READING

Celenza, A. (1991). The misuse of countertransference love in sexual intimacies between therapists and patients. *Psychoanalytic Psychology* 8(4): 501–509.

Coen, S. J. (1994). Barriers to love between patient and analyst. *Journal of the American Psychoanalytic Association* 42(4):1107–1135.

Hirsch, I. (1988). Mature love in the countertransference. In *Psychoanalytic Perspectives,* ed. J. F. Lasky, pp. 200–212. New York: New York University Press.

———. (1994). Countertransference love and theoretical model. *Psychoanalytic Dialogues* 4(2):171–192.

▧▧▧▧

Question 79: Have you ever dreamt about a patient? What does it mean when that happens?

Most therapists reported that they had occasionally had a dream about a current patient or even a former patient. Some practitioners regarded that kind of dream as a sign of some sort of countertransference problem.

> It means I'm thinking about them, that there's some kind of counter-transference going on, that they're important in my life in some way.
> [Male, Ph.D., 15 years practice]

The time I'm thinking of, it was a very clear countertransference to a very beautiful young patient with whom I had a sexual reaction.

[Male, Ph.D., 40 years practice]

At the time, it had to do with what was going on in my personal life, because the patient I dreamt about was sexually attractive but really an unhealthy person. It's an example of how it's about countertransference.

[Female, M.S.W., 5 years practice]

That there is something going on that has been for me too dangerous to look at.

[Female, M.S., 15 years practice]

With patients that I'm currently seeing, it's saying that there's something happening that's not being dealt with as directly as it ought to be. For example, I've been having sexual dreams about a patient, and I'm not consciously aware of any attraction to her. I think that she was unconsciously being seductive with me, and I'm not sure that was dealt with as much as it should have been.

[Male, M.S.W., 25 years practice]

Several people suggested that a dream about a patient indicated some identification with the patient.

There was one person I identified with a great deal, and was very aware of the identification. I dreamt about that patient a lot, and I think I was dreaming about myself.

[Female, M.S.W., 15 years practice]

Even when the dream suggests some countertransference, therapists find it helpful in becoming aware of the problem.

It means the patient gave me a nice gift, and I'm taking the patient home. Sometimes it's sexual dreams or aggressive dreams, there's something I'm not recognizing.

[Male, Ph.D., 20 years practice]

At the very least, it means that there's a certain engagement, and at the same time a certain lack of engagement, in that if I'm having to dream about it there's something I'm keeping away that has to come up in my dreams.

[Male, Ph.D., 20 years practice]

Others had more benign explanations of the significance of such a dream and did not readily accept the idea that it always indicates a counter-transference problem.

> I think it has to do with what the person represents to me at that time in terms of my own issues. Or it can even be a symbol.
>
> [Male, Ph.D., 25 years practice]

> It means that there's something going on in the treatment that I'm trying to figure out, something stressful in some way. It could also mean that the patient is being used to represent someone else.
>
> [Male, M.D., 20 years practice]

> Usually it's a way that there's some issue in the treatment. It could be that the patient is appearing in a symbolic guise and it has nothing to do with them.
>
> [Male, M.D., 15 years practice]

> I've had a few dreams about patients. I really don't know. Not always can I make the connection. Sometimes it's the last patient and something he said that's on my mind. Maybe it's my way of working on the therapy.
>
> [Female, M.A., 15 years practice]

> It obviously means there's something about them I'm trying to tell myself, and I'm not getting it yet.
>
> [Male, M.S.W., 10 years practice]

> It's usually when I'm very touched by something. I tend to get very emotional, and sometimes certain things really stay with me.
>
> [Female, M.S., 15 years practice]

Several therapists mentioned that they regarded dreams about patients as an indication that they were worried about the patient.

> It means I'm worried about them.
>
> [Male, Ph.D., 25 years practice]

> The only times I can think of it was about children, and it always meant I was really worried about them.
>
> [Female, M.A., 20 years practice]

A few people said they found such dreams disturbing.

I've dreamt about a patient in a sexual dream, and was quite uncomfortable about it. It made me wonder if I were acting in an inappropriate fashion, or was about to.

[Male, Ph.D., 5 years practice]

A larger number of therapists found such dreams very useful.

Particular people can penetrate into your unconscious more than other people, and I would want to find out why it was that patient and not somebody else.

[Female, Ph.D., 20 years practice]

Something is going on that I'm not totally aware of and alert to, in my own subconscious. I hopefully give it the credence it deserves, and if I can't seem to fully comprehend it, I discuss it with a colleague or a supervisor.

[Male, Ph.D., 30 years practice]

Occasionally it's told me about some change that's going on in the patient that I wasn't able to formulate in my mind.

[Female, M.D., 15 years practice]

It really helped to get me in touch with who the patient is. The dream was such a vivid expression of who she is that it was very helpful.

[Female, M.S.W., 5 years practice]

I think that it's something about my relationship with that person has touched something very, very deep in me, and there's something I need to know. It's a signal, a message, to myself, and I use it. I even at times have told clients a dream that I've had.

[Male, Ph.D., 10 years practice]

One therapist addressed the special case of dreaming about a patient whose treatment has ended.

Sometimes I dream about them long after I've stopped seeing them. It's one thing when I'm seeing them, but this is different. If I stop and reflect about that patient, there's something unfinished.

[Male, M.S.W., 25 years practice]

Only one person dismissed the significance of such dreams.

It probably means nothing.

[Female, M.A., 20 years practice]

NUMERICAL DISTRIBUTION

Only 8 people said they had never dreamt about a patient. The other 52 said they had at times.

COMMENTS

This issue is: Is dreaming about a patient a sign of a countertransference situation and a problem in the treatment, or is there a more benign explanation?

I remember being taught in training that dreaming about a patient meant some kind of countertransference problem, and this seemed to me even at the time a great oversimplification and a loss of potentially useful information about the patient.

I have dreamt about patients occasionally, and I think it can mean a number of different things. It can mean that I'm really connected to them. It can mean that I'm using them to represent some aspect of myself or of someone else in my life. Of course, it can in fact be an indication of some kind of countertransference, but I wouldn't assume that automatically. Often it turns out to be something significant about the patient that I've missed consciously. For example, I had a dream once about being kidnapped by a patient, and I understood the dream to mean that this patient was much needier than I had consciously realized, which was very useful to know.

RELATED READING

Robertson, B. M., and Yack, M. E. (1993). A candidate dreams of her patient: a report and some observations on the supervisory process. *International Journal of Psycho-Analysis* 74(5):993–1003.

Watson, R. I. (1994). The clinical use of the analyst's dreams of the patient. *Contemporary Psychoanalysis* 30(3):510–521.

❧❧❧❧

Question 80: Do you ever feel envious of your patients?

Another "forbidden" feeling, usually regarded as countertransferential and problematic, is a feeling of envy toward the patient. Yet it seems inevitable that some patients will have enviable qualities or possessions.

Mentioned most often was the financial success or income level of a patient.

> I have patients that are more affluent than me. I feel a little envious. It's not too bad, though.
>
> [Female, M.S.W., 25 years practice]

> Once in a blue moon I have felt competitive with a female patient's financial success. I realize they earn more money than me, and I get a twinge.
>
> [Female, M.A., 20 years practice]

> A lot of them have a lot more than I do, in terms of money. Some of my clients have a ton of money. Those are the only ones I feel envious of.
>
> [Female, Ph.D., 10 years practice]

Other therapists mentioned career success and professional achievement as things that might stir up envious feelings.

> I've been envious of certain patients' intellectual achievements.
>
> [Male, M.D., 20 years practice]

> Career self-activation.
>
> [Male, M.S.W., 15 years practice]

> Sometimes I'm envious of their lives. I have some clients who have pretty exciting lives.
>
> [Female, M.A., 15 years practice]

Some people mentioned patients' success in relationships as something that they envied.

> When I was going through a very difficult breakup of a relationship, it was very hard for me to work with people in very positive, loving relationships.
>
> [Female, Ph.D., 20 years practice]

> There have been times recently, because my husband died recently, when I've envied them running to the Hamptons and dating, all of that.
>
> [Female, M.A., 15 years practice]

A few people mentioned patients' personal qualities as enviable.

A certain social ease, a facility for being able to be extremely articulate and expressive, and be good storytellers and good joke tellers.
[Male, Ph.D., 30 years practice]

I envy some guys their ease with women.
[Male, Ph.D., 25 years practice]

I have patients who are talented, or stunningly beautiful. How could you help but wish you could be like that sometimes?
[Female, M.S.W., 15 years practice]

Some people are very good about making very clear professional decisions, and are creative in their thinking, and I envy that.
[Female, Ph.D., 30 years practice]

A few people, mostly older practitioners, mentioned envying youth, freedom, or opportunity.

Of being young enough to realize a lot of their hopes and plans.
[Female, M.S.W., 45 years practice]

If someone's young and just starting a family, I may envy that second chance.
[Male, Ph.D., 40 years practice]

They're starting younger on what they want to do.
[Male, Ph.D., 5 years practice]

Certain backgrounds that some patients come from, certain opportunities they had that I wished I had had.
[Female, Ph.D., 15 years practice]

There are some patients who seem to have this freedom to do all kinds of things, and I see this profession as being really restricted and confined to an office.
[Male, Ph.D., 20 years practice]

Some people said that envy was not something that they experienced toward their patients.

I'd use a different term, and say I'm admiring of my patients, and sometimes wish I had some of the skills and capacities that they have.
[Male, Ph.D., 25 years practice]

I can't say envious. I feel more maternal.

[Female, M.S.W., 15 years practice]

NUMERICAL DISTRIBUTION

Only 40 people were asked this question because it was added in the middle of doing the interviews. Of these, 33 said that they had sometimes been envious, and 7 said they never had.

Of the 33 who admitted to envious feelings: 15 said it was about money and wealth; 7 said it was around professional success; 5 mentioned youth and opportunity; 6 mentioned their personal lives and relationships; 4 said it was their skills and abilities; and 1 person mentioned freedom (some people gave more than one response).

COMMENTS

The issue here is how best to handle another "forbidden" feeling for the therapist.

Feelings of envy toward a patient can be disturbing. We're not supposed to feel that way about a patient, yet it seems unlikely that any practitioner will have such a complete life that such feelings never come up. There will always be patients who are better than we are at some things or who have more of some quality, and while we may also admire them for that, I think it is normal to have some envy for that skill or ability. There will always be patients with more money, more success, more varied experiences, more time left in their lives. As we age, it becomes increasingly likely that we will envy the youth and opportunity of younger patients.

Feelings of envy toward a patient can be useful for the therapist, because they can bring to awareness a dissatisfaction with his or her own situation. I know that when I become aware of envious feelings toward a patient, it means I'm unhappy with some situation in my own life that needs attention. Such feelings, if induced, can also alert the therapist to something in the patient that needs discussion in the treatment, for example, grandiosity, or feelings of deprivation.

RELATED READING

Allphin, C. (1982). Envy in the transference and countertransference. *Clinical Social Work Journal* 10(3):151–164.

Poggi, R. G., and Ganzarain, R. (1983). Countertransference hate. *Bulletin of the Menninger Clinic* 47(1):15–35.

Spero, M. H. (1988). Countertransference envy toward the religious patient. *American Journal of Psychoanalysis* 48(1):43–55.

Whitman, R. M., and Bloch, E. L. (1990). Therapist envy. *Bulletin of the Menninger Clinic* 54(4):478–487.

ⓡⓡⓡⓡ

Question 81: Which patients are easiest?

While most therapists would agree that no treatment is simple and straightforward, therapists are usually more at ease and comfortable with certain kinds of patients than with others. As one therapist summed it up:

> Patients who don't question the process, who expect to come back, and who don't leave me with indigestion.
>
> [Male, Ph.D., 40 years practice]

Several people mentioned intelligence as the most important feature.

> The ones who are bright and dynamic and want to work on their issues.
>
> [Female, Ph.D., 20 years practice]

> People who are intelligent, and who like to form insights, who like to think about their behavior, look at past issues and present issues and integrate them.
>
> [Male, Ph.D., 15 years practice]

> Somebody who's bright and verbal, and really does have a motivation to try to understand themselves and grapple with their problems.
>
> [Male, M.S.W., 20 years practice]

Some therapists mentioned level of motivation.

> Anxious and depressed patients, and the reason is that they're the most desirous of help.
>
> [Male, M.D., 20 years practice]

> I guess the ones who are working, the ones who bring some energy to the process.
>
> [Male, M.S.W., 10 years practice]

The patients who are very eager to work, that know how to talk, and that are willing to look at themselves and own their own stuff.

[Female, M.S., 20 years practice]

I find people who respond well to the desire for achievement, who are motivated for achievement, the easiest. I have a definite bias toward helping people improve themselves in the pursuit of excellence.

[Male, Ph.D., 30 years practice]

Risk-takers. Creative people in the arts. I think because they're creative with solutions too. They're willing to try something new. Any client who's willing to risk, I'm willing to journey with them.

[Female, Ph.D., 5 years practice]

Several people mentioned verbal expressiveness as most important.

People who talk. I've had people who don't talk and it's really hard.

[Female, M.S., 15 years practice]

Some mentioned level of insight as crucial.

Patients who have a lot of insight, who are very quick to tune in to the process and able to talk about what's going on between the two of us. These are the people I have to work the least with, because they're already tuned in.

[Female, M.S.W., 20 years practice]

The patients who are already introspective, who are interested in their inner lives, and want to talk about it.

[Female, M.D., 15 years practice]

The patient who has the capacity to reflect, an observing ego, who doesn't expect me to give them the right answers.

[Male, Ph.D., 20 years practice]

A number of people said that the healthiest patients are the easiest.

I can tell who the easiest to sit in the room with are: not hostile, with a belief in getting inside of themselves, who do it in a less defensive manner. The easiest are those who are most developed.

[Male, M.S.W., 15 years practice]

Patients who are well-motivated, intelligent, verbal, without any deep pathology.

[Male, Ph.D., 10 years practice]

People who are verbal and expressive are easy to work with. People who are comfortable and trusting. Healthy people. Sometimes people who've been in therapy before know what to expect, and sometimes people who are new to it are more enthusiastic.

[Female, M.S.W., 10 years practice]

Others said that it was the most psychologically sophisticated who were easiest.

The one who's engaging, who doesn't just accept everything I say, but who asks and reflects.

[Female, Ph.D., 30 years practice]

Probably people who've been to therapy before.

[Male, M.S.W., 10 years practice]

Patients who are psychologically hip.

[Male, Ph.D., 5 years practice]

Some people mentioned the emotional relatedness of the patient as being the essential factor.

In private practice, it's the ones who are more anxious and depressed, and less borderline, because they're more related, and you don't have to start at ground zero.

[Female, M.S.W., 15 years practice]

A few therapists said the most important feature was a similarity to themselves.

Those who are most like I am, that I can identify with.

[Male, Ph.D., 50 years practice]

People like me.

[Female, M.A., 20 years practice]

The ones that are obsessive-compulsive, because I am too.

[Female, M.S., 15 years practice]

Some therapists found a particular kind of problem or diagnosis to be the patient they work with most easily.

> Believe it or not, it's easy for me to work with cases of sexual abuse.
>
> [Female, M.S.W., 20 years practice]

> The ones whose issues have to do with separation, to separate and individuate.
>
> [Male, M.S.W., 25 years practice]

> I sometimes find working with depressed patients easier, if they're depressed and talking about it, because when somebody's depressed they spill everything, and I don't have to draw them out as much.
>
> [Female, M.S.W., 5 years practice]

> People with relatively recently developed panic disorder, and not a lot of personality problems and not a lot of depression.
>
> [Female, Ph.D., 10 years practice]

> Patients who don't feel entitled, patients who are depressed, with poor self-esteem.
>
> [Female, M.S.W., 15 years practice]

> The ones who are HIV positive or have AIDS, because they're dealing with significant issues that we can sink our teeth into.
>
> [Male, M.D., 5 years practice]

> The ones with self-esteem issues.
>
> [Female, M.A., 15 years practice]

> The old-fashioned obsessive-compulsive, highly guilty, obedient patient is the easiest.
>
> [Male, Ph.D., 15 years practice]

Sometimes it was a patient from a particular age group, gender, or social background.

> Children and adolescents. I absolutely love teenagers.
>
> [Female, Ph.D., 20 years practice]

> Jewish women ages 28 through 50, who have at least a college degree or are very smart, who are verbal, who are insightful.
>
> [Female, M.S.W., 10 years practice]

Young adults, 22 to 40, either sex.

[Male, Ph.D., 40 years practice]

I like working with late adolescents and young adults.

[Female, M.S.W., 45 years practice]

Your healthy neurotic young single woman.

[Female, M.A., 15 years practice]

Spiritually oriented.

[Female, M.S.W., 15 years practice]

Several therapists suggested that there was really no such thing as an easy patient.

I don't have any patients that are easy.

[Female, M.S.W., 5 years practice]

Everybody is a challenge. Nobody's easy. If I had to choose, it's the person who can take some action after the session.

[Female, M.S.W., 10 years practice]

There's no such thing. Patients who are more verbal and engaged are easier than those who aren't, but no patient is easy.

[Male, M.D., 15 years practice]

A few people pointed out that the patient who is easiest to work with may not be the patient who benefits the most from treatment.

If you mean the bright, verbal, entertaining patients, I enjoy them, and they do all right, but I'm not sure how much I'm actually helping them. I have a borderline patient who's made amazing progress, but I've felt like I'm in the trenches the whole time.

[Male, Ph.D., 25 years practice]

It's tautological, because the ones who get better are the easy ones. Sometimes a patient comes in and uses everything I give him, and it feels like I can't trust it because it's too easy.

[Male, Ph.D., 25 years practice]

In one sense, the easiest are neurotic patients, who are articulate and informed and desirous of change. Although they're sometimes the most painful for me, I do some of my best work with patients in whom the

experience of negative transference is essential in their changing. I know how to work and like to work in negative transference a lot, but it's tough.
[Female, M.S.W., 15 years practice]

NUMERICAL DISTRIBUTION

(Some people gave more than one answer.) Sixteen said bright or intelligent; 12 said verbal and expressive; 11 said insightful and introspective; 9 said motivated; 5 said patients similar to me; 4 said trusting; 3 said patients with previous therapy; 3 said responsive or engaged patients; 3 said patients with a sense of humor; 3 said patients who are adventurous and willing to take risks; 1 said creative individuals; 1 said spiritually oriented people.

Some people mentioned specific groups: 6 mentioned depressives; 5 said neurotics; 3 said anxious patients; 3 said women; 3 said adolescents; 1 said patients with AIDS or HIV; 1 said patients with a history of sexual abuse.

Three people said there's no such thing as an easy patient.

COMMENTS

The issue raised here is: Are patients easy objectively, because of something about them, or subjectively, because of the fit between patient and therapist?

I think the answer to this question is a combination of elements: Some patients have qualities that make them easier to work with, and every therapist works better with some kinds of patients than others.

I think that all of the qualities mentioned above help make treatment easier: intelligence, verbal facility, insight, motivation, and so on. But for me a sense of humor is the most helpful. It keeps things from getting too solemn and bogging down in their own weightiness. I also think it teaches something very important: the fact that we're laughing doesn't mean that we're not serious.

RELATED READING

Berger, A., and Morrison, T. L. (1984). Clinical judgments of easy vs. difficult clients by counselor trainees. *Journal of Clinical Psychology* 40(4): 1116–1122.

Merbaum, M., and Butcher, J. N. (1982). Therapists' liking of their psychotherapy patients: some issues related to severity of disorder and treatability. *Psychotherapy: Theory, Research, and Practice* 19(1):69–76.

℞℞℞℞

Question 82: Which patients are most difficult?

Just as some patients are easier than average, some are more difficult than average. One therapist described the experience this way:

> The more disturbed a person is, the more difficult they are. For me, the more difficult I experience a patient to be, the more disturbed I know that patient is. For me it's diagnostic.
>
> [Male, Ph.D., 50 years practice]

The largest number of responses mentioned the borderline diagnosis.

> The ones who are psychotic or severely borderline. The ones who are so disturbed that they're overwhelmed by panic or hostility or both, or are somewhat delusional because of the nature of the pathology.
>
> [Male, M.S.W., 35 years practice]

> A certain kind of borderline where I can't really understand what they're talking about. I had a professor who said that you know you have a borderline patient when you feel like your brains are scrambled eggs.
>
> [Male, M.S.W., 20 years practice]

> Borderline patients. Those for whom I am not really in the room, but where I start to feel like I'm not really there.
>
> [Female, M.A., 15 years practice]

Another large group mentioned the hostile patient as the most difficult.

> The really angry, aggressive, enraged ones.
>
> [Female, Ph.D., 30 years practice]

Equally difficult can be the resistant, passive-aggressive patient, who can appear in a number of different forms.

> The ones who are like mules, and get me to push them.
>
> [Male, M.S.W., 10 years practice]

> Rigid ones. When people are very rigid, and you have to go at such a slow pace. Or people who aren't coming to change, but are coming here to stay the same, and that's so much the agenda that it takes forever to get beyond that.
>
> [Female, Ph.D., 5 years practice]

People who tend to be very passive in the process, who have enormous expectations that I'm going to make them well magically by knowing what they need and providing it.

[Female, M.S.W., 20 years practice]

The hostile, resistant ones who aren't motivated. And they're not necessarily the deeply disturbed ones. People who are remanded, who come because they have to, are the worst.

[Male, Ph.D., 5 years practice]

People who have an overinvestment in their morbidity, who really want to cling to their pathology. After a while it becomes abundantly clear that they're consciously and willfully holding on.

[Male, Ph.D., 30 years practice]

Obsessional neurotics, not OCD [obsessive-compulsive disorder], but obsessive personalities, because they're always going, "Yes, maybe that's the case, but also, on the one hand but also on the other." After a while you want to clobber them.

[Male, M.D., 20 years practice]

Several people mentioned the over-intellectualized patient, who avoids or is unaware of feelings.

The engineers. The mathematical-minded ones who are always in their heads. I try to get them into the feelings and it's hard.

[Female. M.A., 20 years practice]

I've had several very nonpsychologically minded patients who, nevertheless, wanted therapy. They're very intellectualized and very frightened of more flexibile ways of thinking about themselves, very obsessive.

[Female, Ph.D., 20 years practice]

The most difficult patients are the concrete ones, who have such a difficult time seeing that there's anything possible under the surface.

[Female, M.S.W., 20 years practice]

They're concrete, patients who are looking for external solutions.

[Female, M.D., 15 years practice]

Several therapists cited the depressed patients as the most difficult.

Very depressed patients that are help-rejecting. I prefer patients where the anger can get engaged.

[Female, M.S.W., 15 years practice]

> People who are in major depression and refuse medication.
>
> [Female, M.S., 15 years practice]

> People who are very depressed, and who have realistically horrible lives. So even though you can help them with a lot, the reality of their life is dismal: They're poor; they have little education; they live in a horrible area; and they don't have the financial resources to make changes.
>
> [Female, Ph.D., 10 years practice]

A number of people mentioned the needy, demanding patient as most difficult.

> Whining, kvetching, complaining people.
>
> [Female, Ph.D., 20 years practice]

> The ones who are demanding, who want a different hour every week, who want to make a lot of changes.
>
> [Female, M.S.W., 15 years practice]

> Patients who require a lot of taking care of.
>
> [Female, M.S.W., 10 years practice]

> Those that have an inability to maintain the connection to the therapist. Those who cannot commit themselves to the sessions, who constantly want to change the hour, and they cancel. There's always something happening at the time that you alloted for them. They're very controlling.
>
> [Male, Ph.D., 20 years practice]

A few people said it was the self-destructive patient who was most difficult.

> A suicidal patient who really worried me. Or one with some psychotic features.
>
> [Female, M.S.W., 10 years practice]

> Suicidal patients are very difficult. Patients who tend to self-destruct.
>
> [Female, M.S.W.. 45 years practice]

> Drug-taking young people, especially those who've been smoking pot for a long time. There's an elusiveness, they're not really there with you, and they're very challenging patients. Also chronic cocaine use.
>
> [Male, M.D., 20 years practice]

Several people said that it was the most wounded patients who were the most difficult.

For me, it's the ones without a sense of humor about themselves, and about life. If I can't get them to laugh, I know it's going to be a long, difficult haul. Not coincidentally, these tend to be the most damaged people.

[Male, M.A., 15 years practice]

Very emotionally impoverished, deprived, rageful patients. Very narcissistic patients, even when they're not as deprived, because I can't say anything, I just have to be a total selfobject.

[Female, M.S.W., 25 years practice]

Those who have the most distrust of others.

[Male, Ph.D., 25 years practice]

Narcissistic people who seem to not have the tools to develop insight, who are so wounded that they just seem not to be able to get better, to get past whatever way something is.

[Female, M.A., 20 years practice]

Patients who can be a little boring, who really have had such damaged relationships in their life that they're isolated, and not engaged. The other would be patients who are just really dumb, where I have to explain my words.

[Female, M.S.W., 10 years practice]

NUMERICAL DISTRIBUTION

(Some people gave more than one answer.) Fifteen said the borderline patients; 10 said the oppositional, hostile, or resistant patient; 7 said the depressives; 7 said the rigid, concrete patients; 5 said the needy, demanding patients; 4 said the narcissistic patients; 2 said the boring patients; 2 said the unsophisticated, not-knowledgeable patients; 2 said the substance abusers; 2 said the suicidal patients; 2 said the passive, nonexpressive patients. One person each mentioned these: obsessive patients; patients who frighten the therapist; patients with no sense of humor; patients with no real personality.

COMMENTS

Again, the issue is: Are some patients intrinsically more difficult, or does the difficulty arise from a bad fit between patient and therapist?

And again, the answer appears to be a combination of factors. Since the same kind of patient is described by some therapists as the easiest and by others as the most difficult, the answer in at least some situations must lie in the fit between patient and therapist. On the other hand, since borderline patients appear on almost everyone's list as difficult, perhaps there are also some intrinsic characteristics that are more difficult to work with.

As in the previous question, all of these responses are true for me as well. Therapy is difficult with patients who are hostile, passive, resistant, withholding, and so on. But, again, the most difficult patient for me is the one who can't or won't laugh, and who won't allow me to, either. That can feel like torture sometimes.

RELATED READING

Bongar, B., Markey, L. A., and Peterson, L. G. (1991). Views on the difficult and dreaded patient: a preliminary investigation. *Medical Psychotherapy: An International Journal* 4:9–16.

Brandchaft, B., and Stolorow, R. D. (1994). The difficult patient. In *The Intersubjective Perspective,* ed. R. D. Stolorow, G. E. Atwood, and B. Brandchaft, pp. 407–420. Northvale, NJ: Jason Aronson.

Fremont, S. K., and Anderson, W. (1988). Investigation of factors involved in therapists' annoyance with clients. *Professional Psychology: Research and Practice* 19(3):330–335.

Robbins, J. M., et al. (1988). Therapists' perceptions of difficult psychiatric patients. *Journal of Nervous and Mental Disease* 176(8):490–497.

Smith, R. J., and Steindler, E. M. (1983). The impact of difficult patients upon treaters: consequences and remedies. *Bulletin of the Menninger Clinic* 47(2):107–116.

Winnicott, D. W. (1947). Hate in the countertransference. In *Through Paediatrics to Psycho-Analysis,* pp. 229–242. London: Tavistock, 1958.

🍳🍳🍳🍳

Question 83: What is the hardest topic for you to discuss with a patient?

The therapist has to deal with the full range of human experience. Some would say that an analysis is not complete unless all topics have been addressed. Yet because we are human there may be areas that are harder than others to discuss.

Many of our therapists mentioned money as the most difficult topic, partly because of their own feelings about it, and partly because of the patient's feelings.

Money. It just seems to be. People are more reluctant to describe how much they make, where they put it, what they're doing with it than who they're having kinky sex with. I can't think of anything else that produces the same discomfort.

[Male, Ph.D., 25 years practice]

Money issues. That wasn't always true, but people have become a little more private about that. Some people may not want to tell you what they're making, and they're a little secretive about it.

[Male, Ph.D., 15 years practice]

Probably money. Setting fees, if they owe me money, anything pertaining to money they have to give me.

[Male, M.S.W., 15 years practice]

I don't initiate topics. Money is the difficult one, and that's one I have to initiate.

[Female, M.S.W., 15 years practice]

Money. I find myself giving way.

[Female, Ph.D., 30 years practice]

Others said that death, including the option of suicide, was the hardest topic to discuss.

The hardest topic is death. I have several patients who are HIV positive, and they know they're dying and so do I, and obviously they need to talk about that, so I do, but it's very hard.

[Male, M.A., 15 years practice]

Maybe death. I tend to have very powerful feelings when a patient is talking about somebody who's died, because of loss in my own past, and I tend to lose my objectivity.

[Female, M.S., 15 years practice]

It's not a particular topic. The very hardest thing was to work with women whose child died in childbirth.

[Female, M.D., 15 years practice]

Maybe suicide makes me the most uncomfortable.

[Female, M.A., 15 years practice]

Probably some things related to the Holocaust. They evoke a certain tragic quality and loss in me that is more difficult to deal with.

[Male, M.D., 20 years practice]

Others mentioned issues relating to sex as troublesome.

> Someone who describes a lot of sexual behavior. That can make me very uncomfortable. Patients don't see my discomfort, in fact one told me they could never discuss it with their old therapist, but I feel it.
>
> [Female, M.S.W., 10 years practice]

> When a patient becomes seductive, and it's hard because it's got to be done carefully and gingerly, and not in such a way that you injure the patient's narcissism. You don't just out of the blue say to a female patient, "You're sitting with your legs open." It's got to be done within the context of the material being presented.
>
> [Male, M.S.W., 35 years practice]

> Sex is always delicate. Any kind of sexual topic, especially these days. And it's the most important topic, and it's the hardest to discuss, especially any sexual feelings that might be going on in the session between you and the patient. But if you don't discuss it, it can destroy the therapy.
>
> [Male, Ph.D., 15 years practice]

> The hardest topic for me to deal with is sexual abuse.
>
> [Male, Ph.D., 25 years practice]

Both male and female therapists can have difficulty with patients' sexual feelings toward them.

> When a patient has a sexual dream about me.
>
> [Female, M.S.W., 10 years practice]

> Probably if I sense that they're sexually attracted to me, and I need to address that, it's hard to bring up.
>
> [Female, Ph.D., 10 years practice]

> Probably if they were attracted to me physically.
>
> [Male, M.S.W., 15 years practice]

> Sometimes men's sexual fantasies about me, if they start to talk about that it's hard to listen.
>
> [Female, M.S.W., 20 years practice]

Several therapists said that feelings about the patient and about the relationship with the patient were hardest to talk about.

Although I do it all the time, it's our relationship, what's going on right here in this room at this time. I do it, but it's still really hard.

[Female, M.A., 15 years practice]

I have a very hard time telling people what's bothering me. For example, I have a very grandiose patient who needs to have his ego stroked, and I fall into that, and it's very hard for me to confront him about it.

[Female, M.S.W., 5 years practice]

With any particular patient, there may be aspects of our relationship that are hard for me to explore. For instance, if I'm with a patient who's into demeaning me or demeaning the therapy for reasons that I'm very clear about, but they're doing it in a very skillful way, talking about aspects of how I work that I'm most insecure about, I'm more quiet because I'm afraid that the reaction I'm going to have is too countertransferential. Even though I know there might be other days when I wouldn't feel that way, I'll let them talk and get back to it on a day when I'm feeling stronger.

[Female, M.S.W., 20 years practice]

A negative reaction that I'm having to the patient that I don't feel is necessarily justified or fair, or involves some aspect of the patient that I think is terribly sensitive.

[Male, Ph.D., 5 years practice]

It's when they've done something to hurt me.

[Female, M.S., 15 years practice]

This has only happened once or twice. I had a patient I didn't like, and I tried to figure it out in terms of my countertransference. I spent a lot of time trying to figure it out, and I couldn't find anything, but there was something about him that repelled me, and I felt terrible about it. In no way could I discuss it with him. Fortunately he didn't stay that long. Maybe I should have said that I'm not the right therapist. But I kept hoping that I would be able to overcome it.

[Male, M.S.W., 25 years practice]

The hardest topic is my own critical feelings, my negative, angry, frustrated feelings. Those are the most difficult to manage.

[Male, Ph.D., 50 years practice]

Things between us, like where I'm disturbed about something between us. Like if I have to tell a patient that I'm upset that they're calling all the time.

[Female, M.S.W., 15 years practice]

> Extremely vague is hard for me. A patient who says they want their life to be better, but no matter what I do I can't get them to help me define it, that's really hard for me.
>
> [Male, Ph.D., 20 years practice]

Two people specifically mentioned the question of personal boundaries and information.

> One of the hardest things to do is maintain my personal boundaries, and the hardest thing to discuss is the patient trying to get to know who I am, my personal self.
>
> [Female, M.S.W., 15 years practice]

> Whenever there are inquiries about my own personal life.
>
> [Male, Ph.D., 30 years practice]

Several people said that it wasn't a specific topic, but anticipation of the patient's reaction that might make it difficult to bring up something.

> Probably resistance. Patients don't take too kindly to that being pointed out to them.
>
> [Male, Ph.D., 10 years practice]

> It's hard for me to be firm, to make somebody do something that they don't want to do, whether it's to go to AA, or safe sex. It's hard for me to be firm without being judgmental or autocratic.
>
> [Female, M.S.W., 30 years practice]

> It's not a specific topic so much as what I sense would be very threatening to the patient. Especially if I feel that it's going to raise a dangerous level of hostility or that it's going to hurt their narcissism so much that they'll want to flee.
>
> [Male, M.S.W., 20 years practice]

More than a quarter of the interviewees said there was no particular topic or issue that was difficult to discuss.

> I'll talk about anything.
>
> [Female, M.A., 20 years practice]

> I don't know that there is one.
>
> [Female, M.A., 20 years practice]

> I see myself as being pretty comfortable discussing anything.
>
> [Male, Ph.D., 20 years practice]

NUMERICAL DISTRIBUTION

Twelve people said the patient's feelings about the therapist, especially sexual feelings; 11 said it was money and financial arrangements; 8 said it was their own feelings about the patient; 6 people said death; 4 people said sex; 2 people said suicide; and 1 person said the patient's resistance. Sixteen people said there was no specific topic that was hard to discuss.

COMMENTS

I think that this question again highlights the myth of the totally analyzed analyst, who is completely free of anxiety and conflict and can say or do anything without any difficulty or discomfort. I have trouble believing that so many people find all topics equally easy to discuss and that they could speak with patients about everything with no concern, anxiety, or distress.

I think that for me the hardest topic to discuss is death: not the abstract concept or possibility, but the concrete reality of the impending death of a patient with AIDS. I can do it, but it's hard.

RELATED READING

Adler, J. S., and Gutheil, T. G. (1977). Fees in beginning private practice. *Psychiatric Annals* 7(2):65–71.

Deutsch, C. J. (1984). Self-reported sources of stress among psychotherapists. *Professional Psychology: Research and Practice* 15(6):833–845.

Ginot, E. R., Herron, W. G., and Sitkowski, S. (1986). Therapists' orientation and defensive styles. *Psychological Reports* 59(3):1283–1292.

Prodgers, A. (1991). On hating the patient. *British Journal of Pychotherapy* 8(2):144–154.

🔊🔊🔊🔊

Question 84: When are you disappointed with your work?

Freud called psychoanalysis one of the "impossible" professions, which suggests that some disappointment is pretty much inevitable. What are the circumstances and situations that evoke disappointment?

Many people mentioned the situation of realizing that they had made a mistake, or missed something important.

Sometimes you have a session and bells just don't ring, and it's over and I realize I've missed something I should have picked up, and it could have been better.

[Female, M.S.W., 30 years practice]

If I say something that I shouldn't have said, at a moment when I've been fatigued or not careful.

[Male, Ph.D., 15 years practice]

When I think afterwards at home that I missed the boat on something.

[Male, Ph.D., 5 years practice]

Sometimes I feel I'm off. I'm disappointed when I'm pushing too hard. Not necessarily pushing a client, but pushing myself, when I'm not seeing the forest for the trees, when I know I'm missing something.

[Female, Ph.D., 5 years practice]

When I feel that I'm not tuning in quite accurately, not understanding the patient well enough. Sometimes I go home and think about what they said and I couldn't quite put it together.

[Male, Ph.D., 40 years practice]

When I realize that I made a mistake, and I have to pay for it.

[Female, M.S.W., 15 years practice]

When I make a mistake, especially if it's the kind of mistake I make a lot.

[Male, M.S.W., 15 years practice]

When I don't confront and I should have, when I let things go.

[Male, M.S.W., 15 years practice]

Some mentioned the situation of a patient leaving prematurely.

Sometimes when I feel that somebody just doesn't get better. Once in a while, something totally unexpected happens, like somebody walks in and says they're terminating today and they've been mad at me and they've given up on me, and I've been absolutely unaware. It's very disturbing because it means something very important went completely over my head.

[Female, M.A., 20 years practice]

When I see somebody leave, and I know I wasn't able to help them enough, sometimes I feel critical of myself.

[Female, M.S.W., 20 years practice]

When I fail. When a patient quits on me because I haven't understood them well enough.

[Male, M.S.W., 35 years practice]

Some cited the experience of feeling stuck, thinking that no progress was happening and that they had been overlooking something important.

If I feel bored, and that something is not happening for too long, I feel badly and I don't like that to go on.

[Female, M.A., 15 years practice]

I have been disappointed with myself when I don't feel like I know what's going on with someone, or they're stuck. I get disappointed when they don't change.

[Female, M.S., 15 years practice]

When I think a patient isn't making progress, and I worry that I've not been hearing them right, or that I'm missing something.

[Male, M.D., 20 years practice]

Some mentioned encountering the limits of their effectiveness or their tolerance.

The frustration of not being fully understood. Once in a while, the language is so foreign to the person that they have a genuinely difficult time understanding. I try to translate a concept like resistance, and the person doesn't get it.

[Male, Ph.D., 40 years practice]

When everything I do can't cure poverty, and can't cure racism, and can't cure abuse, so there's a real limit to how much I can help people when they're beaten down by those things.

[Female, Ph.D., 10 years practice]

I feel disappointed if I can't help them to make positive changes in their lives. If the resistances are so great, and the repetition so powerful that they can't move on.

[Female, Ph.D., 20 years practice]

Whenever a patient doesn't respond the way I'm hoping they'll respond. Whenever I'm frustrated in my expectations of myself.

[Male, M.D., 20 years practice]

When I thought that certain things were possible in the treatment, and it turns out they're not.

[Female, M.D., 15 years practice]

I sometimes have a deep feeling that I've failed a situation, that I didn't live up to it out of some personal weakness.

[Male, Ph.D., 10 years practice]

I have a patient who's been rageful at me for so long, and I was trying to tolerate it, but I can't do it. I feel like he sucked me dry.

[Female, M.S.W., 25 years practice]

Some people mentioned becoming aware of countertransference as disappointing.

When I get caught in a countertransference problem of some kind, or when I suddenly find myself behaving or reacting like one of their parents. Which doesn't happen very often, but of course it happens to all of us. I want to scold them, or I want to say, "Cut it out!"

[Female, M.S., 20 years practice]

When I think I talk too much, when I'm too eager to sound smart.

[Male, M.S.W., 10 years practice]

With myself, when I believe I've not made the correct action or move. When I recognize something that has to do with my own dynamics, my own anxiousness or defensiveness.

[Male, Ph.D., 25 years practice]

When I feel stuck, and then I have to ask myself, Who's stuck? Is it me that's stuck? Are they going on okay? When I begin to take too much responsibility for the client, and I realize that and stop myself.

[Female, M.A., 20 years practice]

Several people mentioned being tired or drained as contributing to the feeling of disappointment.

If I'm having a day where I'm tired.

[Male, M.S.W., 10 years practice]

When I'm too tired, when I don't take care of myself enough, when I'm not really present.

[Female, Ph.D., 20 years practice]

A few people mentioned frustration with the business aspects of the work as a factor in feeling disappointed.

> When managed care determines how much you can charge and how many sessions you can have.
>
> [Male, Ph.D., 20 years practice]

> Sometimes when I'm having a consultation with someone who's also interviewing other therapists, and then they don't pick me, and I wonder what I could have done differently.
>
> [Female, Ph.D., 15 years practice]

> Not the work itself. I'm sometimes disappointed with the financial aspect. I don't have control over wanting more patients and getting more patients.
>
> [Female, M.S., 15 years practice]

A relatively new therapist can begin to doubt his or her own abilities.

> I have days that I'm not thrilled. Sometimes I get frustrated with the newness of it, and trying to manage and build it up. I start to wonder if I'm a good therapist, am I doing something wrong, when will I ever get this together, maybe I shouldn't be doing this, maybe I should just go back to the agency.
>
> [Female, M.S.W., 5 years practice]

NUMERICAL DISTRIBUTION

(Some people mentioned more than one situation.) Sixteen people said when they don't see change or results; 11 said when someone leaves treatment prematurely; 10 said when they realize they've missed something important; 9 said when they realize they've made a mistake; 7 said when they realize they've been stuck in some kind of countertransference; 5 said when they encounter the limits of their effectiveness; 3 said when they let things slide or haven't been confronting enough; and 3 said when they're tired. Two people denied that they were ever disappointed with their work.

COMMENTS

The issues here are: What expectations does the therapist have, and what happens when they are not met? Which expectations are reasonable and normal, and which are countertransferential?

Disappointment is almost always directly proportional to expectation. The extent to which we are disappointed with our work depends on what we expect from ourselves. I think most of us expect that we will have some impact on every patient, and we are frustrated and disappointed when a patient terminates unexpectedly because we haven't helped. Every now and then we are confronted with the limits of our effectiveness, which runs right into our feelings of grandiosity and omnipotence.

I can be disappointed in any of the situations mentioned above: when I've made an obvious (or even not so obvious) mistake; when I'm feeling stuck; when I'm mired in some countertransferential reaction. But the most disappointing situation for me happens when a patient quits treatment suddenly, because I know that I will be unable to remedy and repair my mistakes.

RELATED READING

Buckley, P., Karasu, T. B., and Charles, E. (1979). Common mistakes in psychotherapy. *American Journal of Psychiatry* 136(12):1578–1580.

Gilberg, A. L. (1980). Psychoanalysis: hopes, realizations, disappointments. *American Journal of Psychoanalysis* 40(1):27–32.

Kottler, J. A., and Blau, D. S. (1989). *The Imperfect Therapist: Learning from Failure in Therapeutic Practice.* San Francisco: Jossey-Bass.

Saccuzzo, D. P. (1975). Unsuccessful therapy hours. *Psychotherapy: Theory, Research, and Practice* 12(4):353–356.

⬚⬚⬚⬚

Question 85: When do you feel drained or depleted by the work?

Although we are, most of the time, simply sitting and talking, we are deeply engaged in what we're doing and can use up a lot of energy. Certain situations, and certain patients, can be more draining than others. What situations and circumstances create the feeling of depletion for this group of therapists?

The largest number of therapists mentioned working too many hours.

> When I've seen too many patients in a row. I used to see eight people in a row, and I would come home and thinking that the last thing I wanted to hear was another human voice.
>
> [Female, M.S.W., 10 years practice]

> When I go over about thirty-two hours in a week, I'm exhausted. It's too much for me. That's my limit.
>
> [Female, M.S., 15 years practice]

If I'm working too long. Sometimes there will be a day where it's very busy, and I'll have a borderline patient come in and beat me up, and someone who I'm real excited about will say they're leaving therapy, and by the end of the day I feel depleted.

[Male, Ph.D., 25 years practice]

It's not the work, it's that I have to work so many hours to afford to be in the profession: to be in treatment, to be at an analytic institute, to pay office rent. It's an expensive profession.

[Female, M.S.W., 15 years practice]

Many people mentioned a particular kind of patient or a specific kind of interaction.

Certain cases, like when I was working with a multiple personality, that used to totally wreck me.

[Female, M.S.W., 30 years practice]

Schizophrenics are draining because they are so dreadfully needy. The needy people suck you dry.

[Female, Ph.D., 20 years practice]

I feel drained when I work with psychotics. When I'm contaged with toxic feelings.

[Female, M.S.W., 45 years practice]

When I've had two borderlines in crisis on the same day. I'm real tired at the end of the day, I'm quite depleted. I give it all in the office.

[Male, Ph.D., 25 years practice]

With the narcissists.

[Female, M.S.W., 20 years practice]

When they really act out. The borderlines get to me and make me feel like shit, and if that's the last session, I go home feeling that way.

[Female, M.S.W., 15 years practice]

Sometimes if a patient is very depressed or very intractable at a particular time.

[Female, Ph.D., 15 years practice]

Deeply depressed patients I find draining. Some couples work can be pretty exasperating, and it's in my couples work that I've probably had the most failures. That I find draining and frustrating.

[Male, Ph.D., 25 years practice]

Even though I work really well with negative transference, and all the hate and like that, there are times when it gets overwhelming and I feel weighed down by it.

[Female, M.S.W., 15 years practice]

When things don't go well. When a group goes poorly, out of hand, arguing and screaming, I will leave feeling drained.

[Male, M.S.W., 15 years practice]

Mostly when several patients in the day seem to be making no progress for a long time, or if they suggest that their money would be better spent taking a share in the Hamptons. Two or three of those in one day!

[Male, M.S.W., 15 years practice]

Several people said it can happen when they aren't taking care of themselves in some way or because of difficult events in their personal lives.

When I don't get enough sleep. When I'm down. When there's a lot going on in my life.

[Female, M.S.W., 15 years practice]

A few people mentioned the business aspects of the work as most draining.

When I have to call an agency. When I have an emergency and have to do a lot of paperwork.

[Female, M.S.W., 10 years practice]

Mostly by the business aspects of the work, not the work itself.

[Male, Ph.D., 25 years practice]

One person used the feeling of exhaustion as a clue to understanding the patient.

By certain patients, which I regard as countertransferential. I went through a period early in my career which looked like burnout. I was running a unit and it was very stressful. I came out of that experience with the conviction that burnout is a psychological phenomenon, it's not a physical condition. If a patient leaves me feeling de-animated, or de-skilled, or helpless, or like a schmuck, I try to understand that in terms of the patient.

[Male, M.D., 15 years practice]

About 20 percent of the group said that they rarely or never felt drained, depleted, or exhausted by the work.

Very rarely. When I'm working fewer hours, I'm much more prone to get tired at the end of the week than when I'm working a full load.
[Male, M.D., 20 years practice]

Not very often. I've probably taken fewer vacations than anyone I know who does this work. I've never had to cancel sessions. Never missed a day, with the one exception of when my mother died I missed one day.
[Male, M.S.W., 25 years practice]

I have felt tired after a long day, physically tired, but drained? Almost never.
[Female, M.S.W., 10 years practice]

Early on, in the first few years I did, but not any more.
[Male, M.D., 20 years practice]

Finally, one person said that the exhausted feeling was pleasant.

Usually pleasurably so, at the end of a day when I've seen a lot of patients.
[Male, Ph.D., 5 years practice]

NUMERICAL DISTRIBUTION

Twenty-one people said they feel drained when they work too many hours; 17 said they feel drained by difficult patients; 6 said it can happen when they're not taking care of themselves; 3 said they can feel drained when they feel ineffective; and 2 said it can happen from having to deal with the business aspects of the practice, with bureaucracy and paperwork. Eleven people said they rarely or never feel drained by the work.

COMMENTS

An issue here is: Is the work of the therapist inherently difficult, or does something in the personality of the therapist make it difficult?

I think that in some ways the work of psychotherapy is by its very nature difficult. The therapist has to be continuously present and engaged in ways few other jobs require. There is a very high level of responsibility and accountability and few support systems for the individual practitioner. On the other hand, some people are probably better suited temperamentally to the job than others, and each particular therapist has his or her own personal issues.

For me, what makes the job difficult at times has more to do with quantity than quality. I can sometimes, in a sort of grandiose way, schedule beyond my limits. I remember early in my career having a job as director of a residential therapeutic community, which took over fifty hours a week, plus a private practice of fifteen hours, plus three training courses, plus supervision, plus my own therapy twice a week. I kept it up for almost a year, but then I just couldn't do it anymore.

Sometimes now, when I've seen too many people in one day, I can feel exhausted, in the literal sense of emptied out or used up. In general, I know my limits and am careful not to schedule beyond them. Because we do use ourselves so much in our work, it's very important to have activities and relationships outside the office that replenish and refill us.

RELATED READING

Cooper, A. M. (1989). Some limitations on therapeutic effectiveness: the "burnout syndrome" in psychoanalysts. In *Essential Papers on Character Neurosis and Treatment,* ed. R. F. Lax, pp. 435–449. New York: New York University Press.

Goroff, N. N. (1986). The anatomy of "burn-out": the love paradigm as an antidote. *Journal of Sociology and Social Welfare* 13(2):197–208.

Hellman, I. D., Morrison, T. L., and Abramowitz, S. I. (1987). Therapist experience and the stresses of psychotherapeutic work. *Psychotherapy* 24(2):171–177.

Jones, F., Fletcher, B. C., and Ibbetson, K. (1991). Stressors and strains amongst social workers: demands, supports, constraints, and psychological health. *British Journal of Social Work* 21(5):443–469.

Raquepaw, J. M., and Miller, R. S. (1989). Psychotherapist burnout: a componential analysis. *Professional Psychology: Research and Practice* 20(1): 32–36.

Sussman, M. B., ed. (1995). *A Perilous Calling: The Hazards of Psychotherapy Practice.* New York: Wiley and Sons.

⍰⍰⍰⍰

Question 86: When do you feel energized or excited by the work?

Most therapists do the work they do because they enjoy it and find it fulfilling in various ways. Rather than feeling depleted or exhausted (see Question 85), we seem to get some sort of satisfaction from our work and to feel excited by what we do.

Virtually everyone, with only one exception, said that feeling excited or energized was a common experience.

> If I've been working with someone over a period of time, and we finally reach a breakthrough, I have to calm myself down from getting excited.
>
> [Male, M.S.W., 35 years practice]

> There are nights when I've had a series of good things happen, when I've used myself effectively, that I feel refreshed and energized by it, and I feel very good.
>
> [Female, M.S.W., 20 years practice]

> If somebody has really made a connection and really understood something about themself, I find it very exciting.
>
> [Female, M.S.W., 10 years practice]

> When I feel that we've done something really creative, or I've come up with a really creative homework assignment.
>
> [Female, Ph.D., 5 years practice]

> I feel energized when a patient is doing good work in therapy, when we're getting somewhere, when there's a good response to an antidepressant.
>
> [Male, M.D., 5 years practice]

Several people specifically cited group therapy work as creating that experience.

> Especially with group work. I leave it for the latter part of the day, it's almost always interesting and exciting and rejuvenating.
>
> [Male, Ph.D., 30 years practice]

> When a patient really is moving and getting some gratification. When there's a real good group session, I'm flying.
>
> [Female, M.S.W., 45 years practice]

> It's especially group for me. If a group goes well, I will leave feeling high.
>
> [Male, M.S.W., 15 years practice]

Only one therapist said she rarely had the experience.

> Occasionally. Not enough.
>
> [Female, M.S.W., 5 years practice]

NUMERICAL DISTRIBUTION

Only one person said she had the experience only occasionally. Everyone else said it occurred often or all the time.

COMMENTS

The question raised here is: Is the work intrinsically rewarding and exciting, or does the therapist experience it that way because of personality and temperament?

I think that there is something exhilarating that comes out of the intrinsic importance and immediacy of the work we do. When the work goes well, it almost always brings a feeling of excitement with it. I am often excited and energized at the end of a good day, and I'm especially exhilarated by group sessions that go well, because there's so much going on and so many people involved in it.

RELATED READING

Fiscalini, J. (1994). The uniquely interpersonal and the interpersonally unique: on interpersonal psychoanalysis. *Contemporary Psychoanalysis* 30(1):114–134.

Martin, P. J., Sterne, A. L., and Karwisch, G. A. (1976). Affection for patients as a factor in therapists' outcome judgments. *Journal of Clinical Psychology* 32(4):867–871.

Norcross, J. C., Prochaska, J. O., and Farber, J. A. (1993). Psychologists conducting psychotherapy: new findings and historical comparisons on the psychotherapy division membership. *Psychotherapy* 30(4):692–697.

Raskin, N. J. (1986). Some memorable clients and what makes them so. *Psychotherapy Patient* 2(4):107–113.

Vardy, M. M., and Kay, S. R. (1982). The therapeutic value of psychotherapists' values and therapy orientations. *Psychiatry* 45(3):226–233.

℞℞℞℞

Question 87: Do you ever feel competitive toward other therapists?

The reality of our profession is that it is also a business, and we are competing with our colleagues for available patients. It seems inevitable that

ve sometimes become aware of the competition and have some feelings
about it.

Most of the therapists in our group acknowledged some competitive
feelings. One person put it rather graphically.

> At conferences, I want to come in with a machine gun and shoot
> everybody.
>
> [Male, Ph.D., 10 years practice]

Some of the respondents cited specific aspects of the situation. Income
level and professional success were mentioned fairly often.

> Everyone should be coming to me and not to other therapists, to begin
> with, that's number one. And other people make more money, they
> have more hours.
>
> [Male, Ph.D., 25 years practice]

> Definitely. Who's got more hours, and who's practice is up, and who's
> making more money and having all this success.
>
> [Female, M.S.W., 15 years practice]

> Sometimes I'll think that someone else has such a big practice with
> great fees, and I'll envy that. But because of my background relative
> to my siblings, I've learned to translate that and try to figure out what
> they're doing to have what they have.
>
> [Female, M.S.W., 25 years practice]

> That they don't have any trouble building their practice, that they have
> such a great reputation that they can charge one-hundred-and-fifty
> dollars an hour.
>
> [Female, Ph.D., 10 years practice]

> People who are established in the field, and feel self-confident, and
> have an easier time asking for money.
>
> [Female, M.S.W., 15 years practice]

Professional skills and abilities, like writing or marketing, or just general competence, were also mentioned.

> Yes, of course. In terms of wishing I had the facility to write. I'm not a
> good writer.
>
> [Male, M.D., 20 years practice]

I feel it when colleagues of mine are writing, and I feel I should be writing, that I've been lazy.

[Female, Ph.D., 5 years practice]

I have been competitive with other psychologists around editorial output, or political influence.

[Male, Ph.D., 40 years practice]

Sometimes I feel envious when I see someone who has a particular talent or gift that I wish I had.

[Male, M.D., 5 years practice]

I sometimes wonder with senior people who I admire if I'll ever be as good as they are.

[Male, Ph.D., 5 years practice]

Every so often, people talk about previous therapists or friends who are with other therapists, and they say things about them and I think how good that person is and how smart they are, and I feel envious.

[Male, Ph.D., 50 years practice]

Intellectual facility and knowledge were also mentioned.

When I think there's someone who's smarter than I am, or knows more than me.

[Female, Ph.D., 30 years practice]

Mostly around academic issues, like getting recognition for the work you've done, for your thinking.

[Female, M.D., 15 years practice]

I will often envy someone who has come up with a brilliant idea or thought, and I also admire them.

[Female, M.S.W., 45 years practice]

That I had their level of success, or their ability to deal with the professional literature, that they're better read.

[Male, M.S.W., 10 years practice]

Another person described a particular situation which leaves him envious of colleagues' freedom.

Around issues of their lifestyle. I have a good clinical practice, but I also have an evaluation practice that's very draining. There's a lot of paperwork. I don't want to give it up, because I need the money, but it's a full-time job, so in essence I have two full-time jobs. So if I'm jealous of other therapists, it's that they can have the lifestyle of a therapist, with days off, and breaks, and have time for other things, like writing or other projects.

[Male, Ph.D., 15 years practice]

A few people said they were rarely or never aware of any competitive feelings.

I don't give a hoot what anyone else does. I've never been competitive. I think that's what keeps me happy. And I try to use that as a model for my patients. Why do you care what they're doing?

[Female, M.A., 15 years practice]

I feel competitive, but not about therapy. About the things in life.

[Female, M.S., 15 years practice]

It hasn't happened yet. I haven't been in competition yet. The people I know who are also therapists work in a different area of the city, and I respect them and make referrals to them.

[Female, M.S.W., 5 years practice]

NUMERICAL DISTRIBUTION

This question was added in the course of doing the interviews, so only 50 therapists were asked and answered it. Of these, 12 said they were envious around the number of patient hours; 12 said around fees and income; 11 said around others' competence, knowledge, or skill; 10 said around others' professional success and recognition. Five people said they were rarely or never envious.

COMMENTS

The issues here are: Are competitive feelings toward other therapists normal, or a sign of some unresolved pathology? What are the effects of such feelings on the therapist? Do they provide motivation for greater activity, or do they create despair and passivity?

Because in today's marketplace we are competing for patients, money, and professional recognition, I think it is normal to feel competitive at times. Only the most successful therapist can look around and feel completely satisfied. If my patient hours are down, I can easily feel competitive with anyone whose schedule is full, especially if I think I'm a better therapist than they are.

RELATED READING

Persi, J. (1993). Top gun games: when therapists compete. *Transactional Analysis Journal* 22(3):144–152.

℞℞℞℞

Question 88: How do you keep personal crises from affecting your work?

Crises occur in everyone's life, even the therapist's. Sometimes, as in the case of a bitter, drawn-out divorce, or the lingering illness of a loved one, these situations are distracting. What strategies have our interviewees devised to keep crises out of the consulting room?

Most therapists acknowledged that it was sometimes hard to focus on the patient.

> It's not easy. You do the best you can. Maybe for the time being, you have to put up with the fact that you're not quite as attentive as you would have been normally.
>
> [Male, Ph.D., 40 years practice]

A number of therapists said they would try to discuss their distress with others as a way of coping with it.

> By finding the time throughout the day to talk to someone else.
>
> [Male, M.S.W., 15 years practice]

> With a good support system. I make use of my therapist still. Friends, my peer supervision group.
>
> [Female, M.S.W., 25 years practice]

> The fact that I've been in therapy for so long, and am still in, that's the main thing. I make sure that I'm taken care of.
>
> [Female, M.S.W., 15 years practice]

A few therapists said that when the situation was too distracting they would cancel sessions, even whole days, and might sometimes tell patients why.

I've taken time off, if I've felt that it's going to be a real problem. I try to get on the phone with all my friends, my support group. But if I really felt distracted I would cancel appointments.

[Male, Ph.D., 25 years practice]

I don't think you can keep them out. When there have been illnesses in my family and I've needed to leave abruptly, I've needed to tell clients that.

[Female, Ph.D., 10 years practice]

It's only happened once or twice. I'll cancel sessions until I've recovered.

[Male, M.D., 20 years practice]

If there's a major catastrophe, I can't not own up to that. Not necessarily tell them about it, but acknowledge it in some way. I may cancel sessions if I need to.

[Male, Ph.D., 40 years practice]

The way I deal with that is that if it's a crisis that's going to affect me in the office, I cancel the day. And if I think it's not going to affect me, I come to work and deal with the crisis later.

[Female, M.D., 15 years practice]

Most people said they found that their professional roles helped them exclude their own personal concerns from coming into the office and disrupting the work.

I try to keep a professional distance. I can turn it off and turn it on, to some extent. I focus very specifically on the person I'm talking with, and though there may be a lot going on in my life, because of my focus, that all goes away for the time I'm talking with them.

[Male, M.D., 5 years practice]

Something happens when I walk in the office and close the door. It's gone. I don't know exactly how that happens. I guess it's the frame. This is the frame, and anything that's not part of the frame is excluded for the forty-five minutes. When the session is over, it's back.

[Female, M.S.W., 20 years practice]

I can be having a bad day, or be depressed about something, but as soon as the door closes, as soon as the patient sits down, the focus is all outwards. I never find myself drifting off in my own stuff. Because I'm so active. As soon as they leave, it'll come back.

[Male, Ph.D., 25 years practice]

I set boundaries. I have a mindset: this is my office, and this is the time
I see people.

[Male, M.S.W., 10 years practice]

I just go into Professional Therapist mode. You shift gears.

[Female, M.S.W., 15 years practice]

I seem to be able to compartmentalize, and when I'm in this particular
role, I really am out of touch with my own life. I get carried away by
the work.

[Male, Ph.D., 50 years practice]

I'm a professional. I'm supposed to be behaving like one. I take that
very seriously.

[Female, Ph.D., 20 years practice]

Several people pointed out that it was often a relief to be able to go to
work and focus on someone else's situation.

When I'm going through something specific, I find it to be the best
place for me, because I can go to escape myself sometimes.

[Female, M.S.W., 5 years practice]

It really helped me to have this work when I was going through my
crisis. I would have fallen apart otherwise.

[Female, M.A., 15 years practice]

Oftentimes, if I focus on the work I'm doing with patients, that's a relief.

[Male, Ph.D., 25 years practice]

I felt when I was getting divorced that it was my work that kept me
sane, because I had all those hours when I wasn't focusing on how
miserable I was.

[Female, M.A., 20 years practice]

You have to come in and switch gears. In this room, I have to be the
therapist. I have to clearly define my role. It can be difficult, I can still
be hurting, but my role is not to address that part of me right now.
Sometimes it was actually helpful, because I had to focus on someone
else, and it was a way of taking care of myself, to focus on someone
else. Perhaps I'm working better, because I'm working harder to make
sure I'm attentive.

[Female, Ph.D., 5 years practice]

One person pointed out the value of such situations.

> Personal crises add depth and dimension to us as human beings, and therefore can enhance my ability to do the work.
>
> [Female, M.S.W., 45 years practice]

NUMERICAL DISTRIBUTION

Forty people said they found that they were able to focus on the patient and the work in spite of personal crisis; 11 said they would cancel sessions or days if they needed to; 9 people said they make sure they get their own needs taken care of elsewhere.

COMMENTS

Some issues in this area are: What are the effects on the treatment of a crisis in the therapist's personal life? What are the best ways to manage such crises and prevent them from damaging the work with patients?

There will often be situations in the therapist's life that impact on the practice: death in the family, major illness (of the therapist or of someone close), divorce, financial problems, and so on. These events unbalance us and consequently must have some effect on the work we do. On the other hand, having a place where we must think about something else and someone else is often a relief. In not thinking about our own situation, we may actually be more focused than usual on the patient's situation.

Of course, sometimes patients pick up on the situation anyway. I remember that when my father died suddenly, all my patients were talking about death, though only one had seen the obituary in the newspaper. This may have been because I had taken a week off, which might have felt like *my* death to these patients, but I remember thinking at the time, and still believe, that somehow they knew.

It may be useful, without revealing all the personal details, for the therapist to let patients know that he or she is not in a normal state of mind due to such a situation. Otherwise, patients may sense the difference but doubt their own perceptions, which is clearly not therapeutic.

RELATED READING

Flapan, D. (1986). The trauma of the therapist's illness. *Issues in Ego Psychology* 9(2):32–39.

Frankel, A. (1993). Crisis in the life of the therapist. *Contemporary Psychotherapy Review* 8:77–89.

Kilburg, R. R., Nathan, P. E., and Thoreson, R. W., eds. (1986). *Professionals in Distress: Issues, Syndromes, and Solutions in Psychology.* Washington, DC: American Psychological Association.

Pappas, P. A. (1989). Divorce and the psychotherapist. *American Journal of Psychotherapy* 43(4):506–517.

Schwartz, H. J., and Silver, A. L. S., eds. (1990). *Illness in the Analyst: Implications for the Treatment Relationship.* Madison, CT: International Universities Press.

ß ß ß ß

Question 89: What is your greatest asset as a therapist?

Every therapist has qualities that enhance his or her skills and abilities in doing therapy. There was a wide range of specific attributes mentioned by this group as contributing to their success in doing the work.

   More than half our group mentioned the emotional connection: empathy, love, caring, and concern.

> My ability to empathize. And my concern for people. I can really be there. I like to connect in that intimate way.
>
> [Female, M.S.W., 20 years practice]

> This is going to sound awfully pretentious, but I think it's the love.
>
> [Male, M.S.W., 25 years practice]

> I'm very sensitive to how people feel.
>
> [Female, M.S.W., 20 years practice]

> A supervisor told me once that I have a "true heart," and that made me feel good. And it's a place that I operate out of.
>
> [Female, M.S.W., 5 years practice]

> My candor and my warmth, my empathy.
>
> [Female, M.S.W., 15 years practice]

> My sensitivity, my ability to listen and be with the person.
>
> [Male, Ph.D., 15 years practice]

Empathy. An ability to feel what a patient is going through and relate it to what I've gone through.

> [Female, M.S.W., 5 years practice]

Many people mentioned their intellectual attributes, including creativity and originality.

I should say all that stuff about love and my heart, but I think the greatest asset is that I'm very smart.

> [Male, Ph.D., 25 years practice]

Ingenuity, and the ability to improvise on some basic principles.

> [Male, Ph.D., 20 years practice]

I'm creative, and I'm open to doing things or saying things or suggesting things that are unconventional.

> [Female, Ph.D., 5 years practice]

Several mentioned their neutrality and ability to be accepting.

My world view. I don't judge my patients. I have no investment in their living any particular way of life. I can be totally accepting of whatever it is they want to talk about.

> [Male, Ph.D., 50 years practice]

A number of different patients have said that they value the way that I listen. And supervisors have also said something about that, that given what patients say to me, or the ease with which they do, they think there's some way that I convey openness, a nonjudgmental quality, that makes it easy for people to say things to me.

> [Female, Ph.D., 15 years practice]

Tolerance, patience. I won't get ruffled. Also my optimism and hopefulness, that we will figure things out.

> [Male, M.D., 20 years practice]

My tolerance for diversity, sans prejudice.

> [Female, M.A., 15 years practice]

That I'm extremely accepting, and it's genuine.

> [Male, Ph.D., 40 years practice]

Some people said that it was their personal and/or professional experience that was most valuable.

> I think that my greatest asset is that I have overcome my own prob-
> lems, and I therefore can empathize with patients, and help them
> with theirs.
>
> [Male, Ph.D., 15 years practice]

> I guess my training. I've had a lot of training and experience.
>
> [Male, Ph.D., 40 years practice]

> Compassion and knowledge. I'm really experienced at this point, and
> whatever I don't know I'm willing to learn about it.
>
> [Female, M.S.W., 10 years practice]

> I have very good training. I did a residency and two fellowships. Also,
> I care very sincerely, very genuinely, about my patients and about
> people.
>
> [Male, M.D., 5 years practice]

> My life experience, and the frame of reference that gives me.
>
> [Male, M.S.W., 10 years practice]

> I form a link in terms of their cultural underpinnings. I've been exposed
> to many cultures myself, and the patient feels understood, and it makes
> for a very good start.
>
> [Male, Ph.D., 30 years practice]

> I think at this point, and this may sound conceited, is that I have a
> certain amount of wisdom. A patient said to me the other day that they
> appreciate my life experience, and there's something to that.
>
> [Female, M.S.W., 30 years practice]

Several cited commitment and perseverance.

> I'm very reliable. I'm always there.
>
> [Male, Ph.D., 20 years practice]

> My endurance. No matter how angry or upset or disappointed or
> frustrated the person is with me, or I am with them, I don't give up.
>
> [Female, Ph.D., 30 years practice]

A few mentioned some aspect of their personality as most important.

I have charisma. I'm charismatic, and people feel that and they think that something magical and mystical can happen here and it does. I believe that a lucky therapist combines commitment with competence and charisma. If people don't like you they're not going to talk to you. People like me, and they talk to me. There's something about me that engages people and it works, and it's one of my best gifts.

[Male, M.S.W., 15 years practice]

Probably my voyeuristic tendencies. I think I really like life, and there's something about engaging in it with people that's exciting and reward-ing, and maybe I convey that to people, and it allows me to sit through the tough stuff.

[Female, M.S.W., 15 years practice]

My energy. I engage people very easily, and maintain very good pro-ductive relationships that push people. I'm bright and quick and can do all that.

[Female, Ph.D., 20 years practice]

Probably my style. Something about my relative informality. There are probably a lot of people it turns off, but they don't come back and I don't have to worry about them.

[Male, Ph.D., 20 years practice]

Several people mentioned sense of humor as the most valuable asset.

Without putting on a lot of false modesty, I think I have a number of assets: my intelligence, my memory, my creativity, my ability to under-stand a patient's experience, my own personal and professional expe-rience. But I think my greatest asset is my sense of humor, which lightens the work and cuts through so much in such a gentle way.

[Male, Ph.D., 15 years practice]

Finally, several people said that it was their genuine enjoyment of other people that was most valuable.

That I really like people and it's really evident to them. I'm accessible.

[Female, M.S.W., 10 years practice]

I do like people. There are very few people I don't like. And I can laugh at myself. When I don't do things well I can keep on trying, I don't get all upset.

[Female, Ph.D., 10 years practice]

The fact that I like people, and that I like the work.

[Female, M.A., 15 years practice]

NUMERICAL DISTRIBUTION

(Some people gave more than one answer.) Twelve people mentioned their compassion, caring, warmth, or love; 11 people said their sensitivity or ability to empathize; 11 said their ability to connect or be present; 7 said their intelligence; 7 said their personal life experience; 7 said their openness, and ability to be accepting and nonjudgmental; 6 said their knowledge and skill; 3 said their patience; 3 said their sense of humor; 3 said their personality; 2 said their enthusiasm; 2 said their reliability; 2 said their creativity and flexibility; 1 said his integrity.

COMMENTS

The main issue here is: Which therapist qualities and characteristics are conducive to effective therapy, and which are not significant to outcome?

There seem to be some obvious answers to this question: we may assume that friendly is better than unfriendly, or that warm is better than cold, and so on. But the question remains of what qualities really determine the outcome of therapy and which are essentially irrelevant to outcome.

I think that all the qualities mentioned by these therapists are significant to some degree, but I also think it would be very difficult to decide their order of importance, which matters most and which least. How we conceptualize therapy and the way we think it works may determine which qualities we identify as significant and in what order of importance. Ultimately, of course, patients tell us what is and what is not significant, and this may vary from individual patient to patient.

RELATED READING

Baudry, F. D. (1989). A silent partner to our practice: the analyst's character and attitudes. In *Essential Papers on Character Neurosis and Treatment,* ed. R. F. Lax, pp. 397–408. New York: New York University Press.

Carsen, M. L., and Roskin, G. (1984). Empathy from the perspective of the student therapist. *Hillside Journal of Clinical Psychiatry* 6(2):259–270.

Miller, L. (1993). Who are the best psychotherapists? Qualities of the effective practitioner. *Psychotherapy in Private Practice* 12(1):1–18.

Thompson, B. J., and Hill, C. E. (1993). Client perceptions of therapist competence. *Psychotherapy Research* 3(2):124–130.

⧜⧜⧜⧜

Question 90: What is your greatest liability as a therapist?

Just as we each have qualities that enhance the work, we also have qualities that detract from it. With this question, responses appear to split into two main categories: one in which therapists describe a tendency to be too active or invasive; and one in which therapists identify a tendency to back away from the patient and not be active enough.

A number of people said that fear of the patient's anger, upset, or rejection sometimes kept them from doing what they know needs to be done.

> I'm really fearful of upsetting people, and so I'm really held back, and I lose myself out of that fear.
>
> [Female, M.S.W., 5 years practice]

> I'm not as comfortable with anger as I could be.
>
> [Female, M.S.W., 30 years practice]

> The thing that I have come up against, that I hope doesn't affect my work that much but that I have to watch out for, is wanting to be liked myself, and not wanting to be abandoned. So that if a patient starts talking about termination, I have to immediately remind myself that it's for the patient, not for me.
>
> [Male, M.S.W., 20 years practice]

> I have a need to make people feel okay, and that can get in the way.
>
> [Female, Ph.D., 5 years practice]

> Maybe I'm not as active sometimes as I should be. Like confrontational. I might not push in a direction that I feel the patient is hesitant to go in when maybe the patient is more ready than I think. Maybe I follow the patient a little more than I need to.
>
> [Female, Ph.D., 15 years practice]

> My need to be loved sometimes can blind me to things that I need to tell them about. I don't want to be rejected.
>
> [Male, Ph.D., 25 years practice]

> Being gingerly about bringing up stuff between them and me that's going to be difficult.
>
> [Female, M.S.W., 15 years practice]

If I were to talk about the part of treatment I'm least competent at, it's expressing negative feelings. I like things to be easygoing, mellow, and loving. I may therefore fail to attend sufficiently to those feelings.

[Male, Ph.D., 50 years practice]

I think that I'm very good at engaging another person, and I can be very charming and take someone in, but that can work to a patient's detriment, because I don't want them to continue coming to see me because I have a good personality. I may from time to time use that to keep someone in therapy because I'm avoiding bringing up a difficult issue.

[Female, M.S.W., 10 years practice]

Others mentioned tendencies to be too active, mostly by talking too much, or to be too engaged with the patient.

Sometimes I think I talk too much. My own wish to get involved with patients, my own level of interaction. Over the years, I can develop a level of fondness that can be a liability.

[Female, M.A., 15 years practice]

Sometimes I push people too hard, and sometimes, especially with people who are slower-paced, they don't like me. They feel pushed too much.

[Female, Ph.D., 20 years practice]

Maybe being a little too eager to help someone.

[Male, M.S.W., 10 years practice]

I talk too much. I always have to think, "Is it appropriate to say something, or is it not?" That will always, to the day I die, be an issue for me in therapy.

[Male, M.S.W., 15 years practice]

Overly interpreting, not letting something be.

[Female, M.S., 15 years practice]

Impatience, which several people mentioned, is sometimes what motivates the therapist to be too active.

I think probably my impatience. It's hard for me sometimes to let patients go at their own speed. I want to move them along, and that's not always what they want or need.

[Male, Ph.D., 15 years practice]

My wish for patients to get there. If I get into that mode, I lose my patience with the process, and I'll sometimes push where I should be sitting back.

[Female, M.S.W., 20 years practice]

I get impatient sometimes, and talk too much.

[Female, M.S.W., 20 years practice]

I'm a little too impulsive. I sometimes have too short a fuse. If a patient's been busting my chops, instead of planning out a response I'll say something angry.

[Female, M.S.W., 25 years practice]

Several people mentioned their insecurity about their practical or theoretical knowledge as their heaviest liability.

I don't know a lot about many different problems and how to treat them. There are a lot of people I couldn't really work with. I couldn't work with an alcoholic. I don't know how to treat that. My experience has been very specialized.

[Female, Ph.D., 10 years practice]

Sometimes I would like to be more knowledgeable about theory. I'd like to learn more.

[Female, M.S.W., 10 years practice]

Not being up to the minute on current theory.

[Female, M.A., 20 years practice]

My lack of training in psychotherapy.

[Male, M.D., 5 years practice]

Even people with many years of experience can feel anxious and unsure of themselves.

My insecurity and my anxiousness. My fear of being controlled myself.

[Male, Ph.D., 25 years practice]

My own degree of anxiety.

[Female, Ph.D., 20 years practice]

It's doubts about myself, letting concern about my own competence get in the way of the session.

[Male, M.S.W., 10 years practice]

> That I would take something as my fault, I'd take it personally that the person's leaving, and that would be hard on me.
>
> [Female, M.S.W., 20 years practice]

> Maybe I'm not smart enough, I don't have enough information.
>
> [Female, M.A., 15 years practice]

> My lack of self-confidence.
>
> [Female, M.S.W., 15 years practice]

> My own sense of insecurity. My own self-doubts. Am I doing the right thing? What is the patient saying?
>
> [Female, M.S.W., 15 years practice]

> I'm not where I want to be in my own life, and so my lack of confidence sometimes shows. Sometimes when my confidence is really low, it can affect the therapy. It's visible, and I let the patients get to me in a way where they sense it.
>
> [Female, M.S.W., 5 years practice]

A few people said they sometimes had trouble focusing on the patient.

> There's still a lot of areas, things I'm threatened to do with patients, where I can hear what patients are talking about as somehow relating to me as a therapist, as how good a job I'm doing.
>
> [Male, M.S.W., 15 years practice]

> My attention span wanders at times. Of course, I have no idea what other therapists' attention spans are. But I wonder if mine is worse than everyone else.
>
> [Male, M.S.W., 15 years practice]

> I like immediate gratification. Sometimes it's hard to put aside my own needs for care and attention.
>
> [Female, M.S.W., 15 years practice]

One person said that she was too focused on her patients.

> Not taking care of myself—overworking. Being there for other people and forgetting to pay attention to myself too.
>
> [Female, M.S.W., 10 years practice]

A few people said they might be too rigid in some way.

Maybe my rigidity about the frame. I have a rigidity as a person, and it probably keeps me from understanding certain things, and limits me.
[Female, M.A., 15 years practice]

I have to make sure that I hear patients within the context of their own lives and not try to make them fit some preconceived mold of my own.
[Male, M.S.W., 35 years practice]

A tendency to be withholding, a little bit critical.
[Male, M.D., 15 years practice]

Having to be right, being really invested in being right, and getting nervous about the possibility of being wrong.
[Male, Ph.D., 5 years practice]

My patients often criticize me by saying that I'm not flexible.
[Male, Ph.D., 20 years practice]

My obsessiveness, which is probably why the obsessives get to me.
[Male, M.D., 20 years practice]

Intellectualism, a tendency to want to figure things out, a little obsessiveness.
[Male, M.D., 20 years practice]

One person suggested he might not be rigid enough.

Probably my relative informality. At times, it may make me less able to set the boundaries than I should be.
[Male, Ph.D., 20 years practice]

A couple of people said they had the most difficulty with the business aspects of the profession.

I tend to be kind of soft in the financial area, and tend to charge less than other people, and that's a liability for me.
[Female, M.S., 15 years practice]

I'm a lousy businessman, and it's created terrible situations with people because of billing situations, and insurance forms that haven't gotten filled out. I'm also very frequently late.
[Male, Ph.D., 40 years practice]

Finally, one person said something that we all feel at times.

> My greatest liability is that I still have sensitive points, and I can still develop countertransference feelings. Certain things still make me lose it.
> [Male, Ph.D., 15 years practice]

NUMERICAL DISTRIBUTION

(Some people gave more than one answer.) Nine people mentioned their reluctance to deal with the patient's anger; 7 said their impatience; 6 said they talk too much; 6 said their lack of theoretical knowledge; 5 said their self-doubt or lack of confidence; 4 said their tendency to be judgmental; 3 said their difficulty with fees and money; 3 said their need to be loved or liked; 3 said their short attention span; 2 said their oversensitivity; 2 said their obsessiveness or compulsivity; 2 said their rigidity; 2 said their tendency to jump to conclusions. One person each said the following: their anxiety level; their tendency to personalize what the patient says; their tendency to overwork; their impulsivity in responding to patients; their need to be right; their informality; their tendency to intellectualize; their tendency to be too directive.

COMMENTS

The issue here is the same as the previous question: Which therapist qualities determine treatment outcome, and which are not significant factors?

Again, what we identify as an asset or a liability depends a lot on the way we conceptualize therapy and how it works. If I believe that therapy works on the basis of insight, I may not consider it a liability that I deliver my interpretations in an objective, neutral way; if I believe that therapy works via a warm and loving relationship, I may have a different attitude toward such a style of relating.

Every therapist has both strengths and weaknesses, and I think it is important to know what qualities your own categories include. In my own case, I think my greatest liability is my impatience, a tendency I have at times to feel frustrated and to rush people along a little faster than they may be ready to go. Because I know this, I can sometimes control it, but other times I just do it and regret it later.

RELATED READING

Bugental, J. F. (1988). What is "failure" in psychotherapy? *Psychotherapy* 25(4):532–535.

Conte, H. R., et al. (1995). Determinants of outpatients' satisfaction with therapists: relation to outcome. *Journal of Psychotherapy Practice and Research* 4(1):43–51.

Hellman, I. D., Morrison, T. L., and Abramowitz, S. I. (1987). Therapist flexibility/rigidity and work stress. *Professional Psychology: Research and Practice* 18(1):21–27.

Thompson, C. (1988). The role of the analyst's personality in therapy. In *Essential Papers on Countertransference,* ed. B. Wolstein, pp. 120–130. New York: New York University Press.

Welt, S. R., and Herron, W. G. (1990). *Narcissism and the Psychotherapist.* New York: Guilford Press.

ﾂﾂﾂﾂ

Question 91: How do you think patients see you?

Almost every therapist hopes to present himself or herself in a positive way, but patients may have their own views. Given the possibility of trans-ferential distortions, what kinds of images do therapists believe their patients have of them?

One person pointed out that patients sometimes have a limited view of the therapist.

> A lot of patients think that I don't move out of this chair, that I'm there just for them.
>
> [Female, M.S., 15 years practice]

A number of people said that the way the patient sees the therapist changes over time.

> In the beginning they're scared of me and intimidated, and later they see me as very caring and maternal.
>
> [Female, M.S., 20 years practice]

And several others pointed out that patient issues or transference can influence how the therapist is experienced.

> It depends on the transference. Some people tell me that I seem to be very tough, and some tell me that I seem kind, and some tell me that they think I'm very funny, which always surprises me.
>
> [Female, Ph.D., 20 years practice]

Ultimately, I think they see me as a support and someone who wants to help, but going through transferential stuff they see me as someone who couldn't possibly understand.

[Female, M.S.W., 5 years practice]

Some patients see me as the guru, some see me as the mother they wish they had had. Which is sometimes a countertransference problem, trying to be the great earth mother. Some patients just see me as friendly. And some see me as only doing this because they pay me.

[Female, M.S.W., 20 years practice]

For every patient it's different. I'm often surprised at what they see and what they don't see. When I went through a very difficult period, I know I looked horrible, and no one commented on it. And other times people will notice my shoes. I think they see what they need to see.

[Female, Ph.D., 5 years practice]

Some people see me as cold, some see me as warm. Somebody told me I seem like Barbara Walters, and I asked what kind of person that would be, and the patient said it meant very self-assured and articulate.

[Female, M.S., 15 years practice]

Sometimes they're baffled by me. They don't know my age, they don't know anything about me. They tell me that they find me empathic.

[Female, M.S.W., 15 years practice]

Many of our group said they believe that they are seen as caring and trustworthy, as wise and competent.

Generally, as someone who's trying to help, someone benevolent. Sometimes too benevolent, they'll tell me, too gentle or too kind.

[Male, M.D., 20 years practice]

On the whole, as warm, empathic, present.

[Female, M.S.W., 15 years practice]

Generally I think they see me as somebody who really wants to help them, and I listen, and they're amazed at how much I remember of what they've said.

[Female, M.S.W., 5 years practice]

If we've chosen someone to be our therapist, we grant that person some kind of specialness inevitably. I assume that if someone stays with me that they see me in a very positive way.

[Male, M.S.W., 10 years practice]

I've explored it with some of them, particularly at termination. I think they probably see me as somebody who is warm. I've had patients tell me that I seem looser than years before, and they're right.

[Female, M.S.W., 10 years practice]

For the most part, I think they trust me. I look older, and that helps. I'm able to take more of an intergenerational position.

[Male, Ph.D., 25 years practice]

Several people suggested that patients may idealize the therapist.

Some think I'm this high-functioning, very idealized person. And some think I must be a wonderful mother because I'm so nurturing.

[Female, M.A., 15 years practice]

One patient told me she sees me as a "feisty little lady" and she meant that as a compliment. They think that I've got a life and I've got it together. Sometimes they think I've got a house in East Hampton, but I don't. A little idealizing. They seem to think that I'm strong.

[Female, M.S.W., 15 years practice]

Often people think you have a perfect life, particularly if there's something very noticeable like you're pregnant.

[Female, M.S.W., 10 years practice]

I think I'm often idealized, as very bright, that I have my life all together, everything's perfect, I know it all.

[Female, M.S.W., 20 years practice]

Most see me as sympathetic, humanistic, somebody that they know is always there for them. They see me as very intelligent. Some have been in awe of me, and that's something I've had to work on with them.

[Male, Ph.D., 10 years practice]

A few said the patient may also devalue the therapist, at least at times, or be suspicious of the therapist's motives.

Some are afraid that I'm only interested in getting their money, and don't really care about them, that I'm just a businessman.

[Male, M.S.W., 20 years practice]

There are those that idealize me, and those that think that I just do it for the money.

[Male, Ph.D., 20 years practice]

While many people emphasized the distortion in the patient's perception, the transferential influence, a few emphasized the accuracy of patient perceptions.

> On my better days, I think they find me surprising. Generally, I think that people see me for who I am. I find that most of my patients see me as very "on."
>
> [Male, Ph.D., 10 years practice]

> I think most of my patients see me as being empathetic and as being a good listener, and there's where it ends in commonality. Some see me as harsh or serious, as kind of heavy, talking about heavy things. And others who see me as real easy, and they can say anything and I'm nonjudgmental, and I can be funny. And I am different with different people, so it's not just their perception. Different people trigger different aspects of me.
>
> [Female, M.S.W., 20 years practice]

NUMERICAL DISTRIBUTION

Twenty-four therapists said they believe their patients see them in a positive way: caring, engaged, helpful. Nine said that patients sometimes see them in a negative way: cold, distant, only in it for the money. Twelve people said that patients idealize them, and 5 said patients see them as strong and self-confident. Ten therapists said that how patients see them changes over time or depends on the transference.

COMMENTS

The issue this question raises is: Do patients experience us as we want them to? Do they see us as we see ourselves, or do they have very different images of us?

This is a difficult question to answer with any kind of objectivity. In addition, there are always the complications of transference and expectation. I believe that, on the whole, patients see therapists as engaged, as accepting and caring, as smart and knowledgeable, as gentle, as dependable and consistent, and most of the time I believe that my own patients see me that way. Sometimes, however, they see me as passive, disengaged, critical, or impatient, and it is always difficult for me to know how much of that is true and how much is transference distortion.

RELATED READING

Chused, J. F. (1987). Idealization of the analyst by the young adult. *Journal of the American Psychoanalytic Association* 35(4):839–859.

Horvath, A. O., Marx, R. W., and Kamann, A. M. (1990). Thinking about thinking in therapy: an examination of clients' understanding of their therapists' intentions. *Journal of Consulting and Clinical Psychology* 58(5):614–621.

Kavanagh, G. (1994). The patient's dreams of the analyst. *Contemporary Psychoanalysis* 30(3):500–509.

Ortmeter, D. H. (1992). Idealization, gender, and the psychoanalyst. In *Gender and Psychoanalytic Treatment. Current Issues in Psychoanalytic Practice: Monographs of the Society for Psychoanalytic Training,* vol. 5, ed M. Kissen, pp. 59–70. New York: Brunner/Mazel.

ⓢⓢⓢⓢ

Question 92: Do you have religious or spiritual beliefs and values that inform your work?

The area of religion and spirituality is often neglected in discussions of patients and treatment, except as a brief background fact or, in some cases, as part of the pathology. Yet, for many patients, religious and spiritual experience is an important part of their daily lives. Therapists may also have such beliefs and experiences, and these are likely to affect their work in some way.

More than half the therapists in the sample group said they had no such beliefs, but most of these emphasized the importance of respecting patients' faith.

> I hope not.
>
> [Male, M.S.W., 35 years practice]

> Nothing that I can identify. It's all a mystery to me.
>
> [Male, M.S.W., 25 years practice]

> Certainly, I have ethical and moral beliefs that inform my work. I'm an atheist, but I try to be very respectful of religious patients. I've never had a patient accuse me of violating their religious beliefs.
>
> [Male, Ph.D., 40 years practice]

I feel informed about various religions and spiritual beliefs and cultures, but I think I'm pretty open-minded about them, so I don't think my own beliefs affect my work.

[Female, M.S.W., 5 years practice]

I don't, but I'm very respectful of others', and I will use that as a strength. I always ask people what their religious beliefs are, and how do those help them. You need to be very educated. I'll read the Bible, and draw from it, and encourage church or synagogue attendance. I don't have a bias against religion, which I think a lot of therapists do.

[Female, Ph.D., 10 years practice]

The other half of our sample said that they did have religious or spiritual beliefs. Almost everyone who said they have such beliefs said that these beliefs did inform their work in some significant way.

I think that my spiritual beliefs have to do with a profound notion that people can heal themselves by some greater identification with humankind. I find often that the sessions that feel the most profound to me are sessions where we hit something like that together, where the patient feels some kind of spiritual stuff.

[Female, M.S.W., 20 years practice]

I'm very influenced by Louise Hay, and the Course in Miracles. More and more, I'm coming to the belief that we create everything in our lives. That's one of the things my AIDS clients have taught me. That we're drawing experiences to ourselves to release them. And I really believe that a lot of mental illnesses, probably physical too, are spiritual issues. I really think it's important to release hatred, anger and rage. I think those things destroy our psyches.

[Female, M.S.W., 15 years practice]

My belief system, which is a combination of humanism and pantheism, informs my work, in that I believe that you can't wait for God to take care of you.

[Female, M.S.W., 20 years practice]

I've continued in my ministry. I'm fascinated by the similarities. For example, there's a Christian concept of metanoia, a change of heart, to be converted and change your ways, an inner change. I think that what Christians have meant by metanoia is what happens in good therapy. There is some rearrangement of inner dynamics. Also, Jesus said, "What does it profit a man if he gain the whole world and lose his soul?" That's one translation, but you could also substitute "life" for "soul" and I've been thinking lately that you could also substitute "sanity."

[Male, M.S.W., 10 years practice]

The spiritual beliefs that inform my work are a kind of existential spiritualism, that life is a struggle, and each person's struggle is the meaning of their life. You can't avoid the struggle, you have to embrace it.

[Male, Ph.D., 15 years practice]

I believe in the value of a religious or spiritual support system. I often tell my patients that I'm impressed that every religion in the world has the same common theme when they pray, and it's basically: Help! Because living is tough, and if you can believe in some higher power or some cosmic plan, even if it's not specific to you, I find that useful. I also believe in the value of prayer, which is really a form of stress management and relaxation, and a lot of the research supports that. And the research supports that people are happier when they're feeling part of a community rather than isolated and alienated.

[Male, Ph.D., 25 years practice]

I think that working a lot in the recovery field brings a whole aura of spirituality, pro and con, and working with sexual issues people bring a whole mess of stuff from their religious pasts. I try to help people develop their own spirituality.

[Male, M.S.W., 15 years practice]

I'm a Unitarian/Universalist, and they believe in social justice, that you have to make this world a better place since we don't know anything about what comes after. I'd say that informs my work.

[Female, M.S.W., 25 years practice]

I'm Catholic, and I have a strong spiritual side. I don't hold to any particular religion as correct. I'm open to spirituality, to the spiritual side of a person's life, and that enhances my work. I work with a lot of dying people, a lot of people with AIDS, and it certainly comes up.

[Male, M.D., 5 years practice]

Not religious, but ethically. I have a patient who cheated on an exam, and I do take a stand about that. Not that he has to kill himself, but we need to look at what are the consequences personally for him, even if he gets away with it.

[Female, M.S., 15 years practice]

Some people made a distinction between religious and spiritual beliefs.

I'm not religious at all, but I'm very Jewish culturally. I'm a Jewish mother, and bring that attitude to my work, sometimes with detrimental effect. I have to watch my countertransference. Sometimes it's very positive. I also believe in some of the new-age concepts, such as "meant to be" and "learning from experiences" and why someone is in your life, and depending on who I'm working with, may bring that into the work.

[Female, Ph.D., 20 years practice]

NUMERICAL DISTRIBUTION

Thirty-three people said they did have religious or spiritual beliefs that inform their work in some way; 27 people said they did not.

COMMENTS

Some issues in this area are: Are psychotherapy and religious beliefs incompatible? What are the best ways for the therapist to explore this area with patients? How does the therapist distinguish normal religious or spiritual beliefs and practices from those concealing some pathology?

Freud said many negative and critical things about conventional religion and that attitude persists in various ways, for example, in the position that belief in God or a "higher power" may interfere with a sense of personal control. On the other hand, therapists may feel that a patient's religious beliefs are off limits to inquiry and exploration, and some issues may go unexamined.

While our field is not necessarily linked to any particular spiritual beliefs, I think that even the choice of this profession implies certain moral or ethical principles: that individuals matter; that we have a responsibility to others and a duty to relieve suffering; that truth is important. We put these principles into action in every session. While I was raised without religious affiliation, and have no conventional religious beliefs, I do accept and understand those beliefs in others. I think the ethical and moral principles of responsibility to others and concern for truth do guide my own work and provide for me a sense of purpose.

RELATED READING

Goud, N. (1990). Spiritual and ethical beliefs of humanists in the counseling profession. *Journal of Counseling and Development* 68(5):571–574.

Grimm, D. W. (1994). Therapist spiritual and religious values in psychotherapy. *Counseling and Values* 38(3):154–164.

Houts, A. C., and Graham, K. (1986). Can religion make you crazy? Impact of client and therapist religious values on clinical judgments. *Journal of Consulting and Clinical Psychology* 54(2):267–271.

Lewis, K. N., and Lewis, D. A. (1985). Impact of religious affiliation on
therapists' judgments of patients. *Journal of Consulting and Clinical
Psychology* 53(6):926–932.

Norcross, J. C., and Wogan, M. (1987). Values in psychotherapy: a survey
of practitioners' beliefs. *Professional Psychology: Research and Practice*
18(1):5–7.

Shafranske, E. P., and Gorsuch, R. L. (1984). Factors associated with the
perception of spirituality in psychotherapy. *Journal of Transpersonal
Psychology* 16(2):231–241.

🔯🔯🔯🔯

Question 93: How do you deal with a very religious patient?

Is there an intrinsic conflict between psychotherapy and religion? Freud
seemed to think so, and in some ways that attitude persists. In psychotherapy, we try to question everything, and faith may imply accepting
without question. A conventionally religious patient may be difficult to
work with as we are normally used to doing.

The large majority of those responding to the question said that they
did not see any special difficulty working with such patients. They all
emphasized the importance of respecting the beliefs, whatever they might
be, and of being knowledgeable about the religion itself.

> I've worked with someone who was ultra-orthodox Jewish. I work
> slowly, and I have to learn a lot of information about what the belief
> system is. The only difference is that it may be new to me.
>
> [Female, Ph.D., 5 years practice]

> It hasn't been a problem. I never discuss my lack of religiosity. I've had
> two patients who were very angry with God, and I've helped them
> talk about it, and even support their conception of God.
>
> [Female, M.S.W., 10 years practice]

> I can accept anything, even astrology, if it's important to them. I don't
> make a judgment about it.
>
> [Female, M.S.W., 30 years practice]

> I work with a number of ministers. And my very first analytic control case was an Episcopal priest. I just deal with the material as it comes up.
>
> [Male, M.S.W., 35 years practice]

> I've had orthodox Jews in my practice, and worked with them very well, some very interesting work with them. I had a very religious Catholic woman, and I referred her to a therapist who was an ex-nun, because I felt I was the wrong therapist for her. I just didn't know enough about it.
>
> [Female, Ph.D., 20 years practice]

Some therapists stated their belief that religion is sometimes helpful to the patient.

> A lot of times if people take their beliefs seriously, they may feel that someone's out there taking care of them, and it gives them some hope.
>
> [Male, M.S.W., 10 years practice]

> I've had patients who are very religious, where the religion is really a help to them. I've encouraged them to go to church, or seek something within their religious community. If I think it's hindering them, that's a different issue.
>
> [Male, Ph.D., 10 years practice]

> Sometimes people are just looking for a sense of community or belonging because their families were fragmented or disturbed, and sometimes the values of a particular faith are appealing. So I just talk with them about what it means to them, and what the benefits are for them.
>
> [Female, M.S.W., 10 years practice]

> I've gotten more tolerant of religion as I've gotten older. I think it can help people. In the best way, it can make them kinder.
>
> [Female, M.S.W., 25 years practice]

Some therapists said it was necessary when working with very religious patients to step gingerly around the religious beliefs and that doing so may be particularly tricky when the religious beliefs are woven into the pathology.

> They sometimes believe in a fanatic way, and don't want their belief system touched. They don't want to question it, and you have to at least address what is underneath, and what is finding refuge in their religious beliefs.
>
> [Male, M.D., 20 years practice]

Sometimes, especially with someone who's psychotic, I'll reinterpret their beliefs a little bit, reframe them, to make them a little more benign. As a rule I don't even do that, unless it's very negative and they're using it against themselves.

[Female, M.S., 20 years practice]

Sometimes the religious material is simply off limits.

For a while I saw a large number of Orthodox Jewish people, and it was just a separate issue that wasn't brought in.

[Female, M.A., 20 years practice]

A few practitioners said it was difficult to work with very religious patients.

I have seen patients who were very religious, and sooner or later they couldn't continue working with me, because we get to a point where there's a conflict. But some have continued, because they were themselves very conflicted about their fantasies and impulses.

[Male, Ph.D., 20 years practice]

Probably, because their resistance would be so enormous to having to do anything themselves, that change doesn't come out of your own effort.

[Female, M.S.W., 20 years practice]

I have found it difficult to keep Jesuits on track. The irony is they always want to cure me.

[Female, Ph.D., 30 years practice]

NUMERICAL DISTRIBUTION

Not everyone was asked this question but of those who were: 35 said it would not be a problem; 6 said it would be difficult.

COMMENTS

The issue here is: What are the best ways for the therapist to question and explore the area of religious belief and practice while respecting the patient's choices and traditions?

This question was included because, although it happens only rarely, I have encountered several very religious patients over the years and had

great difficulty working with them, not specifically because they were religious, but because some very religious people seem to expect God to run
their lives for them, and they don't see themselves as having either personal responsibility or personal control, which then makes change feel to
them both difficult and unnecessary. I'm still not sure how I would deal
with another such patient.

RELATED READING

Genia, V. (1994). Secular psychotherapists and religious clients: profes-
sional considerations and recommendations. *Journal of Counseling and
Development* 72(4):395–398.
Lovinger, R. J. (1979). Therapeutic strategies with religious resistances.
Psychotherapy: Theory, Research, and Practice 16(4):419–427.
Rayburn, C. A. (1985). The religious patient's initial encounter with psy-
chotherapy. *Psychotherapy Patient* 1(3):35–45.
Spero, M. H. (1988). Countertransference envy toward the religious pa-
tient. *American Journal of Psychoanalysis* 48(1):43–55.

ଛଛଛଛ

Question 94: How has AIDS affected your work?

Not all areas in the United States have the concentration of HIV and AIDS
cases that we have in New York. Many of the therapists in the New York
area have seen HIV positive or AIDS patients in therapy. Even those who
haven't have noticed that there is an increased awareness or anxiety about
sexual behavior among their patients.

A number of therapists described the effect on them personally of working with HIV positive and AIDS patients.

> I've had four patients die of AIDS since I began practice. At any given
> time I have three or four people who are HIV positive. Mostly I've gotten
> a reputation in the gay community for doing some work around grief,
> so I see people who have lost a son, or a daughter, or a lover. It always
> feels like a big shadow over my practice.
>
> [Male, M.S.W., 15 years practice]

> It's affected me as a human being. It's made me want to challenge
> patients more to grow, to be more challenging to them. It's made me
> understand how much pain human beings have, and that we live on

the edge all the time. I work more with people who are afraid of dying, and have to figure out how to manage their lives. What do you work on with somebody who could die in two or three years?

[Male, M.S.W., 15 years practice]

I've not had direct experience with a patient dying, but my gay patients have had many partners die. It's like a big cloud in the sky. It's very sad. Two of my patients are HIV positive, but not ill, no symptoms yet, and I dread it. I care for these people, and I can't stand it.

[Female, M.S., 15 years practice]

That is my commitment as a physician, not totally, but a large part of it, to HIV and AIDS work. That's been an interest of mine since I started training. I've really developed myself professionally to do that work, so it's really affected me profoundly.

[Male, M.D., 5 years practice]

I do have one that's HIV positive. It makes me feel more committed.

[Female, M.S.W., 15 years practice]

I volunteer one hour a week through an agency to see someone with AIDS. So I always have at least one person who has AIDS. I find it extremely rewarding. It's a way to give something. It's almost exciting, some of the things that happen to people at that time in their life.

[Female, M.A., 15 years practice]

One patient profoundly affected my life. He was a very spiritual man, and he taught me a lot about life and death. I admired his courage.

[Female, M.S.W., 15 years practice]

Those therapists who specialize in a substance abuse population are likely to see a larger number of people with HIV.

It's affected it a lot with the substance abuse population. I don't have anyone in my private practice who is HIV positive. In my internship, I had asked not to work with AIDS patients, and within a month I was working with people who were positive. It totally freaked me out, and I left the placement. But in my other clinic, it came up again and I realized I had to grapple with it. If you're going to work in substance abuse, you have to work with AIDS.

[Female, M.S.W., 5 years practice]

Therapists who see many gay patients are almost certain to have encountered HIV and AIDS. One therapist described the issue of "survivor guilt" in gay patients who are still HIV negative.

> I'm working with people who have a lot of survivor guilt, because they've lost so many people through this disease that almost everybody they've had a history with is gone. They're dealing with the kind of issues that we used to deal with in people in their seventies and eighties, where the peer group is gone before them.
>
> [Female, M.S.W., 20 years practice]

Some therapists said that they had changed their approach to dealing with the subject of sexual behavior with patients.

> In the late seventies and early eighties, all my gay patients would come in talking about some kind of "gay plague," some kind of disease. I've lost a number of patients over the years, and it's been very distressing. It's a constant battle to get people to be not so self-destructive. Sex used to be something that people took a while to discuss, and now I have to jump in right away. I know that I have been instrumental in keeping some people alive.
>
> [Male, Ph.D., 15 years practice]

> I feel very fortunate that no patients have been HIV positive yet, but it's around a lot, and the question of safe sex comes up a lot. I think one has to be educating as well as analyzing. I have a lot of anxiety about somebody getting AIDS, and how I would deal with a patient who had it. I would not want to take on anybody who has AIDS as a new patient right now.
>
> [Female, M.S.W., 30 years practice]

> I've had only one patient who was HIV positive, but it has affected my work in that I talk more quickly with patients about their sexual activities than I might have prior to AIDS.
>
> [Female, M.S.W., 10 years practice]

> I'm more careful in getting a sexual history and exploring current sexual behavior. It hasn't affected my technique so much as the issues that patients bring, like the added difficulty that AIDS has presented in dating and the whole social scene. Dealing with social isolation is a lot more difficult because now there's a lot more rationalizations for it.
>
> [Male, Ph.D., 25 years practice]

Many therapists described some of the emotional and practical diffi-culties of working with HIV positive and AIDS patients.

> I have had a couple of patients who were HIV positive, and I'm not sure if they're still alive. There's a time frame problem that comes in, the specter of death and illness, and the tragedy and depression are very difficult to deal with. It's a very challenging and difficult situation. My experience over the past five years is that they leave treatment, they're not ready to continue treatment. It's been disappointing, and it feels like I haven't helped them a lot.
>
> [Male, M.D., 20 years practice]

> I've done a lot of AIDS work at the hospital, and I'm now with an agency where we see a lot of AIDS-related disability. It's been very tough. I've lost several patients that I've been working with, and that's very hard for me. Also, it changes the structure, because you have to be ready at a moment's notice. You have to be ready for emergencies, you have to be ready for absences with no warning, you have to be ready for reduced fees or no fee at all, you have to be ready to do a lot more outreach than you would normally do. It's not a clean therapy any more. You have to do a lot of networking, and a lot of reaching out, if you're going to hold on to the patient. There are often unexpected terminations. Sometimes you have time to prepare, but often it's very sudden.
>
> [Female, Ph.D., 30 years practice]

> I have a few clients who are HIV positive, and one has died. It's very difficult when someone becomes ill, a young person facing death like that, it's very painful to be with.
>
> [Male, Ph.D., 10 years practice]

> I've had HIV positive patients at the clinic. I have my own defense, which is that I deny the fatality, so when I work with them, I give it all I have. I hope that unconsciously my feeling is transmitted, and very often I feel it is. With one patient, the T-cell count rose, although with another it dropped. Two other HIV positive patients left treatment, and I think they left to protect me from their dying.
>
> [Female, M.S.W., 45 years practice]

Both therapists and patients are more aware of the risks of certain sexual behaviors and of multiple partners. Several therapists reported increased anxiety levels in patients when discussing sexual activity, and the thera-pist may also feel more anxious.

None of my patients have had AIDS or been HIV positive. There's been mourning for friends who have died. I see it in the content of certain obsessive ideations, certain patients who see every sore as a sign of it, but other than that, it hasn't affected me.

[Male, Ph.D., 25 years practice]

AIDS has not affected my work, with the exception of the anxiety that it's produced in homosexual patients, and grief. I have no one in my practice who's HIV positive.

[Male, Ph.D., 50 years practice]

I feel more alarmed about patients who talk about having many sexual partners.

[Female, Ph.D., 15 years practice]

Many therapists said that the nature of the treatment changes when someone is HIV positive.

I've had AIDS patients, and the difference with them is that the work has been more supportive.

[Male, M.S.W., 25 years practice]

In the work, I think that we are more reality-based about real-life problems.

[Female, M.A., 15 years practice]

I have a few HIV positive clients that I'm seeing right now. I guess I've gotten used to it. We monitor them, and discuss their T-cell count. I think there are times when I might do a little more enabling than I normally do because of their illness, like allow them to miss a session and not call. Things I might not normally do with someone else.

[Male, M.S.W., 15 years practice]

And one person said the treatment does not change.

I've had several clients with AIDS. The work is the work. It's not different with someone who has AIDS.

[Male, M.S.W., 10 years practice]

One female therapist was very angry at the response of our field to the issues of AIDS.

I've worked in the field of AIDS, women with AIDS, for seven years. There's a lot of denial with many mental health practitioners. They've stayed away from this. They might not accept a patient with AIDS. I don't know what the problem is. There's this incredible crisis going on and our heads are in the sand. I've been at conferences where AIDS hasn't even come up. I'm really amazed. The mental health profession really hasn't responded to the crisis.

[Female, M.S.W., 15 years practice]

A surprisingly large number of therapists said that they had not encountered any AIDS or HIV positive patients in their practices.

So far I haven't worked with anyone who's even HIV positive. I've worked with people who've been tested and they've been negative. It's an issue and people are worried about it.

[Female, M.S.W., 10 years practice]

My work is in such an extremely conservative part of the country that the gay community is extremely closeted. I've not had anyone who's been HIV positive.

[Male, Ph.D., 20 years practice]

NUMERICAL DISTRIBUTION

Sixteen people said they had never seen anyone with AIDS or even HIV, and saw no impact on their practice or their work; 11 others said that while they had never seen an HIV positive patient, they were aware of increased anxiety and concern about sexual activity in patients or even in themselves; 13 had seen HIV positive patients but had not yet dealt with full-blown AIDS or patient deaths from AIDS; 20 had seen AIDS patients up to the time of their deaths.

COMMENTS

Some issues in this area are: What is the nature of treatment with a patient with HIV or AIDS? What is the impact on the therapist of working with such patients?

It's remarkable that in New York City in 1996 there could be practicing therapists who have never see a patient with HIV. Most therapists here, and increasingly around the rest of the country, are likely at some point to have a patient who is HIV positive.

We are used to thinking of our work with most patients as getting them prepared for life, but when someone gets AIDS, the work is often about getting them prepared for death. It is easy to wonder what the point of therapy is with someone who will probably die soon, and it can be very difficult to work with an HIV positive patient who is unable to confront the reality of his impending death.

I believe that the work of helping someone face death is just as significant and valuable as the other work we do. I have had in my practice an increasing number of gay men who are HIV positive. Right now they're all without serious symptoms. A few years ago I went through the whole course of the disease with a patient, from diagnosis to death. I saw him at home and in the hospital, right up to a few weeks before he died. He told me that it was very important to have at least one person in his life that he didn't have to protect from his real feelings. For me, it was very hard because I really liked him and we had done such good work: He was in a good relationship and had gone back to graduate school when he was diagnosed. It took almost two years for him to die. It's hard to think about going through that again but I'm sure that I will.

RELATED READING

Bowers, M. K., Jackson, E. N., Knight, J. A., and LeShan, L. (1964). *Counseling the Dying.* New York: Jason Aronson, 1975.

Dunkel, J., and Hatfield, S. (1986). Countertransference issues in working with persons with AIDS. *Social Work* 31(2):114–117.

Locke, S. A. (1994). *Coping with Loss: A Guide for Caregivers.* Springfield, IL: Charles C Thomas.

Winiarski, M. G. (1991). *AIDS-Related Psychotherapy.* New York: Pergamon Press.

ᴙᴙᴙᴙ

Question 95: How has this career affected the rest of your life? Your marriage? Your children? Your friendships?

The work that therapists do, and the schedule by which they do it, may have effects on significant others in their lives: spouses, children, and friends.

Many people mentioned the demands of both training and work itself as making them less available to family and friends.

> When my kids were young, and I was just starting out, it took too much time away. As things improved, by the time my youngest came along, I was working a four-day week, so that I could spend one full day at

home. As a consequence, we have the best relationship. My older kids were cheated of my time.

[Male, M.S.W., 35 years practice]

The difficulty is in working at night. We work at night. In the beginning, there was a lot of resentment on the part of my husband, who wants me with him. My daughter has said that if I had been working this many hours when she was young, she wouldn't have liked it.

[Female, Ph.D., 20 years practice]

I've got two small kids, and I don't get home until ten, ten-thirty. I don't like that.

[Male, M.D., 15 years practice]

The only people who have suffered from the effects of this career are my family. I'm worn out by the time I get home, and not really interested in hearing about somebody, not even the person I love. I just don't want to hear anything. I just want to relax and veg out.

[Male, Ph.D., 50 years practice]

It certainly has cut down on my social interactions. I really don't have time to socialize, except on the weekends. It has definitely limited my time and ability to have a wide circle of friends. I don't let it affect my personal relationship, my partnership, though in the beginning my partner was occasionally jealous of patients.

[Female, M.S., 20 years practice]

I'm not home in the evenings, and my partner feels lonely. There are times I'd like to do things during the week, and I can't because of my schedule. Especially in the summertime, when it's still light out and I'm still working.

[Female, M.S.W., 10 years practice]

The pressures of the work, and my achievement motivation, have taken me away from them more than I would have liked. Right now, with my children grown up and married, I feel really good about the relationships we have, even though I recognize that if I had been there more, maybe some of the things I see now I wouldn't be seeing.

[Male, Ph.D., 25 years practice]

Taking care of patients all day can make it harder for therapists to feel that they want to do more of that when they get home to the family.

> You're a caretaker all day, and then you go home and if you have children you do it some more.
>
> [Female, M.S.W., 10 years practice]

> It profoundly affects what happens with my daughter. There are many times I come home from my practice feeling drained and talked out and as if I've just spent ten or twelve hours attending to other people's needs, and there are times when I resent my daughter being so needy. Her particular kind of neediness happens to be talking to me in great detail about what's going on in her life. I'm sure there are many times I would be far more attentive and responsive if I were in a job that emotionally isolated me most of the day. It's hard for me to get the kind of space that I need at night to relax, and let my mind go, because it's so interactional at home.
>
> [Female, M.S.W., 20 years practice]

> Except at home with my children, I'm a very patient person, and I'm not with the kids because I use it all up in here.
>
> [Female, M.D., 15 years practice]

Two female therapists said that they thought that being a therapist forced them to focus less on their own lives and their own needs.

> Sometimes I think that the negative effect is understanding too much, and not putting my own needs first. It's a liability anyway in my life, and think there's a way that this profession encourages that, and it's not necessarily good for a relationship.
>
> [Female, M.S.W., 15 years practice]

> I feel like I'm spending a lot of my time listening to other people's lives, and I wonder how much energy I have left for my own.
>
> [Female, Ph.D., 5 years practice]

Others found that the training and experience, as well as the freedom to set their own schedule, actually made them more available.

> The training as a therapist can actually help you with your personal life, your husband and your children. The more you know, the better. You can't analyze everyone, but it helps you understand. Also, I knew it wasn't going to be enough for me to stay home and raise children, so I have this work which I really like where I can set my own hours, then I'm a better wife and a better mother because I'm a happier, more fulfilled person.
>
> [Female, M.S.W., 30 years practice]

As a mother, it's allowed me to make decent money and make my own hours, and I can still do a competent job of mothering. I'm very glad that my husband is not in this line of work, because it's refreshing not to deal with the same issues. He tells me I'm thinking too much, and that gives me a good balance.

[Female, M.S., 15 years practice]

I've felt so much better about myself with the benefit of what the work has given me. I've been a better model and a better resource to my family.

[Male, Ph.D., 25 years practice]

My husband's a therapist, and I think we understand ourselves a lot better than most people do, and understand each other as well. A respect for difference, there's not one best way to be. We're both very flexible. We don't pathologize our children. We've seen a wide range of pathology, which makes what our kids do not so bad. When they start lining up their toys in an obsessive manner, I can say to myself that's very normal for a four-year-old.

[Female, Ph.D., 10 years practice]

It's let me be very involved with my kids. I'm in charge of them three days a week, and my schedule's been designed around that.

[Male, Ph.D., 20 years practice]

With my lover, it's helped me understand some of my behavior in the relationship, and be able to work on it. I have more understanding of my family.

[Male, M.S.W., 15 years practice]

Others said that the personal therapy and growth required by the training and the work enhanced their self-esteem and all their personal relationships.

This career, all the training, the knowledge, even the therapy I've done, everything in this field I've done has helped me to grow, to the point where I've developed better relationships over the years.

[Male, Ph.D., 15 years practice]

Only in the sense that it's given me so much, the self-esteem. It's fed me so well, and I have things to share.

[Male, Ph.D., 10 years practice]

It has changed everything I think and do. I feel like a different person because I trained to be a therapist. My whole belief system changed about who people are and how they operate.

[Female, M.S., 15 years practice]

> I'm very happy doing this work, and that improves all my relationships.
> It allows me to have free hours to do other things. When I talk to friends
> I might tend to slip into this way of relating, because it's how I think
> now, but I usually catch myself.
>
> [Female, M.S.W., 10 years practice]

Conflicts in roles, not being willing to let go of the therapist role, can
be a problem for some.

> My interest in people's feelings and my ability to see what I believe is
> going on an unconscious or behavioral level is just pervasive through-
> out my whole life. Everybody is always experiencing an exploration
> into their own conscious and unconscious lives when they're with me.
> It's because that's what I'm interested in talking about, and what I see,
> and if I see it, and it calls for some kind of observation, I care too much
> about them to be quiet. So I'm a very intrusive friend.
>
> [Male, Ph.D., 25 years practice]

> I've always been tremendously analytical. Sometimes I wish it was less,
> because it can be detrimental. Sometimes I'm not aware that I'm asking
> probing questions with my friends. I can be intrusive.
>
> [Female, M.S.W., 10 years practice]

Some people said that the intimacy of the work created a dissatisfaction with the usual level of social interaction.

> I think that most of my close friends, actually all of them, are analyti-
> cal, or have been in therapy. It affects me in that this is how I see.
> Like a carpenter walks into a room and sees the structure. I meet
> somebody and I see the structure. I'm not interested in analyzing
> them, but in order for something deep to go on between two people
> they have to speak somewhat the same language, or be able to get
> it. So people who like to stay on the surface, I can't really get that
> close to them.
>
> [Female, M.S.W., 20 years practice]

> Sometimes it's hard dealing with people outside the therapeutic situ-
> ation. People are just talking at different levels. If I meet a woman, and
> she has negative ideas about therapy, she immediately invalidates
> herself. And when people are grossly defensive, coming at you from
> defense rather than from relating (and most of the world is that way)
> that sometimes is lonely.
>
> [Male, Ph.D., 25 years practice]

Several people said that the profession gave them a certain status in social situations, sometimes an inhibiting one.

> I think when I meet people, there's always a reaction to my being a therapist. For example, in a discussion amongst my friends about the differences between men and women, one person said that she thought that I would be the most qualified as a therapist to speak to that point. So it's interesting to be looked at as an expert on something like that.
> [Female, M.S.W., 5 years practice]

> It has brought me a lot of respect from the people around me. Whenever anyone asks what my profession is, they're always respectful of it, and that feels good. It's always fodder for jokes, too, about shrinks. Because I've had so much therapy, I've figured out how to be more content with my life.
> [Female, M.A., 20 years practice]

> The only impact I'm aware of is that when you tell people you're a psychiatrist or an analyst, it kills the conversation.
> [Male, M.D., 20 years practice]

Two people mentioned the financial deprivation of this kind of work.

> The training period to become an analyst takes a lot of time and money and effort, and in that sense it's been difficult for my family. It makes me less available. And maybe there's some deprivation financially, because compared to other M.D.'s, psychiatrists are second from the bottom, and analysts probably earn less than most psychiatrists.
> [Male, M.D., 20 years practice]

> The major thing is that I don't have anywhere near as much money as the guys who went into business or advertising, fields like that. They're millionaires. If I was other than a pieceworker, I would have much more material things, and much more to give to my children. I have a little bit of shame that I haven't been more financially successful.
> [Male, Ph.D., 25 years practice]

Only a couple of people said they didn't see any particular influence of the work on family or social relationships.

> Mostly I don't see much effect one way or the other. I approach my work in here the way I approach most other things I do.
> [Female, M.D., 15 years practice]

NUMERICAL DISTRIBUTION

(Some people gave more than one response.) Twenty-six people said their personal therapy and training made them better, happier people and improved all their relationships. Seventeen people said their schedule made them unavailable to family and friends; 4 others said their ability to control their schedule made them more available to family and friends. Four people said they thought the profession was isolating or constricting of freedom, and 4 others said they often feel drained by the work. Seven people said they found themselves taking the therapist role outside the office; none of these thought this was a problem. Four people saw no particular effect on their personal lives.

COMMENTS

Issues raised by this questions include: What are the effects of doing this work on the private life of the therapist? What is the impact on significant others in the therapist's personal life? Does the work make the therapist more available or less so?

I think that doing this kind of work affects a number of aspects of my private life. The most concrete effect is that because of my schedule, working evenings every weeknight, I'm not available to do the usual social things that people do, so I don't see my friends as much as I want to. And when I do go to social gatherings, parties and such, I find that I have little tolerance for the empty kind of cocktail party chatter that goes on. I expect a lot more from human conversation than that, and I can get frustrated and impatient.

The work also affects my main relationship in several ways. Sometimes I think my partner expects me to be as wise and therapeutic as I am in the office, which really isn't possible because I'm not the therapist at home. Of course, if I try to be the therapist and analyze the behavior that I see, that's totally unacceptable. In addition, I think I am sometimes expected at home to behave impeccably, with perfect insight and self-awareness all the time, which is impossible.

RELATED READING

Guy, J. (1987). *The Personal Life of the Psychotherapist.* New York: Wiley.
Henry, W. E., Sims, J. H., and Spray, S. L. (1973). *Public and Private Lives of Psychotherapists.* San Francisco: Jossey-Bass.

Maeder, T. (1989). *Children of Psychiatrists and Other Psychotherapists.* New York: Harper and Row.

Philpot, C. L. (1987). When mother is a family therapist: the impact of being a family therapist on one's family of origin and family of creation. *Journal of Psychotherapy and the Family* 3(2):33–45.

Titelman, P. (1987). *The Therapist's Own Family: Toward the Differentiation of Self.* Northvale, NJ: Jason Aronson.

☙ IV ☙
The State of the Field

This section deals with the field as a whole: what's right and what's wrong with the mental health profession right now, and what it is like to be a private practitioner at this time.

Our profession is currently besieged from several directions. Managed care seeks to control the way we practice. The controversy about recovered memories has helped to create a climate in which therapists can easily be sued for the way they practice. The current drive by the American Psychological Association for prescription privileges on a par with psychiatrists threatens to push practice even further into the medical model. Although this is the shortest section of the book, it is in many ways the most important, because this is where some experienced practitioners tell us what must be changed about the way we do our jobs if our profession is to survive.

Question 96: Have patients ever told you about unethical therapists?

In many cases, the patients who come to us have had previous experiences with other therapists. Often, there are negative feelings toward the previous professional that led the patient to seek someone new. Sometimes the experiences have been very damaging because of clearly unethical behavior by that therapist.

Most of the therapists in the survey reported instances of patients describing clearly unethical behavior. Only 10 out of 60 said that they had never been told of such transgressions, and two of them pointed out that most of their patients had never been in treatment before.

Many of these violations were some kind of sexual activity.

> The most common thing I encounter is therapists who have sexual contact with patients.
>
> [Female, M.D., 15 years practice]

> I've worked with patients who have had previous therapists who had sex with them. I've worked with patients who married their original therapist, and were then abandoned by that husband. I also have worked with patients who were homosexually abused by their therapist.
>
> [Female, M.S., 20 years practice]

> Only one patient has ever come to me and told me about anything major. One man told me that a therapist had masturbated him.
>
> [Male, Ph.D., 15 years practice]

> Therapists seeing them socially, which was acceptable to that therapist's theoretical orientation, which was gestalt from the sixties and seventies, and eventually they propositioned the client and had sex with them, describing this as a growth experience. In one case, I knew the therapist and it was no surprise to me whatsoever.
>
> [Male, M.S.W., 15 years practice]

And the violator is not always a male therapist.

> I had one lesbian patient who told me that a female therapist gradually became very close, and then eventually sexually overt with her. This therapist told the patient that she really needed treatment, that she shouldn't leave, that the therapist could really take care of her and help

her, and encouraged kissing and fondling, saying that it was important to her treatment.

[Female, M.A., 15 years practice]

I had one man who told me about a female therapist that he slept with.

[Male, Ph.D., 20 years practice]

I've heard of one female therapist who dated someone from her group, a male patient.

[Female, Ph.D., 15 years practice]

Several therapists described the difficulty of working with patients who had been sexually involved with a previous therapist.

One woman had had an affair with her psychiatrist, and it made my treatment with her very difficult because she found the limits I set very frustrating. I don't mean she wanted to sleep with me too, but this other guy was so sloppy about everything and she simply got used to that style, that by comparison she said I seemed very distant and aloof, which no other patient has ever told me.

[Male, M.A., 15 years practice]

The one I'm thinking of, I tried to explore what it might mean in terms of the trust that the patient might have working with me as a male therapist. I said flat out that it was not something I would consider appropriate or ethical. The patient didn't seem particularly upset about it. It was a therapist who terminated her treatment, and then said he was in love with her, and they had a brief affair. This was in a different country from the U.S.

[Male, M.S.W., 20 years practice]

I have a total of four patients, two of whom are men, who have been sexually involved with a previous therapist. One of the guys came in with that as an issue, and another took about a year and a half to tell me about it. There were issues about feeling responsible for it, his fear that I might not want to work with him, that I would see him as litigious. And the women, in both cases it was a replay of things that had happened to them as a child. Two of these patients were taking legal action, and two were not, and there it became a therapeutic issue why they weren't. We had to look at them allowing things to happen to them in general in their lives, and wanting to let it go rather than taking care of themselves.

[Female, M.S.W., 20 years practice]

Only two therapists expressed some doubt about the accuracy of those reports.

It's mostly sexual abuse, but that's their reporting and who knows?
[Female, M.S.W., 45 years practice]

I've been told about sexual things, that you never really know if they're true or not.
[Male, M.D., 15 years practice]

These are some of the other things mentioned:

Falling asleep, being drunk.
[Female, M.S.W., 20 years practice]

Financial scams, being used by therapists for personal services and errands.
[Male, Ph.D., 10 years practice]

Therapists who've thrown them out, therapists who didn't know what they were doing, therapists who were drunk during sessions.
[Male, Ph.D., 40 years practice]

One patient arrived at the therapist's door to find a note saying that the therapist had gone away, and the therapist never called the patient again. Abandonment of the worst kind.
[Female, Ph.D., 20 years practice]

Therapists who cross boundaries and talk about their own lives a lot. I've had many patients who've told me about seeing a therapist who told them all his problems.
[Female, Ph.D., 5 years practice]

Someone charged more than the agreed-on fee.
[Male, M.S.W., 10 years practice]

I did have a patient whose previous therapist told her she could not go away for the summer.
[Male, M.S.W., 15 years practice]

I know of instances where people were told that everything was confidential, and then the therapist has called their job and revealed all kinds of things.
[Female, M.S.W., 5 years practice]

A therapist who suddenly decided it was time for the patient to terminate, and it seemed to have to do only with the therapist's own schedule.

[Female, Ph.D., 15 years practice]

Going out to dinner with patients. Being at parties with patients. If I went to a party and there was a patient of mine there, I would leave.

[Female, M.S.W., 10 years practice]

Some financial dealings, like investing in a house with a patient.

[Male, M.D., 20 years practice]

That they were more involved in telling the patient their own problems. Taking advantage of them, for example, by having the patient do clerical work for them.

[Female, Ph.D., 30 years practice]

Soliciting referrals from patients, over and above patients voluntarily saying they'd like to refer someone. I believe their reporting is accurate. And using the dependency to make the patient feel guilty that the therapist's needs weren't met. "I'm lowering your fee, so you ought to send me people."

[Female, M.S.W., 20 years practice]

Occasionally, the therapist seemed reluctant to label the behavior of his or her predecessor unethical.

"Unethical" is a strong word. Patients have told me about behavior that I thought was questionable. Like becoming directly involved in their personal lives. Like seeing two different patients, and introducing one to the other and then counseling them individually using information that one gave to another.

[Female, M.A., 20 years practice]

One fairly lengthy report includes almost every possible violation of the rules.

I know of a psychiatrist who conducted group therapy, and if patients didn't cooperate as he wanted them to or thought that they should, they were fined huge sums of money. He felt that some of his patients were rather inhibited, so to help them with their sexuality, he would have sexual intercourse with one of the female patients in front of the group, or he would take one of the female patients to a private room and have intercourse with her while the group was in session. This therapist had a farm in a foreign country that was within flying distance of New York, and he had his patients fly down there and they lived in a kind of commune, and part of their therapy was they had to work to build silos and whatnot to build up his farm, for which they were paying him money. Then he was under indictment by the U.S. government, so he moved to another country with which there was no extradition, and the group would meet, and he would meet with them via phone and charge them for it. After a while, the people in the group began to recognize that he was a charlatan.

[Male, M.S.W., 35 years practice]

NUMERICAL DISTRIBUTION

(Some people mentioned more than one situation.) Thirty-three people mentioned sexual relationships with previous therapists; 34 mentioned other kinds of unethical behaviors; 10 said they had never been told of such behavior.

COMMENTS

The issues in this area are: How many unethical or incompetent therapists are practicing? How do we control them? What are the best ways to educate patients to make them less vulnerable to mistreatment? How does the current therapist best deal with a patient who has had such treatment in the past?

If this group is representative of the field, then a significant number of therapists are hearing about unethical behavior. That situation can be a dilemma for the current therapist, especially when told of sexual abuse, because patients often protect the transgressors and refuse to name the violators or take any action against them. The effects on the present treatment can be extreme. In a way, it's remarkable that such patients seek treatment again, but even when they do, their trust is severely damaged, and therapy can be difficult.

Other less flagrant violations of ethical principles also do damage, and patients may be surprised by the stricter limits set by the new therapists and see them as punitive or withholding. Over the years, I have had many patients, mostly but not exclusively female, tell me about sexual and other violations by previous therapists. The more flagrant the violation, the more difficult I found the therapy to be.

RELATED READING

Akamatsu, T. J. (1988). Intimate relationships with former clients: national survey of attitudes and behavior among practitioners. *Professional Psychology: Research and Practice* 19(4):454–458.

Borys, D. S. (1992). Nonsexual dual relationships. In *Innovations in Clinical Practice: A Source Book*, ed. L. VandeCreek, S. Knapp, and T. L. Jackson, pp. 443–454. Sarasota, FL: Professional Resource Press.

Gartrell, N., Herman, J. L., Olarte, S., et al. (1987). Reporting practices of psychiatrists who knew of sexual misconduct by colleagues. *American Journal of Orthopsychiatry* 57(2):287–295.

Levenson, J. L. (1986). When a colleague practices unethically: guidelines for intervention. *Journal of Counseling and Development* 64(5):315–317.

Pope, K. S. (1994). *Sexual Involvement with Therapists: Patient Assessment, Subsequent Therapy, Forensics.* Washington, DC: American Psychological Association.

Wood, B. J., Klein, S., Cross, H. J., et al. (1985). Impaired practitioners: psychologists' opinions about prevalence, and proposals for intervention. *Professional Psychology: Research and Practice* 16(6):843–850.

ॐॐॐॐ

Question 97: What are the important problems in our field?

Our field is currently besieged with various problems and issues. The public is often skeptical about both the effectiveness of therapy and the motives of the therapist. What do our therapists identify as problems? What do they think is wrong with our field?

The most significant issue, mentioned by almost two-thirds of the group, was the high incidence of untrained, unethical, or incompetent practitioners. A number of people specifically mentioned arrogant, controlling, or abusive therapists.

> Unethical therapists, that nobody has a window on because it's private. There are boundary violations with patients who need the relationship with the therapist and aren't able to challenge them.
>
> [Female, M.S.W., 10 years practice]

> It attracts people who are natural helpers, who are drawn to this field to rescue, to enable, to fix, and to work out their own issues, and they don't. They come in with so much unresolved stuff going on. Anyone with a high school diploma can call themselves a therapist. One thing I

like about the medical profession is that they force you to do continuing education to get recredentialed.

[Male, M.S.W., 15 years practice]

I think that there are a lot of people in the field who don't have other lives, and for whom this is their main emotional life. To be a therapist, because there's a lot going out, you need a lot coming in. It's dangerous not to have another emotional life, because then you need stuff from the patients that they shouldn't be providing. Also, I think a lot of therapists are kind of autocratic, and believe that they have the correct take on things, and wield their power too much with their patients.

[Female, M.S., 15 years practice]

I think one of the problems in our field is that a lot of people get into this business in order to be loved like they loved their therapist, so that they let their own countertransferential needs to be adored and revered interfere with good work.

[Male, Ph.D., 25 years practice]

There are a lot of people doing this work that shouldn't be doing it. I opted out of teaching at an institute because I felt that they were taking students in that should not have been taken in, and that they had a responsibility to do some screening as to who should be admitted to the training program. There's more to it than just taking people's money and putting them through four years of treatment and training and then at the end saying maybe they shouldn't be there or doing it.

[Female, M.S.W., 15 years practice]

There's a real problem with licensure, and I'd like to see some minimal requirement by the state to be able to hang out a shingle and call yourself a therapist, and that there be some training standards that are understood as a legal requirement. I think there are an awful lot of very stupid people out there doing therapy. I don't mean untrained, I mean stupid. People who haven't been in treatment themselves with someone who knows what they're doing. And there are a lot of people out there who shouldn't be allowed to treat people, just as there are a lot of physicians who shouldn't be practicing.

[Male, M.D., 20 years practice]

I think there's a lot of mental illness in our field that isn't recognized and isn't taken care of. A lot of therapists do a lot of damage to their patients. And we don't have any way of controlling that.

[Female, M.S., 20 years practice]

I see a lot more professionals that are disturbed. I know our patient often see us that way, but I think that a lot of people are going straight from school into doing treatment, who don't understand the process of therapy. People who have boundary problems, who share too much with the patients. And I think that needs to be addressed. I see an attitude toward Medicaid patients and minority patients that's very racist.

[Female, M.S.W., 10 years practice]

There are a lot of very poorly trained therapists who don't know what they're doing and don't really understand the power of the relationship, or the power of the needs people feel when they come to them, the power of their words to the patient. They're doing things that they don't even know they're doing. There are more and more people like that coming out of this or that counseling program, who don't choose to go on and get more training.

[Female, Ph.D., 15 years practice]

There are a lot of therapists who are not very well trained, who do a lot of flaky stuff, and that hurts the profession. The deficiencies in the psychiatric training programs are that residents are not in therapy themselves, and that the emphasis is so much on the biological versus more intensive training in therapy itself.

[Male, M.D., 5 years practice]

The quality of the product is not always very good. There are a lot of people out there who've had very little training, and are not very serious.

[Male, M.D., 20 years practice]

Training is not adequate enough. Therapists are not steeped in the kind of education that is so necessary in this field. I don't think they've taken enough philosophy, enough anthropology. There isn't an understanding of science and the scientific method, and to be able to keep up with important developments in theory and practice. They become more technocrats and technicians than they do therapists. It's okay, but it's limited. Their education is too narrow, and they lack the depth to do the traveling and investigating that's necessary. Students who've taken a course in symbolic logic do better than students who've only taken courses in sociology and psychology. That training is not so difficult, but unfortunately it's absent in most people's repertoire.

[Male, Ph.D., 30 years practice]

A third of our group mentioned the increasing influence and control of psychotherapy by the managed care organizations.

> Managed care is destroying this field. It's a restraint of trade. It's teaching therapists that you can't treat people the way they need to be treated in terms of length of treatment. It's all going to become short-term, even for people who need something else. It's very unsafe for a client not to know that they'll be seen as long as needed, that at any moment their therapy can be cut off. That should be between you and your therapist, not some other person.
>
> [Female, Ph.D., 10 years practice]

> The whole managed care system is horrendous. The intrusiveness, and within that the parameters of treatment are not set by an informed intrapsychic model but are set by a medical model and a model that's based on the monetary functioning of an insurance company. The basic model is completely at variance with a psychotherapeutic/psycho-analytic model, and there's no interest in the comfort and well-being of the patient, but rather the diminution of symptoms. What's important is not that a person is happy and content and comfortable in their life, but that they're symptom-free.
>
> [Female, M.S.W., 15 years practice]

> Managed care is a very big problem, because people's confidentiality is being broken, they want us to break it, and that's very dangerous. Also people are telling our patients how much time they can spend in therapy and what kind of therapy they should be doing, behavioral, cognitive, all kinds of things. And that will fix something external, but not the internal problem, which only manifests in another way.
>
> [Female, M.S.W., 20 years practice]

> I'm concerned about the increasing control and regulation of insurance companies who are going to be pushing for the least sessions possible so that they get the biggest return. I think that will result in inadequate care. We are the one profession around that's talking about personal growth rather than treating a specific disease entity that can be diagnosed according to DSM-IIIR, so that is going to be a loss if it continues in that direction.
>
> [Male, Ph.D., 25 years practice]

> Managed care is a nightmare. We're no longer doctors, we're providers. We don't prescribe the stuff or create it, we just provide it, and we

don't call the shots. It's political, and I'm not a political person. It's very depressing to see this happening and be a victim of it, and to see my clients be victims of it, because they are. What's happening is they're encroaching on our ability to function ethically, because if you can only be renewed for ten sessions each time you apply, and you form an intense relationship with the client, and you don't know whether the treatment will be continued after the ten sessions, then you're in a situation where you might have to contribute to somebody's pain, not healing.

[Male, Ph.D., 10 years practice]

There's too much outside interference. The way things operate now, if they have an insurance policy, they first have to call the insurance company and give reasons why they want to come into therapy. And a patient of mine who did this recently discovered after spilling his guts that he was talking to a clerk in Dallas.

[Male, M.S.W., 35 years practice]

The HMOs and managed care, because it's an impediment to treatment. People don't have free choice, and I have to talk to some little pipsqueak on the phone who's telling me how I have to run my practice, and they're just trying to save money for their company and it has nothing to do with therapy. Too much emphasis on medication, too much Prozac, and not enough working on the person. The quick fix. And there is a trend in that direction.

[Female, M.S.W., 15 years practice]

The idea that you provide fifteen services in three months. That you buy therapy like you go to get a haircut. There's a search for quick answers. Humans in general desperately want short cuts. It isn't a treatment.

[Male, M.S.W., 15 years practice]

Managed care is a horror. It's fraud and deceit. It's a moral crime being committed for profit. They're ripping the public off, as well as me.

[Male, M.D., 20 years practice]

There's the idea that people can get well in eight sessions. The complex issues of someone who's depressed, with absent and rejecting parents, to think you can deal with that quickly devalues the whole process. And then people think there's something wrong with them, because their health plan says they should be better in twenty sessions. I don't believe in quick fixes. And maybe therapists have bought into the quick fix.

[Female, M.S.W., 15 years practice]

Managed care companies can only make money by wiping out psycho-therapy, long-term treatment. We're in a life-and-death struggle right now to survive, and to convince the political community that this is a worthwhile enterprise. I'm very pessimistic that a cottage industry like ours can stand up against the enormous amounts of money that will be made by businesses that have everything to gain by getting rid of psychotherapy. It may become in twenty years a small profession just for rich people. The middle class will be frozen out.

[Male, Ph.D., 40 years practice]

Another large group were concerned about the increasing medicalization of the field of psychotherapy, and the growing reliance on "experts."

The main thing that's wrong with this field is that it's attempted to use the medical model and emulate medicine. The disaster in this field is licensure and regulation, because any efforts to regulate and license are to set standards. Now, what standards do you set, except the standards that are prevailing? Then everyone has to meet those stan-dards, and progress becomes impossible. You've frozen the picture of the profession in whatever state it is, and any departures from that will not be recognized as legally acceptable. We have to begin to move outside the picture of being physicians.

[Male, Ph.D., 50 years practice]

In a major way, too much professionalism. It's true of the whole world, with everything, that there are designated experts who claim to know everything, and they're the people who have the answers. Everything becomes compartmentalized, and the whole person gets lost. I have no problem with differing theoretical beliefs, but that's not the same as the fragmentation of the human being, which is what's happening more and more with the emphasis on diagnosis and expertise and intervention. I don't intervene, I talk to people. This gets driven more and more by the scientific ethos that's around, and managed care and cost containment. Also, it's the medicalization, because I don't think what we do is medical, and we shouldn't be reimbursed from a medical insurance company.

[Male, Ph.D., 20 years practice]

The old question of lay analysts versus medical analysts. It's time that lay analysts and medical analysts were on equal footing in every possible way. I never agreed with the American approach. I don't think psychoanalysis is a specialty of medicine. It's related to medicine, just as it's related to anthropology, and sociology, and history and culture and law and everything else.

[Male, M.D., 20 years practice]

One of the problems is that it's become too professionalized. Freud talked about lay analysis, about the need to train a whole army of people. It's become too exclusive, and too hierarchical. According to managed care now, therapy should be cognitive, behavioral, step-by-step treatment plans, medical model. They've thrown a mechanistic model onto me. I can see a new generation of people doing therapy, and it won't be the psychologists. People used to go into psychology to find themselves, to find their souls, but I don't think that can happen any more.

[Male, Ph.D., 40 years practice]

Related to this last problem is the increasing reliance on medications as the primary treatment.

I am a very strong believer in psychodynamic therapy, and the biggest problem in the field is that it's not dynamic enough. Most of the country is involved in cognitive therapy, and behavioral therapy, and Prozac. I think this is a horrible shame. The total medicalization of psychiatry is a horror, and the growing belief that what people need is the right chemical cocktail, specially made just for them.

[Male, Ph.D., 5 years practice]

Others said that the field of psychotherapy didn't have enough impact on society as a whole, on the social and political conditions in the country.

As a profession, as a whole, we do not address those problems out there in the world that make people come to us. We don't let it be known that there's something wrong with our educational system, with our social system, that things are breaking down in lots of departments, and there's something that needs to be done not on the scale of the one-to-one private practice. I think it's incumbent upon us morally and ethically to do something about that, and I don't see much being done at all. It's just not enough to do one-to-one. I don't feel like this is the answer any more, and that's one reason I'm getting out of the field. There's something too isolated about the whole field.

[Male, M.S.W., 25 years practice]

I think the dimension of how this field can affect society is terribly lacking. Maybe it's not possible, or maybe it's happening in the only way it can, because we're only a professional group.

[Female, M.S.W., 5 years practice]

We don't do enough socially conscious work. There's a lot that's known about how the mind operates, and how people interact, that can be applied to the culture and to social issues in very useful ways that we don't do at all.

[Female, Ph.D., 15 years practice]

A smaller group said that another problem was the proliferation of different theories and techniques, and the lack of a coherent body of agreed-upon theory and practice.

What's wrong with our field is what's wrong with our culture right now, which is that we have a cultural anarchy in our society right now. There is no center. When psychoanalysis first was invented, it had one view. Freud was adamant that psychoanalysis should not be mixed with religion, or with politics, or with anything. It was supposed to be a pure, objective occupation. Nowadays, we have feminist psychoanalysis, we have pastoral psychoanalysis, and psychotherapy has become people's various axes to grind, and that has hurt it.

[Male, Ph.D., 15 years practice]

One of the biggest problems is the absence of a consensus about effective approaches, and there doesn't have to be just one. That's a major problem. There's a problem in the area of psychotherapy research, that in an effort to make it clearer and more unified, is doing it in a way that distorts the process of psychotherapy, and doesn't take into consideration the complexity of the process. So the research is not very useful.

[Female, M.D., 15 years practice]

Theoretically, I sometimes feel concerned that people are working without some kind of theoretical model, and are just sort of winging it. Less foundation. Also I think that there's too much of an attitude that it's just a business, and not enough concern for theory, for a model, for principles.

[Female, M.A., 15 years practice]

Our field is not clear cut. If somebody has diabetes, the M.D. can specify the treatment exactly. In our field, it becomes much harder to justify the treatment.

[Female, M.S.W., 10 years practice]

There's the lack of a standard body of knowledge, and of a consensual standard of competence. The other thing is that, as a result of that, the field lacks credibility. There's a tremendous difficulty demonstrating the value of the work we do.

[Male, M.D., 15 years practice]

A colleague wrote a paper that says, "We're on the royal road to incoherence." There's no consensus about what we're doing. We don't have an agreed-upon technique, or on what constitutes evidence of what we're really looking for. So therapists are listening to patients from the point of view of their theoretical position, instead of as people.

[Female, M.S.W., 5 years practice]

There's competitiveness amongst different schools of thought. A lot of times we're trying to treat something that's physiological in a psychological way. We need a lot more research on what really works. We need to be a lot more scientific in our approach.

[Male, M.S.W., 15 years practice]

We need to be doing more intense research, controlled research, on psychotherapy forms and outcomes, recognizing that there are definitely some ways of doing things that are demonstrably better than others. If you can't prove that you've got something going, then you shouldn't be doing it.

[Male, Ph.D., 20 years practice]

Another portion of the group said the competition and lack of collegiality among different types of practitioners (M.S.W.'s, Ph.D.'s, M.D.'s), and among therapists of different theoretical orientations, was a major problem.

There's also a problem that, although we subscribe to the idea that we are scientists, people adopt their theoretical orientation with religious tenacity, and are as willing to challenge their own theoretical beliefs as a religious zealot is, and people become theoretical zealots, self-righteous, condescending, totally insufferable.

[Male, Ph.D., 25 years practice]

The thing that bothers me most is the hostility among different kinds of therapists, the competition and willingness to discount other points of view, almost a mean-spiritedness.

[Male, M.S.W., 20 years practice]

The thing that worries me is fundamentalism, the religious attitude toward the field, and with that comes rigidity, and people start holding on to their territory. I wish there was more of a dialogue, more openness. People are competitive.

[Female, Ph.D., 5 years practice]

I think the confusion in training is ridiculous, all the different disciplines, social workers and psychologists and psychiatrists, licenses and non-licenses. The power of the medical therapists bothers me, although it doesn't impinge on my daily work. It's not fair that they get more money and are usually less qualified to do therapy.

[Female, M.S.W., 30 years practice]

Therapists, as a rule, become a little too arrogant. This is something I find in my colleagues, even in myself. Arrogant about their knowledge, that they've got it covered, and they can do it all, and they lack the humility. This is a profession where we need to be humble and realize that we don't know it all. It's not only with seasoned practitioners, it's with beginners too.

[Male, Ph.D., 30 years practice]

The field is very fragmented, and there are little pockets where everyone thinks they know what they're doing and this is the only way to do it. And there's not enough intercommunication among those pockets, not enough flexibility and collegiality.

[Female, M.S., 20 years practice]

There's a competition and a disrespect among the professions that do this work, and that's not been helpful to the field: psychiatrists, social workers, psychologists, psychiatric nurses, guidance counselors. There's a breakdown of something, of collegiality and respect and support and recognition of people's talents.

[Female, M.S.W., 15 years practice]

People get very boxed into their points of view, and very judgmental about other people's points of view. There's a lot of fighting and competitiveness that's misdirected.

[Female, Ph.D., 15 years practice]

It would be nice if it wasn't as competitive. There's not enough intermingling, and too much "My way is the right way!" I'm more effective when I can combine and blend different things, and it would be nice if the field were more open to that.

[Female, Ph.D., 20 years practice]

There's a little too much black magic going on, and at the same time there's a lot of dogmatism. There are a lot of therapists who are insecure themselves and uncomfortable with what they don't know about psychotherapy. So they reach for a hook, and the hook is some theory, and they fit patients into the theory. There's too much of that, and I'm very uncomfortable with it.

[Male, Ph.D., 10 years practice]

Two people said that therapy was not available enough to everyone who needs it.

It's difficult for the people who really need it to get it. I started taking clinic patients again, and I got a lot of people I hadn't seen in my practice for a while. I think I'm always going to accept low-fee patients in my practice. People who are not middle class, who can really benefit from having someone in their lives to help with their problems, and who know they're going to get it on an ongoing basis. Too many people don't have the money. It needs to be accessible to the people who could use it.

[Female, M.A., 15 years practice]

Therapy isn't available enough. We haven't helped people see that having therapy doesn't mean you're crazy. We haven't removed that stigma.

[Female, M.S.W., 20 years practice]

There were also some comments about the way therapists try to approach problems, with the goal of getting and keeping patients in treatment.

The thing about therapy is if you or I go to twenty different therapists today and say that we have a bellyache and we're wondering if maybe it's psychological factors, all twenty will accept us as patients. No one will say, "Have you tried a TUMS?" We will pathologize anything. Because anyone can benefit from talking about their life, and also we have to make a living. What insurance salesman is going to tell you that you have enough insurance? We keep people too long, and we don't encourage other kinds of things.

[Male, Ph.D., 25 years practice]

Historically, we've tended to take people on in treatment with the implication, never a promise, but with the implication that if they stick through the process, whatever their stated goals are are going to be met. I think that's not fair. I don't know whether it's our wish or our grandiosity, but we to get some more clarity about what we can do and what we can't do. I think there are a lot of things we don't know.

There are a lot of people we're going to be working with that we know from the outset are not going to get all better. Therapy's not going to be a panacea for them. It may be helpful, it may give them some tools they didn't have before, it may give them greater ease with some of their symptoms, but it's not going to be a panacea.

[Female, M.S.W., 20 years practice]

I encourage termination, when people have been in treatment for a long time, and tell them that this is not a permanent lifestyle, that one should reach an endpoint in treatment. There are a lot of practitioners who allow it to go on ad infinitum.

[Female, M.A., 15 years practice]

I think there tends to be, among many of our colleagues, an over-emphasis on intellectualization and understanding and not enough of a willingness, both in their lives and their patients, to encourage change. So that people can stay in therapy interminably. I'm talking particularly about analysis.

[Male, Ph.D., 25 years practice]

Several people said that the effectiveness and the importance of the work that therapists do was not generally understood or appreciated by the public.

If I keep someone out of the hospital, or keep a family together, or keep a kid from killing himself, then I'm performing an invaluable service to society, but I don't think we're appreciated enough.

[Female, Ph.D., 20 years practice]

I don't think we do an adequate job of public education. We fail in helping people to understand the breadth of the field, and the ability to do preventive kinds of things, both in the emotional and physical conditions.

[Male, Ph.D., 20 years practice]

One thing wrong is that the public does not appreciate the fact that well-trained therapists can really help a lot. So we live in an era where there are very powerful forces against psychotherapy, that may prevail. Thirty years ago, the intellectual community was very involved in psychoanalysis. Everybody had to go into analysis. Today, there is for some reason a turning away of the intellectual community, and there's a hostility now against psychoanalysis, and this is part of the whole problem.

[Male, Ph.D., 40 years practice]

Finally, one man discussed the problem of the therapist's role.

> Sometimes we take ourselves too seriously, and believe our own bull-shit. We participate in this notion that there is a well-analyzed person, or a together person, and that's crazy to begin with, but then we walk around acting like we're it. So we perpetrate a lie to our patients which fosters shame. We can hide behind our role, and there's a fraudulence built in, a shame-enhancing mechanism. We're overly institutionalized. We have all these institutions and papers and titles and licenses and credentials, which all work against the very basic thing we're trying to do, which is to help people be natural with each other, be authentic, be there without all that stuff.
>
> [Male, Ph.D., 25 years practice]

NUMERICAL DISTRIBUTION

(Some people gave more than one answer.) Thirty-eight people mentioned untrained, incompetent, or unethical practitioners; 20 people mentioned managed care; 12 people said the lack of a consistent body of theory and treatment; 8 people said the lack of collegiality and the fragmentation of the field; 8 people said there was not enough public awareness or enough impact on social and political realities; 8 people said the arrogance of certain therapists and abuse of power; 7 said the medicalization of the field and the tendency to overtreat; 3 said the increasing reliance on medication; and 2 said that it was not available enough to people.

COMMENTS

Some issues in this area are: What is wrong with our field? How do we remedy these problems? What is our best response to managed care? How do we control unethical and incompetent practitioners? How do we address the larger problems of society as a whole? How can we reach basic agreement among the different schools of treatment and different professional backgrounds?

We have a lot of work ahead of us in addressing the problems in our field. We need more concrete experimental research to demonstrate what is effective and what is not. The nature of the work, private and usually irreproducible, makes such research difficult. Right now, we have no effective way to control the unethical or incompetent practitioner, since he or she usually has all the necessary credentials. I think the solution to the problem of the lack of external monitoring of private practitioners is best solved not by other professionals but by better educating patients about what is and what is not good therapy.

Right now, the attempt to take over the field of psychotherapy by the medical insurance establishment is probably the biggest threat to our survival and must be addressed first. If the field doesn't survive as a viable, energetic, autonomous discipline then it seems unlikely that any of the other problems can or will be addressed. I think that the increasing medicalization of the field, with the proliferation of diagnoses and psychiatric "disorders," is having a detrimental effect on psychotherapy in particular and society in general. Every human condition, every problem, every disruption, is now a psychiatric illness, and people are left feeling less and less responsible for their behavior and less and less in control of their lives. The whole managed care situation is a direct outgrowth of this medicalization, and psychotherapy, which is really just two people talking, is now required to behave as if it were a medical procedure, which it is not and was never designed to be.

RELATED READING

Dryden, W., and Feltham, C., eds. (1992). *Psychotherapy and Its Discontents.* Buckingham, England: Open University Press.

Gabbard, G. O., and Smith, W. O. (1982). Psychiatry–psychology conflict: origins in training. *Journal of Psychiatric Treatment and Evaluation* 4(3):203–208.

Pope, K. S., and Tabachnick, B. G. (1993). Therapists's anger, hate, fear, and sexual feelings: national survey of therapist responses, client characteristics, critical events, formal complaints, and training. *Professional Psychology: Research and Practice* 24(2):142–152.

🐚🐚🐚🐚

Question 98: What are the positive trends or developments in our field?

While there may be significant problems in the field nowadays, there may also be aspects that are changing and improving. Which elements in the profession do our therapists identify as a positive development?

Half the group saw improvements in theory, a wider acceptance and exploration of new ways of thinking and practicing. People said that the field seemed more flexible, less rigid and authoritarian, more open to divergent theories and approaches.

People are freeing themselves from the rigid, Freudian approach and exploring other ways of working, and doing very creative things, particularly these relational-developmental people who are all over, in every section of the field.

[Female, M.S., 20 years practice]

I think that things are getting looser, and I see more people working in an eclectic fashion, even people from institutes who started out with more rigid training, are letting go of some of that and expanding their armamentarium of what they can use.

[Female, M.S.W., 20 years practice]

I'm glad to see the American Psychoanalytic Association coming to its senses a little bit, and opening its mind a little bit to neuropsychiatry, to people without M.D.'s, to Kohut. There's a greater ecumenical sense.

[Male, M.D., 20 years practice]

There's more conversation between the different schools, more effort to integrate, and dialogues are better now.

[Male, M.D., 20 years practice]

The trends in family therapy are wonderful. They're much more open, much more feminist-oriented, much more women-oriented, much more open to gay issues.

[Female, Ph.D., 20 years practice]

People are willing to question things that were formerly sacrosanct. There are many more legitimate theoretical schools, and that's healthy, unless it becomes the new expert and just replaces the old with the new, the new ultimate truth.

[Male, Ph.D., 20 years practice]

Several people specifically mentioned the new emphasis on the relationship between patient and therapist.

The way in which therapists work who focus on the relationship in the room is finally being recognized as the way to work, and acknowledged by patients as what helps them the most.

[Female, M.S., 15 years practice]

I think some of the newer theories are very useful, where they pay more attention to the relationship between patient and therapist. Not just transference, but the real relationship.

[Female, M.S.W., 30 years practice]

Some people saw an increased awareness of certain social issues, such as sexual abuse or alcoholism.

> I think it's good that people are talking about abuse, how prevalent it is, even if they're fighting about it. At one time we didn't even talk about alcohol abuse. Twenty years ago, doing an intake, you would ask about drinking, and the person would say, "Socially," and that would be it, you wouldn't even ask any more questions, and you didn't write it down on a person's hospital chart. It was thought that it was too private.
>
> [Female, M.S.W., 10 years practice]

> We're becoming much more aware of the prevalence of sexual abuse, and that's a good thing.
>
> [Female, M.S.W., 20 years practice]

Several therapists mentioned a different attitude toward the patient, more adaptive to what the patient needs.

> The move toward being more where people are, and what their needs are, and not standing on the old analytic rules and limitations.
>
> [Female, Ph.D., 30 years practice]

> In psychoanalysis, it's becoming so much more human and relational, that's been a tremendous plus. It used to be so dry, and inhuman, and people were taught to practice in horribly rigid and stultified ways.
>
> [Male, Ph.D., 5 years practice]

> The field is paying more attention to patients. We're coming more and more to listen to experience of patients within the treatment and within their lives, and using theory in a different way to respond to that, rather than imposing the theory on the patient.
>
> [Female, M.S.W., 15 years practice]

Others mentioned an increased amount of creative, thoughtful published work.

> There are a lot of good teachers, a lot of good books, a lot of dedicated people trying to improve their skill and knowledge. If it isn't wiped out, it will become more and more effective as a treatment.
>
> [Male, Ph.D., 40 years practice]

> There's an influx of new ideas.
>
> [Male, M.S.W., 10 years practice]

There are some brilliant clinicians and theoreticians, who are writing and talking and contributing great wisdom.

[Male, Ph.D., 10 years practice]

Several people said that they were happy that assumptions are being questioned and challenged.

The things that people take for granted are breaking down, and it's a good thing to happen.

[Male, Ph.D., 30 years practice]

I think more and more, with a lot of conditions, we're talking about physiology and organicity. We're having to ask new questions and to risk having to change. What we thought was right isn't necessarily true.

[Female, Ph.D., 5 years practice]

A quarter of the group saw increased availability to the public and increased acceptance of being a patient.

I think psychotherapy is really becoming integrated into the mainstream of our society now. Everybody's in therapy, and they are public figures saying that. I think we're basically doing a good job.

[Male, Ph.D., 25 years practice]

Universal health care could make it easier for people to access at least some therapy. Maybe more people would avail themselves of it if everybody had access to it.

[Male, M.S.W., 20 years practice]

The idea of people knowing that talking to someone else helps, and establishing a relationship where you can get things out. More people seem to know that.

[Female, M.A., 15 years practice]

Over the long term, people are much more tolerant of psychotherapy. The stigma is practically eliminated, except probably in certain ethnic and cultural and socioeconomic groups.

[Female, M.A., 15 years practice]

People joke about Oprah and Geraldo, but there's a kind of public education happening. They're learning that our childhoods impact on us. It's more acceptable to say you're in treatment, and almost everybody can benefit from treatment.

[Female, M.S.W., 25 years practice]

The one positive thing I see is that therapy is much more accessible to people, with not such a big stigma attached. People don't have to sneak around to be in therapy. It's much more humane than it used to be, too. Years ago it was much less interactive than it is now. Plus now people call each other by their first names.

[Female, M.S.W., 10 years practice]

It's become much more mainstream to be in therapy. I see a lot of lower-middle-class people now who I would have never expected to go into therapy.

[Male, Ph.D., 10 years practice]

Another segment of the group mentioned improved professionalism or increased accountability and responsibility of individual practitioners.

On the whole, I think most people in the field are pretty good, and most try to be helpful, and are not overbearing or controlling. There's a professionalism that I think has grown. I like that we're being held accountable.

[Male, M.S.W., 10 years practice]

Those therapists who are well trained, and who keep up, and who continue to grow as people and as therapists, are doing wonderful work. They're making a great contribution to their field. There are a lot of good things being written, a lot of exciting work being done.

[Male, M.D., 5 years practice]

This is a field that's constantly checking itself, and we are now being bombarded by consumers that are more educated. This good because it empowers the clients and it's less likely that the relationship will become abusive.

[Male, Ph.D., 20 years practice]

Some people mentioned the improvements in medication, the development of new pharmacological treatments.

I think there's more acceptance of medications by clinicians and that's a good thing.

[Female, M.A., 15 years practice]

The developments of new medications are tremendously positive, that things we used to routinely prescribe years of psychotherapy for are becoming tremendously helped by medications, which either alleviates the person's distress, or helps them to get into treatment. People aren't coming up with major new psychological theories. In fact, it's just the opposite: The pressure is to trivialize or to bastardize treatment. Overall, the combined therapy is a very positive thing.

[Male, M.D., 15 years practice]

A few people said that they thought managed care would make therapy more available or would help define appropriate treatment for specific conditions.

In a way, the whole trend toward managed care and shorter treatment is having some positive effects. I don't think someone who comes in with a history of sexual abuse can be treated in two sessions by burning a picture of the offender, which is what some people are doing. But to tell them they have to be in analysis for nine or ten years may be just as fallacious. We have to think about not just what's going to work, but also what's the quickest way we can help somebody.

[Female, M.S.W., 20 years practice]

I happen to be an advocate of the brief psychotherapeutic approach. We need to be more goal-oriented, and managed care has influenced us to be. I think it's a good trend.

[Male, M.S.W., 15 years practice]

I like the short-term outcome-based efforts of the managed care. I think that makes us look at what we're actually doing and the assumptions we've been making.

[Male, Ph.D., 25 years practice]

There is a growing understanding that empirical and experimental research is of great importance. There is the beginning of an understanding that certain diagnostic groups work better with some kinds of interventions than others. Obsessive-compulsive disorder is the most obvious example, where it's quite clear that medication plus a behavioral approach is the most effective way of dealing with it, and that anything else borders on the unethical.

[Male, Ph.D., 20 years practice]

Some of those therapists concerned about the influence of the insurance companies said that they saw increased willingness to oppose the imposition of managed care and to organize toward that goal.

We're gathering together to fight this managed care business, which is positive.

[Female, M.S.W., 20 years practice]

Managed care may crystallize a strong countermovement. There may have to be a strong and more unified statement to the public of what psychotherapy is and is not. Sometimes having an enemy helps.

[Male, M.S.W., 15 years practice]

Some people saw an increased awareness and attention to the spiritual dimension of the patient's experience, and less pathologizing of every aspect of human behavior.

Centuries ago, the priests and the rabbis were the people who dictated what man thought and what he did. Then we moved away from the churches and synagogues and into science. Now we're thinking more about who man is, and we're the ones who are responsible for this look inside.

[Male, M.S.W., 15 years practice]

Eclecticism, and humanism, and moving into a broader frame of reference. Moving more in the direction of education, and spiritual pursuits, and not looking at everything from the disease model.

[Male, Ph.D., 50 years practice]

We're not looking for pathology as much, and that's positive.

[Female, M.S.W., 10 years practice]

Only five people said there were no improvements or positive developments in the field.

It's too relative, and only temporary. We can improve behavior, but we don't touch the soul.

[Male, Ph.D., 40 years practice]

NUMERICAL DISTRIBUTION

Thirty-one people saw improvement in theory and practice; 13 mentioned improved availability to the public and more acceptance by society; 5 people saw more professionalism and improved accountability; 4 mentioned the improvements in medication, and their increasing acceptance by nonmedical therapists; and 2 people mentioned the increased awareness of specific issues, such as sexual abuse and alcoholism. Five people thought there were no positive developments or trends.

COMMENTS

The issues in this area are: What is currently improving the practice of psychotherapy? What can we do to maximize this improvement? What else needs to be improved?

All of the things mentioned above are significant developments in the field as a whole, but I think that the shift from a one-person dynamic, where the patient has all the issues and problems and the therapist is a neutral blank screen, to a two-person dynamic, where therapist and patient look at the relationship together and the therapist can acknowledge his or her own contributions, is the most important improvement.

RELATED READING

Evans, L. A., Acosta, F. X., Yamamoto, J., and Skilbeck, W. M. (1984). Orienting psychotherapists to better serve low income and minority patients. *Journal of Clinical Psychology* 40(1):90–96.

Friedman, L. (1982). The humanistic trend in recent psychoanalytic theory. *Psychoanalytic Quarterly* 51(3):353–371.

Heimann, H. (1991). Psychiatry at the end of the 20th century. *European Psychiatry* 6(1):1–6.

Pulver, S. E. (1991). Psychoanalytic technique: progress during the past decade. *Psychoanalytic Inquiry* 11(1–2):65–87.

⬧⬧⬧⬧

Question 99: What do you like about private practice?

Everyone in private practice is there by choice, and consequently there are aspects of the arrangement that they like (Question 100 addresses difficult or problematic aspects).

A large majority mentioned that they like the freedom, being free to set schedules, fees, vacations, and so on.

> You can set your own schedule, you have a lot of flexibility, take vacations you want. You don't have to report to anybody. The freedom.
> [Female, M.S.W., 20 years practice]

> The opportunity to work independently, to set my own hours, to have a family and a practice.
> [Female, M.A., 15 years practice]

That I can pick and choose with whom I'm going to work, and refer out the people I'm not. That I'm in my own space, where I feel taken care of, and don't have immediate needs that might get taken out on the patient.

[Female, M.S., 20 years practice]

The ability to control my own time, the flexibility. Nobody's telling me what to do. I couldn't work any other way anymore.

[Male, Ph.D., 25 years practice]

Another large group said they like the autonomy and the independence, not being accountable to anyone except the patient.

Not having to answer to a higher authority, except that's changing. I like the independence, I like being able to depend on myself. Structurally I like being able to say, "Well, I don't want to work on Monday mornings, so I won't."

[Female, M.S.W., 15 years practice]

I must have known my whole life that I needed to be on my own. It satisfies my need to rule my own world in as many ways as possible.

[Female, M.S., 15 years practice]

You're your own boss. You have the opportunity to practice along the lines and principles that you think are the best. My experience working in hospitals and clinics is that they're set up for the benefit of the people working there, and not for the benefit of the patients.

[Male, M.D., 20 years practice]

A number of people said they like the lack of bureaucratic requirements, such as paperwork and meetings, often found in agency settings.

I like that there's no bureaucracy, no paperwork, no writing silly treatment plans for the auditors.

[Male, M.S.W., 15 years practice]

I like not going to staff meetings. That's why I did this to begin with. I never have to go to a meeting that I don't want to go to. And I like that when I work, it's real work. I never liked schmoozing, and down time. This way, when I work I work, and when I don't work it's my time.

[Female, M.S., 15 years practice]

> I like being my own boss. I like not having to go to meaningless bureau-cratic meetings and fill out forms.
>
> [Male, Ph.D., 5 years practice]

Again in contrast to agency or clinic settings, a number of others emphasized the privacy of the relationship with the patient and that patients are there by choice, not assigned.

> I like working individually with patients, and that they really opted to come to me. The flexibility of hours is very important to me.
>
> [Female, Ph.D., 15 years practice]

> That the hours are my own, that I have more of a direct feeling that I'm being paid for what I do. It's a much cleaner kind of one-to-one balance in terms of what your accomplishments are.
>
> [Female, M.S.W., 20 years practice]

> Being able to work independently, come to my own awarenesses, decisions, put them into effect, grow with them. That I determine how the thing goes. I can take risks when I'm able to. That I'm doing the treatment.
>
> [Male, M.S.W., 15 years practice]

> The purity of the way in which I can work. That was true up till this year, and managed care. There are no intrusions whatsoever.
>
> [Male, Ph.D., 10 years practice]

> I like that it's my own, my own office. I think there's a different level of patients in private practice than in an agency, more motivated.
>
> [Female, M.S., 15 years practice]

One person, whose clinic works with a particular population, welcomed the opportunity to work with other types of patients in her private practice.

> It's nice to work with people who are more like me, in terms of the possibilities they have in life, where the potential is better. It's a nice balance to dealing with people who are living in poverty.
>
> [Female, Ph.D., 10 years practice]

Others liked best the importance of the work, its intellectual and emotional challenge, and the variety of situations it includes.

I'll go to my grave knowing that I've made a difference. That I've really helped some people so that their lives are changed, and I can look back and know that I did work that made an important difference. That's so satisfying.

[Female, M.S.W., 30 years practice]

After working at an agency, where my income was based on a salary, I really liked that people are coming to me and want to pay me for what I can do for them, what I am doing is really valuable. I really like to be able to sit with somebody and have a relationship where I'm also trying to help them. It's intellectually stimulating but it's also emotionally in touch in a way that's actually relaxing.

[Male, M.S.W., 20 years practice]

I like meeting different people. One of the fringe benefits of my work has been learning about the lives of people who are so different from me. It's brought me into worlds that I would have otherwise never known about.

[Female, M.A., 20 years practice]

I really do enjoy working in a deeper way, to help people unlock parts of themselves. It's really interesting and stimulating and exciting.

[Female, M.S.W., 15 years practice]

A few people said they liked the income level and the status of the profession.

I like the money.

[Male, M.S.W., 15 years practice]

It's more lucrative than if I were working at a clinic.

[Female, M.S.W., 25 years practice]

Finally, two people said that for them it doesn't feel like work in the conventional sense.

I don't feel like I'm working. I feel like I just hang out. I set my own time schedule, I don't have to answer to a lot of people who don't respect me.

[Male, Ph.D., 25 years practice]

You don't have to go to work. I get dressed, I walk down the hall, and I'm here. I don't have to prepare.

[Male, Ph.D., 20 years practice]

NUMERICAL DISTRIBUTION

(Some people mentioned more than one aspect.) Thirty-two people mentioned the freedom, with hours, and fees, and patients; 15 people mentioned the independence or the autonomy; 10 people included the lack of bureaucracy and paperwork; 7 mentioned the privacy and intimacy of the relationship; 4 said the significance and importance of the work; 3 said the income; 3 said the variety of experience; and 2 said that it was intellectually stimulating and challenging.

COMMENTS

Some issues in this area are: How is private practice different from agency work? How does the therapist balance the privacy and autonomy against the isolation of individual private practice?

Clearly, most therapists who are only in private practice, without an agency affiliation, like the freedom of working for themselves. I think I also love the freedom, independence, and autonomy most of all. I'm accountable to no one except the patients themselves. Nobody asks me where my paperwork is. I work when I want to and set my own schedule.

To use the medical model just for a moment, private practice creates a sterile field in which to work. It's only the patient and me, so it feels clean and pure, uncontaminated by outside influences or third parties. I also like the feeling of accomplishment, that I get to take credit for the success of the practice that I've built up and developed over the past fifteen years.

RELATED READING

Brown, P. (1990). Social workers in private practice: what are they really doing? *Clinical Social Work Journal* 18(4):407–421.

Freudenberger, H. J., et al. (1986). The private practice of psychology: four variations. In *Innovations in Clinical Practice: A Source Book*, vol. 5, ed. P. A. Keller and L. G. Ritt, pp. 233–244. Sarasota, FL: Professional Resource Exchange.

Levin, R., and Leginsky, P. (1990). The independent social worker as entrepreneur. *Journal of Independent Social Work* 5(1):89–99.

🐚🐚🐚🐚

Question 100: What are the difficulties of private practice?

While those in private practice are there by choice, they do not necessarily like everything about the situation.

Over half the group said that the isolation of being alone in the office all day, seeing only patients, can be difficult or even dangerous.

> I'm concerned about isolation. I'm moving into a group practice, but I would be terrified of isolation if it were just me on my own. I think there's a real problem with private practice that too many people get isolated, don't get challenged in what they do in their work, and sometimes become dangerous.
>
> [Male, Ph.D., 25 years practice]

> It is isolating. You don't have contact over the coffee urn or the water cooler, so it can get lonely.
>
> [Female, M.S.W., 20 years practice]

> I miss the people. There's no one else to talk to, even to say hello, not to mention someone to share issues and problems with.
>
> [Female, M.S.W., 10 years practice]

> You're isolated. Not really, because you're in company all the time, but you're isolated from your peers. I really enjoyed being part of a faculty or in a hospital setting. I liked the stimulation of other people. It's too lonely.
>
> [Male, Ph.D., 50 years practice]

> I miss, although I have two different peer supervisory situations, conferences where a number of people are involved with the same patient, the team approach at the hospital. The whole dimension of professional pride, having other people observe what I do, is something I miss in private practice.
>
> [Female, M.S.W., 20 years practice]

> I hate the isolation, I really hate it. When I was working in a hospital setting, that was the saving grace: the team and the other clinicians, and a chance to talk things through. I've relieved that a little bit by teaching, so at least I'm in an academic environment where I'm with other people.
>
> [Female, M.A., 15 years practice]

A few people said specifically that they were not troubled by feeling isolated or that they even enjoyed it.

> Isolation is not an issue because I've always worked in my home, and can come up and see someone, or make a phone call. There are times I like being isolated, when I can hide downstairs.
>
> [Male, Ph.D., 40 years practice]

Most who were troubled by feeling isolated suggested a number of different solutions to the problem.

> I talk to people, make lunch dates, go to the gym, take workshops, join groups, those kinds of things.
>
> [Female, M.S.W., 15 years practice]

> I teach, I coach my kid's soccer team. I balance it by doing other things. I write music. I go running.
>
> [Male, Ph.D., 20 years practice]

> I develop a social life, take seminars and courses.
>
> [Male, M.S.W., 10 years practice]

> I try to build in activities: I do a peer supervision group; I try to have a lunch date at least twice a week; I'll call people on the phone.
>
> [Female, M.S.W., 25 years practice]

> I try to get out and walk around. I try to meet people for lunch. I've learned how to be alone with myself.
>
> [Female, M.A., 20 years practice]

> I'm in a peer group, and a supervisory group. I go to conferences. And I try to live a rich life.
>
> [Female, M.S.W., 20 years practice]

One person pointed out the danger of not finding ways to compensate for the isolation of private practice.

> I don't feel isolated because I do a lot of other things beside psychotherapy. Also, I have a very full personal life, and that's very important. Therapists who don't have a personal life are dangerous. You have to make sure you take care of your own personal needs, and not isolate themselves with their patients.
>
> [Male, Ph.D., 10 years practice]

Almost a third of the group mentioned the financial uncertainty.

> I struggle with hoping that this doesn't get reflected in what happens with patients, but I have far more anxiety with the whole area of whether somebody's going to stay or go than I would like to have. I would like to be far more neutral than I actually feel. Sometimes I worry that my own anxiety creeps into what I choose to focus on. I try to counter that, but I'm sure it infects the treatment in some way.
>
> [Female, M.S.W., 20 years practice]

> Sometimes, especially as I look forward to retirement, there are lapses in practice, patients not coming in. Also, patients showing up with all different kinds of insurance, restrictions, and whatnot. Uncertainty about being paid.
>
> [Male, Ph.D., 40 years practice]

> The uncertainty of the schedule, and the referrals. It isn't easy getting new patients. I don't have a connection with doctors and hospitals.
>
> [Female, M.A., 15 years practice]

> Having to make sure that you're maintaining referral sources, doing the billing, paperwork.
>
> [Male, M.D., 20 years practice]

> I find it very insecure money-wise. Also, it's becoming more and more entrepreneurial, which goes against my personality and my values, to have to market myself.
>
> [Male, M.S.W., 15 years practice]

> I don't like not being able to fill hours, the uncertainty. The bills appear whether there's somebody in the other chair or not.
>
> [Male, Ph.D., 20 years practice]

One person spoke at some length about the difficulty of carving out a territory as an individual practitioner.

> It's more anxiety-producing to be out there on your own, facing all the forces that are out there when the forces are much stronger than you. You have to find a way to find your niche, to fit in a way that gives you some influence.
>
> [Male, Ph.D., 25 years practice]

Several people mentioned having to provide all the fringe benefits (insurance, vacation, sick time) for oneself.

You don't have a pension plan that they deduct, you don't have a retirement plan, you don't have sick time, you don't have medical coverage, you don't have vacation time. Those are really big drawbacks.

[Male, Ph.D., 15 years practice]

You don't get paid vacations. You never can take a sick day without planning it in advance and rescheduling all your patients.

[Female, Ph.D., 20 years practice]

The isolation. The financial uncertainty. All the crap: paying your own taxes; paying health insurance; handling every detail. As much as I complain about bureaucracy, they do take care of some things. Nobody takes care of anything for me. Sometimes I wish that someone would take care of me more.

[Male, Ph.D., 25 years practice]

When I first went into private practice, I wanted to go to a conference, and I realized that I had to pay for it myself. I hadn't thought about that. And if you're at a conference for a few days, nobody does your work for you, and you don't get paid. And you don't have health insurance. Things like that.

[Female, M.S.W., 10 years practice]

If you're ill, there's no one who pays your sick leave. In private practice, I've come in with a one-hundred-and-three degree temperature, my back was out and my head was killing me, where in a social agency I would just call in sick.

[Male, M.S.W., 35 years practice]

Several people said they had problems with managed care (see also Question 9), and the way these organizations were beginning to dominate the field.

In our state, solo private practice, for all intents and purposes, is dead here. Everybody's moving to group situations. It's the only way you're going to be able to contract with insurance companies.

[Male, Ph.D., 20 years practice]

I have only a small private practice because I don't want a large one. There are a lot of hassles I don't want to be bothered with, such as dealing with the insurance companies, the managed care companies.

[Male, M.D., 5 years practice]

A couple of people had difficulty with the responsibility for the patients in one's care.

Responsibility, a lot of responsibility is all on you. As I grow older, this is something that's very much a part of practice now, to worry about medications and suicide.

[Male, M.D., 15 years practice]

A large private practice carries with it a very large twenty-four-hour responsibility which I don't want. My lifestyle requires a balance between professional and private life, and for me, having a large practice would make that difficult.

[Male, M.D., 5 years practice]

Several therapists said they were unhappy with the demands of the schedule that a therapist has to keep.

I work every evening, and one evening in the summer I had to cancel for some reason, and I realized I was missing the sunsets, and how beautiful the days can be in the summer.

[Male, Ph.D., 20 years practice]

I have to work when the patients can come. I don't like working early in the morning, but sometimes I have to.

[Female, M.S.W., 5 years practice]

I have a tough time taking time off, of not feeling that I have to be the Energizer Bunny, and just keep going and going.

[Female, Ph.D., 5 years practice]

I'm disappointed that I have to work so hard to be in this profession. It's hard to work so many hours.

[Female, M.S.W., 15 years practice]

The biggest difficulty is that your schedule is so set. Once your schedule is set, it's hard to start disrupting the schedule to accommodate special events.

[Female, M.S.W., 15 years practice]

A few people said they liked everything about private practice.

There's nothing I don't like. The isolation isn't a problem because I'm a reclusive person. I think that therapists who tend to feel isolated in private practice are therapists who aren't really connecting with their patients. This is probably one of the only professions where being intimate is the actual job. Your job is to try to achieve intimacy, and help people who can't be intimate achieve it. So I don't feel isolated because there's always such an intense intimacy in the therapy.

[Male, Ph.D., 15 years practice]

NUMERICAL DISTRIBUTION

(Some people gave more than one answer.) Thirty-two people mentioned the isolation; 18 mentioned the financial uncertainty; 7 mentioned the lack of benefits like insurance, sick leave, paid vacations, pension plans, and so forth; 3 disliked working so many hours or in the evenings; 3 mentioned the difficulties of working with managed care; 2 mentioned the paperwork; and 2 said they didn't like having so much responsibility. Three people said there was nothing they didn't like about private practice.

COMMENTS

Issues here include: Are certain aspects of private practice objectively troublesome, or does difficulty arise from the personality of the individual practitioner? Are training programs effectively preparing therapists for the difficult aspects?

One of the basic rules of life is that freedom comes only with responsibility, and the freedom of private practice comes with the additional responsibility of taking care of everything oneself: health insurance, vacation time, finding patients, collecting fees. Sometimes these requirements can feel burdensome.

For me, the most difficult aspect of private practice is the financial uncertainty. Even after years of having an established practice, I've had periods where a number of patients terminated at the same time and my income dropped precipitously, albeit temporarily.

Although the work is very intimate, it's not a relaxed, casual intimacy. The therapist is in a professional role at all times and needs other relationships and other activities outside of that professional role. Isolation can also be a problem, and I make certain to arrange other activities to stay in contact with others outside the office.

RELATED READING

Dryden, W. (1985). *Therapists' Dilemmas.* New York: Harper and Row.
Garber, B. (1987). The isolation and loneliness of the child analyst. *Annual of Psychoanalysis* 15:193–208.

Steiner, L. R. (1939). Case work as a private venture. *Journal of Independent Social Work* 1987, 2(1):57–70.

Strom, K. (1994). Clinicians' reasons for rejecting private practice. *Families in Society* 75(8):499–508.

🔁🔁🔁🔁

Question 101: Do you like being a psychotherapist? What do you like best?

Almost everyone in this sample said they like being a therapist (see also Question 99). Many said they love it and can't imagine doing anything else.

> I love it. I'd do it even if I wasn't being paid. Don't tell anyone.
>
> > [Male, Ph.D., 25 years practice]

> I love it. I wouldn't know what else to do with myself.
>
> > [Male, M.S.W., 35 years practice]

> I love it. I'll never retire, they'll have to drag me out by my heels. I get better as I get older.
>
> > [Female, M.S.W., 30 years practice]

> I love my career. I go to work every day and I can't believe I roll out of bed and love what I do.
>
> > [Female, M.S.W., 5 years practice]

> I love it. Philosophically, given that we're born and we die, what happens in between is the only thing we can control. If you think that you've had impact on people's lives, and they feel better about themselves and have benefited from knowing you, that's a marvelous thing.
>
> > [Female, M.A., 20 years practice]

Some emphasized specific aspects of the work.

> I like working with people, being intimate. It's gratifying to be able to help people.
>
> > [Male, Ph.D., 15 years practice]

> I like working with people. I feel privileged to be present at someone's growth.
>
> > [Female, M.S., 15 years practice]

I like being part of a process that has deep meaning, the sharing of that sense of deep meaning.

[Male, Ph.D., 10 years practice]

I love finding out what people think and feel. It's the most interesting thing about people. I like being highly paid for what I do.

[Female, M.S., 15 years practice]

I like that it's something that changes, that it's a new story all the time. It's like a new chapter every hour in a different book.

[Female, Ph.D., 5 years practice]

It's always interesting. Someone is allowing me to know them in a way that they're not even aware of. It's a kind of voyeurism. The process is so fascinating.

[Female, M.S.W., 10 years practice]

I find it fascinating, and sometimes I sit here and think, "Wow, I'm getting paid for this." You have to take very good care of yourself, but I love it.

[Female, M.S.W., 25 years practice]

It's fascinating. Also, you can turn that interest into a way of helping people improve their lives. I really feel blessed that I've always loved it, and with all the ups and downs and pains I've always loved it. It's a gift I got, to be able to do this, and most people don't get this about work, and it's the biggest curse in the world. People who can't get it together about work, that is the pits, because work is so crucial to our identity.

[Male, Ph.D., 25 years practice]

I don't think there are many professions where you don't get bored doing it after twenty years.

[Female, Ph.D., 10 years practice]

It's a profession where you have no choice but to get better, because the more you do it, the more you grow. That doesn't happen in many professions. If you don't become senile, you keep getting better.

[Male, Ph.D., 20 years practice]

I like best that it really makes me work, and makes me think, and it doesn't make me so secure that I march to my own tune.

[Female, Ph.D., 30 years practice]

I like the fact that I've been doing it for a long while, and that I have people of all different ages, and they'll know me through their lives, that I'm a stabilizing factor in people's lives, that they come to me and find a place to feel safe.

[Male, Ph.D., 15 years practice]

Very few people expressed reservations about the profession. Even with these reservations, most are happy in their choice of career.

I like the therapy part of it. The rest of it really sucks. I like best the idea of having a positive impact on somebody's life. There are days where I'd do it for nothing because it's just so good.

[Male, Ph.D., 20 years practice]

I wish I didn't have to do as much as I have to do in order to make a living. The work would be more enjoyable if I had to do less of it.

[Female, M.S.W., 15 years practice]

I like being effective in my work with patients. I like being able to use my mind and be stimulated regularly. At times I might feel too responsible for others, and feel a weightiness on me.

[Male, M.S.W., 15 years practice]

I have mixed feelings about it. I like it when it's easy, and someone comes in and we have a good time together, when I don't feel bored. I would like not to have to see thirty to forty hours. Would I keep doing this if I became successful at something else? I probably would.

[Male, Ph.D., 20 years practice]

One person was glad to be retiring.

I have liked it, but I'm very happy to be getting out.

[Male, Ph.D., 25 years practice]

NUMERICAL DISTRIBUTION

Only 4 people said they had serious doubts or reservations about being a therapist. Everyone else said they loved it or liked it very much.

COMMENTS

Some issues here are: Is psychotherapy inherently a satisfying profession? What are the effects on the patient and the treatment of having a therapist who loves the work or of one who does not?

I love being a therapist. It's the only job I ever had that didn't get boring and repetitive after a year. It's constantly fresh and new, each new hour and each new patient. I consistently feel challenged and engaged by what I'm doing. The work is intrinsically meaningful, unlike many other jobs that seem to consist mainly of moving papers around an office.

The *New York Times* only a few years ago reported a poll taken among lawyers, and almost two-thirds of those interviewed were seriously unhappy with their work and said that they wished they had chosen a different profession. If the therapists interviewed for this book are a representative sample, our level of job satisfaction is considerably higher.

RELATED READING

Burton, A. (1975). Therapist satisfaction. *American Journal of Psychoanalysis* 35(2):115–122.

Nash, J. M., Norcross, J. C., and Prochaska, J. O. (1984). Satisfactions and stresses of independent practice. *Psychotherapy in Private Practice* 2(4): 39–48.

Conclusions and Recommendations

So what do we make of all this? There is a tremendous amount of material in this volume—how shall we regard it? What does it reveal about the state of the field of psychotherapy? What does it suggest about changes and improvements?

I think there are a few surprises in the material, and also a few implications about the future.

SURPRISES

1) Gaps in Training

I was surprised to realize when I designed the questionnaire how many of these topics and areas were unaddressed during my own training and (it appears) many other therapists' training as well. Whitaker (Whitaker and Bumberry 1988) said that "because the primary tool of any therapist is himself," in a certain sense "we all must reinvent the wheel in order to be therapists" (p. 40). But I think much of this reinvention might be unnecessary if these specific areas were at least discussed in graduate schools and training institutes. The current state of affairs, a situation in which everyone comes to his or her own conclusions, may also contribute to the second surprising discovery, namely,

2) Total Disagreement

I expected to get a lot of divergent opinions about matters of theory and metapsychology. I did not expect to see the total lack of agreement even about such seemingly concrete and straightforward questions as whether to answer the phone during a session or what to tell patients about confidentiality. If as a field we can't even agree about such simple matters, how are we ever to settle the more difficult questions of how therapy works and how best to conduct ourselves with patients? There currently are some three hundred different kinds of psychotherapy, and we have no agreement about which of them is effective and which is not, or why.

3) Bad Therapy and Bad Supervision

Another surprise for me was to realize how many therapists had experienced bad therapy and bad supervision. Although most of them seem to believe that they know what was bad in those treatments, I wonder how many other aspects of their experiences were also negative or harmful but are not identified as such. How much are they unconsciously perpetuating by modeling on their bad therapists without even knowing that it's happening?

4) The Primacy of the Relationship

A fourth surprise was discovering how many therapists believe that psychotherapy works because of the connection between the patient and the therapist. Even some very psychoanalytically oriented therapists and some very behaviorally oriented therapists gave this explanation, which in both cases seems to contradict the basic beliefs of those theoretical approaches that the techniques and the interventions produce the change.

SOME IMPLICATIONS AND SOME RECOMMENDATIONS

Because the field of psychotherapy is in such crisis right now, specific recommendations for concrete action are necessary. Before making these recommendations, let me summarize the current situation.

A recent study of the effectiveness of psychotherapy conducted by *Consumer Reports* magazine resulted in a number of encouraging findings, as reported and analyzed by Seligman (1995, 1996). He found that "patients benefited very substantially from psychotherapy, that long-term treatment did considerably better than short-term treatment, and that psychotherapy alone did not differ in effectiveness from medication plus psychotherapy. Furthermore, no specific modality of psychotherapy did better than any other for any disorder" (Seligman 1995, p. 965). In addition, he found that "respondents whose choice of therapist or duration of care was limited by their insurance did worse" (Seligman 1996, p. 24), and that "long-term treatment produced better quality-of-life scores than short-term treatment" (Seligman 1996, p. 24).

In spite of these indications, "evidence shows that managed health companies limit treatment to an average of 8.2 sessions or less per client, whereas the positive outcomes for brief therapy as reported in the research averaged 15 to 30 sessions" (Walls and Scholom 1996, pp. 17–18). Apparently, even brief therapy is not brief enough for the managed care companies.

Long-term therapies, especially psychoanalysis and psychoanalytic psychotherapy, are even more likely to be proscribed. "Increasingly, managed care providers not only are opting for shorter treatment and for medication over psychotherapy, but they are also actively opposing long-term psychotherapy or psychoanalysis" (Bollas and Sundelson 1995, p. 92). These pressures are not limited to therapists already in practice, but are already affecting training of future therapists. "Graduate and professional schools of psychology already are steering students into courses that teach the short-term symptom-oriented behavioral therapies in demand by the managed care companies, and away from courses in the more intensive psychological therapies. Thus, managed care marketing propaganda is now shaping our graduate school curricula as well as APA policy . . ." (Walls and Scholom 1996, p. 20).

At the same time that these pressures are distorting the duration and type of treatment, legal incursions into the privacy and confidentiality of the psychotherapy office are changing the nature of treatment and the role of the therapist. New laws now require the therapist who suspects child abuse, or anticipates that a patient may become violent, to report these situations to the proper authorities. Bollas and Sundelson (1995) suggest that "psychoanalysis cannot function if the patient does not have complete confidence that what he says to his psychoanalyst is privileged" (p. 59) and that the analyst cannot function in his neutral role if he has become an agent of the state.

For some unknown reasons, the professional organizations are not fighting these changes but appear to be accepting the changes as inevitable and even positive. In writing about the American Psychological Association's Task Force on Psychological Interventions, which has developed "guidelines" for treatment of specific diagnoses all of which promote medication and short-term behavioral treatment, Walls and Scholom (1996) remind us that "what is not clear is why the APA is doing what insurers want and not what is in the best interests of the public and the professionals it represents" (p. 18). Walls and Scholom also warn that "managed care companies are certain to use the authority of these lists to rationalize their exclusive use of short-term therapies, and to justify their exclusion of non-behavioral therapists from their panels, claiming that they are doing so because they only want to pay for 'scientifically proven' therapies" (p. 21). In another aspect of this problem, in the area of reporting suspected child abuse to authorities, ". . . the APA actually lobbied the state of California to be put on the list of those professions mandated to report child abuse cases when they discovered that psychologists had for whatever reason not been included!" (Bollas and Sundelson 1995, p. 146).

What can we do to combat and even reverse these trends? Some specific reponses, some of which can begin to be implemented now, occur to me.

1) Change the Training

One possible conclusion we can draw from these interviews is that training in psychotherapy needs to be expanded or even radically changed. First, we need to include in the training *all* the areas and aspects of being a psychotherapist, not just theory, metapsychology, and technique. Second, we may need to put more emphasis in training on how to form the relationship and less on how to formulate the intervention. Technique and theory are important, and every therapist must be well grounded in both, but we may have neglected what most of the therapists in this group believe is the crucial aspect of good treatment. Unfortunately, in order to do this, we need first to know some facts.

2) Answer These Questions Once and For All

In order to teach all the different areas of practice, we need to know what to teach, and in order to do that we have to establish some facts. Psychotherapy research is perhaps the most difficult of any to do, and, as Heisenberg suggested, observation changes what is observed. But somehow we have to determine what is true and what is not, what works and what doesn't, what is significant and what is immaterial to treatment outcome.

I also think that some of this research needs to consist of talking to patients and asking them directly what worked for them and what did not, how they felt and what they thought about the way their therapists did therapy, just as *Consumer Reports* (1995) did. I plan in my next book, which will be a kind of companion volume to this one, to do just this: interview a substantial number of former and current patients about the same topic areas covered in this survey and see how the patients' experience compares to the therapists' beliefs about it.

3) Educate the Public

I think we need to educate patients about what good therapy and bad therapy are, at least insofar as we know now. Many in our survey were concerned about unethical and incompetent practitioners and how they can damage and abuse patients. Such abuse would not be possible if patients knew more clearly and concretely what they could reasonably expect from a competent and ethical therapist. I think there has been for too long a cloud of mystery about therapy, and one of the main reasons I did this book was to help dispel that fog so that patients might better educate themselves about what therapists do and what therapy is.

I think many practitioners have been unnecessarily afraid of better educated, more sophisticated patients, that they'll somehow give us a difficult time or be harder to treat, that they'll see through our techniques and challenge our authority. I suppose this is possible in some cases, but in general I think more knowledgeable patients would actually be easier to work with and more trusting of a good therapist.

4) Speak Out in Public and Affect Society at Large

A number of therapists suggested that we in the field of psychotherapy don't have as much impact on society in general as we could have, and I think that is true. In spite of certain gaps in our knowledge, there are many things we do know about people and the effects of different experiences on them. We seem to think that we can save the world one patient at a time, but that approach does not seem to be sufficient. I think that therapists get used to working in private, and this is an area in which we need to be very public.

I think also that we need to make room in our private practices for other kinds of patients than we are currently used to seeing. Poor patients, who are usually seen in crowded clinics, can also use good treatment. How many white therapists, who make up the vast majority of the field, treat black or other ethnic patients? How many set aside one or two hours a week for very low-fee patients or volunteer in some other setting? I think we need to start doing this more consciously and more deliberately.

5) Restore Complete Confidentiality

Recently, increased public awareness of child abuse has led to the passage of laws that require reporting of suspected instances to the authorities. *Tarasoff* and other such legal decisions have saddled the therapist with "duty to warn." Somehow, therapists have been made agents of political and social authority to the detriment of the therapy. Psychoanalytic treatment is not possible in this environment. "Were there to be a restriction of this basic process . . . then the entire procedure would come to a halt" (Bollas and Sundelson 1995, p. 61). Once a specific topic is off-limits, "[the patient's] self-censorship not only means that a specific area of conflict is not addressed, it also means that he is from this point incapable of free-associating" (Bollas and Sundelson 1995, pp. 61–62).

There is no compelling reason for psychotherapists to be placed in the role of policemen. In terms of duty to warn, no therapist, no matter how expert, is capable of predicting a patient's behavior in any area with any certainty. As heinous as child abuse is, other adults, such as teachers, family physicians, and neighbors, are actually in a much better position to notice or suspect such abuse. The state recognizes the necessity for complete confidentiality for lawyers and priests; there is no good reason not to extend that same privilege to therapists.

6) De-medicalize Psychotherapy

Most of all, I think we need to get out from under the medical model. Many of the problems mentioned by the therapists in this book are a direct or indirect outgrowth of the medical model of treatment. Over the past fifty years in this country, psychotherapy has become more and more part of the health care system, and the large insurance companies have more and more demanded from clinicians justification for treatment and proof of efficacy on a medical basis. No insurance company will reimburse for psychotherapy without a diagnosis from the DSM. Insurers are requiring more and more paperwork and clinical records, often to the point where confidential material must be revealed. The privacy of the treatment is compromised, and clients may hesitate to reveal controversial material to the therapist.

Length of treatment has also become an issue, with many insurance carriers allowing only short-term treatments of ten or twenty sessions. Treatment of this length must be geared to a specific concrete complaint or symptom, which again is part of the medical model: Identify the symptom and "cure" it. But a therapist doing dynamic therapy often works with a patient over the course of several years, not only on specific symptoms but on more global personality exploration and restructuring.

I think the trend of increasing medicalization of psychotherapy is a dangerous one, both for therapists and for patients. As early as 1926, Sigmund Freud, in *The Question of Lay Analysis*, warned against the possibility that psychoanalysis could become the exclusive domain of the physicians. Freud believed that the training a physician received was not only of little value in doing psychoanalysis but was actually at odds with basic psychoanalytic principles and techniques. More and more, however, psychotherapists of every background are being required to justify their treatments in medical terms. Recently, Ph.D. psychologists have been lobbying strongly to be granted the legal right to prescribe medications, as if becoming more like physicians would offer them more legitimacy.

If psychotherapy were really a medical procedure, this all might be reasonable. But it stretches the definition of "medical" beyond all clarity to include what psychotherapists actually do. What we do in psychotherapy is talk: We sit in a room and we talk. We do this once or several times a week, for 45 or 50 or 60 minutes. We meet as briefly as one time or for several years. By what definition is this a medical procedure?

Part of the confusion is due to the fact that many psychotherapists (particularly psychoanalysts, and all psychiatrists) are M.D.s first. When they prescribe medication, for schizophrenia or panic disorder, that is by definition a medical treatment. But when a physician paints a room, or makes a cup of coffee, that is not a medical procedure, and psychotherapy is not a medical procedure simply because many physicians do it.

Although psychotherapists are required to make a diagnosis, most people seeking therapy do so not because they are ill but because they are unhappy. "DSM-IV demands that all clinicians fit their patients into categories that experienced analysts know to be spurious" (Bollas and Sundelson 1995, p. 134). The medical model requires that we speak in terms of "mental illness" and psychiatric "disorders," but most people are not ill and do not experience themselves that way. They are discontented, frustrated, unhappy, tired of repeating the same self-destructive patterns. They seek therapy because they recognize that their own behaviors and choices are somehow creating this unhappiness, and they wish to change. By attempting to force psychotherapy into the world of medicine, we are distorting both the process and the outcome.

I think one solution would be to eliminate psychotherapy entirely as an insured medical procedure. Only the medical portion, that is, any drugs or medications, would be covered. Individuals wanting psychotherapy would have to pay for it themselves, and no outside agency would have the right to request records or violate confidentiality. We clinicians would have to adjust our fee schedules to support this new system of individuals paying for treatment entirely on their own, but I think many clinicians would be happy to do this if they never had to deal with the insurance companies again.

It is possible, however, that the trend has already gone too far to be reversed. I know a number of clinicians who have already told me of patients who will not consider beginning treatment unless they can get their insurance companies to pay for it or who have stopped in the middle of ongoing therapy when insurance benefits have run out. Perhaps the "mental health" field will have to live with increased interference from insurers and employers, but there is a price for this, and I believe that the price is actually a diminishing effectiveness. Short-term treatments may seem more cost-effective, but as the saying goes, "It's the stingy man who spends the most."

References

Bollas, C., and Sundelson, D. (1995). *The New Informants*. Northvale, NJ: Jason Aronson.

Consumer Reports (1995). Mental health: does therapy help? November, pp. 734–739.

Freud, S. (1926). The question of lay analysis. *Standard Edition* 20.

Seligman, M. (1995). The effectiveness of psychotherapy: the Consumer Reports study. *American Psychologist* 50:965–974.

—— (1996). Good news for psychotherapy: the Consumer Reports study. *Psychologist Psychoanalyst* 16(1):23–25.

Walls, G. B., and Scholom, A. H. (1996). APA Practice Guidelines Template jeopardizes clinical autonomy of practitioners. *Psychologist Psychoanalyst* 16(1):17–21

Whitaker, C. A., and Bumberry, W. M. (1988). *Dancing with the Family.* New York: Brunner/Mazel.

Postscript

know that other questions not included in these interviews will occur to many readers. Several have already occurred to me, such as, "Do you accept gifts from patients?" or "Do you reply to cards or letters from former patients?" If I can collect enough additional questions, a second book may be possible. Please send such questions or any other comments to me via e-mail at Lkassan@aol.com or by regular mail, care of the publisher.